MARITAL COUNSELING
Psychology, Ideology, Science

MARITAL COUNSELING
Psychology, Ideology, Science

Compiled and Edited by

HIRSCH LAZAAR SILVERMAN, Ph.D., Sc.D., L.H.D., LL.D.

Professor, School of Education, Seton Hall University
South Orange, New Jersey
President, Academy of Psychologists in Marital Counseling
President-Elect, New Jersey Association of Marriage Counselors

With Forewords by

JOHN H. CALLAN, Ed.D.
Dean, School of Education
Seton Hall University
South Orange, New Jersey

REBECCA LISWOOD, M.D.
Founder and Director
Marriage Counseling Service of Greater New York
Adjunct Professor, Adelphi University
Garden City, New York

DAVID R. MACE, Ph.D.
Executive Director
American Association of Marriage Counselors
Madison, New Jersey

CHARLES C THOMAS · PUBLISHER
Springfield · Illinois · U.S.A.

Published and Distributed Throughout the World by

CHARLES C THOMAS • PUBLISHER

BANNERSTONE HOUSE

301-327 East Lawrence Avenue, Springfield, Illinois, U.S.A.

NATCHEZ PLANTATION HOUSE

735 North Atlantic Boulevard, Fort Lauderdale, Florida, U.S.A.

© *1967, by* CHARLES C THOMAS • PUBLISHER

Library of Congress Catalog Card No.: 67-16117

With THOMAS BOOKS *careful attention is given to all details of manufacturing and design. It is the Publisher's desire to present books that are satisfactory as to their physical qualities and artistic possibilities and appropriate for their particular use.* THOMAS BOOKS *will be true to those laws of quality that assure a good name and good will.*

Printed in the United States of America

N-1

To My Sisters and Brothers:
Lucille, Elliot, Emanuel, Rosalind, Helen and Muriel

CONTRIBUTORS

Hirsch Lazaar Silverman, Ph.D., Sc.D., L.H.D., LL.D., *Editor*

Usha Anand, Ph.D.
Jules Barron, Ph.D.
Alexander Bassin, Ph.D.
Hugo G. Beigel, Ph.D.
James A. Brussel, M.D., F.A.C.P.,
    F.A.P.A.
George Calden, Ph.D.
William L. Carrington, M.D.
Thomas E. Connolly, M.S.W.,
    A.C.S.W.
Arthur Eisenstadt, Ph.D.
Albert Ellis, Ph.D.
Gerhard Falk, M.A.
Henry H. Foster, Jr., LL.M.
Allan Fromme, Ph.D.
Martin Goldberg, M.D.
Hilda Goodwin, D.S.W.
Edward F. Griffith, M.D., M.R.C.S.,
    L.R.C.P.

Henry Guze, Ph.D.
Robert A. Harper, Ph.D.
Sylvia B. Herz, Ph.D.
John W. Hudson, Ph.D.
Warren R. Johnson, Ed.D.
Rabbi Leo Jung, Ph.D., D.D., D.H.L.
Rev. Gordon J. Lester, C.SS.R., L.C.L.
Eleanore B. Luckey, Ph.D.
Thomas C. McGinnis, Ed.D.
Emily H. Mudd, M.S.W., Ph.D., D.Sc.
Gerhard Neubeck, Ed.D.
Robert Plutchik, Ph.D.
William R. Reevy, Ph.D.
H. L. P. Resnik, M.D.
Victor D. Sanua, Ph.D.
Alexander A. Schneiders, Ph.D.
Jeshaia Schnitzer, Ed.D.
Morton A. Seidenfeld, Ph.D.
Leo Wollman, M.S., M.D.

BIOGRAPHICAL NOTES

USHA ANAND earned her Ph.D. in psychology from Lucknow University. From 1959 to 1962 she was an assistant professor in psychology at her alma mater. She served in 1962 as a Fulbright Visiting Scholar in the United States. At present she is a counselor with the Association for Moral and Social Hygiene in India, and helped in the establishment in New Delhi of the Family Life Institute.

JULES BARRON, Ph.D., is in the practice of psychotherapy that includes individual and group process, couples, marital and family therapy. He is a group therapist and training supervisor at Bergen Pines County Hospital, in New Jersey; and is consultant on the mental health team of the Riverdell Regional High School Mental Health Services. Dr. Barron is past president of the American Academy of Psychotherapists (1964-66); and served as Director of Publications and Editor of its Newsletter. Currently, Dr. Barron is a member of the Executive Board of the Psychotherapy Section of the American Psychological Association, and is past editor of its *Bulletin* and chairman of its Publications Committee. He has written professional papers, poetry, edited monographs and given innumerable presentations before professional organizations, and has been on the faculties of Long Island University, The City College of New York, and Fairleigh Dickinson University.

ALEXANDER BASSIN, Ph.D., is Director of Research and Education at the Probation Department of the Supreme Court. For the past decade he has been Director of Group Therapy at the Civic Center Clinic. He is Adjunct Associate Professor of Education and Psychology at the Ferkauf Graduate School of Education of Yeshiva University. He is a consultant to the Board of Directors of Daytop Village, a treatment facility for drug addicts.

HUGO G. BEIGEL, Ph.D., is a marriage counselor and consultant in personal and sexual problems. Among his professional associations are the American Psychological Association, Diplomate of the Society for Clinical and Experimental Hypnosis, Fellow of the Society for the Scientific Study of Sex and the Advisory Council, Institute of Rational Living, in New York City. He is the author of a number of books, including *Architectural Beauty, Encyclopedia of Sex Education* and *Advances in Sex Research.*

JAMES A. BRUSSEL, M.D., F.A.C.P., F.A.P.A., is Assistant Commissioner, New York State Department of Mental Hygiene. During World War II and the Korean Conflict he served in the United States and overseas, always as chief of a neuropsychiatric service. He is certified in both specialties by the American Board of Psychiatry and Neurology (since 1937). He is a Fellow in the American Medical Association, the American Psychiatric Association, the American College of Physicians and the New York Academy of Science. He is Associate Editor of the *Psychiatric Quarterly,* and has been a consultant, at various times, to *Life, Medical Economics* and to Saunders Publications (Philadelphia). Dr. Brussel is the author of a number of books, including *The Layman's Guide to Psychiatry, The Layman's Dictionary of Psychiatry* and *Home Medical Encyclopedia.*

GEORGE CALDEN, Ph.D., received his doctorate at the University of Michigan. He is a clinical psychologist with the Madison (Wisconsin) Psychiatric Associates. He has thirty published papers, mostly in the field of the psychology of physical illness.

WILLIAM L. CARRINGTON, M.D., is an Australian psychiatrist who has taken a leading part in the development of family-life education and marriage-counseling services in Australia. Since 1962 he has been the Director of the Marriage Guidance Council of Victoria. Dr. Carrington has written a number of books, two of which, *Psychology, Religion and Human Need* and *The Healing of Marriage,* have been published in America. In addition to his work in marriage counseling, Dr. Carrington is well known throughout Australia as a lecturer and broadcaster, and for twenty-five years was Honorary Lecturer in Pastoral Psychology and Practice at the main Episcopal Theological Seminary in Melbourne.

THOMAS E. CONNOLLY, M.S.W., A.C.S.W., was Executive Director of the Onondaga Health Association in Syracuse, New York. He is active in community affairs in upstate New York, and serves on various social-welfare committees. He is with accreditation by the Academy of Certified Social Workers. He has been a featured speaker before the American Association of Clinical Counselors. Mr. Connolly is now Director of the Alcoholism Project of the Community Welfare Council of Schenectady, N. Y.

ARTHUR A. EISENSTADT, Ph.D., was educated at Brooklyn College, and at Cornell and New York Universities. His areas of specialization are speech, education and psychology, and he has taught these subjects at Cornell, Rutgers and St. John's Universities. He has served as President of the New Jersey Speech and Hearing Association, and is currently Editor-in-Chief of its *Journal*. Dr. Eisenstadt has lectured and taught in Europe under Fulbright Plan sponsorship and is now Director of the Speech and Hearing Center at St. John's University.

ALBERT ELLIS, Ph.D., holds a bachelor's degree from the City College of New York and M.A. and Ph.D. degrees in clinical psychology from Columbia University. He has taught at Rutgers University and New York University, has been Chief Psychologist of the New Jersey State Diagnostic Center, and later Chief Psychologist of the New Jersey Department of Institutions and Agencies, is a consultant in clinical psychology to the Veterans Administration, is Executive Director of the Institute for Rational Living, and for the last two decades has been in the private practice of psychotherapy and marriage and family counseling in New York City. He is a Fellow (and Past-President) of the Society for the Scientific Study of Sex, and a Fellow of the American Association of Marriage Counselors, the American Sociological Association, the Society for Applied Anthropology and the American Association for the Advancement of Science. Dr. Ellis has published over two hundred papers in psychological, psychiatric and sociological journals, periodicals and anthologies, and has authored or edited twenty-four books and monographs.

GERHARD FALK, M.A., is Associate Professor of Sociology at the State University College at Buffalo. He previously taught at South Dakota State College and the University of Pennsylvania. He is Past-President of the Western New York Sociological Association, President-Elect of the Group Psychotherapy Association of Western New York and Board Member of the Anti-Defamation League and the Buffalo Area Council on Alcoholism. He is the author of a dozen articles in professional journals.

HENRY H. FOSTER, Jr., LL.M., Professor of Law and Director of the Law-Psychiatry Project at New York University, earned the LL.M. from Harvard University and an LL.M. from the University of Chicago. He was a Senior Fellow in law and behavioral science, at the University of Chicago from 1958 to 1959. He is the co-author of *Society and the Law*, and is Chairman of the Research Committee, Family Law Section, American Bar Association, and Chairman of the Family Law Committee, Association of American Law Schools.

ALLAN FROMME, Ph.D., author of *Sex and Marriage, The ABC of Child Care* and *The Ability to Love*, taught psychology at the City College of New York, Sarah Lawrence College and Columbia University between 1937 and 1960. He served as Chief Psychologist, Child Guidance Clinic, St. Luke's Hospital, as well as Director and Chief Psychologist, Mental Hygiene Clinic of University Settlement House. He is a member of the American Psychological Association, the Eastern Psychological Association, the American Association of Marriage Counselors and the New York Academy of Science. He is in private practice as a psychotherapist.

MARTIN GOLDBERG, M.D., Assistant Professor of Psychiatry, Family Study Division, University of Pennsylvania School of Medicine, is an attending psychiatrist at the Institute of the Pennsylvania Hospital. He is a Diplomate of the American Board of Psychiatry and Neurology and a member of the American Psychiatric Association and the American Association of Marriage Counselors. He has been active for the past ten years in teaching marriage counseling to medical students and graduate physicians and is the author of a number of papers on marriage counseling and psychotherapy.

HILDA M. GOODWIN, D.S.W., is Assistant Professor of Family Study in Psychiatry at the School of Medicine of the University of Pennsylvania, and Director of Training with Marriage Council of Philadelphia. She has been a consultant, on marriage counseling, to family agencies and to the Clinical Social Work Service of the Veterans Administration (Philadelphia) Regional Office.

EDWARD F. GRIFFITH, M.D., M.R.C.S., L.R.C.P., was born in Los Angeles, California, and had his early education in England and Lausanne, Switzerland. He trained at St. Mary's Hospital, London, and qualified in 1922 for his M.R.C.S. and L.R.C.P. He has been for the past fifteen years in general practice in Devonshire and Aldershot. He is an honorary member of the American Association of Marriage Counselors. Dr. Girffith gave up general practice in 1938, came to London and specialized in marital problems from the gynecological and psychological point of view. He was appointed to the staff of the Department of Psychological Medicine at the Middlesex Hospital in 1938. Trained as a Jungian analyst in Zurich during 1946 to 1947, he has since devoted much time to marriage, marriage preparation and marital disharmony, about which subjects he has written extensively in nine published books and many articles.

HENRY GUZE, Ph.D., is Adjunct Professor of Psychology, Long Island University Graduate School of Arts and Sciences, and is Research Associate of the Harry Benjamin Foundation. He is a practicing psychotherapist in New York City, with particular emphasis on psychosomatic disorders and schizophrenia. Dr. Guze is a charter member and is Director of Publications of the American Academy of Psychotherapists, charter member of the International Society of Comprehensive Medicine, charter member and President-Elect of the Society for the Scientific Study of Sex and Diplomate of the American Board of Examiners in Psychologic Hypnosis. He holds Fellow status in the Academy of Psychosomatic Medicine, the American Association for the Advancement of Science and the Society of Clinical and Experimental Hypnosis. His special research areas are: endocrine functions in sex differences; instinctual behavior in mammals with special reference to hoarding, maternal and sex behavior; postural aspects of pathology; and transsexualism and transvestism.

ROBERT ALLAN HARPER, Ph.D., was trained in psychology, anthropology and sociology at Ohio State University, where he received his Ph.D. degree in 1942. He then took postdoctoral training in psychotherapy in Detroit, New York and Washington. He has taught at several leading universities, and has directed counseling clinics and counselor-training programs at both Ohio State University and the Merrill-Palmer Institute in Detroit. During World War II, Dr. Harper served as a psychiatric social worker in the United States Army. Since 1953 he has been in the private practice of psychotherapy and marriage and family counseling in Washington, D.C. Dr. Harper is former President of both the American Academy of Psychotherapists and the American Association of Marriage Counselors. He is a Fellow of the American Psychological Association and a Charter Fellow in the Society for the Scientific Study of Sex. He is also member of approximately twenty other professional organizations, in many of which he has served in some leadership capacity. Dr. Harper has written extensively for professional journals and for popular magazines. He is the author of two books: *Marriage* and *Psychoanalysis and Psychotherapy: 36 Systems;* and is co-author of three others: *Problems of American Society, A Guide to Rational Living* and *Creative Marriage.*

SYLVIA B. HERZ, Ph.D., is a social psychologist and marriage counselor in New Jersey. She is a Director-Founder of The Marriage Institute in Cranford (New Jersey) and is a radio lecturer on marital problems. She is a member of the American Psychological Association, the Academy of Psychologists in Marital Counseling, the Society for the Psychological Study of Social Issues and the American Association for the Advancement of Science.

JOHN W. HUDSON, Ph.D., received his doctorate in sociology from Ohio State University. He was on the staff of the Marriage Counseling Clinic at Ohio State University from 1950 to 1951;

Grant Fellow in Marriage Counseling at the Merrill-Palmer Institute in Detroit from 1951 to 1952; Training Therapist and Supervisor of Marriage Counseling Interns at The Merrill-Palmer Institute from 1952 to 1964; Chairman, Graduate Program in the Study of Family Life at the Merrill-Palmer Institute from 1956 to 1962; Associate Professor in the Department of Sociology of Wayne State University in Detroit in 1963; and has been Associate Professor in the Department of Sociology of Arizona State University in Tempe, Arizona, since 1964. He has been in part-time practice in marriage counseling and psychotherapy from 1957 to the present. His professional affiliations include the American Association of Marriage Counselors, the American Academy of Psychotherapists, the American College of Neuropsychiatry, the Board of Directors for the Institute of Rational Living, the American Psychological Association, the American Sociological Association, the National Council on Family Relations and the Arizona State Psychological Association.

WARREN R. JOHNSON, Ed.D., is Professor of Health Education, University of Maryland, and has been a member of the University's graduate faculty since 1951. Also, he is Coordinator of Health Education and Director of the Children's Physical Developmental Clinic, a research and demonstration program in child rehabilitation. He was elected to Fellowship in the American College of Sports Medicine, the American Academy of Physical Education, the American School Health Association and the Society for the Scientific Study of Sex. Among his books are *Human Sex and Sex Education, Science and Medicine of Exercise and Sports* and *Health Concepts for College Students.*

RABBI LEO JUNG, Ph.D., D.D., D.H.L., was born in 1892, in Moravia, the son of Dr. Meir Jung, later Chief Rabbi of the Federation of Synagogues of London. His universities include Berlin, London and Cambridge. He holds the degrees of Hon. B.A. of London and Cambridge, M.A. of Cambridge, Ph.D. of London University, D.D. of Yeshiva University and D.H.L. from New York University. Since 1931 he has been Professor of Ethics at the Rabbi Isaac Elchanan Theological Seminary of Yeshiva University. Since 1950 he has been President of the Jewish Academy of Arts and Sciences. He was President of the Rabbinical Council of the Union of Orthodox Jewish Congregations of America from 1928 to 1934, and has been a trustee of the Jewish Welfare Board since 1928. His writings have been translated into French, Dutch, Hebrew, German, Yiddish, Norwegian and Hungarian, and have appeared in magazines and newspapers in every continent. He is the author of a number of books, including *Foundations of Judaism, Fallen Angels, Crumbs and Character* and *Rhythm of Life.* Dr. Jung holds the distinction of being the only American rabbi who participated in the Great Soncino Translation of the Talmud into English, the Tractates of Yoma and Arakhin having been translated and annotated by him. He has sponsored eight volumes of the Halakhic yearbook, *Noam,* appearing in Jerusalem.

REV. GORDON J. LESTER, C.SS.R., L.C.L., was educated at Holy Redeemer Jr. College, Oakland, California, and St. Joseph College, Kirkwood, Missouri, both seminaries of the Redemptorist Fathers. He studied philosophy, psychology and theology at Immaculate Conception Major Seminary, Oconomowoc, Wisconsin. He professed vows as a Redemptorist in 1940, and was ordained as a priest in the Redemptorist Order in 1945. He did postgraduate work in canon law at the Pontifical College of the Angelicum in Rome, Italy, and obtained Licentiate in canon law summa cum laude in 1949. From 1949 to 1956 he held the position of Lector and Dean of Students at Holy Redeemer College in Oakland, California, where his chief work was counseling young men preparing for the Redemptorist priesthood during their undergraduate years. From 1956 to the present, Father Lester has devoted almost all of his time to preaching missions, retreats and novenas on the Pacific Coast and in the Hawaiian Islands. This work consists of giving a series of lectures on human problems and the Christian answers to those problems, and counseling people, especially in marriage and family problems. Besides dealing with lay people in these matters, Father Lester has worked extensively with religious sisters in problems of their vocation. Father Lester is consultor to the Provincial of the Far West Province of the Redemptorist Order, and is also a judge on the diocesan tribunal of the diocese of Oakland, California.

ELEANORE B. LUCKEY, Ph.D., Professor and Head of the Department of Child Development and Family Relations at the University of Connecticut, was previously on the faculty of the Iowa Child Welfare Research Station at the University of Iowa, and also taught at the University of Minnesota. She is an associate editor of the *Journal of Marriage and the Family* in the area of research in marital adjustment and person-perception. Her recent publications include a number of articles in professional journals. She is an active member in the American Psychological Association and the American Personnel and Guidance Association.

THOMAS C. McGINNIS, Ed.D., is a graduate of the William A. White Institute of Psychiatry, Psychoanalysis and Psychology in New York City. He is a founder and is Director of the Counseling and Psychotherapy Center, Fair Lawn, New Jersey, and is an instructor in marriage and the family at the New York University Graduate School of Education. Among his professional positions are Treasurer of the American Association of Marriage Counselors and President of the New Jersey Association of Marriage Counselors. His memberships include the American Association of Marriage Counselors, the American Academy of Psychotherapists, the American Psychological Association, the Academy of Psychologists in Marital Counseling and the National Association of Social Workers.

EMILY H. MUDD, M.S.W., Ph.D., D.Sc., is Professor in Family Study in Psychiatry at the University of Pennsylvania. Since 1936 she has been Director of the Marriage Council of Philadelphia. She is a Fellow and Past-President of the American Association of Marriage Counselors; Consultant to the *Encyclopedia of Mental Health* from 1961 to 1963, and is author of *The Practice of Marriage Counseling* and *Success in Family Living*. Dr. Mudd is also co-author of *Readings on Marriage and Family Relations, Man and Wife, a Sourcebook on Family Attitudes* and *Sexual Behavior and Marriage Counseling: A Casebook*.

GERHARD NEUBECK, Ed.D., is a professor of family studies, member of the Department of Psychology and the director of the Postdoctoral Marriage Counseling Training Program at the University of Minnesota. He is a Fellow of the American Association of Marriage Counselors and the author of numerous articles on marriage and marriage counseling. As a Fulbright Lecturer in Denmark during 1960 to 1961 he was able to observe marriages in the Scandinavian setting, providing him with an increased perspective on the relations between the sexes.

ROBERT PLUTCHIK, Ph.D., is the author of two books: *Small Group Discussion in Orientation and Teaching* and *The Emotions: Facts, Theories and a New Model*. He is editor of *Controversy*. Now in preparation is his *Foundations of Experimental Psychology*. He was a Special Fellow at the National Institute of Mental Health from 1961 to 1963, and Project Director for research sponsored by the Office of Naval Research. Currently he is Associate Professor of Psychology at Hofstra University.

WILLIAM R. REEVY, Ph.D., is Associate Professor of Psychology, State University of New York at Cortland, New York, and Consultant, Department of Mental Hygiene, State of New York (Clinical Psychologist, Auburn State Prison, Auburn, New York). Formerly, he was Associate Chief Psychologist, District of Columbia General Hospital, Washington, D.C. He has contributed chapters or articles to *Encyclopedia of Sexual Behavior, Advances in Sex Research* and *Sixth Mental Measurements Yearbook*.

H. L. P. RESNIK, M.D., earned his medical degree from the College of Physicians and Surgeons of Columbia University. He is a member of the American Psychiatric Association, the American Association of Marriage Counselors and the American Group Psychotherapy Association. At present he is: an instructor in the Departments of Psychiatry, School of Medicine and Graduate School of Medicine, at the University of Pennsylvania; Lecturer for the Marriage Council of Philadelphia; and on the medical staff of the Hospital of the University of Pennsylvania, the Pennsylvania Hospital and Philadelphia General Hospital. As of 1967, he is Associate Professor of Psychiatry, School of Medicine, State University of New York, at Buffalo.

VICTOR D. SANUA, Ph.D., received his doctorate from Michigan State University, with a major in clinical psychology and minors in sociology and anthropology. After interning at the

N.Y.U.-Bellevue Medical Center, he was awarded a postdoctoral fellowship by the Russell Sage Foundation. For approximately two years he worked as a psychologist in the Midtown Manhattan Mental Health Study. Subsequently he became a research fellow in the Department of Social Relations at Harvard University, where he initiated studies in the sociocultural aspects of schizophrenia. He has taught at Michigan State University, Brooklyn College, Suffolk University and Massachusetts University. Since 1960 he has been an associate professor at Yeshiva University Graduate School. During the academic year 1965 to 1966 he was a Fulbright Lecturer at the University of Paris (Sorbonne), where he conducted research and taught at the Center of Social Psychiatry and at the International Center of Intergroup Relations. He is a Fellow of the American Psychological Association and of the American Sociological Society. For a number of years he was Secretary-General of the Interamerican Society of Psychology.

ALEXANDER A. SCHNEIDERS, Ph.D., is Professor of Psychology and Student Counselor at Boston College. His previous positions include Professor of Psychology and Director of Psychological Services at Fordham University from 1953 to 1961 and member of the Board of Directors of the Astor Home for Children from 1957 to 1961. His publications are many, including: *Personal Adjustment and Mental Health; Proceedings* of the First Institute for the Clergy on Problems in Pastoral Psychology (Editor); articles on psychology for *World Book Encyclopedia; Personality Development and Adjustment in Adolescence; The Anarchy of Feeling; Personality Dynamics and Mental Health;* and *Adolescence and the Challenge of Maturity.* He is a member of the American Psychological Association, the New England Psychological Association, the Massachusetts Psychological Association, the Academy of Psychologists in Marital Counseling and the Society of Sigma Xi.

JESHAIA SCHNITZER, Ed.D., is rabbi of Temple Shomrei Emunah, in Montclair, New Jersey, and has been a marriage counselor for many years. He has been a member of the American Association of Marriage Counselors since 1957. He is actively engaged in important communal services, and has contributed widely to professional journals and periodicals. He lectures widely on marriage topics. Dr. Schnitzer is serving also as Jewish chaplain at the East Orange Veterans Hospital. He has been affiliated, and does special community and national field work, with many organizations, including the Montclair Chapter of the American Red Cross, the Montclair Child Guidance Clinic, the Tri-State Family Relations Council, the New Jersey Chapter of the United Nations and the National Association of Social Workers.

MORTON A. SEIDENFELD, Ph.D., since 1960 has been Special Assistant to the Assistant Commissioner for Research and Training, Vocational Rehabilitation Administration, Department of Health, Education, and Welfare, in Washington, D. C. His former positions include: Director of Rehabilitation at National Jewish Hospital in Denver, Colorado, from 1938 to 1940; Chief of Psychological Services, United States Army, Surgeon General's Office, from 1940 to 1945; and Director of Psychological Services, National Foundation, from 1945 to 1960. He is a Fellow of the American Psychological Association, the American Orthopsychiatric Association, the American Academy of Psychosomatic Medicine, the Royal Society of Health (England), the New York Academy of Sciences, the American Public Health Association and the Society of Public Health Educators.

HIRSCH LAZAAR SILVERMAN, Ph.D., Sc.D., is Professor in the School of Education of Seton Hall University, and also serves on referral as a clinical and consulting psychologist. He is the author of eight books and over seventy papers in professional journals. He holds Fellow status in national and international societies and professional associations, including the American Psychological Association, the New Jersey Academy of Science, the American Association on Mental Deficiency, the Philosophical Society of England, the Gerontological Society, The American Association for the Advancement of Science, the New York Academy of Sciences, the Royal Society of Health (England), the World Academy of Arts and Science, the Royal Society of Arts (London), the American Medical Writers' Association and the International Council of Psychologists. He was elected an Honorary Fellow of the Association for the Advancement of Psychotherapy. He is a certified psychologist in New York and New Jersey States. He has taught at Yeshiva University, Rutgers University, Mohawk College of the State University of

New York and Long Island University, and has lectured extensively throughout the United States and overseas, including talks at New York University, Harvard University and the University of Honolulu. His biographical data appears in *American Men of Science, Directory of American Scholars, Leaders in American Science, Who's Who in the East* and *Who's Who in American Education.*

LEO WOLLMAN, M.S., M.D., is a gynecologist and obstetrician at the Maimonides, Caledonian and Coney Island Hospitals in New York City. He is an affiliate of the American Association of Marriage Counselors, a trustee of the American Society for Psychoprophylaxis in Obstetrics, a member of the American Association of Planned Parenthood Physicians, the National Council on Family Relations, the International Fertility Association, the American Fertility Society and the Canadian Society for the Study of Fertility. He is Secretary of the National Association on Standard Medical Vocabulary, a life member in the American Medical Writers' Association and Past-President of the Royal Medical Society. He is current President of the Society for Clinical and Experimental Hypnosis, New York Section, and former President of the Metropolitan New York Society of Clinical Hypnosis. He is Secretary of the Academy of Psychosomatic Medicine, and a member of the Association for the Advancement of Psychotherapy, as well as a member of the Brooklyn Psychological Association. Some editorial positions that Dr. Wollman holds are Editor-in-Chief of *News Letter* of the American Society of Clinical Hypnosis, Consulting Editor of the Society for Clinical and Experimental Hypnosis *Newsletter*, Advisory Editor in Hypnosis to *Psychosomatics* and Associate Editor of the *Journal of Sex Research*. He is the author of twenty-four scientific articles and a contributor of chapters in books on sex and marriage.

FOREWORD

Democratic society has traditionally recognized the importance of family life. Through religion, custom, and law, man has attempted to provide resources for strengthening and protecting the family unit as an essential foundation of our society. The basis for a sound family life is a sound marriage between individuals who accept both the rights and responsibilities incumbent on each of the marriage partners. As marriage and family are strengthened, our society is strengthened and prospers.

In recent years marital counseling has assumed a major role as an important means for helping individuals adjust to the increasing tensions and pressures that beset marriage and modern society. Marital counseling serves to help individuals recognize the nature of their problems, discover acceptable alternatives for solving them, and gain a higher degree of personal insight or self-knowledge. Because of the complexity of human relationships there is no single formula for a successful marriage. That which is effective and desirable in one situation might be ineffective and undesirable in another. As a consequence, the marriage counselor must be a person of unusual talent and competence. Professional skill, intelligence, dedication, empathy, a sense of humor, and deep sensitivity to the needs of individuals are all attributes of the effective marital counselor. He must be a person who can relate well to others — who is, in effect, a skilled listener. He must be mature, well-adjusted, and free from prejudice. The ability to see the problems of others objectively and to know the degree of personal involvement necessary in a particular situation are also important. In sum, the marriage counselor must be a person of skill, integrity, patience, and basic good will. His success in dealing with clients will depend on these, and more.

Marriages work or are successful only when individuals are determined to make them so. Perhaps the true mark of a mature marriage is the growing selflessness which becomes increasingly evident as each of the partners assumes the full measure of identity in the marriage — where they become truly as one.

The tensions and seeds of failure in a vast number of marriages today can be traced to the breakdown of communications between husbands and wives — where the ability to "talk things out" is no longer present — where one or both parties in the marriage have given up any attempt to verbalize the reasons for their hostility or "hurt." Another important function of the marriage counselor, therefore, is to assist the parties in effecting a reestablishment of communications. Once this has been accomplished, a basis for further remedial effort has been established.

Husbands and wives who experience happy, contented, successful marriages have certain common characteristics. For the most part these are personality and character traits which the serious and dedicated married person can try to develop. While this listing is not intended to be complete, it may suggest some attitudes and attributes which are worthy of attention and emulation by the person who is determined to work for a satisfying marriage. First of all, the successful marriage is one in which the partners have a deep and abiding respect for each other — where there is an acceptance of the fact that although man is an imperfect creation he is capable of adjusting to a variety of situations and able to modify his behavior accordingly. In addition, they have a respect for the sanctity of marriage. They take seriously their marriage vows and will make a genuine effort to live up to them. Secondly, they are mature and have a mature attitude toward life. Their actions are guided by reason and reasonableness. Third, they have an appropriate sense of values wherein they are able to distinguish between what is truly important and what is unimportant. Fourth, they are capable of loving and being loved. Recognizing the importance of physical love they also have an understanding of what may be termed spiritual love. Fifth, they are willing to hear as well as be heard. They recognize the importance of keeping open the channels of communication and are willing to accept the necessity for compromise which results in the important "give and take" exchange in marriage. Sixth, they will make a sincere effort to understand each other — to forgive each other's fault and recognize that each of us is imperfect at best. Seventh, they are individuals who have personal dignity. They live by a code which extends to each other the common courtesy desired by all. Finally, they are persons who are sensitive to the needs of each other and seldom fail to recognize and give credit for the unique contribution that each makes to the marriage. Conversely, the marriage "in danger" is one where the partners, either through neglect, immaturity, indifference, or ignorance have failed to understand the importance of these attributes or have refused to make a sincere effort to develop them.

This book can serve many purposes. As one reads the contributions of these outstanding scholars, he should gain greater insight into the problems faced by married couples and the counselor. Few problems, if any, are unique. The problems of marriage and everyday living are remarkably similar among individuals in our culture. The dissimilarity is mainly in the methods used or accepted to solve these problems. It is important, in the final analysis, to understand that the marriage counselor can only serve as a catalyst to help individuals gain the insight, self-knowledge, understanding, and confidence to solve their own problems — in their own time and in their own ways.

Marital Counseling: Psychology, Ideology, Science is a noteworthy contribution to the psychological literature in the field. It includes scholarly contributors of national and international repute. The chapters run the gamut of the major phases of counseling in marriage from the sociological to the psychological to the religious, and the writers as men and women of professional competency and experience stimulate the imagination and thinking of the reader. The work of editing this volume has been accomplished in a masterful manner. Professor Silverman, an experienced writer himself, is the author of eight books and numerous articles and studies published in professional journals.

The volume is psychological-philosophical and scientific-humanistic in content and scope. Dr. Silverman combines in his excellent compilation of chapters, reality and professionalism, the "why" and "wherefore" of the profession of counseling and guidance in marital areas. He makes the profession pause to examine and re-examine the validity of its goals and its practices. Without stating it directly in his prefatory remarks as educator and psychologist, Professor Silverman makes his readers think — a most unusual and disturbing accomplishment for an editor. While the argument throughout the book is inherently on objective and scientific levels in marriage counseling, the editor sedulously makes a sound argument for true professionalism and moral integrity in the field and its ancillary tangents. I strongly recommend this book to behavioral scientists, teachers, counselors, psychologists, medical practitioners, sociologists, social workers and all adults interested in marital relationships. It is a book written and edited with incisive scholarship and erudition.

JOHN H. CALLAN, ED.D.
Dean, School of Education
Seton Hall University

FOREWORD

MARRIAGE IS A SERIOUS BUSINESS that must be entered into with careful thought and preparation. It should be the most wonderful relationship any human being can ever experience. As a physician and marriage counselor of long experience, I wish every newlywed could start out with more preparation in the way of knowledge about what marriage does — and can — mean.

For marriage is a challenge. People have to work at it with love and sensitivity and humor. And to make it work, marriage partners must be emotionally mature. Marriage is for *adults* — not for children. The most common cause of marital disharmony is the failure to understand and accept the realistic value of marriage. Some of the most important basic facts that married people must learn to accept should include the following concepts: One does not come into this world understanding the needs of the opposite sex; one is not born with the ability to communicate effectively with another human being; and, also, one is not endowed with a good sexual adjustment and sexual technique at birth.

Marital Counseling: Psychology, Ideology, Science, so ably edited by Dr. Hirsch Lazaar Silverman, is a sound text for the practitioner in the field. But it also will serve well as a reference for the intelligent adult concerned with preparation for improved marital relationships. Throughout this comprehensive text is the intimation that the entire field of marital counseling demands high academic training, professional experience of a broad yet refined nature, and personal qualifications that are predicated on substantial emotional and psychological quality.

The contributors to this volume were selected wisely by the editor. They add immeasurably to the ever-growing field of marital counseling with their knowledgable views and attitudes. So many of them recognize sensibly, even brilliantly, that a *good* marriage counselor interprets people to themselves and to each other, gives people an insight into the true nature of their problems, introduces a fresh perspective on people's problems, works with both husband and wife conjointly as well as independently, never sits in judgment on a patient or merely gives advice, and will call in other competent specialists if necessary.

I feel that *Marital Counseling: Psychology, Ideology, Science* is a very fine accomplishment, and constitutes one of the most penetrating discussions in the whole field that has come to my attention. Dr. Silverman as editor and contributor himself to this important volume has produced a very remarkable book, combining hopefulness with realism, scientific method with a humanistic spirit. This book will do a great deal of good as a contribution to the literature in marriage counseling, its theory and practice.

REBECCA LISWOOD, M.D.
Founder and Executive Director
Marriage Counseling Service of
    Greater New York
Adjunct Professor in Marriage and
    Child Care
Adelphi University

FOREWORD

T HE IDEA OF THIS VOLUME WAS conceived some years ago by my friend, Hirsch Silverman, and he has labored long and diligently to translate it into action. Now that the chapters have been gathered together, he has sent them to me and asked me to write an Introduction. I am delighted and honored by this request. My task, as I understand it, is to provide a broad overview of the development of marriage counseling in our time.

It so happens that I have been involved to a considerable extent in this process of development. I have been deeply interested in marriage counseling for most of my professional life. I can claim to have practiced it for at least thirty-five years, and to have assisted in its organized development for thirty of these years. The growth and direction of the marriage counseling services in my native Britain was my primary professional responsibility for a seven year period, and I have now been similarly involved in the United States for exactly the same length of time. In addition, I have been drawn into helping to establish, or consulting about the needs and possibilities of establishing, marriage counseling services in fifteen countries in Europe, ten in Asia, ten in the American Continent, and five in Africa. I have therefore had a good opportunity to observe the global development of this new personal and professional service to troubled married couples.

It can be said that marriage counseling is at once very old and very new. Someone has said that the first marriage counselor was the serpent in the Garden of Eden; and someone else has remarked that the troubles that shattered the peace of that idyllic spot were caused not so much by a red apple, but by a green pair! What is manifest is that the marriage relationship, by its very nature, is charged with potentialities for conflict; and it seems reasonable to assume that as long as marriage has existed, in any shape or form, there must always have been disappointed and disillusioned husbands and wives who welcomed the opportunity to weep on some sympathetic shoulder and to pour out their troubles into some receptive ear. It is equally certain that there have always been people willing to make their shoulders and ears available for this purpose; and indeed that some at least of these people have found opportunities to tidy up the domestic lives of their neighbors and friends not wholly unwelcome. We may therefore conclude that the basic situation has always existed wherein a person in marital trouble has gone to another person to seek comfort and counsel; although there have been periods in which prudence has dictated that such interchanges be kept strictly within the family. In Tolstoy's novel, for example,

xxiii

Dolly is skillfully reconciled to her husband Oblonsky, after his infidelity, by the good offices of Anna Karenina; while Levin, less successfully, seeks to unburden himself to his brother Koznyshov concerning his relationship with Kitty, and is put off instead with an irrelevant philosophical discussion.

Today, our marriage counseling is more sophisticated and probably on the whole more successful. But we need to remember that while we bring new resources to our task in the era of dynamic psychology, the old-time counselor was not without his store of traditional wisdom. The shrewd perception into affairs of the heart revealed by some of the great novelists and biographers of the past can match the insight of our best clinicians today.

However, our modern situation represents significant and substantial departures from that of the past; and these departures have made the services of the trained marriage counselor today both necessary and possible.

First, there has been a radical change in marriage itself. It is indeed not too much to say that marriage has been literally turned inside out; in the sense that the familial considerations that were at the center are now on the periphery, while the achievement of interpersonal fulfillment which was on the periphery is now at the center. Under the old system, when marriage was essentially a family duty, and personal fulfillment a hoped-for but not guaranteed bonus, spouses were able to exercise enormous tolerances of frustration and disappointment — tolerance even unto death, for until recently, in the traditional Oriental cultures, the proper and correct solution for the wife who found her marriage unendurable was suicide. If this sounds outrageous to us, we must remember that in those traditional cultures personal fulfillment was a forbidden goal to all but the privileged few; and one of the great roles of religion in the past was to inculcate uncomplaining acceptance of one's lot and the renunciation of personal ambition.

By contrast today, and in American culture to a greater extent than elsewhere, self-realization and personal fulfillment have become so much a primary right that the quest of such goals is often held to justify even the neglect of social duty and the disregard of conventional morality. Today, marriage must make people happy or they won't stay in it; which means that the marital bond can no longer be sustained in most cases by external coercion, and finds durability only through internal cohesion. The achievement of such durability is an enormously difficult task for many, and probably impossible for some. So marriages are failing on a large scale; and yet some at least of these failures could undoubtedly be prevented and arrested by the intervention of a skilled person — not, as in the past, by persuading them to go on tolerating unacceptable situations, but rather by showing them that their situations can in fact, through appropriated processes of readjustment, become acceptable to them.

Another event that has led to the development of modern marriage counseling is the study of human personality and human relationships that has burgeoned through the growth of the behavioral sciences. Human culture possesses, as we have noted, an accumulated tradition of ancient wisdom about the ways of men and women; and our ancestors were neither as stupid nor as indifferent as we sometimes suppose. They were, however, severely handicapped in certain directions. Their thinking was encumbered by superstitious beliefs which caused them frequently to reason from false premises. They lacked the scientific instruments that now enable us to measure the functioning of body and mind. And they had limited opportunities to make comparative investigations of behavior patterns and emotional reactions. Today, by contrast, all is wide open to investigation, and the means for investigation are refined and sharpened. Organized study and research, together with the rapid and widespread sharing of the knowledge they bring to light, and the opportunity to use that knowledge and to observe the results, have provided us with resources we never had before for understanding and helping men and women in their legitimate search for marital happiness.

New needs, based on new expectations; met by new knowledge made available through new methods of understanding and helping people: this is the combination of events that has brought about the rapid and dramatic growth of marital counseling in our world of today. I have seen that growth take place, sometimes beginning with nothing and leading to well organized services, in a comparatively short period of time in country after country in our modern world.

In the less than forty years in which organized marriage counseling has been made available to the public in these United States, much has been achieved. But much still remains to be done. Out of the comparatively simple idea of helping husbands and wives to adjust more comfortably to one another has emerged a bewildering variety of complications. Questions have been raised to which we do not know the answers. Differences of opinion have stimulated vigorous and healthy questing for the best ways of serving our clients. The result is that marital counseling today is in a state of considerable fluidity. Let me illustrate this by discussing four of the basic issues that are continually under consideration.

1. *What is the goal of marriage counseling?* Two rather different answers have been given to this question. In the early days, public interest in marriage counseling was aroused largely because it was seen as a means of "saving" marriages — and almost at any price. Divorce has been viewed until comparatively recently as either an unmitigated evil or at least a highly regrettable necessity. The spectacle of increasing numbers of couples wending their way to the divorce court aroused alarm, because it looked like

an ominous sign of the disintegration of the culture. Consequently, any-thing that might promise to turn these married couples back from the abyss could be certain to gain public support; and it was in this light essentially that the early development of marriage counseling was seen. The counselor was viewed as a conciliator, making full use of his powers of per-suasion, sometimes laced with overtones of coercion, to get couples to stay together and maintain social stability.

In due course, however, this concept gave way to another — that of en-abling a currently malfunctioning married couple to discover hidden poten-tials in their relationship, and through the development of these to be able after all to meet each others' needs. These were marriages that needed im-proving rather than saving, because they were not necessarily about to break up. The couples concerned might have been disappointed because their expectations were unreasonable, and had to be scaled down to attain-able reality. They might have been out of effective communication with each other, and needed help in exploring deeper levels of their shared life. They might have been blocked by conflicts that could be resolved through the learning of better problem-solving devices. But these couples were not necessarily headed for the divorce court. They could have jogged along as they were; but they were sufficiently motivated to want more out of marriage, and to seek help in order to achieve this goal.

This shift in the concept of what marriage counseling sets out to do, and the corresponding willingness of couples to see the counselor's role as being routine repair work, has made the task of the counselor more satisfying and more often successful. But at the same time, the concept of what success means in marriage counseling has had to be modified. Since saving a marriage at all costs is not now the primary goal, it is recognized that the marriage counselor may also provide for the couple a more humane and enlightened way of ending a hopeless marriage, which if continued could only prove unhealthy and destructive both for the spouses and for their children. Acceptance of this view has of course been greatly hindered by the outmoded adversary system of divorce procedure in our courts; but the growing weight of evidence is inevitably bringing us to recognize that when two people cannot, despite their most earnest efforts, live together in harmony, this is not necessarily due to any iniquity on their part, but simply a human misfortune that had best be recognized and terminated. Support and guidance from a competent counselor as people pass through this ex-perience may be highly therapeutic.

There are a few marriage counselors who claim to adopt a strictly neutral attitude to the outcome of their counseling, and would regard with suspicion even the view that the counselor's task is to explore all practicable ways of making the marriage work. They would suggest that this reveals a bias, and that the only proper position for a marriage counselor to adopt is that he will help the couple to see their marriage in perspective, in order that they may decide whether they want to mend it or to end it.

There has been some controversy as to whether the marriage counselor should even actively *recommend* separation or divorce to his clients. The general view has been that this would be inconsistent with the nature of the counseling process. But voices have been raised on the other side, indicating that it is the counselor's responsibility to offer what he believes to be the best solution to the problem the clients have brought to him, even when this in his opinion is the termination of their union.

2. *What is the scope of the marriage counselor's task?* Discussions of marital breakdown have frequently identified three major areas in which causes are likely to be found — hostile environmental factors; relational failure due to inadequate role functioning; and personal inadequacy. The question then arises — does a marriage counselor operate in all of these areas? Or does he focus his attention upon one or more of them and call on other specialists to aid him?

The environment of a marriage is hard to define. Clearly it would include a great variety of influences outside the actual relationship of the husband and wife — the culture in which they live, the values accepted in their community, the life of their immediate neighborhood; their conditions of work, their religious affiliations, their social life, their immediate relatives and friends. It might also include such factors as income, housing, and physical health. Some of the forces in the environment are supportive to the marriage, while others are destructive.

While environmental influences can never have the same central importance for the marriage counselor as the inner relationship of the couple, he knows well that external factors may easily have a profound and even decisive effect on the marriage. Yet essentially the areas involved cover a wide variety of fields of specialization; and the counselor, if he is to offer his couple the best help obtainable, may be under the necessity of calling in the social worker, the pastor, the lawyer, the physician, the vocational counselor, the real estate agent, the home economist, and many more besides. Certainly no marriage counselor could claim expertise in more than one or two of these varied fields.

It is primarily with the dynamic interaction between the two married persons, however, that the marriage counselor is concerned. There seems to be general agreement that this is his true area of specialization — the manner in which the couple communicate, cooperate, and strive to handle the complex problems arising out of their partnership as persons on the one hand, and their emotional complementarity on the other. These matters are treated extensively, as we would expect, in a number of the chapters of this book.

Behind many marital problems, however, lie stubborn conditions of personal inadequacy. Much can be done (probably a good deal more than the traditionally oriented psychotherapist is willing to admit) to change the attitudes, and even the behavior patterns, of husbands and wives through re-education, rational therapy, and other devices which simply provide the client with deeper insight and clearer perspective. But when all these resources have been exhausted, there are marriages that cannot function because husband or wife simply lacks the interior integration of personality necessary for sustained functioning in the primary marital roles. To achieve the intrapsychic orientation that is called for in such cases, deeper and more intensive forms of individual therapy have so far proved to offer the best solution.

Today, an increasing number of practicing marriage counselors are qualified also in psychotherapy; and this equipment obviously provides them with an additional resource that will prove to be of great value to them in their work. But whether, as some believe, a marriage counselor is not properly qualified unless he has this skill, is a controversial question on which there is deep division of opinion at the present time.

3. *What configurations of persons involved bring the best results?* Marriage counseling usually begins when a threatened or disturbed spouse turns to a helping person. This means that the primary pattern is normally a one-to-one relationship between counselor and client. Since this conforms to the classical concept of psychotherapy, most marriage counseling has been undertaken on this basis. But a distinctive emphasis has been made by insisting that the *focus* of the counseling is not upon the person being counseled, as in personal counseling, but upon the marriage relationship. And although the marriage counselor is normally willing to work with one partner only, if necessity demands, it is his hope and indeed his expectation that he will in time draw the other spouse into the counseling process.

For long years the accepted pattern of marriage counseling was that the counselor worked with each partner separately, and encouraged them both, as a result of the insights they were gaining, to undertake new ventures in communication and readjustment when they were at home together. However, in time, the idea began to take hold that there might be some decided advantages in interviewing them both together. This had been discouraged in the early days as a procedure involving some disadvantages and even some hazards. As experiments began to be made, however, the consensus grew that the gains involved in conjoint counseling are likely in most cases to exceed any risks that may be taken.

It is my impression that a decided shift of emphasis has now taken place, and that, in the United States, though not yet elsewhere, conjoint counseling now has the edge as the preferred method. A few purists even refuse to see marital partners except conjointly. The majority, however, now tend to make flexible use of both separate and conjoint interviews; generally seeing spouses separately at first until rapport has been gained with each, then moving them into conjoint interviews to foster and facilitate the restructuring of the interaction process.

A further development has appeared in the form of group marriage counseling. The application of the principles of group dynamics to marital counseling began to be made some time ago; but it is my impression that acceptance of this approach has been more reluctant than has the changeover to conjoint counseling. Nevertheless there is evidence that, in competent hands, group marriage counseling has proved to be a highly effective method. It has been undertaken with groups of husbands separately, and groups of wives separately; but the pattern that has been most widely accepted involves groups of married couples together. Some counselors have worked on the assumption that a couple must be pre-selected for readiness to be moved into a group; while others consider that almost any couple can benefit from group counseling.

Wider extensions of these newer methods are being experimented with. The family therapy movement, developed initially as a resource tool in studying patterns of interaction among family members, has been put to use as a therapeutic method. Initiated largely by psychiatrists and social workers, this approach takes the whole family — normally husband, wife, and children of all ages — into a conjoint group, and works flexibly with the entire complex of interrelationships.

A controversial extension of group marriage counseling makes use of the principal of marathon therapy. A group of couples are brought together in an ongoing process of intensive interaction that may extend continuously over a period of some thirty hours, with minimal time out, on an individual basis, to eat and sleep. It is probably too early yet to evaluate the long-term effectiveness of this novel approach.

Various configurations of counselors have been employed. The traditional psychotherapist will frequently handle a marital problem by taking one partner into therapy and allocating the spouse to another therapist. Normally this is little more than parallel individual therapy; but attempts have been made to build collaborative elements into the process. Some limited experiments have used two marriage counselors together, working as a foursome with the same couple. Sometimes this has been undertaken as a training experience which pairs an experienced counselor with a beginner. In one instance that has come to my notice, a husband-wife counseling couple have worked intensively in "foursome" interviews with a client couple.

4. *What are the theoretical principles underlying marriage counseling?* It can be said without fear of contradiction that marriage counseling is a field in which practice has far out-run theory. This is not a very satisfactory state of affairs, and needs to be remedied.

The marital dyad can be seen as representing a point of critical confrontation for the behavioral sciences of psychology and sociology. Marriage could be viewed by the psychologist as a primary arena for the meeting of ego needs, and for personality functioning. The sociologist could view it as a nuclear social system in which human interaction processes take place in a highly concentrated form.

Up to the present time, the marital relationship seems to have received decidedly more attention from sociology than from psychology. There are however evidences that this is changing. Some promising beginnings are being made in the formulation of theoretical frameworks to explain what takes place in a marriage. Several chapters in the book deal with aspects of this subject.

As we look to the future, we may confidently predict that we shall see a steadily increasing emphasis both on the study of marriage as a primary human relationship with enormous power to influence the life both of the individual and of society; and on the development of effective means to release the great potentials for growth and fulfillment that lie in the shared life of the married pair. In short, there can be no doubt that marriage counseling has a highly significant future.

This being so, it is of considerable importance that the voices of those who have had extensive experience in this new field, and have reflected seriously upon the implications of their experience, should be heard. The literature of marriage counseling has been slow in developing. Among the earliest writings I have been able to identify in English are a small and now quite out-dated volume of my own, published in England in 1948, and a similar volume written quite independently by John Cuber, and published in the United States in the same year. The volume of writing in the intervening period has been quite sparse. It is possible that this is due in part to the fact that clinicians do not write as readily as do theorists; and that many who may have considered contributing to the literature modestly decided that their ideas were as yet too inchoate and untried to be worthy of publication. Whatever the reason for the small volume of published material up to now, I am convinced that a considerable burgeoning of communication and exchange among practitioners of marriage counseling is greatly needed if we are to make substantial progress.

This being the case, I believe that all who are genuinely interested in the development of marriage counseling will join me in acknowledging our debt to Hirsch Silverman for the production of this volume of essays. The project must have involved him in much painstaking toil. I have read the material he has assembled with considerable interest. No less than 22 of the writers are known to me personally, my professional association with one of them going back to 1938. The geographical development of marriage counseling is well demonstrated by the fact that the writers represent the European, the Asian, and the Australian continents as well as the American. The variety of professional disciplines they represent is too great to enumerate.

Dr. Silverman has wisely not attempted to regiment either his material or his writers. Rather he has established an open forum, in which an impressive assembly of specialists in the field have been given the opportunity to contribute their best thinking on some aspect of the subject. The material has not been narrowly confined. It covers, in roughly equal proportions according to my estimate, four major areas — the nature and functioning of the marriage relationship; the methods and techniques of counseling with married couples; various aspects of marriage counseling viewed as professional practice; and a miscellany of related issues such as sex, love, communication, mental health, and divorce, which have important implications for the marriage counseling field.

The editor of any symposium has a difficult choice to make. He must either try to achieve conformity to a plan at the cost of constricting his authors; or he must give them wide freedom and accept an inevitable diversity. Hirsch Silverman, rightly as I think, has chosen to direct his team with a loose rein, and has respected their right to use to the full their individual patterns of self-expression.

The result should provide, for the experienced marriage counselor, a valuable opportunity to compare his own attitudes and methods with those of a selected and experienced group of his colleagues. In my reading of the volume, I myself found much that was stimulating and enlightening. For the beginner who wants to find his way in the marriage counseling field, the book should provide a gold mine which he can explore extensively and profitably.

It has been my privilege for some thirty years to work closely with marriage counselors all over the world; and I have found them, with the rarest exceptions, to be men and women who manifested in a striking degree warm humanity combined with high integrity and a deep sense of dedication to their task. Marriage counseling is not easy work, and those who approach it superficially find that the glamour soon fades. It may often prove exhausting and disappointing, and one needs a genuine sense of vocation to stay the pace. But those who do so find themselves to be members of a rich and rare fraternity. They are sustained, again and again, by the realization of the fundamental nature of their task; for it is not too much to say that the marriage counselor is engaged in nothing less than the strengthening and renewing of the elemental foundations of the entire structure of human society. The counselor may often find his work arduous, and sometimes costly; but he will never have the experience of feeling that what he is engaged upon is worthless or irrelevent. It is this faith, this confidence, and this sense of enduring purpose that renew in him constantly the springs of true charity and of altruism. I have valued nothing in life more highly than the good fortune that has been mine in working with such people and claiming them as my personal friends.

DAVID R. MACE, PH.D.
Executive Director
American Association of
Marriage Counselors

PREFACE

T HIS IS TRULY A BOOK *on* marriage counseling. It deals with human beings. In this sense, it is a subjective book. There is no attempt to represent all aspects (despite the fact that practitioners from all branches of thought were invited to contribute chapters) .

This volume is concerned with the development of marital counseling, especially in the United States, its present status and significant trends that are already manifesting themselves to the point of reshaping the field. Consideration also is given to those significant innovations that are influencing thought in marital counseling.

The point of view dominating the entire book is that the best clinical and theoretical experiences must be provided for those being trained and working in marital counseling.

In a sense this volume is an effort in conceptual itinerary, a formula, a theorization. It presents a series of interrelated investigations, all bearing upon a common set of problems. This makes it a kind of guided overview of a field which encroaches upon the self-consciousness of most people, and I hope that it may be widely read by younger as well as older people, by clinicians as well as laymen, by students as well as teachers.

In the revision of the individual chapters the Editor sedulously tried to maintain the author's own flavor of presentation. For the most part he has not taken the liberty of altering the emphasis, the outlook or the mode of expression of any of the contributors—not that he necessarily agrees with all that has been written or implied by all the contributors; however, each has a message worthy of study and rumination.

The chapters vary in quality: Some are brilliant in concept; others are mostly fluent in expression. It is hoped that the strength of this volume may be judged rightly in a broad, intelligently emancipated manner, with enlightened viewpoint and conceptualization.

This is an unpretentious book, written intentionally without jargon or pedantry, with descriptive and illustrative material cut to a minimum. But I hope it will be among the books which will change men's minds about the field of marital counseling. If some of the ideas developed in these chapters may in time (if not now) seem self-evident, it is because, hopefully, they may become part of our thinking in the field.

It is the Editor's opinion that no one text can provide enough material in an area such as marital counseling. Practitioners, teachers, clinicians and students are therefore urged to supplement this book with appropriate collateral and supplementary reading.

My own interest now, as always, is the way people organize their lives. That is why I particularly enjoyed the work of editing this volume and contributing my thoughts to it.

HIRSCH LAZAAR SILVERMAN

ACKNOWLEDGMENTS

IN THE COMPLETION OF THIS BOOK I benefited from the help of a number of individuals. I am grateful to them.

My publisher deserves thanks for consistent encouragement, for the complete freedom granted and for remarkable patience with me as Editor. My gratitude goes to Mr. Payne E. L. Thomas, particularly, for constant helpful advice. I also wish to express my thanks to Mrs. Betty S. Woodward, of the Editorial Department, for suggestions that were always valuable. The entire staff of my Publisher has been most cooperative, and I thank them sincerely, individually and collectively.

I am indebted to the authors of the individual chapters for their indulgence in accepting ideas and criticism graciously, and for their cooperation and interest.

I am appreciative for the patience and understanding of my wife, Mildred, and for her reasonableness, no less, in the many months of work and time in preparation of the manuscript.

My daughter, Hyla, in her own inimitable way gave me encouragement, with frequent prodding, to finish my work on the book and (hopefully) spend some time with her.

I am especially indebted to my two sons, Morton and Stuart, for their creative thinking. Despite their youthfulness they evidence potential of high order in this regard.

In the preparation of the manuscript I have had the invaluable assistance of Mrs. Catherine Sedlak. Not only for her secretarial help but for her sound suggestions I am indeed very grateful.

To Dean John H. Callan of the School of Education, Seton Hall University, I express my appreciation for his inspiration to continue research and contribute to knowledge.

H. L. S.

CONTENTS

SECTION I
MARITAL COUNSELING: PSYCHOLOGICAL FACTORS

SECTION II
MARITAL COUNSELING: IDEOLOGICAL FACTORS

SECTION III
MARITAL COUNSELING: SCIENTIFIC FACTORS

SECTION IV
SUMMARY
COMPREHENSIVE EVALUATION:
MARITAL COUNSELING CONCEPTS

MARITAL COUNSELING
Psychology, Ideology, Science

SECTION I

MARITAL COUNSELING:
PSYCHOLOGICAL FACTORS

Chapter I

EDUCATIONAL AND PROFESSIONAL TRAINING
OF THE MARITAL COUNSELOR

WILLIAM R. REEVY

HISTORICAL INTRODUCTION

IN ALL LIKELIHOOD, CASUAL, unconventional marriage counseling has existed from time immemorial—perhaps for as long as the institution of marriage (11, 20). People have always been ready to advise others and to seek advice, to consult and be consulted, and there is no reason for assuming that marital problems would not have come under the fascination of this natural tendency of man. In any form remotely resembling a profession, however, it is no more than three or four decades old in the United States.

It reflects a degree of pedanticism to set the exact date when marriage counseling had its origin as a profession, but the approximate date can be set and the major currents in which it originated can be noted. Ellis (11) is of the opinion that marriage counseling began in the 1920s "with the investigations and teachings of Professor Ernest R. Groves." Mudd (21) avers that, "in the United States, formalized marriage counseling services whose chief focus is the promotion of partner adjustment before and after marriage began when two clinics opened in 1928." Abraham Stone (30) states that he, together with Dr. Hannah Stone, opened the first marriage consultation center in the United States in 1929. This center was established at the Labor Temple in New York City and had as its aim providing information and guidance to those about to be married or already married. This pioneer venture was followed by the founding of the American Institute of Family Relations in 1930, with Paul Popenoe as director, and the founding of the Marriage Council of Philadelphia in 1932, with Emily Mudd as director (30, 21). Whether the origin of marriage counseling begins with the work of Groves, who counseled as a result of his teaching marriage and family courses, or whether its beginnings start with the formal establishment of marriage consultation centers, councils and institutes is a moot point. But it is a certainty that formal marriage counseling is not old. And we can be certain of the fact that other sociologists and instructors of marriage and family life were doing as Groves was doing, counseling in conjunction with their courses and urging that others do likewise (7, 23). So we see that, in the early '30s, sociologists, social workers, gynecologists, geneticists and others, independent of each other, were formally recognizing the need of giving help on premarital and marital problems.

Very shortly after the founding of the aforementioned marriage counseling centers, the American Association of Marriage Counselors was formed in 1942. Robert Latou Dickinson, the internationally known gynecologist, had been meeting for several years with other physicians in New York City in order to discuss sexual and marital problems. The Association was the outgrowth of these meetings. At the time of the Association's formal launching, these physicians united with Drs. Ernest Groves, Emily Mudd and others. Dr. Kinsey, of the famous Kinsey reports, joined the Association soon after its establishment.

From its outset the Association had represented in its founding body and membership distinguished persons of varying professional backgrounds, and the pioneers in the Association were pioneers in other respects. For example, and as previously mentioned, Dr. Groves was probably the first person to teach a marriage and family course at a university, and perhaps one of the first to counsel in conjunction with his courses (30). Dr. Mudd, as we have seen, was one of the first directors of a marriage counseling center.

Some of the original members of the Association were, a few years later, to be members of a Joint Subcommittee on Standards for Marriage Counselors of the National Council on Family Relations and the American Association of Marriage Counselors. The report of this subcommittee, which Abraham Stone chaired and on which Dr. Janet F. Nelson, a psychologist, served as secretary, made its final report at the tenth annual conference of the National Conference on Family Relations in 1948 (4). The other members of this subcommittee were Gladys H. Groves, Sophia J. Kleegman, Robert W. Laidlaw, Herbert D. Lamson, Emily H. Mudd, Rev. Otis R. Rice and Anna Budd Ware. Nearly half of the membership of this committee consisted of persons who were also among the first members of the American Association of Marriage Counselors.

One is struck with the fact that a core of names keeps recurring in differing but related events. Further, it is clear that a nucleus of persons were deeply interested in fostering and steering the emergence of a new profession, since they were involved in all sorts of interlocking activities and pursuits relating to marriage counseling. The same core of persons is seen to be founding or directing the first counseling centers, to be involved in the founding of the first professional organization representing the discipline of marriage counseling, and in serving on and even chairing committees dealing with highly professional concerns, such as the setting of standards to be met by those who would serve the public. As demonstrated by their activities, these professionals were from the start immersed in dealing with the question of what standards are to be acceptable for one to qualify as a professional marriage counselor.

These standards were briefly spelled out in terms of academic training, professional experience and personal qualifications in the Joint Subcommittee report of 1948 referred to above and are quoted below in entirety, as this remains the basic statement.

MARRIAGE COUNSELING
Report of the
Joint Subcommittee on Standards for Marriage
Counselors
of the
National Council on Family Relations
and
The American Association of Marriage Counselors
Abraham Stone, M.D., Chairman
Janet Fowler Nelson, Secretary
Gladys H. Groves
Sophia J. Kleegman, M.D.
Robert W. Laidlaw, M.D.
Herbert D. Lamson
Emily Hartshorne Mudd
Rev. Otis R. Rice
Anna Budd Ware

Marriage counseling is here regarded as a specialized field of family counseling which centers largely on the inter-personal relationship between husband and wife. It involves many disciplines and is inter-professional in character. Those who wish to enter this field however, whether physician, clergyman, psychiatrist or social worker, require a common body of scientific knowledge, techniques and qualifications.

Standards for acceptable and recognized marriage counselors, are herewith presented in terms of academic training, professional experience and qualifications, and personal qualifications.

1. Academic Training
   a. Every marriage counselor shall have a graduate or professional degree from an approved institution as a minimum qualification. This degree shall be in one of the following fields: education, home economics, law, medicine, nursing, psychology, religion, social anthropology, social work, and sociology.
   b. Whatever the field of major emphasis, there shall be included accredited training in: psychology of personality development; elements of psychiatry; human biology, including the fundamentals of sex anatomy, physiology and genetics; sociology of marriage and the family; legal aspects of marriage and the family; and counseling techniques.

2. Professional Experience and Qualifications
    a. The candidate shall have had at least three years of recognized professional experience subsequent to obtaining his degree. In addition, he shall have had actual experience as a clinical assistant in marriage counseling under approved supervision.
    b. A candidate's qualifications shall include:
        1. Diagnostic skill in differentiating between the superficial and the deeper level types of maladjustment, and the ability to recognize when the latter type requires referral to other specialists.
        2. A scientific attitude toward individual variation and deviation, especially in the field of human sex behavior, and the ability to discuss sexual problems objectively.

3. Personal Qualifications
    a. The candidate shall possess personal and professional integrity in accordance with accepted ethical standards.
    b. The candidate shall have an attitude of interest, warmth, and kindness toward people, combined with a high degree of integration and emotional maturity.
    c. The personal experience of marriage and parenthood is a decided asset.

Revision of this statement as represented in the 1958 Report of the Committee on Standards and Training of the American Association of Marriage Counselors is minor insofar as it relates to the matter of a marriage counselor's qualifications (18).

Prior to the presentation of this report, individuals who were centering their counseling "largely on the inter-personal relationship between husband and wife" and premarital problems were stating their considered opinions as to what academic, professional and personal qualifications a marriage counselor should have. Cuber (7), Foster (12) and Groves (13) presented their opinions in considerable detail, and certainly these and other views influenced to a considerable degree the thinking which culminated in the formal committee report. We find, for example, these men mentioning course areas which would be highly desirable in the educational background of a marriage counselor. A surprising number of these areas of accredited academic training found their way into the Joint Subcommittee Report and are recommended today.

Groves (13) was of the opinion that formal instruction in marriage counseling "must draw upon all the sciences that contribute significant information concerning marriage and family experience . . .," and he suggested that the highly desirable fields of knowledge in the counselor's background would be: (a) social work; (b) anthropology; (c) biology; (d) medicine; (e) law; (f) psychiatry; (g) psychology; (h) sociology; (i) religion.

Foster (12), in asking if family counseling is a profession, averred that "no person should undertake to become a marriage counselor without considering and answering for himself some of the questions raised in this paper," a paper in which he asked how essential were a number of course areas in the education of the counselor. He listed some ten, among which were: (a) biology; (b) sociology-anthropology; (c) political science (law in relation to the family); (d) psychology; (e) family life; (f) home economics; (g) economics, etc. There is a considerable overlap of his academic disciplines in comparison with those of Groves (1945). Apparently there was, sometime before the establishment of any professional organizations to represent the field, considerable agreement on certain matters among these first promulgators of marriage counseling as a profession. They were in accord on such points as: (a) the need for marriage counseling to establish itself as a profession; (b) fields of knowledge which contribute information vital to the background of the counselor; and (c) formative and tentative ideas as to what the academic training, professional and personal qualifications, and professional experience of a marriage counselor should be.

EDUCATION IN MARRIAGE COUNSELING

Introduction: Diversity in Educational Background of Pioneer Marriage Counselors

In the pioneering period just prior to and at the time when marriage counseling was emerging as a profession, men and women who were involved in the activity came to it with varying backgrounds (13, 20, 30). A number of the pioneers have already been mentioned, and these pioneers were of such educational backgrounds as genetics, biology, medicine, psychiatry and psychology. It was the conviction of many of the pioneers that, as Groves (13) averred: "Marriage covers a wide area of human experience and the causations of its problems are distributed among all the specialties that deal factually with human nature." Therefore, "no member of a profession can safely as a counselor rule out insight gathered from some other line of investigation or the experience that comes from applying this knowledge to problems of conduct." The pioneers of the marriage counseling profession, partly by reason of the fact that they were persons of such varying educational backgrounds who interacted with one another in a true interdisciplinary approach, saw clearly that the mysteries of as complex a relationship as the marital one could not be unraveled by one scientific discipline alone. They perceived that our understandings of the sex factor in marriage, of the physiological, social and psychological factors in marital relations, of the effects of interpersonal relations within a family group upon its individual members and many related understandings could

not possibly be developed from the framework of one type of research conducted by a single discipline. These pioneers, therefore, favored the emergence of marriage counseling as developing within an interdisciplinary
professional context. And so the original development of marriage counseling took place within such a conjoining. Statistical breakdown of the
membership of the American Association of Marriage Counselors by type
of profession for the eighth and twelfth years after its inception shows this
variety in education and professional background. This is still true of the
membership in the present day, as the following table shows.

	1954	1950
Professions of A.A.M.C. Members	*Per Cent*	*Per Cent*
Educators	18.0	10.0
Social workers	15.0	12.5
Clinical psychologists	13.0	8.5
Sociologists	12.0	12.5
Ministers	12.0	8.0
Gynecologists	11.0	27.0
Psychiatrists	9.0	17.0
General medicine	9.0	2.5
Urologists	1.0	2.0
	100.0	100.0

Professions of A.A.M.C. Members *as Reported in the 1966 Directory*	*Per Cent*
Social work	29.0
Psychology	24.0
Ministry	18.0
Medicine	12.0
Sociology	11.0
Education	5.0
Law	1.0
	100.0

These figures cannot be taken as representative for the entire United
States, as many persons who do marriage counseling are not members of the
Association. While, for example, some of the members of the Academy of
Psychologists in Marital Counseling are also members of the Association,
many are not. All members of the Academy, however, are members of the
American Psychological Association and as such come from backgrounds in
psychology, being graduates either of departments of educational psychology
or of psychology. Further, many psychiatrists, social workers and other
professionals who do marriage counseling have not affiliated themselves with
any professional group representing marriage counseling, *per se*. Nevertheless, these figures in the foregoing tables illustrate concretely the diversity of
the educational backgrounds from which professionals come who were
affiliated with the organization which first represented marriage counselors
in a unified body.

Diversity in Educational Background of Marriage Counselors to Continue into the Future

Stone (31), in making predictions with respect to marriage counseling as a profession, stated on December 31, 1949, that "the counselor of tomorrow will be well grounded in the anatomy and physiology, the psychology and sociology of marriage and of human relations, as well as in the skills and tools of counseling." In stating this he was not only predicting that marriage counseling would become a full-fledged profession, but alluding to the fact that future marriage counselors will continue to arrive at marriage counseling from a wide diversity of backgrounds. Certainly it is an opinion in which Groves would concur were he alive today. Rutledge (26), in a more recent predictive view of what should and probably will happen in marriage counseling, indicated that, in the future, candidates to become marriage counselors would be selected "primarily [from] those who have attained the doctorate or equivalent, and who have functioned adequately in their professions." Since he endorses most of the American Association of Marriage Counselors' functioning philosophy as to membership requirements, standards for individual practitioners, training standards, etc., it is clear that he is suggesting that future marriage counselors will continue to come from a variety of academic disciplines. In the past, the facts have been so, and in all probability marriage counselors will continue to come from a variety of academic and professional orientations.

General Description of the Academic Programs in Marriage Counseling: Introduction

In discussing the education and training of the marriage counselor there is no need for describing the various academic disciplines which are found to impinge upon marriage counseling and to be represented in the background of marriage counselors. It will be assumed that the reader has familiarity with these or can avail himself of that information elsewhere. But mention should be made of the fact that, as Groves (13) has pointed out ". . . each of these experts (professionals of varying academic backgrounds) will naturally tend to over-emphasize the value of the contribution of his profession to the training program, (but) no particular group can rightly claim a monopoly." And, as Reevy (25) has pointed out, academic discipline, insofar as it influences the thinking and activity of a man in the profession he finally enters, will continue to exert an influence on the orientation he takes toward marriage counseling. For example, he points out that the psychiatrically oriented marriage counselor will have a proclivity to handle many cases of marital conflict "from the point of view that he is actually dealing with individual neuroses which are determined by their own particular causes." There is no doubt that the academic training a professional has when he enters the specialty of marriage counseling will continue to influence his approach to the handling of premarital and marital problems. However, the purpose here is not to describe the variety of academic disciplines but to give some picture of education in marriage counseling *per se.*

Types of Education in the Academic Programs of Marital Counseling

Academic exposure to the concepts, theories and techniques of marriage counseling may take place in four general ways, by way of: (a) some mention of and education about marriage counseling in a course in counseling; (b) one or several courses in marriage counseling taken in some academic department, as psychology and sociology, usually at the graduate level; (c) part of a graduate program leading to an advanced degree with either a major or minor in marriage counseling; and (d) part of a post-doctoral program at various types of centers, institutes or foundations, with a concentration in a marriage counseling training program. The first two types of exposure are not important for discussion in the topic at hand. Perhaps the only good purpose such courses serve is in interesting some students in exploring the possibilities of becoming professionals in marriage counseling. The latter two types of experiences lead directly to the educating, indoctrinating and training of trainees for the professional field and need description in some detail.

As of a recent date (1961), eight colleges in seven universities offered programs with a major in marriage counseling, and at seven institutions a student was able to minor in the field (22). The seven universities offering a major were Brigham Young University, Teachers College, Columbia University, The University of Southern California, The University of Pennsylvania, Purdue University, Florida State University and Boston College. At two of these universities there have been recent shifts of the marriage counseling major from one academic department to another. At Teachers College the major was shifted from the Family Life Department to Counseling Psychology, and at Purdue the transfer was from Sociology to Family Life.

Courses of Study in the Academic Programs of Marriage Counseling

The areas of study offered in these programs vary somewhat in comparison to one another, but the most frequently offered courses are human development, personality theory, counseling and psychotherapeutic theory, research methods, community organizations, marriage and the family, psychology, sociology and religiocultural forces. These courses are offered in nearly all the programs with a major. Less frequently offered are anthropology, sexology and domestic relations law. Courses offered by only one or two of the programs are psychological medicine, genetics, child welfare and physical medicine. As might be expected, the same academic areas of study are available for students minoring in marriage counseling, as, if a department offers a major in marriage counseling, it will generally offer a minor.

Nearly all the programs with a major require a practicum in marriage counseling, with these practicums varying over a period of one to three years and with a range of four to twenty hours per week of marriage counseling. Almost half of these programs use off-campus agencies for supervision, and one-half require that a dissertation or project be done in the marriage counseling area.

The programs are housed within a variety of academic departments, such as education, family life education, psychology and sociology. Usually, the student must fulfill the requirements for the doctorate in the department in which he is registered. He will then earn a doctorate, as in sociology "with specialization in marriage counseling." This emphasis then means that the prospective marriage counselor is to be first "thoroughly trained in all the theory and methodology that marks a competent sociologist," psychologist, educator, etc. The would-be marriage counselor is first to be a thoroughly trained and educated psychologist, for example, and a marriage counselor in addition.

The specific course requirements in marriage and family counseling of one department of sociology will illustrate what it is that a student must study in this special area while at the same time grounding himself well in the science of sociology. As has been said, the emphasis in these academic graduate programs is to produce a scientist with mastery of theory and methodology and requisite skills in a particular science, who, in addition, pursues special work in marriage and family counseling. It is assumed that such a person will then be able to use his knowledge and skills in the basic scientific disciplipne in order to apply them to the specialized field of marriage and the family and marriage counseling.

The Ph.D. Program for Marriage and Family Counseling, Department of Sociology, University of Southern California

Specific Course Requirements

    (1) *The Seminar in the Family* and *Sociology* are required to give the student a knowledge of the history of the family and a mastery of research efforts in the analysis of the family and of marriage. In addition, any lack of understanding of psychological or sociological background must be met in additional courses.

a. *The Developmental Family Cycle*
b. *Seminar in the Family*

(2) Specific courses to give to the student specialized knowledge of marriage and family counseling are given in the following sequence of courses and are required of all persons in this specialization.

a. *Marriage and Family Counseling*
b. *Diagnosis in Marriage and Family Counseling*
c. *Diagnosis in Marriage and Family Counseling*
d. *Practicum in Marriage and Family Counseling*. This course is generally taken for four semesters and begins as soon as final screening is successfully completed. The student finishes this course when in the judgment of the staff he has successfully completed his internship which ordinarily runs for one thousand hours of supervised practice. However, the staff may decide that this is not sufficient and additional internship may be required before the degree will be granted. Internship practice is given at the marriage counseling clinic on the University campus with students and in a service setting in Los Angeles.

General Nature of the Academic Programs with Specialization in Marriage Counseling

If a doctoral program with a major in marriage counseling is under the auspices of some other department, the same general philosophy will hold; the student will be developed primarily as a psychologist if his doctorate is in psychology, as a family life educator if his degree is from a family life department. In whatever department he is matriculated, however, he will experience intensive additional study in marriage and the family, personality and human development, personality theory, counseling and counseling theory, and practicum in counseling.

Building on the core of knowledge provided within the framework of a well-established scientific discipline, and experiencing intensive work in the course of study as mentioned above, the student will have had an interdisciplinary experience, having been exposed to medical, psychological and sociological knowledge and the ways of thinking and of analyzing problems of these scientific disciplines. The hope is to steep the person in the interdisciplinary nature of this field of study.

Though the doctoral programs with a specialization in marriage counseling are few and, therefore, the opportunities are limited for students to avail themselves of such doctoral training, the existence of these programs in the form just described lends credence to the notion that marriage counselors as professionals will in the future continue to come from a variety of scientific disciplines.

Description of an Ideal Graduate Training Program in Marriage
Counseling

Rutledge (28) has written about graduate training in marriage counseling, and as a member of the 1958 Committee on Standards and Training of the American Association of Marriage Counselors is well qualified
to describe one version of an ideal doctoral program in marriage counseling. In his view the candidates who come from the sorts of disciplines
we have mentioned and who wish to enter the field of marriage counseling
—which he considers as having, since 1955 risen as a profession—should, he
declares, become expert in certain fields of knowledge. In the following
fields their knowledge should be thorough: (a) human development and
function, including the mechanisms of individual adjustment; (b) personality theory; (c) broad fields of sociology and cultural anthropology; (d)
social changes which have affected the family and the new literature referred
to currently on marriage and family relations; (e) sexology; and (f) behavioral dynamics, normal, pathological and neurotic. In certain other
subjects he needs "intensive orientation":

1. Medicine, including psychosomatic, biochemical, and psychiatric processes and procedures;
2. Genetics;
3. Domestic relations law;
4. Religiocultural forces;
5. Cultural anthropology;
6. Economics;
7. Statistical methods and research;
8. Philosophy and ethics;
9. Community forces: community organization; educational resources;
   service resources.

Included in the doctoral program should be extensive practicum experience
amounting to fifteen clock hours spent in practical work the second year (of
a 4-year program), twenty hours the third year, and the fourth year ending
in a full-time internship. The practicum training should cover the gamut
of case work-up and handling from intake to write-ups of case records, that
is, including staffing consultation about cases and therapy, with the "heart
of the process" being interviewing and supervision. The doctoral candidate
should also be required to complete a thesis as part of the doctoral requirements, and the topic should be some phase of marriage counseling. This
idealized program incorporates most of what was being referred to in the
Joint Subcommittee Report as being desirable in the professional qualifications of the counselor. This program, however, among other things, emphasizes strongly that a marriage counselor should become an expert

sexologist. It also places great stress on practicum, both emphases which are not undue. Also, this program requires much more by way of preparation for this specialty than was required of the pioneers. But the day of self-taught marriage counselors is coming to a close. This is as it should be, for, as Rutledge (26) notes, as accrediting organizations come into existence, "the tendency then is to set standards much higher than those required of the earlier members" but, as he further sees it, "that is the way a profession must develop if it and the public are to be protected."

The doctoral programs described in this section closely parallel the program outlined by Rutledge (28) and the day may well be at hand when future marriage counselors all will have met the rigors of a stern academic program and the type of practicum experience he describes.

Postdoctoral Training in Marriage Counseling

Description of Postdoctoral Training as Recommended by the American Association of Marriage Counselors

A number of postdoctoral training programs in marriage counseling exist, and these centers serve as the major source from which professional marriage counselors have been recruited. The number of these centers has always been small, the number of persons enrolled in each of the programs has been few, and so the profession of marriage counseling has not grown by leaps and bounds. Rutledge (26) noted that the American Association of Marriage Counselors numbered approximately 160 members; today the number is approximately 500.

Most of the postdoctoral training programs align themselves to the standards of the American Association of Marriage Counselors as set forth in the 1958 Committee Report on Standards for Training Centers. These standards spell out the requirements as to the type of general setting in which the training program is placed. Included is a description of what is required by way of organizational structure of the setting, what the staff of the training center should consist of, and how professional "housekeeping" as to such matters as record keeping, fees, evaluation, etc. should be conducted. Also, the Report spells out in some detail what the requirements are which are to be met by the trainee as a candidate for a program and what his program and activity should be when he is at a center.

A training center, to meet the Association's approval, must have been run for at least one or two years by a responsible governing body that has proved that it can direct and develop a service by reason of the fact that it is able to and does employ competent professional staff, has developed sound personnel practices, has a sound financial structure which reasonably guarantees a life of the program of three or more years, and is a program which is able to interpret itself to the community. The center must meet certain requirements in relation to professional staff. A multidisciplinary approach must be insured by having at least one marriage counselor on the staff (who is a member of the Association), with representatives of at least two other professions as psychiatry, psychology and social work, and by insuring that consultants of these fields are available. If consultants are not regular members of the center they must be always available or come on scheduled visits. There should be on the staff at least one person who is able to supervise the practice of marriage counseling.

Standards are specified as to the way records must be kept so that marriage counseling can be taught properly to the trainees, and to insure that trainees will be given a sufficient number and variety of cases and to evaluate how the trainees' work is progressing.

The report also sets forth conditions and standards to be met by the trainee to be eligible for a program. These standards also relate to activities and work in the program once training is in progress. The trainee must come to the center with the degree that is accepted as the usual professional degree in his field, e.g., Ph.D. in psychology or sociology, M.A. in social work. In addition to fulfilling degree requirements he must have practical experience of at least two years duration in working with people in the field of his speciality. Before being accepted in a program each candidate must have been examined in a face-to-face interview, if feasible, by members of the center to evaluate his personal qualifications. Also, he is to submit a plan in which he tells realistically how he will use the marriage counseling training he undertakes in the center.

At the training center the trainee, ideally, is to spend a full year in residence, but a residence of one academic year (nine months) is acceptable if no less than two and one-half days a week are spent at the center, during which time the candidate should spend a minimum of:

1. Six to eight hours a week in direct marriage counseling interviews with patients;
2. Six hours in classes, seminars and case conferences per week;
3. One and one-half to two hours per week in being supervised, and
4. Plenty of time to get case interviews into record form.

According to Mudd (21), three major programs of the type described above were in operation at the time she wrote: one at the Marriage Council which she directs; another at the Merrill-Palmer Institute in Detroit; and a third at the Menninger Foundation, in Topeka, Kansas. Since that date the program at the Menninger Foundation has been transformed into a program in pastoral care and training, and, according to Leslie (18), it is uncertain how much emphasis there will be on marriage counseling training.

According to Leslie (18), at the time that he wrote, three programs at the postdoctoral level had applied for and received approval when the above standards were applied. In 1964, two centers thus approved were in existence, and five additional centers were awaiting evaluation and were likely to be approved.

Brief Description of the Training Program of the University of Minnesota

The Post-Doctoral Marriage Counseling Program at the University of Minnesota, which is administered by the Family Study Center, is an example of one of these programs. In order to be eligible for the program, which is designed to provide preparation in marriage counseling for professionals without previous training in this field, a doctoral degree is required for all professionals except social workers, where an M.S.W. is acceptable.

The course offerings consist of seven seminars meeting three hours a week, as follows:

1. Three courses in psychology of marriage.
2. Three courses in marriage counseling.
3. One course in counseling psychology.

This latter course consists of practicum experiences which take place in a variety of professional settings, as the University Counseling Bureau, a family service agency, a mental hygiene clinic. Trainees are assigned to at least two different agencies during their traineeship and, in addition, participate in a three-hour seminar where their case material is discussed. This seminar has as its purpose the training of the students so that they become "more sensitive in the use of their own personalities in counseling."

In addition to pursuing study in the above seminars, a trainee must take another six units (two 3-credit-hour courses) in courses selected so as to supplement his knowledge in areas germane to marriage counseling. For these courses the trainee might select from ones such as family and child development, statistics, tests and measurements, anthropology.

During the traineeship these students are assigned for supervision to experienced supervisors in the agencies. These supervisors may be from a profession such as social work, psychiatry or psychology. Further, trainees are expected to function as members of the professional staff, participating in staff meetings and other in-service programs.

Outlook for the Future for Training and Standards in Marriage Counseling

When the matter of standards for the individual practitioner or standards for training centers in marriage counseling has appeared for consideration, the American Association of Marriage Counselors has always been the professional body that struggled with this problem. Since its existence, and perhaps because of the role it plays in credentialing practitioners and in approving training centers, there are increasing numbers of persons whose specific training is in marriage counseling, whereas before, nearly all experienced marriage counselors had come to the specialty from one of the clinical and social sciences as medicine, clinical psychology, social work, sociology (11). Some few practitioners of marriage counseling who maintain that marriage counseling is, basically, a form of psychotherapy have not been pleased about this trend (9, 14, 29). They think that only clinically trained persons are candidates for recruitment into this field, because the majority of persons coming for marriage counseling are severely disturbed people, most usually neurotic, prepsychotic or even psychotic. Few, if any, are normal persons with only a problem in marriage or with problems that can be solved by information or education. They view the personality disturbances and personality maladjustments of the patients as being the major source of marital problems and view psychotherapy as the way of relieving these persons of their difficulties. It must be said that whether or not the contention of this group is correct, were they to set up training programs, standards for accreditation and individual certification, much of what has been written in this paper would be different. For one thing, training in psychotherapy would be much more emphasized. The nature of the supervision of the trainee would also be different and along more traditional psychotherapy lines. Also, it might be that individual therapy of the trainee would be a requirement in addition to the requisite degrees.

However, it is most likely, as Rutledge (28) predicts, that the American Association of Marriage Counselors will continue to play a leading role as the "clarifying organization" both for training programs and certification standards. In this effort it may be joined by the recently formed Academy of Psychologists in Marital Counseling, Inc. which has a number of standing committees, one of which is a Committee on Training and Standards. Certainly this group, with its membership requirements of "prior membership in the American Psychological Association" and with the capacity of meeting the requirements for being titled Certified Psychologist of the State in which the candidate resides if that state has a certification law for psychologists, will take a forward looking role in the matter of standards. This group will take, also, a role in stimulating among psychologists an interest in marriage counseling. While through its efforts more psychologists will become involved in marriage counseling, members of a wide variety of "helping" professions will continue to enter marriage counseling. Marriage counseling will not be limited to one specialty, as sociology or psychology or psychotherapy. And therefore, in the revising of standards of education and training for the future, this multidisciplinary approach which was stressed by the pioneers will continue to be much in evidence.

REFERENCES

1. ALBERT, GERALD: Advanced psychological training for marriage counselors—Luxury or necessity? *Marriage and Family Living, 25:*181-183, 1963.
2. AMERICAN ASSOCIATION OF MARRIAGE COUNSELORS, COMMITTEE ON STANDARDS AND TRAINING: *Report on Standards and Training.* New York, American Association of Marriage Counselors, Inc., 1958.
3. BAILEY, MARGARET B.: Social casework training for marriage counseling. *Marriage and Family Living, 13:*166-168, 1951.
4. THE COMMITTEES MAKE THEIR CONTRIBUTIONS, REPORT OF THE JOINT SUB-COMMITTEE ON STANDARDS FOR MARRIAGE COUNSELORS OF THE NATIONAL COUNCIL ON FAMILY RELATIONS AND THE AMERICAN ASSOCIATION OF MARRIAGE COUNSELORS. *Marriage and Family Living, 11:*5-6, 1949.
5. CONSTITUTION OF THE ACADEMY OF PSYCHOLOGISTS IN MARITAL COUNSELING, INC., 1962, pp. 1-9.
6. CRIST, JOHN R.: An experiment in marriage counseling training. *Journal of Counseling Psychology, 2:*35-37, 1955.
7. CUBER, JOHN F.: *Marriage Counseling Practice.* New York, Appleton, 1948.
8. DIRECTORY OF MEMBERS: American Association of Marriage Counselors, Inc., Madison, New Jersey, 1966.
9. ELLIS, ALBERT: A critical evaluation of marriage counseling. *Marriage and Family Living, 18:*65-71, 1956.
10. ELLIS, ALBERT: Neurotic interaction between marital partners. *Journal of Counseling Psychology, 5:*24-28, 1958.
11. ELLIS, ALBERT: Marriage Counseling. In Ernest Harms and Paul Schreiber (Eds.): *Handbook of Counseling Techniques.* New York, Macmillan, 1963, pp. 147-153.
12. FOSTER, ROBERT G.: Is family counseling a profession? *Journal of Social Hygiene, 22:*125-129, 1936.
13. GROVES, ERNEST R.: Professional training for marriage and family counseling. *Social Forces, 23:*447-451, 1945.
14. HARPER, ROBERT A.: Marriage counseling: art or science? *Marriage and Family Living, 13:*164-166, 1951.
15. HARPER, ROBERT A.: Should marriage counseling become a full-fledged specialty? *Marriage and Family Living, 15:*338-340, 1953.
16. HOLLIS, FLORENCE: Evaluating marriage counseling. *Marriage and Family Living, 12:*37-38, 1950.
17. KARPF, MAURICE J.: Marriage counseling and psychotherapy. *Marriage and Family Living, 13:*169-178, 1951.
18. LESLIE, GERALD R.: The field of marriage counseling. In Harold T. Christensen (Ed.): *Handbook of Marriage and the Family.* Chicago, Rand McNally, 1964, pp. 912-943.

19. MACE, DAVID R.: What is a marriage counselor? *Bulletin of the Menninger Clinic, 18:*92-96, 1954.

20. MUDD, EMILY H.: *The Practice of Marriage Counseling.* New York, Assn. Pr., 1951.

21. MUDD, EMILY H.: Marriage counseling. In Albert Ellis and Albert Abarbanel (Eds.): *The Encyclopedia of Sexual Behavior.* New York, Hawthorn, 1961, pp. 685-695.

22. NEUBECK, GERHARD: Academic programs in marriage counseling. *Marriage and Family Living, 23:*276-278, 1961.

23. NIMKOFF, MEYER F.: Counseling students on premarital problems. A function of the sociologist. *Mental Hygiene, 19:*573-585, 1935.

24. ORMONT, LOUIS R.: The use of group psychotherapy in the training of marriage counselors and family life educators. *Marriage and Family Living, 24:*144-150, 1962.

25. REEVY, WILLIAM R.: The structure of marriage counseling. In William C. Bier and Alexander A. Schneiders (Eds.): *Selected Papers from the ACPA Meetings of 1957, 1958, 1959.* New York, Fordham, 1960, pp. 121-127.

26. RUTLEDGE, AARON L.: Marriage counseling today and tomorrow. *Marriage and Family Living, 19:*386-390, 1957.

27. RUTLEDGE, AARON L.: Discussion of Atlee L. Stroup and Paul Glasser, The orientation and focus of marriage counseling. *Marriage and Family Living, 21:*27-28, 1959.

28. RUTLEDGE, AARON R.: Developing doctoral programs in marriage counseling. *Merrill-Palmer Quarterly, 5:*125-131, 1959.

29. STOKES, WALTER R.: Discussion of Atlee L. Stroup and Paul Glasser, The orientation and focus of marriage counseling. *Marriage and Family Living, 21:*25-26, 1959.

30. STONE, ABRAHAM: Marriage education and marriage counseling in the United States. *Marriage and Family Living, 11:*38-39, 50, 1949.

31. STONE, ABRAHAM: Marriage counseling today and tomorrow. *Marriage and Family Living, 12:*39-40, 1950.

32. STROUP, ATLEE L., and GLASSER, PAUL: The orientation and focus of marriage counseling. *Marriage and Family Living, 21:*20-24, 1959.

33. UNIVERSITY OF MINNESOTA, MINNESOTA FAMILY STUDY CENTER: Brochure, Postdoctoral marriage counseling program. University of Minnesota, Minneapolis, Minnesota.

34. UNIVERSITY OF SOUTHERN CALIFORNIA, MIMEO: Graduate program for the degree of doctor of philosophy and post-doctoral training program in sociology with a specialization in family life education and marriage counseling.

Chapter 2

OBSERVATIONS ON MARRIAGE COUNSELING, FAMILY LIFE AND SEXUAL EDUCATION IN MEDICAL CURRICULA

H. L. P. RESNIK

ALTHOUGH IT IS IMPOSSIBLE to corroborate, all current estimates indicate that the majority of overt marital problems comes initially to the attention of the physician. When one adds the myriad of functional and psychosomatic complaints that are the covert presenting symptoms of marital disharmony, then the necessity for the physician's familiarity with marital problems and marriage counseling techniques becomes apparent. Witness the cartoon in which the patient asks the physician: "Did you ever think of taking me off marriage?"

Family life education involving sexual education and marriage counseling training is a relatively new emphasis in medical curricula (1, 2, 7, 8, 10, 13). The first program, which originated at the University of Pennsylvania School of Medicine fourteen years ago, was an elective course available to senior medical students to orient them to the many personal problems of their patients. Marital problems do not respect specialty practice, and their symptoms are so ubiquitous as to involve every system. Headaches, muscular pains, cardiac concerns, gastrointestinal complaints—all can result from an inability to resolve marital stresses. Although general practitioners, gynecologists, internists, pediatricians and psychiatrists (probably in that order) see more such problems, any physician may be consulted.

Inherent in the ideal physician-patient relationship is the premise that no problem is too minute or too personal to discuss. Duvall (3) has indicated that this relationship has in it some essentials for good marriage counseling (or psychotherapy) that the nonphysician counselor must work to achieve before obtaining an optimal therapeutic position. These assets are the traditional respect of the community, the readiness for help with which the patient comes to the physician, his willingness to explore such difficulties completely with the physician and the other physical healing services offered to the patient and his family. The patient's familiarity with the concept of serial visits tends to curb unrealistic and magical expectations.

ACKNOWLEDGMENT: John P. Kotis, D.S.W., who for many years has taught marriage-counseling techniques to University of Pennsylvania medical students and psychiatric residents, was helpful in discussing and critically reviewing this manuscript.

Thus, the beneficial result of marriage counseling by properly trained physicians is a more immediate and intensive confidance and willingness to dig in. The prerequisite here is "properly trained." The current medical student is rarely so trained or exposed; his physician instructor often less so. Herndon and Nash (7) asked 514 practicing North Carolina physicians to evaluate the effectiveness of their formal training in preparing them to cope with marital problems. More than half (55%) reported that little in their medical school training had been helpful, and two-thirds reported that neither their internship nor residency had further prepared them. The outstanding exceptions were obstetricians and psychiatrists, whose training focuses more on intramarital relationships.

In his clinical education, the medical student learns to obtain a history, make a diagnosis and begin an active therapy program to bring the patient's uncomfortable symptoms under control. The whole regimen is one of action, whether it be examining a throat, delivering a baby, ordering laboratory tests or writing a prescription. The student can master his own anxiety more easily by identifying with an active doing and helping approach than he can with a more passive and introspective one. Clinical psychiatry is oriented toward assisting the student with such a transition. This less active, more listening and clarifying attitude was initially applied to understanding clinical problems in terms of intrapersonal psychopathology. There has been a gradual metamorphosis of this viewpoint as we have witnessed the increasing acceptance of group and family therapies and, more recently, community therapy programs. We have been participant observers of the gradual shift from the individual alone to his interaction with his peers, his family and his society. It is only natural that, on this continuum, therapists should focus upon a particular interrelationship—with the spouse —that is called marriage therapy (6). This has a legitimate and proper place in the study of human behavior as it is taught to the medical student and physician.

STATEMENT OF THE PROBLEM

What, then, are some of the variables that influence this discrepancy between marriage counseling services requested of the physician and the paucity of training and experience with which he is prepared? I believe there are three contributory problems whose roots lie in the basic postulates of medical education. They are so deep that their denial contributes to the fantasy that present-day medical training equips the young graduate to serve as the ideal marriage counselor as well as family physician. Offered in the form of questions to be discussed in detail, they are:

1. What are the personality and character attributes that medical schools

find attractive in applicants? What effect does this have upon their potential ability as marriage counselors?

2. What personal experiences with marriage are medical students likely to have?

3. What specific training is offered to medical students and physicians to prepare them for their role as family and marital counselors?

1. The personality characteristics and sexual attitudes of medical students have been reported by Lief and his associates at Tulane University (10, 11). Obsessive-compulsive personality features characterized half the students, and were manifested by denial of emotions, intellectualism, self-control and mastery. Of course, these traits tend to be those selected and rewarded by medical schools and stand a student well in the program. This personality is also restricted in terms of its interaction with the opposite sex. It is not by chance that Doctors Casey, Kildare and Morgan work hard, romance infrequently and remain bachelors. Contrary to popular expectations, Lief found that medical students did not have the wide sexual experience that the laity believes they have. He found frequent conflicts over such questions as masturbation, virginity and premarital sexual relations. Such conflicts are rarely considered in course work material, and thereby must only become further isolated and denied (15). The Tulane studies led to a characterization of the medical student as over controlled sexually rather than promiscuous, casual and under controlled. They revealed a significant amount of anxiety about sexual matters which Lief felt interfered in a variety of ways with the students' ability to manage the sexual problems of their patients. He states that "the relative isolation from outside pursuits, his attempt to model his behavior on the image of the good doctor, and his basic personality pattern, in which a degree of emotional isolation has been present anyway, not only interfere with sexual experimentation but likewise interfere with the development of intimacy . . . [which] is inhibited unless there is *time* for meeting potential mates and developing such relationships." These attributes, although conducive to withstanding the rigors of facts, figures and procedures, are not particularly adapted to understanding patients' emotional problems. As students move to their psychiatric clinical work a wholly new frame of reference is opened to them. Some are capable of feeling and introspection; others will deny their emotions more intensively. The former will be able to incorporate the psychological model into their medical practices, while the latter only become more objective and isolated by their apparatus and ritual.

What basis does this afford for mature counseling concerning sexual matters? The faculty, products of the same selection and training milieu, often fosters this omission of highly charged material because of their own unresolved conflicts and misinformation (5). To state that sexual education of medical students is too personal and intimate for medical school curricula is to project these personal values upon the teaching situation. That they will pick this up on the wards is reminiscent of the parental attitude allowing children to learn through street experiences rather than through frank discussions with their elders. To state that the question is too controversial is to dodge the responsibility of the medical educator. To state that the student picks this up in his progress through life and especially through the four years of medical school is to deny the superspecialized and time-consuming character of medical education. Several examples come immediately to mind. There are enlightening lectures concerning the biology of menstruation without mention of the girls' traumatic discovery experiences, lectures on reproductive physiology without mention of sexual and anatomical differences in the orgasm, and lectures on genital anatomy and function without mention of masturbatory activity and its fantasied effects upon these structures.

There are also medical problems with less obvious marital counseling overtones. Consider for a moment the psychic or real effects of genital surgery upon the libido. The patient with a hysterectomy or mastectomy may have strong feelings about her integrity as a female that explain her unwillingness to expose herself to her husband. Colostomy patients and their spouse need help in terms of preferred positions for intercourse to avoid undue pressure and "dirty body" fears. Patients with severe dermatitides may also feel physically rejected by the spouse. The most frequently *un-*masked question by the recuperating coronary or hypertensive patient is that of limitation of sexual activity. Unless the physician is sensitive to his patient's embarrassment and raises the question himself, the unposed and unanswered question can be stressful. In these situations a few moments in individual and joint discussion of the interpersonal stresses raised by such an illness can be excellent prophylaxis. The responsibility of teaching such forthright confrontation with the questions of sexual information and marital enlightenment must fall within the province of the psychiatrist, who has examined his own attitudes and experiences and is more free to discuss them with students as well as his fellow physicians.

2. The second influence upon the medical student is his personal experience with marriages. These would include his parents' marriage in which he was raised, his own marriage and in-laws', if any, and his observation of his teachers' relationships in their marriages. There is no relevant information to lead us to believe that the marriages from which physicians come differ substantially from others. We do know that physicians tend to beget physicians, so that an identification process involving

attitudes toward family surely is at work here. Suffice it to say that this most important arena greatly influences role expectations for both the student's spouse and for those marriages he might be called upon to counsel.

It behooves us to examine closely the circumstances involving the other two sources of influence about which more can be said. First is the medical student's own marriage. The folklore picture is that of the conscientious student who deigns not to marry until graduation or, more frequently, until his practice is successful. He then sacrifices self, spouse and family for his patients. When the new physician struggles to conform to the public expectation, it certainly places a strain upon both his spouse and his progeny. The relationship with his children, initially hampered by the fact that he is more often a physically older father, is compounded by the fact that he is an exceedingly busy one. Often he abdicates much of his responsibility to his spouse because of this. This may make a fine dedicated physician but a poor father and husband. What marriage counseling would come from such a man?

Lief (11) reports that the percentage of those married in one medical school class increased from 20 per cent in the first year to 57 per cent at the beginning of the senior year. Presently, national figures indicate 60 to 65 per cent of medical students are married at the time of or shortly after graduation. Given the educational demands upon their time, one can only extrapolate the stresses upon the courtship and subsequently upon the marriage of these 40 per cent. The physician's wife and her attitudes have also been studied (4). Unmet dependency needs and unfulfilled oedipal rescue expectations are frequent. Role identification struggles follow the working wife upon whom the student is ambivalently dependent. The intrusion of children, whether planned or accident, wreaks havoc with the student's study schedule and sows the seeds of conflict over responsibility to medical education or to family. Such stresses do not promote the most fertile soil from which harmonious marriages spring. Many are successful despite such stresses, but it is obvious that the platitude that the physician is the best marriage counselor, at least on the basis of his own marital and courtship experience, is untrue (9). He may be in the optimum position, but his personal credentials may greatly bias his clinical efficacy.

The last aspect to be considered is the young physician's identification with those more advanced than he in the medical hierarchy. Working beside the intern in the emergency room, assisting the resident obstetrician at a delivery, scrubbing with the surgeon or making a house call with the pediatrician in the early morning hours all tend to reinforce the image of medical practice first and the marriage and family second. The Hippocratic oath to many suggests service at the expense of sacrifice. To the uncritical the system tends to perpetuate itself. The selfless surgeon or the denying obstetrician may be utilizing his medicine to flee an unhappy marriage. The student sees only the externals and identifies with these.

Certainly, I am not advocating the elimination of such training experiences, but I feel strongly that the student and his wife should witness the physician's marriage under other circumstances also. He should be invited into the home of his medical preceptor. In small groups, students, residents and their wives should be encouraged to participate in discussions of marriage and medicine with the physician and his wife. Here will be one of the best learning experiences and most solid foundations for future marriage counseling with patients. The insight one derives from evaluating one's own role and responsibility in a marital relationship surpasses any didactic lecture. Although any perceptive physician could lead these discussions, the psychiatrist skilled in psychodynamics, group process and marriage counseling is the natural leader. One trusts that he has utilized these skills to relate to a wife who must be involved in this process also. I am convinced that the medical wife would like to share some aspects of her husband's professional training. This affords us an ideal opportunity and exemplary learning situation. A program such as I will outline below evolved from such observations at the University of Pennsylvania. An elective for senior medical students rapidly by student request became an elective for the student and his wife, fiancée or girlfriend. Saturday morning lectures were preceded by breakfast and transportation together and were often followed by lunch and continued discussions with other couples. This leads us naturally to our last question.

3. In their survey, Herndon and Nash (7) indicated that few physicians had any marriage counseling training in their undergraduate or postgraduate programs. In 1952, the first formal course dealing with love, marriage and sexuality was offered to medical students by the University of Pennsylvania School of Medicine. This course, and the establishment of the Department of Psychiatry's Division of Family Study and its clinical service, the Marriage Council of Philadelphia, were the results of the insight and administration of Dr. Kenneth E. Appel and Dr. Emily H. Mudd (2, 12). The evolution of the program is detailed elsewhere (13), but, briefly, there are separate orientations to the medical student, to the psychiatric resident and to the interdisciplinary doctoral program candidate. The student program consists of a senior lecture elective entitled Family Attitudes, Sexual Behavior and Marriage Counseling, a one-way mirror counseling case presentation and discussion for all students as part of their outpatient psychiatry clinic experience, and a research elective in Family Life and Marriage. The psychiatric resident elective program involves supervised clinical instruction one day weekly for six months to one year. The doctoral candidates in marriage counseling taking a program in the Graduate School of

Education include teachers, ministers, school counselors and physicians. The latter group merits special attention, for it is the only source of supervised marriage-counseling trained graduate physicians, other than cursory exposures in brief psychotherapy courses for graduate physicians.

The program at the Bowman Gray School of Medicine (14) embodies classroom instruction in the first three years and diagnostic experience in the third and fourth years. Premarital and marital counseling are available for students and house officers. As yet, a supervised clinical program has not been offered. Other medical school curricula offering different programs are gradually evolving (8).

A SUGGESTED PROGRAM MODEL

I believe a synthesis of the Pennsylvania and Bowman Gray approaches would serve as a model for marriage counseling instruction within the medical school curriculum. It should be administered by a discrete marriage counseling unity within the department of psychiatry and should have direct liaison with the other departments in the medical school and university.

1. For the medical student.
    a. Academic program.
        Second year—the family unit as a clinical experience.
        Third year—lecture and case material.
        Fourth year—supervised clinical experience.
    b. Personal experience.
        Fourth year—a series of four to six small group meetings of married students and their wives, and of single students with their fiancées or girlfriends to be conducted at the home of an experienced faculty member and his wife.
2. For the intern and resident.
    a. Presently, the psychiatric and probably the gynecologic residents are most frequently aware of marital problems. An ongoing case managed by a house officer and a group discussion led by a psychiatrist and/or marriage counselor (the former is preferred to reinforce the medical identity) should be held biweekly and made available to all specialty groups.
    b. The same psychiatrist and/or marriage counselor should meet with interested house staff and their spouses with the generally stated aim to discuss "doctor-wife problems." One will speedily learn what direct marriage counseling is needed for this group! It is certainly an important adjunct to the inevitable wives' defensive groupings (Hospital Widows, Wives Anonymous, The

Physicians' Wives' Club or whatever you will call them) which only tend to reinforce the ladies' isolation, masochism, denial of dependency and loneliness. Some of this is normal coping with a difficult situation. However, the physician-husband should be involved and not allowed to hide behind his Hippocratic shield.

3. For the practicing physician. More focus on marital problems and sex information in the increasing numbers of intensive courses on short-term psychotherapy currently being offered to physicians through existing clinical resources. Any such program will need as instructors physicians with accepted marriage counseling training. The American Association of Marriage Counselors has set forth rigid clinical and educative criteria for their more than five hundred members. Currently, there are only twenty-nine physicians residing in only nine states who have qualified for membership. Clearly, these small numbers must speak out in an attempt to have formal marital counseling lectures and demonstrations incorporated into medical school curricula.

REFERENCES

1. APPEL, K. E.; GOODWIN, H. M.; WOOD, H. P., and ASKREN, E. L.: Training in psychotherapy: The use of marriage counseling in a university teaching clinic. *Amer. J. Psychiat., 117*:709-12, 1961.
2. APPEL, K. E.; MUDD, E. H., and ROCHE, P.: Medical school electives on family attitudes, sexual behavior and marriage counseling. *Amer. J. Psychiat., 112*:36-40, 1955.
3. DUVALL, E. M.: The physician as marriage and family counselor. *Western J. Surg., 62*:443-52, 1954.
4. EVANS, J. L.: Psychiatric illness in the physician's wife. *Amer. J. Psychiat., 122*:159-63, 1965.
5. GREENBANK, R. K.: Are medical students learning psychiatry? *Penn. Med. J., 64*:989-92, 1961.
6. HALEY, J.: *Strategies of Psychotherapy.* New York, Grune, 1963.
7. HERNDON, C. N., and NASH, E.: Pre-marriage and marriage counseling. *J.A.M.A.* 180 (No. 5) : 395-401, 1962.
8. KLEMER, R.: *Counseling in Marital and Sexual Problems. A Physician's Handbook.* Baltimore, Williams & Wilkins, 1965.
9. LEWIS, J. M.: The Doctor and His Marriage. *Texas J. Med., 61*:615-19, 1965.
10. LIEF, H. I.: Sex education for medical students and doctors. *Pacif. Med. Surg., 73* (1A) :52-58, 1965.
11. LIEF, H. I.: Sexual attitudes and behavior of medical students: Implications for medical practice. In E. Nash, L. Jessner, and D. W. Abse (Eds.) : *Marriage Counseling in Medical Practice.* Chapel Hill, U. of N. C., 1964.
12. MUDD, E. H., and KRICH, A.: *Man and Wife.* New York, Norton, 1957.

13. Mudd, E. H.: Marriage counseling instruction in the School of Medicine Curriculum University of Pennsylvania. In *Marriage Counseling in Medical Practice*. Chapel Hill, U. of N. C., 1964, pp. 319-327.

14. Nash, E.; Jessner, L., and Abse, D. W.: *Marriage Counseling in Medical Practice*. Chapel Hill, U. of N. C., 1964.

15. Woods, S. M., and Natterson, J.: Medical education and sexual attitudes. Paper presented at American Psychiatric Association, 122nd Annual Meeting, May, 1966.

Chapter 3

MARITAL PROBLEMS AND MARITAL ADJUSTMENT*

EMILY H. MUDD *with* HILDA M. GOODWIN

What Are the Most Frequent Problems That Disturb the Functioning of a Marriage but Do Not Necessarily Lead to Divorce?

PโROBLEMS OF MANY DIFFERENT kinds may be cited as the immediate cause of marital difficulties—money, sexual maladjustment, inlaws, children, infidelity, etc. However, the problems essentially complained of fall within the broad category of lack of consideration by one spouse for the other. The lack of consideration may be in the handling of money—selfishness about money or failure to support; it may be in the area of affection and sex—failure to respond or perform adequately sexually or undue demand or withholding; it may be in the area of work or recreation—overactivity which leaves out the spouse or laziness in meeting responsibilities; it may be in ineffectual communication or complete absence of attempt to let the partner know what is going on. But, essentially, the basic complaint is that a person fails to consider his spouse's feelings, needs, values and goals, or acts in disregard of them.

Failure to meet the other partner's preconceived ideas of how a husband or wife should act, and failure to agree with his standards of behavior or value systems, i.e., the idea that the other is "different," with difference interpreted as "undesirable," may cause misunderstanding and difficulty. Any difference from one partner's preconceived ideas of how his spouse should function in marriage may be regarded as a failure to perform satisfactorily or in a socially acceptable way and may be considered an affront by the other partner.

How Can Marriage Partners Adjust to Differing Temperaments, Desires for Socializing, Values, Ideals, etc.?

Basic to adjusting to different temperaments, desires, values and ideals is an acceptance by each partner of the right of the other person to be different, and a willingness to work out a compromise in terms of the long-run welfare of the marital unit—rather than a demand that one's own expectations and happiness come first.

For example: Mrs. Brown may desire to continue with her career after

---

*Reprinted with authors' permission from *The Encyclopedia of Mental Health*. New York, Watts, 1963, pp. 965-978.

marriage because her feelings of achievement and self-worth are closely tied in with her career. Mr. Brown may feel that his wife's first responsibility is to her home and children, and may expect her to discontinue her career. It is quite possible that a solution satisfactory to both can be arrived at through part-time work, with Mr. Brown lending some support and help with the home and children. Mutual willingness to consider the feelings of the other may not resolve the conflict, but it makes for an environment where a resolution of conflict is possible. There are several elements involved in resolving a conflict: first, ability to communicate with each other with the expectation that the communication will be listened to and be understood; second, ability and willingness of at least one partner to make concessions; third, understanding and support by each partner of the other's efforts to make a change in expectation and behavior.

How Can Jealousy Become a Problem in Marriage?

The concept of monogamous marriage is emphasized in the ethics of Christianity and Judaism and is reflected in the laws of the United States. Therefore, when either partner steps over the culturally prescribed limits of marital fidelity, it is to be expected that anxiety and resentment on the part of the other partner will ensue. This anxiety or resentment is or might be interpreted as jealousy.

Jealousy not founded on fact is the outward manifestation of a deep insecurity of the jealous partner in his or her sexual role and in his or her concept of self, especially in the capacity to evoke and keep the affection and fidelity of the other partner. Often this leads to attempts to limit or control the behavior of the partner with inevitable hostility, doubt and fear in the jealous spouse, so that a destructive spiral may be set up between the partners.

Is Selection of Friends (Separate and Mutual) Often a Problem in Marriage? How Should Husband and Wife Attempt a Solution?

Selection of friends may, but need not, be a problem in marriage. Marriage essentially links two networks of friends, and marriage partners with ability to establish good personal relations gradually get to know each other's friends. In general, in compatible marriages, people who appeal to one partner appeal to the other partner also. The sexes differ substantially in their interests, and each partner has need for both individual and joint friendships. Separate friendships and activities threaten a marriage only when they absorb too great a proportion of a person's leisure and interest. The question is one of balance. Difficulties may arise when either partner, out of personal insecurity, feels threatened by the other's friendships, or if there exists a misconception about "togetherness" in marriage, leaving no room for diverse interests and activities. The mutually held group of friends may be enlarged as each tries to share his individually held friends with the other, and through joint activity in community and church groups.

How Can the Division and Spending of Money Become Problems? How Can Husband and Wife Adjust to This Problem?

Individuals develop their attitudes toward money from their early home associations, and money can mean very different things to different persons. To one person the accumulation of money may represent emotional, as well as practical, security; to another the control of money may represent power; and to yet another it may reflect dominance in the family, etc. If the individuals' attitudes are relatively healthy, money problems may be solved by setting up a mutually acceptable budget and bank account that represent the operating funds of the new unit—the marriage. Whether the money is in a joint bank account or in separate accounts, and how the various types of financial indebtedness are handled, are unimportant provided the method is mutually agreeable and practical. If one system proves impractical, open-mindedness by both partners toward revision is of great assistance to marital harmony.

How Can Either Individual's Dependence on, or Dislike of, Certain Relatives Become a Problem?

A wife's overdependence on her parents may provoke frustration for her husband, who may feel that decisions are never made by himself and his wife, but by the wife and her parents. If this situation continues, anger is aroused because the wife seems to care more for her parents than for her husband and the marriage. A similar situation may arise between a husband and his parents. If a marriage is to be successful, it is essential that the partners separate themselves from the child role in relation to their parents and accept an independent, adult role, both in their marriage and with their parents. In some situations where a person has remained dependent on his parents, therapeutic help may be necessary for him to achieve reasonable independence.

However, it is also important for the small nuclear family to have connections with the larger kinship groups, and for each partner to have some willingness to accept and adjust to, and at times even to implement, the need of the other to maintain adult contact with the larger family groups.

In *Modern Introduction of the Family*, edited by Norman W. Bell and Ezra F. Vogel,[1] the nuclear family is defined as "a structural unit composed, as an ideal type, of a man and woman joined in a socially recognized union and their children. Normally, the children are the biological offspring of the spouses, but as in the case of adopted children in our society, they need not necessarily be biologically related. This social unit we shall call the nuclear family or simply the family."

Which Books Do You Recommend for Information on the Problems of Adjustment to Marriage?

Listed below are a few books that have been helpful in our work at the Marriage Council in Philadelphia.[2] There are many other excellent books dealing with various aspects of preparation for, and adjustment in, marriage in any well-stocked public or university library:

1. *Facts of Life and Love,* by Evelyn M. Duvall;
2. *Toward a Successful Marriage,* by James A. Peterson;
3. *Being Married,* by Evelyn M. Duvall and Reuben L. Hill;
4. *Love and Marriage* (revised edition) , by F. Alexander Magoun;
5. *The Happy Family,* by John Levy and Ruth Monroe;
6. *Man and Wife:* A Source Book on Family Attitudes, Sex Behavior, and Marriage Counseling, edited by Emily H. Mudd and Aron Krich;
7. *Sex Life in Marriage,* by Oliver M. Butterfield;
8. *Sexual Harmony in Marriage,* by Oliver M. Butterfield;
9. *Marriage Manual,* by Hannah M. and Abraham Stone;
10. *Sex Attitudes in the Home,* by Ralph G. Eckert;
11. *The Dynamics of Aging,* by Ethel Sabin Smith.

Is It Possible To Estimate an Individual's Readiness (including maturity of outlook) for Marriage?

The most important considerations that have to do with readiness for marriage are the degree of psychological maturity attained by each partner, plus the way in which each individual's needs, temperaments, social background and values mesh with those of the intended mate, according to James A. Peterson in *Toward a Successful Marriage.*[3] Physical health and the adequacy of approach to love and affection are also important aspects of readiness. There are definite criteria of maturity that may be utilized in assessing readiness to assume an adult role in marriage. Inventories and projective tests for ascertaining the degree of maturity of an individual have been prepared by various authors. One such outline, in *Marriage for Moderns,* edited by Henry A. Bowman,[4] has specific reference to maturity for and in marriage. An individual may utilize this outline to study his own degree of maturity and that of his intended mate. However, it is our conviction, based on clinical experience, that the attitudes, values and goals, and the abilities, skills and daily performance level of each individual concerned (as these interrelate with the partner) , are of major significance.

What May Cause Major Crises in Marriage and When Are They Most Likely To Occur?

What may precipitate a major crisis in one marriage may be handled adequately by the partners in another. The first year of marriage is a year of new adjustments for both partners, and, depending upon their maturity and temperament, may be completed without undue stress, or, on the other hand, may foment serious problems. The largest number of divorces is reported in the first year of marriage, the next largest number in the third and fifth years. Adjustment to the role of parent, in addition to that of husband and wife, imposes additional strain. How severe the strain and whether or not the birth of a child may be disrupting to the marriage depend upon the marital stability of the couple and their readiness for the responsibilities of parenthood.

What Are the Special Marital Problems of the Working Woman?

Special marital problems of the working woman depend in the main upon the individual situation and the attitudes of the husband and wife concerned. Generally speaking, questions of overfatigue, pressure and strain from attempting to carry two functions, and resentment toward necessity for employment, might all be anticipated. In a study of working wives by Artie Rianopulos and Howard E. Mitchell ("Marital Disagreement in Working Wife Marriages as a Function of Husband's Attitude Toward Wife's Employment," as elaborated in *Marriage and Family Living, XIX* (4), November, 1957),[5] it was found that the wife's working became a problem only when the husband did not approve. When both the husband and wife approved, the fact of the wife working in itself did not constitute a problem. Eleanor E. Marroby, in a study, "The Effects Upon Children of Their Mothers' Outside Employment,"[6] concludes: "Some mothers should work while others should not, and the outcome for the children depends upon many factors other than the employment itself."

What Are Likely To Be the Problems of a Marriage Between Individuals of Different Religions? Races? Economic Levels? Age Levels? Educational Levels?

Marriage requires an adjustment of the feelings, attitudes, behavior, ideas and value systems of the two individuals. Anything that creates a great discrepancy in any one of these factors may intrinsically place greater stress on the adaptive resources of the partners.

People are not just individuals—they are members of groups—and in any marriage between individuals of different groups both intrapersonal and interpersonal pressures exist. The strength of the pressures will vary from individual to individual, depending upon the degree of identification each partner has with his own group. In some situations the inner ties may be minimal, and only external or social involvements conflict; in other situations the outer group involvement may be minimal, and the inner identification strong. Partners of divergent backgrounds bring conflicting values, expectations and behavior into marriage and hence have less common ground on which to build. More consistent effort is therefore necessary to establish a mutual basis of understanding and functioning. When troubles arise, the sense of difference magnifies the difficulty. Insofar as the partners remain tied to their own groups, the solidarity of the marriage is threatened. When children come, the question arises as to which group they shall be reared in, and any resolution involves either compromise or renunciation by one partner. "Mixed marriages" are vulnerable to all the usual inlaw problems, and their resolution is more difficult.

In interclass marriages, it is usually the woman who marries upward. Studies have shown that this type of marriage is, on the whole, less successful than homogamous ones. However, when the wife holds the higher position, an even greater strain is placed on the marriage, because the wife tends to assume the husband's social position in the community. The husband may feel a constant strain to "get ahead," may resent financial assistance from his wife's family and may feel both inadequate and inferior, and thus handicap his capacity to cope successfully with career and work situations.

Mixed marriage involves greater psychological strain; and the greater the disparity between group identifications, the greater the potential problems and effort necessary to bring about a satisfactory adjustment.

How Does Great Friction in Marriage Affect the Child?

A child's basic need is for a feeling of love and security. Where parents are continually quarreling, the child's sense of security may be adversely affected, both by fear of the breakup of the home and because of divided loyalties. It is difficult for a child to live in a situation where he needs the support and affection of both parents, and where one parent may try to use him against the other or may try to secure his loyalty, with the result that he feels guilty toward the other parent.

How Does One Parent Sometimes Use a Child As a Weapon Against the Other Parent?

Parents who are having marital difficulties are often adept in mobilizing a child's anger or fear against the other parent. Frequently, a parent may suggest to a child that the other partner will leave home unless the child is a "good" child or behaves in a particular way. Obviously, if more trouble ensues, the child thinks he is responsible for the difficulty and feels guilty. One parent may subtly indicate that the other parent is "cranky," "mean," "stingy," etc., with an idea that the child will, therefore, turn to him or her for affection and loyalty. Children may be used by the mother as a means of extorting additional financial outlays from the father. If the father refuses or is unable to meet the demand, the deprivation to the child of whatever he may have wished may be attributed to the father. Often a child is threatened with the displeasure of the absent parent if he does not comply with some request or if he misbehaves. If separation or divorce threatens, one parent may use contact with the child as a means of controlling the other's actions and decisions.

Could Some Problems in Marriage Be Eliminated if Women Were To Marry Men Younger Than Themselves?

In his studies of the sexual behavior of the human male and female, Alfred C. Kinsey[7] indicates that the peak of orgastic sexual outlet occurs at very different ages for the two sexes—in the male usually between the ages of eighteen and twenty-two, and in the female between the ages of thirty and thirty-seven. Thus, it might appear that a woman in her thirties would have a better sexual adjustment with a man between the ages of eighteen and twenty-two. There are, however, many other factors to consider in marriage. Culturally and traditionally, it has been the accepted custom for men to marry women considerably younger than themselves. This partially had its origin in the days when it was necessary for a man to establish himself economically before he could assume the responsibilities of marriage. It was also related to the higher death rate of women in past generations during their childbearing years, with the consequence that a man might have had several wives. There is a trend at present for couples to marry within a narrower range of age difference—usually from two to five years— with the male the older. In terms of present values held for marriage— companionship, affection, children and a way of life in the community— couples tend to choose mates within the same general age decade. Nowadays, the acceptance of marriages in which the man receives financial help from his parents or his wife enables men to marry at a younger age.

Why Does It Seem That Problems Begin When One Individual in a Marriage Becomes Famous or Successful? Does One Individual Sometimes "Outgrow" the Other?

There are many marriages in which one partner becomes famous, and the other partner adjusts to the situation and may in fact be one of the bulwarks that enables the "famous" partner to achieve and function. In some instances the achievements of one partner may enable the other to bask with comfort and delight in reflected glory. In other situations one partner may grow beyond the other in achievement, learning or sophistication, and the difference creates discomfort and unhappiness for both. Where the wife outstrips the husband it is obvious that, in a culture which is still close to the patriarchal, the feelings of competition and frustration would in most instances be more intense than where the husband outshines his wife. Obviously, there are differences in capacity to learn and to achieve, differences in motivation and, frequently, in the opportunity to grow and change. The adjustment made, in each instance, would depend upon the individuals involved; it might be to separate, to divorce or to accept the difference and live with it, perhaps even to enjoy it.

Do Marriages Have a Better Chance for Success Where the Partners Have Distinctly Different Personalities and Interests Rather Than Where There is a Similarity of Personalities?

In all societies married couples are found to have many characteristics in common, particularly those status characteristics that are structurally central in that society. Marriages are likely to be more stable if the partners have somewhat the same conception of the role of each in the marriage as well as similarity of personality characteristics and interests.

Each person brings to marriage a need for maintaining his own identity and a need for a complementary relationship with another. Where there are great differences in personality and interests, the problems involved in adjustment to each other are inevitably greater and demand more of each partner than in a marriage where like interests and like values lend themselves to easier adjustment and complementarity. A study, "Impressions of Personality as a Function of Marital Conflict," in the *Journal of Abnormal and Social Psychology, 47* (2), April, 1952, undertaken by Malcolm G. Preston, William L. Peltz, Emily H. Mudd and Hazel B. Froscher, indicates that when partners in marriage each feel that they love each other and feel that the marriage is happy, they rate their partner (on a list of personality characteristics) as more like themselves than do partners who rate themselves as unhappy in their marriage. This happens whether or not the self-ratings of each partner are more or less similar. It can therefore be seen that realistic differences of the kind referred to in this question might tend to promote and sustain stress and even conflict.

Is a Marriage Headed for Trouble if One Partner is Psychologically Dependent on the Other?

There is no one pattern of marriage that is essential for a satisfying union. There is reason to believe that the choice of a marital partner represents the merging of many needs and motives. When a person approaches marriage, he is likely to select a person who seems to meet his needs on both an unconscious and a conscious level. The quality of satisfaction in a marriage is closely related to this meeting of each other's needs. Whether the marriage can weather the adjustments necessary when children arrive depends to a large extent on how each partner has been able to develop into a more independent individual, to readjust to the changed configuration of the family, and yet to maintain needs that the other partner is able to meet to some satisfactory degree.

Is a Marriage Due for Trouble if One Partner Insists on Complete Responsibility or if One Partner Refuses To Take Part in the Responsibilities of the Marriage?

It would seem improbable that a marriage of this kind could exist without conflict and disintegration. Marriage assumes a certain mutuality of satisfactions, duties, functions and responsibilities. If one partner insists on assuming complete responsibility for decisions, budgeting, child-spacing, etc., it demotes the other person to the role of an object; he is no longer an equally participating adult. At this point the partner thus treated has no opportunity to express his individual needs and preferences within the marriage relationship and is faced with acceptance of the role of a child or with frustration and conflict. Conversely, if a person refuses to take part in the responsibilities of marriage, he or she is functioning at the level of the child who expects to be cared for and wants to make no decisions. This, too, almost inevitably creates anger and frustration for the partner.

Do Late Marriages Create Fewer Problems Than Early Ones?

This is a relative question; "late" would need to be more clearly defined. There is evidence that in very early marriages, i.e., teen-age as compared with those entered into a few years later, the partners tend to show less understanding and less sympathy for each other's needs and problems. In American culture, persons under twenty are also more likely to be both emotionally and economically partially dependent on their parents. This then involves divided loyalties and involvement of six rather than merely two persons in the marriage—surely a complicating factor in adjustment. William J. Goode, in *After Divorce*,[8] found that the average marrying age for the divorced group was substantially younger than that of the "married once only" segment of the general population.

What Are Likely To Be the Problems in a Marriage Where One Partner Is Dedicated Almost Exclusively to his Work, and his Family Comes Second in his Time, Interest and Consideration?

The problems that arise in this type of situation depend, to a large extent, on whether or not the man's conception of his role in the marriage coincided or conflicted with the conception held by his wife. One of the cultural values in the United States is a demand for activity that results in accomplishments. In the medical, religious and scientific fields, a work dedication that places the family in a secondary position is quite common, and members of the family tend to recognize this as a universal factor and to adjust to it. This implies a value orientation to, and identification with, the particular kind of work by both the man and the members of his family. In other situations where career and business pressures are great and the burden of maintaining the marriage and rearing the children falls on a wife whose value orientation and identifications are dissimilar, anger and frustration often result. The particular problems depend both on the personalities involved and the specific situation. Loneliness, frustration, feelings of deprivation, anger at too much one-sided family responsibility, difficulty in the management and discipline of teen-age children, difficulty for the children in relating comfortably to masculine or (if the mother works) feminine figures could arise.

What Problems Are Likely To Arise When a Man's Work Takes Him Away From Home Frequently and for Long Periods?

The problems of any married couple must be understood in terms of their mutuality and the interdependence of the particular family-role adaptations. The values sought in marriage are satisfaction of sexual needs, reciprocity of emotional and social companionship, the sharing of authority and a division of labor.

Emotional loneliness, lack of companionship, individualized and overburdening responsibility, as well as the unavailability of the sexual partner, may all create dissatisfactions and conflicts. Vulnerability to involvement with persons outside the marriage is inevitably increased. Boredom for the man who must spend long hours in the impersonal atmosphere of hotels, and for the woman confined to the home with young children, is an added problem. Each couple must find individual solutions. If the couple together faces frankly the difficulties and deprivations inherent in the situation for each one, emotional sharing and understanding can do much to mitigate the situation. Decisions regarding independent social activity should be made jointly and be based on consideration of each other's feelings and attitudes. When possible, the man might arrange to take his wife with him on trips to conventions, etc. to reinforce their relationship as husband and wife.

What Are Likely To Be the Problems of the Career Girl Who Marries and Gives Up Her Job?

"Career" girl implies that much of the woman's sense of self and identity has been found within her career, and that one of her basic values has been in accomplishment in her career. Moving into marriage and giving up her job will mean a period of major adjustment, because she will be faced with a reevaluation and reintegration of what constitutes her value and worth as an individual. In addition, she will be faced with increased household tasks —probably working alone—that often appear to carry less long-range challenge and satisfaction. Problems of boredom and loneliness and of the "waste" of education are frequent complaints heard from this group of young women as they attempt to adjust to becoming wives and homemakers. Actually, contemporary conditions indicate that the choice between marriage or a congenial career is no longer necessary. Historically there has been a dramatic increase in employment of women outside of their homes, usually on the basis of economic need. Robert O. Blood, Jr., in his book, *Marriage*,[9] states that the following is the emerging life-cycle pattern of the employment of married women:

1. Nearly all wives are likely to work after marriage until their first pregnancy;
2. Very few mothers of preschool children (mostly hardship cases of of severe economic necessity) will work even part-time away from their children;
3. When the last child enters first grade, employment will rise sharply and continue to increase until the last child leaves home or reaches adulthood, when employment will reach a second peak.

The impact of the wife's employment on the marital satisfactions of both husband and wife therefore depends on the balance between: accruing gains, in terms of less financial strain; losses, in terms of housekeeping and mothering time; and changes in division of labor within the home. All these variables are influenced drastically by whether the husband's attitude is favorable or unfavorable toward his wife's employment.

What Are Likely To Be the Reasons That Either Partner Would Seek Outside Sexual Interests?

It has come to be an accepted fact that there is a two-way cause-and-effect relationship between sex and the rest of marriage. Success in marriage does not rest on a satisfactory sexual relationship alone, but on many other factors. It is hoped that in marriage a couple may be able to integrate the sexual and nonsexual aspects of their relationship into a deepened sense of belonging and security, which involves the whole of their personalities. The capacity to do this depends not only on the reciprocal relationship between the partners but also on the relative state of maturity of each partner. Prior to marriage, being in love is a state of mind that tends to idealize and overestimate the loved one, to overlook or minimize faults or flaws, and to satisfy the need we all have for an uncritical and all-embracing love. When the couple goes on into marriage, reality must be faced, and, unless each partner has the capacity for integrity and responsibility in the handling of frustration and the acceptance of differences, fidelity in all areas is threatened.

Cooking, cleaning and financial responsibility, are a far cry from the early illusions of being "in love," and, as irritation, dissatisfaction and frustrations increase, there may be a search for another "all-giving" love. In every marriage critical times will come to threaten the relationship. As the man's energies are taken up more with his job and a woman's attention with childbearing and caring for children, one or the other may feel deprived or rejected, or as if he or she does not matter. Unresolved immature longings become more insistent, and either partner may seek a relationship outside of marriage hoping to find a "more understanding" or "more giving" partner. Usually this kind of behavior has its roots, not in mature capacity for sexuality, but in the areas of unmet childhood needs for love, receptivity and dependency. In marriages where one partner has a mature capacity for love and the other has remained at a childish stage of development, such outside interests are more likely to occur. Sometimes they are absorbed within the marriage framework with resultant difficulties. Sometimes they lead to the decision to end the marriage.

Why Does Either Partner in a Marriage Seek Excessive Outside Interests?

When marriage partners seek excessive outside activity, it might reasonably be assumed that they are finding their life together unsatisfactory, and are using this form of activity as an escape and essentially as an "emotional divorce." In attempting to understand the reasons for the difficulty, it would be necessary to assess the particular marriage and the individual partners. It could be that either partner (or both) is finding continuous dissatisfaction in the marriage, but that neither wants to run the risk of actual dissolution because the relationship is of some real or potential value.

What Factors in Marriage Could Cause the Partners To Reach the Point Where "They No Longer Have Anything To Say To Each Other"?

Breakdown of communication between partners is frequently one of the first symptoms of a disturbed marital relationship. Communication is not only an exchange or interchange of thoughts and ideas. Communication that brings about true understanding conveys not just thoughts, but the feelings behind the thoughts. To be aware of someone else's feelings, we must be able to recognize our own and have the courage to discuss them.

In every marriage there are anger-provoking situations. Resentments grow and build. When, because of fear of anger, fear of ability to control anger, or hopelessness in making the other understand, anger is repressed, denied or blocked off, it gradually builds a wall between the two partners, so that each essentially feels he or she has nothing to say to the other.

BIBLIOGRAPHY

1. BELL, NORMAN W., and VOGEL, EZRA F. (Eds.) : *Modern Introduction of the Family*. The Free Press of Glencoe, Illinois, 1960.
2. *Books Recommended*
    Facts of Life and Love for Teenagers, Duvall, Evelyn M., Association Press, New York, 1956.
    Toward a Successful Marriage, Peterson, James A., Scribner's Sons, New York, 1960.
    Being Married, Duvall, Evelyn M., Hill, Reuben L., Association Press, New York, 1960.
    Love and Marriage, Magoun, F. Alexander, Harper & Brothers, New York, 1948.
    The Happy Family, Levy, John and Monroe, Ruth, Alfred A. Knopf, New York, 1938.
    Man and Wife, Mudd, Emily H., and Krich, Aron, W. W. Norton & Co., Inc., New York, 1957.
    Sex Life in Marriage, Butterfield, Oliver M., Emerson Books, New York, 1953.
    Sexual Harmony in Marriage, Butterfield, Oliver M., Emerson Books, New York, 1953.
    Marriage Manual, Stone, Hannah M., and Abraham, Simon & Schuster, New York, 1935.
    Sex Attitudes in the Home, Eckert, Ralph G., Association Press, New York, 1956.
    The Dynamics of Aging, Smith, Ethel Sabin, W. W. Norton & Co., Inc., New York, 1956.

    — — — — —

3. PETERSON, JAMES A.: *Toward a Successful Marriage*. New York, Scribner Sons, 1960.
4. BOWMAN, HENRY A. (Ed.) : *Marriage for Moderns*. New York, McGraw-Hill Book Co., 1942.
5. RIONOPULOS, ARTIE, and MITCHELL, HOWARD: Marital disagreement in working wife marriages. *Marriage and Family Living, XIX:4,* November, 1957.
6. MARROBY, ELEANOR E.: The effects upon children of their mother's outside employment, Chapter 41. In: Bell, Norman W., and Vogel, Ezra F., (Eds.), *Modern Introduction of the Family*. The Free Press of Glencoe, Illinois, 1960.

7. Kinsey, Alfred C., *et al.*: *Sexual Behavior of the Human Male and Sexual Behavior of the Human Female.* Philadelphia, W. B. Saunders & Co., 1953.
8. Goode, William J.: *After Divorce.* The Free Press of Glencoe, Illinois, 1956.
9. Blood, Robert O., Jr.: *Marriage.* The Free Press of Glencoe, Illinois, 1962.

Chapter 4

THE PSYCHIATRIC IMPLICATIONS OF LOVE*

JAMES A. BRUSSEL

Whether in the limited sense of the sex act or in the lofty sense of reverence for a Supreme Being, the human phenomenon called "love" has captured the imagination of poets, philosophers, moralists and even scientists from time immemorial. The concept of love has been oversweetened by advice-to-the-lovelorn columnists and soured by cynical essayists. Perhaps more than any other word in our language, "love" has suffered from misuse, as in such ridiculous phrases as "I *love* strawberries" and "Don't you just *love* Brahms?" Principally, though, it suffers from a multiplicity of meanings: sexual excitation and copulation; the mating experience; the total relationship between husband and wife; the feeling of parent for child and child for parent, sibling and other family relations; love of one's neighbor or fellowman (so-called "brotherly love") ; and the love of God— although these do not exhaust the list.

The English language is noted for its ambiguities, and there is often confusion between the original meaning of a term and its popular connotation. In psychiatric usage, love is ordinarily associated with heterosexual adjustment, since this usually signifies that the individual has reached maturity. There can be little argument against the thesis that it should be the goal of every individual to progress through several preparatory stages (the autoerotic, narcissistic and the homoerotic) to the mature state in which he or she finds a mate with whom physical, emotional and intellectual satisfaction can be achieved and with whom children can be raised, cared for and, in their turn, also guided to maturity. Oversimplified or platitudinous as it may sound, this is the ideal pattern of a human life.

Maturity or heterosexual adjustment is not, however, achieved without overcoming several hurdles. First, there is the need to pass the normal stages of development successfully. Next, there is the ever-present factor of the biological and intellectual differences among individuals. Last, one must cope with the infinite variety of environmental experiences, which individuals interpret and react to in so many different ways. Just how many people ever do achieve complete maturity is open to question. To have married and raised a family is not necessarily proof that one has divested oneself of all the elements of the pre-mature personality. Nor has it been

---

*Reprinted with authorization from *The Layman's Guide to Psychiatry*, New York, Barnes & Noble, 1964, Chapter 16, pp. 173-182.

shown that unmarried or childless individuals suffer from more than their share of psychiatric problems. Nevertheless, the attainment of a stable life, with established home and family, is a goal to be sought; the personality shows the fullest development when the individual has achieved this ideal, assuming of course that he or she is emotionally and otherwise well adjusted.

AN HISTORICAL REVIEW OF LOVE

Just as "the course of true love never did run smooth" in the individual case, neither has the role of love in the social structure remained constant through the ages. Ours is not the first era to regard love with cynicism, nor are the saccharine approaches of the nineteenth century the first such recorded in literature. At some risk of generalization, one can count off certain historical intervals and characterize them on the basis of the contemporary attitudes toward love.

Thirty centuries ago a lovesick Egyptian post bemoaned an "illness" no doctor could cure but which yielded to his sweetheart's embraces. Marital bliss—and discord—were lampooned in the early Greek comedies, but were given more significance in the Bible with the story of Adam and Eve. One of the oldest and most beautiful love stories is that of Rachel and Jacob, recorded in Genesis: ". . . and Jacob served seven years for Rachel; and they seemed unto him but a few days, for the love he had to her." Ancient history and literature contain many tales of supreme sacrifice to preserve marital love, such as the story of Orpheus, who descended into Hades to regain his wife, Eurydice.

On the other hand, there are accounts of philandering—the wife who leaves her husband for a lover or the husband who deceives his wife. Helen of Troy's elopement with Paris was the direct cause of the Trojan War (yet afterwards she was received at home again by her spouse, Menelaus!). The first wife whom we know was unfaithful while her mate was "away on business" was Clytemnestra. Ulysses engaged in several romantic interludes on his adventurous voyage home, while Penelope, the classical picture of the patient wife, repulsed all suitors.

The so-called "double standard" was popularized when, in the time of Socrates, women were supposed to be faithful while their husbands supported concubines, the original "kept women." When Plato wrote of the lofty love between human beings, regardless of sex, founded on a timeless love of Good and Beauty, he brought us the expression "platonic love." Christianity introduced into the picture a paradoxical concept that was both a boon and a curse, accounting in no small measure for contemporary confusion. While religious doctrine made the first attempt to unfetter women by preaching equality between the sexes, it also introduced the concept of sin into love; thus, love could be both profane and sacred.

In the Middle Ages this concept was reflected in two diverse pictures presented by the literature. On the one hand, a knight was a personification of the romantic ideal, dedicated to the protection of the weak and all women. An individual knight sought the hand of a young, unmarried girl or bound himself hopelessly in service to another man's wife. Women were pedestaled in verse and song, yet the concept of love included cohabitation, although each such love usually ended tragically, as in the cases of Lancelot and Guinevere, Tristram and Isolde.

The Renaissance brought an open element of sensuality to love. Chivalry was ignominiously slain by Cervantes' tongue-in-cheek mockery. Somewhat later the French wallowed in an abundance of flowery prose and poetry in an over sentimental approach to the subject. A certain amount of cynicism carried over, however, and French literature included derision for the husband unaware of his wife's infidelity. Shakespeare and Molière endowed literature with the term "cuckold."

England's Puritan Protestants emphasized the danger of sin attached to love with all the implications of eternal damnation and endless suffering for the unrepentant. This concept migrated to the American colonies and found expression in early colonial literature, particularly in Nathaniel Hawthorne's *The Scarlet Letter*.

Early in the eighteenth century the melancholic aspect of love was virtually laughed out of existence. People pursued *affaires du coeur* openly with no thought for moral obligations. Don Juan and Casanova were models for young men in emulate and types young women secretly desired. The role of woman had changed; no longer a symbol of love, she became primarily a means for pleasure.

The nineteenth century saw three distinct attitudes toward love. The early part of the century was the period of the great Romantic movement, when Shelley, Wordsworth and Keats were the prominent figures and lyric poetry the dominating form in literature. The ideal of love and beauty which had been woven from the time of Plato and before reappeared again with the same strength it had shown during the Middle Ages. A stronger movement than the earlier French attempt, the Romantic period in England also incorporated something of the earlier styles; the satire of the Neoplatonists found expression in such works as Byron's *Don Juan* and *English Bards and Scotch Reviewers*. The magnificence of medieval tradition was replaced by exotic Eastern influences and religious symbolism, outstanding examples of which can be seen in the works of Coleridge.

The Victorian era which followed had a restraining influence on the imagination of its writers. Sentimentality returned but was channeled toward an ideal of good men and good women, and the social scene gained prominence as a literary background. Despite the *rigeur* of Victorian comportment, in the latter part of the century there were the Oscar Wildes, the translations of the Rubáiyát of Omar Khayyám, and the unadulterated sensuality of the *Indian Love Lyrics* proclaiming:

> For this is wisdom; to love, to live,
> To take what Fate, or the gods, may give,
> To ask no question, to make no prayer,
> To kiss the lips and caress the hair,
> Speed passion's ebb as you greet its flow—
> To have—to hold—and—in time—let go!

The candy coating around love was swiftly and finally eradicated with the advent of World War I. Poetry, prose and song emphasized realism; idealism and romanticism became associated with the past. Thus, we had John Held and F. Scott Fitzgerald, followed by John Steinbeck, Tennessee Williams and Arthur Miller.

CONTEMPORARY ATTITUDES

Today the concept of love may be estimated as somewhere between sentiment and sex without inhibitions or excessive restrictions. Yet what is alleged to be liberal thinking and unrestrained discussion on the one hand is accompanied by a general lowering of moral attitude on the other. We are plagued by a record-breaking divorce rate. Writers reap fortunes through articles which give pseudo-solutions to sexual problems in marriage but which are predominantly expositions on how to enjoy sex—read by young and old, married and unmarried. Sex is too frequently set apart from love in so-called "frank" plays and movies, lewd literature and loose talk. There is emotional satisfaction and benefit from frank discussion, but there is irrefutable harm when frankness is a veneer for arousing unnatural curiosity, temptation and crime through unscrupulous bypassing of social decency, such as is presented to all ages via the printed word, stage, screen, radio and television. According to police statistics, prostitution flourishes as never before. Out of indiscriminate sexual activity by adolescents, by their philandering parents (married, divorced or widowed) and by other adults, mental and emotional reactions—outgrowths of insecurity and guilt —have developed.

The present perplexity about love has received additional impetus from the insecurity of modern life and, to some degree, from the misrepresentation of and failure to comprehend the philosophy and dynamic approach of such investigators as Sigmund Freud. Endocrinology has revived the Ponce de Leon interest in sexual restoratives and encouraged manufacturers of nostrums to give false hope to the ever-increasing army of impotent oldsters. Religion battles birth-control agencies on the issue of contraception. Drug stores sell pregnancy-thwarting devices to teen-agers; gynecologists prescribe contraceptive pills and diaphragms for their unmarried female patients. Abortionists, lay and medical, do a land-office business. In some states adultery is a statutory crime. While the streetwalker is subject to arrest, the economically independent woman who uses her body to assure herself of male companionship is not a prostitute—she is merely lonely.

PSYCHIATRIC CONSIDERATIONS OF LOVE

The most sensible approach to a consideration of love comes to us from the gifted pen of Dr. Félix Martí-Ibáñez, probably the ablest editorialist in the medical profession:

> Stendhal evolved the 'crystallization' theory in love: the sedimentation on one person of imaginary perfections projected by another. Just as a twig cast into the Salzburg salt mines, he said, is slowly coated by a myriad tiny iridescent salt crystals until transfigured into a vision of graces by the lover's imagination.
>
> Stendahl was wrong. True love is born suddenly and lasts forever. It is a motion of the soul towards something incomparable. To be in love is to feel bewitched by someone who is or seems perfect. Love first starts with a centripetal stimulus aroused by another person, which when it finally strikes the core makes love blossom centrifugally until it becomes a psychic current flowing endlessly towards that person.
>
> We all carry deep within us [in the unconscious] a preformed imaginary profile of the beloved that we try on most persons we meet. Therefrom springs the arrow, the French *coup de foudre* . . . love at first sight, when we suddenly meet someone who fits this ideal model.
>
> Although love is a dynamic feeling, it narrows our world; it is a psychic angina that begins with a change in our attention, which becomes obsessively fixed on one person. The image of the beloved fills our world completely. Hence, we do not "crystallize" on the object of our love, but set it apart and stand hypnotized before it as a lion before a lion tamer. [This, in Freudian parlance, would be the supreme ego ideal.] A lover's soul, filled with one single image, is like a sick man's room filled with the smell of flowers. In this sense, love impoverishes "horizontally" our world, while enriching it "vertically" with knowledge of another human being.
>
> Love, however, is not the same as sexual instinct. Whereas love is born from another being whose qualities trigger the erotic process, sexual instinct pre-exists the object of desire, cares not for perfection, and insures only the continuation of the species, not its improvement. *Sexual instinct is sometimes selective; love is always so* [italics ours] and excludes all desired objects but *the* one. There is no love without the sexual instinct, but in true love such instinct merely serves the same purpose as the wind in sailing.
>
> Love, Ortega y Gasset said, is "surrender by bewitchment," not a will to surrender, but surrender despite oneself; one is engulfed as if by

magic by the beloved. This is not so of desire, which entails no surrender, only the capture of the quarry. In desire the object of desire is absorbed; in love the lovesick one is absorbed. We can desire without loving, but we cannot love without desiring. Desire dies with fulfillment; love is never fully satisfied. Thus, love is the most delicate reflection of a person's soul, a wondrous talent granted to only a few.*

With each succeeding generation taking an about-face attitude toward the meaning of love, there can be no surprise that our present civilization is like the neurotic child, the product of an emotionally insecure background. Psychiatrists are defied to produce a definition of love. That challenge will never be met. Search though you may through endless library shelves of standard psychiatric texts and tracts dealing with marriage, the term "love" is neither defined nor indexed!

Stendhal attempted, over a century ago, to specify four varieties of love: passion-love; sympathy-love; sensual-love; and vanity-love. The first is valid, but the idea of "crystallization," described above, falls short of serving either as a definition or an explanation. All forms of love, however, have certain features in common. In heterosexuality it is an extraverted drive (as opposed to self-love or autoeroticism). Love must be reciprocated to be fully gratified; unrequited affection spells frustration. Love is individually selective in the higher forms of life; it arouses the impulse to give which supersedes but does not necessarily eliminate the desire to take. It stimulates curiosity for the love object—both psychological and physical. Certainly sexual contact is a natural corollary of love, but it follows, it does not precede or immediately accompany it. This statement at once provokes the question: Can not clandestine, illicit love precede a full love life? It can, but the true and maximum appreciation of the emotion cannot be achieved while a sense of guilt, unconscious and/or conscious, detracts from the complete libidinal concentration on love. This guilt is the result of the illicit lovers ignoring their superego's complaints, the heritage of family, the dictates of society, of religion, etc.

Love, as we have presented it, exists in persons before the desire to have sexual intercourse. Thus, true lovers become more and more inseparable as they continue to learn each other's assets and liabilities. A couple genuinely in love may initially experience sexual difficulties. Were they not in love, these handicaps would be seized as an excuse and magnified until they were accepted as a reason for dissolving the union. To the contrary, under the revealing light of love, two people can frankly, cooperatively and successfully overcome these difficulties. The emotionally mature

---

*Marti-Ibanez, Felix: De l'amour (editorial). *MD*, 2:11, April, 1958.

woman, for example, who marries for love will experience thoroughly satisfying sex. The emotionally immature woman who goes from one liaison to another solely for physiological gratification thereby prostitutes herself in the search for male companionship.

A SANE "SLANT" ON SEX

Says A. H. Maslow of Brandeis University: "One of the deepest satisfactions coming from the healthy love relationship permits the greatest spontaneity, the greatest naturalness, the greatest dropping of defenses and protection against threat. In such a relationship it is not necessary to be guarded, to conceal, to try to impress, to feel tense, to watch one's words or actions, to suppress or repress. My people report that they can be themselves without feeling that there are demands or expectations upon them; they can feel psychologically (as well as physically) naked and still feel loved and wanted and secure" (1).

At the outset of this chapter we synonymized love and heterosexual adjustment. The healthy attainment of mature love is another way of saying achievement of good mental hygiene. If we subscribe to the tenet of prevention rather than cure, then the proper point to launch a program of mental hygiene is at the beginning—when life commences. No one, regardless of age, is ever so richly endowed, intellectually and emotionally, that nothing remains to be learned. Instruction and guidance are of the utmost importance before puberty. Reaction patterns, personality traits, interpersonal relationships—these are in the making from the first breath of life.

Sex is more than the physiological satisfaction of desire. It is an important component and offshoot of love; it also implies the need to adjust, after psychosexual development has been completed, to a universe of man and woman. Parents, therefore, have an obligation beyond providing the necessities for existence. If they feel that anything more than this can be purchased or is guaranteed by law through payment of taxes, then they fail in their responsibility to their families. The teacher and the chaplain are important influences in a child's development. However, they cannot do the entire job without parental cooperation—any more than the nursemaid, baby-sitter, grandparents or television can be expected to serve as surrogates for mother and father.

First and foremost the child should be given every reason to feel secure and wanted in the home. Honesty is the keystone in the arch of family love. Every minute brings a youngster something new that he wants to learn about; he will ask questions. If he is impatiently brushed aside—rejected—

---

*Maslow, A. H.: *Motivation and Personality*. New York, Harper, 1954, pp. 239-240.

if the reply is untrue or veiled with mystery so as to connote wickedness or fear, not only do doubt and insecurity result, but confidence in the parent is shaken. If conversation threatens to turn to delicate topics, changing the subject is far better than the forefinger on the lips, the wink, the warning glare or the foreign phrase that cautions the speaker. If you cannot answer a child's question because you lack the knowledge, say so, but then seek the information with the child. He will respect your honesty and when you do have the data to satisfy his queries he will believe you unconditionally.

Sex instruction deserves priority in child training. Properly administered and maturely handled, this feature of a youngster's upbringing will go far in molding a good citizen with healthy interests. All sex knowledge is not imparted to a child at any one age, any more than Euclid is taught before the student masters basic arithmetic. Simpler facts are explained at first, such as the age-old question: "Where do babies come from?" As time goes on and the child's mind develops, further instruction is given. There is no need to dread this responsibility, which, in fact, is a happy experience for both teacher and pupil. Brochures, pamphlets and books are available in public libraries, from the American Medical Association, local mental health societies and other agencies.

No household has to be a citadel of unnatural prudery. Neither should it be a center for vulgarity or off-color stories. A healthy, sincere, modern attitude of respect for sex, ever properly linking it to genuine love, will go far in advancing good mental hygiene. Such a home never has to worry when the teen-age daughter begins to date, or when the boy's voice changes and his chin sprouts a stubble. Sensible parents, earnest and moderate in attitude, fostering an atmosphere of family togetherness, will raise children who find complete satisfaction in scouting, hobbies and athletics, and who will be untempted by narcotics, liquor, zip guns and clandestinely pursued sensuality.

Sex should be neither emphasized nor ignored as a component of love. It is important to know the limitations of sexual attraction and to be able to distinguish it from real love; it should be a part but not a whole. George Santayana expresses the philosophic viewpoint in *The Life of Reason:* "There can be no philosophic interest in disguising the animal basis of love, or in denying its spiritual sublimations, since all life is animal in its origin and spiritual in its possible fruits."

Finally, an excellent literary appreciation of love is given us by Thornton Wilder in *The Bridge of San Luis Rey:* ". . . we ourselves shall be loved for a while and forgotten. But the love will have been enough; all those impulses of love return to the love that made them. Every memory is not necessary for love. There is a land of the living and a land of the dead and the bridge is love, the only survival, the only meaning."

REFERENCE

1. MASLOW, A. H.: *Motivation and Personality.* New York, Harper, 1954, pp. 239-240.

Chapter 5

THE PHILOSOPHICAL AND PSYCHOLOGICAL
IMPLICATIONS OF MARRIAGE AND WOMANHOOD

HIRSCH LAZAAR SILVERMAN

IN VIEWING MARRIAGE RATHER objectively, with honesty free from sentimentality, flowery language or patronizing approval, I maintain that, for the most part, it is from man's side that the greatest hindrances come to the realization of marriage—unity, positive purity, complete oneness of life and work between man and woman; but, it must hastily be added, woman increases man's difficulties if she gets into the man's way, through not understanding his hopes and aspirations and by not learning to cherish a noble respect for his fight.

Some poets sing of "ideal love" in regard to marriage. Philosophers, from time immemorial, have felt that marriage involves human dignity, responsibility, community and mutual trust. But man seemingly has inherited more than woman has of the disordered instincts that result from disrupted marriage in countless previous generations.

Love and understanding are perhaps the two basic forces in marriage. Expanded, these words as concepts mean the union between two people is only true according as they love and understand each other in thought, feeling and will, tasks of duty and sources of joy, and are consequently able to fight life's battles, bear its pains and enjoy its glory together; and this by having directed, forwarded and *freed* each other's development.

Of course a woman can exercise influence in various possible ways in a man's life; but if it be not that of a free and living being, it drags down: It is an influence of somnambulism and retrogression, a return to the oriental idea of the relation between the sexes. Marriage, in its widest sense, is the common work of a man and woman. Nothing is justifiable in either person that is one-sided.

I protest against a trivial social view that marriage is something altogether practical, that for two to become one and thereby blessed, is a mere dream. I regard the view that "there is no such thing as love" as shallowness and cynicism of belief. Most if not all of the conditions for a moral marriage may be laid down in this concept of "Love".

At present, "love" may be an idea to which no clear meaning attaches. Love presumes youth, as a rule; but it is not the same thing as youth, or even as youth with warm and mutual liking into the bargain. Youth is a glorious thing, but it has its own dangers, and the chief of them is self-deception. It is only too easy for two young people to rock themselves in dreams of bliss without real love as a basis. Love is confidence, and means life in the future with mutual understanding. For marriage is really a state of being awake to life and activity, in all its forms.

Just as a poetical work reveals an idea, a truth that has a perfect right to its place among the truths of the world—a truth that is so permanent and indestructible, that, if a time has come for that truth, it cannot be injured or neglected, evaded or turned aside, though he who attempts to injure it may thereby injure himself—so is it with marriage, I believe. A good marriage sets forth and even enhances an idea perfectly.

The object of marriage should be to make each human personality *free*, in the sense of emancipation, of liberation. I do not say this axiomatically, and I maintain this thesis: Marriage should confer the power of giving expression in real life and living to both husband and wife. Until the relation between them turns sufficiently in this direction, the relation is not yet love. Perhaps mankind has yet to arrive at a newly reached awakenedness in its moral conscience in this regard no less.

Women certainly are not weak creatures. This is one of man's delusions. Women certainly can take steps without man's help; they have will and conscience of their own. It cannot be overemphasized that morality in love really is the effort to make the beloved one free, awakened, responsible, true, pure-hearted, noble and strong, instead of enslaving and making the beloved dependent, irresponsible, needing help, slavish-minded and clinging. Modern husbands—too many of them, from my observations—have an intense psychological wish to be a patron and have an artificially developed gift for patronizing. Too many husbands wish to go on hugging that untrue view of half-humanity to their breasts just as a child hugs its doll.

Detestable is the husband who permits his principles to dry up into mere maxims, his duty, honor, taste and judgment into routine, until he ends in being one of these faultless persons whom no one would care to exchange ideas with on any subject, great or small, but who, on the contrary, is listened to by tacit understanding with a respectful smile when he is so "obliging" as to communicate any view which he happens to hold.

I feel that the husband or wife who even attempts to be will and conscience to the other is indeed foolish, for the usual results will come to the surface—deception, hypocrisy, crooked ways, duplicity, loss of trust, absence of ease, joy and healthiness in daily intercourse, and a habit of covering the abyss with artificial liveliness that seems to have taken root in time. Boredom then settles down on the house that should have been their home.

Some men like to think that a woman never grows (or that it is happier for her not to grow) old. Amid all this new order of things, man yearns for the lark in woman, the careless gaiety of the girl in the woman, the person that used to be. A glance around shows us many women arrested thus, many young souls prevented from ever becoming real women. This is social murder, psychologically, on a grand scale, results of which are most disastrous for human destiny. It means that homes often get amiable hostesses, without husbands getting loving wives or children loving mothers.

Absence of ideality often makes married life in later years grotesque. Also, the education of the husband and wife is a determinant; the selfishness that is more or less in every natural woman's heart—which unchecked and suppressed destroys either her whole woman's personality or the happiness and honor of all around her, but, raised to the moral plane of freedom, in the philosophical and psychological sense, would, on the contrary, save both husband and wife—this selfishness must also be a determining factor; the husband's egoism of his sex, with satisfaction that he is a man and not a woman—this exaggerated individual egoism must be understood; in essence, the world of consciousness of the spouses is no less a fundamental determinant in marriage.

The kernel, then, of every home is its principle of *womanliness* and *manliness*. Modern homes too often go to pieces before our very eyes from some necessity *within itself*. Our homes must contain everything that can attract, if marriage is to succeed—simplicity, gladness, power of work, good temper, gentle yet strong regard, love of beauty, happy children, friends, good habits, an earned reputation, a position of the husband that has at length been won by praiseworthy endeavors.

The husband's view of his wife must be an ennobled one, and he must have manly dignity. Indispensable conditions for mutual healthy development must not be wanting. The wife must not be a "passive" woman, whose will is either dead or stubborn, or one with a "broken heart," or a superficial person, who is satisfied with trifles, or one who openly suffers, weeps and sighs, or one of those who combine any of these characteristics with that of a prude or a coquette, who lives life with a half-conscious longing for the unnecessary and the artificial.

Basically, weakness is most often nothing but destroyed power of thinking and doing. No form of weakness can ever enter the lives of the husband or wife, for any appreciable length of time, if harmonious existence is to continue. We must recognize and come to admire individuality in the person—in the woman and in the man.

Chapter 6

MARRIAGE AND THE ADULT PERSONALITY

ALLAN FROMME

I<small>N OUR SOCIETY, GETTING</small> married is almost as inevitable as growing up. In fact, growing up, in the sense of merely coming of age, seems to be its major requirement. However dull and prosaic this may sound, it remains a simple incontrovertible fact of life. Getting married is not nearly so romantic a matter as we like to think it is. The choice of *whom* to marry is another issue, and it is this which lends itself more appropriately to the romantic process of falling in love. But love and marriage go hand in hand not nearly so reliably in fact as they do in the sweet realm of hope and desire. It is an ideal, rather than a real, connection. At bottom, less is required of us to get married than to exercise our franchise to vote. As a result, more and more people keep getting married, largely independent of their understanding of what lies ahead for them and equally independent of their emotional readiness to face their own domestic future.

The consequence of this lack of understanding and readiness is what one might expect it to be—chagrin, disappointment, unhappiness. People blame each other, not themselves, and often find fault with the structure of marriage itself. This latter is easy to do, because, unlike other human associations, marriage has no constitution or charter with which to defend itself. It merely places two people together in the expectation that they will "live happily forever after." Although marriage unquestionably affects our happiness, the influence is much stronger the other way around. By the time we reach marriageable age, we have already developed long-practiced habits of response which mark us as happy, confident and optimistic, or unhappy, anxious and worrisome. The way we handle ourselves generally is the way we handle ourselves in marriage. Our capacity for happiness, in short, may be tapped by marriage, but never created by it.

This places the burden of the outcome of any marriage not on the institution but on the individuals who marry. The quality of a marriage reflects the emotional habits and resources of people far more than the supportive or destructive forces of society. These habits of perception, feeling and response in people are not easy to change. In fact, they are not even easy to discern clearly enough for most of us to make the effort to change them—until we bring them repeatedly into conflict with others. Marriage supplies the most common arena for such conflict. By placing two people together in the most unvarnished relationship, where the lack of structure invites them to be completely themselves, and where they are already unusually susceptible to hurt because of the promises and tender sentiments shared, marriage has come to be the widest testing ground of personality.

It was not always this way. In previous centuries, marriages were not only arranged by others but a structure existed which is now rapidly disappearing. Roles were defined with clarity and unyielding rigidity. Men and women knew what they had to do—and did it. Marriage was convenient and necessary, often fulfilling, but it never was the emotional free-for-all it is rapidly becoming. People neither entered marriage with the huge hopes they now have for gratification, nor did they enjoy our present-day opportunities for freeing themselves for the purpose of starting all over again. Marriage was more a way of life than a self-elected opportunity for the pursuit of happiness.

It is a most curious fact that marriage should have become the major treasure chest—and all too often the cemetery—of our most romantic hopes and desires in view of its utterly unromantic beginnings and more recent history. Up until a mere yesterday ago, marriages were arranged. Even dragon-slayers of fabled note were *awarded* the hand of the princess. Neither she nor they were given the luxury of choice. Marriages were more often *socially* acceptable arrangements than *personally* acceptable ones. They expressed social convenience and conformity rather than romantic selection. Yet, today, the very opposite seems to prevail. People in love rush headlong into marriage, regardless of the uncongenial forces surrounding them. In fact, these very forces, rather than exercising a negative and discouraging influence, frequently add motive power to the decision to marry.

Why should this have happened? How did love come to dominate marital choice and even the very decision to marry? How did we come to expect so much romantically of marriage? As always, many factors contributed to the change, and unfortunately we have little more than mere opinion for the evaluation of the relative efficacy of these factors. The phenomena elude both experimental control or statistical isolation.

The beginnings of our modern attitudes toward marriage probably go back as far as the Middle Ages. Chivalric notions about women were a prominent part of the mystique developed when knighthood was in flower. Although this may well have laid the groundwork for a romantic approach to women, there remained altogether too many other forces in society which prevented more than poetic lip service to such romance. Women continued to be chattel because governments were dominated by men and men were dominated by economic forces. It took many centuries before the social structure yielded to the latent needs of people—most people—who remained unsatisfied by it. Huge political and industrial revolutions preceded the smallest changes in attitude toward women and only since World War II have women finally begun to think differently of themselves.

In ever-increasing numbers, women today are availing themselves of the opportunity for advanced education, fitting themselves for more significant participation in the whole economy. At one time, they worked exclusively at home; then they worked *for* men; now they work *with* men. They are wage earners, they are voters, they are independent members of the community largely enjoying the right of self-direction and decision. Their own needs and desires—even their most romantic ones—can now finally be examined not merely in the framework of fantasy. Women are eminently capable today of *acting* on their needs and desires in a manner unknown to previous history.

The growing freedom of women was aided and abetted by a psychological revolution at least as influential in its consequences as the major political and industrial changes which preceded it. Man's understanding of himself had been remarkably limited up until very recently. His attachment to religious and moral concepts seemed to substitute for his pervasive ignorance of himself. The appearance and acceptance of Freud's writings finally had the effect in less than half a century of forcing both men and women to recognize the reality and imperative quality of their needs. No psychological system had ever before placed its primary emphasis on human needs. No system ever traced the intricate ways we do ourselves in by failure to express these needs. Because of this stress on human need and desire, the more realistic our understanding of ourselves became, the more fully was the basis laid for romantic choice and behavior.

What is the essence of romance, after all, but unbridled self-expression? The whole history of romantic literature is basically an expression of protest against the restraint and orderliness of more classic forms. Experience, feeling, desire—these are the words which figure most prominently in romantic works of literature. The harmonies imposed upon us by moral or institutional forces are rejected for the more chaotic but deeply personal needs we feel within us. Personal experience becomes more important than social compliance. The self becomes more important than the group. The freedoms decreed historically in the Declaration of Independence and the Bill of Rights have finally been made available on a level deep enough to affect our love life. It makes an interesting psychoanalytical aside to recognize that now that these freedoms are truly available, we express them more in our behavior than we do in our literature. Romantic literature apparently *was* a substitute for the real thing.

Although men everywhere have always fought for freedom, its rational use is at least as difficult as obtaining it in the first place. Back in grade school, one of the most difficult assignments came when the teacher told us all merely to write a composition—a composition on anything. Immediately she was besieged with questions such as: On what? How long shall it be? Is it all right if . . .? On the other hand, if she asked us to write a composition on Columbus's first mate during his second voyage, we'd know where to do the research on the subject even if we had never heard of the individual before. In the same way, many people complain a lot more about their weekends than the more structured time they spend during the week. This is not to say that people cannot use and enjoy their freedom. This is merely a reminder that wishing is a lot easier than acting on our wishes. The relationship between men and women is finally free, selective, open to choice. But this is only half the battle. The results today clearly indicate the difficulties which remain.

There are many reasons for this, but most important of all is the simple fact that marriage is not a simple ordinary relationship between a man and a woman. It is a very grown-up relationship, and unfortunately many people are simply not adult enough for it. We don't give our thirteen- or fourteen-year-old children the keys to our automobile just because they express the desire to drive. In fact, we don't even give our twenty-one-year-old children the keys to our automobile under those circumstances. Not until they learn how to drive and pass certain tests necessary to obtain a license do we then feel free to give them the privilege of driving. In the same way, we don't turn over the U. S. Savings Bonds we have accumulated for our children merely on their request. In many areas of their behavior we wait until we see the signs of readiness and responsibility before we allow our children to indulge themselves. Love and marriage are notable exceptions. If they are of age, there is little we can do to prevail on them to consider whether or not they are grown up and ready enough for the relationship they are about to enter.

But it is not the fault of our children. Nor is it any one's fault specifically. The fact is we have no tests, no clear-cut marks of readiness. The skills involved in a good marital relationship are not so specific as they are in other areas of our behavior. It's much easier to become a good driver, a financial expert, a good doctor, lawyer, almost Indian chief than it is to develop the grown-up qualities necessary to get the most out of the pervasive, intimate relationship of marriage. The word "intimate" is the key to some of the great difficulties people face in marriage.

From all the evidence, we begin our lives in a fairly detached though dependent state. As a result of the care we receive, we become increasingly aware of the person or persons around us. We build up a more and more dependent and intimate relationship with them. Dependency and intimacy go hand in hand for many years during the first stages of our life. But before too long, the weaning process sets in. We're encouraged to give up bits and pieces of our dependency. As we grow more rapidly, during the years from six to twelve, particularly, a great deal of our intimacy is given up as well. We begin to keep secrets from our parents, the very people with whom we have enjoyed the greatest intimacy. This goes on at an ever-increasing rate so that soon the child regards his parents' questions as unwarranted invasions of his privacy. Although he may come to enjoy many friendships, there is still an overall loss in his ability to develop and sustain intimacy in a relationship. Even when he finally falls in love, it is difficult for him to reveal all areas of his being and share them completely with the person he loves.

What this means is that, as we grow, we get little experience in being intimate. In our daily relationships, we have little opportunity for intimacy. We are better at more formal, structured relationships. We know people best in terms of some of their more obvious characteristics, namely, their occupational status, their political interests, even their golf handicap. We hesitate, no matter how genuine our interest, to ask many personal questions of them for fear they will think we are prying. The simple result of all this is that we are not very good at being intimate—and yet this is what marriage demands.

There are many men, who, despite the ardor of their courtship, find it extremely difficult in marriage to confide in their wives. There may be many reasons for this, some good, some bad, but the fact remains that something is missing in the relationship. Often such a man feels that his wife simply cannot understand the subtleties of the kind of financial manipulation which occupies him during his working day. Or he may feel that his worries will be misunderstood by his wife, who cannot understand his investments or the quality of the risks he may have taken. More generally, whether his wife can or cannot understand these matters is not his prime consideration. He does not expect her to understand and settles the matter on that level. Some men even feel that it is unmanly to unburden oneself to a woman—even one's wife. Other men frankly distrust their wife and see marriage more as a limited partnership. In other cases, a man claims that every time he has taken his wife into his confidence, she winds up trying to boss him.

Women are by no means exempt from the same difficulty. They too feel and often decide in advance that a man—even their own husband—cannot understand many things. The result is that they do not even attempt to help him understand some of these matters. The reason for withholding or diluting the intimacy of their relationship frequently is an expression of hostility and vindictiveness. They put things on a *quid pro quo* basis. If my husband is not going to share such and such with me, they argue, then I will also keep things from him. The more simply we isolate and state all of this, the more childish it sounds. This is exactly the point. It takes adults to enjoy intimacy; children easily sulk, withdraw and destroy their intimacy. On a physical level, intimacy is even more difficult to achieve. Despite the fact that we talk more about sex these days than probably ever before in our history, there are many areas of deep sexual difficulty which remain in the marriages of most people. It is worth examining this in some detail.

The simplest way to clarify what we mean by sex is to take our clue from Sigmund Freud. He defines sex as the use of the body for the purpose of pleasure. As a national and cultural group, we have beset ourselves with all sorts of obstacles for the use of the body for the purpose of pleasure. In the first place, altogether too many of us have been more influenced by medieval theology than we know. At one time, we were persuaded to believe that pleasure was the royal road to hell, and we still believe that hard work is a far greater virtue than pleasure. Pleasure at best is the Saturday night reward for a week's hard work. Pleasure is not what settled the West, built empires or created a great nation. We are still wary about our pleasures, even centuries after the initial doctrine was foisted upon us.

The second factor of importance is also a matter of history. When our Pilgrim forefathers came to this nation, they brought with them the notion that cleanliness was next to godliness. Some 250 years later, we find ourselves a nation with more tiled bathrooms than any other in the world. Although there are unquestionable virtues associated with this turn of events, we can expect some problems to emerge as well. This emphasis on cleanliness and privacy also has the unfortunate effect of eating into our ability to develop and maintain an intimate physical relationship with others. Consider, for example, the way in which we develop such habits of cleanliness as are involved in bowel control in our own children. Although everybody develops this sooner or later on his own, parents all too often, despite the writings of psychologists on the subject nowadays, continue to urge their infants and children to develop sphincter control in many cases even long before the nerve endings have grown out to make such control possible. Parents will prop an infant up on the potty, in some instances, even before he can sit up. Others will keep a child on the stool for as long as an hour or two in the imperative effort to make him perform. Worse yet is the case of the child who has been "trained" and then begins to have "accidents." Add to this the overly strong lessons in modesty and the concealment of private parts which parents impose on their children, and we begin to see that bathroom activities and that portion of our body associated with them become the loci of anxiety. The final *coup de grace* is delivered when parents take a strongly punitive attitude towards early masturbation in their children.

Not only does all this eat into the psychological intimacy of parent and child, but the child comes to fear those very portions of the body which later in life will ideally be brought into the service of pleasure and love. Instead, he will be left with the vague though disturbing feeling that any activity involving those portions of his body is somehow dirty or wrong. Since we are dealing with vegetative habits and unstriped muscles, the reinforcement of such feelings during the early years can be enough to ruin the healthier use of this portion of the body forever. Of course, there is always the possibility that when a person looks upon sex as dirty or wrong, his own hostility will take over the sexual function. Sex then gets to be not an intimate expression of love but rather of defiance, self-assertion and frank hostility. It is no accident that our idiom itself catches this. The person who is seduced is taken advantage of sexually or otherwise.

The persistence of sexual difficulty in marriage was not nearly so deleterious to the relationship as it has recently become. In the loosening of sexual mores, the very real emancipation of women and the importance we now attribute to need all conspire to render lack of gratification a very serious threat. At one time women may have secretly hoped for sexual gratification in marriage; now they actively demand it. Despite the fact that orgasm in the female is still largely a medical and psychological problem, women express their disappointment and chagrin about the lack of sexual fulfillment in no uncertain terms. But children easily express disappointment too. It takes a great deal of grown-upness to sit down and examine what one complains about. And all too frequently one or both of the marital partners are still unable to develop the intimacy necessary for such examination.

This lack of physical and psychological intimacy between husband and wife unquestionably dilutes the quality of their marital relationship. Many times people have difficulty developing intimacy in marriage because it is not at all uncommon for them to discover that they have not married the person they thought they did. During her courtship a young woman frequently sees her beau as gallant, attentive, fun loving. Once they marry and he finds himself deluged with the financial problems involved in setting up a home, he easily becomes overworked, irritable and worrisome. During his courtship it is easy enough for the young man to find the girl of his choice to be the very quintessence of sexual attractiveness. Attractiveness, however, is at best the promise of fulfillment, and promises are more easily made than realized. Once they marry it is just as easy for him to find that this woman, now his wife, is interested in many things other than his sexual gratification. In short, we make mistakes about each other, and we also change from one situation to another.

Making mistakes about each other is easy the younger and the more emotionally involved we are. A woman sees a man premaritally as strong and assertive only to find out later that he is domineering. Or she may find him appealingly sensitive only to discover later that he is helpless and dependent. Similarly, a man may find a young woman to be gay and carefree only to find her later to be careless and silly. On the other hand, the serious and responsible young woman might turn out to be humorless and more interested in domestic chores than domestic pleasures. The fact is that it is extremely difficult to separate our value judgments of people from what the facts really are. It's an old story; if you like someone you say he has the courage of his convictions, whereas you describe the same behavior in someone you don't like as stubborn, unyielding and rigid. The people on our side are always fair and just; the others are unthinking and wrong.

These errors of judgment are common indeed. There is no specific way of guarding against them. The more adult and mature we are, the less given we are to making such errors. But becoming truly adult is by no means the inevitable accompaniment of mere chronological growth. We even say: "There's no fool like an old fool"; or "The older a lamb gets the more sheepish it gets." A certain amount of age and experience are both necessary, but it is largely the emotional freedom to reflect on experience and correct our errors which promotes our emotional grown-upness. This is a hard thing to come by. Emotional freedom really means that we are not driven by inner forces which we habitually fail to recognize. Yet, more often than we realize, many of us are driven in exactly this fashion.

Let us see how this too can affect the quality of marriage. A woman who is unsure of herself and anxious about the impression she makes on people may choose from all her suitors a man who is a Johnny-sit-by-the-fire type. Once married and assured of his devotion she gains somewhat in security. Over the years she comes to express growing impatience with the fact that her husband shows no inclination to do any large-scale entertaining of friends. She blames him for her inability to make a social breakthrough when actually she married him in order to avoid the fears she nurtured about people. Her inability to recognize this prompts her to use her husband as a scapegoat. This is one of the most common functions of the marital relationship; i.e., to blame each other for problems which may have their origin actually in ourselves.

We're all familiar enough with the history of hostility toward minority groups expressed by making them scapegoats. What we fail to see, all too often, is the more personal domestic variety of the same psychological mechanism of projection taking place under our very noses. Although it is obviously smaller in scope, it is just as invidious. Relationships are spoiled again and again in marriage and are frequently driven beyond repair not merely because of the rancor expressed, but because, as in all scapegoating, the causes of difficulty are constantly misplaced. One cannot remedy what has been incorrectly diagnosed, and all cases of misplaced blame represent such faulty diagnosis.

Yet one might well ask why marriages in which the major faultfinding is with each other rather than ourselves survive at all? Not only our clinical reports, but our plays, movies, even our humor all remind us of how commonly married people blame each other for the problems and unhappiness that seem to be their wont. Do these people remain together in wedlock merely because of the children, the price of divorce or the inertia we can count on in human nature? Unquestionably these are powerful forces maintaining the fact of marriage if nothing else. But there is something else. Oddly enough, there is the satisfaction involved in having someone to blame. It's like what Sartre said of the Jews: God made them because if he didn't, pepole would have been at a loss to explain away their personal and national difficulties. From a clinical standpoint we know that either we have scapegoats or we have symptoms. Many a marriage gets to be the displaced dumping grounds for hostility which people cannot express acceptably elsewhere. Men and women may be unhappy in such marriages, but they remain relatively symptom-free.

And so we hurt each other by becoming targets of convenience. Not that there is no hostility or disappointment married men and women actually find in each other. Of course there is, but more often than not the *expression* of this is far greater than that which is initially felt. The marital relationship provides us with a kind of automatic transmission stepping up our feelings into a higher rate of expression entirely without our control. A slice of burnt breakfast toast which can be replaced in two minutes can set off a chain of emotional reactions which might leave the man and the woman both burning all day. The reason is that things which bother us quickly join forces, so that what we express involves much more than meets the eye. We take the whole thing out on each other and blame each other unknowingly, irrationally and with irresponsible abandon. The man feels he is unhappy, not because of his job frustrations, but because his wife is inattentive enough to burn his slice of toast. The woman feels she is unhappy, not because of her own difficulties in being something other than her own mother taught her to be earlier in life, but because her husband is impatient with her efforts to please him at breakfast.

It becomes clear that marriage does in fact offer us the opportunity for self-expression. The trouble is that we abuse this opportunity all too often. Elsewhere in life we are not permitted the same vigorous expression of disappointment and anger. Marriage, on the other hand, allows us more freedom than perhaps is good for us in this area. Elsewhere we can rave just as enthusiastically, demonstrate the deepest approval and show almost the same amount of devotion as we do in marriage. Many a man behaves exactly this way about his job, a favorite athlete or team or his automobile. By comparison, his wife occupies an accepted but unexciting part of his life. Yet this is the same person he found before marriage more exciting than anyone or anything else he had come upon in his life. His romantic attachment to her made her absolutely imperative for him. Like most people who marry today, he saw in this choice the best of all possible women.

Why do these romantic feelings change in so many people after they marry? Although marriage imposes rigors which are more or less absent from a premarital amatory relationship, the fact of the matter is that the marital state is only secondarily responsible for this change. It is the people who are important, not the institution. Even if they did not marry, their intense feelings of excitement about each other would dwindle anyway. The reason is simple. Intense feelings about anything are maintained only very rarely and very exceptionally. Even an artist's devotion to a great and important work is probably diluted from time to time by periods of waning interest. One might well wonder whether Michelangelo, during the seven-year period it took him to paint the ceiling of the Sistine Chapel, did not get even more excited about other projects which came to his attention. Human beings are complex organisms with many needs, desires and interests. It is the rule rather than the exception that at one time we are partial to one thing and, at other times, to another. This is not fickleness; it is our complexity.

There are many advantages to being this way provided we learn how to handle ourselves. The child merely sits and cries for what he wants as though life itself depended on it. He is thrown into paroxysms of joy and despair depending almost entirely on the means and abilities of others. He is aware of his simple but pressing needs; he remains unaware of the forces which must be put together to satisfy these needs. The result is a dependent existence with little affective continuity from moment to moment. Just as we expect, there is little stability in the feelings and emotions of children.

There are many grown-ups who are not much better off than children in this respect. They too suffer, if not from moment to moment, from day to day, and are so buffeted about by their own needs and desires that they cannot maintain stable relationships with anyone. Like children they remain poignantly aware of what they want and almost as ignorant of the techniques by which these desires could be satisfied.

Many of these people are like children in still another significant respect. A child has to be reminded to put his toys away. He is notoriously careless with some of the things he cried for the most. He knows little about maintaining and safeguarding from loss those things which do not capture his fancy at the moment. Since we cannot indulge ourselves in all our interests simultaneously, taking care of our possessions gets to be almost as important as obtaining them in the first place. Of all the possessions we accumulate in our life, people are by far the most important.

We enter marriage these days with such high hopes of what we will get from the relationship, we are easily hurt when we are momentarily set aside for other interests. Certainly it is natural for men and women to brush each other aside despite their romantic promises. They do not and in fact cannot make ardent love to each other uninterruptedly from the time they marry. In romantic literature the quality of any love has always depended on its most overt expression. If Romeo said good night briefly and not "till it be the morrow" no one would have been impressed. Although married love depends on its overt expression also, the quality of this love is often even more clearly established by less obvious means. Like a fine long-playing record, the pauses in the music must yield true silence rather than noisy rumblings and hisses. A good therapist must learn to hear the eloquence of what is *not* said by his patients. Similarly, the quality of a marital relationship will depend on what a man and a woman do when they are not actively expressing their devotion to each other. A man can make a woman feel rejected by his interest in his work, or contrariwise he can have her feel that his work is never more than a necessary chore which removes him from her most unwillingly.

This is not at all a matter of deceit. Love has little supportive or romantic value if it does not give one a sense of its continuity through periods of absence. When a great ape is taken from the cage of his friends, they cry—but only until he is out of sight. Human beings of course are very different. Romantic literature bulges with descriptions of the great amount of crying when lovers are apart rather than together. Since life demands a great deal of us today, it is utterly inconceivable for a married couple to be together all of the time. As a matter of fact, if they are, they could not even serve each other well. The subtle division of labor of which a man and woman are capable demand periods of absence as well as periods of togetherness. In a good relationship, the striving characteristic of absence is maintained when they are together and the promise of gratification survives their periods of absence. In other words, a happy couple remains convinced that they are always each other's first choice no matter what else they may have to do. Romantic as this may sound, the greatest part of this is achieved not so much by our romantic efforts. It is one of the more effortless, happy consequences of being truly adult.

There are many significant ways in which adults differ from children, and virtually all of them are relevant to the quality of the marriage people eventually make. It goes without saying that the decision to get married, the choice of whom to marry, the wedding and the honeymoon, and many times even the early years do not necessarily reveal the kind of marriage people eventually have. Despite the growing frequency and acceptance of divorce, marriage is still not thought of as a kind of interim arrangement. Yet it is not merely the durability of a marriage which testifies to its excellence. A marriage can last even though its participants continue to live a highly mercurial life with each other. Marriages even survive the persistent lack of satisfaction. A marriage is a good one when people continually want it. This means that, given the real and hypothetical choices and alternatives we continue to find, imagine and dream about in our lives, the marriage we have is the one we continue to want.

This is a lot more realistic than it sounds at first blush. Certainly any grown-up realizes that there is always the possibility of something better than what he has. He does not have to feel that he has the outstanding marriage of the millennium in order to prefer it to some hypothetical alternative. It is merely that he is grown-up enough to be happy with what he has accomplished and with what he has. And so he prefers it. He does not remain restive and striving, constantly seeking something beyond his grasp. We do not consider it smug for the Lord at the end of each day's work to have looked at it and said, "It was good." True, he might have said, "I'll try to do better tomorrow," but the standard of satisfaction he set for us should serve as a model. It has always been far more realistic to work with what one has in ability than in desire.

It should be perfectly obvious that it takes a good deal of grown-upness to reconcile oneself to the differences between dreaming and doing. Children are far too inexpert at doing to guarantee tomorrow's satisfactions. The most grown-up adults cherish what they have and spend as much effort caring for it as they did in obtaining it. There are of course other characteristics of their childhood which they might hold on to with advantage. The spontaneity, enthusiasm and even the ability to dream itself are all worth preserving into adulthood. But unless the ability to act on their dreams becomes the most important part of their adjustment, things slip away from them too easily. They remain emotionally like children—sulking, petulant and easily discouraged.

One of the major distinguishing characteristics between children and adults in this context is the amount of narcissism in their makeup. Children live in a small, solipsistic world dominated by intense self-awareness. Their interest in themselves is so strong and so central that the rest of the world merely gravitates around them like mere planetary bodies. It were almost as though the world existed for them. One of the great accomplishments of growth, on the other hand, is that ideally it frees us from this slavish attachment to self. The world and the people in it command our attention very much more than the small narrow demands of self. Not only is life very much more interesting for the individual as a result of this, but he becomes free enough to give himself and of himself to others. This is a basic requirement for any important human relationship which is not essentially a dependent one.

Of all the characteristics that separate adults from children this is probably the most important for the marital relationship. The ability to give of oneself is the very thing which makes human attachment desirable. This is different from the imperative attachments developed by infants and children. Their attachments are necessary for survival. Adult attachments express the luxury of choice. The difference can be recognized easily enough provided we do not allow ourselves to become romantically over-whelmed. In the latter instance, need dominates the relationship. This itself should make it suspect. But, once out of hand, we do anything to justify the decision made. More rational choice involves fact more than it does promise. Grown-up lovers do a great deal for each other and have a good time with each other *here and now* rather than merely in the happy never-never land of the future.

This is another way of saying that adults have oriented themselves to reality sufficiently to enjoy a good deal of it. When they fall in love, the object of their love is part of the reality to which they have adjusted. They do not take such enormous romantic license as to change the love object so that they mistake you for one of their dreams. They may be fond of their dreams but they like you better. Secondly, they are free enough of them-selves to be truly interested in you. As a result they pay attention to you. They care for you even when they cannot share your exciting presence. Thirdly, they see life not as some poetic dream but as a very real opportun-ity to fulfill oneself. Such fulfillment takes work and work takes many forms. Sometimes we work hard by sweating at the brow in a huge physical effort; sometimes we work every bit as hard by holding our breath, biding our time, exercising patient restraint and waiting for the tides to change before we move.

All people have their ups and downs. Adults have fewer of them than children. By virtue of their capacity for empathy they can help each other over many of these emotional hurdles. Inevitably there are many of them in marriage because we expose more of ourselves in this relationship than in any other known to man. The rewards are eminently worth the effort. In a world in which man is being separated from others more and more by the increasing division of labor, men reach out more wantingly than ever for others. In a world in which many of our primary face-to-face groups no longer exercise the hold over us they once did, man feels an increasing sense of alienation from others. The increasing parity between men and women make their relationship together a potentially richer one than ever before in history. Certainly they are attracted to each other; certainly they want each other; what remains now is for them to learn how to live with each other. Our clinical records strongly suggest at this point that what this means is that they learn how to live with themselves. Growing out of childhood into the emotional maturity of adulthood is the best guarantee for men and women to enjoy a durable and deeply satisfying marriage.

Chapter 7

THE NATURE OF DISTURBED MARITAL INTERACTION

ALBERT ELLIS

Let me begin this chapter with a typical example of disturbed marital interaction; then I shall try to show what the essential nature of this kind of neurotic interaction is; and, finally, I shall try to indicate some of the remedies that can be taken to interrupt and minimize it.

The husband of the couple I saw for marriage counseling was 32, very bright and artistically talented, and desirous of having a mate who would (a) be stimulating to live with and (b) give him sufficient time to be by himself when he was home to pursue his writing. The wife was 30, warm and beautiful, but interested far more in close ties with her husband and two children than in intellectual pursuits. She also wanted sex relations three or four times a week, while her husband was perfectly satisfied to have intercourse about once every two or three weeks.

The husband was so unhappy over his wife's persistent demands for companionship that he constantly criticized her, belittled her in front of others, neglected his relations with his children and became so depressed on many occasions that he worked only sporadically at his writing. The wife, in her turn, carried on side affairs with men for whom she had little love or liking, constantly told the children what a poor father they had, and found excuses to keep interrupting her husband on those days when he finally did come out of his depressed moods and begin to do some work on the novel he was desperately trying to finish. The mates fought viciously over sex, and had highly unsatisfactory coitus on those relatively rare times when they did agree to copulate.

Both these individuals were obviously disturbed in their own right. The husband was needlessly condemning himself for not consistently buckling down to his writing, and was consequently becoming more and more depressed and doing less consistent writing. The wife was so direly in need of being loved, in order to sustain her own worth as a human being, that she was having side affairs with men whom she did not care for and who had no great feeling for her. Both mates, therefore, were foolishly sabotaging their own main life goals and were needlessly creating self-hatred and hostility to others.

Maritally, they were neurotically interacting because, after seeing that they were frustrated in some of their main marriage goals, instead of stoically facing and intelligently trying to minimize their disappointments, they were insanely raging against these thwartings and thereby only balking themselves all the more. Thus, by denigrating his wife for not being more self-sufficient and for demanding more of his time, the husband was encouraging her to be still less able to be by herself and to be more upset about his wanting more time to himself. And by angrily interrupting her husband's writing, the wife was helping to aggravate his desire for solitude; by excoriating him for being a poor father and bedmate, she made fatherhood and sexual copulation even less desirable to him.

Disturbed marital interaction, in other words, arises when one mate reacts badly to the normal frustrations and the abnormal and unrealistic demands of the other mate and in this process helps accentuate the frustrations and demands. Then the other mate, in his or her turn, also reacts poorly to the sensible requests and the unreasonable demands of the first mate; and increasing low frustration tolerance and outbursts of temper on the part of both spouses ensue. Disturbed individuals tend to respond anxiously or angrily even to relatively good life-situations, since they have basically irrational or illogical attitudes or philosophic assumptions (2, 3, 4, 5, 6, 7). When external pressures are difficult, then they react even more neurotically or psychotically (8, 10, 13).

Disturbed people particularly often respond badly to marriage because, at best, monogamic mating is an unusually difficult business and because our expectations in regard to it are exceptionally unrealistic. It should be obvious to almost any sound-thinking person that, while friends, lovers and business associates are often on their best behavior, and consequently will treat one politely and hypocritically, spouses and children are *not* likely to be able to maintain the same kind of urbane pretense for any length of time. Consequently, domestic partners are almost certain to be frequently irritable, short-tempered, unresponsive and difficult. Yet the average husband thinks that just *because* he is married, his wife should be consistently kind and mannerly, and the average wife thinks that just *because* her husband is married to her, he should be invariable sweet and responsive. Thus, two people who, if they were in the least realistic, would frequently expect the very *worst* kind of behavior from their mates, are quite irrationally asking—nay, demanding—the very best conduct from the other. The result of these highly untenable assumptions about what the married state *should* be can only lead to clear-cut disappointment and disillusionment on the part of those who hold these assumptions; and this especially is true for basically disturbed individuals, who tend to invent and cling to unsound premises in the first place, and then roundly to give themselves a pain in the gut when reality proves these to be unwarranted.

The first and foremost cause of disturbed marital interaction, then, is the utterly unrealistic expectations which husband and wives tend to have, not merely about themselves and about others (as is the case with non-maritally upset individuals), but also about the marriage relation itself. They senselessly cling to the supposition that a spouse absolutely *should be* continually loving and forgiving—when, if they were wiser, they would believe that *it would be lovely* if a spouse were that way, but the chances very much are that he or she simply won't be. Then, after somehow imbibing this nonsensical belief, married individuals usually do one more thing that insures their neurotically interacting forever: Namely, they pigheadedly cling to, and utterly refuse to work at eliminating, this self-defeating value system.

This is the real tragedy, and in a profound sense the main cause, of all emotional disturbance: human drifting or goofing. Granting that human beings acquire, usually early in their lives, major self-defeating philosophies and pernicious conditioned patterns of response, the fact remains that they theoretically are capable of changing these philosophies and of reconditioning themselves—and they usually don't. This, in fact, is why we usually refer to an irrational person as neurotic or disturbed rather than as stupid or incompetent: because he presumably *can* behave better than he currently is behaving. Neurosis, as I pointed out in my book, *How to Live with a Neurotic,* is essentially stupid behavior by a *non*-stupid person. The neurotic can do better, but he doesn't. Because, in regard to his self-defeating conduct, he drifts or goofs.

Take, for example, the husband of the couple I mentioned in the beginning of this paper. He was an unusually bright, well-educated and artistically talented individual. Nevertheless, he easily surrendered to several forms of idling in his disturbed relations with himself and his wife. First, he uncritically accepted the hypothesis that he *had* to succeed as a writer and that he was a worthless slob if he didn't. Second, when he became depressed about his sporadic attempts at writing, he lazily allowed himself to wallow in his depression for days or weeks at a time, without making any real effort to see what nonsense he was telling himself to cause this depression and to vigorously challenge and question this nonsense. Third, he made little effort, even though he expected to remain married indefinitely, to strive for true *marital* interaction with his wife and children, but instead largely tried to do exactly what he wanted to do, just as if he had no marital responsibilities. Fourth, he refused to make any allowances, along the lines we mentioned above, for the reality that marriage *is* the kind of a relationship where one is not overpolitely responded to by one's wife and children, who are generally preoccupied with normal and abnormal problems of their own. Fifth, when this husband's wife acted badly, he failed to let any of her mistakes go by, but felt constrained to open his big mouth and point all of them out to her in considerable detail. Sixth, when he observed that his wife was using his negative barbs against her to shatter herself with,

he stubbornly stuck with the belief that his defamation of her would somehow, magically, do good rather than harm. Seventh, when he could have
pacified his wife to some extent by having more frequent sex relations with
her, he vindictively chose to have them even less than he personally desired.

In many ways, then, this husband not only acted ineffectually in his relationships with himself and his wife; but when his main premise—namely,
that he *should* be happy in marriage, no matter how different from his wife
and no matter what her and his emotional hangups were—obviously bore ill
fruit, he did nothing to see, examine or change this premise. On the contrary, he rigidly held on to it and preferred to believe that it was his wife's
fault that his philosophy of life and marriage was not working out too well.

This tendency toward human drifting is so pronounced among disturbed people and their marriages that even the followers of Carl Rogers
(12), who tend to believe that humans have an almost infinite capacity for
self-actualization, have had to recently take cognizance of it. Thus, in the
Rogerian-oriented course of programmed instruction in improving communication in marriage, the Human Development Institute of Atlanta (11)
notes that both mates are responsible for poor communication: "Either one
of them could do something to change things, but instead of doing so, they
concentrate on blaming the other person and hoping that he will change.
Naturally, nothing happens—and nothing *will* happen until one of the two
stops trying to blame the other and asks himself, 'How can *I* be different?
What can *I* do about this?' " Obviously, even the Rogerians have, albeit
reluctantly, come around to the view that human drifting and blaming will
indefinitely perpetuate marital discord and that therefore husbands and
wives who are interacting in a disturbed fashion must somehow be persuaded not merely honestly to express their true feelings to each other—but,
much more importantly, to work their heads off at *changing* the blaming
assumptions that create and perpetuate these feelings.

The more disturbed people and their negative interactions with each
other that I see in my psychotherapy and marriage counseling practice, the
more I am convinced that *all* forms of psychopathology are largely perpetuated by various kinds of drifting or goofing. Neurosis and psychosis, as I
began to point out a decade ago, are so-called emotional disorders which
are largely caused by crooked thinking (1, 3). The origin of this irrational
cognizing is interesting, but not too important in its treatment. Many
patients, even before they come for psychotherapy, know full well just how
they originally started having crazy thoughts and what they must do to give
them up—just as most cigarette smokers know how they started smoking
and what they must do to discontinue it. But, in spite of their insight, they
continue their cognitive goofing and they refuse to work very hard at giving
it up.

This is particularly true in marriage, where husbands, such as the one mentioned above, see clearly that their treatment of their wives is short-sighted and foolish, but nonetheless stubbornly continue this marital-de-feating treatment. In the case in question I was able to show the husband that his expectations about marriage in general and his wife in particular were highly unrealistic and that he had no chance for a happy home life if he kept maintaining them. Somewhat to my surprise, he quickly went to work to challenge and question his own assumptions, began to hold his tongue when his wife and children behaved badly, concentrated more on solving his own writing problems than demanding that his wife change to suit him, and deliberately started to satisfy his wife sexually two or three times a week, whether or not he himself wanted coitus. His concerted work in this connection soon began to pay off. His wife stopped her outside affairs, encouraged the children to be more affectionate toward him and voluntarily got herself absorbed in painting, so that she easily was able to let him have more time for his writing. Although she did not significantly change her own basic assumptions that she direly needed his love to consider herself a worthwhile person in her own right, and hence remained fundamentally neurotic, she at least was able to live more successfully with her disturbance —largely because her husband tackled his own neurosis and stopped blaming her for being disturbed. Hard work on the husband's part, therefore, led to a considerable reduction in his own disturbance and in the disturbed marital interaction; while some, though limited work on the wife's part led to a better marriage in spite of the maintenance of many of her own negative premises about herself.

Similarly, I find that, whenever I can induce any of my psychotherapy patients or marriage-counseling clients to *work* at changing their underlying neurosis-creating assumptions, significant personality changes ensue, and their interactions with their mates, families or other intimate associates almost always improve. More specifically, this work usually consists of: (a) fully facing the fact that they themselves are doing something wrong, however mistaken their intimates may *also* be; (b) seeing clearly that behind their neurotic mistakes and inefficiencies there are invariably important irrational, unrealistic philosophic assumptions; (c) vigorously and continually challenging and questioning these assumptions by critically examining them and by actively doing deeds that prove that they are unfounded; (d) making due allowances for the intrinsic difficulties and frustrations of certain human relationships such as monogamous marriage; (e) learning to keep their big mouths shut when one of their close associates is clearly behaving badly, or else objectively and unblamefully pointing out the other's mistakes while constructively trying to show him or her how to correct them in the future; and (f) above all, continually keeping in mind the fact that a relationship *is* a relationship, that it rarely can spontaneously progress in a supersmooth manner, and that it must often be actively worked at to recreate and maintain the honest affection with which it often starts.

To sum up: Disturbed marital interaction arises when a marital partner is neurotic or psychotic in his own right and when he consequently has unrealistic expectations of what his mate's behavior *should* be. Whatever the original source of these irrational premises may be, the important thing is that the individual usually does not clearly understand what they are, and, even when he does, he stubbornly refuses to work against them and give them up. Basically, therefore, he is a drifter or goofer, and his disturbed marriage will usually continue until he realizes that cognitive goofing simply does not pay, and that there *is* no way out of individual and human releationship dilemmas other than work, work, work.

REFERENCES

1. BECK, A. T.: Thinking and depression. *Arch. Gen. Psychiat., 9:*324, 1963.
2. ELLIS, A.: *How to Live With a Neurotic.* New York, Crown, 1957.
3. ELLIS, A.: *Reason and Emotion in Psychotherapy.* New York, Lyle Stuart, 1962.
4. ELLIS, A.: *The Origins and the Development of the Incest Taboo.* New York, Lyle Stuart, 1963.
5. ELLIS, A., and HARPER, R. A.: *A Guide to Rational Living.* Englewood Cliffs, Prentice-Hall, 1961a.
6. ELLIS, A., and HARPER, R. A.: *Creative Marriage.* New York, Lyle Stuart, 1961b.
7. ELLIS, A., and SAGARIN, E.: *Nymphomania: A Study of the Over-sexed Woman.* New York, Gilbert Press, Inc., 1964.
8. FREUD, S.: *Collected Papers.* London, Imago, 1924-1950.
9. FROMM, E.: *The Art of Loving.* New York, Harper, 1962.
10. GORDON, R.; GORDON, K., and GUNTHER, M.: *The Split-Level Trap.* New York, Bernard Geis Assoc., 1961.
11. HUMAN DEVELOPMENT INSTITUTE, INC.: *Improving Communication in Marriage.* Atlanta, Human Development Institute, 1964.
12. ROGERS, C.: *On Being a Real Person.* Boston, Houghton, 1961.
13. SELYE, H.: *The Stress of Life.* New York, McGraw, 1956.

Chapter 8

ROLES AND ROLE RELATIONSHIPS IN MARRIAGE

ALEXANDER A. SCHNEIDERS

THE IMPORTANCE OF DEFINING ROLES IN MARRIAGE

Every psychologist, psychiatrist, sociologist and marriage counselor is keenly aware of the most serious psychological crisis in contemporary society, namely, the *identity crisis*. This identity crisis has its roots in many facets of recent history and in many changing sociological patterns; and it has been nourished by the changing needs and aspirations of contemporary man and woman. What these patterns are, and how they have contributed to the identity crisis will be a major task of this study (6, 8, 21).

One prominent element underlying the identity crisis is the changing structure and function of the family, particularly in America. Along with this change, and in part reflecting it, is the rapidly shifting pattern of society. This change has been particularly noticeable since the Great Depression of the thirties, and even more so perhaps during the war years of the forties, but the process has been long in the making. Students of these phenomena, including the identity crisis, are aware that such remote factors as the industrial revolution, the evolution of modern education and more recent factors like the growth of psychology, psychoanalysis, urbanization and religious upheavals have contributed materially to the changing pattern of the family and of society.

Because the family is an essential part of the social structure, and thus is constantly modified by it, whatever changes occur in the latter are sure to filter down into the family, affecting both its makeup and its functional significance. For example, the growing acceptance of family limitation, whether by direct birth control, abstinence or other method, has, during the past one hundred years, materially affected the size and the composition of the family, and therefore the impact of the family on the individual members. This factor has been intensively studied in a number of empirical investigations, and the results show quite clearly that family size and composition have a direct bearing on personality development, and therefore on role definition (1, 16).

Perhaps the easiest way to understand and to interpret these tangled variables and mutually dependent interrelationships is to view them in terms of the *continuously changing value systems* in contemporary society. Human values have a great deal to do with role definitions and personal identity; and therefore any significant changes in value systems are bound to affect the individual role perceptions, role expectations and role activations. If, for the sake of discussion, we define values as those more or less stable personal and social ideas, concepts, traditions and mores that determine and shape basic attitudes and practices of both individuals and groups, we can see how important they are, or at least can be, both to personal identity and to role definition.

Among these numerous and common values and attitudes there are few more important that those relating to marriage and family life. We are all too keenly aware of what the erosion and disruption of certain values have done to the family as a social institution, and to marriage as a way of life. This is not the place to plead for or against such practices as divorce, separation, family limitation and other modes of social behavior that characterize contemporary society. We are merely emphasizing the fact that the easy acceptance of such practices in large segments of our society, and their incorporation into our value systems, have changed the functional significance of family life and the structure of the marital union. To speak of roles and role relationships in marriage without adverting to this deep and pervasive influence could only result in a lopsided perspective of the whole problem. Similarly, the impact on family life, on marriage and on society itself of the values created by affluence, and by increased emphasis on material things and their importance to our way of life, has certainly played a leading part in our definitions of basic roles. As Cottrell says in his article, "Roles and Marital Adjustment":

> We are interested in marriage as a problem of adjustment of roles that people tend to play, these roles being conceived of as results of the past experiences of the marriage partners. We shall go a step farther in defining our problem and limit it to a study of marriage as an adjustment between roles that have developed in the childhood and adolescent family experiences of husband and wife. . . . Such a concentration of attention is due to the fact that so many of our case studies, both of well-adjusted and of poorly adjusted marriages, picture people who seem to be seeking to re-enact in their marriages, relational systems or situations which obtained in their parental families. These efforts are sometimes conscious and sometimes unconscious (3, p. 107).

A striking example of this influence is the influx of women into the labor market in ever-increasing numbers, millions of whom are married women with one or more children of preschool and school age. This phenomenon is to an important extent a reflection of the emphasis on affluence, since a large proportion of working wives and mothers have deserted the home for the factory or office in order to supplement the family income. The privately owned home, the two-car garage, the expensive wardrobe, the unbelievably costly college education and plush summer vacations are phenomena (or values) that are taken for granted by a large segment of our society. Once these values are accepted, it becomes mandatory for the married couple to increase the family income, and thus the working wife or mother becomes an essential component of family life. Once this practice is condoned, marriage roles and role relationships undergo a profound change, and this change often interferes with successful marriage careers (18, 20).

The data on working wives and mothers indicate clearly the possible impact of this phenomenon on marriage and family living. The full-time working wife accounts for as much as 40 per cent of the average family income, and she is often referred to as an "incomer." The incomer and her husband spend 40 per cent more on alcoholic beverages, clothing, house furnishings and appliances than when the husband is the sole earner, a third more on recreation and automobiles, and 20 per cent more on food and medical care. According to Labor Department figures, in October, 1963, there were over 24,107,000 women at work, which includes one out of every three women in the country. Three out of every five of these women are married, and one out of every three has children under eighteen. Since 1951, the number of working wives has increased by nearly 5,000,000. The effect that this absence from the home has on the family and children is indeterminate, primarily because empirical studies are yet inconclusive. Whether related to adjustive difficulties or delinquency patterns in children is debatable at the present time, but certainly the incomer does contribute to affluence of the family.

These changing roles, and others like them, have led to deep-seated alterations in the ideas that modern man and woman have of the correct or proper role they are supposed to play in and out of marriage and family life. This phenomenon is closely bound up with another one that is part of our contemporary social order, and that is the changing concepts of male and female, of masculinity and femininity. In fact, the changing social values already referred to have had a strong effect on these different concepts. The terms "male" and "female" or "masculinity" and "femininity" cannot mean the same in a society in which there is widespread role reversal, role diffusion or role confusion (7). Masculinity, for example, is not as easily defined in a society in which what was thought to be a primarily male role is preempted in large numbers by women. If, as in ancient times, the man in the family was supposed to be the head of the family—and we are not arguing here that he should be—and it turns out that in all literal truth the wife is the actual head of the family, then poor role definition or role confusion is an extremely likely result (3, 11, 14).

It need hardly be pointed out in this connection that a great deal of this confusion and diffusion of masculine and feminine roles has resulted from another familiar phenomenon—*feminine emancipation and egalitarianism.* Again, we are not entering here into any argument regarding the "goodness" or "badness" of this phenomenon. We are merely recognizing the fact that the feminine role and the definition of femininity have changed markedly in the past one hundred years, with the result that many women, and perhaps even larger numbers of men, are no longer sure of their own basic roles (19). All marriage counselors and counseling psychologists are aware of the widespread failure of role definitions in the marital situation. That is the reason why such a topic as this would find its way into a marriage manual. As we shall see, where there is no clear-cut definition of roles in marriage, the marital union itself is very likely to erode and fall apart.

Other outcomes of role confusion and role diffusion are increased homosexuality, psychic impotence and frigidity in marital relationships. The mechanism of this development need not concern us at this point. But experts in family life and in psychosexual development know from clinical experience and from well-accepted theory that *role confusion* in the areas of masculinity or femininity is a strong determinant of homosexual tendencies, of inadequate sexual relationships and of orgastic inadequacy. This is particularly true in situations where there is *role reversal,* and the mother becomes the dominant figure in the family pattern, and the father passively accepts the role of a meek follower. It is this kind of psychosocial matrix that generates role confusion in children, particularly adolescents, who are striving for self-identity and a reduction of the identity crisis (7, 21).

These facts serve to emphasize the close relationship between *personal identity and role definition.* In the absence of a clear-cut sex identity there can be no personal or self-identity; and without personal identity there can be no real social identity, and no interpersonal relationships so important to a successful marital union. Sex identity, followed by personal identity, is necessary to adequate role definition and to *a projection of self* into future roles and future situations. When marriage is regarded correctly as a continuing process of self-realization and of continuing interaction, its relationship to role definition and projection becomes quite clear (9). As Erikson says clearly: "The term identity expresses such a mutual relation in it that it connotes both a persistent sameness within one's self (selfsameness) and a persistent sharing of some kind of essential character with others" (8, p. 102).

There is therefore the real need for, and a precise function of, role definitions in marriage. They are necessary to the satisfactory fulfillment of the most basic commitments of marriage. There are several such commitments that stand out prominently in the ongoing process of continuing marital adjustment. First of all, there is the commitment to love, to cherish and to be faithful to the marital partner. Secondly, there is the commitment to protect and to nourish, to complement as much as possible the loved one's needs and characteristics, to communicate effectively with one another and to support the other partner in sickness and in health. There is thirdly the commitment to gratify the most basic sexual and affectional needs of husband or wife, and thus in all respects to function effectively as a friend, as a lover and as a companion. And, finally, there is the commitment, by implication if not by outright promise, to function effectively as a father or a mother when children become part of the family structure.

In brief, therefore, role definitions are necessary to fulfilling the intrinsic as well as the extrinsic functions of the marital union, and to meeting the adjustive demands of the marriage relationship. These definitions, therefore, are important to *the mental health aspects of marriage* and to the kind of *personal growth* that is necessary to a continuing, stable union. That such commitments depend deeply and essentially on the effectiveness with which the married couple go about defining their precise roles is clearly attested by marital failures and maladjustments. When the husband fails to understand and therefore to enact his role as a man, as a lover, as a sexual partner or as a father, the marriage will soon fall apart. And, similarly, when the wife assumes a role that properly belongs to the husband, or fails to enact the role that the husband rightly regards as essential to marriage, erosion will quickly set in and the marital union will begin to disintegrate (12).

ROLES AND ROLE RELATIONSHIPS

Adequate and realistic role definitions are of deep importance to role relationships in marriage. This concept is part of the broader principle that all human relationships are determined in part by each person's perception of himself—in other words, by what he conceives himself to be and by what he imagines himself to be. These self-perceptions are referred to as the *body image* when perceptions are directed toward the physical makeup of the person, and the *self-concept* when the reference is to a much broader inclusion of personal characteristics as perceived by the person himself (10). Important here is the fact that whatever role a person plays in the drama of daily life, or whatever role he intends to play, will be in some degree a projection of his body image and of his self-concept. It is very difficult, for example, for a shapeless, sexless woman to project herself into the role of a wife or a mother; it is equally difficult for a weak, emaciated male to project himself into the role of an ardent lover. This is the basic reason why it is practically impossible for a homosexual boy or girl to think constructively and realistically of marriage. The homosexual impulse so beclouds the self-concept that it is beyond the person's capacity to project himself into the role of husband or wife, father or mother.

The same kind of difficulty is encountered by persons with inadequate self-concepts and poor role definitions when they enter into relationships that are largely determined by certain roles. The person who has difficulty thinking of himself as a male will find it extremely uncomfortable to relate effectively to a member of the opposite sex; and, obviously, the same holds true for women who doubt their own femininity. When, therefore, it occurs, as often it does, that a person with serious doubts regarding his own identity and his own role definition enters into relationships of marriage, the marital union soon begins to erode. Such persons find it impossible to maintain adequate and healthy role relationships with the partner whom they have chosen to share their life (1). In such instances communication quickly breaks down at every level, and the marriage relationship sinks to a point where there is little if any mutual understanding, cooperation or mutual support.

The following case clearly illustrates these several points:

Jim Brown and his wife were referred to the marriage counselor because of serious difficulties in marital relationships generally, and sexual relationships in particular. Six months prior to the first interview with the counselor, the husband had become completely impotent, even though the marriage had endured for six years, and Jim had fathered two children. An interesting sidelight was the fact that the wife, Mary, was exceptionally good looking, beautifully groomed, shapely, and very feminine. In addition, she loved her husband and her children, and experienced strong sexual inclinations toward her husband.

Jim reported to the counselor that the erosion of sexual desire and potency had been going on for several years prior to the onset of impotence. During this time he became less and less interested in his wife as a sexual object, and also experienced a growing aversion to her as a person. This was the basis of the wider marital conflict. At the same time that the erosion was occurring, a morbid interest in pornographic material increased, and it was the discovery of this material that led the wife to insist on professional help for her husband.

Analysis revealed that Jim had poor sex identity, and an inadequate image of himself as a male, and was deeply anxious about relationships with the opposite sex, including his wife. Significantly, Jim's father had deserted the family when Jim was less than one year old, leaving the boy to the tender mercies of an overpossessive and overprotective mother, aunt and grandmother. This situation, of course, would only breed sexual confusion and diffusion, and a failure of sex identity.

After a year of counseling with both husband and wife, and intensive psychotherapy with the husband, the potency was restored, and is still intact after five years. Jim still has doubts regarding his role as husband and father, but is functioning much more adequately.

As the reader can easily see, Jim's marital problem hinged completely on poor role definition. His failure in self-identity not only impaired his relationships with his attractive wife, but also made it impossible for him to function effectively as a father. He tried desperately to be a good father to his children, but simply did not know how to enact the role. As a result, the children turned more and more toward the mother for emotional gratification and support, and began to show signs of uneasy dependency on the mother. In all such instances, encountered so frequently in marriage counseling, the effort to project one's self into various roles that depend essentially on sex identity is doomed to failure. Not until the person sees himself and then accepts himself as a man (or as a woman), and at the same time divests himself of the anxiety that invariably is associated with poor sex identity and with interpersonal relationships, will he be able to achieve effective role definition (4).

ROLES AND THE NATURE OF HUMAN PERSONALITY

The foregoing interpretation of roles and role relationships, set within the framework of marriage or outside of it, can be sharpened and strengthened by defining the relationships between the different roles that a person assumes and the structure of human personality. As one writer says (3, p. 107), personality "is the organization of the roles the person plays in group life. This definition connotes two aspects of the phenomenon we term personality. One is the aspect of traits or characteristics belonging to a person —one might say the content of personality . . . . the second is the integrative aspect. For example we think of stable and unstable, rigid, and flexible persons, persons who are the same or nearly so in all situations and persons who are chameleon-like in their variability. These terms indicate the texture of the fabric or structure of the personality. In many, though not all, personalities there is a predominant or central role that tends to be most characteristic of the person, while other roles, while present, are organized in subordinate relationships."

Significantly, the history and etymology of the term *"personality"* indicate a close correspondence between the two concepts. The word "persona," from which the term personality is obviously derived, referred in the early days of the Greek theater to the mask worn by the actor which enabled him to assume a particular role on the stage. And, even today, in numerous theatrical situations, a mask of sorts is worn by different actors when, for example, they don a beard, affect a particular hair style, grow a moustache, wear glasses and in various other ways change their personalities to suit the roles they wish to assume.

Also, in less dramatic situations, persons alter their personalities from day to day, or even from hour to hour, in order to suit the peculiarities or demands of a particular situation. The riotous teenager, for example, twisting and cavorting with the twist or the watusi, is quickly transformed into an image of piety when he enters church. Similarly, the housewife, some-what careless of her appearance when alone in her own familiar environ-ment, transforms herself into a portrait of beauty and loveliness when din-ing out. These two perhaps oversimplified examples of the relation between personality and role definition serve to exemplify an important fact, which is that personality is not a constant, unchanging reality, but rather *a con-tinuously changing, developing and emerging phenomenon,* well suited to the demands that life imposes on people to assume different roles at different times (1).

This viewpoint of roles in relationship to human personality points up most precisely the importance of personal identity and of role definition to *the realization of selfhood,* and to *the actualizing of personal existence.* Without self-identity, and in the absence of clearly defined roles, the im-portant qualities of individuality, selfhood and personality itself are difficult if not impossible to achieve. Moreover, these factors have a great deal to do with the realization of maturity and adulthood, qualities that are indis-pensable to a successful and happy marriage. All such intrapersonal elements are so deeply entwined, and interpenetrate at so many points, that the development of one is always in some way related to and dependent on the other. It is this quality of *interpenetration* that makes a careful definition of roles and of role relationships in marriage so important.

Let us raise one more issue in this connection. Apart from factors already isolated and discussed, what are the determinants of the various roles that married persons (or single ones for that matter) learn to assume? Are these roles *culturally* determined for the most part, or are they basically *ontological* in nature? Are they the outcomes of *existential* growth, or are they the result of *ontogenetic* development? These questions are not merely academic, for they have deep, practical significance. To the extent that roles are culturally or environmentally determined, they are much more modifia-ble and manageable than if they are the result of ontological or develop-mental determinants. Erickson (8, pp. 110-111) makes a point in this con-nection that is of considerable importance.

> Adolescence is the last and the concluding stage of childhood. The adolescent process, however, is conclusively complete only when the in-dividual has subordinated his childhood identifications to a new kind of identification, achieved in absorbing sociability and in competitive ap-prenticeship with and among his age-mates. These new identifications are no longer characterized by the playfulness of childhood and the experi-mental zest of youth: with dire urgency they force the young individual into choices and decisions which will, with increasing immediacy, lead to a more final self-definition, to irreversible role pattern, and thus to com-mitments "for life."

It will of course become clear very quickly that the answers to these questions will depend partly on the role whose background is being studied. Some roles, for example, appear for a time and then largely disappear. This is true of the student role assumed by the majority of persons in our culture. Similarly, but for different reasons, the role of housewife and even the role of mother may be ended by divorce; or the role of mother might terminate with the death of an only child. However, let it be noted that the mother-role is more deeply embedded in ontological and developmental substrata than is the role of student. What we wish to indicate is that some roles are *adventitious* and *are likely to disappear,* whereas other roles are more *con-natural* but *may be terminated* by adventitious factors (5).

In order to come to grips with this important question, let us begin with the assumption that self-identity and role definition are inseparably linked to the basic qualities and the basic distinctions within human nature. Both of these factors depend *intrinsically* on the distinction between male and female, and reflect at every point the inescapable *ontological* fact that the two sexes are *constitutionally* different. We have no desire to press this issue too far and thus alienate all those ardent disciples of feminism who never seem to tire of trying to eradicate differences between the two sexes. We are quite aware of the gains in equality and emancipation achieved in the name of modern womanhood; and we are not arguing that it should be otherwise (11). But the fact is that an unyielding nature has decreed for all times, as far as we know, that motherhood *per se* will be restricted to women, and fatherhood (however vague that term may be) to men. Only the male of the species *can impregnate* the female; and only the female of the species *can be impregnated.* This is an ontological, genetic and physical fact that sets the pattern for later role definition.

This primary datum regarding the two sexes sets the stage for the emergence of other differential characteristics that in turn contribute to role definition. These characteristics include the distinctive masculine and feminine forms, breast development in the female, which contributes not only to physical form but also to the role of mother, the possession of a penis by the male, which contributes to a clearer definition of the self-concept and to sex identity, and such less important features as height, weight, body proportions, strength and endurance. All these differential qualities are used for both self-identity and role definition (14).

To this ontological and developmental determination of sex identity and sex roles are added a number of social, cultural, religious and environmental determinations that also contribute to role definition for both sexes. The use of different names and styles of dress, hair styling, divisions of labor, the application of differential criteria for productivity and creativity,

and religious attitudes that differentiate the one sex from the other contribute in a smaller way to sex differentiation and to the defining of roles.
Anything, therefore, which tends to obscure these differences, as is happening to some extent in the labor market, in the business world and in
politics, will make sex identity and role definition more difficult to achieve.
There are undoubtedly many masculine women who are confused regarding
their basic sex identity, and there are just as many men of the passive variety
who are equally confused regarding their roles. This is what the present
writer attempted to show in his definition of "the feminine protest" in a
recent book, *The Anarchy of Feeling* (19).

ROLE DEFINITION AND THE PROCESS OF IDENTIFICATION

Before considering basic roles in marriage, there is one other important
social and environmental determinant of role definition that must be
studied most carefully. This is the *process of identification* which binds one
individual to another, and the individual person to various groups, such as
the family, the peer group, the high school or college class, the church or the
local Kiwanis Club. The primary identification that influences role definition as well as role relationships more strongly, perhaps, than any other
factor is that between two persons whose lives are linked in some way that
fosters identification. The following case is illustrative of this point.

> Bill was a young man, 28 years of age, who had been married for one
> year when he was referred for counseling and therapy. The basic reason
> for referral was a total inability to achieve sexual relationships with his
> wife, despite the fact that he loved her very much, and she was physically
> and sexually attractive. Bill was totally incapable of erection and penetra-
> tion, despite his wife's nudity, sexual play and other efforts to stimulate
> sexual excitement and arousal in her husband.
>
> Bill related that his father was absent a great deal from the home,
> and that he always had been strongly identified with his mother, who
> was a strong, dominant and possessive personality. Bill reported repeated
> dreams of emasculation by his wife, from which he would awaken with a
> great deal of fear. After months of therapeutic treatment, with little posi-
> tive result, the marriage was annulled.

The prototype of this identification is exemplified in the relationship
between father and son, and between mother and daughter, although there
are many other important identifications that can develop as a result of
church membership, school experiences or peer-group relationships. It is a
truism of contemporary psychological theory that *positive identification* of
the boy with a significant male figure during the early developmental stages
is practically a *desideratum* of normal, healthy sex identity in adolescence;
and the same rule would hold for the young girl in relationship to the

mother. It is this identification that helps to complete the process and to confirm the fact of sex identity, and, without it, as happens so strikingly in children without parents, sex identity is likely to be badly confused or almost totally lacking (8).

The deep significance of adequate and healthy identification with the like-sexed parent or other important figure is attested by failures or distortions in identification. Everyone is aware today that *cross-identification,* in which the girl identifies with the father and the boy with the mother, can have serious detrimental effects on the developing personality. Likewise, with *negative identification,* by which the boy rejects the personality of the father, and the girl rejects that of the mother, there is likely to be poor sex identity and confusion. In both of these instances role definition, especially where marriage is concerned, becomes very difficult. Intense identification of the boy with the mother will, of course, lay the groundwork for an effeminate psychic structure or homosexual trends, and the same thing can happen to the girl who cross-identifies with the father. For its part, negative identification tends toward role confusion because of the rejection of the personality of the significant figure. In both instances the roles of husband and wife, as well as the roles of father and mother, tend to be rejected or perceived in a confused manner because of the distorted relationship that exists between the child and his parents (19).

This statement does not mean that all positive identifications are salutary to role definition. It quite often happens that the growing boy or girl will positively identify with a member of the same sex, but one who possesses qualities that are inimical to healthy role definition. The boy who identifies with the local gang leader or with a dyed-in-the-wool racist may find it difficult to assume healthy roles in any vocation later on. For identification to contribute effectively to role definition, it must be positive and directed toward the kind of personality that can serve as an effective model for the assumption of healthy roles. We can see from this brief description that role definition is a many-sided thing, and must be studied most carefully in order to determine its relationship to marriage.

BASIC ROLES IN MARRIAGE

We come finally to the problems of identifying and defining those roles in marriage that are basic to this relationship. In other words, what must a person be like, what roles must he assume and fulfill, if the marriage is to endure? Having discovered what these roles are, it will be an easy matter to determine more precisely what role relationships are likely to emerge out of the union (3).

The definition of marriage roles hinges upon the primary fact mentioned earlier regarding the ontological and developmental characteristics of certain roles. In the case of the male partner to the marriage, his role *will always carry the stamp of masculinity,* and it is this quality that determines *the emergence of other roles.* It is only because he is masculine that the male partner can be, first of all, a *husband,* and then secondly, a *lover,* the two primary roles for the male partner. Too often these primary roles are relinquished to an important extent, or emasculated by reason of *feminine domination.* This is what happens with the passive husband. He is a husband in name only, and a lover not at all. The husband should be a dominant figure in the life of his family, even though he should not be dominating. He should be a leader, without being a dictator. He should be the titular head of the home, while carefully preserving the equal rights and privileges of his wife. He should be the decision-maker, after careful and thorough consultation and agreement with his partner. Without these basic characteristics, it is *extremely doubtful* whether any man can fulfill the role of husband.

Equally as important, the male partner must be a *lover* to his wife in the fullest sense of the term. He must not only share with her the important qualities of love, fidelity and mutual respect; *but he must actively make love to her.* To be a real lover, he must continue to pursue her, seek her charms, possess her in the best physical sense of that term and, if necessary, seduce her, so that she will know with unshakable certainty that the man she married is a lover in the most complete sense. It is only this active fulfillment of the role of lover on the part of the husband that makes it possible for the woman to sense deeply and enjoy completely her essential femininity.

By fulfilling these two primary roles, it is easy for the male partner to fulfill a third role—the *partnership role.* Both husband and wife should regard themselves as partners in the most important venture of their lives. As partners, they should be companions to one another in different ventures and areas of behavior, and in this way they should complement each other in many phases of their personalities; and this complementation *should lead to mutual completion.* In a sense, therefore, each partner should derive a portion of his existential being from the other. This is the basic psychological meaning of the ancient phrase, "They shall be as one."

In his role as husband, the male partner to the marriage should also function as a *protector* and *provider,* first to his wife, then to his children. These are important roles that are often attenuated in our contemporary society, partly because of widespread *passivity* among males, and partly because of the more dominant role being played by women in the economic and social world. It is rather difficult to be a provider if the wife's salary equals or exceeds that of the husband. It is equally difficult to be a protector if the family situation is such that there is no one to protect, or if there is a deep conviction that the female partner is stronger than the male.

Finally, the male in the marriage partnership will usually, in the course of time, have to assume the role of *father*. Success in fulfilling this role will also depend essentially on the quality of the husband's sex identity. The concept of *fatherhood* has little or no meaning apart from the quality of masculinity; and the more that masculinity is unrealized because of a faulty sex identity, the more difficult it becomes to assume the role of the father. It is because of this deep and intrinsic relationship that we so carefully defined the process of identification, and the achievement of identity, in the foregoing pages (15).

We need hardly emphasize that the several roles of the male partner have a close parallel in the roles assumed by the female partner in the marriage relationship. Here we can distinguish five primary roles—*wife, lover, partner, nourisher* and, finally, *mother*. As with their male counterparts, each one of these roles will be largely determined in their efficacy by early *identification,* by *sex identity* and by *the conviction of femininity.* To paraphrase what we have said before: *To be a wife one must first of all be a woman.* But also, to be a wife the woman in marriage has to be a *lover* in the fullest sense of that term, and a full partner in the marital relationship. If she is also to be a mother she must first of all qualify as a wife, as a lover, and then as a nourisher to her husband and her children. Here we see clearly how all marriage roles interpenetrate each other, and how each one is in its own way dependent on the other. This is a fact too seldom and too little realized by many married persons. They tend to dissociate one role from another, with the result that each one suffers in the process of fulfillment. It is only when all of the roles assumed by both partners in the marriage are carefully defined and related to each other that the highest goals of marriage can be realized. When there is role confusion and role diffusion, as happens always in cases of inadequate sex identity, the marital ship will quickly flounder (7, 19).

REFERENCES

1. ACKERMAN, N. W.: 'Social role' and total personality. *Amer. J. Orthopsychiat., 21:*1-17, 1951.
2. ACKERMAN, N. W.: *The Psychodynamics of Family Life.* New York, Basic Books, 1958.
3. COTTRELL, L. S.: Roles and marital adjustment. *Publications of the Amer. Sociolog. Soc., 27:*107-115, 1933.
4. EISENSTEIN, V. W. (Ed.): *Neurotic Interaction in Marriage.* New York, Basic Books, 1956.
5. ERICKSON, E. H.: *Childhood and Society.* New York, Norton, 1950.
6. ERICKSON, E. H.: The problem of ego identity. *J. Amer. Psychoanal. Assoc., 4:* 56-121, 1956.
7. ERICKSON, E. H.: The syndrome of identity diffusion in adolescents and

young adults. In J. M. Tanner & B. Inhelder (Eds.): *Discussions on Child Development.* New York, Int. Univs., 1958, pp. 133-154.

8. ERICKSON, E. H.: Identity and the life cycle. *Psychological Issues, No. 1,* 1959.

9. FISHBEIN, M., and KENNEDY, RUBY J. R. (Eds.): *Modern Marriage and Family Living.* New York: Oxford U. P., 1957.

10. FISHER, S., and CLEVELAND, S. E.: *Body Image and Personality.* Princeton, Van Nostrand, 1958.

11. FRIEDAN, BETTY: *The Feminine Mystique.* New York, Norton, 1963.

12. LANDIS, J. T. and LANDIS, MARY G.: *Building a Successful Marriage,* 4th edit. Englewood Cliffs, Prentice-Hall, 1963.

13. MAY, R.: *Man's Search for Himself.* New York, Norton, 1953.

14. MEAD, MARGARET: *Male and Female.* New York, Morrow, 1949.

15. MERRILL, F. E.: *Courtship and Marriage: A Study in Social Relationships.* New York, Sloane, 1949.

16. MUDD, EMILY H.; KARPF, M. J.; STONE, A., and NELSON, JANET F. (Eds.): *Marriage Counseling: A Case Book.* New York, Assn. Pr., 1958.

17. PEARSON, G. H. J.: *Adolescence and the Conflict of Generations.* New York, Norton, 1958.

18. PRESIDENT'S COMMISSION ON THE STATUS OF WOMEN: *American Women.* Washington, D. C.: Supt. of Documents, 1963.

19. SCHNEIDERS, A. A.: *The Anarchy of Feeling.* New York, Sheed, 1963.

20. SHINN, R. L. (Ed.): *The Search for Identity: Essays on the American Character.* New York, Harper, 1964.

21. WHEELIS, A.: *The Quest for Identity.* New York, Norton, 1958.

22. ZIMMERMAN, C. C., and CERVANTES, L. F.: *Marriage and the Family.* Chicago, Regnery, 1956.

Chapter 9

PSYCHIATRIC PROBLEMS IN MARITAL COUNSELING

MARTIN GOLDBERG

Some years ago, I received a telephone call one day from an anxious young man. He explained that he had been referred to me by another psychiatrist, a psychoanalyst, with whom he had had analytic treatment for many years. "Now, I have finished with my therapy but I have some problems involving my spouse and myself," he explained. "My doctor suggested that I contact you, since you are especially interested in marriage counseling and he felt you would be able to help us." Such requests are not uncommon in my practice, so I agreed to see this man and his spouse and gave them a joint appointment for the next week. When the designated time arrived, I emerged from my consultation room into the waiting room to find, seated there, *two* handsome, anxious young men. As I attempted to swallow my surprise, one of them said to me, "I neglected to explain to you on the telephone that I and my mate are homosexuals. But we consider ourselves married, and we do need your help with our marriage problems."

This story, which I am sure sounds like a manufactured anecdote or joke, happens to be entirely factual. And I believe it exemplifies very well a truism with which I would like to begin this consideration of psychiatric problems in marriage counseling: Any and all kinds of people can get married and have problems. Consequently, the marriage counselor, at various times in his work, may have to deal with people of every conceivable psychological sort—from so-called "normal" individuals to very ill, chronic schizophrenics. (As it turned out, the two young men who came to me for help with their "marriage" did not need marital counseling in the ordinary sense, at all, for one of them was quite unhappy with the relationship, wanted to terminate and grow past it, and actually needed and received intensive psychotherapy.)

It is always an important part of the counselor's role to be able to recognize and understand the psychological makeup and problems of his clients, and to be able to identify the psychopathology that may exist in them. If severe psychopathology is evident in either or both spouses, it may often necessitate referral for psychiatric evaluation and treatment. But there are other instances where, even though deep intrapsychic conflict is present, marital counseling may be the treatment of choice for one of several possible reasons.

One such instance is the situation in which a married couple are troubled by clash and difficulties chiefly in their interpersonal relationship, and want and need to concentrate on resolving this, rather than dealing with intrapsychic conflicts that also are present. I think here of a middle-aged woman, whom I will call Carol, referred to me for psychiatric evaluation by a marriage counselor some years ago. She described her problem as being one of feeling indifferent to her husband's sexual advances. As I questioned her about this, she revealed that her husband was a very passive sort of man, who never pressed the issue if she rebuffed his approaches and who had a very stereotyped idea of the sex act which allowed for little or no lovemaking or sex-play and for virtually no variation in sexual technique. I also found that Carol was a very outspoken, aggressive sort of woman. She tended to identify with, and both resent and admire, her father, whom she described as a very strong, aggressive man, although she had married someone quite the opposite. Obviously, both Carol and her husband had inner psychological problems, and I suppose that one approach to their difficulties would have been to suggest that each of them undergo individual psychotherapy. However, although her husband was passive in the marriage he was quite a successful and happy individual otherwise, in his business efforts, etc. And, although Carol was obviously quite aggressive for a woman, she had put this into useful channels as a good homemaker and mother, and as a leader in the activities of various women's organizations. My clinical evaluation led me to feel that individual psychotherapy, with its emphasis on probing and insight, might be more disruptive than helpful to this couple. Since they were both distinctly requesting help with their *marriage* and not asking for an opportunity to remake or improve their personality structures, I recommended that they return to the counselor who had originally seen them and continue with an effort to resolve their marital problems by joint counseling.

Another sort of situation in which marital counseling may definitely be indicated is that in which one or both spouses may already have had psychiatric treatment, but severe conflicts are still present in the marriage. This may be the case where the individual psychotherapy has not been particularly effective, but it may also happen even where psychotherapy has been quite successful, for the completion of psychiatric treatment by no means guarantees a resolution of marital problems, nor does it always serve to prevent their developing in the future. Sometimes, also, psychiatrists will refer patients with whom they are currently working in individual psychotherapy, for concurrent marital counseling. In my own dual professional role, of psychiatrist and marriage counselor, I have experienced this in two ways. Not infrequently, I will suggest that a patient whom I am seeing in individual psychotherapy should go with his spouse to a marriage counselor for counseling, while continuing in therapy with me. On the other hand, I occasionally have couples referred to me in which one or both of the pair are in psychiatric treatment with another doctor, and their psychiatrist has suggested that they also undergo marital counseling with me. Such an approach is a bit complex in nature, but it is sometimes quite appropriate in very difficult situations—where psychotherapy or marital counseling alone will not provide a solution.

There is yet another instance in which an approach to marital counseling may be clearly indicated, even though deep psychic disturbance is present in one or both of the marital pair. This is the sort of case in which it is clear that psychiatric treatment would be indicated and possibly helpful, but is also equally clear that the spouse or spouses are far too frightened or resistant to accept referral to psychiatric resources. As anyone who has had any degree of experience in working with disturbed people can attest, such situations are far from rare. It is generally wiser, in such an instance, for the counselor to attempt to keep contact with the couple and offer them counseling, with the aim of preparing them and bringing them to a point where referral for individual psychiatric treatment can be made and accepted.

A twenty-eight-year-old man, whom I will call Alvin, came with his wife to a marriage counselor, who was trained in social casework. The wife was responsible for initiating the contact, complaining of being very depressed and feeling hopeless about their marital situation. A few interviews with this couple revealed to the counselor that there was considerable psychological disturbance in both of them. Alvin had persistent difficulties in sexual potency, and was only able to sustain an erection after dressing himself in women's undergarments. He also had several fetishes—for women's gloves and shoes, etc.—and a need to be markedly sadistic at times in both his general emotional and sexual relationships with his wife. She, on her part, was a withdrawn, overintellectualized girl who had never related well to men and had suffered from recurrent periods of depression throughout most of the twenty-six years of her lifetime. The counselor was well aware that both Alvin and his wife were in need of individual psychotherapy, and he very gently explored this matter with the couple. The wife was mildly receptive to the idea, but Alvin strongly protested that this was *not* what he wanted, that he was happy with his sexual propensities as they existed, and that all he desired was some help in getting along in his marriage.

Obviously, in such a case any real help for the marriage was impossible, in the face of the spouses' individual problems, but the counselor was wise enough not to press the issue at the time. Instead, he continued to see Alvin and his wife regularly for several more months. By the end of this time,

Alvin was able to say that his real objection to psychotherapy was not that he did not desire change, but rather that he was afraid that his problems were too severe and chronic and no psychiatrist would be able to help him. Shortly after this, the counselor was able to effect referral, sending Alvin to me and his wife to another psychiatrist. Alvin's problems proved to be severe and chronic, as he had feared, but I am happy to say that he was able to stay with intensive psychotherapy over a number of years and effect the very change and improvement in himself that he had thought was impossible.

It must be evident, from the instances I have thus far discussed, that the marriage counselor's professional role calls for a good deal of psychological knowledge, training and expertise. The counselor's primary task is to help his clients assess the difficulties in their interpersonal relationships and attempt to resolve them. But, in addition to this, a really competent counselor should be capable of understanding the individual personality and intrapsychic makeup of each spouse, so that he can utilize this knowledge where it is helpful in the counseling process and also so that he can carry out referral to a psychologist or psychiatrist when and where such is indicated.

A particular situation, in which the recognition of psychiatric disturbance may be of vital importance, is that of the client who is suffering from *depression*. The depressed man often suffers from difficulties in sexual potency and may get involved in marital infidelity. Likewise, the woman who is depressed may become sexually cold and unresponsive, or may enter into an affair outside the marriage. Since more obvious signs of depression are often hidden or lacking, it happens, not uncommonly, that such people find their way to a counselor, looking for help with their marriages. The counselor should be alert to the characteristic symptomatic picture of depression, which often presents with several or more of the following complaints: fatigue; loss of appetite; lack of energy and interest; constipation; difficulty in sleeping—particularly in the early morning hours; impairment of sexual functioning; and various vague aches and pains, as well as depression of mood and thought. The depressed person often states that he feels his worst on first awakening (usually in the very early morning hours) and then improves in mood and energy during the day, so that by night he is feeling relatively well.

If a client presents some of the symptoms of depression, it is well for the counselor to suggest an immediate psychiatric consultation, for the purpose of diagnosis. In some instances, a client may be suffering from a *masked depression*, which makes recognition more difficult, for there is no evident depression of mood in such a person, and the disturbance may be expressed only in slight changes of behavior or in some physical symptoms.

However, skillful interviewing will usually elicit some feelings of hopelessness, intense boredom or lack of interest in life.

Certain other well-recognized facts about psychological depression may be helpful to the counselor in recognizing these disturbances. Depressions are more apt to occur in the *involutional* period of life—after the menopause for women, and in the fifties or sixties for men, when the latter have often passed their peak in business or professional achievement. A depression *may* occur at any age of course, and is often preceded by some experience of personal loss, threat of loss or fear of attack. Examples of these include the loss of a close relative through death, the loss of a job, and reactions to surgical operations involving the loss of organs or special senses, etc. Depression is more likely to occur in the *compulsive* type of personality—the sort of person who is generally hard-working, hard-driving and possessed of a fair amount of hostility, often unexpressed. A family history of depression may also increase the likelihood of its occurrence in an individual.

The reason that I devote a fair amount of concern in this chapter to the recognition of depressions is that these illnesses are generally very responsive to proper psychiatric treatment and are also very dangerous if untreated. In any depression, the threat of suicide is a very real one. Hence, it becomes doubly important that a marriage counselor be able to recognize the possibility of such an illness in his clients and carry out the speediest possible referral for proper medical evaluation and treatment, if such is needed.

I would also like to emphasize the fact that the depressed person is generally full of guilt and self-hatred and has a terribly low opinion of himself. Any strong censure from outside sources may only tend to increase these feelings to the dangerous point where suicide becomes likely. This has obvious importance in some marital situations. For instance, the depressed man who becomes involved in an extramarital affair may subsequently suffer much guilt over this. If his infidelity is discovered, and he is then attacked or reviled by his wife—or strongly criticized by a friend, minister or counselor, or doctor—his already low self-esteem may well sink to a hazardous level. Consequently, the counselor's role in such a situation must be to help both the man and his spouse to an understanding approach of his behavior—while hastening, needless to say, to get the man to psychiatric care.

Suicide is a definite danger in some individuals, other than the depressed spouse, who may come for marriage counseling. I would like to make particular mention of the spouse who uses the *threat* of suicide or the *suicidal gesture* as a weapon and manipulation in a disturbed marriage. Eve, a twenty-eight-year-old suburban housewife with two children, was such a spouse. She and her husband consulted a marriage counselor over problems ostensibly stemming from her husband's infidelity and her discovery of this. To Eve, who was a very dramatic, overemotional sort of woman, this infidelity seemed to be a horrible personal insult and betrayal, and she was obviously concerned with making her husband suffer for what he had done to her.

In the course of a few joint interviews with the marriage counselor, she several times made the threat that she would kill herself if her husband did not abjectly apologize for his actions and promise his unswerving fidelity for the future. These threats were so obviously intended to coerce her husband and the counselor and were so little accompanied by genuine depression or emotion that the counselor did not feel compelled to refer Eve for psychiatric evaluation. However, a few days after one of the joint interviews, following an episode of arguing and pleading with her husband, Eve swallowed fifteen sleeping pills. She immediately phoned her husband and told him what she had done and prompt hospitalization was carried out. Eve did not lose her life—but she came about as close to it as is possible; she was unconscious for thirty-six hours, and intensive medical and surgical attention was necessary to pull her through.

I was called in to see this girl after this episode and from my interviews with her, I believe that she had harbored no intention of killing herself. She was making a suicidal gesture, intended to gain her the sympathy and attention of others and to force her will on her husband. Such suicidal gestures or threats are particularly common in people whom psychiatrists classify as hysterical personalities—very self-centered persons with marked tendencies to dramatize themselves and to manipulate their relationships and environment. However, the important point to draw from this incident is that any suicidal gesture *may succeed* in taking a person's life just as well as a genuine suicidal attempt. Had Eve been unable to reach her husband on the telephone immediately after she took the sleeping pills, her "gesture" would have surely meant her death. Consequently, the marriage counselor must regard *any* mention of suicide by a client as potentially serious and should always seek psychiatric consultation or advice for such people.

I would like now to consider some special psychological problems that may be encountered in counseling marital couples. One of the most interesting of these is the situation in which one spouse is either in psychotherapy or psychoanalysis or has been in such treatment. It often happens, in such a case, that the spouse who is in therapy becomes increasingly self-centered. Moreover, since there are many complex neurotic interactions in any marriage, any change or improvement in the spouse who is in individual treatment is likely to disrupt some of these interactions. The other spouse is then apt to try to restore the former neurotic balance and undo the bene-fit of any change. It is precisely here that concomitant marriage counseling can be of great value, for the counselor can focus on helping the couple to accept a new and healthier interaction rather than returning to the old one.

At other times, a spouse who is in individual therapy may try to use his new-found insights, perceptiveness, and knowledge of human behavior as weapons in the marital conflict. I have known this situation to occur so many times that I regard it as an almost inevitable, though unfortunate, concomitant of psychotherapy. It is terribly easy for a husband with a smattering of psychiatric sophistication to accuse his wife of being "castra-ting," if she stands up to him in an argument; or to tell her that she is "projecting her own impulses," if she charges him with interest in another woman; or to tell her that she may be a "latent homosexual," if she has women friends of whom he does not approve. Moreover, some couples may get into a game of psychiatric one-upsmanship. Such a couple were Grace and Ed, whom I saw for counseling with their marital problems. Grace had supposedly completed a "psychoanalysis" some years previously. Although I had some doubts as to whether she had really done so or had left analysis before a successful termination, I could not check on the situation, since the psychoanalyst who treated her was now deceased. In any case, what I found was that in all of the many conflicts that she had with her husband, Grace always managed to hold a trump card. This was her declaration that, "after all—I'm well! I've worked out my problems." The implication was always very clear that Ed was "sick" and could not possibly have "worked out" his problems since he had not had analysis. Ed, in turn, could only retort feebly that he had never been "sick" enough in the first place to require a psycho-analysis.

Such games as this one, played by Grace and Ed, are not uncommon in our culture, where people are generally raised with an attitude of regarding matters as either black or white, either right or wrong. It then becomes a simple step, with a bit of psychological learning, to substitute for "right or wrong" the characterizations of "sick or healthy," "mature or immature," "normal or abnormal," etc.

Another sort of marital situation which has considerable psychiatric interest and complexity is that in which one spouse presents very obvious, overt psychiatric difficulties, and, while the other appears to be relatively more stable, it soon becomes evident that the pathology is present in both of them. Perhaps the most classic example of this can be seen in couples where one spouse has a severe alcoholic problem. I am intrigued at the frequency with which I have found that the nonalcoholic spouses in such marriages share, vicariously or latently, the very problems that contribute to the alcoholism. I recall one man, with a terrible drinking problem, who was in psychotherapy with me some years ago. He went through long, intensive treatment, during which I occasionally saw his wife. She seemed like a veritable Rock of Gibralter emotionally—very sound, very stable, very dedicated to her husband's recovery. After many years of therapy, her husband finally seemed to have conquered his alcoholism. Several years later, I ran into him on the street and inquired about his condition. He told me that he was doing just fine, except for one thing: His wife had now become a severe alcoholic.

I know, from discussions with other doctors and counselors, that such a situation is *not* a mere happenstance. The nonalcoholic spouse may erupt when the problem is "cured" in the other spouse, as happened here. Or, more commonly, the "well" partner may sabotage—subtly or openly—the recovery of the "sick" one, since both have a stake in preserving the disturbed marital interaction.

Moreover, this type of marital relationship is not unique to the alcoholic. I have seen it frequently, also, where one person is homosexual, or sociopathic, or addicted to drugs, or schizophrenic, etc. I have seen instances in which people of all these sorts were married to seemingly stable individuals and where closer knowledge of the couple revealed that the psychopathology was very much a shared feature of their marriage.

Of course, I believe that this is one extremely strong reason why marital counseling, as well as the joint psychotherapy of couples, has a great deal to offer apart from that which individual therapy can achieve. As the joint approach to disturbed couples becomes more widely used, I believe we will learn considerably more about how psychological illness is shared in marriage.

I think that everything I have written thus far may serve to emphasize certain relevant conclusions. The first of these is that any person attempting to do marital counseling needs a good deal of psychiatric training and knowledge as part of his professional skills. I happen to also believe that psychiatrists and psychologists, who are more accustomed to dealing only with individuals, should have a good deal of knowledge and training in marital interaction and problems, to equip them for their work. Thirdly, there is a need for close cooperation between all the helping professions, and this should be reflected in the more widespread use of psychological and psychiatric consultations and referrals by marriage counselors. Here again, I believe it would also be highly desirable if psychiatrists more often availed themselves of the possibility of referring their patients for marital counseling, concomitant with or subsequent to individual therapy. Finally, I would like to stress something that I believe is evident in my approach to this entire chapter, and that is my belief that it is always best to have a completely flexible approach to any therapeutic or counseling situation. Rigid, sharply delineated systems of psychotherapy or counseling which set down "rules" as to the manner in which people can be worked with and *what* people we can work with may be comforting and reassuring to the therapist or counselor. But the best interests of the people who consult us are served when we devise and improvise our approaches to fit *them* and their special, often unique, situations.

Chapter 10

IRT THERAPY IN MARRIAGE COUNSELING: THE POWER OF INTEGRITY, RESPONSIBILITY, TRANSPARENCY

ALEXANDER BASSIN

Marriage counselors will probably react with moans of protest to what must sound like the presentation of another new method of treatment: "IRT Therapy? Who needs it! We're having enough trouble trying to digest the thirty-six systems of psychoanalysis and psychotherapy Robert A. Harper (1959) wrote a book about."

We respond: In New York there is a subway line also called the IRT. It is neither new nor modern. On the contrary, it is distinctly old-fashioned, noisy, inelegant—no shiny chrome, fluorescent lights, air-conditioning—but it will whisk you anywhere from Flatbush through Times Square out to the far-reaches of Flushing Meadows quickly, dependably, safely.

So with IRT Therapy. It isn't new, but comes from the distilled wisdom of the socializing procedures relating to the Judeo-Christian ethic going back some two thousand years. And it isn't fancy, but it delivers a therapeutic payload with considerable more consistency than the 60 per cent or so reported by Eysenck (3) as the apparent batting average for conventional psychotherapy. Or, as Dr. John W. Drakeford exclaims (2, p. 143) with excitement unusual for a professor of psychology, "It works! It really works!"

IRT Therapy emerges from three concepts which engage and separate at various points depending upon the personality, background and life style of the practitioner, but the three concepts are intrinsically related, and are found with different degrees of emphasis in the writings of O. Hobart Mowrer, William Glasser and Sidney M. Jourard.

INTEGRITY THERAPY

Mowrer is the champion of Integrity Therapy, which will be described first in this report. He is research professor of psychology at the University of Illinois and a graduate of the University of Missouri. He received his doctorate from Johns Hopkins University, has taught at Yale and Harvard, and in 1954 was president of the American Psychological Association. His name crops up with amazing frequency both in the body and footnotes of virtually every major text on psychology. In 1953, after more than seven years of psychoanalysis by three analysts, he suffered a severe depression

100

which brought on a three-month experience in a state hospital, as a result of which his name is now joined to that of Clifford Beers and Anton T. Boisen as founders of seminal new movements in the treatment of the mentally disturbed.

Mowrer argues that psychoanalysis with its emphasis on *removing guilt* is engaging in a basically incorrect procedure. Rather than being a villain, the accepted approach in conventional analysis, guilt serves a healthy purpose in intrapsychic reactions, Mowrer asserts.

One may make a crude analogy. The symptoms of guilt could be compared to a flashing "idiot light" on an automobile dashboard, signaling that something is amiss in the mechanism. Likewise, the guilt which gives rise to a depression, for example, fulfills a useful and necessary function by reminding the sufferer of his past misdeeds, and, until he discontinues concealing the shortcomings and makes useful amends, he will continue to experience discomfort and uneasiness. In other words, guilt is to be reevaluated and conceptualized not as an enemy, but as a friendly, motivating force for good. The stifling or eradication of guilt feelings, to return to our metaphor, would be similar to tearing out the wires leading to the warning light on our automobile panel.

Mowrer was interested in developing the theoretical foundation of his experience and testing his theory with troubled people. He started with small groups in his own community in Illinois, and later introduced them to the State Research Hospital at Galesburg, Illinois, using ex-mental patients as his therapeutic co-workers, along with seminary professors and ministers on sabbatical leave working under a grant from the Ely Lilly Foundation.

Mowrer agrees with Lewin that there is nothing so practical as good theory, and he has been constantly at work turning out vast quantities of extremely well-written material flowing from a highly facile pen. His first two books in this field, *The Crisis in Psychiatry and Religion* (13) and *The New Group Therapy* (14), have served as the cornerstone of what he has dubbed Integrity Therapy.

The distinctive features of Integrity Therapy have been delineated by Drakeford (2, p. 14) under a series of postulates.

1. Deterministic theories which make man a victim of heredity, environment or any other force are rejected. The individual is answerable for himself and exercises his responsibility in making personal decisions.

2. Each person has a conscience or value system which gives rise to guilt when violated. This condition should not be considered a sickness or disability but a result of the individual's wrongdoing and irresponsibility.

3. When the individual responds to personal wrongdoing by concealment, as most of us do, his guilt throws up symptoms of varying degrees of severity ranging from vague discomfort to depression and
   then to complete immobilization.
4. The road back to normality for the individual is to engage in acts of
   openness with "significant others."
5. The person in trouble needs to become involved in a group which
   would offer a microcosm or small world exercising both a corrective
   and supporting function for him.
6. Openness by itself is not enough, and the individual is under obligation to undertake some activity of *restitution or penance* appropriate
   to his acknowledged failure in life or act of deception.
7. To remain a truly authentic person it is not enough to remain open
   and make restitution. It is also necessary to feel a responsibility to
   carry the message of Integrity to other people in trouble.

Mowrer joins the growing movement which maintains that most perceptive and interested people can play a part in helping their troubled
neighbors. In this respect he agrees with the Marriage Guidance Movement
of England which uses specially trained laymen and women as cotherapists
and discovered, according to an evaluation by psychiatric supervisors that:

> . . . In the quality of work done there has been no difference at all
> between the lay counselors and the professional counselors. They simply
> had to admit against their prejudices that properly trained lay counselors
> who were properly selected in the first place can do every bit as good a
> job as professional counselors (12).

Elliott's Case

The operation of Integrity Therapy in marriage counseling may be
understood by referring to a specific case situation described by Elliott
(1966).

> A young man of 24, married about a year, joined with five others in
> the new therapy group I had formed. His main presenting complaints,
> offered in the first session, were depression and confusion about personal
> and professional goals. In the process of getting acquainted with the other
> group members and making himself and his own concerns for therapy
> known, he spoke of the fact that his wife's pregnancy had recently inter-
> rupted sexual relations and that he experienced this as a severe emotional
> deprivation. Because of his own unloving childhood family, he said he
> felt an especial need for emotional closeness and reassurance from his wife
> and found this forced sexual separation very difficult to bear.
> In the flat, discouraged tone of his voice and in his defeated and de-
> pressed posture and bearing, it was tempting to see him as one who more

than anything else needed some strong affirmation and loving support from the group. Members of the group initially tended to respond to him in this way, sympathetically inviting him to talk more about his feelings, which seemed mostly to be blurred and confused.

After an interval I suggested a new tack. Perhaps, I said, we ought to invite him to talk more about his living than about his feeling, about the day-by-day structure and pattern of his life, and I added that I had come to believe that troubled feelings often follow troubling behavior. He was able to respond to this invitation by disclosing that for some years he had been taking small things from stores without paying for them. He had acquired enough psychological sophistication to connect this behavior with emotional deprivation and his need for signs of love. But his attitude towards these acts, as he reported them, was less one of defensive justification than of a kind of helpless confusion. "I know it's wrong, but I don't feel guilty about it."

I suggested that maybe he had come to the stage where his feelings had become a very unreliable guide to behavior, and that while his conscience did not function clearly enough to check his stealing or to produce clear feelings of guilt about it, it apparently was making itself known in painful and indirect fashion in his symptoms of degression and distress. To find a guide for repairing his life I suggested he would have to look to some other resource than "feelings." After some further conversation about this pattern of theft, I somewhat startled him and the other members of the group by giving him an assignment. Before the next meeting, he was to have undertaken to repay the store owners or managers for these recent thefts and was to report back the following week, his successful completion of this assignment as a condition of his good standing in the group. The unexpected character of this approach from the leader caught the whole group somewhat by surprise, but they and he quickly responded to it in a positive way as a signal of seriousness and concern for the man and for his life. At the next meeting he reported that he had carried out the assignment and already had begun to show signs of recovery from his depression and of the emergence of more positive self-feelings.

The above case illustrates Mowrer's basic concepts that psychopathology stems from: (a) tangible acts of misbehavior, deeds done in violation of one's conscience, of the standards one has accepted as valid for his life; and (b) the concealment of such misbehavior from the significant others in one's life in order to avoid the pain of disapproval, punishment or rejection. When this sequence is repeated often enough, the duplicitous behavior brings about one form or another of emotional trouble. In other words, symptoms should be read as disguised and distorted conscience signals registering a genuine, though often well-concealed, moral conflict in the person's past and present life. This view of the nature of emotional troubles requires that a program of treatment or repair would tend to reverse the process. The concealment is repaired by acts of confession, by the honest disclosure of one's self to others and ultimately to the "significant others" in one's life. The step of self-revelation must be followed by an alteration of one's behavior and by undertaking tangible reconstructive steps towards the repair of injuries done to others and to one's own self-respect.

A Case of Marriage Counseling by Integrity Therapy

A marriage counselor practicing this form of treatment was confronted by the following situation:

A crack salesman of 40 appeared for a private session stating that his marriage was breaking up. He wanted to save it, but was very dubious about the prospects. His wife was a slob, a stupid, uncultured woman and had moved away from him as his own success and affluence increased. He would have left her long ago, he told the counselor, but for the children.

The marriage counselor came directly to the point: Was there another woman in the picture?

Rather offhandedly, the client nodded affirmatively but attempted to assure the counselor that this was not a factor in their marital disagreement.

The counselor engaged in an act of "modeling." He suggested that his own life experience indicated that a satisfactory marriage must be based on mutual trust and confidence. On an occasion in his own life when he had strayed from the path of marital fidelity, he also found that all sorts of symptoms had developed and were removed only after he had revealed himself to his spouse. Yes, sooner or later, the client would have to call in his wife for a confrontation and an admission would be in order. The client blanched.

In the first place, his wife would never agree to come to the counselor, and secondly, she would "die" if she learned of the other woman.

The counselor asked if his client would be ready to participate in an experiment that seemed to work in at least 90 per cent of all marital conflict cases. Would he go to his wife and say to her: "Our marriage is falling apart. I would like to save it. I visited a marriage counselor and he indicated it was probably my fault and I would have to change by behavior and attitude if our marriage is to be salvaged. Will you come with me to see him so I can tell you about some of the bad things I've been doing that are driving us to a divorce."

It is a rare spouse that can resist the offer to hear her husband be open and self-critical!

In this case the client was finally able to confess his infidelity—whereupon the wife admitted that she had suspected this situation during the past three years (over which period the husband was certain his wife was blissfully ignorant about what was going on) , and she is glad that at long last it is out in the open. She then released a flood of self-critical material about the neglect of her husband, her meanness towards him, her neglect of the home and the children. Within six sessions this marriage, which seemed headed straight toward a breakup, was placed on a more solid foundation than ever. Periodically, the counselor calls on the couple in his work with new clients to provide testimony about the benefits of being honest, open, authentic, transparent in their relations with one another.

Basic Concepts of Integrity Therapy

Any wrongdoing, past or present, that an individual decides to keep secret causes him to become walled off from others in various ways. He feels he is on guard all the time to keep from being exposed as a type of person he doesn't want to be. He feels anxious, ill-at-ease, uncertain, depressed, always uncomfortable because of his dread of what others would think of him if they knew the facts of his behavior. Integrity Therapy insists, however, that what the person must do is to work up enough courage to admit frankly to others the mistakes he has made—and he will frequently find that they accept him more completely than he ever thought possible—and he will then begin to feel better himself. The more he actually begins to practice honesty with others, the easier life will become, and his symptoms will slip away. He will also be surprised to notice that others become more open to him—that they also have been holding secrets of their own which they would like to get off their chests and thus feel better, too. One person dropping a curtain of secrecy encourages another to do likewise.

Listen, say the Integrity therapists, to that "still, small voice" within us, because what it "tells" us will help keep us psychologically satisfied. Unfortunately, this "voice" can be throttled to such an extent that it grows all but silent. Then we have no internal gyroscope to guide us, and we are in trouble. All sorts of symptoms emerge with a message: "Get back on the Integrity track!"

Integrity Therapy emphasizes the need for self-revelation, confession to significant others. It also insists that confession must be followed by restitution and good works. Mowrer has explored the history of primitive Christianity and notes how frequently public confession was a required ritual of group living; and he believes the original vitality of early Christianity may well be related to this procedure which insures honesty and integrity in interpersonal relations. He notes how frequently the most effective of the self-help groups, Alcoholics Anonymous, Gamblers Anonymous and others succeed where more conventional approaches fail dismally in rescuing a victim from a life of shame and despair.

The Swami Who Ate Gur

Of course, an obvious difficulty related to the practice of Integrity Therapy is the personal strain placed on the therapist. He no longer sits in detached, faceless judgment, employing his superior knowledge of psychodynamics to effect personality alterations upon his hapless patient. He must now act as a *model* of openness about his own less-than-perfect past and must demonstrate in the existential *now* that he is a person of honesty, integrity and responsibility. Dr. Santokh S. Anant, a Sikh psychologist who was a Lilly Endowment Fellow at the University of Illinois during the summer of 1965 in Mowrer's program, tells an anecdote to illustrate this requirement.

> I remember a story from one of the ancient Indian books. A mother was worried about her son's habit of eating *gur* (balls made of raw brown sugar). She was very much concerned that excessive eating of gur might affect the health of her son. She took the boy to a swami who was famous for his success in healing. When she had described her problem to the swami, he asked her to return after two weeks. At the end of two weeks she again took her boy to the swami. When her turn came to see the swami, he told the boy, "Son, you should not eat gur. It is bad for your health," and asked them to return to their home. Probably this woman was expecting more than just a brief communication to the boy. She became quite angry and asked the swami why he could not say the same thing during her earlier visit and save her the trouble of another trip. The swami told her that his words would not have had any effect at that time because he himself was in the habit of eating gur. During these two weeks, he had given up the habit and now he was in a better position to advise the boy. The moral of the story is that one should not preach what one does not practice himself. For this reason psychotherapists have to be very careful in their own personal lives. Before they can expect their patients to live responsible lives, they have to learn to do the same themselves (1, p. 7).

The Role of Confession in Integrity Therapy

The word "confession" stirs many unfortunate connotations in the contemporary mind. One imagines a prisoner in a police backroom, lights shining in his face, and two burly detectives are questioning him in turn until, weak and exhausted, he whimpers a "confession."

Or, as the word impinges on our eardrums, we visualize the Chinese brainwashing procedures and finally the kind of ceremonial confession related to the practices of the Roman Catholic Church.

However, what the proponents of Integrity therapy have in mind is a confession on an entirely different style which has been described by Mowrer in a paper called "How to Talk About Your Troubles" (15).

1. *Complaining is not confessing.* Some people are under the impression that they are engaged in confessing when they are merely reciting their difficulties and problems and telling how unbearable their life has become. The complainer is discussing how he *feels* rather than what he has *done*. Complaining irritates, bores and depresses the listener and leaves the complainer as isolated and lonely as he was before beginning his dirge.

2. *Blaming other people for our problems and difficulties is not confession.* Much that passes for confession is actually a process of justifying a current state on the grounds that other people have caused the problem. If an individual continues to blame others it is highly improbable he will ever face himself for what he is, according to Drakeford (2, p. 93). In an Integrity therapy group meeting, sooner or later an experienced member is likely to speak up, "Never mind about what others did to you. What did you yourself do?" One odyssey of self-discovery is reported by a group member, "I thought I really had it made. My husband had been unfaithful and I was going to make the most of it. But the group wouldn't let me do this. They insisted that I was to blame somewhere, and it wasn't long before I came to see they were right."

3. *We should confess our faults, not our virtues.* A member is wasting the group's time if he concentrates on trying to unearth his "hidden nobility." Groups develop an alertness to people whose apparent faults are virtues. The woman who says, "I suppose I'm just too sweet and kind. I just let them walk all over me," is quickly reminded that being patient and long-suffering is not a crime. As a matter of fact, Mowrer, both in the paper quoted and in his more formal writings, argues for a strategy of (a) confessing misdeeds only and (b) concealing present and future "good works." He makes repeated reference to L. C. Douglas, the author of *Magnificient Obsession* (1929) and *Dr. Hudson's Secret Journal* (1939), whose leading characters engage as a primary therapeutic measure in what Mowrer calls "charity by stealth."

4. *We confess for ourselves, not for others.* Many people are altogether ready to be very honest about *someone else*. Mowrer insists that if confession is to be effective it must be about the speaker and not someone else.

Mowrer deals with the danger of confession, with the likelihood of a story being repeated outside the group and thus compounding the basic problem. But in Integrity Therapy there is constant emphasis on *integrity*, and therefore all understand that what is heard must be kept in the strictest confidence. Yes, it is a calculated risk, but the risk decreases as the group members become increasingly open in their own lives. Most Integrity groups, as a result, have only participants, no observers. But, in the last analysis, we guess Mowrer would say that the risk of irresponsible people talking outside the group in no way compares with the real dangers of the secrecy kept bottled within the individual.

5. *Confession must denote a willingness to come under the judgment of our fellows.* Part of the expectations of our society is for a person to be reliant and strong, with no indication of weakness. Other people are inhibited by the fear that, if they become open and acknowledge their failings, the persons to whom they confess will not understand and possibly look down on them in contempt.

This precept has particular application to marriage counseling. An erring husband is fearful that confessing misdemeanors will provide his spouse with a club to hit him over the head. Thus, many well-meaning marriage counselors observe husbands and wives deceiving each other and even encouraging them not to tell, to keep their duplicitous behavior a secret. The proponents of Integrity Therapy, on the other hand, suggest that most often the counselor must have confidence that honesty, responsibility and transparency in the marital bond is more important than in other relations. Therefore, it is intrinsically incorrect as a therapeutic maneuver to permit any continuation of deceit or deception.

6. *Confessions are made to "significant others" in our lives.* No one suggests that therapeutic confession is accomplished by standing on a rooftop and bellowing one's misdeeds to every passing stranger. Integrity Therapy does not advocate indiscriminate confession. The appropriate subjects for confession are individuals important and significant in our lives, "significant others," as the phrase picked up by Mowrer from Sullivan goes.

William James, more than fifty years ago, provided additional testimony about the benefit of confession:

> For him who confesses, shams are over and realities have begun; he has exteriorized his rottenness. If he has not actually gotten rid of it, he at least no longer smears it over with a hypocritical show of virtue—he lives at least upon the basis of veracity (9, p. 89).

Jung joins James with a similar fine turn of phrase: "In keeping the matter private . . . I still continue in my state of isolation. It is only with the help of confession that I am able to throw myself into the arms of humanity, freed at last from the burden of moral exile" (1933, p. 35).

REALITY THERAPY

Now that we have finished with the "I," we move to the "R" of IRT therapy.

Reality Therapy, the main component of which is emphasis on *responsibility*, is the brainchild of Dr. William Glasser, an extraordinarily warm, friendly, unassuming young psychiatrist who writes in a smooth, lively style remarkably free of the polysyllabic jargonese which makes the writing of his colleagues such a strain on readers in the field. He is an even better extemporaneous lecturer, his platform presentations being full of homespun anecdotes, down-to-earth illustrations liberally sprinkled with wit and humor. He is engaged in private practice in Los Angeles and acts as consultant for the Ventura School for Girls of the California Youth Authority. He is the author of *Reality Therapy: A New Approach to Psychiatry,* which contains a lengthy foreword by the same O. Hobart Mowrer who is the father of Integrity Therapy. Mowrer writes: "This is an extraordinarily significant book. Readers will themselves discover that it is courageous, unconventional, and challenging. Future developments, I predict, will show that it is also scientifically and humanly sound."

A recent review of the volume in *Social Casework* (8) is on a similar enthusiastic level. "'Once in a while there comes a book with ideas that prove revolutionary. *Reality Therapy* is such a book. It is a profound and entirely new conception of mental health and psychotherapy. It will disturb those with set ideas, but those who are uncertain about final answers will welcome it."

Glasser's book contains a slashing, no-holds-barred attack on conventional psychiatry and its current psychodynamic Freudian foundation.

First of all, Glasser argues that mental illesss, as a diagnosible, treatable illness which is somehow like physical illness, does not exist; it is a myth. He questions the usefulness of the elaborate nosological systems that are employed in psychiatry and suggests that this type of labeling has a deadly, nontherapeutic impact.

Glasser asks if there is really any usefulness in one of the essential postulates of conventional psychiatry—the one which holds that one must probe into the patient's past life to search for the psychological roots of his problem in order to help the patient understand these beginnings so that he can change his attitude towards life.

Glasser attacks the concept of *transference.* Conventional psychiatry maintains that the patient must relive with the therapist his past difficulties so that a forum can be provided to explain to the patient that he is repeating the same inadequate behavior. On the whole, Glasser asserts, the therapist's interpretations of transference behavior and the subsequent alleged insights are not effective in getting patients to give up old attitudes and learn new ways to relate to people and solve their problems.

What about the unconscious? What about this basic concept of psychodynamic theory? Glasser suggests that concern about unconscious mental conflicts, which are considered in conventional therapy more important than problems of the here and now, is a waste of time. He argues: "Because no one lives a life where his needs are always fulfilled, it is impossible not to find a wealth of buried conflicts which being similar to present difficulties, seem to explain the person's inability to fulfill his needs now" (p. 42).

The conventional therapist attempts to remain completely detached and uninvolved, making no moral judgments about the behavior of his patient. Glasser, on the other hand, insists on the necessity for an emphasis on the right and wrong. Clients must be confronted with their behavior so they can judge its quality by their own standards; then they must decide what to do about it.

In conventional techniques of therapy, the main task of the therapist is to assist the client in gaining *insight*. Having gained insight, it then becomes the client's responsibility on his own to learn better ways of behaving. Glasser says: "We spend much time painstakingly examining the patient's daily activity and suggesting better ways to behave" (p. 43) rather than trying to develop insight. In other words, Glasser sees the therapist as a sort of teacher involved in a special type of education with his pupil learning to live more effectively. In concluding about the differences of his own approach and that of conventional therapy, Glasser states: "Reality Therapy is not a different variety of the same approach, but a different way to work with people. The requirements of Reality Therapy—an intense personal involvement, facing reality and rejecting irresponsible behavior and learning better ways to behave—bear little resemblance to conventional therapy and produce markedly different results" (p. 43).

Theory of Reality Therapy

"I can explain all I know about psychiatry in about fifteen minutes," Glasser told a recent meeting of Chicago schoolteachers. In essence, every human being, whether a Chinese infant girl or a Swedish king have the same two basic psychological needs: *the need to love and be loved and the need to feel that we are worthwhile to ourselves and to others.* Helping people fulfill these two needs is the goal of Reality Therapy.

The Meaning of Responsibility

The basic concept of Reality Therapy, *responsibility*, is defined by Glasser as the *ability to fulfill one's needs, and to do so in a way that does not deprive others of the ability to fulfill their needs.* A responsible person does that which gives him a feeling of self-worth, a feeling that he is worthwhile to others. He strives for self-respect and even endures privation to attain a self-image that is worthwhile. When a responsible man says he will perform a job for us, for example, he will try to accomplish what was asked both for our sake and for his own. An irresponsible person may or may not do what he says, depending upon how he feels, the effort he has to make and "what is in it" for him. Thus, he gains neither our respect nor his own, and in time he will suffer and cause others to suffer.

The Reality Therapist

The therapist within the framework of Reality Therapy suffers some of the difficulties experienced by our righteous swami described earlier. He must be a highly responsible person—tough, involved, sensitive and human. He must be willing to fulfill his own needs and must be willing to discuss some of his own struggles so that the patient can see that acting responsibly is possible, even though difficult. He is neither aloof, superior nor sacrosanct, nor would he ever imply that what he does or what he stands for or what he values are unimportant. He must have the strength and courage to become involved, to have his values tested by the client, and to withstand intense criticism by the very person he may be trying to help. He must submit to have every fault and defect of his picked apart by the patient. He must be willing to admit that, like the client, he is far from perfect, but he is a person who can act responsibly even if it takes effort.

Furthermore, the Reality therapist must be strong and not expedient or opportunistic. He must be able to withstand the patient's request for sympathy, for sedatives, for justification of his actions, no matter how the patient pleads or threatens. He does not condone an irresponsible action and must be willing to watch the client suffer if this helps him grow towards responsibility. "Therefore, to practice Reality Therapy takes strength, not only the strength of the therapist to lead a responsible life himself, but also the added strength both to stand up steadily to patients who wish him to accede to their irresponsibility, and to continue to point out reality to them no matter how hard they struggle against it." (5, p. 23) .

The Technique of Reality Therapy

In various addresses, Dr. Glasser has explained the methodology of his treatment procedure. He warns, however, that, in contrast to conventional psychiatry, the theory of which is difficult to explain but the practice easy, Reality Therapy has a simple, fifteen-minute theoretical base, but a treatment procedure that is extremely difficult to follow.

1. *Involvement.* The first and most difficult phase of Reality Therapy is the gaining of the *involvement* that the client so desperately needs but which he has been unsuccessful in attaining or maintaining up to the time he presents himself for treatment. Unless the requisite involvement develops between the responsible therapist and the irresponsible client, there can be no therapy, Glasser asserts. The guiding principles are directed towards achieving the proper involvement: a completely honest, human relationship

in which the client, for perhaps the first time in his life, realizes that someone cares enough for him not only to accept him but to accept him in order
to fulfill his needs in the real world.

> How does a therapist become involved with a patient so that the pa-
> tient can begin to fill his needs? The therapist has a difficult task, for he
> must quickly build a firm emotional relationship with the patient who
> has failed to establish such relationships in the past. He is aided by
> recognizing that a patient is desperate for involvement and is suffering
> because he is not able to fulfill his needs. The patient is looking for a
> person with whom he can become emotionally involved, someone he can
> care about and who he can convince cares about him, someone who can
> convince the patient that he will stay with him until he can better fulfill
> his needs (5, p. 21).

Unless the client is convinced that the therapist genuinely cares about
him, there can be no prospect for change. Glasser extends this thesis to all
areas of human interaction, whether it be in marriage, school or work.

2. *Reveal yourself.* Glasser differs from Mowrer in terms of emphasis of
confession as an essential ingredient for therapy, but he does insist that
involvement cannot be obtained if the therapist maintains the aloof "stone
face," the impersonal posture that is taught in conventional psychotherapy.
On the contrary, the therapist must be prepared to *reveal himself* as a
person, with a family, with a car, with his own ups and downs. "If a patient
asks if you have any children, don't freeze over and say, 'I'm not supposed
to talk about things like that.' Tell them about your kids. Take the pictures
out of your wallet and show them" (6).

3. *Be subjective and personal.* Glasser feels that orthodox psychiatry, in
its insistence on being objective and impersonal, is laboring under an
almost impossible handicap. People simply do not change in that kind of
interpersonal situation. Furthermore, not only should the therapist be subjective and highly personal, he must demonstrate this attitude by constantly
speaking of himself using first person pronouns. For example, in working
with a student who is not handing in his term papers, the reality therapist
does not say, "The school administration expects you to do your homework," but "I would like you to work."

4. *Emphasize behavior, not feeling.* Unlike conventional psychiatry,
which is very much concerned with providing a forum for the expression of
feelings, Glasser notes: No one ever explains what the therapist is supposed
to do with these feelings once they've been expressed. Glasser, on the contrary, suggests that the person speak about concrete behavior and deeds
rather than philosophy and rumination. He holds that feelings are beyond
our control; behavior is not. We can't tell ourselves to start feeling happy,

for example, but we can tell ourselves to *do something.* Best of all, if we can do something responsible rather than irresponsible, our behavior may help us feel better. The Reality therapist does not mind discussing this and other concepts of his craft with the client, rather than acting as though he were in possession of some great esoteric final truth that is beyond the comprehension of mere laymen.

5. *Force a value judgment!* The most important single component of Reality therapy as a method, next to obtaining involvement, is to so direct the conversation that the client makes a value judgment about his behavior. For example, to use a situation mentioned by Glasser, if a kid punches a teacher in the nose, we ask him, "Now, did that behavior do you any good?" If the student responds that it did, there is very little you can do about it. Drop the matter for discussion at a later date. But, Glasser insists, in ninety-nine out of one hundred cases, the boy will think for a moment and then respond, "Naw, I guess it didn't. Just made a big hassle and now I'm in more hot water than ever." The client must be pressed, again and again, to evaluate the responsibility of his behavior. Is it helping him meet his needs? It is interfering with other people meeting their needs? Is it doing him or others any good? These are the inquiries the Reality Therapist throws at the client after a firm involvement has been achieved.

6. *Don't accept excuses.* Glasser means this literally. Even if a client presents the most heartrending explanation for his behavior, simply don't accept it, he argues. Disregard excuses. In this area, Glasser borrows a motif from the work being done at Daytop with drug addicts. Here, it has been found that the acceptance of excuses tends to lead to an evasion of responsibility. It is better to be firm and demanding than indulgent and forgiving (19, 20).

7. *Work in groups.* Glasser indicates that the most effective way of working with people, particularly delinquents and students, is in groups. In the first place, the group provides an opportunity for the member to act as a change agent, and, secondly, it is easier to accept a perception of a situation from a peer rather than an authority figure.

Along with Willard A. Mainord (1962), Dr. Glasser is convinced that the treatment of individuals with all kinds of syndromes is best accomplished in a group.

8. *Never give up.* The ability to stay with a client through thick and thin, never to give up, to retain confidence in his capacity to work out a solution is a characteristic of the Reality-therapy method. The client may be testing the sincerity and the depth of involvement of the therapist and the therapist must be sufficiently responsible in his own right to stay at the client's side no matter how difficult and unrewarding the experience may appear to be.

Reality Therapy in Marital Counseling

The precepts and procedures of Reality therapy appear to be ideally suited for the practice of marital counseling. Here the emphasis should be, as we see it, on current behavior, evaluation of the behavior in terms of its contribution towards a satisfactory marriage, and the working out of plans to correct any deficiencies that may become apparent even after a small number of interviews. Reality therapy then contributes to the notion that counseling can be relatively quick, effective and satisfying both to the client and counselor.

TRANSPARENCY THERAPY

Now for the final letter of the insignia. Transparency is the concept presented by Sidney M. Jourard, an associate professor of psychology at the University of Florida and the author of *The Transparent Self: Self-Disclosure and Well-Being* (10).

> I became fascinated with the phenomena of self-disclosure after puzzling about the fact that patients who consulted me for therapy told more about themselves than thay had ever told another living person. Many of them said, "You are the first person I have ever been completely honest with." I wondered whether there was some connection between their reluctance to be known by spouse, family and friends and their need to consult with the professional psychotherapist. My fascination with self-disclosure led me on an empirical and conceptual odyssey. . . .

A chapter in Jourard's book is of particular interest to marriage counselors. "Sex and Openness in Marriage," he calls it and he deals in a remarkably frank, uninhibited way with the problems that develop in the marital situation and what can be done to improve matters. In terms of IRT Therapy, one comment deserves repetition:

> I think that pastoral counselors will be most helpful in their task of midwifing marital well-being when and if they have themselves been able to face the breadth and depth of misery and joy in their own marriages, if they are growing persons rather than starch collars wearing the mask of a minister. There is surely nothing about being a minister that precludes being a person.

How natural it is, then, to move into the work of another outstanding exponent of honesty and transparency in human relations, Carl Rogers, whose latest volume is fittingly titled *On Becoming a Person*. What emerges from that text is the same emphasis we obtain from Jourard, that we respond affirmatively to those individuals who are prepared to be open about themselves, *congruent* at all aspects of their being in interpersonal relations.

Research on Transparency

The concept of Transparency may remain a vague abstraction immersed in a mystical aura that would make it difficult to recognize and visualize this characterological trait. However, when one attempts to translate a concept into the hardware of research, we are compelled to add skeleton, blood and muscle to what might be little more than a flight of fancy. Jourard, while pursuing the notion that accurate portrayal of self to others is an identifying criterion of healthy personality—while neurosis is related to inability to know one's "real self" and to make it known to others— engaged in research that is helpful in concretizing the transparency concept. He followed the characterological studies of Fromm (4), Riesman (16) and Horney (7) relating to the tendency common among persons in our society to misinterpret the self to others. This trend is central to the "marketing personality," the "other-directed character," and the "self-alienated" in- dividual as they have been described by Fromm, Riesman and Horney respectively. On the other hand, much of social science is founded upon the self-disclosures of respondents; the conditions, dimensions and circum- stances relating to self-disclosure bear directly upon the very validity of many purported facts in the social sciences. Jourard concluded that a systematic analysis of self-disclosure holds promise of yielding information that is relative to many diverse areas of theory and method.

Jourard discloses that he was particularly puzzled about Karen Horney's concept of the "real self." He might have noted also the intense interest aroused by public figures when a situation develops which promises even a slight disclosure of the real person rather than the elaborately programed public relations mannequin that is manufactured for mass consumption. The popularity, for example, of the television star of a few years back, Jack Paar, who constantly joked with his audience about their interest in the "real" Paar. Carl Rogers comments wryly about the tremendous response to a lecture which contained a hint that he would speak of himself as a person.

Jourard wondered how he could adopt the concept of the "real self" for purposes out of research; and out of his thinking came the idea that the kind of personal data we all put down on an application form when we are applying for a job might have the makings of a research tool. Some applica- tion forms, labeled "confidential," asked for detailed data about oneself. Jourard asked himself, "Who would an applicant tell these things to besides his prospective employer or teacher?"

And then he was off, itemizing classes of information about oneself which could only be known by another person by direct verbal telling. After much fiddling this way and that, as Jourard confesses (10), he wound up with a sixty-item questionnaire listing ten items of information in each of six categories which he called "aspects of self." He devised an answer sheet with rows corresponding to the items and columns headed by target-persons.

The questionnaire itself reveals Jourard's attempts to concretize the transparency concept. He asks: To what target-persons—mother, father, male friend, female friend or spouse have you expressed your attitudes and opinions on: (a) what I think and feel about religion; my personal religious views; (b) my personal opinions and feelings about other religious groups other than my own; (c) my views on the question of racial integration in schools, transportation, etc.; (d) my personal views on drinking; (e) my personal views on sexual morality; how I feel that I and others ought to behave in sexual matters. (I have selected the questions at random to obtain the flavor of the basic approach.)

Another portion of the questionnaire asks questions of taste and interest: (a) my favorite foods; the way I like food prepared; my food dislikes; (b) my favorite beverages and the ones I don't like; (c) My favorite reading matter; (d) the kinds of movies that I like to see best; the TV shows that are my favorites; (e) my taste in clothing; (f) what I would appreciate most for a present, etc.

The third area involves work or study. He asks: (a) what I find to be the worst pressures and strains in my work; (b) what I find to be the most boring and unendurable aspects of my work; (c) what I enjoy most and get the most satisfaction from in my present work; (d) what I feel are my shortcomings and handicaps that prevent me from working as I'd liked to; or (e) that prevent me from getting further ahead in my work.

Jourard has prepared a questionnaire along these lines dealing with the area of the person's attitudes and feelings about money, personality, body. He asks that the self-disclosure rating scale be marked on the following continuum: *zero*—have told the other person nothing about this aspect of me; *one*—have talked in general terms about this item (other person has only a general idea about this aspect of me); *two*—have talked in full and complete detail about this item to the other person (he knows me fully in this respect and could describe me accurately); and *X*—have lied or misrepresented myself to the other person so he has a false picture of me.

The results of Jourard's investigations are interesting but not directly related to the focus of this paper. His particular contribution, however, is in assisting people who may be wondering about what is meant by self-disclosure—what does Paul Tillich (1952) have in mind by the title of his volume *The Courage to Be*. Jourard's answer is that being transparent means making ourselves known, expressing our viewpoint, being honest in our interpersonal relationships.

CONCLUSION

All this might strike many marriage counselors, as I know it impinges on the sensibilities of psychologists, social workers and therapists, as the meanderings of some long-winded philosopher who has somehow popped into the middle of the twentieth century without benefiting from the accumulated wisdom that began with Freud and his disciples. But one need merely examine the professional scene with special reference to the practice of marriage counseling to suggest that the conventional approach based on so-called psychodynamic principles is not leading us toward becoming better practitioners in working with people who are behaving irresponsibly. Perhaps these suggestions coming from Glasser, Mowrer, Jourard and an ever-increasing number of professionals and laymen should be given a more respectful hearing.

In the last analysis, however, we will stick to our beliefs and practices unless we become reasonably assured that there is something better in the offing. I would humbly suggest that my own experience in marriage counseling indicates a measured echo to Dr. Drakeford's exclamation: "It works! It really works!"

REFERENCES

1. ANANT, SANTOKH S.: *Psychotherapy, Morality and Belongingness*. Mimeo, 1966.
2. DRAKEFORD, JOHN W.: *Integrity Therapy: A New Direction in Psychotherapy*. Mimeo, Fort Worth, Texas. 1965.
3. EYSENCK, HANS J.: The Effects of Psychotherapy: An Evaluation. *J. Consult. Psychol, 16*:319-324, 1952.
4. FROMM, ERICH: *Man for Himself*. New York, Rinehart, 1957.
5. GLASSER, WILLIAM: *Reality Therapy—A New Approach to Psychiatry*. New York, Harper, 1965.
6 GLASSER, WILLIAM: Unpublished address to Chicago School Teachers, Jan. 28, 1966.
7. HORNEY, KAREN: *Neurosis and Human Growth*. New York, Norton, 1950.
8. JACOBS, GORDON L.: Review of *Reality Therapy: A New Approach to Psychiatry. Social Casework*, June 1966, p. 388.
9. JAMES, WILLIAM: *The Varieties of Religious Experience*. New York, Modern Lib., 1902.
10. JOURARD, SIDNEY M.: *The Transparent Self*. Princeton, Van Nostrand, 1964.
11. LONDON, PERRY: *The Modes and Morals of Psychotherapy*. New York, Holt Rinehart, Winston, 1964.
12. MACE, DAVID R.: Marriage guidance in Britain. *Southern Baptist Family Life Education,* April, June, 1959, p. 4.
13. MOWRER, O. HOBART: *The Crisis in Psychiatry and Religion*. Princeton, Van Nostrand, 1961.

14. MOWRER, O. HOBART: *The New Group Therapy*. Princeton, Van Nostrand, 1964.

15. MOWRER, O. HOBART: How to talk about your troubles. Unpublished paper, 1965.

16. RIESMAN, D.: *The Lonely Crowd*. New Haven, Yale, 1950.

17. ROGERS, CARL R.: *On Becoming a Person*. Boston, Houghton, 1961.

18. SALZMAN, L., and MASSERMAN, J.: *Modern Concepts of Psychoanalysis*. New York, Citadel, 1962.

19. SHELLY, JOSEPH A., and BASSIN, ALEXANDER: Daytop Lodge: Halfway house for drug addicts, *Federal Probation*, Dec. 1964.

20. SHELLY, JOSEPH A., and BASSIN, ALEXANDER: Daytop Lodge—A new treatment approach for drug addicts. *Corrective Psychiatry, II* (No. 4) : 186-195, 1965.

21. TILLICH, PAUL: *The Courage to Be*, New Haven, Yale, 1952.

Chapter 11

MARRIAGE COUNSELING AND THE COUNSELOR— AN OVERVIEW

ELEANORE BRAUN LUCKEY

In order to talk about marriage counseling, we need definitions. Marriage counseling is different from individual counseling and is usually distinguished from family counseling in that it centers primarily on the marriage pair and the problems arising from this pair relationship. Marriage counseling involves two individuals plus the *relationship* between them, and is concerned not only with the growth of two individuals as separate persons, but with growth of these individuals as they relate to each other in a very special and intimate way involving close emotional interaction and a sexual relationship.

It is sometimes said that counseling is different from education in that marriage education and guidance involves the process of giving information, presenting new material and correcting misconceptions, is usually a group situation and is preventive rather than therapeutic. Counseling is more often individualized and tends to be concerned with problems involving a conscious decision-making process. Therapy goes beyond and deals primarily with the unconscious, deeper probing into what may be crippling neurotic or psychotic conditions. It is difficult to draw any kind of dividing line between these processes and to know with certainty when the client is involved in an educational rather than a therapeutic experience. Marriage counseling includes from time to time and, within one client, all three different levels.

Perhaps the main reason for drawing lines between these levels is to help the educator, counselor or therapist to stay within his area of competency. A general classification of the case (a diagnosis if one prefers to call it this) which is made as early as possible in the counseling relationship should indicate whether we are dealing with normal people with problems too difficult for them to solve, or if we are confronted with a marriage in which one or both of the spouses are emotionally disturbed beyond the limits of normality. This kind of recognition is more important in relation to the counselor's abilities than to the treatment of the case. Few marriage counselors have developed any defined system of diagnosis with specified treatment, but practically all know their own limits of training and experience. The educator and social worker recognize that they may sometimes give guidance and counsel, but they are not equipped to give therapy. The well-

119

trained therapist, on the other hand, may be woefully lacking in educative techniques or sources of information. The counselor most often represents a kind of middleman between these two. In any event, a proper classification of a marriage case early in the counseling process may save many hours for the clients as well as the counselor by indicating that an appropriate referral to some other professional should be made when factors exist which are outside the scope of the counselor's ability.

SPECIAL AREAS OF KNOWLEDGE

Although the actual techniques in marriage counseling depend considerably more on the counselor than on the marriage problem itself, there are numerous areas of special knowledge over which the marriage counselor must have mastery. In addition to the basic concepts of individual personality development and behavior, the marriage counselor needs to have a ready knowledge of the dynamics of interpersonal relationships. He needs to know why one is attracted to certain individuals and feels uncomfortable with others—to know what this neurotic-compulsive state of "falling in love" is, what its relationship to marriage is in our society and how it differs from what Fromm calls "productive love."

He is something of a sociologist as well as a psychologist—understanding man as he lives as a member of his specific social group as well as an individual. This means he needs a knowledge of current social trends such as the increasing number of teenage marriages. He needs to understand the forces that bring such trends into being, what factors permit them to exist or encourage them. He needs an awareness of contingent problems, such as the growing number of children of divorce in our society. He needs knowledge of the "social norm" and what constitutes departures from it and the associated penalties. Taboos, sanctions, status symbols, values and attitudes vary among different socioeconomic groups, and in order to understand the individuals and the marriage, the counselor needs a knowledge of the milieu from which they come.

Religious values and attitudes also vary widely within American society. A devout Roman Catholic couple will approach their marriage and the difficulties that they encounter with quite a different outlook than the atheist. The Protestant from a rigorous fundamental sect will differ from the Protestant with a liberal viewpoint, and the Orthodox Jew holds to commandments laid aside by the Reform Jew.

Important as awareness and knowledge of these social and philosophic differences are, respect for the individuals who hold them is even more crucial, and it is difficult to respect that which we have inadequate knowledge of.

The counselor needs to be able to read and apply the findings of research, its interpretations and the implications growing out of it. He must keep up with research in at least two fields, that which is pertinent to marital behavior and family life and that of counseling. He should be familiar with studies of marital interaction and decision-making, with investigations of counseling techniques and outcomes and with materials related to marriage and sex practices such as the Kinsey (2, 3) reports.

The counselor needs special information regarding sexual behavior, the psychological uses of sex and the range of sexual standards existing in our society. Although it is generally believed that the sexual relationship of a pair is as good or as poor as their personal relationship, a counselor can improve that relationship by helping a couple learn better sex techniques. Sex is a way of communicating—a way of self-expression that is unique and different from the verbal level. Because sex is a communicative channel, couples need to learn the techniques of conveying meaning adequately to each other through the sexual medium. Coitus is an art, and the arts are, at least in part, learned.

Within our present complex society there exists an exceptionally wide range of sexual attitudes and values and a lack of agreement about what is and what is not moral. A knowledge of this gamut and its resultant confusion within the individual, as well as within the society, is essential to the counselor. He must be aware, too, of attitudes and practices that are typically held by the male and by the female, especially as these differ from each other. Men and women frequently have misunderstandings because they belong (and have all their lives) to different sexual subcultures within the society.

Because marriage problems sometimes have very mundane and practical facets, the counselor needs to be something of a jack-of-all-trades or at least have ready referral sources. He will want to have special information regarding finance and money management, as well as an understanding of the importance of how the use of money relates to the expression of total personality. Although financial squabbles may be symptoms of deeper rifts in the marital relationship, they frequently originate from just what they appear to—poor management of money. If a counselor doesn't himself know about insurance, investment and installment plans, he needs to know where to send his clients for such information competently given.

Home management means the management of human resources within the family, as well as the selection and use of material resources such as the washer, the dryer and the jillion other things that go into the modern home. Time management—especially when there are small children at home—can swamp an inexperienced housewife. There may never be enough time, enough energy or enough skill to convert the family house into the husband's castle! And commuting husbands, tired from the push of too many people, too many machines and too much traffic may make a disheveled household the target for all their annoyances. Although a poor marriage was probably never saved by a handful of household hints, poor marriages can be improved by a wife's developing the necessary techniques of managing her home and her children in a way that makes her feel like, and appear to be, a more adequate person. Knowing where to send clients for information on home management and child care stands the marriage counselor in good stead.

Special problem areas such as alcoholism and drug addiction increasingly confront the marriage counselor. Wherever his knowledge is scant, he needs to have a ready roster of community referral resources, and he needs to make his referrals with sufficient skill that cases will not be "lost," but will follow through to the help they need.

The marriage counselor is not content with understanding only the intricacies of the dyadic relationship; he must have a knowledge of the total family constellation and the stages of family development as they progress from the newly wedded to the retired and the widowed. He must have a great deal of special information about general family problems such as sibling rivalries, inlaw complications, job mobility, problems of the working mother, out-of-wedlock pregnancies and problems of early childhood and adolescence.

A final down-to-earth kind of skill a counselor needs is that of being able to keep records. The kind of records kept will, of course, depend very much on the structure of the situation in which the counselor works. In a social agency the record keeping may be well defined and prescribed; when a counselor is in private practice, his records may depend entirely on his own judgment. Few, if any, counselors can afford to substitute their memories for the written word, and most have developed their own most efficient method of keeping track of the diagnosis, the planned treatment, the progress, and the evaluation. Some counselors must also be concerned with bookkeeping aspects—the payment or nonpayment of the counseling fees. And, of course, if any kind of research is going on, very careful and specific records must be kept.

THE BACKGROUND OF THEORY

What may be called the counselor's "technique" will depend not only on the kind of personality the counselor has and the philosophy of life that he ascribes to but also to a large extent on his training—on that which he has learned *about* counseling and about personality development. He has to have a pretty good idea in his own mind as to just what he thinks counseling is and what the nature of man is; in other words, he needs to know what it is that he is attempting to do in the counseling relationship and how he is going to bring it about. In addition, if he is a *marriage* counselor he must be cognizant of the special conditions of marital interaction and how these are influenced. There is no one theory that has developed its accompanying techniques and proved itself to be *the theory* best designed to accomplish the goals of marriage counseling.

A quick review of some of the more prominent psychological theories will permit an examination of what these have in common and in which respects they are diverse.

Stimulus-Response Theory

Stimulus-response (s-r) theory (which is no one theory but a cluster of theories) concerns itself with the process in which the individual mediates between his array of responses and the tremendous variety of both external and internal stimulation to which he is exposed. It is objective and functional and places a heavy emphasis upon empirical and laboratory research. In spite of the fact that, as a basis for learning theory, the principles of stimulus and response have probably been developed into the most explicit and concrete of any of the theoretic formulations, little has been applied directly to the process of counseling—and that only fairly recently. Counselors who rely on the s-r theory emphasize behavior as a result of learning; they think of habit as representing the stable and enduring characteristics of the person and as the link between a stimulus and a response. Response learned to one stimulus object may be transferred or displaced to another object. Upon these and similar assumptions the counselor sees his main job as helping his client to unlearn undesirable responses and to learn new ways of behaving that are not in conflict with each other or with the society in which he lives.

The counselor with an s-r orientation tends to be directive with his client; he sees himself as a teacher—informing, drilling, assigning homework and exercises.

Psychoanalytic Theory

Psychoanalytic theory bases its highly complex principles upon the assumptions of Freud, who was first to emphasize the developmental aspects of personality and the decisive role of infancy and early childhood. Sex and love are held to be primary forces in the development of personality, as are the inborn forces of hate and destruction. Of primary concern are the deep recesses of the unconscious and its power to direct the behavior of the individual.

The counselor versed in psychoanalysis tends to use the traditional techniques of free association, dream analysis, interpretation and the forces of transference.

Psychoanalytic theory has contributed the bulk of basic concepts regarding interpersonal relationships within the family. Concepts such as identification and the oedipal complex figure prominently in most studies of the dynamics of familial interaction.

Expanding on and deviating from Freud, a group of neoanalysts have modified both analytic theory and techniques through their insistence that the social milieu exerts a powerful influence on personality development.

Alfred Adler (1) insisted that man is primarily a social rather than sexual creature and that he is motivated by social interest—primarily his need to succeed and his desire for superiority. His doctrine of the creative self holds that man makes his own personality, which is structured of the raw material of his heredity and the sum total of his experience. Man is a conscious being, ordinarily aware of his behavior and the reasons for it; he is capable of planning his actions in the direction of self-fulfillment. The Adlerian counselor deals forthrightly with the events, the fears and the plans of his client's life. The client is encouraged to see himself as a creature of worth and uniqueness who can achieve mastery over himself and his fate. The counselor may use all the techniques common to psychoanalysis plus a rigorous directiveness in keeping with a strong-willed philosophy.

Harry Stack Sullivan (6) considered personality as a purely hypothetical entity which cannot be studied apart from interpersonal situations, and for this reason it may be that the most definitive theory of marriage counseling will eventually be based on the constructs that Sullivan brought into being. He consistently emphasized the unique contribution of human *relationships* on personality development and behavior. Like many other personality theorists, Sullivan conceives of the organism as a tension system which can vary between absolute relation (euphoria) and absolute tension (extreme terror). Tension arises from two main sources: needs of the organism and its anxieties (threats to its security).

Believing that the human being is extremely plastic and malleable and is subject to change primarily through new interpersonal relationships, the counselor relies primarily upon communication between his client and himself to effect the necessary reduction of tension that permits more adequate functioning. What takes place in the psychiatric interview is of fundamental importance and is characterized by four stages: (a) the formal inception; (b) the reconnaissance; (c) detailed inquiry; and (d) the termination. Much of what has come to be known as "self" theory and relationship theory reflects Harry Stack Sullivan.

Self Theory

Self theory has had many proponents and as many facets, but the clearest statement of position, as well as the most complete formulation of accompanying counseling methods, has come from Carl Rogers (4). Rogers has drawn freely from the work of others. He has built on Sullivan's interpersonal theory as well as on phenomenological concepts which are related to Lewin's field theory, and he incorporates many of the concepts of holistic and organismic theory as it has been developed by Goldstein, Maslow and Angyal. Through a synthesis of these theories and a proposed method of psychotherapy with a substantiating body of research, Rogers has probably made a greater impact on counselor techniques (client-centered or non-directive) than any other single person.

The primary concepts of Rogers' theory are these: (a) the organism is the *total* individual; (b) the phenomenal field is the totality of experience; (c) the self (a differentiated portion of the phenomenal field) consists of a pattern of conscious perceptions and values of the "me." The organism reacts as a whole to the phenomenal field in an attempt to satisfy its needs which are to actualize, maintain and enhance itself. The personality unfolds along lines dictated by the nature of the organism which is growth, self-actualization (differentiation, expansion, autonomy and socialization). A person progresses toward his goal only when he can see his choices clearly and can adequately symbolize them.

Because the client is the best source of information about himself and because it is *his* perceptions that must be entered into and *his* symbolization that makes his choices clear to him, the counselor's function is to find an effective way to permit this process to take place. The counselor creates the climate of acceptance and permissiveness necessary to free the client to verbalize his perceptions and to correct them, and to see and to select among his choices. The essence of therapy is in helping the client to *be* in a more unified fashion what he organismically *is*.

The counselor who is a true Rogerian has accepted a *philosophy* rather than developed *techniques*. He has a faith in man and in the experiences of life. He believes in both himself and his client, and this belief is evidenced by his *acceptance* of both self and client through his attitude of *positive regard* and his ability to be *congruent* in the counseling relationship.

Although these and other theories differ in varying degrees and aspects, there are important identifiable concepts that are common to all. The relationship between counselor and client is central in that it provides the opportunity for the client to develop an intimate relationship without encountering the danger of getting hurt. Through the counselor's conduct the client is able to express (symbolize) his anxieties, perceive his predicament and grow more comfortable (or make changes). The counselor allows the client control over his situation, expects him to assume the responsibility for his choices and retires from the relationship as the client takes over the management of his own life.

THE COUNSELOR

There is little question that the key to all counseling is the counselor himself and that counseling skill (or art) is no entity apart from the counselor as a person, his knowledge and training, his life experience, his attitudes, values, perceptions and feelings.

The marriage counselor brings to the session his self plus his ideas about what man is, what counseling is, and his set of values and attitudes specifically toward marriage and families. The counselor has to face for himself the same kinds of questions that his clients bring him. Does marriage have a value in itself such that it should be preserved? Are the marriage vows sacred? Should the husband "wear the pants"? Is is "wrong" for the mother of young children to work outside the home? Is it "bad" to be in debt? Who should compromise if a husband and wife don't share the same interests and activities? Who should give in when the pair is deadlocked in conflict? What about attitudes toward children—when is a father too strict and a mother too lenient? What standards should the parents agree on with regard to adolescent Susie? He faces these *not* in order to take a stand himself or to sell his special brand of beliefs, but in order to be aware of how his own feelings are entering into the relationship between his clients and himself.

An integral part of the feelings about oneself are derived from one's role within the community, a role that is determined by such factors as occupational or professional function, status, age and sex. Many marriage counselors are primarily ministers, social workers or professors who also do marriage counseling. Connected with one's specific position may be a whole set of feelings about oneself that may enter strongly into the way he functions as a counselor. For example, ministers may feel that they are the representatives of the church or of God when they counsel, and must therefore advocate a prescribed course of action. Whether counseling is seen as an important part of one's job, as a frill or as a bother also colors the picture, as does the sense of pride or shame that the counselor has in his professional position. The counselor's age and sex—and his feelings about these in relation to his client—may set up certain barriers or destroy them. The counselor's marital status or his marital history may color his feelings about himself with regard to certain marriage cases. Any of the feelings about oneself that are associated with social role may contribute or detract from the relationship with the client, and these will vary from time to time and certainly from case to case.

Most persons who are counselors see themselves as being strongly oriented toward social service; they feel a special responsibility to humanity and are concerned about "doing good" in order to meet their own need to maintain their self-respect and sense of self-worth. When one is in a position where others ask help of him, and where his expectation for himself is that he will render such help, it is difficult not to be anxious about fulfilling this expectation and appearing to advantage. Such anxiety is often heightened by both the overt and the subtle pressures to succeed that abound in our society. We don't want to fail and when clients ask for advice and opinions and answers, it is difficult to resist trying to meet their expectations.

Often connected with role and position is a given value system and set of beliefs about marriage. Some counselors are committed to saving the marriage at almost any price; others believe that the individual is of first importance, and, if necessary, the marriage can or should be dissolved for the benefit of one or both of the partners in it. Because counselors, too, are a product of their society and its value system, the majority of them in our culture believes there is a "rightness' about an existing marriage, and they tend to believe it should be preserved.

The counselor's role within the community determines many things other than his feelings about that role. To a degree *which* people approach him depends on his position; the private marriage counselor and the psychiatrist have a very different clientele from the social worker in a family agency or the minister. *How* the counselor is approached and what is expected of him are also often "built into" his role to a considerable extent. A client is very likely to reveal himself quite differently to his minister than to a stranger he has never seen before and expects to see only in the counseling interviews. The client who is paying a good-sized fee may hold different expectations than the one who is asking charity. And, naturally, the counselor's response is partially dependent on who and how and with what expectations his client approaches him.

An awareness of oneself in terms of needs and the ways he seeks to fulfill his needs is as essential to the counselor as his awareness of his social role with all its expectations. The counselor understands his own set of values and beliefs and knows how these may enter into his perceptions of his clients and of the situations in which they find themselves. A great deal of *knowledge of self* is the prerequisite for the counselor's wise use of himself. And knowledge of self exists only where there is a sense of *acceptance* and comfort with oneself. The counselor of necessity is a person of integrity and maturity; inasmuch as these are lacking, there will be flaws in his counseling relationships.

CONGRUENCY

There is a very close link between the kind of "technique" that a counselor chooses to use and his own personality; if the technique is not a true expression of the counselor's self, the relationship lacks genuineness. This implies that, because the counselor is a unique personality, the technique which he employs is specific unto him; it is his own, just as his need pattern, his life experiences and his mode of expressing himself are uniquely his own. Only he can know how it is that he feels and how he can best express these feelings so that his client has the advantage of a secure, intimate relationship that is therapeutic.

Within the interview situation the counselor must be constantly as aware of his own feelings as he is those of his client. This often means that in the initial interviews at any rate, the counselor will work as much with himself as with his client. He will work toward defining what it is he feels and what may be the barriers within him that will keep him from closeness with his client.

Acceptance of another human being—even in the artificial situation of a counselor's office—is difficult. Overcoming one's aversions and one's "right's and wrong's," putting aside one's own preferences and dealing with one's own problems of transference can sometimes keep a counselor so busy that he can hardly listen with even half an ear to his client. When it is a married couple that the counselor must work with, the complications are more than doubled. He has need to relate simultaneously to two individuals —each of whom he may feel quite differently about.

The most important aspect of counseling is the degree and quality of communication that takes place. Communication not only reveals the client's problems and feelings but provides the clues to the counselor's feelings; it is the way in which the counselor makes himself known to his client. It is the way in which the counselor takes his client "unto himself."

Too often, communication within the counseling interview—like that within the social setting—is used to conceal people from each other rather than to reveal. The interview may be a series of intellectualizations, abstractions, evasions and defenses carried on by the clients and the counselor in some kind of a role-playing game, with each being intent on trying to impress each other.

Learning *how* to make oneself understood honestly is sometimes a problem even when one is willing to be so understood. Some counselors verbalize; some use facial expression and gesture; some seem to make contact with their clients in a kind of silent sensitivity that may be empathy. Experienced counselors use all these media.

Receiving the communications of the client—cutting through to what it is that the client is *really* saying—demands a concentration that is beyond mere listening. Basically, the counselor must *want* to know what it is that the client is expressing and must be willing to be alert and to focus on it.

When communications go astray—and they frequently do—it is the responsibility of the counselor to try to bring them back to the target. There may be times where the counselor is "lost," and, when this happens, he should not find it difficult to admit he doesn't know what his client is talking about. By striving for more clarification for the counselor, the client may do a great deal of clarifying for himself.

Pretenses and cover-ups and avoidances of the issues are some of the "phonies" that can be insurmountable barriers in the counseling relationship. They are often the defenses that the client brings with him—and brings necessarily as a part of his problem and himself, but they have no place in the repertory of the counselor.

SOME SPECIFICS OF MARRIAGE COUNSELING

All the factors that we have discussed as being pertinent to counseling situations "in general" are pertinent to marriage counseling—the counselor's knowledge, training and philosophical orientation, his maturity and use of himself in the counseling relationship. There are, however, additional factors to be considered in dealing with a couple and their marriage problems.

In contrast to individual therapy in which the counselor centers his attention primarily on the individual, the marriage counselor must keep track of *two* personalities, with not only the *intra* conflicts but also those between the two; there are two sets of inconsistencies, indecisions and interpretations; and there is a whole array of perceptions in the interplay of feeling and action between the spouses.

Because of this complexity some counselors prefer to work with only one of the married pair; counselors with a psychoanalytic orientation almost always work with only one spouse, and only if it is absolutely necessary will they have contact with the other or his therapist. However, counselors who consider themselves primarily *marriage* counselors usually want to work with *both* of the partners, and in cases where only one spouse comes for help, the counselor will try to induce the other to come in. By experiencing the interaction between the partners as well as learning of the perceptions and expectations that each partner has, the marriage counselor has much more knowledge of his case and a much better "feel" of the situation. Some counselors believe that to counsel only one of the married pair is as ridiculous as it would be to read the lines of only one character in a Shakespearian drama!

Each partner needs to be evaluated or "diagnosed" as if he were an individual counseling case. The counselor enters into each individual's feelings, his perceptions and his needs. Marriages are sometimes out of kilter because one partner's neurotic demands cannot be met or because one spouse is psychotic or on the verge of a psychotic break.

In addition to the assessment of each individual, the counselor looks at the couple as a *pair*—noting what each "does to" the other and in what kinds of situations. He notes how they support and encourage each other, and how and where they destroy. Probably the most important area the counselor concerns himself with is that of the clients' *perceptions*.

Each spouse has a set of: (a) perceptions of himself; (b) perceptions of his spouse, and (c) perceptions of his spouse's perceptions of him. In other words, he holds three sets of ideas: (a) his own self-concept; (b) his concept of his spouse; and (c) his concept of what the spouse's concept is. These may be in close agreement or widely disparate.

The client also holds a set of *expectations* of: (a) what he "ought" to be; (b) what his spouse ought to be; (c) what their relationship ought to be; and (d) what his spouse's expectations are on all these.

The counselor has to keep track of the wife's perception of and expectation for herself and her feelings about herself, her perception of and expectations for and feelings about her husband, and what she thinks her husband's perception of her is, his expectations for her and his feelings about her! The husband, too, has this same "field" in which to operate.

It is the meshing of these perceptions and expectations of both the individuals that is the basis of the *relationship;* these plus what might be considered the basic needs of each individual account for feelings and behavior of the couple. To encompass this tremendous amount of action as well as emotion means the counselor must be extremely alert and himself be *open* to the experiences of the counseling sessions.

There are dangers inherent in this kind of dual counseling whether it is done in conjoint sessions or with only one client present. The counselor has to be extremely careful never to take sides or seem to be more partial or more understanding or empathic with one spouse than the other. This is sometimes extremely difficult, because normally the marriage counselor tends to see one person's side a little more clearly; he may find one of the pair more attractive and admirable than the other, or he may himself tend to identify with one and not the other. Part of the success in establishing a good relationship is being able to convey to *each* of the pair the counselor's sense of genuine *caring* for him, of being *with* him yet *not* being *against* the spouse.

It is also difficult not to betray the confidences of each individual to the other. It is important never to reveal to one partner anything that the other has said, or in any way to use the statements of one to manipulate the other. The counselor cannot permit himself to be used as a channel of communication between the two; essentially *they* must establish their own channel. The counselor's responsibility is to permit and aid in interpretation and clarification, and to encourage the two to communicate with each other as fully and through as many media as they can.

Counseling with both of the spouses presents the hazard that either one or both of them will use the counselor as a club or a pawn. When this happens, the counselor can no longer be useful to them. If either of the pair attempts this, it needs to be brought into the open and dealt with.

Frequently, only one of the spouses will seek counseling, and although any marriage counselor would prefer to have both spouses concerned and involved, it is better to have one than none! Frequently, the solo client is helped to see himself in a new perspective; and by gaining a new perception of the marriage relationship and his role in it he can modify his own feelings and behavior enough to bring about reactions which are more positive on the part of the partner who is not in counseling. Whenever it is possible most counselors try to bring the reluctant partner into counseling in some way. This always has to be a voluntary process and not one in which the nonparticipating spouse is made to feel compelled or imposed upon. Probably the most successful way of involving the unwilling spouse is to enlist his aid in helping the counselor gain a more complete picture of the marriage situation and its conflicts. This must be a genuine appeal and not simply a gimmick to bring the spouse into a counseling situation. If the counselor creates a genuine, warm and accepting atmosphere, the unwilling spouse often becomes willing. He finds that here is someone who will listen to his side of the story as well as "the other" side. Once he discovers that it is easy and safe to talk about himself, he, too, may be eager to work with the counselor.

Counseling sessions may involve one spouse at a time or both, depending on the strength of the marital relationship and on the willingness of each partner to reveal himself before the other. Often when a couple first comes to counseling there is so much bitterness, so much need to attack or so much withdrawal that conjoint sessions are not the best use of the counselor's time. When the clients have learned to trust the counselor and are secure enough to reveal themselves to each other, the counselor can be of tremendous help in encouraging communication and in clarifying feelings when the three work together in one interview.

Conjoint sessions can be risky, but they also can be occasions of tremendous growth. The counselor may have to take safeguards so that a situation does not become too devastating. He may find himself sometimes protecting one client from the other, sometimes supporting one so that he can make himself heard by the other. It may be that the counselor will need to keep one of the pair from revealing himself too soon or too bluntly, or from striking too often or in a too vital territory. The counselor himself has to be cautious that he does not snatch away defenses or emotionally disrobe either of his clients before the eyes of the other. Because the counselor must take on these additional responsibilities which are somewhat of the nature of a referee, conjoint sessions tend to be more structured and the counselor more active.

CLIENTS LEARN ABOUT MARRIAGE

A part of marriage counseling is helping the clients learn not only about themselves but about their partner and about the marriage relationship itself. Almost always, clients come initially with complaints about their partners; usually they want *advice*—and frequently it is advice about the other spouse. Often the first one or two sessions may be spent by the clients "wading through" their complaints and expelling some of their anger and anxiety. Early in the process the counselor needs to help them understand that he has no little pink pills that he can prescribe in order to make their troubles go away. He needs to destroy the illusion that he is an advice-giver and will solve their problems for them. With help, clients usually can understand that their problems have been developing over a very long period of time and that the process of "growing out of" them may be almost as long and certainly more painful than "growing into" them. They can realize that the problem is *their* problem and not the counselor's; this doesn't mean that the counselor isn't deeply concerned, but it does mean it is *they* who must find *their* solution. They need to know that the counseling process is not something that is done *to* them; progress that is made is made *by* them with the counselor's help.

Most clients have little idea of what to expect of marriage counseling or the counselor. Although through the extended period of the counseling sessions they begin to see and understand the process, they are usually more comfortable if the counselor defines his role and his work to them at the outset. Because each counselor sees himself differently and works within his own specific framework, his definition will be uniquely his. Most marriage counselors, however, direct their efforts toward three general goals: (a) the client's perception of himself to be as clear and as complete as is possible (his needs and expectations and his ways of trying to meet these needs); (b) The client's perception of the spouse to be as the spouse perceives himself—with his needs and expectations and way of meeting these; and, finally, (c) open communication regarding these sets of perceptions so that each understands the other better, so that decisions can be made, compromises affected or accommodations made.

In many respects the marriage counselor serves in the capacity of the *teacher,* in that he is helping his clients to discover a great deal of knowledge about self and the other as well as what marriage in this society is. Understanding their own feelings—and that of the spouse—involves some basic information about personality development and the influence of early childhood, information about defense mechanisms and how they protect, information about personality needs of human beings and a great deal of information about how the society in which we live determines the "right" and "wrong" ways of meeting these needs. Most clients need to have their romantic ideas of marriage challenged; they need to understand love as something other than the mystical, omnipotent force that they fall prey to. If they have a specific area of conflict, they may need information that will help them make decisions about such things as job choice, finances, sex, treatment of the inlaws or of the children.

Clients learn how to assess the dynamics of their married relationship by asking themselves: How do I feel about myself, and what is it that my spouse does to me that either violates a good feeling that I have about myself or reinforces a bad feeling that I have about myself? They learn that most of their behavior is in defense of the self-concept or toward enhancing that concept; they learn that when there isn't enough freedom to grow in the marriage because one spouse does not permit the other to develop a self-concept in keeping with his own needs, there is conflict. For example, the wife who makes her husband feel like a little boy when he wants and needs to feel like a man is likely to find that he *acts* like a little boy, that he becomes resentful and wants to strike back, or that, in spite of her, he may try to feel like a man and prove it by buying himself a new car, getting drunk or finding himself a woman or two that does make him feel like a man. Or he may simply pull himself away from his mothering wife and become distant and indifferent. If he is one who has learned to turn anger and disappointment inward, he may hate himself for not being the man that he wants so much to be, and he may find a variety of ways in which to destroy himself or a part of himself. Relationship dynamics such as these can be explained to clients and understood by them, and soon they learn to look at themselves in these new ways. One doesn't have to be a psychologist to be insightful.

Identifying feelings and verbalizing them often leads to a husband's saying such things as, "My wife makes me feel like the man who pays the rent," or "her star boarder," or even "the worm that's been caught." A wife may say, "He makes me feel like a waitress," or "a prostitute" or a "moron." Once these feelings are verbalized, the client can deal with them more rationally; he can explore the *why* of them, and such explorations frequently lead to broad insights about self and spouse.

People can be taught—at least to some extent—to be open-minded. Almost always, people in marriage difficulties are eager to fix the blame—and usually to fix it on the spouse! One of the first questions a client asks is often, "Who is wrong? Me, or the other fellow?" Couples can learn that disagreement doesn't necessarily mean that one of them is right and one is wrong; it means each is different; each holds a different point of view or may be seeking a different goal. Both of them may be "right," yet conflict persists.

Giving a spouse the freedom to differ is a principle that can be learned more easily perhaps than learning to give him the right to *fail*. This is probably true because one spouse's failure reflects on the other or may inconvenience the other, and when the self-image is damaged or imposed upon, there is protest.

Clients soon learn to look at themselves in these terms. They learn to examine themselves beyond the first layer of their complaints and feelings to discover if these are symptoms or basic causes of conflict. Finances, sex, the wife's working—these problems are the visible ones and are usually the ones that are first presented to the counselor, but couples often discover, as they try to clarify these, that they are only the surface layer, beneath which are much more basic discontents and unmet needs.

Teaching clients to communicate and to use all the channels of communication that are at their disposal is another of the marriage counselor's tasks. It is remarkable how obscurely we make ourselves known! Counselors can point out that clarity can often be gained by just a switch of words or a changed vocal inflection or a restatement in different terms. Spouses can increase communication by eye contact, gestures, touches and most certainly and perhaps most meaningfully through coitus. With the counselor's help the couple can examine the meaning—or the lack of meaning—in their sexual relationship. By working at the business of making themselves understood outside the counseling session, as well as in it, clients often make far greater progress than seems possible. Counselors will encourage the couple to spend time together talking, working and having fun.

Once the spouses begin to move toward a reconciliation, they can apply the same basic techniques with each other that the counselor has used with them in the counseling relationship—acceptance and understanding, congruence of feeling and expression, a willingness to listen and a willingness to reveal oneself. These are the fundamental principles working in all close and meaningful relationships—whether it be counseling or marriage.

The ultimate objective of the marriage counselor is the same as that of any counselor—to work himself out of a job. With the marriage counselor, however, the "job" involves one of two additional steps beyond helping each individual to "find himself in life." One is the complicated process of helping two human beings live together in the most intimate, intensive and permanent relationship existing in our society; the other is the often sordid and depressing business of helping two human beings separate, divorce and reestablish themselves as single persons, or sometimes as single parents. Such a counselor must be a mature person who has learned to use himself so effectively that his clients are free to reach their maximum growth; he must have a command of special areas of knowledge and information, and he must sometimes be a teacher as well as sometimes a therapist.

REFERENCES

1. ADLER, A.: *The Practice and Theory of Individual Psychology.* New York, Harcourt, 1927.
2. KINSEY, A. C.; POMEROY, W. B., and MARTIN, C. E.: *Sexual Behavior in the Human Male.* Philadelphia, Saunders, 1948.
3. KINSEY, A. C.; POMEROY, W. B.; MARTIN, C. E., and GEBHARD, P. H.: *Sexual Behavior in the Human Female.* Philadelphia, Saunders, 1953.
4. ROGERS, C. R.: *Client-Centered Therapy; Its Current Practice, Implications, and Theory.* Boston, Houghton, 1951.
5. ROGERS, C. R., and DYMOND, ROSALIND F. (Eds.) : *Psychotherapy and Personality Change: Co-ordinated Studies in the Client-Centered Approach.* Chicago, U. of Chicago, 1954.
6. SULLIVAN, H. S.: *The Interpersonal Theory of Psychiatry.* New York, Norton, 1953.

Chapter 12

THE DIMENSIONS OF THE "EXTRA" IN EXTRAMARITAL RELATIONS

GERHARD NEUBECK

IMPLICIT AND EXPLICIT GROUND RULES

Anyone who writes about marriage must deal with the problem of ground rules. Men and women who have agreed to live together in that relationship we have called marriage are bound by such ground rules, be they implicit or explicit. The evolution of these ground rules is well known, and they have remained relatively stable for centuries. Though often questioned, in recent years more serious doubts about such ground rules have been raised. Experiments engaged in by married men and women showed that transgressions of ground rules did not necessarily end up in the destruction of the marriage. The writer has previously suggested in other research (7, 8) that the problem of ground rules be further investigated.

One must start with the assumption that whatever ground rules exist they are subject to local cultural as well as overall sociological/psychological deviation. The ground rules, of course, have been shaped and refined by religious institutions, and in almost all societies are codified by governmental authority. Again, interpretation of the rules will differ from person to person, from couple to couple. Variation within the marital pair—for whatever reason, be it culture or sex-linked—is a problem which will be discussed later. As Foote (2) suggests, marital dynamics also may vary according to developmental phases of the marriage.

It is certainly difficult to extrapolate from this complex set of rules (which for the individual before he or she is married exist in the abstract) a set of personal, marital expectations. Yet, individuals do grow up with personal goals to be fulfilled through marriage, which will determine to a large degree the interpretation they will make of the ground rules and the decisions they are going to make to live by them or violate them.

We know, of course, that, with rare exceptions, ground rules are hardly ever specifically discussed before marriage, but they are nevertheless *assumed* to be the same for both spouses. Rarely is there an explicit agreement ahead of the marriage ceremony. Jokes, cartoons and commentaries about the violation of ground rules by some one person occasionally give people an opportunity to think about the rules, but only infrequently is this a serious and weighty thought. Only when the moment has come that a ground rule has been violated does the consideration become critical. For most persons the rules agreed to during the marriage ceremony or in discussions of the rules by the clergy in premarital instruction are taken for granted. I doubt that many individuals really internalize meaning at this, the so-promising stage of marital union.

This is not to say that in the fantasy life of individuals ground rules are not dealt with. To whom one is married forever and ever or what other heroes may appear on the scene may indeed occupy the dream world of our lovers. But after all *this* kind of world is not for real. One thing is certain, though; ground rules have never included the realm of fantasy; ground rules govern behavior. (It also follows that there are no external penalties for transgression of rules when transgressions take place in fantasy.)

In today's world the problem of ground rules receives a great deal of attention. Stage and television, film plays, novels, real-life events of the neighbor next door present us with frequent examples of how the rules work or fail to work. Occasionally this leads to an actual challenge as to the validity of the rules though, the discussion is usually faint-hearted and abortive; it is taboo territory except for iconoclast writing in offbeat journals. The only serious attempt that I know, one which received a good deal of public attention, was Albee's *Who's Afraid of Virginia Woolf?"* But the problem of ground rules does deserve our attention.

WHAT ARE THE GROUND RULES?
1. Individuals enter marriage on a voluntary basis.
2. Marriage is a permanent relationship.
3. In monogamous marriage one man is married to one woman.

While partners marry voluntarily, these marriages take place in a culture which places high value on marriage and in which an ever-increasing number of the population does marry. While marriage is assumed to be permanent, divorces are permitted in a majority of cultures, and the contract, "till death us do part," remains unfulfillable. The third rule, in which marriage is regarded as an exclusive relationship—the seventh commandment—implies that marital parties are assumed to be sufficient unto each other in the areas of human functioning to the marked exclusion of outsiders (4). It is this third rule on which this paper's attention is focused.

Jackson also has commented on what he calls the "Achilles paradox." Though a voluntary act to begin with, marriage continues on the basis of "having to want to stay together." As Torbett and I have pointed out earlier (8) "We must examine how this voluntary relationship, this regulated coming together, fulfills the expectations of meeting needs for both of the participants, the spouses." Winch and his associates (9) investigated this problem, and a host of others since have addressed themselves to the question of complementary needs. Torbett and I asked the question: "How well does *marriage* do the job of meeting the expectations of the spouses?" The term "efficiency" was then introduced, which Webster defines as: "Serving to effect the purpose, or producing intended or expected results." We went on: "How effectively is marriage then working for those who enter it? . . . effectiveness in marriage can only then take place when both spouses behave toward each other in certain ways. Marital effectiveness is a product of the effectiveness of both spouses. The institution of marriage can only be effective when both spouses behave in these certain ways." We further claimed that "effectiveness can only be produced if, when one partner expresses a need for a certain satisfaction from the other, this other assumes the obligation to meet that need." This is Jackson's Achilles paradox. The obligation to meet spouse's need starts out as a "means to an end." But as a behavior it develops quickly into an "end in itself," and possibly into a need. If I assume an obligation to meet my spouse's need for closeness—however that is felt—and come close, I have also met my need for wanting to please. My behavior is means and end at one and the same time. Obligation and need-fulfillment are so closely linked that it is probably impossible to distinguish between them in most marital situations.

MARRIAGE AS A GROUP SITUATION
Significance

The environment in which the needs of marital partners can be met mutually can best be described by referring to the marriage situation as a group situation. The work of Lewin (1940) has been helpful in conceptualizing marriage as a group, and Levinger more recently has used this concept also. Lewin's essay, called "The Background of Conflict in Marriage," dates to 1940 and was published in his book, *Resolving Social Conflicts* (6). He begins this essay by saying: "Marriage is a group situation, and, as such, shows the general characteristics of group life." Levinger (5), in a piece called "Marital Cohesiveness and Dissolution: An Integrative Review," declares that "the marriage pair is a two-person group." I am borrowing this concept from Lewin and Levinger to describe further the environment for which the ground rules are operative.

Lewin declares that married group life has greater significance than ordinary group life since "marriage is very closely related to the vital problems in the central layer of the person, to his values, fantasies, social and economic status. Unlike other groups, marriage deals not merely with one of the aspects of the person, but with his entire physical and social existence." Lewin further describes the adaptation of the individual to the group. He declares that "belonging to a certain group does not mean that the individual must be in accord in every respect with the goals, regulations and the style of living and thinking of the group. The individual has, to a certain degree, his own personal goals." It can be readily seen, however, that, in a two-person group, deviation from group goals may be much more catastrophic than in a group in which there are greater opportunities for a pooling of personal goals. Deviation in a group of two obviously has greater consequences than deviation in a group of six or twelve. Lewin himself says later on that, "because of the small number of members in the group, every move of one member will, relatively speaking, deeply affect the other members, and the state of the group. In other words, the smallness of the group makes its members very interdependent."

Social Distance

Another aspect of the marital situation as a group situation is the variation in social distance. Lewin says: ". . . willingness to marry is considered as a symptom of desire for the least social distance." What is said here, then, it seems, is that the willingness to marry itself is an admission of the willingness to lose a degree of privacy and accept permanent proximity. It obviously follows that privacy is restricted in marriage. Levinger also quotes the work of Festinger, Schachter and Back, when he refers to their definition of group cohesiveness as "the total field of forces which act on members to remain in the group." So with the lack of privacy, the quest for permanent proximity, cohesiveness is established which in itself, then, is a constant reinforcer of the maintenance of the group situation, i.e., the marriage situation.

Free Movement

Closely related to this is Lewin's reference to the amount of space of free movement of a person. He goes on to say: ". . . too small a space of movement generally leads to a high state of tension." This confinement to the small space of the two-person married group quite likely leads to the seeking of less-confining situations, though again this may be dependent on how much free movement is required by an individual.

Jealousy

Lewin, in his 1940 analysis of the marriage group situation, is not afraid of suggesting some ideas about jealousy. His explanation of jealousy is based partly on the feeling that one's property is taken away. Lewin suggests that a great amount of overlapping exists; "from the tendency of love to be all inclusive, this feeling may be easily aroused if the relation between two persons is very close." He goes on to say that "the intimate relation of one partner to a third person not only makes the second partner 'lose' the first one, but the second partner will have, in addition, the feeling that something of his own intimate life is thrown open to a third person." By permitting his marriage partner to enter his intimate life he did not mean to throw it open to the public. The relation of the partner to the third person is felt as a "breach in the barrier between one's intimate life and the public."

If I understand Lewin correctly, he suggests that, whatever the marriage environment furnishes in line with need-satisfactions, the environment itself is confining and will force group members to make certain kinds of sacrifices in order for these needs to be met. The sacrifice includes not only a lack of freedom but also the sharing of property, in this case the properties of one's spouse, and the giving up of relationships with a variety of other peripherally related individuals.

Abstraction and Reality

Again it must be emphasized that the degree of deprivation and the degree of frustration are highly individualized and can be measured only on an individual basis in line with the kinds of conditioning and building of expectations that we have described earlier as a function of early upbringing and learning. The hypothesis that suggests itself, however, is quite clear. The greater the need for freedom, the more confining the marriage environment might be, and the subsequent wish to escape from it; the greater the need for the possession of property and subsequent unwillingness to share property, the greater the jealousy and willingness to be faithful on one's own part. It must be understood, however, that these are highly abstract expectations and that they may be discarded in the wake of impulses that are triggered by tempting situations. We also know that the double standard has applied here, so that faithfulness is expected more of women than of men. Again I would think, however, that this is a result of the ability to control superego functions in regard to impulse stimuli (7).

Marriages Have Developmental Phases

Lewin, in the essay, contributes an idea that has not been developed by anyone else until rather recently. He spoke of marriage as a group in the making. This refers to what now is called the life cycle of a marriage (though he did not lay down any rules in the essay which would describe in more detail the various cycles such as early marriage, marriage in the thirties and later marriages). He suggests, however, that, in the young marriage, "the situation is not clear in regard to the balance between one's own needs and those of the partner. That leaves typical conflicts, but at the same time allows greater flexibility for their solution."

OBLIGATIONS AND ROUTINES

I discussed earlier some aspects of the voluntary *versus* the obligatory responsibilities among marital partners. The hopes from premarital days that "hubby" will do all these nice things develops quickly into an expectation that hubby has a duty to do them. But there is more that takes place than a change in expectations: Need-meeting behaviors become routinized. They become routine duties. It is from this shift from the voluntary "wanting to" to the obligatory routinizing that we can explain the feelings voiced that "our marriage has gone stale." The fun has gone out of the relationship. Fun depends in this case on more spontaneous actions, decided on when and how the mood strikes me rather than when I am "schedulized" to perform these acts. With such "fun" missing it is likely that relationships are sought which by the very fact that they are outside of the marriage promise voluntary and spontaneous responses. This may be similar to or accompanied by a need for "playfulness," to which I will refer shortly.

OVEREXPOSURE AND VARIETY

Other dynamics of the marital situation can be viewed as overexposure and subsequent satiation. Since marriage is expected to extend over the total life span, exposure will be constant, and there is no escaping from the presence of the other person with whom one "lives together." This permanent togetherness results in quantitative and qualitative exposure that may lead to satiation, since there is only a finite number of personality aspects available. These traits or characteristics may be exhausted, though occasionally they can be altered enough to serve as a new challenge. When the scenery remains constant, however, after a while one may have seen enough, and new scenery looks desirable. On the other hand, it may not be impossible that, in some cases, marriage partners who seek escape avenues from the steady, taken-for-granted confrontations with their mates, once recognizing this need, can develop within their marriage such conditions that would offer them new glimpses at each other under new circumstances and in different environments, with new horizons than from what life was like before. But even such attempts are governed by the limitations within the very nature of personality and personality interaction; there is only a certain degree of variability. When needs for variability are not met sufficiently, a new person with a new set of characteristics will seem attractive. Not only is the grass greener on the other side, it is also of a different sort.

Closely connected with this is the feeling of boredom. If all the "tunes" upon the instrument of our personalities have been played, and even the variations have been exhausted, and even when, after having given the instrument a rest, a taking up of the old exercises and the playing of the well-known tunes has brought temporary satisfactions, will they not soon yield to the resignation that it is "the same old thing, all over again"? Bored, one turns away from an instrument that offers no new discoveries and turns to one that offers them.

PLAYFULNESS

Playfulness itself, implying lack of seriousness and, to a degree, lack of responsibility, is in many ways incompatible with married life. Individuals with psychopathic personalities do not fit into the restricted space of marriage. Because marriage calls for responsibilities and seriousness, the playful personality cannot find enough opportunity for play and will look for such opportunities where they can be found. Outside of those persons who are outright psychopaths, however, there are many whose playfulness is not socially destructive. For them marriage can become a playground where games of many varieties can be played. To what degree such couples can build into their life experiences which momentarily have a minimum amount of seriousness and responsibility, such as "evenings out," vacations —depending on the age of the children and other phases of the marriage— or conduct that includes a certain degree of playfulness, will be a result of a shared system of values that regards playfulness as not only legitimate but even wholesome. Traits such as flirtatiousness may also be related to the kind of game-playing mentioned above. If flirtation according to the dictionary means "making love without meaning it," it is obviously not possible to flirt with a spouse. A spouse is not a candidate for consummation; spouses have already consummated. Reintroducing elements of courtship into one's life can only be accomplished by the courting of someone new.

With such courting may also go a degree of anxiety, a noncrippling type, which a person needs to sustain an emotional momentum. Such anxiety-provoking moments are hard to find in a relationship with a mate of long standing, and newcomers will seem attractive. This anxiety will then be fostered by situations which make one live more dangerously, live with ambiguity, live in a vacuum rather than in the well-defined, well-circumscribed, as well as predictable, marital environment. Only those marital situations which open themselves up to experimentation among spouses will bring enough security to prevent experimenting on the "outside" for the experimentally minded person.

SEXUALITY

There is no special reason why sexual needs should not be seen in a vein similar to that of other marital dynamics. That it has received and maintained a special loading, however, is clearly traceable to the taboos surrounding sexual conduct. These are likely to remain with us, and will, therefore, give the sexual area an aura that it really does not warrant. Let us look at the phenomenon of sexuality in greater detail since it does have a complexity all its own.

A good deal of recent writing has attempted to see sexual appetite as related to an exclusively physiological base, appetite for both spouse or other-than-spouse partner. Other writers and researchers, notably Ford and Beach (3), produced evidence that sexual response is a physiological/social/psychological phenomenon, and extramarital sex activity should be seen in this context. (Even enormous sexual appetite, let us say a few standard deviations away from the Kinsey norms, cannot be understood simply as mere physiological drive.)

Sexual relations with "outsiders" can then be seen against the background of the earlier discussion. The relative importance of sexual expression will leave the individual to concentrate on that aspect of the "outside" relationship rather than on another. Sexual relations may become inevitable, not necessarily because one "lusts" sexually after the "outsider," but because one believes sex belongs in the relationship. This is true in the light of the fact that sex carries with it a symbolic function. So while sexual activity serves basic physiological needs, the psychological ones are not far behind. Our culture makes manifold uses of sexual stimuli, and it is easy to fall for the sex thing even if sexuality is not what is primarily wanted. Sex is "in," and one better have it. This is not to say that there are not perhaps a great many individuals who are naturally and simply desirous of sex partners who may be other people's spouses. And again, in fantasy such pairings are often imagined and consummated. Men more so than women are given to fantasy couplings. By the mere fact that we are men and women attraction is a constant. Our ground rules of long standing forbid us to go further than fantasy, but the rules are often broken, and some cultures do not include rules that forbid sexual enjoyment of other people's mates. A few more primitive cultures actually encourage it. Unfortunately, there are also a set of individuals, notably the psychopaths already mentioned, whose emotional and sexual impulses are not governable by either internal or external controls. The objects of their impulsivity are seldom aware that they are simply utilized for essentially exploitative purposes, sexual ones in this case, though there is probably a good deal of mutual exploitation in existence as well.

In the sexual area, temptation has greater significance than in others because we value sex so greatly today. But Oscar Wilde's bon mot, "I can resist everything but temptation," really points to what is regarded as the "right opportunity." Opportunities which bring one together alone with a nonspouse are almost expected to produce an extramarital sexual involvement. Partial opportunities of this sort are built into our social life.

Party ritual calls for a degree of flirtation. There are seductive moves, first tentative "dares," then more pronounced invitations that end up in full-fledged sexual episodes. Our culture, while explicitly "puritan," promotes social affairs which in fact are institutionalizing men-women opportunities. There is the case of social dancing, for instance, where close body contact is "allowed," leading not infrequently to sexual relations as a matter of course.

The "seven-year itch" phenomenon or the middle-age adventure refers to a yet different aspect of extramarital activities. Linked to the age of the marriage, it is implied that, periodically, sexual appetites arise which have as their target a person outside of the marriage. But, since we have assumed earlier that this sexual appetite really encompasses a variety of other motivations, these "itchings" should then be understood as the arising of new needs over the life span of the marriage which, if not met by the spouse—and a good deal of testing may go on with the partner inside the marriage first—are pursued in outside relationships.

CAN MARRIAGE MEET ALL THE NEEDS?

In an earlier comment I discussed one of the corollaries to the ground rules of marriage, namely, that marriage is an exclusive relationship in which mates are expected to be sufficient unto each other to such a degree that satisfaction given by or sought of third parties is not included. That marriage should serve all the needs of the spouses is built into our marital expectations, yet anyone who examines this proposition realistically is struck with its impossibility. Marital lives are not conducted in isolation, and husbands and wives are in contact with numerous other people during each twenty-four-hour day. So, as a matter of course, spouses will experience satisfactions from a great many other men and women. The quantity and quality of these satisfactions will determine to what degree they are tolerated by the spouse, though the tolerance level of the spouse is at least as much of a determinant.

TOLERATION OF "OUTSIDE" SATISFACTIONS

We also know that marriage cannot serve to meet all of the needs of both spouses at all times. Many marriage partners define at least implicitly —certainly discretely—what area of satisfactions they will leave to outsiders, and they are not only *not* disturbed that outsiders serve in this capacity, but probably relieved that they themselves are not called upon to have to address themselves to each and every need or whim of their mates. In this sense the extramarital relationship becomes a supplement to the marriage relationship. The "extra" is no longer referring to the geographical outside, but to something additional. Again, the degree of tolerance depends on what these satisfactions are like, how and when and how often they take place, and what meaning is read into them. Meaning obviously is a function of individual taste and value system, or is connected with psychological mechanisms such as projection. The trouble over meaning usually arises from lack of understanding or from not having made one's point of view more explicit. To some degree, feelings of jealousy can be explained in this way, and clarification of meaning may enable spouses to be more tolerant about involvements with outsiders. In fact, some relationships of this kind are acceptable to everyone, perhaps even taken for granted. A co-worker of the other sex with whom one shares many hours during the day (thereby having available opportunities for personal communication) is common-place in today's world of work where men and women work side by side. And on a social level we assume that friendships extended to other couples will include intimacies on a verbal or even affectional level between differ-ent sex friends. For housebound wives, however, outside relationships be-come immediately suspect, while for men these bonds, office and work linked as they are, have a more neutral quality. In a study by Babchuk and Bates (1) called "The Primary Relations of Middle-Class Couples: A Study in Male Dominance," a hypothesis was tested that "the husband will initiate a greater number of mutual primary friendships shared by the couple than will his wife." While the nature of that study is not primary to my investiga-tion here, dealing as the study does with male dominance, it is of interest to see that, in the case of their couples, both the husband and the wife ac-quired friends with whom they both shared intimate confidences.

It is possible then to maintain relationships with both spouses of another pair, and even though it has been usually assumed that there will be less of a "threat" when both partners share these confidences, it seems from the Babchuk and Bates study that, in successful marriages, differential degrees of intimacy between spouses and outsiders, in this case members of friend-ship pairs, are maintainable. Side by side with a substantial and satisfactory level of communication between mates can go a sharing of "intimacies" with outsiders.

So, with meaning understood by both spouses, and under an umbrella of an acceptance that marriage for them is not an all-inclusive relationship, it is feasible to have outsiders taking care of needs which cannot be met within. But does this include sexual needs as well? Faithfulness is ordinarily seen as faithfulness in the flesh, and transgressions of sexual nature have always been seen as the most crucial kind. So, to allow sexual relations be-tween one's mate and an outsider seems to call for more than an intellectual willingness. The momentousness of sex—however artificially fanned by the culture—produces emotional roadblocks which cannot, so it seems, be over-come by realizations that parallel those mentioned earlier, that is to see sexual relations simply as an area of general needs and to deal with them in line with a point of view that sees marriage as a not-all-inclusive relationship. Sexual relationships outside of marriage are not tolerable by such individuals as if they were just another unshared area, since guilt is great and they are unable to tolerate the burden inflicted upon them by religious and cultural mores. Persons must either experience relatively little guilt or a high degree of guilt tolerance to participate in extramarital sexual affairs.

To tolerate any kind of outside involvement—and probably sexual involvement more than any other—an ability to compartmentalize is of vital importance. To separate out one personal relationship from another seems absolutely necessary if these outside experiences are going to result in anywhere near meaningful satisfactions.

FAITHFULNESS AND LOYALTY

I have discussed at some length the tendencies of marital partners to seek satisfactions outside of their marital bonds, and I have tried to delineate the dimensions of these extramarital relations, trace their motives and suggest mechanisms by which they can be tolerated by spouses. Concommitant to these behaviors, however, are forces of contrary nature. While it is, perhaps, not possible to separate out ideas fed to us by our superegos, spurning us to behave "morally" and be trustworthy, there are in most of us substantial ingredients of conservatism. We want change, but we also want to preserve; we like the new, but we cherish the old as well; we desire thrill and excitement, but calmness is also welcome; ambiguity seems interesting, but lack of it feels so secure; we may be bored, but familiarity also breeds content. But, most of all, human beings have an affectionate nature which makes for loyalty and a continuing concern for the welfare of the other (spouse). A momentum built up during years of intimate marital contact is not only the result of "having to stay together," but stems also from innumerable reinforced mutual need satisfactions which "pay off" over and over again. And, last but not least, there are those husbands and wives who simply want to do right, for whom virtue has its own reward.

The mechanism of marriage as a means to regulate the relations between the sexes has limitations and imperfections which need constant repair and readjustment. To fit one's expectations into the confines of the marital scheme and limitations which are imposed on it by its very nature is never easy. That so many spouses are able to make use of the mechanism of marriage and make such good use of it is a tribute to the invention itself. One should not only deplore failures, as demonstrated in divorces, but should also applaud the successes of those who over time provide each other with pleasure and are able to conduct their joint affairs effectively. At the same time it is now clear that marriage can work out successfully for both of the spouses even when it is not an all-inclusive relationship, when either in reality or fantasy there are other persons who share one's life.

REFERENCES

1. BABCHUK, NICHOLAS, and BATES, ALAN P.: The primary relations of middle-class couples: A study in male dominance. In William J. Goode (Ed.): *Readings on the Family and Society.* Englewood Cliffs, Prentice-Hall, 1964.
2. FOOTE, NELSON N.: Matching of husband and wife in phases of development. In Marvin B. Sussman: *Sourcebook in Marriage and the Family,* 2nd Edition. Boston, Houghton, 1963.
3. FORD, CLELLAN S., and BEACH, FRANK A.: *Patterns of Sexual Behavior.* New York, Harper, 1951.
4. JACKSON, DON D.: Family Rules: The Marital *Quid Pro Quo.* Unpublished paper delivered at Conference on Family Process and Psychopathology, Eastern Pennsylvania Psychiatric Institute, Philadelphia, Pennsylvania, October 9, 1964.
5. LEVINGER, GEORGE: Marital cohesiveness and dissolution: An integrative review. *Journal of Marriage and the Family.* 27 (No. 1) : 19-28, 1965.
6. LEWIN, KURT: *Resolving Social Conflicts.* New York, Harper, 1948.
7. NEUBECK, GERHARD, and SCHLETZER, VERA M.: A study of extra-marital relationships. *Marriage and Family Living,* 24 (No. 3) : 279-281, 1962.
8. NEUBECK, GERHARD, and TORBETT, DAVID: Dynamics of marital effectiveness. Part of a paper delivered at the Groves Conference, 1962, in Baltimore, Maryland.
9. WINCH, ROBERT F.: *Mate-Selection.* New York, Harper, 1958.

SECTION II
MARITAL COUNSELING: IDEOLOGICAL FACTORS

Chapter 13

OBJECTIVE OF MARRIAGE COUNSELING: FAMILY UNITY *VERSUS* INDIVIDUAL HAPPINESS

USHA ANAND

MARRIAGE COUNSELING AS A SPECIFIC area in the general field of counseling psychology needs its own philosophical roots, theory, technique and practice. This seems particularly true when we try to see the problem in a cross-cultural perspective. Marriage counseling, in certain respects, has not only to be different from other types of counseling, but the practice of marriage counseling itself may also differ from culture to culture, depending upon the value system existing in any particular culture. Despite the cultural differences, when it comes to the basic philosophy we find there can be and is a certain amount of common professional sharing among those working in the field. For example, in marriage counseling the fundamental aim of the counselors is to bring happiness to marriage and thus restore the lost equilibrium of marriage. The means may be different, but the end is the same. Thus, we find a common thread running through it all, despite cultural differences; and yet, one's thinking is a product of the cultural influences to which one is exposed. The views expressed in this chapter are a product of the author's counseling practice in the Indian cultural setting. The topic itself is a product of her experience with a certain case during her counseling practice.

It is difficult to say how applicable the views expressed in this chapter will be for other cultures. But for the Indian culture—which has given the author the very thoughts for the chapter—they certainly seem to be relevant.

INTRODUCTION

Marriage counseling as a specialization is relatively recent even in more advanced countries, and it is in the earliest stage of infancy in the Indian cultural setting. Considerable theoretical and practical research is needed in the field before one can come to any standard procedure in the practice of marital counseling in this culture. And yet, before one concentrates on the practice, one has to be clear about the basic theoretical stand one would wish to take. Much as one may emphasize the practical, empirical research side of the picture, all these would be incomplete until one decides on the theoretical framework and philosophical orientation. In the context of the present chapter, an important basic issue in terms of the objective of marital counseling is happiness of the individual, perhaps at the cost of the family.

151

In other words, the question arises: As counselors, are we trying to help towards uniting families or breaking them? In order to discuss the problem, it is necessary first to understand the basic objective of marriage counseling, the types of problems one comes across in marriage counseling, the approach to be adopted by the counselor and the like. All these points will be discussed in the following pages, upon which will then be based the decision regarding objectives of marriage counseling in terms of family unity and individual happiness.

MARRIAGE COUNSELING

Marriage counseling at best can be defined as a helping discipline through which the counselor aims at helping the client—who comes with some problem in his marriage and family living—to see and realize the constructive side of the marriage and thereby overcome the difficulty which was the cause of the problem and which was exercising a negative influence on marriage and married life. Some people may like to think of marriage and family counseling as two different forms of counseling, but to this author they seem to form a continuum. It is only for the sake of classification and categorization that one talks of marriage counseling as different from family counseling. Otherwise marriage counseling is only a part of family counseling; and the basic approach in terms of philosophical roots and theory will be the same in the two cases. There is a natural transition from marriage to family, and the problems in marital life will include family problems also.

TYPES OF PROBLEMS IN MARITAL COUNSELING

Some of the problems which one comes across in marital counseling are disturbed interpersonal relationships, sexual incompatability leading to sexual dissatisfaction, lack of economic adjustment, infidelity leading to disharmony in married life, unhappiness or disturbance due to inlaws or other relatives, religious problems due to religious differences between the spouses (particularly in cases of interreligious marriages), lack of emotional understanding and adjustment, and problems of sterility. Normally, none of these problems exists in isolation, and any one problem is related to and has its repercussions on various others. There is a complex interrelationship between and among the various factors. Moreover, problems in any one of these spheres are only symptoms and manifestations of the basic fact that there is something wrong in the marriage and marital life. Whether the difficulty is in interpersonal relationship or in sexual compatability, the end result will be unhappiness in marriage and dissatisfaction of the partners with each other. That way the various problems mentioned above are various aspects of married life and are very closely interlinked with each other. A disturbance in any one of them will have an effect upon all others and on the marriage in general. When there is some disturbance or difficulty in any one sphere, it mars the total marriage. In cases of couples with children, it will not only affect happiness of the two partners but that of the children also. So the marriage counselor's concentration is not on the couple, or on one of the spouses—the one who comes for help—but on marriage as a totality and the family as a unit. Regardless of whether he* is working with one partner, with both partners or with the whole family, what he is attempting is restoration of happiness to the total unit, consisting of various members of the family.

AIM OF MARRIAGE COUNSELING

The author agrees with Mudd and Goodwin (3) in what they say about the goal of marriage counseling on the basis of their experience at the Marriage Council of Philadelphia. According to them, "the goal of marriage counseling is to help each partner, through his relationship to the counselor, come to some awareness of the appropriateness or inappropriateness of his own feelings, attitudes, demands, expectations and responses, as they are related to his marriage, and to help him resolve or handle more adequately those factors that are causing trouble within the marital interaction. . . . The focus in counseling is thus on learning to understand the reciprocal interaction between the two partners rather than on each person's intrapsychic conflicts as in individual therapy" (3, p. 29).

The fundamental aim of marriage counseling, therefore, is to bring the constructive aspect of marriage to the notice of the couple, or one of the partners, as the case may be, and thereby strengthen and increase happiness in marriage. This end can be achieved by making the couple realize the root cause of the problem in a sympathetic, understanding and nonjudgmental climate, at the same time bringing to their notice the fact that *improvement in marriage and married life* is possible. Sometimes the couple is not aware of their own potentialities in making a success of marriage. With the help of the counselor the couple get a new insight into their basic potentialities and thereby realize the contribution that can be made by both the partners in making the marriage a success. The counselor plays more or less an instrumental role in bringing back the happiness in marriage to the couple. The focus throughout, in marriage counseling, is *the couple and the marriage as a unit, not the individual as such.* As stated by Popenoe (4): "Marriage counseling . . . means counseling the marriage. Even though this is accomplished by dealing with an individual or with two or more individuals, the focus must be on the marriage rather than on

---

*"He" here represents both male as well as female counselors.

the individual. The purpose is to make a marriage successful or more successful." The counselor's attempt is to save the marriage from being destroyed and to bring about a new orientation for the couple which will change unhappiness in marriage into health and happiness in marriage. It is here, too, that a counselor's role becomes different from that of a lawyer. The counselor's first attempt is toward bringing and restoring unity and happiness to the couple and thereby saving the marriage and a family from destruction.

THE COUNSELOR'S DILEMMA:
FAMILY UNITY OR INDIVIDUAL HAPPINESS

This aspect is only the theoretical standpoint in counseling. In some cases, the whole process takes the anticipated shape. But this is not so in all cases. In certain others we find that things are not so easy and smooth as their theoretical description makes one believe. Sometimes the counselor may face difficulty not only during the counseling process but at the very outset when the client approaches the counselor. One important consideration is: What brings the client to the counselor? Does the client want the counselor to help him build the marriage or dissolve it? Does the client approach the counselor for the unity in marriage or does he approach the counselor as a means for seeking a divorce? The initial problem and approach can sometimes be extremely baffling for the counselor.

It is difficult, of course, to say what the experience of counselors in other countries has been in regard to this problem, since the discipline of marriage counseling is not quite so new there as it is in India. Perhaps elsewhere the clients who come to the counselor are also quite well-educated about the nature of counseling service. Consequently, the expectations with which they enter counseling situations may be very much in conformity with what the counselor believes and practices. But, in a culture like in India, where counseling services have just started and people enter the counseling situation with all sorts of expectations, sometimes the counselor finds himself faced with a dilemma. The expectations with which the client enters the counseling situation are quite different from the nature and philosophy of the service being offered. Even in other countries, the goal of marital counseling is to save marriages. It is even more so in an Oriental culture, such as the Indian, where marriage is a sacrament, and family—the institution of family—the highest value.

According to Kapadia (2), "Hindu marriage is a sacrament. As marriage is said to be sacred it is irrevocable. The parties to the marriage cannot dissolve it at will. They are bound to each other until the death of either of them; and the wife is supposed to be bound to her husband even after his death. This concept of marriage, that it is indissoluble, is a lofty one, because it means that the husband and wife after marriage have to adjust their tastes and tempers, their ideals and interests, instead of breaking with each other when they find that these differ. It thus involves sacrifices on the part of both husband and wife as each is called upon to overcome the incompatibility of the other. Hindu marriage, thus viewed, is not an ordinary affair wherein the weakness of flesh plays a dominant part. On the contrary, demands of personal gratification and pleasures are subordinated, and the individual is called upon to make marriage a success by means of compromise and adjustment" (2, pp. 168-169). Consequently, in terms of basic philosophy and nature of the service, counseling in Indian conditions is likely to be more marriage- and family-"unity" oriented rather than "separation," or breaking oriented. It is such difficult, or should one say different, cases which set the counselor thinking. He finds his roles and responsibilities clashing with each other. One such instance is the client who comes to the counselor for help in regard to separating the couple, rather than uniting it. In such cases the counselor may sometimes feel that the particular client who approached him may be happier without the partner he now has. What should be the counselor's approach in such cases? Should the counselor help in separating the two? Should he attempt to unite the two? Or should he remain indifferent? This is a vital problem confronting counselors practicing in the field of marital counseling. A decision has to be reached by them in regard to the basic objective in marital counseling. They have to decide about the goal of marriage counseling as well as the objectives of such counseling.

As mentioned earlier, the thinking expressed in this chapter is based on a case study which the counselor came across during her experience. It seems worthwhile to mention the case briefly and throw light on the expectations with which the client had come to the counseling situation. In this case only one spouse—namely, the husband—approached the counselor. According to the history of the case, the couple had been married for practically twelve years but had never enjoyed what one may call "happiness in marriage." From the very beginning they could not get along with each other and found themselves unsuitable for each other. The wife had not even been living with the husband for some years. (In fact, the total time spent together was about three to four months.) According to the report of the husband, he had made all possible efforts to bring his wife home and make her stay with him. But she did not want to come, and stayed with her parents instead. While in the beginning the husband made attempts to make his wife stay with him, when he failed he wanted a divorce. But the wife would not even agree to that. The husband was prepared to give whatever monetary compensation was required, and he just wanted to dissociate himself from his "partner," as he was neither living a happy married

life, nor a married life at all, and yet he was not even free under the circumstances from the bondage of marriage. It was this situation which was contributing to his mental agony, and he was very much disgusted and depressed when he approached the counselor. The wife was not even living in the same town. The role the client wanted the counselor and the agency*
to adopt was that of a mediator between him and the wife, to persuade the wife to agree to divorce without the wife's knowing that he wanted the agency to take initiative in the matter.

This is only a single instance, but one is likely to come across such cases during one's counseling practice. Cases such as mentioned above set the counselor thinking—what role is he supposed to play? What should be the responsibility of the agency? What should be the counselor's responsibility? Is his task the same as that of the lawyer, or is it much different? There are various questions which confront the counselor and he finds himself entangled among the following conflicting roles:

A Psychologist *Versus* a Psychologist Practicing Marital Counseling

The role of the counselor purely as a psychologist would differ from his role as a marital counselor. His concern, as a psychologist, is more with the individual as an individual. On the other hand, his concern as a marital counselor is more with the marriage and the relationship and interaction pattern within the marriage. A psychologist can confine himself to the restoring of happiness to the individual, but a marital counselor or a psychologist practicing marital counseling concentrates more on the unit — the couple and the institution of marriage. His basic duty is directed toward saving the marriage (which consists of two individuals), along with all its aspects, rather than saving just the individual. Thus we find that the role of a psychologist simply as a psychologist is different from his role as a psychologist practicing marital counseling.

A Private Practitioner *Versus* an Expert Attached to a Certain Agency

The role of the psychologist as a private practitioner is different from his role as an expert attached to an agency working in the field of marital counseling. A private practitioner primarily is guided only by his individual thinking—from whatever school of thought it may be influenced. On the contrary, an expert attached to an agency has not only to take his own thinking into consideration, but he has also to be guided by the objectives and philosophy of the agency to which he is attached. His existence becomes a part of the agency within which he operates. The type of help he provides will be governed by the philosophy of the agency in relation to marital

---

*At that time the counselor was attached to the Family Life Institute, Association for Moral and Social Hygiene of India, at New Delhi.

problems. In a country like the USA, where marital counseling is not only more common but practiced on a larger scale, there may be numerous psychologists in marital counseling who are in private practice. But, in a country like India, marital counseling is a new field of specialization, and due to various social and economic factors, marital counseling as a rule is practiced in an agency setting. In such a setting the aims and objectives of the agency acquire considerable importance, and the approach followed by the counselor is to a large extent influenced by them. Although a private practitioner in all probability will channelize his efforts in uniting the couple and saving the marriage, it is expected even more so in the case of a psychologist practicing within an agency setting. Most of the agencies in the field of family welfare, family relations and marriage guidance aim at restoring happiness in marriage and family, thus opening the constructive aspect of marriage to the couple. In the case of such a practitioner the approach is likely to be all the more "unity oriented" than the case otherwise may be.

As Belonging to a Certain Sociocultural System

The practice and theory of marital counseling cannot be in contradiction to the existing sociocultural system. Cultural relativity is an integral part of any type of counseling. But it is even more so in case of marriage and family counseling where the issues in question are also social. One's basic theoretical standpoint as a counselor cannot be contradictory to the existing system of norms and values in any culture. The type and extent of encouragement given to the client will be governed by the social system of the country. The same approach may prove effective in one culture and ineffective in another. In deciding the basic theoretical standpoint or course of action, the counselor has to take into consideration the particular culture in which he is practicing. What one has to bear in mind is not "what is proper for the client as an individual" but what would be proper for the client as a member of a certain sociocultural group. The counselor's approach, instead of being "absolute" or "culture-free" has to be "relative" and "culture oriented."

Out of the whole list, some roles are mutually compatible; others are incompatible. For example, the counselor's role as a psychologist and his role as a psychologist practicing marital counseling are different from each other. As a psychologist, the focus may be on individual happiness, but as a marriage counselor the emphasis may be on total family unity and marriage. The end here would be bringing individual happiness along with family unity, rather than apart from it. Similarly, as private practitioner his role may be quite different compared to that of an expert who is practicing within the framework of an agency which itself has some basic theoretical standpoint. From the point of view of professional ethics, the policy of the counselor becomes an ethical issue. It seems that the counselor's policy will not be determined by any single factor but a combination of various factors mentioned above, as well as interrelation and balance between those factors. The counselor will have to weigh his respective roles and decide on the basis of a balance between them. Yet it seems that any marriage counselor will have more or less the same basic philosophy or ideology.

Apart from the different *roles* of the counselor, he will also have to judge the situation from the point of view of his *responsibility* and professional ethics in relation to the following considerations.

The Client as an Individual Versus the Client as a Part of the Unit— The Couple

The responsibility of the counselor in case of marital counseling is different from his responsibility in case of personality counseling. In marital counseling he owes responsibility not only to the two individuals as individuals, but to both of them as part of a unit. In personality counseling the counselor's concern and responsibility is confined only to the individual in his own right. But the pattern of responsibility the counselor has in the case of marital counseling is different in the sense that the responsibility of the counselor towards the individual/individuals is not only in their own right but as part of the unit consisting of both of them. The counselor's approach has to be beneficial for both (rather than for any one of them), and to both in relation to each other.

The Client as a Part of the Institutions—Marriage and Family

Related to the first point is the present one. The repsonsibility of the counselor to the client consists of the realization on the part of the counselor that the client does not have an isolated existence but exists as a part of the institution of marriage and the family. The decision of the client as a result of marital counseling will have its effects not only on him and his partner but also on the institutions of marriage and the family. The consequences of marital disharmony, rather than being confined to the two individuals alone, are much more extensive. So it is one of the basic points which has to be very intensively and carefully thought through by the counselor as far as his responsibility and professional ethics are concerned.

The Client as a Part of Society at Large

Though no culture or society values marital disharmony, the specific values and standards related to marital and family life differ from culture to culture. In his counseling practice the counselor has also to consider the client in terms of his cultural or subcultural group membership. The counselor's responsibility towards the client is not confined to his existence in a vacuum. Instead, his responsibility to the client has relevance to the particular society or culture to which the client belongs. Therefore, the type of help provided by the counselor needs to be governed by the existing pattern of norms and values in the culture in which he is practicing.

The Agency Within Which the Counselor Operates

This point has already been discussed in relation to the role of the counselor as an expert attached to an agency. But the specific point to be mentioned here is that, just as the counselor has responsibility to the client as a member of the unit—the couple, and the group—and the society and culture to which he belongs, as well as relative to the institutions of marriage and family, the counselor's responsibilities also include the agency to which he is attached. This would depend upon the aims and objectives that the agency has and the cause for which it stands. Actually, the role of the counselor as an expert attached to a certain agency is also determined by his responsibility to that agency. Hence, the agency within which the counselor operates is one of the important aspects to which the counselor owes responsibility.

Again, we find the basic decision to be taken by the counselor is between his responsibility to the client as an individual and as part of the unit—institution and society. It is at this point that one finds marital counseling is different from personality counseling. Whereas the emphasis in personality counseling is on the individuals, in marital counseling the emphasis is on marital relationship, the relationship pattern and the interaction between the couple. The following statement by Bordin makes it absolutely clear that the root cause of marital difficulties lies in the relationship between two personalities rather than any other factor: "Marital counselors who talk to couples already in difficulty are more likely to find the roots of these difficulties in the relationship between the two personalities . . . (1, p. 18)." Hence it is this relationship which is to be helped, rather than anything else.

HOW TO RESOLVE THE CONFLICT

As has been said earlier, the decision of the counselor regarding his role and basic approach will depend upon the factors mentioned under the various subheads pertaining to the counselor's role and responsibility and professional ethics. Taking the latter as an example, one finds that the type of responsibility the counselor owes to the client as an individual is slightly different compared to the responsibility he owes to the client as part of the unit or as a part of the institution. Moreover, even the individual as an individual does not exist in isolation and apart from society. This is even more true when it comes to dealing with the individual as a member of the unit.

Even in restoring or providing happiness to the individual as an individual, some amount of social control and consideration may become necessary, particularly in terms of factors which are responsible for his unhappiness. And it is more so in case of marital counseling, where the two partners are very largely and closely responsible for making each other happy or unhappy and where the unhappiness thus caused does not remain confined to the two individuals as individuals only, but is extended to the family as a whole and affects the total functioning of the family unit. So in marital counseling, looking at the client from the point of view of a part of the unit, the counselor has to keep *the interest of the family as a whole in focus* rather than that of the individual.

Some amount of individual or personal happiness sometimes has to be sacrificed for the greater and larger interest of the family. The attempt of the counselor in such cases should be to restore the happiness of the individual in the total family setting rather than at the cost of it. Although when one tries to think deeply about it, one feels that the approach of the counselor will depend upon the interrelationship between, and the balance of, various factors already discussed. Unless all the factors are weighed properly, the counselor may not be quite justified in taking a decision regarding his basic approach. And yet, when one tries to view the problem of marital counseling taking all the factors together, the role and responsibility of the counselor seems to be slightly bent towards family unity rather than individual happiness.

For a counselor practicing counseling in general, the approach and basic policy may be slightly different. But for a marriage counselor, for whom the focus is not two individuals or a group of individuals as individuals but as forming a unit, which has its own characteristics, it seems the aim will be more "family unity" than "individual happiness." The two are not completely opposed to each other, for one cannot have family unity unless the individuals composing the family are also happy.

So the question becomes slightly modified in the sense that one has to decide about individual happiness not *per se* but *with* or *without* family unity. In marital counseling it seems more justified to have family unity as its goal of which individual happiness should be a part. In other words, *it should be family unity with individual happiness.* The efforts of the counselor should be directed toward making the total family unit happy in such a way that the individuals composing the family do not feel unduly burdened or unhappy. If we attempt to solve the issue with individual happiness alone, it would be practically diametrically opposite to the basic aim of marriage and marriage counseling. On the contrary, if we aim at family unity alone, then the individuals within the family unit will find themselves under a sort of constant pressure.

The attempt, therefore, has to be to make the individual somewhat happy and at the same time retain family unity. Complete loss of either seems to be psychologically detrimental for either the person or society. The individual who is constantly giving away his own wishes for the family, almost like a martyr, may do so to start with but will not be able to receive any happiness in doing so, even if he continues to do it all his life. This extremely conformist attitude, in course of time, may shatter and disintegrate. On the other hand, if we only see to individual happiness the family and society may almost cease to exist. During the course of one's existence one has to make a series of adjustments, all of which demand some amount of giving in and sacrifice. Rather than making it an ordeal, if the same thing is undertaken with some amount of mental readiness, understanding and acceptance, it may come spontaneously to the individual.

In such situations one will not be confined to his individual interests and happiness only, but will have some consideration for the total unit, too. The ideal situation seems to occur when one can retain family unity without affecting his own happiness. And it is towards this end, this goal, that the counselor has to strive. Through his counseling he has to bring the client to a point where he is prepared to contribute to family unity without completely sacrificing individual happiness or even feeling that he is doing so.

Having discussed the desirability of family unity with individual happiness as the objective of marriage counseling, the writer is not blind to one specific category of cases where the choice is not family unity *with* individual happiness but *either* family unity *or* individual happiness. In such cases the decision has to be in terms of either/or. But, one wonders, even after feeling convinced about the desirability of the individual's breaking away from the family in certain cases as the desirable course of action, is this what the marital counselor should help or encourage his client to do?

First, such a role may be adopted by other experts, like lawyers, etc. The very fact that marital counseling as a profession does exist, and that the profession is more popular in countries where the divorce rate is high and marriages are easily broken up, is sufficient proof for making one realize that there is *need for a constructive approach* to marital problems. The very reason a couple or one of the partners seeks counseling probably seems to be due to their realization that there still is some possibility for holding the marriage together. Before one lands in a divorce court one would like to tap all other resources for the unification in marriage. In other words, before trying one's hands at a destructive approach or path, one would first try the constructive one. The role of a marital counselor, whether within or outside an agency, is to unite the couple, to save the marriage, to prevent the marriage from breaking up, and not vice versa. So, in terms of the basic objective of marriage counseling, the role of the counselor is to build the marriage through a constructive approach rather than to allow it to disintegrate and dissolve through a destructive approach.

Second, even if in certain cases it becomes necessary—depending upon the merits of the case—to separate the couple from each other in view of the total harmony of the family, it should be treated more as an exception rather than the rule. Exception, if anything, only proves the rule. So the goal or aim would still be family unity, even though in some cases the counselor may have to help the client make a decision in terms of his or her happiness, without keeping family unity as the focus.

CONCLUSION

Therefore, the ultimate aim of marital counseling, and consequently of a marriage counselor also, is *to strengthen the family unit and family unity*. It is the constructive aspect of marriage which is brought to the attention of the couple and which provides them with new insight into their marriage. This in turn helps to make a marriage more successful and happy. In general, *the objective of marriage counseling is family unity*. In specific cases, depending upon the merits of the case, the course of action may have to be changed. But such cases are more exception than general rule. The general rule would still remain unchanged and the ideal basic aim of any individual or agency in the field of marital counseling seems to be family unity with individual happiness. The individual happiness is not overlooked, but efforts are made to help the individual achieve this end in the context of family unity.

SUMMARY

Marriage counseling as one aspect in the general field of counseling psychology needs its own theoretical framework and philosophical roots. The fundamental aim of marriage counseling is to help the client gain a new insight into marital difficulties and thereby come to a healthy solution to his marital problems. The role of the counselor lies in bringing the constructive aspect of marriage to the notice of the couple and thereby helping in saving, building and strengthening the marriage. But sometimes the counselor comes across difficult situations, when the couple or one of the spouses approaches the counselor for a destructive rather than constructive approach to marriage. What should be the goal of marital counseling in general, and what should be the role of the counselor in specific cases? The thesis of the writer is that, in general, the goal of marital counseling is family unity with individual happiness. In certain cases, the counselor has to make the decision on the basis of a balance between his different roles as well as different aspects of his responsibility to the client. His roles include that of a psychologist, private practitioner, marriage counselor, an expert operating within a certain agency and one belonging to a certain sociocultural system. His responsibilities include the client as an individual, as part of the unit—the couple—and the institutions—marriage and family, the agency to which the counselor belongs, and society at large. In some cases the counselor may have to decide in terms of individual happiness as the encouraged course of action, but such cases are only exceptions to the rule rather than the rule. The general rule still remains *family unity with individual happiness as the goal of marital counseling.* The choice is not in terms of *either/or* but *with,* i.e., not either family unity or individual happiness, but family unity with individual happiness.

REFERENCES

1. BORDIN, E. S.: *Psychological Counseling.* New York, Appleton-Century, 1955.
2. KAPADIA, K. M.: *Marriage and Family Life in India,* 2nd Ed. London, Oxford, 1958.
3. MUDD, E. H., and GOODWIN, H. M.: Counseling couples in conflicted marriages. In Greene, B. L. (Ed.) : *The Psychotherapies of Marital Disharmonies.* New York, Free Press, 1965.
4. POPENOE, P.: What is counseling? Unpublished pamphlet. California, American Institute of Family Relations, 1954.

Chapter 14

VALUE ISSUES IN MARITAL COUNSELING

JOHN W. HUDSON

A CONSIDERATION OF THE VALUE issues in the field of marriage counseling must include looking at the problem from at least four points of view: (a) the field of marriage counseling; (b) the definition of a marriage counselor; (c) the orientation and training of the marriage counselor; (d) specific problems in the field of marriage counseling. In this chapter I will attempt to deal with each of these areas and some of their value implications in some detail, with the hope of raising questions which will encourage further inquiry by the reader.

The forces which converged to bring about the formalization of the field of marriage counseling included: (a) the marriage education movement, with its emphasis on getting to know the prospective marital partner and understanding the personality factors necessary for marital success; (b) the sex-education movement and the research in animal and human sexual behavior; (c) the increased complexity of modern, urban living. Many individuals, including teachers, ministers and physicians, had been engaged in marriage counseling as the direct result of the requests of the groups with which they were working.

> A particularly important development in the field of marriage counseling in the United States was the organization in 1942 of the American Association of Marriage Counselors, the first national group to recognize marriage counseling as a distinct social and scientific discipline (18).

In its early years the American Association of Marriage Counselors met with the hope of meeting more effectively the needs of those seeking their help. Marriage counseling was viewed principally as a specialized field designated to deal with problems which were primarily on the conscious level. Cuber (2), in his article "Functions of the Marriage Counselor," lists the four functions of the marriage counselor as: (a) the advice-giving function (the giving of information, sometimes technical and sometimes lay); (b) the decisional function (assisting the client in making a decision); (c) the definitional function (if some act comes to be defined as "bad," "sinful" or "indecent," and then, somehow, one commits that act, he may acquire a serious maladjustment); (d) reorganization of behavior (this type of case frequently grows out of the preceding type and becomes possible only when the client has already partly defined the given behavior as wrong or inexpedient but cannot break the old "habit" by mere volition alone). Clark Vincent, commenting on Cuber's article, points out that the marriage counselor performing Functions a and b would define marriage counseling in a manner different than the counselor performing primarily the function in the fourth category. Cuber set forth what was then, and continues to be, one of the major value and philosophical issues in the field of marriage counseling— the value issue concerning whether the marriage counselor should limit himself to those marriage problems which are principally of a conscious or situational nature or whether he will deal with problems involving personality disturbances and emotional conflicts which may involve the unconscious. The lines here are fairly well delineated. They seem to arise from whether a marriage counselor can be effective in many of the situations with which he is confronted without going into what has historically been the province of the psychologist and psychiatrist. Marriage counselors themselves are divided on this question. Each side has its vociferous spokesmen.

Laidlaw, then Chief of Psychiatry at Roosevelt Hospital, New York, and Past President of the American Association of Marriage Counselors, gave his point of view at the 1949 meeting of the American Psychiatric Association:

> Marriage counseling is a form of short-term psychotherapy dealing with interpersonal relationships, in which problems relating to marriage are the central factor . . . it is an approach carried out essentially at a conscious level. . . . If, as therapy progresses, unconscious factors are discovered which necessitate long and involved psychotherapeutic techniques, the case ceases to be in the field of marriage counseling (10).

Foster, formerly Director of Marriage Counseling Service and Training Program, Department of Social Applications, The Menninger Foundation, stated in 1950: "Marriage counseling is primarily and essentially an educational job," (6).

The New York Academy of Sciences, recognizing the need for clarification of the fields of psychotherapy and counseling, established five commissions to explore the subject. The following statement is relevant here:

> We can express the difference in emphasis, then, by saying that counseling looks more often toward the interpretation and development of the personality in the relations characteristic of specific role-problems while psychotherapy looks more often toward the reinterpretation and reorganization of malignant conflictual elements with the personality through the relation with the therapist (15).

As recently as 1957, marriage counseling was placed by Mace in the general category of one of "the services which help the individual, at the conscious level, to achieve a better understanding of himself and of his destiny. This broad category includes all functionally directed education

—teaching, preaching, and propaganda. It also includes all counseling in the generally understood meaning of the word" (12) .

In *Marriage Counseling: A Casebook,* edited for the American Association of Marriage Counselors, the authors state:

> The marriage counselor can best make his important contribution by equipping himself to function not as a pseudo-psychiatrist or analyst, but as one who has made a special study of the problems and interpersonal relationships of family life: the bonds, loyalties, and conflicts; the loves, rivalries, and hostilities; the need for identification and independence, on the one hand, and the conflicting desire for independence, on the other; the wish for security and the urge for adventure; in brief, the stresses and strains involved in membership in a marriage and a family and the psychosocial factors and influences of such membership on the personality (13, pp. 40-41) .

The authors of the *Casebook* define marriage counseling:

> Marriage Counseling may be defined as the process through which a professionally trained counselor assists a person or persons to resolve the problems that trouble them in their interpersonal relationships. The focus is on the relationship between the two persons in marriage, rather than, as in psychiatric therapy, the reorganization of the personality structure of the individual (13) .

Throughout the literature there are also individuals who point out: (a) that marriage counseling is a form of psychotherapy; (b) that the effective marriage counselor needs to be able to recognize and differentiate between psychotic and neurotic problems; (c) that many of the difficulties within marriages are the result of personality conflicts within or between marriage partners; (d) that the marriage counselor will be dealing with problems of the unconscious as well as the conscious, and at times will be involved in efforts at basic personality reorganization. Spokesmen for the marriage counselor functioning as a psychotherapist have become more outspoken as the profession has developed.

Stokes (19, p. 25) , psychiatrist and marriage counselor, in his discussion of an article entitled "The Orientation and Focus of Marriage Counseling," states:

> Marriage counseling is a form of individual psychotherapy in which there is a special concern with the ways in which marriage partners interact with each other. . . . Although I deeply believe in marriage counseling as a worthy and needed profession, I would reject the idea that my primary interest is really counseling in marriage. It so happens that marriage is the chief proving-ground of emotional maturity, as well as the arena in which the parent-child relationship so critically affects the emotional development of human beings. Therefore it is in marriage that the symptoms of

emotional immaturity and neurosis most strikingly appear. . . . Thus I see the marriage counselor of the future as primarily a student of the human life cycle, with emphasis upon its emotional aspects. He will be a therapist concerned with the application of his knowledge to all members of the family, at every age.

Rutledge, Director of Marriage Counseling and Psychotherapy Training at The Merrill-Palmer Institute and former President of the American Association of Marriage Counselors, has long been a champion of the idea that marriage counseling represents the most advanced and highly technical form of all psychotherapies. Commenting in *Marriage and Family Living,* Rutledge says:

> It is deceptive to believe that the marriage counselor does not deal with the unconscious just because he does not intend to. Clients bring themselves, including their unconscious motivation, to the counseling hour, whether they come for personal problems or because of marital difficulties. This certainly means the counselor should have a basic understanding of and be able to recognize evidences of the unconscious in the daily married life and in the counseling session (16, p. 28).

Rutledge, in a discussion of "The Use of Dreams in Premarital Counseling" went a step further in his opinion of the counselor dealing with the unconscious:

> (1) The use of dreams in counseling and therapeutic contacts is a legitimate function for many specialists in human behavior, not just for the psychiatrist or psychoanalyst, as has often been claimed. (2) This automatically underlines the fact that, whether or not they know it, all counselors are dealing with unconscious material (20, p. 260).

Ellis, in his discussion of the use of rational-emotive psychotherapy as a technique for use in marriage counseling, states:

> Very possibly, most of these troubled individuals should come for intensive psychotherapy rather than for "counseling," but the fact is that they do not. It therefore behooves the counselor, and especially the marriage counselor, to be enough of a trained and experienced therapist to be able to deal adequately with the individuals who come to him for help . . ." (4).

Albert, in his article in *Marriage and Family Living,* adds a significant note in his conclusions:

> But it does appear highly worthwhile to urge that universities and other training centers require that marriage counselors-in-training receive a thorough grounding in motivation, personality development, abnormal psychology and diagnostics, as well as a working knowledge of psychoanalytic theory (including perhaps, not only Freudian concepts but also

such more recent approaches as those of Sullivan, Reich, Rogers and the Neo-Behaviorists). This would be in addition to courses in the specific area of marriage counseling, and such other relevant subjects as family dynamics and the sociology of the family (1).

Obviously, a marriage counselor with the type of training that Albert is recommending is not going to limit himself to advice-giving and dealing with only conscious, reality-oriented problems. The philosophical and value question of the role of the marriage counselor is at present unclear. The field of marriage counseling and its practitioners are faced with the value question of whether marriage counseling is to remain primarily an educational, advice-giving, reality-oriented service for "normal" people or whether it is to be a profession of highly trained, competent therapists prepared to deal with a wide variety of marriage problems, including those which have their roots in individual personality disturbances.

Marriage counseling from its inception has been a multidisciplinary profession. Among others, the disciplines have included psychology, sociology, medicine, social work, law and religion. Each profession has been adamant in insisting upon the importance of its own special contribution to the field of marriage counseling. We find the psychologist frequently emphasizing psychological factors, the physician emphasizing physiological factors, the minister, spiritual factors, the sociologist, cultural factors, etc. Although specialized internships and training in marriage counseling may reduce these tendencies, it is usually not difficult to spot the principal theoretical bias of the marriage counselor. Undoubtedly, one of the major factors which contributes to a counselor's theoretical bias is the lack of a systematic theoretical structure for marriage counseling.

Related to the theoretical bias of the counselor are the methods and techniques of counseling and psychotherapy that he employs. We find individual marriage counselors who are identified with the Freudian approach, the Rogerian approach, Ellis' approach to psychotherapy, as well as with many others. Initially, most psychotherapeutic approaches were designed to be used in working with an individual client; consequently, they must be modified when applied to the interpersonal marital situation.

It is not the purpose of this chapter to analyze the underlying value assumptions of various theoretical approaches. It should be clear to the reader that a marriage counselor operating from a Freudian frame of reference, with its emphasis on instincts, drives, repressions and unconscious conflicts, is going to reflect a different set of values than the therapist who operates from a Rogerian point of view. Marriage counselors who utilize Rogers' system will turn more to their own thoughts and attitudes. Rogerians hold to the value that the thoughts and feelings the therapist has toward the client are the most crucial antecedents to effective therapist behavior. Rogerians assume "that if the therapist holds the 'right attitude', if he has a fundamental faith in the patient, the appropriate statements and expressive gestures by the therapist will follow" (5). If the marriage counselor subscribes to the theoretical position of Ellis' rational-emotive therapy, he will take a more active and direct role than either of the counselors described in the preceding therapeutic approaches. It is clear that the choice of personality theory and the method and techniques for the marriage counselor are not based solely on an objective analysis. His choice reflects his own conscious and unconscious values and biases.

Most schools of psychotherapy agree that the ideal theoretical model describes the counselor as one who: (a) takes a serious interest in the client and gives him his undivided attention; (b) does not respond or react to either the client's affectionate or hostile feelings; (c) does not pass moral judgment; (d) maintains neutrality both affectively and intellectually; (e) keeps his own emotional life separate from that of the client's; and (f) keeps his own biases and predilections out of the counseling situation. Obviously, as all ideal models are theoretical, it is highly doubtful that any counselor can measure up to the foregoing list. There is also the question of whether the counselor who holds rigidly to these standards can be effective.

The marriage counselor is a product of his culture and, as such, reflects his own values in the counseling relationship (whether he is aware of it or not). It is important, for both theoretical and therapeutic reasons, for the marriage counselor to be cognizant of his values and how they operate in the therapy. If the marriage counselor risks revealing himself from behind the professional shroud of the passive, reflecting, nonjudgmental mummy, it is inevitable that he will express his values, attitudes and opinions on a wide variety of subjects. This is particularly true when working with married couples, as the basis for much marital disharmony lies not only in the neurotic pattern of the individuals involved, but in their philosophical and value conflicts. The philosophical and value conflicts of husbands and wives arise frequently from their different sociocultural backgrounds. The marriage counselor first must face the fact that he is a human being and, as such, holds values. Second, if he is going to be effective in his counseling, much of his therapy with couples is going to involve the exploration and discussion of values, including many of the therapist's. Third, the counselor will consciously or unconsciously communicate his own values, and it may as well be done openly. Fourth, the more open the counselor is regarding his own values, the freer and more spontaneous the counseling can be.

A factor which influences the value position of the marriage counselor is that marriage counseling has tended to be problem-oriented and has directed its attention principally to the resolution of conflict situations. Although it is not explicitly stated, it is clear from reading the literature in the field of marriage counseling that one of the central values is that of adjustment.

This concept is not unique to the field of marriage counseling, but is particularly significant for the marriage counselor because he is frequently working with two or more individuals. In many cases the marriage counselor cannot hold equally to the value of the integrity of both individuals where adjustment is the value. It makes a difference whether one is talking about adjustment in terms of the integration of self or adjustment in terms of the compromising of self for the value of others. The value of adjustment seems to have been adopted by many marriage counselors. Where adjustment means the acquisition of new knowledge or skills which will further facili-tate the growth and development of an individual, it may be appropriate, but where adjustment means the compromising of self-values for the values of others for the sake of a marriage or family, the value is dubious.

Green states; "Therapists who advocate any specific type of adjustment are prone to sociological naivete. The institutional bases of their own specific values are shifting ground so rapidly in modern society that it is a rare combination of value and structure that is itself in adjustment" (8). The conflict between self-values and the values of others is many times erroneously thought to be resolved by the marriage counselor by shifting the focusing of the counseling from the individual to the institution of mar-riage. Adjustment may become an end in itself without regard to the in-dividual. The "well-adjusted" person is all too frequently seen as the individual who adapts himself to any situation, person or marriage for the sake of avoiding personal or social disorganization. When the focus is shifted from individual values to the institutional values of marriage and family it may implicitly or explicitly convey to the client that there is a value which transcends his personal wishes or desires. This may represent an unconscious rejection, on the part of the marriage counselor, of divorce as an acceptable solution to marital discord.

It is important for the marriage counselor to be aware of his position on the value issue of divorce. Much harm can be done to an individual by the counselor who insists that the only satisfactory solution to marital conflict is adjustment and reconciliation. He is apt to find himself in the position of contributing to far greater personal and family disorganization by his unrelenting value stand. An obvious case is the situation involving the married couple where one of the partners finds the marriage relationship to be no longer meaningful and wishes a divorce so that he can pursue his own personal interests. This picture may be further complicated where there are children. If the counselor is committed solely to the values of marriage and the family he is apt to violate the integrity of the individual wishing to get out of the marriage, viewing his behavior as neurotic, disturbed or immature.

Although the professional code of ethics of the American Association of Marriage Counselors does not state saving marriages as one of the goals of marriage counseling, the individual counselor may nevertheless find himself in this position either as the result of his own personal values, those which are imposed upon him by the agency for which he works or by the client who seeks his help. Because the marriage counselor is working within an interactional system, that is, the relationship between husband and wife, as well as other family members, he may be less able to disregard the effects of one individual's behavior on another.

One of the clearest statements of the value issue of divorce is made by Stokes in the February, 1959, issue of *Marriage and Family Living:*

> I have small concern with the preservation of the marriage as such. My primary focus is upon the dignity and satisfactions of the individual spouses and only secondarily upon the sociological values associated with the marriage. I cannot conceive of accomplishing enduringly successful marriage counseling upon any other terms.
>
> I suspect that because marriage has been for so long entrenched as a religious sacrament that many marriage counselors still feel impelled to preserve marriage at any cost. . . . I often have a feeling that too much emphasis upon the sociological factors and values of marriage is just a rationalized hangover from the ancient mystical concept of marriage as an inviolable sacrament" (19, p. 25) .

Rutledge, in his article, "Should the Marriage Counselor Ever Recommend Divorce?" says:

> If a marital diagnosis reveals that continued marriage of a couple not only promises nothing in the way of a healthy relationship but points to marked personality destruction for one or both, it is the marriage counselor's responsibility to underline this prognosis. To be sure, one of the couple must make the decision to separate or not to separate, to divorce or not to divorce. But the counselor may be derelict in some cases unless he gives his professional opinion of the advisability of ending, with as little hurt as possible, a relationship that can bring only continued destruction of personality" (16) .

Barrier discusses Rutledge's article, quoting Section 14 of the proposed Code of Ethics of the American Association of Marriage Counselors which states:

> While the Marriage Counselor will feel satisfaction in the strengthening of a marriage, he should not feel obliged to urge that the married partners continue to live together at all costs. There are situations in which

all resources fail, and in which continued living together may be severely damaging to one or several persons. In such event it is the duty of the Counselor to assess the facts as he sees them. However, the actual decision concerning separation or divorce is a responsibility that must be assumed by the client and this should be made clear to him. If separation or divorce is decided upon, it is the continuing responsibility of the Counselor to give further support and counsel during a period of readjustment, if that appears to be wanted and needed, as it often is.

Barrier concludes her discussion of Rutledge's article with the statement: "It is not the role of the marriage counselor to recommend dissolution of the marriage" (16, p. 325).

In the thirteen years that I was affiliated with the Marriage Counseling Service and Psychotherapy Training Center of The Merrill-Palmer Institute I was repeatedly struck with the infrequency with which divorce was recommended as a solution to an unsatisfactory marriage. With the system of courtship and mate selection that is used in our culture it would seem that a certain percentage of individuals seeking the services of marriage counselors would be poorly mated and that, unless the counselor were committed solely to the values of adjustment or the sacredness of the marriage relationship, divorce would more frequently be recommended.

Related to the counselor's value system is the setting in which the counseling takes place, and this may influence the investment that the marriage counselor makes in the individual client. If he is in private practice the selection of clients is more apt to be based on values reflecting his own financial welfare, professional status, prestige and personal and therapeutic biases than if he operates in an agency setting where his salary is fixed. In an agency, the size of his case load, the clients and his preferences for particular types of marriage counseling problems may not be given consideration. The counselor working in an agency may find himself under more direct supervision and his personal investment in his clients may not be as great. If the counseling is part-time and an adjunct to his primary responsibility it will have an effect on the relationship between the marriage counselor and his client. The college teacher who does counseling as an outgrowth of his teaching is faced with different value issues than the minister who does counseling as a part of his pastoral functions.

The teacher is frequently faced with the value dilemma of separating the roles of the critical evaluation and judgment of academic performance from the accepting, nonjudgmental role of counselor. The minister may find himself caught in a value dilemma arising out of theological precepts and religious convictions. When his theological precepts and religious convictions clash with the reality situations of his counselees the minister may have to sacrifice either religious values or secular values.

Fees are one of the major value dilemmas for the marriage counselor. The problem of fee-setting is one which many counselors would prefer to avoid. In agencies it is frequently handled by administrative decision, but for the private practitioner there is no neat ready-made solution. In discussions with many marriage counselors (both those working in an agency setting and those in private practice) I wonder at their inability to face this issue squarely. The amount of uncollected fees frequently equals the sum of a few years' annual collections. The counselor who has difficulty in setting and collecting his fees has many "valid" explanations. He may rationalize his failure to deal realistically with the issue on vague therapeutic grounds. He may set his fees low because of doubt about his own adequacy, or he may set his fees arbitrarily high on the sole assumption that if an individual is unwilling to pay a high fee he is not sufficiently motivated to get help. There is little doubt that money has a variety of meanings to individuals, including marriage counselors, but it is an integral part of the counselor-client relationship and, as such, must be dealt with realistically. The arbitrary setting of fees without regard to the financial situation of the client, excessively large uncollected fees, refusal to see an individual at a reduced fee—all reflect values conflicts of the marriage counselor.

The sources of the marriage counselor's referrals poses value questions which cannot be dismissed casually. The marriage counselor may find himself being cast in the role of a clearing house for lawyers, courts and physicians. He may find himself being used by other professional persons who are attempting to avoid their responsibility in helping their clients to face crucial issues. Under certain conditions referral to a marriage counselor may be a form of coercion. The coercion may be by a spouse, lawyer, physician or other professional. Care must be taken by the counselor not to impose his value of counseling on the person. It is important to know the terms under which the client presents himself to prevent being caught in a power struggle. A value dilemma may arise if a client has been under some other therapist's care prior to his coming to his present counselor. If one uses the simple interpretation that this is a form of resistance or hostility on the part of the client toward his previous therapist, the value issue is resolved. It may be that the client is resistant or hostile, but there are other valid reasons for changing therapists. Among other valid reasons for changing therapists include: (a) inability to establish rapport with previous therapist; (b) fees of previous therapist prohibitive; (c) transportation to and from previous therapist inaccessible; (d) time of appointments inconvenient or not feasible for client; (e) previous therapist's theoretical and psychotherapeutic techniques unacceptable to client; and (f) incompetency of previous therapist. Care must be taken at all times to insure the rights of the client to choose his therapist.

Depending upon the particular state in the United States, or upon professional affiliations of the marriage counselor, he may or may not have privileged communication. The issue of privileged communication is being clarified for the marriage counselor in many states which have certification or licensing acts. Although this handles the technical problem, it does not handle certain value issues that arise in marriage counseling. Because of the unique position the marriage counselor occupies, he frequently becomes apprised of information which may seriously affect a marital relationship. In most situations he is committed to the confidentiality of interview material given by each spouse. Situations arise where he might be able to facilitate the relationship or help to avert unnecessary complications if he were to divulge information given in confidence. Where privileged communication does not exist it is important to inform the client in order to avoid future complications or legal involvement.

SUMMARY

Part of the reason for the formation of the American Association of Marriage Counselors and for its rapid growth arose from one of the assumptions of analytic therapy which had generalized itself into almost all psychotherapies. The assumption is that effective therapy can take place only in those situations where the relationship between the therapist and the client is not encumbered or complicated by contacts with any other members of the client's family. This position has been carried to ridiculous lengths by some therapists, including the refusal to talk to or see any other member of the family, even when permission has been granted to the therapist by the client. Some of the pioneer marriage counselors recognized that the interaction of husbands and wives frequently brought about problems which could be resolved only by a therapeutic approach to the couple rather than to an individual.

In recent years there has been an increasing recognition on the part of marriage counselors that values are both implicitly and explicitly operative in the counseling relationship. The very notion of counseling implies a value system. The particular theoretical orientation of the practitioner carries with it certain value assumptions. The circumstances under which the therapy occurs may denote certain value considerations which are functioning for both therapist and client. The value issues with which marriage counselors are faced become increasingly complex when the therapy involves a married couple.

The value position of the marriage counselor is probably more complex than that of any other individuals working in the helping professions. This comes about partly as a result of: (a) confusion in the minds of the individuals seeking the services of the marriage counselor regarding the role of the marriage counselor; (b) the orientation or capacity in which the marriage counselor functions; (c) the particular theoretical framework of counseling to which the marriage counselor subscribes; and (d) the source of referral. One of the best methods a marriage counselor may employ in examining his own values is the careful questioning of the underlying assumptions he makes to support his diagnosis of the individuals he is seeing. Psychological jargon and diagnostic categories are all too frequently rationalizations for more fundamental personal values on the part of the counselor. Whenever a marriage counselor finds himself viewing all marital conflict as the result of immaturities, neurotic patterns, personality disorders or psychopathology, he is probably deluding himself regarding his own objectivity and value positions. Marriage counseling has adapted the methods and techniques of individual psychotherapy and has principally relied on existing theories of personality development. As a consequence, the marriage counselor must frequently force the problems arising out of marital interaction into theoretical systems which were originally constructed to explain individual behavior. The methods and techniques of therapy which he employs are likewise those originally designed for application to individuals.

With the implementation of standards of training and the establishment of training centers the professional marriage counselor is coming into his own.

Marriage counseling is evolving from an educational advice-giving, conscious, reality-oriented service to a scientific highly specialized form of psychotherapy. The prestige of the profession is reflected in the increased number of individuals now referring to themselves as marriage counselors with psychological or sociological backgrounds, rather than as "psychologists or sociologists who do marriage counseling."

The further growth of the profession will hinge on the effectiveness with which we marriage counselors can deal with value issues, not only those of the client but, more importantly, our own.

REFERENCES

1. ALBERT, GERALD: Advanced psychological training for marriage counselors — luxury or necessity? *Marriage and Family Living, 25*:181-184, 1963.
2. CUBER, JOHN F.: Functions of the marriage counselor. *Journal of Marriage and Family Living, 7*:3-5, 1945.
3. EHRLICH, DANUTA, and WIENER, DANIEL N.: The measurement of values in psychotherapeutic settings. *The Journal of General Psychology, 64*:359-372, 1961.
4. ELLIS, ALBERT: Reason and Emotion in Psychotherapy. New York, Lyle Stuart, 1962.

5. FORD, DONALD H., and URBAN, HUGH B.: *Systems of Psychotherapy*. New York, Wiley, 1963.
6. FOSTER, ROBERT G.: Marriage counseling in a psychiatric setting. *Marriage and Family Living, 12*:41-43, 1950.
7. GINSBURG, SOL W.: Values and The Psychiatrist. *American Journal of Orthopsychiatry, 20*:466-478, 1950.
8. GREEN, ARNOLD W.: Social Values and Psychotherapy. *Journal of Personality, 14*:198-228, 1946.
9. GREENE, B., Editor: *The Psychotherapies of Marital Disharmony*. New York, Free Press, 1965.
10. LAIDLAW, ROBERT W.: The Psychiatrist as Marriage Counselor. In Vincent, Clark E.: *Readings in Marriage Counseling*. New York, Crowell, 1957, pp. 52-61.
11. LESLIE, GERALD; NEUBECK, GERHARD; GREENE, KARHARINE; HILL, THEODORE, and LUCKEY, ELEANORE: Who are your untreatables? *Marriage and Family Living, 22*:333-341, 1960.
12. MACE, DAVID R.: What is a Marriage Counselor? In Vincent, Clark E. [Editor]: *Readings in Marriage Counseling*. New York, Crowell, 1957, pp. 29-35.
13. MUDD, EMILY; KARPF, MAURICE J.; STONE, ABRAHAM, and NELSON, JANET F., editors: *Marriage Counseling: A Casebook*. New York, Assn. Pr., 1958.
14. MUDD, EMILY H.: *The Practice of Marriage Counseling*. New York, Assn. Pr., 1951.
15. PERRY, WILLIAM G.: On the relation of psychotherapy and counseling. *Annals of the New York Academy of Sciences, 63*:319-432, 1955.
16. RUTLEDGE, AARON L.: Should the marriage counselor ever recommend divorce? *Marriage and Family Living, 25*:319-326, 1963.
17. SCHOFIELD, WILLIAM: *Psychotherapy: The Purchase of Friendship*. Englewood Cliffs, Prentice-Hall, 1964.
18. STONE, ABRAHAM: Marriage education and marriage counseling in the United States. In Vincent, Clark [Editor]: *Readings in Marriage Counseling*. New York, Crowell, 1957, pp. 12-19.
19. STROUP, ATLEE L., and GLASSER, PAUL: The Orientation and Focus of Marriage Counseling. *Marriage and Family Living, 21*:20-25, 1959.
20. WHITLOCK, GLENN E.: The use of dreams in premarital counseling. *Marriage and Family Living, 23*:258-263, 1961.

Chapter 15

THE INSTITUTIONS OF DIVORCE

HENRY H. FOSTER, JR.

INTRODUCTION

T HE BONDS OF ACRIMONY NO LONGER are willingly endured by most of mankind, and an escape from what A. P. Herbert called "Holy Deadlock" will be discovered when a marital situation is sufficiently intolerable. Marriage and divorce long have been favorite subjects for study by theologians, behavioral scientists and lawyers. It is noteworthy, however, that, like the inspection of the elephant by the three blind men of Hindustan, their reports usually have been fragmentary; dogma has been confused with reality; custom with fact; and *de jure* with *de facto*. This is because modern man has an essentially ambivalent attitude towards marriage, divorce and the family. He agrees that these intimate interpersonal relationships have, and for others should have, social, religious, legal and private facets and dimensions, but he insists upon his own inalienable right to the "pursuit of happiness." Although it is right that divorce be difficult for the impetuous, the typical American who no longer enjoys the privileges and dividends of a happy marriage often feels he has a right to a divorce and that he should be freed of further duties and responsibilities. If he doesn't have the *quid* he doesn't want to pay the *quo*. The result is that there are at work several social and legal institutions of marriage and divorce (1).

This phenomenon of variance and gap between statute and "living law" and the proliferation of social institutions has been for many years a favorite subject of study by sociological jurisprudence and sociology, and the discrepancy between matrimonial law and what people in fact do about family breakdown has received repeated attention (2). It is not our purpose "to beat a dead source" of sociological insight. Rather, we will direct our attention to the background of the modern law and practice of divorce, and will try to delve into its antecedents in the hope that by that means we may better understand the current reality of divorce.

PRIMITIVE LAW

Since marriage and its termination are among the outstanding events in the lives of most people, it is not surprising that each is a focal point for diverse consequences. In addition to its sexual and child-rearing function, marriage may be the event seized upon for the transfer of wealth (3). The form regulation takes, its laxity or rigidity, depends upon many factors, some of which may be relatively unique to the particular culture (4). What matters most and is prized most highly tends to find expression in matrimonial events. A culture which stresses magic, invocation of the supernatural and religious values produces exaggerated forms and rituals for marriage ceremonies, and that relationship may be viewed as entailing a complex of religious duties. An acquisitive society may utilize marriage and divorce as a means for the transfer of wealth. Warlike people often devise rules as to exogamous marriages in order to plant allies or spies among neighboring tribes. In short, many ancillary or incidental social, religious and legal purposes may be served by marriage or its termination, and such may become predominant as compared with the sexual or child-rearing function that we tend to view as the essence of marriage.

Perhaps the "bride-price" is the best known economic consequence of marriage among many primitive people. One authority reports that the bride-price was found to exist in 79 per cent of the several hundred cultures examined (5). Marriage arranged by parents, marriage by capture, exchange of gifts or by the exercise of public control followed in that order of frequency. Another anthropologist refers to systems of compulsory payments as "perhaps the most widespread and basic of all methods of distribution [of property] among primitive peoples—more important than trade or free gifts or warfare or tribute" (6).

We mention bride-price and its significance as a medium for the distribution of property for two reasons. First, there has been a sad neglect by most scholars of the economic aspects of marriage and divorce, even though in fact economic factors may be decisive as to custom and practice. Second, there is an obvious interrelationship between family finances and family stability. In both preliterate societies and in modern America, socioeconomic considerations are significant factors in the choice of a mate and in the termination of unsatisfactory marriages. The amount of the bride-price limits the choice of a mate, and if "divorce" requires the bride's parents to return the bride-price they received, easy divorce may be discouraged in fact, even though readily available in theory. In the United States, ordinarily a suitor's means affects his eligibility, and, as any lawyer will tell you, the negotiation of the financial terms of settlement is the crux to that consensual divorce that is our prototype. Furthermore, divorce rates generally increase during prosperity and decrease during depression years (7), and divorce is much more common among the lower than the higher occupational groups (8).

Insofar as it is somewhat safe to generalize at all about the primitive law of marriage and divorce, and it is duly noted that no generalizations are safe (9), it may be observed that the social, as distinguished from the legal, institutions of marriage and divorce tend to reflect the predominant values of a given culture. If this is a sociological fact, it is not surprising that our own matrimonial institutions change, adapt and proliferate according to the values of the given time and place. Moreover, diversity is inevitable because of the clash of conflicting multiple interests that must be reconciled and satisfied at least in part. Neither the disgruntled spouse nor the canonist will achieve total victory because neither can dictate the terms of both *de facto* and *de jure* settlement of family problems.

THE SECULARIZATION OF LAW

One of the most momentous events in the history of a people is the secularization of law (10). Among primitives this occurs when law emerges from custom and a specialized group is charged with the administration of rules promulgated by chiefs or wisemen. At least in some measure the history of Rome and the history of England may be surveyed in terms of the secularization of law. In Rome, when legal institutions evolved, and a law craft was differentiated from the priesthood, there was a progression to freedom for marriage and divorce (repudiation), and wives eventually secured equal rights. In England, William the Conquerer in 1086 fulfilled his vow to the Pope, made in exchange for the latter's blessing for the 1066 invasion, and established the ecclesiastical courts with jurisdiction over matters spiritual, including marriage and divorce, that was to endure until 1857 (11). *Curia regis,* the ancestor of both Parliament and the king's courts, achieved jurisdiction over temporal matters. The ecclesiastical courts were presided over by bishops trained in civil and cannon law, but the king's courts by the time of Henry II developed what came to be called the "common law." Training in the common law became the function of the celebrated Inns of Court, and a distinct law craft emerged that functioned pragmatically and developed its own "knowhow." Concrete problems rather than abstract principles, solutions rather than postulates, were the focal points for study, so that an empirical and pragmatic approach to law was engrained in barristers. A problem-solving technique was developed that stressed the individual case but gathered analogies from past decisions.

For our purposes, it is important to note that the clergy continued to have primary jurisdiction over marriage and divorce, except for the brief interval of the Cromwell period (12), for almost eight hundred years. Moreover, to the extent that statutes were significant, they were usually dictated by clerical pressure. Not lawyers but clergymen formulated the canons and the laws pertaining to marriage and divorce. For the most part the law of the ecclesiastical courts, if not egregiously unsuitable, was transplanted to these shores and became the basic value system for American statutory and decisional law on marriage and divorce. Although we established no ecclesiastical courts, but rather proclaimed a wall of separation between

Church and State, the principles formulated by the bishop's courts and the dogmas of our own lobbying theologians continue to be the dominant strains in our law of divorce. In functional terms this is significant, because lawyers are conditioned to give priority to human needs and are skilled at effecting compromise, whereas, historically, the clergy all too often has placed religious dogma or principle above human interests and salvation above legitimate human needs. It is the intransigence of the clergy, not the stupidity of lawyers, that accounts for most of the anomalies of our divorce law.

THE CHURCH, THE REFORMATION AND "LIVING LAW"

We have said that total victory is never achieved by disgruntled spouses or the clergy in matrimonial matters, and that the intransigence of the latter occasions anomalies or gaps between law and custom. On the surface, however, it would seem that, during the period of feudalism and from the Middle Ages down until 1857, the clergy had its way. What had the superficial appearance of victory for religion and morality, however, was far from such. In fact, there were many escape hatches for misunderstood or too-well-understood husbands. As you know, desertion ever has been the poor man's form of divorce. At least from the time of the urbanization of London, disappearance served as a substitute for divorce, and it was not until 1829 that a metropolitan police force was established in that fair city. Sherlock Holmes came much later.

But, to return to our history, there is clear and convincing evidence that, before the Reformation, dispensations for marriage and annulments were subjects of great abuse. Grounds for annulment, including degrees of consanguinity and affinity, were construed so as to make the termination of an unsatisfactory marriage readily obtainable (13). Although during the feudal period prohibitions against the remarriage of persons divorced *a mensa et thoro* were extended so that in theory there was no divorce as we know it, remarriages did in fact take place, and such was the subject of scandal and comment (14). Moreover, certain groups, for example the street mongers of London, formulated their own rules as to marriage and divorce. After the Reformation, dissenting sects likewise developed their own extralegal rules without regard to the official law, which recognized only Parliamentary divorce. And, in rural England, wife sales at county fairs continued well down until the latter part of the last century, and *The London Times* even gave market quotations on what wives were selling for at such auctions (15). Divorceless society indeed!

Thus, we have an inherited dichotomy between the law in theory and what people actually do when the marital situation becomes intolerable. True, to a great extent, it was only the husband who had an effective means of self-help, but then there is always the problem of whether or not his resort to self-help was not engineered by the wife.

For many centuries, apparently, the Church did not greatly concern itself with either the formalities of marriage or the effective securing of its indissolubility. Although the doctrine that marriage is a sacrament can be traced to St. Augustine, it was not until the Council of Florence, in 1439, that it became officially established as such, and it was not until the Council of Trent (1543-1563) that the devout were required to marry in the face of the Church (16). In England, legal requirements for marriage were not imposed until 1753, when Lord Hardwicke's Act was enacted. Thereafter, elopments to Gretna Green became popular and replaced the notorious Fleet Street marriages that Hardwicke's Act was intended to eliminate. In any event, simultaneously with the regulation of marriage and divorce, there arose a "living law" of custom and practice that served the felt needs of that substantial portion of Englishmen who could not afford the vast fortune required for Parliamentary divorce, or the sizable sums needed for divorce *a mensa et thoro* or annulment (17). The law was priced out of the market for nine-tenths of the population, and the fact that, upon occasion, they resorted to extralegal means had no great consequence because there was no police force to interfere, no property to be probated, and the matter never came to the attention of the authorities. The same situation exists today in our own urban centers, and in America each year the number of desertions is approximately equal to the number of divorces—some 400,000 in number.

It should come as no surprise that the most intimate of human relationships—marriage—has both a public and private aspect and that there are many levels of legal, religious and social validity and significance. Self-interest engenders self-help when satisfaction cannot be obtained through regular channels, and if the law obstructs and religion inhibits, either custom will arise to compete, or legal and religious institutions will adapt in fact, if not in theory, to answer pressing human needs (18). Such has been our history both as to the formalities of marriage and its termination.

OUR CURRENT AMBIVALENCE

If in the past there has been great difficulty for both Church and State in attempting to regulate marriage and divorce effectively, the changing values and complexity of modern life make it all but impossible to thwart self-help, assuming that to be desirable. We have no real Federal law of marriage and divorce. Each of the fifty states has comparative freedom as to the formulation of marriage requirements and grounds for divorce. Some diversity is to be expected, and may or may not be a "good thing." Out-of-state elopements and migratory divorce must be reckoned with in promulgating local laws. Max Rheinstein has pointed out that there is a sort of perverse Gresham's law at work in the field of divorce—if it is possible for a dissatisfied spouse to obtain a divorce with some difficulty in one place, but with greater ease and speed in another, "cases tend to accumulate in the place of the easy, and to dry up in the place of hard divorce" (19).

Divorce reform is no easy matter. In many, if not most states, organized religion and powerful churchmen, who may or may not reflect the actual beliefs of their parishioners, usually succeed in blocking any substantive reform of the divorce laws. In a sense this is ironical, for the "fault" premise of our divorce laws is more a product of the Protestant Reformation than of Roman canon law. It was Martin Luther and Calvinist Scotland that introduced adultery and malicious desertion as grounds for divorce and fashioned the fantastic fiction of an "innocent and injured spouse" and a defendant who was wholly to blame. An experienced lawyer would never be the author of such a fable (20). The lawyer's approach would be in terms of solving the family's problem, dissolving the marital partnership if it is devoid of meaning, or trying to make it a going concern if the marriage is viable.

It should not be assumed that the lawyer is wholly without influence. In effect, what he often does is to bypass the written law or adapt it to his functional purpose. Divorce law as practiced in metropolitan areas, and in many villages as well, is not what it appears to be in theory. Since 90 per cent of divorce cases are uncontested, and usually only the plaintiff and counsel are present, there being no danger of cross-examination or dispute, the presentation of evidence becomes a formality. It is a ritual. It may take five to fifteen minutes. A referee who is himself a lawyer may hear the "case." Thus, the actual institution of divorce becomes something quite different from the postulated adversary procedure and that clear and convinving proof the statute calls for. The real contest, if any, occurred at the lawyer's office where financial and property matters were negotiated, and the legal rules, such as the defenses of recrimination and condonation, were of practical importance only as they gave leverage regarding the terms of settlement—the horrible cost of all this being perjury, trumped-up cases, fraud, collusion and the debasement of the judicial process in an area where the public most often comes into contact with law and the courts (21).

We will be forced to suffer from ambivalence and will be tormented by the hypocrisy of divorce procedures as long as we perpetuate the anachronistic vestiges of ecclesiastical law that are ill-suited to the twentieth century. Although we have been long-suffering in this regard, and ways have been found to circumvent theoretical barriers against consensual divorce, the practical expedients, escape hatches, and social institutions of divorce are not satisfactory and are inadequate if we wish to promote family stability and really value honesty, integrity and respect for the judicial process. In the name of a doctrinal morality, a much grosser immorality has been perpetrated that undermines law and order. Spinoza's warning that imposing legal wages for sin may be the death of the law is very much in point. He said: "He who tries to fix and determine everything by law will inflame rather than correct the vices of the world."

Affirmative help for families in trouble, constructive aid, should be provided by our public courts. Sin, as such, should be left for ecclesiastical sanctions and private conscience. The destructive and demoralizing legal processes we accept but subvert, based upon discredited notions of human depravity and a fatuous optimism as to virtue, should be replaced by the problem-solving technique that is so characteristic of good counseling.

CONCLUSION

An attempt has been made to outline some observations about the legal and social institutions of divorce. In summary, we wish to make the following points.

1. There is both a theoretical law of divorce and a "living law" of divorce, and any inquiry into the realities of family stability must reckon with both (22).

2. Inevitably, current social values press for acceptance, and undue rigidity of legal institutions will be overcome by the creation of competing social institutions or by a resort of self-help (23).

3. Although scholars have concentrated on the moral, religious and social aspects of marriage and divorce, the economics of marriage and divorce has been a neglected area.

4. In fact, economic considerations to a large extent determine the actual process of marriage and its termination. In most states divorce is readily obtainable once the terms of financial settlement have been fixed. For example, among New Yorkers, economic rather than legal considerations largely determine whether an annulment or divorce is sought in New York, a divorce is obtained in Mexico (at the cost of plane fare for one plus legal fees for two), or Nevada or Idaho (expenses for six weeks at a dude ranch plus legal fees), or resort is had to the extra legal device of desertion (24).

5. The "fault" element that permeates the law of divorce is unrealistic, unworkable and nefarious. On an operational level, it is equivalent to the metaphysical pastime of counting the number of angels that can sit on the head of a pin. This preoccupation with "fault" brings to mind the comparison of the philosopher, the clergyman and the lawyer: A philosopher is a man who goes into a dark cellar at midnight to look for a black cat that isn't there; he is to be distinguished from the clergyman who sees the cat; and from the lawyer who enters the cellar with a cat hidden in his pocket, then emerges to produce it in triumph!

6. Proponents of divorce reform and a therapeutic approach to family problems must overcome the entrenched opposition of some moralists and some churchmen who enjoy inordinate prestige with legislators. Legislators must be educated to the realities of divorce and the needs of families in trouble. Insofar as the substantive law of divorce is concerned, the most efficacious reform of divorce grounds is to add and implement a ground providing that estranged couples who have lived apart by mutual consent for two or more years may procure a divorce if the court is satisfied that their marriage is dead. Such a ground eliminates the perjury, fraud, corruption and abuse of traditional grounds and attaches no stigma—it becomes unnecessary to wash dirty linen in public (25). In addition to providing for a "living apart" ground, divorce reform calls for a change in focus from "fault" to the problem of whether or not attempts at reconciliation are practicable and in the best interests of the family. With this change of focus, it becomes essential that a professional staff be provided for the family court in order to further efforts at reconciliation.

7. Courts and lawyers also should not lose sight of the practical importance of providing community services for marriage counseling. Since the litigation stage is late in the history of family breakdown, counseling has less chance of success once suit has been filed, and it is essential for lawyers to cooperate by referring clients to professionally qualified persons at prior stages, when reconciliation has a better chance.

8. One of the greatest obstacles to divorce reform is the ambivalence towards divorce that is so typical of our society. Those who are not concerned about the integrity of our judicial process may find it acceptable to have a theoretical strict control of divorce but laxity in practice, thus having one's cake and eating it too. Such acceptance, however, entails a terrible cost. We are paying too great a price in family breakdown, fraud, perjury and collusion.

9. In a democratic society we must have faith in the educational process and assume that if we can establish a case for a better system of administering family law, it will win public support.

10. If a family court is established, in order to function and fulfill its purpose, a staff of competent experts is needed, and liaison must be maintained with other public and private agencies that are concerned with family problems. Interprofessional cooperation is essential.

In our opening paragraph we referred to the three blind men from Hindustan. After these peregrinations through the shallows of divorce it may be fitting to return to that fabled land. Legend has it that over the principal gate of the city of Agra there is the following inscription, perhaps written by the three blind men:

In the first year of the reign of King Julief, two thousand married couples were separated, by the magistrates, with their own consent. The emperor was so indignant, on learning these particulars, that he abolished the privilege of divorce. In the course of the following year, the number of marriages in Agra was less than before by three thousand; the number of adulteries was greater by seven thousand; three hundred women were burned alive for poisoning their husbands; seventy-five men were burned for the murder of their wives; and the quantity of furniture broken and destroyed, in the interior of private families, amounted to the value of three million rupees. The emperor re-established the privilege of divorce (26).

REFERENCES

1. See FOSTER: Common Law Divorce, 46 Minn. L. Rev. 43 (1961). ". . . evasions of the law governing divorce in New York comprise only a special and conspicuous case of the general pattern of institutionalized evasions of institutional norms. The pattern develops whenever the laws governing a political jurisdiction or the formal rules governing an organization have lagged behind the changing interests, values, and wants of a substantial part of the underlying population. For a time, the evasions make the law tolerable, although hardly liked. . . . the existence of Reno can be said to make for the persistence of severe divorce laws in New York. . . . if these laws [in New York] were stringently enforced rather than liberally interpreted through legal casuistry and illegal connivance, the bottled-up pressure for divorce would probably make for a major change in the laws sooner than is apt to be the case under current conditions. . . . Institutionalized evasions, it appears, tend to persist only so long as they are kept tacit. . . ." Sociologist Robert K. Merton in Foreword to O'Gorman: *Lawyers and Matrimonial Cases,* 1963, p. xi.

2. Ibid. See also, MUELLER, *Inquiry Into the State of a Divorceless Society,* 18 U. Pitt. L. Rev. 545 (1957) and Ehrlich, FUNDAMENTAL PRINCIPLES OF THE SOCIOLOGY OF LAW (Moll transl. 1936). "The evasion of matrimonial laws throughout the country is manifested in four patterns of behavior: (1) The laws explicitly refuse to allow divorce through the mutual consent of the spouses, but most divorces appear to be based on mutual consent; (2) collusion between parties is prohibited, yet some degree of collusion is probably present in nearly every [uncontested] divorce action; (3) the law assumes that matrimonial actions will be contested, but most [typically, over 90 per cent] are not; (4) matrimonial actions are decided on the basis of evidence presented in court, but such evidence usually bears little relationship to the actual causes of marital disruption. In brief, every major premise underlying most matrimonial laws is persistently denied in the majority of matrimonial cases." O'Gorman: *Lawyers and Matrimonial Cases,* 20-21, 1963.

3. BENEDICT: *Patterns Of Culture.* Mentor Books, 1957, p. 39.

4. *Ibid.*

5. Hobhouse; Wheeler, and Ginsberg: *The Material Culture And Social Institutions Of The Simpler Peoples,* 1930, p. 154-155, 216-227.

6. Bunzel: The economic organization of primitive peoples. In: General Anthropology, [Edited by Boas], 1938, pp. 77-78. See also Linton: The Tree of Culture. Vintage Books, 1959, pp. 326-408.

7. Goode: After Divorce, 1936, p. 39.

8. Monahan: Divorce by occupational levels. 17 Marriage & Family Living 322, 344 (1955).

9. Benedict: *Patterns of Culture.* Mentor Books, 1957, p. 220.

10. This is because, according to Pound, the "immediate task" of law is to "adjust or reconcile or harmonize conflicting and overlapping claims or demands or desires." Pound, THE HISTORY AND THE SYSTEM OF THE COMMON LAW 162 (1939). Unfortunately, it is generally true that the life of ecclesiastical law was dogma, not experience. Established doctrine, in clerical hands, tends to become an end in itself, without regard to the wisdom "that the law exists not for itself, but to serve human ends." Holmes: Collected Legal Papers, 1920, p. 186.

11. *The Matrimonial Causes Act* of 1857, 20 and 21 Vict. c. 85 (1857), provided that absolute divorce might be granted for adultery and abolished the jurisdiction of the ecclesiastical courts over divorce and conferred it upon a special court that also handled cases of probate and admiralty.

12. Civil divorce by regular courts was granted for a brief period under Cromwell.

13. The most important detailed study is that by Powell: *English Domestic Relations,* 1917, p. 64-65. He quotes from Style, to the effect that remarriage after annulment or divorce *a mensa et thoro* was frequent. See also Conset: *Ecclesiastical Courts,* 2d ed., 1700, and Ayliffe: *Paregon Juris Canonicic Anglicani* 2d ed., 1734, both of whom comment about widespread fraud in obtaining annulments and upon illegal remarriages after bed-and-board divorce.

14. Powell, *op. cit.* at p. 87 quotes Godolphin to the effect that the canons of 1603 sought to bar remarriage after divorce *a mensa et thoro* by requiring that bond be posted by the husband, but the law was interpreted to mean that if the husband did remarry, forfeiture of the bond was the only penalty that might be imposed. Consequently, abuses continued.

15. Mueller: *Inquiry into a divorceless society,* 18 U. Pitt. L. Rev. 545 (1957). Some of the ladies fetched but a shilling, and one was transferred for a dram of gin.

16. It should be noted, however, that penances might be imposed for informal marriages although the marriage itself was valid before the Council of Trent. Of course, the Council of Trent's decree Tametsi had no force or effect in Protestant England.

17. Mueller, *op. cit.* at pp. 550-551, estimates that a Parliamentary bill of divorcement and the other suits it entailed cost between six hundred and one thousand pounds. Between 1715 and 1775 there were but sixty

such bills, between 1775 and 1800 around seventy-four and between 1800 and 1836 there were eighty to ninety. Although annulments and divorce *a mensa et thoro* were far cheaper, they, too, were beyond the means of the average Englishman.

18. "In fact, whenever a rule of law lay across the path of human progress, or failed to give an adequate satisfaction for human needs, we may feel reasonably sure that human progress and human wants have found their way under its barrier by means of legal fiction or around it by equity. They have flowed over it sometimes in the form of legislation, but the barrier has rarely been so high and strong in our race as to cause a pressure sufficient to result in revolution." Page, *Professor Ehrlich's Czernowitz Seminar of Living Law,* Proceedings of the Association of American Law Schools 46, 68 (reprint 1914), reprinted in Hall: *Readings In Jurisprudence,* 1938, pp. 825, 834.

19. RHEINSTEIN: *The law of divorce and the problem of marriage stability,* 9 Vand. L. Rev. 633 641 (1956).

20. The lawyer's view has been expressed by JAMES BRYCE: "The effort to base legal rules on moral and religious principles leads naturally to casuistry, and away from that common-sense view of human transactions and recognition of practical consequences which ought to be the basis for law." BRYCE, *op. cit* at pp. 421-422. See also BRADWAY: The Myth of the Innocent Spouse, 11 Tul L. Rev. 377 (1937), and LLEWELLYN: Behind the Law of Divorce, 33 Col. L. Rev. 249 (1933).

21. For a fuller development of this view, see Foster, "Family Law in a Changing Society," Chap. 7 of DAVIS, FOSTER, JEFFERY, & DAVIS: *SOCIETY AND THE LAW,* Free Press, 1962. "When evasion becomes common practice among large numbers of law-abiding citizens, the determinants of such evasion are to be found . . . in institutionalized inconsistencies rather than in individual immorality. The extraordinary prevalence of evasion in matrimonial actions plainly points to a cultural conflict in which the legal norms governng the dissolution of marriage are incompatible with norms held by a large segment of American society. The law prohibits what the public permits. Under these conditions patterns of evasive behavior have developed by which the law is obeyed in theory and denied in fact." O'GORMAN: *Lawyers and Matrimonial Cases,* 1963, p. 21.

22. MALINOWSKI: *Crime And Custom In Savage Society,* 1951, p. 127, points out that "the true problem is not to study how human life submits to rules — it simply does not; the real problem is how the rules become adapted to life."

23. "The fact that the evasion of law is known to officers of the court symbolically legitimatizies the behavior; it is given institutional approval . . . the general absence of punitive action structurally stamps the evasion as acceptable . . . ." O'GORMAN: *op. cit.*

24. ". . . only one out of fourteen peripheral practitioners, and only two out of nine major practitioners reported that their clients' divorce actions

unusually took place in New York; in contrast, 15 out of 22 minor practitioners said they handled most of their divorces in local courts." O'GORMAN: *op. cit.* at 79.

25. Some twenty-seven American jurisdictions recognize some form of "living-apart" as a ground for divorce. In states such as Alabama, Connecticut, Maryland, North Dakota and Utah, a judicial separation may be converted into an absolute divorce if there is no reconciliation after the stipulated period of time. See McCURDY, Divorce — A suggested approach, 9 Vand. L. Rev. 685 (1956), and Note, Divorce: Living apart statutes as a replacement for fault, 1959 Wash. U. L. Q. 189.

26. Quoted, with tongue in cheek, by Blake: *The Road To Reno,* 1962, pp. 80-81, from 28 Niles Register 229 (June 11, 1825). See also Palmer, Fact against fiction in divorce, 38 Amer. Bar Ass'n J. 652 (1952) where he states: "We realize that it [divorce] is a safety valve, and that without it thousands of persons who now are living free and reasonably useful lives otherwise would be in graves, jails, sanitariums and asylums." On the other hand, see Ernst and Loth: *For Better Or Worse,* 1952, where follow-ups on clients revealed that, typically, those procuring divorces later decided that they were worse off than they had been during the broken marriage.

Chapter 16

LAWYERS AND SOCIAL WORKERS: COLLABORATORS OR COMPETITORS IN RESOLVING MARITAL CONFLICT*

EMILY H. MUDD

T HE GREAT PSYCHOLOGIST, William James, commented that, as soon as a young person enters upon his formal professional training, marks of his profession are upon him. He tends thereafter to think and feel as a lawyer, a physician, an engineer or whatever. It is natural and important that most professional individuals find their primary identity within the realm of their own professional background. However, this in no way precludes, in fact in my concept it requires, an understanding of the commitment to those seeking assistance and the major goals of other professions with which involvement occurs in the pursuit of daily responsibilities.

This chapter is delimited to two specifics. We are concerned with the relationship between two professional groups—lawyers and social workers —and to one aspect of their work—that of resolving marital conflict. I shall attempt to discuss:

1. Something of the background and responsibilities of social workers functioning in the area of marriage counseling;
2. A few illustrative cases;
3. Some implements to constructive cooperation; and
4. Suggestions for collaborative efforts between social workers and lawyers aimed toward prevention of some of the causes of marital disintegration.

TRAINING AND RESPONSIBILITIES OF CASEWORKERS

It is my understanding that social workers involved in family-relations counseling will be those who have elected to be trained in their university sequence as caseworkers, and who in all probability have had supervised field placement in a family agency or child-guidance clinic. Certain of these caseworkers have gained further specialized experience by being assigned in their agency primarily to marriage-counseling cases under skilled supervision, or by placement for a third year of advanced training or doctoral work in a recognized marriage council. Some caseworkers with specific interest are associating themselves with the American Association of Mar-

---

*Paper presented by invitation at the National Conference on Social Welfare, Atlantic City, N. J., May 26, 1965.

riage Counselors—a national interprofessional organization whose main purpose is the promotion and maintenance of training and standards in this field of specialization.

Counseling with couples or individuals in marital conflict is regarded as a complex and difficult responsibility by social caseworkers. This task, according to the excellent guide put out in 1959 by the Family Service Association of America, is "to help individuals and families mobilize the resources within themselves and society to cope with many problems in everyday life (1). Please note again the words *to mobilize* resources, not only within themselves, but *in society* to cope with problems. Clearly, family caseworkers, over and beyond their assistance in helping the troubled person mobilize his or her inner resources, have a primary obligation to seek out the community resources needed by their clients. Within this framework legal consultation and service are often essential to the welfare and future stabilization of those husbands, wives and children immersed in marital conflict. Examples from our daily experience are familiar to us all.

CASE EXAMPLES

Case 1

Recently I had a follow-up visit from a college woman (and her 3-year-old son) whom I had seen with her boyfriend when she was pregnant and unmarried. At that time vital decisions concerning the financing of the birth and rearing of the child faced us with obvious legal implications. While we helped this young woman with her anger, her natural anxieties, her ambivalences and plans for the future, we suggested that she also talk with a wise and socially minded lawyer. This consultation provided advice for the young woman concerning her rights and those of her unborn child. It also brought realistic legal pressures on the unmarried father, and eventually his family, for support of the child. In this instance (and we all like to report constructive outcomes), there was a happy ending. The young mother subsequently married a fine man who knew the entire situation. Following the marriage her lawyer helped to effect a final settlement with the little boy's father so that monthly support checks would no longer bring routine reminders of a difficult past.

Case 2

In another instance a prominent lawyer called. He represented the parental family interests of a young man already separated from his wife. This lawyer had urged his client to seek marriage counseling and to ask his estranged wife also to come to the same agency for counseling before he, the lawyer, proceeded to draw up a separation agreement. After some weeks of interviews it became clear that this marriage would not continue. With both clients' written permission, a conference was held between the counselor and the lawyer for the purpose of discussing details which hopefully would assist the lawyer in drawing up legal papers to serve the interests of husband, wife and children as reasonably as possible.

We are all familiar with frustrated and angry clients who threaten impulsive action or are adamant in their determination to act unwisely. We know that if these actions are followed our clients may jeopardize their legal rights. In such instances the marriage counselor has grave responsibility, and hopefully will make every effort to steer the client to reliable legal services.

Case 3

For instance, the young wife who packs up in anger and leaves home needs to know how proof of desertion can influence her later divorce action or custody of the children. Discussion with this wife of referral to reliable legal sources to ascertain these facts can often bring reality into turbulent plans, postpone hasty decisions and permit time to explore the overall needs and goals of both partners.

ADDITIONAL ORIENTATION TO LEGAL PROBLEMS

From these and many other possible illustrative cases, it is clear to you that, in my thinking and experience, *lawyers are essential collaborators to caseworkers.* It can, however, be questioned whether every caseworker receives sufficient orientation in professional training to be alerted to those many and often-complex situations which may involve clients in legal complications. There are times also when, because of these lacks, a caseworker may be uncertain or unknowing or confused between his responsibility for alerting a client to the need for obtaining adequate legal advice and his equally important responsibility *not to attempt to give specific legal information to his client.* This seems to be an important distinction. *Caseworkers are not trained in law even though they should be oriented to the types of legal problems which involve families in conflict.*

How can such further orientation be achieved if and when it is needed? We have found so many legal matters of importance to marriage counselors that we feel that such training should be included in a supervised graduate training program in marriage counseling (2, 3).

If a case with legal problems is presented, the discussion on practical issues may serve as a springboard for the lawyer to bring in related material of mutual benefit. For instance, there are matters in which the counselor as well as the client may need legal protection. The possibility of subpoena with the counseling records in a contested divorce case is an unpleasant hazard for all caseworkers. Records may be respected and not called on by the court if legal counsel is considerate, but we all know social-agency records do not yet have the confidentiality accorded those of the physician and clergy. Caseworkers in private practice usually are advised to carry heavy malpractice insurance, and of course the whole matter of state licensing for marriage counselors of various professional backgrounds will undoubtedly be explored further, and even pressed, in the next decade.

Discussions and conferences with marriage counselors and lawyers sharing together both information and problems obviously serve an educational function. This educational function can also be supplemented by having available in the office more than one of the excellent manuals prepared by lawyers and others (4, 5). These reference works offer comprehensive information about separation, divorce, support, custody of children, etc., and can be helpful to staff and selected clients. When wisely used with clients they will be suggested with the comment, "Of course each situation has personal elements which it is important for you to explore individually with your lawyer."

CONSTRUCTIVE COMMUNICATION

Discussion during which members of both professions participate also contributes to an even more neglected function, namely, *constructive communication* between professional persons from these two different backgrounds. Several recent articles have emphasized problems of communication and indicated the need for increased understanding between lawyers and social workers (6, 7, 8).

National associations, interested perforce in interprofessional contacts, have appointed committees, held conferences and edited books focused on family conflict and divorce (9, 10). For example, Committee appointed in 1950 by The Family Law Section of the American Bar Association under Judge Paul Alexander of Detroit had as its purpose the recommendation of revisions of state and Federal laws. Judge Alexander had established the first marriage-counseling service as a definite adjunct of a divorce court (11). Again, the Joint Committee of the American Association of Marriage Counselors and the Family Law Section of the American Bar Association has held two yearly meetings and a conference in 1965 on "A New Look at Divorce Practices in U.S. Culture" (12). Our work in Philadelphia, we claim, has exposed our staff to both serious difficulties with some members of the bar and essential constructive and supportive relationships with other lawyers. In fact, Marriage Council of Philadelphia owes its very existence to the efforts of an outstanding jurist, Mr. Henry Drinker, who drew up our Charter, chaired our Legal Supervisory Committee of five prominent lawyers,* assigned members of his firm to represent our casework staff when

---

*Since Mr. Drinker's illness and death, Marriage Council of Philadelphia's Legal Supervisory Committee has been chaired by the Honorable Nochem S. Winnet. Members include Robert D. Abrahams, George F. B. Appel, Ralph C. Busser, Jr., and Wilbur N. Haines, Jr.

subpoened, wrote agreements for supervised field work with Columbia University and, finally, drew up an affiliation agreement between Marriage Council of Philadelphia and the Department of Psychiatry, University of Pennsylvania. There has been constant referral of clients by our staff to legal resources and an increasing number of referrals from lawyers to Marriage Council of Philadelphia—in fact, 9 per cent of all cases in 1963-1964. In the last decade it is perhaps significant that there have also been self-referrals to us of lawyers and their spouses involved in marital conflict.

POSSIBLE NEW APPROACHES

Because of our feelings of support and freedom of interchange, I would like now to suggest that work in marital conflict can and perhaps should involve both caseworkers and lawyers in new cooperative investigation. Can we together devise and promote different approaches to ameliorate or remove certain existing conditions in our culture which contribute to anger, humiliation and disorganization in family living? Can we release some of the time and energy now spent by both professions with pathetic, irritating, pathological and unhopeful case situations and invest it in efforts at prevention?

One such approach might be aimed at more realistic and adequate premarital preparation through discussions with individual young adults in small groups or counseling with groups of engaged couples. Divorce figures make clear the vulnerability of the young, the unprepared, the immature to the stress of marriage and children. People contemplating marriage, for all their radiant happiness, are people in crisis, if for no other reason than that they will shortly experience a major change in social and personal role. We suggest that longer waiting periods between obtaining a license and the marriage would make possible a routine exploratory interview. This in turn might uncover facts and feelings of an unhealthy nature. If explored further these might raise questions in the minds of the couple as to the advisability of the marriage. The expressed interest of the community in every marriage through such a requirement would vastly extend the work now done by committees of religious institutions, such as the Committee on Marriage of each Friends Meeting. This committee meets with each couple who desire to be married in the meeting and explores with them their plans and goals before deciding as to the suitability of the marriage taking place in the Meeting House.

Medical examinations which include mental as well as physical health assessments would add another dimension to the discovering of pathology and indicate possible postponement of marriage. Each of these approaches could serve as effective first steps. Uniform marriage, divorce and reciprocal-support laws throughout the country might also discourage a number of undesirable unions and later disintegration. A potentially good marriage can only benefit from the concern and scrutiny of the community. Marriage and its consequences are, in reality, by no means private affairs.

Another important cornerstone for the promotion of mental health in marriage could be laid by welcoming facilities through churches, PTAs, clubs, Chambers of Commerce or Better Business Auxiliaries, for each new bride and groom or family who move to a strange community. Kindly attention from interested local couples would go far to allay the loneliness, isolation and depression so often experienced by the wife and mother who does not go out to work, and who spends most of her hours within her own walls. A helpful approach at a latter stage in the marriage would be for each community to have available special apartments for families with children in which the mothers are employed. If these apartments offered suitably staffed day nurseries for infants and recreational activities for teenagers after school and before mother returns from work, continuing anxiety for mother and child would be greatly relieved. Conceivably, this could accomplish wonders in preventing resentment and deprivation to young children, and unsavory gang influence upon teenagers that so often lead to juvenile delinquency.

I present one other idea for your consideration: Much thought is going into care for older citizens. More imaginative approaches might link the vital need of young parents for an evening out with the urgency of older men and women to feel useful, wanted and in contact with the stimulation of youth.

The profession of law has been honored through the ages. Social work, as a profession, is still relatively young. As the United States, with its vastly increasing population, moves toward intensive and continuing services for larger segments of its citizens, these skills of the social caseworker will be further intertwined with those of the lawyer. Patience, persistence and goodwill will be needed to foster continuing mutual understanding and reciprocal non-time-consuming cooperation in the almost overwhelming load that lies ahead. Mutual trust between lawyers and social workers should engender the confidence essential to frank and constructive communication. It does not seem unrealistic to predict that from this union will emerge the courage, vitality and daring essential to the initiation of new concepts of prevention.

REFERENCES

1. FAMILY SERVICE ASSOCIATION OF AMERICA: The lawyer and the social worker: A report of the Committee on Lawyer-Family Agency Cooperation. 1959.
2. MUDD, EMILY H.; GOODWIN, HILDA M., and YOUNG, DONALD R.: Mental health teaching in professional education. *J. of Medical Education, 37* (No. 1) : 36-43, 1962.

3. ROSENBERG, EDWARD B.: Marriage counseling and the lawyer. Unpublished lecture given to Marriage Council of Philadelphia, Graduate Training Program, 1960.

4. PILPEL, HARRIET, and ZAVIN, THEODORA: *Your Marriage and the Law.* New York, Rinehart, 1952.

5. GOODE, WILLIAM J.: *After Divorce.* Glencoe, Free Press of Glencoe, Inc., 1956.

6. WINNET, NOCHEM S., and TROMMER, EVELYN M.: Meet the marriage counselor, his place in the sun, his role as a specialist, use of marriage counseling. *Shingle,* Philadelphia Bar Assoc., *XXIII* (No. 9), (Dec.) 1960, *XXIV* (No. 1), (Jan.) 1961, *XXIV* (No. 2), (Feb.) 1961.

7. SMITH, CHARLETON S.: A lawyer's guide to marriage counseling. *Amer. Bar Assoc. J., 56:*719-722, 1964. Reprinted by the Family Service Association of America.

8. MUELLER, EDWARD E., and MURPHY, PHILIP J.: Communication problems: Social workers and lawyers. *Social Work, 10* (No. 2) :97-103, 1965.

9. MUDD, EMILY H.: The social worker's function in divorce proceedings. Law and contemporary problems. *School of Law, Duke University, 18:*66-71, 1953.

10. MUDD, EMILY H.: Conflict and conflict-resolution in families: In *Conflict Resolution and World Education,* edited by Stuart Mudd, Vol. III, World Academy of Art and Science. The Hague, Netherlands, Dr. W. Junk Publishers, 1966.

11. Bridgman, Ralph: The processes of discord and estrangements, divorce and reconciliation. *Pastoral Psychology, Sept.-Oct.,* 1958.

12. American Association of Marriage Counselors and Family Law Section, American Bar Association: A new look at divorce practices in U. S. culture. Unpublished report, Conference, Detroit, March 5-6, 1965.

Chapter 17

THE CHANGING AMERICAN FAMILY PATTERN AND ITS EFFECT ON MARITAL STABILITY

SYLVIA HERZ

WHEN ANALYZING THE CONTEMPORARY marital relationship, it is necessary to examine the social controls which formerly molded the man-woman relationship within the family unit. While, in the past, marriage and the family derived their stability from social, economic and religious expectations, the willingness of persons to continue their marriage today depends greatly on whether or not they personally find marriage satisfying and the family relationship a meaningful one.

In meaningful and constructive relationships, each person has the opportunity to grow intellectually and emotionally. Giles sets forth the "growth-belonging" theory which, in effect, summarizes man's drives or needs in relation to human interaction.

> It says in effect that the constant struggle of man in all climes and times has been to achieve freedom to grow, to develop all abilities, to contribute to his society. It says that the human sciences support the idea that growth and the desire for it characterize the human individual and the social group. It expresses strong support for the democratic goal as stated: to promote the maximum growth of all, and to foster the chief condition for that growth-belonging (9, p. 96).

To understand the motivations for behavior within the family unit, we must explore the socioeconomic changes which have taken place within society from early American to contemporary times and their effects upon marital relationships. A family pattern that appears to be "natural" may nevertheless be created by cultural and social forces. Therefore, in analyzing family systems and patterns, we study not only the social relations internal to a given family, but also between family and society.

EIGHTEENTH-NINETEENTH CENTURY EARLY AMERICAN FAMILY

The pioneer, rural, old-fashioned large family in early America was imperative in its all-absorbing demands of economic productivity, cooperative practicality, protection, religion, education, medical attention and marriage.

Rural, Cooperative and Self-sufficient Family Unit

An agricultural economic base with traditional values formed the foundation for the typical early American family. The rural family unit was a self-sufficient one, since the basic needs of its members, such as food, clothing, shelter, protection, recreation, education, religion and health, were fulfilled within the home. Since in many areas there were few if any outside sources such as stores, theatres, medical authorities, churches and schools, the family had to provide these essentials from within. Full cooperation by all family members was the method employed.

Marriage—An Economic Arrangement

Within this framework of the family setting, great emphasis was placed upon practical and materialistic goals. The early American family marriage was itself an economic arrangement. Securing a daughter-in-law or son-in-law by the head of the household was governed by such practical concerns as having a sturdy constitution, good working habits and the ability to perform household duties (3, Vol. I, Ch. 3). These traits made up the essentials of good working marriage.

It may be noted that various other societies employed the market system of mate selection as well. The system varied from one society to another, with respect to who controlled the transactions, the rules of exchange and the relative evaluation of various qualities. In traditional Arab societies, a man's family—controlled by the elders—paid a bride-price for the woman; while in the Brahmin castes of India the woman's family paid a groom-price. The rules may also have required counter-gifts of some kind (12, p. 32).

In America, as in other earlier societies, marriage for love and affection was considered unimportant in the hierarchy of the values of family life.

Family Unity and Demanding Solidarity

Economic ties and personal loyalties among its members emerged within the self-sufficient rural family. Familism and authoritarianism were the two guiding principles which governed the family's internal organization (18, Ch. 2).

The Family Über Alles

Familism represented the subordination of the individual's interests, needs and desires to those of the family as a whole. There was pursuance of family goals for the good of all rather than goals that the individual set for himself. The primary obligation of a family member was to carry out the assigned and well-defined goal, set by an elder, which fit into the overall pattern of family goals. For example, if a son wished to become a teacher within the family, he would have to forego his ambition in order to farm if the latter work was more needed by the family group. Therefore, the type of training one received, dictated by an elder and conducted within the family, had little regard for one's individual aptitudes and tastes, but primarily was based upon skills needed by the family in its strivings for self-sufficiency.

Father Knows Best—Always

The early authoritarian household was one in which power was centralized within one individual, who ruled with an iron hand in demanding immediate obedience. There was little opportunity for individual decision-making. Patriarchal authoritarianism meant that the power to rule lay with the eldest male of the family, who was viewed as being its head and leader. Therefore, the power of the husband or father was both accepted and unquestioned, and the main duty of a good wife, along with other family members, was to obey and carry out responsibilities.

Some behavioral scientists, however, question the extent to which the patriarch alone determined the family unit's course of action (27). It is noted that the wife-mother frequently influenced the patriarch's decisions by feminine persuasive tactics in the use of subtle suggestions. This is not to say that she argued with him or told her husband what to do outright. This was unthinkable in the patriarchal household.

In addition, there also existed a mother-centered or mother-dominated home where the wife-mother actually determined the family's course of action. This type of home developed when the husband was no longer able to perform his role adequately, due to injury or death as a result of the cultural and occupational hazards during this period of history (18, Ch. 2). Nevertheless, the authoritarian nature of the family was pronounced, regardless of whether the father or mother was in control. There was no overt disagreement among family members since it was necessary to follow goals set by the head of the household in order to maintain successful operation of the family unit.

In order to command obedience, it was necessary that the decisions and commands of the head of the family always be viewed by the family as right. If questions were raised by the others, the authoritarian won on the basis of custom and tradition that he was right. Thus, the authoritarian was able to maintain his power since traditions were highly valued and not subject to critical examination or change (7, pp. 12-13).

Emotionally, the authoritarian felt he had to be viewed as always right by all members alike. Any implication to the contrary would be shattering to him psychologically (5). The authoritarian, therefore, used whatever means necessary—shouting, berating, humiliating, mocking, etc.—to win his point and keep the disobedient or questioning member in line.

Since custom and tradition dictated that the eldest male or the father rule the family, it did not follow that he was the most competent to rule nor that he had competency or ability at all. Therefore, the authoritarian's right to govern was not based on demonstrated ability but rather on irrational authority (18, p. 19).

Inequality of Family Members

The composition of the authoritarian family was looked upon and treated as a group of unequals—superior and inferior members. First and foremost, the authoritarian figure was superior to all. Among the other family members, the physically weak and fearful were treated as basically inferior. In contrast, those possessing physical prowess and lacking fear— except fear of the authoritarian and God—were greatly revered and admired (19, pp. 401-411). Age and sex played a part as well in regard to family status. Males and adults were considered and treated more favorably than women and children.

Family members were treated as commodities. Each was regarded in relation to how much he could contribute to the family's economic well-being rather than being valued for his intrinsic worth as a human being. Family members were, therefore, considered as things to be used and exploited for the material benefit of all members.

It is, therefore, comprehensible that we find encouragement of marriage and increase in family size in early America. The tradition of large families continued, since a high birthrate meant a more adequate labor supply, a necessity for survival in an economy which had little or no mechanization (3, Vol. II, p. 17).

Family Stability

Due to economic interdependence of family members and ensuing loyalties, the early American family had stability with little divorce.

External forces in the community itself also had stabilizing effects upon family integration. It was a natural expectation that wives obey their husbands and children their parents. If there was family conflict, the community viewed the situation, despite circumstances, as being caused by an ungrateful wife or a disobedient child. Consequently, persons did not wish to be regarded with disfavor in the eyes of the community and suffer the shame and disgrace that would accompany a divorce. Marriage was considered to be a permanent and religiously holy union. Separation or divorce were both socially and religiously unacceptable as adjustments to marriage conflict (1, pp. 443-444).

Although the early American family unit has been described as a permanent and socially stable one, the happiness and emotional development of its members are questionable. There is evidence that suggests that personal adjustment in the authoritarian family was similar to that found in a dictatorial society, where the individual is subjugated to the demands of a powerful leader (3, Vol. I, Chs. 5-6). One may conclude, therefore, that there was little opportunity for individual growth and creativity or reaching one's full potential in the authoritarian family relationship.

TRADITIONAL FAMILY PATTERNS ALTERED BY SOCIAL CHANGE

Social factors helped to influence changes in the personal relationships within the family constellation as well as outside it. America's shift from a rural to an urban society and various sociohistoric components were responsible for family changes in attitudes and behavior.

America Becomes Industrialized

The shift from an agricultural to an industrial economy in America's last 150 years has brought with it large migrations to the city, away from the country. There was great appeal in the city: better working conditions; higher wages; and more adequate educational, cultural and medical facilities (10, pp. 90-92).

Changing Family Relationships

Three major family changes were effected by America's industrialized cities: First, the family became less self-sufficient; second, the authoritarian lost some of his power; and third, the individual tended to undergo attitudinal changes toward his family (18, pp. 22-23).

The Fading Self-sufficient Unit

The family no longer had to depend solely upon its own resources for survival and satisfaction of its needs. Provision of clothing, food, shelter, protection, recreational and medical facilities, and instruction in education and religion were taken over by agencies and institutions outside the home. Home chores such as cleaning and cooking were simplified through the use of machines and appliances. Consequently, the family was freed from many duties which at one time were vital to its survival (20, Vol. II, Ch. 13). Time and energy, saved by elimination of family chores, could now be devoted to the interests and needs of the individual.

Gradual Collapse in Authoritarian Power

With the rise of factories and mills, the work unit was no longer in the home but, instead, employment was gained outside it. The authoritarian was, therefore, released of the hold he previously had on the work lives of his family members. Not only did he no longer have the power to command, but, unless he had his own business he too probably worked in a factory and took orders from others rather than gave them. Thus, the very core of authoritarian familism was struck by industrialization.

Change in Family Attitudes

As a result of the individual's mobility within the urban setting, he became exposed to and interacted with persons of different backgrounds with different rules of conduct and values. Daily contact with nonfamily members, both in the factory and at school, heightened the individual's awareness of these new and different cultural patterns.

Also, religious and community controls were not as stringent or binding as before. The individual came to realize that his family pattern was only one of many, and perhaps there was merit in further examination of varying existent social patterns. As a result, the previously held strong loyalty to his family's standards was being challenged and reexamined in the light of new and different value systems.

Sociohistoric Forces Affect the Family

The existence of such sociohistoric factors as secularism, scientific humanism, democracy in politics, the emancipation of women and the American frontier (18, pp. 24-27) over an extended period of time contributed greatly to the creation of a new social and psychological family setting.

Secularism

Under secularism, man started to question customs, traditions and values, and realized that they were not God's invention. The individual started to modify and create new social standards. With the advent of secularism, life was constantly being examined, and if traditional family patterns needed revision they were subjected to scrutiny and change without fear of divine punishment. The secular doctrine therefore challenged traditional authoritarianism by allowing the individual to alter his life pattern to suit his needs (2, pp. 361-376).

Humanism

The humanism of the period, evident in philosophy, literature and political development, projected the importance of human values and faith in the individual as a human being. Emphasis on the individual and trust in his ability became popular. Thus, humanism further helped to break the tradition of authoritarianism which revered only custom and the patriarch (8, pp. 384-397).

Democracy in Politics

Spreading of democracy and democratic ideals, both within the American government and abroad, helped to instill democratic values within the family. The consequent rise in individual democratic thinking led to overt rebellion against the authoritarian patriarch in his dictatorial and undemocratic familial setting.

Emancipation of Women

When woman left the home to work in the city's factory or mill, her status as being subservient and inferior underwent change. She now utilized her contribution to the family income as bargaining power for more equalized treatment both in and outside the home. The wife-mother was now released from some of her household duties and obtained a certain amount of power within the family council and its more democratized decisions. Male dominance within the family was thereby curtailed.

Family Organization on the American Frontier

Young marrieds frequently migrated to frontier territories which offered them greater economic opportunities and new patterns of conduct. Since the frontier family was removed from parental control, opportunities presented themselves that challenged traditional values. Hardships and battles of frontier life constantly threatened the life of the husband-father who actively protected his family from the ravages of attacking Indians, beasts and bandits. Consequently, by necessity, the wife took over the role of the father in decision-making and otherwise created mother-centered patterns in the household. Therefore, changes in concepts and behavior of the traditional way of life were inevitable in the American frontier family.

CHANGING VALUES ON THE AMERICAN SCENE

The new urban society—with influences of secularism, humanism, political democracy, emancipation of women and frontier life—emerged. With it developed new social patterns, accompanied by changing values in family living and relationships. Family members no longer were motivated to obey the traditional patriarch's authoritarian mode of behavior. After a long period of intensive struggle between the old and the new, reorganized family units appeared in new types of interpersonal relationships.

Respectful Individualism

An individual was now able to pursue goals and interests that he himself had selected to suit his needs and desires without being forced to accept goals set by the patriarch or the family. However, this newly found freedom was accompanied by a respect for the rights, needs, desires and dignity of others rather than self-concern alone.

Democratic Organization of the Family

Regard for Competence

The newly emerging family organization regarded competence rather than tradition as the important factor in granting family authority. Consequently, the power to make decisions was delegated to those members who possessed ability, according to the consensus of opinion. One or more persons in the democratically oriented family could make decisions at different times, depending upon skill, competence and experience.

In contrast to the authoritarian patriarch, the person who is democratically selected to pass judgment is not considered to be automatically "right" in his decisions. Although he has a desire to be right, he can accept the possibility of error.

Equality of Members

A democratic family with individualistic orientation does not categorize members into superior or inferior groupings, but instead respects the equality of all. Besides emancipated women, the position of children has undergone significant change within the family's framework. There is ever-increasing recognition of their needs as children as well as an awareness of the importance of their opportunity to grow emotionally, intellectually and physically.

Concern for the Individual

There exists a concern for the intrinsic worth of each family member as an individual rather than for his ability to produce towards the family's income. This attitude has brought with it a decline in the birthrate (6, pp. 33-34), since another child is not viewed as another "hand," but instead is afforded every opportunity by the family for broad individual development in reaching his fullest potential.

In general, values in the democratic family are frequently examined, reexamined and subjected to change to fulfill the individual needs of the various members.

PROBLEMS OF THE CONTEMPORARY AMERICAN FAMILY

Transitional Conflicting Values

The contemporary American family may be described as being in a state of transition between two sets of values. In short, Americans are in transition from authoritarian familism to democratic individualism and the corresponding values that accompany both cultural patterns of behavior.

In the patriarchal-authoritarian family the individual is unimportant in comparison to the group, while in the democratic-individualistic family the importance of the individual is of supreme concern. There exists, therefore, a schismatic mixture of traditional and emergent values which too often conflict and confuse the family members, who are militantly developing in this transitional period (26, pp. 18-23) .

Effect Upon Family Conflicts

In interpersonal family interaction the issues centering around the clash between authoritarian and democratic values affect not only the husband-wife relationship but the parent-child rapport as well. Too often the parents' clinging to the old, nostalgic and traditional view, as opposed to the child's desire for the new and experimental, leads to overt conflict. Debatable and conflicting points of view in everyday family living, depending upon one's authoritarian or democratic background and exposure, are largely responsible for family crises evident in contemporary American society.

Changing Values: A Challenge to Marital Stability

The source of much conflict between the spouses is frequently dependent upon the degree of authoritarian and dictatorial demands made by one spouse and the respondent unacceptance by the other, particularly if the latter is of a democratic-sharing orientation. Emergence of new and experimental value systems, therefore, has had a marked effect upon a marriage's stability. Forces have come into play that facilitate and result in marital separation or dissolution.

Need for a Meaningful Marital Relationship

In regard to expectations from marriage, the notion of a successful marriage has converted from that of an economic arrangement to an emphasis on the importance of a meaningful relationship including individual growth and a satisfaction of one's personal needs. Therefore, if the marital relationship does not provide these satisfactions, it is threatened and often terminated.

A More Condoning Society

The religiously oriented community's demand for traditional, strict obedience of the "inferior" wife to her husband's exactions eventually gave way to a regard for her rights as a person and an equal. Gradually, both the community-at-large and the Church, for the most part, with notable exceptions, e.g., Catholicism, granted reprieve and condoned dissolution of the marriage if a partner was wronged or basically deceived by the other. The evolution of current divorce laws implies acceptance of marriage dissolution by the State as well. This enlightened view by society as a whole facilitates divorce and separation without fear of being shunned by friends, relatives and the Church.

Economic Independence of Women

When the long-held concept of "woman's place is in the home" began faltering and was replaced because of the participation of women in industry and in the professions, shouldering responsibility alongside men, marital stability started rocking. Heretofore, the wife's total economic security depended upon her husband as a breadwinner. Today, approximately one-third of wives are working wives. During the first year of marriage some 40 per cent of all wives work outside the home (11, p. 8).

It follows, therefore, that, as more and more women enter the labor force, and bring home their pay checks, decisions about spending the family income will become more democratic and will result in joint decision-planning by both marital partners. If autocratic rule by the husband still prevails, causing dissatisfactions for the wife, she can more easily dissolve the marriage without fear of losing her economic security or becoming a ward of the state. The wife's ability to support herself entirely, if need be, is a great factor in the disappearance of unhappy clinging to an unacceptable and often-hated husband because of economic fears.

Research studies dealing with marital conflict and dissolution have recognized the working wife as a contributory factor.

> Does this indicate that, in some cases, at least, in which wives are self-supporting and independent of their husbands, the need for financial security is met for these wives? Further, does the fulfillment of this need for economic security, in such cases, militate against the desire or need to live together? (13, p. 26).

Status-Seeking: A Style of Life (22)

Frugality and the early American traditional value of "a penny saved is a penny earned" are a far cry from the concurrent "keeping up with the Joneses" mode of living. The middle-class American dream of living in the suburbs, in a one-family home, including a one- or two-car garage—"filled" —has almost become a reality for many. However, the high price being paid by the family in frantically "living beyond its means" isn't without its struggles, suffering, tensions, conflicts and, ofttimes, dissolution. Either one or both marital partners can wreak havoc with the marriage in this runaway type of spending. Frequently, futile attempts by one spouse to balance the budget, as opposed to the other's social-ladder-climbing attempts, are contributory symptoms of a "sick marriage."

Absenteeism in the Home*

In the past, not only did parents and children eat, pray, learn and work together, but their leisure time also was enjoyed in the home as a group. Family-participating musicales, recitals and lectures, in addition to pleasurable visitation of relatives as a family unit, were expected and normal pastimes. Family members' amusements and diversions were sought and obtained as a family.

For the most part, it is rare to find similar interests and activities occurring, simultaneously, among all its members within a typical urban middle-class American family in today's busy community. At a given time, chances are that each family member is in a separate place. Parents are seldom at home, particularly when the children arrive home from school. The father is working or "out-of-town on business." If the mother isn't at work, she, too, is absent due to her golf, bridge, committee work, beauty parlor and the like. Husband and wife alternate on individual nights out during the week. This varies from one to more evenings, depending upon the arrangement. He goes bowling with "the boys," and she has at least one night out "with the girls." On weekends, both spouses may be on the golf course or just "out" all day, terminating the evening's festivities with other similar sets of parents at "the club," theatre or entertainment spot.

Offspring, too, lead their individual lives and are encouraged to do so to conform socially. They group together, first as children, then as teen-agers and finally as engaged and married couples, only to start the "family-isolation cycle" of their parents.

The home becomes a place from which to start and then come back. Family members grow apart emotionally—siblings from each other, children from parents and husbands from wives. Potentially strong family and marital ties become loosened and estranged, and often break apart.

Parental Confusion and Conflict on Child-rearing

The equality of treatment that children have more recently gained, within the family unit, has been discussed previously.

New theories (25) concerning advisable techniques that encourage fuller growth of the child into a happier, better adjusted and functioning individual have become popular with modern parents and are applied in childrearing. The entire concept of "permissiveness" to avoid frustration in sponsoring creativity and individuality has, by the large, replaced the authoritarian "iron hand," "spare the rod and spoil the child" type of earlier parental behavior. However, much conflict between mother and

---

*Much of the data cited here has been amassed, by the author, as a result of studying current middle-class case histories in connection with marital counseling situations.

father is prevalent when there are dissenting views, in general or in specific instances, of which method to employ for maximum child-rearing effectiveness. The spouses' differing concepts of parenthood and their respective roles also militate against marital cohesiveness. Resultant destructive episodes of conflict often pitch parent against parent, parent against child, child against parent and siblings against each other. Ofttimes, devious ways are uncannily devised by children to keep such a conflict alive, thereby ensnaring their parents in a struggle of vying with one another for their children's love.*

Pressure of the Romantic Love Concept

Current jargon of "falling in love," "love at first sight," "marrying for love" and "love conquers all" are popular clichés more or less accepted by our present culture. Popular and overly advertised romantic novels, in addition to the prevailing "love" theme of movies, theatre, television and other media, reinforce the overidealized, overromanticized notion of love in its varying aspects. Needless to say, this romantic idealization of love is at the other end of the spectrum of the earlier economic-arrangement basis for marriage, already discussed.

Accompanying this idealized, romantic-love expectation from marriage, is the heartbreaking disillusionment of discovery that the spouse is, indeed, "human"—possessing weaknesses and frailties of other humans. The romantic hero image that was visualized before marriage has faded into oblivion, only to be regretted by its viewer. Everyday problems and stresses emerge in the marital relationship, and the magic somehow vanishes.

In addition, since the feat of marriage has been accomplished, the spouse finds it unnecessary to put his best foot forward as he did during the courtship or engagement period. Consequently, in place of the realization of the popularly idealized wish to "live happily ever after," the interaction between two individuals, who practically "see one another for the first time," takes place in the marital situation.†

Conflict in Role Interpretations

In early America, the wife-mother's place was definitely established in the home, and her household duties were strictly delineated. Similarly, the role of the husband-father who ruled the house and made all decisions was also clearly defined. There was no question as to what the duties and obligations of the wife-mother and the husband-father were in an authoritarian setting.*

---

*Study of family case histories in depth by the author has evidenced this interaction.

†*Loc. cit.*

*Description of the early American authoritarian setting was discussed at the beginning of the chapter.

Today's confusion in roles partially stems from the fact that, while an equal in the outer labor market, the woman—at times—wishes to be treated as an "inferior" or "weaker sex," both in and outside the home, and also wishes to be treated as an equal or even "superior" when either role suits her advantage. She wishes the male to be dominant and aggressive in their sexual relations and to cater to her in the role of a defenseless woman in courtesies, priorities, etc. On the other hand, she demands her right as an equal and, frequently, as the leader in planning and decision-making, based on experience, education, background or merely because she has a need to dominate (14, Ch. 12).

The husband, on the other hand, may have a background that instilled in him a need to be "boss" and, from exposure or lack of exposure to patriarchal-authoritarian familism, demands that the man in the family "wear the pants" (13, p. 147).

Also, when husband and wife both work and come home tired, questionable and unanswered problems arise. Who cooks? Who does the dishes? Who gets up with the baby at night? Whose right is it to be the aggressor in sex? Who has the final word? Who reprimands the children?

Based upon necessity and practicality, at times the husband takes over the wife's role and vice versa. Along with role-overlapping and -swapping come confusion and conflict between marital partners concerning the status and extent of each one's role, as viewed by the other, according to a predisposition toward authoritarian or democratic family interaction.

Some of the aforementioned changes in values and behavior patterns as a result of emergent values in a transitional period are but a few examples of the varied changes that have resulted within the marital structure, leading to conflict and, finally, disintegration.

Rise in the Divorce Rate

Despite great personal unhappiness caused by divorce, divorce rates have been rising in all Western countries. In most, the rates have been rising faster than in the United States, where the increase began a century ago.

The following table indicates the rise in divorce rate for selected Western countries. According to the statistics, although the United States divorce rate for 1956 is cited as being approximately one out of four marriages, the additional view is presented that this statistic is an underestimation.

Summation of Current Familial Maladies

Need for Understanding an Important "Why" of Conflict

Not only does each marital partner bring to the marriage his particular motives, wishes and his own personality traits but also, as outlined in this

DIVORCE RATES, 1910-1956, SELECTED WESTERN COUNTRIES

Country	Number of Divorces Per 1,000 Marriages	
	1910	1956
United States	87.4	246.2
Germany	30.2	89.2
England and Wales	2.2	74.4
	1911	
Australia	12.9	90.4
France	46.3	100.5
Sweden	18.4	175.4*

*Data from official sources. A ratio between the number of divorces in a given year and the number of marriages in a given year does not, of course, state the changes of *eventual* divorce. Obviously, the divorces in a given year do not primarily come from the marriages in the same year. On the other hand, a more correct figure, the number of divorces for each year per 1,000 existing marriages, is obtainable in only a few countries. When the divorce rate is *rising*, divorces in any given year come from marriages in the prior decade for the most part, and thus the ratio of divorces to marriages in a given year underestimates the likelihood of those marriages ending in divorce (12, p. 94).

chapter, his attitudes and learnings from the past. Therefore, an understanding of an individual's past orientation, authoritarian or democratic, and his reaction to it—accepting or rebellious—will give considerable insight into the dynamics of his marital conflicts. A democratic home offers possibilities for personal growth, individualization and possibilities of reaching one's potential. Difficulties arise in the autocratic and dictatorial home where rigid rules are made to be unquestionably obeyed, and where there is little latitude for individual expression or experimentation.

Inadequacy and Confusion of Traditional Behavior

Traditional patterns of family living and child-rearing, derived from an earlier period and yet still existent, no longer are adequate or even tolerable for today's families. However, most families have been or still are exposed, to a greater or lesser degree, to the traditional pattern with its nondeviating, dictatorial demands. Consequently, family members feel emotionally torn between the two value systems and resultant behavior of each. They feel harassed, anxious or guilty, beset with perplexities and burdened with conflicts, both within the family unit and its surrounding social life. Each family is additionally pressured by agencies, professions and programs to modify, change and reorganize its living habits on the basis of modern, desirable, scientific knowledge (6, pp. 489-490).

More confusion and conflict within the family has been caused by the breakdown in the traditional definition of the masculine and feminine roles by which men and women were previously guided to the performance of their obligations and enjoyment of their privileges. Today, men and women come to marriage with divergent, conflicting and often clashing beliefs in expectations of themselves and their spouses, both as mates and parents.

Children, growing up in this type of social situation, where changes in beliefs, expectations and conduct are progressing so rapidly, are themselves confused along with their parents. Parents are, therefore, unable to understand—let alone accept—their adolescents' attitudes and modes of behavior. The normal cleavage between generations has been broadened and accentuated, often resulting in bitter conflicts and rivalries. It is markedly evident that a more effective development of parent-child understanding, cooperation and communication, in addition to love, reassurance and comfort by the parent, are vital to the family's integrative stability.

HOPE FOR THE AMERICAN FAMILY

The foregoing discussion has shown that the marital relationship in contemporary America is undergoing a severe crisis. However, it is the belief of many social scientists that there will arise out of this transitional period an integration at a new and more significant level than ever before in American society. It is believed that marriages will succeed not only because of external social pressures but also because people will discover that, in the interaction of being married, they will experience satisfaction of their most basic wishes (16, pp. 151-153).

Also, it is hoped that there will be extensions of programs of proven worth and opportunity for creative innovations that will assist families in integrating and in carrying out more cooperatively and efficiently the burdens of twentieth-century living (6, p. 512).

REFERENCES

1. BABER, RAY E.: *Marriage and the Family*. New York, McGraw, 1953.
2. BECKER, HOWARD: Sacred and secular societies. *Social Forces, 28*:361-376, 1950.
3. CALHOUN, ARTHUR W.: *A Social History of the American Family from Colonial Times to the Present*. New York, Barnes & Noble, 1945.
4. CAVAN, RUTH SHONLE: In: *American Marriage: A Way of Life,* Fitting your marriage to the times. New York, Crowell, 1959.
5. CHRISTIE, RICHARD, and JAHODA, MARIE (Eds.): *Studies in the Scope and Method of the Authoritarian Personality*. Glencoe, The Free Press, 1954.
6. DUVALL, EVELYN MILLIS: *Family Development*. Philadelphia, Lippincott, 1957.
7. FROMM, ERICH: *Man for Himself*. New York, Rinehart, 1947.
8. GEIGER, GEORGE R.: *Philosophy and the Social Order*. New York, Houghton, 1947.

9. GILES, H. HARRY: *Education and Human Motivation.* New York, Philosophical Lib., 1957.

10. GIST, NOEL P., and HALBERT, L. A.: *Urban Society.* New York, Crowell, 1956.

11. GLICK, PAUL C.: The life cycle of the family. *Marriage and Family Living, XVII* (1) :8, 1955.

12. GOODE, WILLIAM J.: *The Family.* Englewood Cliffs, Prentice-Hall, 1964.

13. HERZ, SYLVIA: *An Analysis of the Expressed Needs of Married Couples in Recognized Conflict.* Ph.D. Dissertation, New York University, 1964.

14. HORNEY, KAREN: *Our Inner Conflicts.* New York, Norton, 1945.

15. JACO, E. G., and BELKNAP, IVAN: Is a new family form emerging in the urban fringe? *Am. Soc. Rev., 18:*Oct., 1953.

16. LANDIS, PAUL H.: The changing family. *Current History, 19:*151-153, 1950.

17. LANDIS, PAUL H.: Female roles in transition; Male roles in transition; Unsolved problems in role behavior. In: *Making the Most of Marriage,* 2nd Edition. New York, Appleton, 1960.

18. LANTZ, HERMAN R., and SNYDER, ELOISE C.: *Marriage, An Examination of the Man-Woman Relationship.* New York, Wiley, 1962.

19. MASLOW, A. H.: The authoritarian character structure. *J. Soc. Psychol., SPSSI Bulletin, 18:*401-411, 1943.

20. OGBURN, WILLIAM F.: *Recent Social Trends in the United States.* New York, McGraw, 1931.

21. OGBURN, W. F., and NIMKOFF, M. F.: *Technology and the Changing Family.* Boston, Houghton, 1955.

22. PACKARD, VANCE: *The Status Seekers.* New York, McKay, 1959.

23. PETERSON, JAMES A.: Marriage in transition. In: *Education for Marriage.* New York, Scribner, 1956.

24. SIMPSON, GEORGE: Toward analysis of marriage and the family in the United States. In: *People in Families.* New York, Crowell, 1960.

25. SPOCK, BENJAMIN: *Dr. Spock Talks with Mothers.* Boston, Houghton, 1961.

26. WINCH, ROBERT F., and MCGINNIS, ROBERT (Eds.) : *Selected Studies in Marriage and the Family.* New York, Holt, 1953.

27. YOUNG, MICHAEL, and WILLMOTT, PETER: *Family and Kinship in East London.* London, Routledge and Kegan Paul, 1957.

Chapter 18

LANGUAGE AND COMMUNICATION IN MARRIAGE COUNSELING

ARTHUR A. EISENSTADT

WHEN GOD DECIDED TO PUT an end to the Tower of Babel, the Bible tells us, he loosed no flashes of lightning, nor hosts of angels, nor did He brandish His "terrible swift sword." There was no need to do so. He simply commanded, "let us go down and there confound their language, that they may not understand one another's speech" (1). And the tower remained unfinished, and the people themselves were scattered, eternal testimony to the power of maladroit communication. This view of the deistic basis of language is shared by John Locke, who wrote: "God, having designed man for a sociable creature, made him not only with an inclination and under a necessity to have fellowship with those of his own kind, but furnished him also with language, which was to be the great instrument and common tie of society" (2). How vital are language and communication? Thomas Mann has observed that "speech is civilization itself. It is silence which isolates." The extent to which silence "isolates" may be inferred from the fact that, in a recent study of marital friction and divorce, despite the many varied reasons and circumstances which surrounded the unhappy couples, one factor was noted again and again. In many instances, after a period of violent disagreement and quarreling, the husband and wife spoke less and less to one another, finally gave up trying to explain themselves to one another and eventually went to a marriage counselor or a divorce court in an attempt to resolve their problems. To restate these lamentable events in linguistic terms: First they failed to communicate effectively; then they abandoned the communications bridge that formerly connected them; and finally they established communications with a third person in order to repair or dissolve entirely the communicative impasse that had grown up between them.

Here, then, is the rationale of this chapter. Fundamental to society, to human interrelationship and to harmonious living are *communication* and *understanding*. The medium for achieving this understanding through communication is *language,* which exists in many forms and modes. But language and communication are not the same, nor does fluency in language guarantee success in communication. It is therefore of value to examine the nature and makeup of each of these sociopersonal phenomena, the connections between them, the barriers which arise both within and between them, and to offer some suggestions for their more effective use. In order

212

to do so we shall consider the internals and externals of language, the elements which comprise language, the formative influences on language, and language and the communicative process.

ASPECTS OF LANGUAGE

Let us first consider basic linguistic concepts. What do we mean by the term *language*? Pei defined it as "a system of meaningful transfer, involving two or more individuals . . . language depends upon a convention, a common agreement among members of the speaking community to the effect that language sounds will convey certain pre-established meanings" (3). That language requires spoken sounds is open to question, as we shall see, but that it involves a system of agreed-upon meanings and the attempt to transfer messages would certainly seem valid. A more comprehensive description of language is that of Ellis (4), who described linguistic communication as a system of signs, signals and symbols about which people have common agreement. Again we note the prior agreement as to meaning and the idea of a system or code of units, but more properly we find that language consists not only of spoken words or symbols, but of signals and signs as well, often neither verbal nor uttered, as in the instances of gesture, facial expression and significant bodily posture or movement. Indeed, considerable divergence exists over which came first, oral or silent language, and the relative importance and function of each.

Dewey, the educator-philosopher, thought that "language, signs and significance, came into existence not by intent and mind but by overflow, by products [sic], in gestures and sound" (5). That language is an organic and virtually involuntary output of man is supported fully by Mill (6), writing on the "*spontaneous* growth of languages" [italics mine], and by Hastings, who wrote that "language is not simply words, but rather a structure of experiences and meanings which we learn and use. Thus we do not speak our language, we live our language. And if our language is faulty or inefficient, then to that extent so are our lives" (7). Furth pointed out that in the acquisition of language by the developing child, language is not only intellectually learned, but is sensorimotor (perceptual) and operational (actively internal) in its growth, and only later evolves to the stage where it uses the signs and symbols of one's culture (8).

Thus far, it can be seen that language, which is seemingly an overt code or system used to transfer messages to others, actually builds on the foundations of a silent language which is autonomic, sensory and perceptual in part. However, language must also make use of the thought processes and the cultural influences which shape both the thought and the personality of the language user. In his *Life and Growth of Language,* Whitney postulated that "there is obviously mental training and shaping, as well as mental equipment in the process of learning to speak. The mental action of the individual is schooled into certain habits, consonant with those of his community" (9). Pei observed that "the crux of the speaking operation lies in the link established in two minds between a thought-concept and a series of speech sounds that symbolize that concept" (10), which again stresses the intellectual nature of the use of language. A more realistic balance between the various influences on language acquisition is that offered by Furth, who holds that the child assimilates formative factors through sensory and experiential channels long before he begins to be capable of learning through verbal and linguistic avenues, but concedes that "linguistic competence is rooted in the beginnings of intellectual life as an acquired symbolic medium and frame of social expression" (11). The heavy weight placed by society on linguistic skill is attested to by Arnaud, who wrote: "A man may be as intelligent, clever, profound as you will; but be he not glib of speech . . . he may count on being little esteemed by the vulgar world throughout his whole life . . ." (12).

In a more positive vein, Johnson noted that "we are the talking tribes. The tongue is the most mobile structure of the human body, and to fetter its symbolic gestures is to dry up the deep springs of our humanness" (13). Supporting this view is Hayakawa (14), who believes that man, "the talking biped," can not only talk his way into difficulties, but also out of them, and that talk can also be a functioning means of leading mankind to new heights of achievement in poetry, philosophy and science.

In sum, it would appear that language is a means of transfer of thought and feeling from within the individual to one or more listeners, or on occasion, simply to the "outside" of the sender, that it involves a preaccepted system, and that it is intellectual, emotional, visceral and experiential in its acquisition. It makes use of signs, symbols and signals which may be audible or silent, verbal or visual, and conventional or original. Clearly, it was a mature and perceptive mind which produced the lines "language most showeth the man; speak, that I may know thee."

THOUGHT, WORDS AND MEANING

How, then, does man go about using language to gain the esteem of society, to talk himself either into trouble or out of trouble, or to achieve the lofty and concerted goals of mankind? From our analysis thus far it would seem that modern, articulate man experiences certain inner thoughts or feelings which he clarifies internally to a greater or lesser extent by rendering them into a code of signs and symbols which we call language. In order to carry on this activity, which may include a gathering together of facts, values and goals, together with thought processes such as analysis, evaluation, synthesis, selection and decision-making, he must assemble and mentally manipulate a host of symbolizations, each invested with a discrete quality called *meaning.* Customarily, these meaning units are in the form of audible or visible units called *words,* which may use an infinity of combinations to produce phrases and sentences to make up what may be considered an internal *message.* It follows logically, then, that one of the most crucial elements of the processes of developing and using language properly is the selection and use of words, in terms of their meaning. To this problem of meaning in language and the factors affecting meaning, scholars such as Malinowski, Sapir and Whorf have directed their attention, as have Welby, Whitehead and Russell. Their writings may be said to have stimulated and given impetus to the development of the fields of semantics, in which Korzybski, Hayakawa and Walpole are prominent, and cybernetics, which Norbert Wiener named and expounded upon and to which Aldous Huxley and Anatol Rapoport (15), among others, have made contributions.

As might be expected from the efforts of the researchers just enumerated, much analysis and investigation into the nature and influence of words, since they represent perhaps the largest subdivision of language, has been carried out. D. B. Fry (16), a British scholar, has pointed out that it takes three levels of synthesis to produce a word: first the phoneme, which is the smallest recognizable distinctive sound unit (such as *uh* or *ee*); then the morpheme, which is the smallest recognizable meaning unit (such as the prefixes *re-, post-* or *con-*); and finally a combination of morphemes which produce what we call a word. This series of combinations is not merely of interest to the student of phonetics, but to the practical linguist as well, for it poses the problem of additional variations of combination and error which may help to defeat the successful transfer of meaning from the internal being to the outer world. Preceding this problem of the correct combinations of morphemes to produce the appropriate words there comes the need to receive those experiences which become our reservoirs of attitudes, and words. Wendell Johnson describes us as "peering through the tiny, dusty windows of our senses, we see far less clearly than we imagine. Yet dim as our vision may be, our destiny depends heavily upon it . . ." (17). Hans Furth has also concluded from his study of language development in deaf children that nonverbal learning of a neurosensory nature is more influential than we tend to recognize. In addition, we know that many nonverbal signals are included in our code language. Some are autonomic, such as pallor or flushing, increased respiration rate or clamminess. Others are visual and voluntary, such as a smile, a frown, a gesture of welcome or acceptance. Nevertheless, it is in the study of words that many useful concepts and needs for improvement have been discovered, and it is this area which requires considerable examination.

The intimate, perhaps organic connection between words and behavior has been copiously noted. Young (18) deems the use of words one of the "essential biological features" of man, and Dewey (19) characterizes words as "a release and amplification of energies of the individual," while, to Chase (20), "words are what hold society together; without them we should not be human beings." Despite this agreement on the profound nature of the word, we seem obliged to accept the somewhat disheartening fact that words "just growed," for the most part, as the result of a rather incomplete and inconsistent potpourri of custom, etymology, accident and invention. Plato, for example, has one of his characters say: "I . . . cannot conceive myself that there is any principle of correctness in names other than convention and agreement; any name which you give, in my opinion, is the right one . . . and the newly-imposed name is as good as the old . . . all is convention and the habit of the users. Such is my view." (21). He is seconded by Thomas Hobbes, who believed that words turn our thoughts from mental discourse into verbal, and thereby enable us to record our thoughts or pass them along, while that of the four abuses of words, the first occurs ". . . when men register their thoughts wrong, by the inconstancy of the signification of their words, by which they register for their conceptions that which they never conceived; and so deceive themselves" (22). It is this arbitrary and subjective nature of words, both as they are created and as they are used, which helps to account for their misuse and the consequent misunderstandings to which they give rise. It is not surprising that Dag Hammarskjöld pleaded for "respect for the word, to employ it with scrupulous care . . . essential if there is to be any growth in a society or in a human race" (23).

Inherent in the appropriateness of the word, as we can see from the foregoing, is the clarity of its meaning. Profound concern with the importance of meaning and its presence or absence in efforts to think, to express, to share and to influence is precisely what produced volumes like Ogden and Richard's *The Meaning of Meaning*, Hayakawa's *Language, Meaning and Maturity* and Osgood's *Verbal Meaning and Verbal Behavior*, to name a few. Dissatisfaction with the current understanding of meaning initiated many studies in behavioral linguistics, etymology and comparative philology, and stimulated the appearance of certain relatively new sciences which treat the problems created by the need for accurate meaning-transfer. Indeed, Osgood writes: "As for myself, I am convinced that meaning is the most important variable in human learning — verbal or otherwise — that human adjustment is mainly a matter of acquiring and modifying the significances (meanings) of signs and learning how to behave in ways appropriate to these significances" (24), certainly a broad evaluation of meaning. Further analysis of what happens when meaning and significance attach themselves to problems and subject matter brought Dewey to the belief that "things in acquiring meaning thereby acquire representatives, surrogates, signs and implicates, which are infinitely more amenable to management, more permanent; and more accommodating, than events in their first estate. . . . Events turn into objects, things with a meaning" (25). Thus, we can postulate that thought depends upon words for expression, and that words depend upon their received meaning for accurate formulation and transfer. And it is in the attempt to comprehend the various links in this chain — each a vital part of the whole — that a new field has arisen. The student of social behavior and interaction, the teacher of effective language usage and the professional who helps those whose verbal interaction has resulted in confusion and unhappiness — all these have taken a keen and practical interest in this burgeoning area of inquiry and experimentation known as semantics.

SEMANTICS AND LANGUAGE

Semantics has been variously defined. One of the most lucid explanations of semantics is that of Hayakawa (26), who presented the term as covering three major aspects: (a) a study of meaning changes in words with the passage of time; (b) a study of signs and symbols and the conditions which make them meaningful; and (c) an inquiry into the interrelationships among thought, language and behavior, notably the influence of words on human action. Semanticists hold that (a) the name is not the object being named; (b) all general names refer to a general category but are frequently received as meaning a special, single member of that group; (c) "word magic," or uncritical acceptance of general symbols, and automatic response to them create unhygienic linguistic behavior (Korzybski's "signal reactions"); (d) words can be used to analyze and explain other words, which produces healthy modification and flexibility; and (e) such premises applied to language and meaning produce emotional balance, greater maturity, more realistic utility and lessen the likelihood of misunderstanding between individuals and groups. This summary, which is necessarily an oversimplification, nonetheless serves to pinpoint several valuable aspects of language as it is utilized within the individual and as a means of transferring meanings to others. First, it reiterates the essentially artificial and intransigent nature of the word, whether used as internal translator of thought or as external transmitter of message. Humpty Dumpty's famous dictum: "When I use a word, it means just what I choose it to mean — neither more nor less" is a regrettably apt description of much linguistic activity. We misuse words through ignorance, pride, indifference or lack of awareness of other meanings or shades of meaning involved. Does "politician" mean statesman or charlatan? Does "servant" mean job category or inferior person? Frequently, it means "just what I choose it to mean —

neither more nor less." But regardless of what we choose it to mean when we say it, by what meaning is it received? Again, by what the person addressed chooses it to mean — neither more nor less. This is why Norbert Wiener observed that "speech is a joint game between the listener and the forces of confusion" (27), and why Miller found that "words signify only what we have learned that they signify" (28). And what happens when different individuals have learned different "significs"? The answer is brief and melancholy: semantic confusion, misunderstanding and conflict.

Semanticists also believe that not only is difference of meaning a cause for verbal mix-up, but that our own social customs or our uncritical intellectual habits may add to semantic difficulties. Social gesture language — what Malinowski called "phatic communion" — in which the response is automatic, habitual, and inaccurate abounds in our society. The power of suggestion also distorts and deflects. Someone asks, "You'll go along with the rest of us, won't you?" And the reply is "Yes, of course," — after which you wonder why you allowed yourself to be "roped in"; and resentment, a sense of injustice and discord begin to appear. What Hayakawa called "psittacisms," a parrot-like repeating of what has been read or told, without using one's own critical thinking before its use, is still another cause of inaccuracy and conflict. Johnson's term, "The enchantment of words," and the labels "spellbinder," "demagogue" and "word-artist" all suggest how widespread is the havoc wrought by skillfull, ill-intended words and their uncritical acceptance. These and similar clichés give weight to Korzybski's view that symbolic malfunction and the consequent failure of communication are basic factors in the evolution of human conflict.

It would appear to be a staggering task to bring about common understanding regarding word meanings when we consider that there are well over 600,000 words in the English language, and that 70,000 words make up the average college-level vocabulary. However, various studies show that man tends to use actively only a small percentage of his populous world of words. Surprisingly enough, about 85 per cent of the words actually used by most college students in theme-writing are found in the list of the one thousand most commonly used words compiled by E. L. Thorndike (29). This indicates that the vast majority of words in current, workaday use are largely the same ones, used repeatedly in different contexts. These inferences may be drawn from this statistical finding: We do not use the greatest part of the potential word bank at our disposal; there is not really an impossibly large number of words which require common definition and use by our own people; and since we use the same words for so many different situations and subjects, one would suspect that we must be using the same words for many different meanings and interpretations — a most uncomfortable surmise. It is not hard to see why one student of language reached the cheerless conclusion that each of us is imprisoned on our own little island, obliged to shout inaccuracies at one another across veritable seas of misunderstanding, or why Plato, when discussing understanding, used the figure of humans destined to try to understand events only by regarding the shadows they threw on the wall of the cave in which they were chained. It is these barriers to liberating the thoughts within ourselves, and these obstacles to trying to convey these thoughts with accuracy, purpose and effectiveness to others, that bring us to the next area of our problem: communication and how it may be successfully practiced.

COMMUNICATION: NATURE, FUNCTION AND EFFECT

The thought has been variously presented in this study that the same word is frequently given many different meanings. The term "communication" is no exception. When one sends a message one is not communicating, but is going through actions which constitute only a part of communication. When one receives a message, he too is only playing a role which represents another segment of communication. It is of crucial importance to understand what communication is *not*, in order to appreciate fully and realistically what communication actually is. It is not *symbolization* or the use of signs and signals which serve to articulate or bring into cerebral existence a series of units, for this can only represent the mind and mood of the sender. It is not the use of *language* — silent or verbal — which serves rather as a system or code of symbols about which there is rather faulty common understanding as to meaning. It is not the process of *expression*, which may simply be a matter of output to ease tension rather than "revealing" to transmit a message.

Hoch and Zubin (30) come closer to the holistic nature of communication when they described it as "any action on the part of individuals which evokes response in others," although this concept leaves out several factors which characterize most communication situations. Oliver and Barbara suggest the cyclical nature of communication in the phrase "a dynamic, circular process" (31), while Chase (32) approaches the organic and involuntary nature of communication in the observation that it is a basic and almost as involuntary as man's circulatory system.

We can now clarify the basic elements of communication. It becomes evident that not only a message and its transmission are involved, nor can the addition of a receiver, who ingests a meaning via code of symbols, qualify the act as bona fide communication. There must also be present a reaction to the ingested message, which is perceived by the sender, a reception by the sender of evidence of the success or failure of the message by which he initiated the communication cycle, and subsequent modification of behavior by the sender and the receiver in reaction to the message and its reception. "We create reactions and consequences far beyond the mere release of words, for we involve others and release external forces" (33), often far-reaching effects. In essence, then, when we describe communication, we are describing a process between two or more individuals in which not only messages but reactions and counteractions of physical, emotional and social import all play an integral and ongoing part. A schematic representation of their conjoint action is:

1. An individual (sender) experiences
2. Thought or feeling (message), accompanied by a
3. Desire to externalize (motive), requiring a
4. Means to project (language), passing through a
5. Medium of transfer (speech, writing), which reaches a
6. Listener-observer (receiver), who then
7. Assimilates and internalizes (hears, understands), proceeds to
8. React externally (replies or takes action), which returns to
9. Original sender (receives feedback), who now
10. Adjusts behavior accordingly.

This sequence may be recycled indefinitely until one or both individuals decide to break off contact and communication.

KINDS OF COMMUNICATION

As might be expected of a complex process used by complex beings, communication tends to take many different forms. The most obvious form — and for that reason the most often misinterpreted — is that of *verbal communication*. We have earlier touched upon the highly arbitrary, ambiguous and emotionally or culturally influenced nature of words. It was pointed out that this made it difficult for an individual to be sure, even within himself, that he could find the words with which to think through a given proposition with accuracy. Now arises another problem: If we grant the dangers of inaccuracy which arise when using words within oneself, how much greater becomes the possibility of incorrect reception when one uses these same words to convey meaning to other individuals who are themselves affected by still another set of arbitrary, ambiguous and emotional or cultural influences. We are familiar with the difficulty of internal verbalization as expressed in phrases like "It's on the tip of my tongue but I just can't say it." We are also familiar with instances of the difficulty of external verbalization expressed in phrases like "Let me see if I can get you to see what I mean," or "Look, let me put it to you this way." In so doing, we admit that the process of verbal communication is fraught with misunderstanding, and so we preface the message with the hope that we will be able to use language which will have the same meanings and moods for the receiver that it has for the communicator. It is in this context that semanticist Wendell Johnson observed that "only those who are wise to the words are the wise to whom words are sufficient" (34), and it is to compensate for this weakness that man turns to supplementing the verbal code with other means of communication.

Among the other kinds of communication is the extensive use of silent, *nonverbal* language. In our previous consideration of language, two major classes of nonverbal symbols and signs were described. These included the use of autonomic and involuntary signs, such as pallor, flushing and changed respiratory rate, on one hand, and such semi-voluntary, more overt signals as gesture, facial expression and bodily movements, on the other. The use of silent language is virtually universal, since much of it is involuntary, and even the alleged "poker-faced" in our society reveal by the very act of suppression of overt signs that there is more to their message than the verbal symbols they are permitting themselves to expose. It is a truism that the manner of utterance frequently is given more weight than the verbal code itself. "Smile when you say that" is merely another way of saying that your words may convey less meaning than the silent language which accompanies them. What has been called the kinesics of expression, the "accessory meanings," to use Arnaud's term, are not only ever-present in the communicative process, but may also be the uncontrollable elements which alter the meaning, influence the reception and produce the exact opposite of the effect desired by the sender.

Another type of communication may be labeled *anticipatory* or *bypass communication*. We may receive a message in terms of what we anticipate will be the follow-up to our reply; in other words, we bypass the remark actually made and answer the response we think the speaker will make if we do answer him directly. By this procedure, the question, "When are you coming back?" when intended as a simple query for information, may receive the bypass response "When I'm good and ready, that's when!" because the respondent anticipated that a direct answer would have elicited criticism, whereupon he chose to seize the initiative by answering the criticism aggressively even before it appeared in verbal form. However, whether or not the original question was intended as a lead-in to an argument, both members of this conversation will be speaking to covert interpretations of intent rather than to overt expressions of thought, and an entirely different level of communication will be utilized in the process.

Allied to this anticipatory or interpretive communication is that which builds on the autonomic or visible speech, coupled with *vocal nuance* and intonation, and then proceeds to answer neither the verbal portion of the message nor the anticipated next remark, but the meaning present in the oral message as determined from its nonverbal signs. Irony, sarcasm and ridicule are prime example of such communication, and again the logical elements tend to be supplanted by reactions of an oppositional and frequently highly emotional nature. Manifestly, in a communication where two opposing meanings are present in the same message, uncertainty, misunderstanding and clash are very likely end products. Here is an actual communication segment recorded by the writer, illustrating such ambiguous interpretation and clash:

> "When's dinner?" (Meaning: When should I be at home.)
> "When's dinner? Not for at least another hour!" (Meaning: Why do you expect dinner whenever you feel like it?)
> "Well for Heaven's sake! All I did was ask a question." (Meaning: How unreasonable and irritable you are!)
> "Well, that's when dinner will be!" (Meaning: It serves you right. Next time be more considerate.)

That still another kind of communication exists is posed by Cameron (45), who holds that it is possible for signals to be produced and received without the conscious awareness of either the transmitter or his listener. Repeated playback and analysis of messages revealed a range of communication which was apparently shielded from both speaker and receiver, and which tended to elude the upper-level perceptions and concepts. Cameron considered this phenomenon to be an *ultraconceptual* or *unconscious communication* of which very little is known, a type which demands further investigation. That such an unperceived communication can have marked effect on both the individuals and their message is fairly obvious, but what is of greater impact on social behavior is that it may distort or restructure both the message as sent and the message as received, entirely without the knowledge of either party to the act.

We have thus far demonstrated that the internal formulation and the external transmission of a message may create many areas of doubt and confusion. Now let us examine the final steps of the original communicative cycle: listening (reception) and feedback (reaction). It is of great significance to consider the recipient's role and the problems involved therein, for effective communicating, as we shall see, must include effective receiving no less than effective sending.

LISTENING AND FEEDBACK

Superficially, the process of listening would seem to consist of an adequate auditory mechanism, the presence of a message to attend to and a knowledge of the code being used by the transmittal agency. In point of fact, this is a dangerous and misleading oversimplification. For one thing, we receive messages via visual perception, intuitive reaction, subconscious signals and nonverbal signs, as we have already discovered, quite apart from auditory recruitment of signals. For another, we hear and retain more successfully those matters to which we attend with a favorable emotional and mental set, and the converse is often disastrously true as well. In addition, we understand language and meaning units largely in terms of our own culture, concepts, semantic habits and personal frame of reference. And finally, we hear partly what we have ourselves influenced and even evoked from the sender, due to the way we listened and reacted to his earlier messages. It is no overstatement to say that listening is not merely the reception of a message, but is in part its adaptation and even its creator. Let us examine these concepts in some detail.

First, there is an *inner listening* which takes place in the sender of a message. "We ask ourselves . . . . We say unto ourselves . . . . And, listening in, we come, if we are watchful and reflective to know shade by shade, though never wholly, the persons we have been and are and are becoming" (35). It is wholly reasonable to conclude that such listening has a profound influence on the individual and helps to shape his thoughts, his desires, his actions and, ultimately, his message. Such listening helps to direct, to alter and even to create communication.

Listening is equally intimate within those who listen to an external transmission. Meerloo's view that listening is "an inner translation into one's own language" (36) again points up the highly subjective and individualized nature of the behavioral phenomenon we call listening. Oliver and Barbara (37) have indicated that mental growth and listening are both integral parts of the communication process, and that either one affects the other, with far-reaching consequences. Studies by Nichols, Lacklider and others (38) have affirmed these beliefs in the essentially dynamic nature of listening, and counter vigorously the traditional belief in the passive indrawn character of the process of reception. We can infer from the foregoing that, like sending, receiving is also a complex, animistic and variegated activity.

Various students of listening have identified many kinds of listening behavior. *Token* or *social listening*, in which only the overt and visible aspects of listening are utilized, is one of the more obvious forms. When we demand of the daydreamer, "Are you listening?" we know that he is present, awake and hearing, but we really mean, "Are you token listening?" and fear he is actually giving only the outer appearance, with none of the inner activities which must be functioning if comprehension and response are to be expected. We prefer that he favor us with *attentive or reflective listening,* for then we can see by overt signs on his part that our words and thoughts are receiving the compliment of close attention and inner evaluation of our message.

However, we may sometimes meet or even bring about *counter-stimulated listening,* to our sorrow. Here the counter-minded auditor does several things besides listening: He may be at once comparing the speaker's ideas and concepts to those he holds dear, calculating the extent of aggression against his own values and beliefs and mentally preparing a proper defense or counterattack of his own. In so doing, his listening threshold and comprehension tend to lower themselves, and he is less the thinker and more the soon-to-be opponent than harmonious communication can tolerate. Better for both our ego and our message is the practitioner of *creative listening*. He, by his attentive manner, his approving mien and his overt signals of interest, appreciation and respect, stimulates and encourages the communicator to greater heights of self-expression, fluency and enthusiasm. This type of reception presents what is known in drama circles as "a good house," and many a grateful performer can attest that he excelled himself in communicating his words and emotions because of the beneficial and encouraging "feedback" which reached him from his audience.

Just what is meant by the term "feedback"? Students of communication, of semantics and of cybernetics seem to be in general agreement that it consists of those signs or symbols which are evoked by a message and received by the sender thereof. Applause, catcalls, general restlessness in the auditor, frowns or smiles, as well as verbalized comments of approval or disagreement, are all examples of feedback. Too, as remarked upon earlier, the careful withholding of any sort of facial or verbal reaction may also be an eloquent species of feedback, somewhat in spirit of being "damned with faint praise." Norbert Wiener, in discussing cybernetics, the science which treats society's use of messages and communication facilities (including those between man and machine), describes feedback as "the control of a system by reinserting into the system the results of its performance . . ." which is a conventional enough description of the term. However, he then adds: ". . . if the information which proceeds backwards from the performance is able to change the method and pattern of the performance, we have a process which may be called learning" (39). If we add to this that the learning frequently takes the form of adapting or of reshaping words and behavior in conformance with this information which "proceeds backward," we have both the essential role and value of feedback in its practical, humanistic application. Feedback, then, is the last activating segment of the initial communication process, and often alters or initiates the beginning of still another communication cycle, as Berlo and others (40) have noted.

BARRIERS TO COMMUNICATION

Some of the barriers to communication are mechanical, some are psychological, others are intellectual or semantic, while still others are clearly cultural or experiential in basis. Frequently, there may be a combination of several barriers, and there may also be a dual-sided barrier in which both sender and receiver contribute to the problem.

Mechanical difficulties are often overlooked in our attempt to grapple with the semantic or social impediments to communication. It is regrettable but true that the physical circumstances alone may defeat message reception. External noise of a distracting or sound-masking character, distance between sender and receiver and inadequacies of volume, diction or hearing acuity may all account for inaccurate or incomplete message reception. Population size, too, creates difficulties, for tests have demonstrated that the larger the number of people involved, the less effectively a communication system tends to operate.

What has been called internal noise, in the form of anxiety, fancied threat to security, belligerence or other potential psychological insult, can create a most obdurate barrier. Emotionalism may color not only the message and the tone and the autonomic aspects of language, but also the reception, interpretation and resultant feedback of the recipient. Emotionally charged messages invite emotionally charged reactions, and may thereby prevent objective and accurate listening. Excessive involvement of personality and emotion can not only distort a message but give it an entirely different content as perceived. Speech which excites defensiveness or emotional barrier may be termed unethical in the Aristotelian sense, since the integrity and good intent of the speaker are seriously questioned by the listener in such communicative situations (41). On the other hand, a relatively unemotional message may be received by a highly emotional listener, who then proceeds to erect his own barriers to communication. Either way, the presence — real or fancied — of emotionalism which gives added and sometimes false dimension to the message creates a formidable obstacle to communication.

On the intellectual side, if the thinking process is defective the results are inimical to proper formulation and transfer. "Either-or" thinking, when the situation is one where far more than two possibilities exist, may create difficulty. Incomplete analysis, fallacious reasoning, vague and oversimplified synthesis, inaccurate data used in consideration of the subject; all represent faulty thought which results in faulty presentation and consequent confusion or avoidable misunderstanding.

Perhaps one of the most common intellectual barriers to effective transfer is that of disorganized thought and expression. The failure to arrange one's ideas in logical recognizable sequence, the error of presenting material with a decision first and reasons for so deciding after the listener has already reacted negatively to the premature conclusion, the confusion created by haphazardly arranged thoughts — all lead to ineffective and often highly unattractive communication. Consideration of the power of order in communication led Wiener to declare that "a measure of information is a measure of order" and to pose an adaptation of the second law of thermodynamics in the words: "A message can lose order spontaneously in the act of transmission, but cannot gain it" (42). Both statements attest to the need for organized thought followed by organized verbalization for effective transmission to occur.

Semantic barriers arise, with many variations, in the dynamics of communication. Some are due to obscurantism, to verbal excess or its opposite, cryptic and crabbed verbalization. Some are due to the identification of the concrete referent with the abstract term, or the word-is-not-the-thing duality. Allied to this is the erroneous consideration of inferences and implications on the same level as facts and valid evidence. The importance of speaking and listening on the same level of abstraction is underlined in this semantic confusion between word and thing, or between inference and fact.

Still another source of semantic difficulty is the use of the sweeping generalization — "catch-all statements" — and their linguistic mates, the stereotype and the word-label. Here the communicator may very loosely consign a specific subject to a general category, e.g., "It's just one of those things," or may equally improperly give a judgment in the form of a stereotype, "What can you expect from a Victorian stick-in-the-mud?" In both instances, analysis and calm, cogent examination have been supplanted by vagueness and the spurious notion that if you label it, you've solved or at least helped the matter under discussioin. This conclusion is not only illogical but may lead to the false impression that something valid and useful has been accomplished.

That cultural and experimental barriers to communication exist has been alluded to in our consideration of words and language. Not only the same words, but even the same phrases may convey different meanings to different individuals, each acting in the light of his own cultural upbringing. Also, not only the speaker's intellectual level, but his background and culture must be considered and adapted to by the effective communicator. What to one individual is a harmless, neutral term may be extremely vivid and offensive to another. "That dress makes you look older" may have been meant to convey that it conferred maturity and dignity, but it may be received as "It makes you look more lined and tired and drawn," as many a dismayed husband has discovered. Our newspapers tell us that international bitterness due to encroachments on democratic rights frequently boils down to a furious discussion of exactly how one defines the term and the concept "democratic rights." So it would seem that amid all these many potential barriers to clear and effective communication, one must be alert to the manifold possibilities of error, and sensitive to the nature and makeup of the intellectual, psychological and cultural apparatus of both sender and receiver. It behooves both the lay practitioner of communication and the specialist in communicative disorders to be able to recognize the specific nature of the semantic or linguistic difficulties in each situation, so they may then consider a solution to these difficulties.

COUNSELING ASPECTS OF COMMUNICATION

We have been considering, up to this point, some of the theoretical and broad aspects of thought, culture, language, transfer, reception, feedback and reaction. Using these considerations as a basis for perspective, we are now able to approach the question of how this material can be specifically applied to the field of marriage counseling. There are three major areas which involve both the counselor and communication problems. These are: (a) the counselor and his own communicative techniques; (b) the diagnostic clues afforded the counselor by the dynamics of communication; and (c) the use of communication itself as a therapeutic technique.

The medium whereby the counselor makes contact with the patient is generally that of verbal communication. The same medium is employed by the counselor to bring out details, to elicit responses and to convey comments and observations from the counselor to the interviewee. Under these circumstances, the counselor's own skill in verbal communication becomes an extremely important factor in his relationships with and his effect upon those with whom he must work. It is not within the scope of this paper to do more than merely point out which interviewing skills dealing with the selection of questions and comments, and their timing and sequence, are of crucial significance to the counselor.

In addition to the choice and timing of the subject matter, however, are many major considerations which this study has already indicated are inherent in all communication, no less so in those situations which the counselor seeks to create between himself and his client. The proper use of language level, the avoidance of confusing and inhibiting professional terminology, the use of phrases and referents which are appropriate to the client's educational and cultural background are all highly useful desiderata. Further, the counselor must refrain from using or allowing himself to be led astray by catch-all terms, disorganized sequences of expression, value statements unsupported by sound and sufficient reasoning, evidence discrepancies which may arise between verbal and nonverbal language when used simultaneously, and ambiguous or variously defined words and phrases.

Of equal importance is the counselor's skill in listening and feedback. Token or superficial listening, and anticipatory or counteraction listening, are to be avoided scrupulously, while reflective, attentive and creative listening habits must become consistent parts of the counselor's approach. Feedback which is encouraging, warm, stimulating and eventually creative is as much to be desired in the interviewer as it is to be looked for in his client. When the counselor does not use effective feedback himself, he weakens the rapport and the communicative harmony between himself and client, and so diminishes his own effectiveness.

The diagnostic clues which verbalization affords to the counselor are many, as Freud, Sullivan, Rogers and Lowenstein have all attested. Lowenstein writes: "Affects expressed in words are henceforth external as well as internal realities . . . the words denoting these realities are henceforth perceived by both patient and analyst. . . . We must conclude that in the formation of analytic insight, verbalization is an essential step" (43). Tonal patterns, pitch variation and other vocal attributes have also been studied by Moskowitz, Moses, Glauber and others (44), and the neurotic and psychotic tendencies suggested by these variables have received specific and revealing analysis. A study of these research findings will reward the counselor who seeks to add to his deductive powers. Not only vocal but verbal patterns as well have received considerable investigation. The consensus is clearly that various types of pressures producing psychoneurosis tend to make themselves evident in the rate, vocal factors, word groupings and conversation patterns of many troubled individuals who come to the counselor for help.

The semantic difficulties present in the interviewee may also furnish clues to certain areas of the patient's difficulty. If the counselor, forewarned by his knowledge of semantic barriers, can identify an inadequacy to handle and interpret ideas on the part of the patient, then one trouble-producing area manifestly has been exposed. Similarly, if the patient's language displays transfer weaknesses, in the form of entropy, progressive disorganization in the communicative process, anticipatory attitudes, or a tendency to use bypass responses, then the informed counselor may reasonably conclude that these improprieties must be corrected and treated as an important aspect of the patient's overall problem.

No less than errors or weaknesses in talking and expressing himself, the patient's level of competence in receptive performance must also be observed and evaluated. We have elsewhere described various kinds of injurious and ineffective listening; these must be held clearly in mind and their presence in the patient duly noted as factors in need of rehabilitation. Feedback is another fruitful source of diagnostic material for the counselor. When a client gives unmistakable evidence that he habitually sends out message reactions which are negative, preoccupied, hostile or anticipatory, it is reasonable to assume that he creates similar communication barriers between himself and his spouse. It would seem judicious to take steps to corroborate the presence of such injurious practices and to investigate their effects. For example, preoccupation or anticipatory feedback suggests the probability that the original message was incompletely or inaccurately received. Under such circumstances it is not difficult to surmise that misunderstanding, improper response and consequent discord are at least partly due to faulty reception and reaction. We may say that ineffective listening results in the relay of unfavorable influences to the speaker, resulting in disturbed relationships and gradual communication breakdown. This is not to say that communication error *per se* accounts for most of the problems and unhappiness that come before the marriage counselor, but it is definitely a contributing factor in many instances, and may be a primary and major factor in many others. It has been the author's experience, when called upon to mediate industrial disputes, that a procedure in which one aggrieved party was directed to state fully and without interruption the sequence of events which led to the dispute, and the other disputant then was allowed to restate the entire situation as he saw it, the points at issue were frequently narrowed down to simple errors of transmission and understanding by one or both parties, and the friction was speedily and simply resolved. In short, communicative error may not be the entire reason for clash, and yet may well be the hinge-pin around which the trouble revolves.

One rather elusive diagnostic technique should also be noted. Cameron has been elsewhere cited as suggesting that signals unconsciously sent and received may be present in some interpersonal communication. He has also stated that "it may also be that regularly made signals by individuals having certain unconscious needs and certain conscious deficits will serve to explain some of the otherwise hard-to-understand selections in friendship and marriage" (45). Interestingly, Freud seems to have suspected a phenomenon of somewhat the same nature when he advised listening to the patient's words while at the same time trying to understand a second kind of coded message also being conveyed by that person (46). The implication for the counselor would be to reexamine the thoughts expressed by his client during the interview, perhaps by tape-recorder analysis, with an eye to locating the substance of this second, subsurface message.

Finally, having given some examination to communication as both a series of skills to be practiced by the counselor, and as a source of diagnostic material to be evaluated by the counselor, let us examine the aspect of the therapeutic techniques which communication makes available to the counselor. It should first be recognized that the opportunity to "get it off his chest" gives the client a feeling of relief from the burden of keeping his thoughts and emotions "all cooped up." Thus, a very definite catharsis takes place when clients are encouraged to verbalize their experiences freely and fully. Fenichel (47) and Sullivan (48) have mentioned the therapeutic value of interpersonal communication among patient and professional.

There is also an inherent value in what has been called client-centered therapy. Here the client is enabled, through his communicative efforts with the interviewer, to formulate, articulate and clarify his problems. In so doing, the client may gain additional insights and maturity, since he feels that he has brought himself to these realizations by his own efforts. This "discussion therapy" approach has been used with considerable success in social-work areas such a mental hygiene, community health and emotional imbalance. The tendency has been noted for such activities to generate empathy and stimulate a certain amount of psychic recognition and understanding.

Furthermore, it is the contention of semanticists Alfred Korzybski, Norbert Wiener and Francesco Barone (49) that a better grasp of how to transfer thoughts accurately and with greater mutual satisfaction between sender and receiver, promotes understanding and harmony among individuals and society. It would seem worthwhile to provide such "semantic therapy," to use Barone's term, by encouraging the use of sound semantic practices, both among counselors and their clients. To do so would be in keeping with Ashley's (50) observation that the brain tends to learn by experience and then to produce adaptive behavior based on those remembered experiences. Unquestionably, individuals whose communicative errors could be made evident would then be in a position to adapt future communicative behavior in such a manner as to avoid misunderstanding and conflict.

Whorf, Newman and others (51) have pointed out that the tendency to conform to labels or verbal stereotypes exerts a very strong influence on many individuals. They tend to react to these word-images in a somewhat "self-fulfilling" way, and thus incline to make their patterns of thought and behavior consistent with this terminology. For example, the individual who gains a reputation as a "wit" may strive to justify the label, sometimes going for beyond the bounds of reason to live up to his sobriquet. The "strong and silent," or the "cool, calm and collected" may also perform self-consciously — and unnecessarily — to enhance and maintain their reputation. And it is in this readiness to respond to outside suggestion that the counselor may find himself in possession of a useful therapeutic technique. If the client has demonstrated his suggestibility to improper or harmful stimuli, it is clearly to the counselor's advantage to build, also by suggestion, a more socially acceptable image by using the same medium of verbal stimulation and transfer.

And so we come full circle to our original point of investigation into thought, language, behavior and communication: the intimate, complex interaction between the individual and his communicative needs and problems. It is by inner communication that we formulate reasoning, insights, attitudes, desires and, ultimately, behavior. It is by outer communication that we seek to liberate, transfer and influence, and in so doing, create either harmony or discord among others. To the extent that we understand the elements of the communicative situation and the possible sources of communicative breakdown, we may hope to improve and manipulate successfully these vital elements of interaction and concord in society. And as we learn well this skill and understanding, we are better able to avoid becoming hapless victims of the conflicts of our own creation.

REFERENCES

1. *Genesis, 11*:7.
2. LOCKE, JOHN: Of works. In: Hayden and Alworth, *Classics in Semantics.*
3. PEI, MARIO: *Invitation to Linguistics.* N.Y., Doubleday, 1965, p. 6.
4. ELLIS, M. J. K.: In *Signs, Signals & Symbols,* Ed. by S. E. Mason, Springfield, Thomas, 1963, p. 109.
5. DEWEY, JOHN: Nature, communication and meaning. In Hayden & Alworth, New York, Philosophical Library, 1965.
6. MILL, JOHN STUART, In *Of Definition,* Ibid.
7. HASTINGS, A. C.: In *Semantics and Communication,* by J. C. Condon, Jr., N.Y., Macmillan.
8. FURTH, HANS: *Thinking Without Language.* N.Y., Free Press, 1966.
9. WHITNEY, W. D.: The life and growth of language. In Hayden, Alworth, *op. cit.*
10. PEI, MARIO: *op. cit.,* p. 7.
11. FURTH, HANS: *op. cit.,* p. 209.
12. ARNAUD, ANTOINE: *The Art of Thinking.* N.Y., Bobbs-Merrill, 1964, p. 281.
13. JOHNSON, WENDELL: *Your Most Enchanted Listener.* N.Y., Harper, 1956, p. 20.
14. HAYAKAWA, S. E.: *Language, Meaning & Maturity.* N.Y., Harper, 1954.
15. See suggested readings.
16. FRY, D. B.: In Mason, Stella, *Signs, Signals & Symbols. op. cit.*
17. JOHNSON, WENDELL: *Verbal Man: The Enchantment of Words.* N.Y., Collier Books, 1965, p. 70.
18. YOUNG, J. Z.: *Doubt and Certainty in Science.* N.Y., Oxford, 1951.
19. DEWEY, JOHN: *op. cit.,* p. 272.
20. CHASE, STUART: *The Power of Words.* N.Y., Harcourt, 1954, p. IX.
21. PLATO: *Cratylus.* In Hayden & Alworth, *op. cit.,* p. 21.
22. HOBBES, THOMAS: *Of Speech, Ibid.,* p. 31.
23. HAMMARSKJÖLD, DAG: *Markings.* N.Y., Knopf, 1965, p. 112.
24. OSGOOD, CHARLES E.: In *Verbal Meaning & Verbal Behavior,* C. N. Cofer, [Ed.]. N.Y., McGraw, 1961, p. 21.
25. DEWEY, JOHN: *op. cit.,* p. 266.
26. HAYAKAWA, S. I.: *op. cit.,* p. 29ff.

27. WIENER, NORBERT: *The Human Use of Human Beings.* Boston, Houghton, 1950.
28. MILLER, GEORGE A.: *Language & Communication.* N.Y., McGraw, 1951.
29. THORNDIKE, E. L.: *The Teacher's Word Book.* N.Y., Columbia, 1921. See also Johnson, Wendell, *op cit.*
30. HOCH, P. H., and ZUBIN, J.: *The Psychopathology of Communication.* N.Y., Grune, 1958.
31. OLIVER, R. T., and BARBARA, D.: *The Healthy Mind in Communion and Communication.* Springfield, Thomas, p. 91.
32. CHASE, STUART: *op. cit.,* p. XI.
33. NILSEN, THOMAS R.: *The Ethics of Speech Communication.* N.Y., Bobbs Merrill, 1966.
34. JOHNSON, WENDELL: *op. cit.,* p. 15.
35. JOHNSON, WENDELL: *Ibid.* p. 29.
36. MEERLOO, JOOST A. M.: *Conversation & Communication — A Psychological Inquiry.* N.Y., Int. Univ., 1952.
37. OLIVER, R. T., and BARBARA, D.: *op. cit.*
38. DUKER, SAM: *Listening Bibliography.* N.Y., Scarecrow, 1964.
39. WIENER, NORBERT: *op. cit.,* p. 71.
40. BERLO, DAVID K.: *The Process of Communication.* N.Y., Holt, Rinehart, and Winston, 1960.
41. ARISTOTLE: *The Rhetoric.* [Ed.] Lane Cooper. N.Y.: Appleton, 1932.
42. WIENER, NORBERT: *op cit.,* p. 19.
43. LOWENSTEIN, R. M.: Some remarks on the role of speech in psychoanalytic technique. In: Barbara, D., *op cit.*
44. *Ibid,* Voice and personality, by C. F. Diehl.
45. CAMERON, D. E.: In Hoch and Zubin, *op cit.,* Ch. 2.
46. LOWENSTEIN, R. M.: *op. cit.,* Ch. 30.
47. FENICHEL, OTTO: *The Psychoanalytic Theory of Neurosis,* N.Y., Norton, 1953.
48. SULLIVAN, HARRY STACK: *The Interpersonal Theory of Psychiatry.* N.Y., Norton, 1953.
49. BARONE, FRANCESCO: *Semantic therapy.* In: Hayden and Alworth, *op. cit.,* pp. 355 ff.
50. ASHLEY, W. R.: *Design for a Brain,* N.Y., Wiley, 1952.
51. WHORF, B. L.: In: *Language, Culture, and Personality,* S. Sapir, A. I. Hallowell and S. S. Newman, [eds.].

Chapter 19

SOLO PRIVATE PRACTICE: THE ULTIMATE GOAL?

THOMAS C. McGINNIS

THE ATTRACTIONS OF PRIVATE PRACTICE

PRIVATE PRACTICE IS AN APPEALING IDEA. It holds as much attraction for marriage counselors, clinical psychologists and psychiatric social workers as it does for physicians and lawyers, and there are very good reasons for this. To many it appears as an ultimate goal. Yet, because the mental-health field is unique in a number of ways, private practice in this field has characteristics of its own that cannot be ignored by anyone aspiring to practice for himself.

It is natural and probably inevitable that a clinician in an agency or institution will find himself, at some time or other, chafing at the restrictions and frustrations with which he has to deal daily. Sometimes it is the case load that discourages him. He may be pressed to accept one urgent case after another. To make room for these cases, he may have to discontinue prematurely the counseling or treatment of other cases not in quite so much distress, but nevertheless not ready to be cast adrift. On the other hand, he may suffer frustration at times because people who need immediate help are being forced to wait their turns, possibly for months, while their problems become more and more difficult to overcome, and may in the end become insoluble. While entry into private practice may not necessarily eliminate painful conflicts of this kind, the private practitioner can at least make his own determination of the total case situation and come to his own conclusion regarding a course of action.

Clinicians who have had broad experience and have developed their knowledge and skill to a high degree often look for a way to make more effective use of their growing capabilities. As employees of an institution or agency, they may not find a sufficiently satisfying outlet. Also, in a culture like ours, in which personal initiative is generally highly rated and well rewarded, private practice would seem to have undeniable prestige value. This, no doubt, has as much appeal to a clinician as it has to anyone else.

Along with the prestige is the attraction of a possibly higher income. Here a warning is in order. A comfortable income is not as easy to achieve in the mental-health fields as in some other professions, and cannot be assumed to be an inevitable or assured result of moving into private practice. Also, there is another difficulty even more fundamental: The qualities required to succeed in the disciplines of marriage counseling, psychology and social work are, to a greater extent than most of us realize, incompatible with the acquisitive viewpoint of the person whose principal aim in life is to make money.

This is not to say that the successful practitioner in these fields cannot make a comfortable income. Often he can; but, when he does so, the increased income is likely to be a by-product of his professional excellence and general competence, not a goal in itself to which he has consciously given high priority in his scheme of living. This may seem like a rather fine distinction, but it is a significant one, nevertheless. This puts the practitioner in the mental-health fields in a somewhat different position than the ordinary businessman who is frankly out to make money, or even than a member of some other profession in which the qualities which lead to success can more easily be blended with acquisitiveness.

Still another type of warning related to money and private practice is the fact that any kind of profit motive may be viewed by many people, including professionals in the mental-health field, with suspicion and criticism. In some instances, one may even encounter open hostility and rejection. This can occur because the personal characteristics of selflessness and willingness to accept financial sacrifice are frequently interpreted by these people as most essential for achieving excellence in the helping professions. Yet, our society generally rewards the attainment of greater occupational skills with increased compensation. It might well follow, therefore, that the potential of higher income from private practice can be a healthy and constructive motivating force for the achievement of greater professional excellence in the mental-health disciplines. Unless the mental-health practitioner understands these circumstances, his initial entry into solo private practice may fall far short of his expectations.

The main point in this brief look at the profit motive is that all the issues must be identified, evaluated and effectively dealt with if one is to be clinically productive, emotionally comfortable and financially successful.

There are other important attractions of private practice besides the ones of self-satisfaction, prestige and income. Perhaps the strongest attraction of all is the broadened opportunity for service which private practice offers. It is easy to make the error of assuming that state or county institutions and family-service agencies, which offer a free or low-cost service, are making a more significant contribution to the community than do private practitioners who generally charge much higher fees. But is this necessarily true? There is a tendency for institutional and agency people to assume that it is; and, in questioning their assumption, I do not wish for a moment to minimize their contributions. On the contrary, their contributions are very great indeed. The point I wish to make is that the private practitioner has a valuable contribution to make also — a fact too often overlooked by those wedded to the free or low-cost service concept. For a great many people, the obligation to pay for a service increases the value of that service. If such people get the service cheaply, they tend to appreciate it less and benefit from it less.

There are a number of ways in which private practice, working in *co-operation* with the public services, can make a greater contribution than either could make alone. These we will now explore.

NEED FOR BOTH PUBLIC AND PRIVATE MENTAL HEALTH SERVICES

There is a great need in the mental-health professions for a greater understanding and cooperation between the publicly supported and the privately operated services and between any established agency and the solo practitioner. Each has a contribution to make. Without the publicly supported services, great numbers of people who cannot afford counseling and psychotherapy would go without help. But, without the contributions of private practice in its various forms, people who could afford to pay the costs of treatment would be competing for time with those of smaller incomes, causing everybody to wait longer. Moreover, the service offered by the private practitioner can aim at much more than the immediate solution of an acute problem. The private practitioner can take the time required to delve deeply — to go to the roots of a person's problem; and those roots are often found to lie in unconscious processes. Such deep psychotherapy requires more time than most publicly supported agencies are able to give any individual case. This is where the private practitioner, either in group practice (where he and one or more colleagues practice together in a privately organized endeavor) or in solo practice, can render an immensely valuable service which the publicly supported agency or institution is less well adapted to offer.

The more thorough and intensive treatment which the private practitioner can offer is of the utmost importance to the development and maturation of the mental-health professions. The future of these professions does not depend so much on their ability to help as many people as possible with specific problems as it does on the growth of basic knowledge and new techniques in uncovering and altering the personality patterns and unconscious processes that produce such problems in the first place. The private practitioner is in a particularly good position to contribute to this basic knowledge and to help evolve the improved techniques. He has no institutional inertia to contend with. Fixed policies do not hamper his experiments and innovations. He has much more freedom to try new therapeutic approaches. Out of this must come the new growth of ideas and maturing of concepts which our professions so badly need.

GRADUAL MOVEMENT FROM PUBLIC TO PRIVATE PRACTICE

The clinician, then, who sees himself as eventually broadening his goals and the scope of his work can find valid reasons, quite aside from selfish ones, for effecting a gradual redistribution of his time. Although he will probably continue to spend a good part of his time in institutional or agency work, he will also want to devote some time to the development of part-time private practice.

The logical first step in this move, if he can manage it, is to associate himself with colleagues in the same or related professions to establish a group practice, or to join a group already established. By dividing his time between the public and the private agency, he is able to benefit from and contribute to both associations. He gains the greater freedom which the private practice affords, yet retains a close connection with the community through the public agency. He needs both; and the public agency, if it recognizes the need for a parallel growth of both kinds of practice, would itself benefit, in the long run, by encouraging him to do this rather than by standing in his way.

As his capacity and experience grows, he may eventually be ready to open his own office for part-time solo practice. An attempt to move, all at once, from public or private group practice into *full-time* solo practice is ill advised for a number of reasons. In the first place, a nonmedical practitioner moving suddenly into full-time solo practice is unlikely to receive enough referrals on a continuing basis to maintain himself. It takes time to develop a private practice.

Secondly, to carry total clinical responsibility for every case in full-time practice can be an exceedingly heavy burden which needs to be undertaken gradually. In a state hospital, mental clinic or family service agency, the clinician is primarily responsible to the organization's board of directors, and often shares work on a case with colleagues. A psychologist, a psychiatrist and a social worker may work together as a team. The same may be true in proprietary group practice, except that there is no board or administrative body to which the practitioner is responsible; the several practitioners share responsibility for the entire operation. In solo practice, on the other hand, the practitioner carries total responsibility himself. Even though he may contract with practitioners in allied professions for supervision or consultation, the responsibility is finally his. This is the "burden" he carries; and, unless he has worked into it gradually, it can deflect the practitioner from successful pursuit of his objective.

LIMITATIONS IN THE DEVELOPMENT OF A PRIVATE PRACTICE

The mental-health disciplines are rather new as professions go and are certainly not as well understood or accepted by the public as, for example, the medical, dental or legal professions. All sorts of misconceptions exist. Few people understand the true functions of a marriage counselor or social worker. Even fewer understand what a psychologist or psychotherapist does or would know the difference between either of these and a psychiatrist. This confusion has a direct relevance to the opportunities for private practice. Though needs for therapy and counseling may be widespread and acute, people are less likely to go to a practitioner if they are unclear as to his function.

Part of the difficulty arises from the nature of mental and emotional problems themselves. A man with a toothache or one who is threatened by a lawsuit knows, or can easily find out, where to go for help. But a man with an emotional problem is in a quandary. He may not even know he has such a problem. All he may know is that he is unhappy, or that his marriage is falling apart, or that he cannot seem to keep a job. He does not know why. He is apt to place the blame on someone else. And it may never occur to him that the mental-health professions exist to serve him.

There is a quality of nebulousness or mystery about the mental-health disciplines that contribute to misunderstanding. For some of this, the disciplines themselves are responsible. We have not yet conceptualized our objectives and approaches with enough precision to present a clear, unclouded picture to the public. To make it even more confusing, various disciplines overlap. Thus, some or all of the functions of a marriage counselor may also be performed by a social worker, a psychologist or a psychiatrist. It is not at all surprising that the public is confused; and, as long as this confusion persists, it is quite possible for a fully competent private practitioner to languish in an empty office.

Another difficult problem faced by the competent practitioner is the loss of public confidence in his profession caused by inexperience of his less competent colleagues who may have entered private practice prematurely. This is an exasperating situation with which the mental-health professions, sooner or later, will have to deal. Tighter standards of training and performance must be proposed, agreed to and enforced if broad public acceptance is to be earned. Laws licensing all mental-health practitioners must require high professional competence. These are still evolving, and much work remains to be done.

PERSONAL REQUIREMENTS OF PRIVATE PRACTICE

Perhaps no profession requires as much training and experience for successful solo private practice as does that of mental health. Clinicians whose training and experience have been limited to a single discipline and who have not had a personal analysis and achieved a healthy emotional adjustment themselves are probably not yet ready for the step.

It is my opinion that none of the individual disciplines — neither marriage counseling nor psychology nor social work — by *itself* provides a broad-enough training for solo practice. For example, the clinical psychologist may have acquired considerable skill in the diagnosis of intrapsychic processes and the conducting of individual psychotherapy, but may have had only limited experience in dealing with the problems of a strained marriage or disturbed relationships among family members. The marriage counselor may be skillful at helping married partners solve their problems of relationship, but may have inadequate knowledge of the diagnosis and treatment of personality disorders which are rooted in unconscious phenomena. The social worker may be skilled in interviewing, in bringing out pertinent information in such types of therapy as family-oriented therapy and family-unit therapy; but he, like the marriage counselor, may lack the training and experience required to treat effectively unconscious processes.

The solo practitioner will find it difficult to function successfully within the limitations of traditional preparation in any one of these specialities. His primary experience may have been in any of them, but, unless he has acquired further clinical experience in each of the others, he will find himself inadequately prepared to assume the wide responsibilities that will almost certainly be thrust upon him.

Fortunately, the trend in modern clinical practice is toward just such a broadening of experience. The distinctions between the disciplines are less sharp than they once were. Less than a decade ago, rather rigid professional roles were implicitly, if not explicitly, followed. For instance, it was a routine expectation in child-guidance clinics for the psychologist to test the child, for the social worker to see the parents for a social history and for the psychiatrist to make a clinical diagnosis of the child. In the course of therapy the psychiatrist would treat the child — who was clearly seen as the primary patient — and the social worker would, under the direction of the psychiatrist, consult and advise the parents. This approach, frequently identified as the "psychiatric team approach," was in vogue for many years, but is no longer considered to be the only approach to the effective treatment of a disturbed child. In fact, the child's total family group may now be viewed as the "primary patient." The conceptualization and development of family-oriented and family-unit therapy and the refinement and expansion of marriage-counseling techniques, coupled with the increased competence of psychotherapists, have greatly changed our clinical course. It has changed so much, in fact, that in many clinics virtually any staff member may be expected to work with almost any type of case and in almost any approach — individual, group or family therapy, marriage or family counseling, or child guidance.

In order to do full justice to these new opportunities for experience, clinicians are increasingly stimulated to achieve additional preparation which focuses on psychoanalytic theory and practice. With adequate psycho-analytic orientation and training, a practitioner is furnished with new knowledge to understand and evaluate better the psychodynamics of individual development, marital and family interaction. He develops new skills in dealing with both conscious and unconscious processes. He learns to make constructive use of his own personality in the therapy of a variety of characterological styles and neurotic patterns. Even if he begins with limited counseling in environmental or symptomatic situations, his awareness of long-term growth potentials can be shared in ways to interest his counselees in a more thorough involvement in psychotherapy.

Perhaps the most important single factor in signaling a readiness for solo practice is personal maturity and healthy emotional adjustment. If these are not present, the clinician may be unobservant of certain dynamics; he will often unconsciously become defensive or, perhaps, punitive in his attitude; he will be unaware of his disguised "therapeutic" inputs which serve to meet his own needs; he will invariably be trapped in the neurotic processes of the patient; he may undermine a marriage relationship; he may reject or be hostile to the patient or other family members; he will, without awareness, become jammed by countertransference binds; he will inadvertently impose his own value systems or be excessively shy in exposing himself; and so on.

While maturity and healthy emotional adjustment require a combination of many constructive experiences and relationships in life, a successful personal analysis often ranks as the most rewarding of all. Aside from the purely personal gains received by a clinician, he also gains a direct, first-hand involvement in what his patients will experience in a therapeutic process. He becomes well acquainted with psychological defenses, with resistances to therapeutic intervention and with transference responses. He knows the strain and pain when one tries to change old behavioral patterns, ways of feeling and cherished but distorted value systems. He has a personal "feel" for the overall therapeutic experience, its stages and interrelationships. He has a "sense" which helps to anticipate therapeutic regressions and the skill to use these regressions for growth when they do occur. Most important is the fact that he has confidence in the ability of persons to grow emotionally and can enjoy his role in accomplishing this task.

SPECIAL CIRCUMSTANCES OF PRIVATE PRACTICE

Anyone who enters private practice discovers soon enough that many of the new problems he meets are one for which his training has not prepared him. He has problems in obtaining referrals in a field where treatment often takes a long time; he has some of the problems of the businessman, including variable income and uncertain hours; he is in some danger of isolating himself from his colleagues. These problems will now be considered.

The mental-health disciplines have one characteristic that has no counterpart in any of the other professions: that is the quality and intensity of the personal relationship required over a long period of time to carry out fully and successfully the service offered. The medical and dental professions do not require as intensive a personal relationship, nor do they have a significant number of patients whose conditions require repeated visits over a long period of time. A majority of medical and dental treatments can be completed in a small number of visits. This, alas, is not true in the mental-health disciplines. This fact alone discourages many people from undertaking counseling or psychotherapy. It, in turn, makes the solo practitioner uncomfortably dependent on a small number of long-term paying clients. Thus, a few dissatisfied clients could injure him much more severely than a few dissatisfied patients could hurt a physician.

With such dependence on a small number of clients or patients, the practitioner in the mental-health field may have difficulty in keeping his case load large enough to provide a satisfactory income. If his case load is too small, he may be tempted into unwise actions, such as persuading people to remain in treatment longer than necessary, cutting his fees to discourage discontinuance of treatment or unwittingly fostering dependency on him instead of helping a person to become his own therapist. Errors such as these will undermine private practice in the long run.

One of the principal difficulties faced by every private practitioner, regardless of his profession, is that he must function as both a professional man and a businessman. He is, of course, in business for himself — a situation that requires certain talents and abilities associated with business competence. Obviously, he has to maintain a comfortable, convenient and attractive office, keep orderly accounts and case records, make and keep his appointments, pay his taxes and bills, collect his fees and see to it that his income is adequate.

Unfortunately, business ability and professional ability do not always go together. Lack of elementary business judgment can interfere with the most capable practitioner's ability to do an effective job. However, the most difficult problems of all may have nothing to do with his business judgment, but with his self-concept. How he sees himself and how he feels about himself as a person and as a professional become crucial issues when he takes full responsibility for determining the fee charged, how and when it will be collected, what cancellation policies will be followed and how incurred debts will be managed. If he formerly worked in a service or institution where fees were handled by an administrative person, he may never have shared with a client or patient the feeling that "This is my money for the service you have given." This direct and highly personal exchange of money for services is a continuous reminder to both of them to evaluate the value of the service and, more specifically, the worth of the therapist. This process, be it conscious or unconscious, goes on all the time and may increase the quality of involvement of both because their commitments of giving to and receiving from each other are clear. There is no organizational structure to blur or screen out the primary importance of this one-to-one affair. It is within this personal-clinical framework that the solo practitioner can emerge as a professional in his own right.

Whoever enters private practice quickly discovers that the income from fees is not comparable to fixed salary. Fees, unfortunately, stop when the practitioner is sick or on vacation or for any reason is not on the job. His expenses, on the other hand, do not stop; his office rent, his telephone bill, the salary of his office assistant have to be paid whether he is on the job or not. And, finally, when he retires, the only pension he will receive (outside of Social Security) is the one he may have had the foresight to plan and fund himself.

A man accustomed to regular hours may find it a shock to be plunged into the long, uncertain hours of private practice of either the group or solo type. To one who has never experienced it, private practice may look like a situation where he can set his own hours; but the facts are otherwise. Many persons seen in private practice have to fit sessions around their own working hours; and, as most of them work in the daytime, the clinician may find himself forced to see many people in the evening. There just may not be enough hours to do what has to be done. He is tempted to skip meals or eat them on the run, neglect his family, pass up vacations and, perhaps, even endanger his health.

The pressures under which the private practitioner works may tempt him to avoid professional meetings, advanced training courses and seminars which he needs in order to keep up with his profession. If he succumbs to these temptations, he may gradually isolate himself from his professional colleagues. He may temporarily earn more dollars by staying on the job; but his failure to stay in touch with his profession and colleagues can be exceedingly costly. It is most important for him to keep in close association, not only with his professional associates, but with nearby clinics, agencies, hospitals, school systems, medical doctors, etc. All this takes effort, time and sacrifice.

BLENDING OF THE SEVERAL MENTAL-HEALTH DISCIPLINES INTO A SINGLE PROFESSION

It is increasingly evident that private practice of either the group or solo type cannot be expected to evolve very far on the basis of competing disciplines, each imbued with a narrow, unrealistic conception of its function. A single broader and more inclusive profession must emerge. Nor can the development of private practice reach its optimum without better understanding and cooperation between community agencies, private services and private practitioners. There must be more stress on the common elements and interdependence of the different disciplines and agencies. The disciplines of marriage counseling, psychiatric social work and clinical psychology are not as different and distinct as some of their practitioners believe. A few of the common elements of all three are:

Establishing a therapeutic relationship with the client or patient;
Diagnosing individual psychopathology, marital conflict and family disturbances;
Formulating tentative treatment procedures and goals;
Identifying and dealing with emotional resistances, feelings, personal values, transference and countertransference phenomena; and,
Treating both intrapersonal and interpersonal processes.

I believe that effective counseling and psychotherapy must include essentially the same processes whether it is performed by one profession or another. Where the several disciplines differ from each other is principally in the emphasis they place, respectively, on individual, marital or family functioning, and in the intensity with which they pursue intrapersonal or interpersonal functioning. Thus, one clinician may treat a person, marriage or family for the alleviation of certain specific symptoms, whereas another clinician may treat the same situations by paying little attention to the symptoms, but focusing instead on the psychological forces which are blocking emotional growth. In both approaches, the clinician must be aware of the complex therapeutic processes, whether he treats them directly or not. The maturation of our profession cannot really go forward until all the disciplines are prepared to learn from each other and accept one another's contributions.

This mutual sharing and cooperation will not be easy to bring about. Any broadening or merging of functions will look like a threat to those individuals and institutions which have built their status and programs on keeping the disciplines separate. The psychiatrist has not always welcomed the practice of psychotherapy by nonmedical practitioners. The clinical psychologist may not welcome having the social worker and marriage counselor make use of his diagnostic and therapeutic techniques. The social worker may be contemptuous of psychiatrists who claim exclusive credit for the "discovery" of family therapy. Nor may the marriage counselor want psychologists to establish a subspecialty in marriage counseling. Inertia and old ways of thinking tend to keep each group in its own niche. But this must change, and is, in fact, beginning to change.

The reason it is changing is that the distinctions that have separated the disciplines are artificial and not realistically based on the nature of people's problems and therapeutic needs. The interpersonal conflicts of a collapsing marriage cannot be separated from the neurotic patterns of the spouses that are bringing it about. Situational difficulties are exacerbated by unconscious processes, and vice versa. It is not a single isolated difficulty that usually needs to be treated; it is a whole person or a group of persons (in a marriage dyad or family unit) with a complex of problems. Whatever his discipline happens to be, the competent practitioner is ultimately dealing directly or indirectly with persons with *all* their problems, conscious and unconscious, individual and marriage, family and community. This fact is more impressive than, and will eventually overshadow, all differences between disciplines and between different schools of psychoanalytic theory and practice.

The therapeutic needs of people virtually beg for a reappraisal of the respective roles of public and private agencies for mental health. There is a great need for the building of mutual respect among community and private practitioners, free from undermining professional jealousies and ideological conflicts. Together, they must establish cooperative referral arrangements that work both ways. It is most unfortunate that able private clinicians sometimes struggle with small practices because community services are reluctant to make referrals to them. Yet, by holding back from cooperation with the private practitioner, community personnel are retarding the maturation of their own profession. The result can only be to deny mental-health services, not only to people capable of paying a reasonable fee, but also, because of burdensome waiting lists, to many persons unable to pay a private fee. On the other hand, some private practitioners may accept or continue to see patients in extended treatment because they incorrectly assume that long waiting lists or inferior practice at community clinics make referrals to the latter undesirable.

A time is fast approaching when members of the several disciplines, both public and private, will have to get together, reappraise their roles, standardize their qualifications for private practice and cooperate in bringing about legislation for their mutual protection and the protection of the public. As their problems are objectively examined, I believe it will become increasingly clear that the need is not for separate competing disciplines, but for a single mental health profession which might simply be called "psychotherapy." It could include all the functions now performed by marriage counselors, clinical psychologists, psychiatric social workers and psychotherapists. Its practitioners could be qualified to engage in all forms of psychotherapy: individual, joint and group, including family-oriented therapy, family-unit therapy and marriage therapy. They could be required to have psychoanalytical training, a personal analysis and clinical experience in all these forms of therapy. The academic training for this single discipline could begin at the graduate level and proceed to a doctorate in psychotherapy.

There is likely to be, in the next few years, an expansion of proprietary group private practice as well as solo private practice in the mental-health field. A private mental-health center can offer an ideal intermediate step for the practitioner who would move from a public agency or clinic ultimately to solo practice. It can fill a need in the community for a service for those people whose incomes are too high for public clinics, but not high enough to cover the fees charged by solo private practitioners. The growth of group private practice should enable the community agencies to do a better job by relieving them of part of their heavy case loads. Individual private practitioners could affiliate with the group and thus divide their time between solo practice and group practice, enjoying some of the advantages of each.

It seems very probable that group private practice and solo private practice will develop concurrently and that the two will depend, to a considerable extent, on each other. Most solo practitioners, I believe, do not want to be completely severed from group practice and are better off with some form of group affiliation, at least on a part-time basis. In the group setting, they receive the stimulus of collaboration with colleagues. The group practice relieves them of total financial dependence on the clients they personally attract. Through the group practice, they may be able to work with a wider variety of cases and so broaden their experience. They can participate in a broader clinical program, which may include group therapy, family therapy, etc. There may be opportunities to participate in research programs or to gain experience in supervision and administration.

CONCLUSION

Private practice in the mental-health disciplines is growing and will continue to grow. It has obstacles to overcome, but many of these obstacles are similar to those which were faced by other professions in their early development. Better training is necessary for those who would take this pioneer path. A tightening of standards is essential and probably inevitable. New forms of practice will almost certainly evolve. Proprietary group practice will develop along with solo private practice, drawing on the strength of the solo practitioners and contributing values to them in turn. Community services, far from fearing this as a competitive development, should welcome it because it will strengthen the entire mental-health movement and help the community agencies to solve some of their most difficult and persistent problems, among which is lack of public confidence and support.

Finally, as marriage counselors, psychiatric social workers and clinical psychologists become more aware of the need of each for the contributions of the others, a single profession — call it "psychotherapy" — will evolve, blending the essentials of them all. This kind of psychotherapist will be qualified to treat the whole person and the whole array of his problems (exclusive of medical ones) at whatever therapeutic level is appropriate.

Chapter 20

THE IDEALS OF JEWISH MARRIAGE:
PERSPECTIVES OF THE MAN-WOMAN RELATIONSHIP

JESHAIA SCHNITZER

THE RECORD HAS SHOWN THAT Jewish marriage and family life in the past, and even in present-day society, has had a fine record for stability and for creating domestic happiness. From the earliest of days, the teachers and sages of Judaism, through thought and example, endeavored to elevate the status of marriage, to emphasize its sacredness and to provide ways and means for beautiful and creative relationships between a man and his wife.

According to rabbinic authorities, the first positive commandment of the Torah (the Pentateuch) is related to marriage. For the biblical verses and commandments of the Book of Genesis direct man toward the wholesome pattern of marriage and family life.

> And God created man in His own image, in the image of God created He him, male and female created He them. And God blessed them, and God said unto them: Be fruitful and multiply and replenish the earth (Genesis 1:27).

The early story of Genesis goes further in underwriting the value and worthiness as well as the need of the primary relationship between a man and a woman in marriage as expressed in the second chapter of Genesis: It is not good for man to be alone, I will make a fitting helper for him (Genesis 2:18).

The teachers of the Bible always found support for their basic beliefs and concepts from the very words of the Bible. One rabbinic explanation based on a text proves that man without a wife is not really a whole man. It is written in the Bible: ". . . male and female created He them and blessed them and called their name Adam (man)."

The two of them were called "man," not just the one partner.

From the very beginnings of the life of the Jewish people, marriage was exalted. The union of a husband and a wife was not a compromise with Satan and evil, but the highest of Jewish ideals. In Judaism, marriage is the completion of God's creation which He called Adam, man. In a very real psychological and spiritual sense the collective enterprise of husband and wife can be the climax of God's creative spirit in human life. Marriage for the Jew is not only considered as the norm for the average individual; but the philosopher of Jewish values goes even further and evaluates marriage as a divine state. Marriage stands for the highest ideal in Jewish life and the Hebrew term for marriage, *Kiddushin,* means "making holy" or "sanctifying."

The concept of *Kiddushin,* or the sanctification of marriage, reveals the place and the height to which marriage is raised in the value system of Jewish life, as well as the true meaning of a husband-wife relationship in marriage. The root of this term, *Kiddushin,* comes from the word *Kodosh* meaning "to be separated" or "to set aside." This is what a real marriage demands in its relationship to two people. The man, in making a legal and spiritual contract with a woman, must set himself apart for her. In turn the woman, too, must assume a new relationship and must separate herself from others for her husband. The Pentateuch is explicit about this relationship: Therefore shall a man leave his father and his mother, and he shall cleave unto his wife, and they shall be one flesh (Genesis 2:24).

The Genesis story of the creation of man and woman provides another basic principle in the human relations between husband and wife. Judaism upholds that every human being is made in the image of God. When a man and a woman approach each other with sincere respect for this ideal, then an important ingredient has been added to the relationship. When one looks upon a mate and can say with reverence, "This woman or this man whom I have chosen for myself is created in God's image," a basis has been set not only for respect and reverence, but also for love. Judaism recognizes the power and the influence of love in this highest form of human relationships. Innumerable expressions in Jewish law testify to the place that love most hold in marriage, and in the family. It is man's obligation not only "to love his wife," but "to honor his mate." He must not only "consider a good wife far more precious than rubies," but he must "consider himself blessed for acquiring a virtuous woman."

Rabbi Akiba, one of the greatest of Jewish sages, said of his wife: "I owe everything that I am to her" and that "if the whole Bible is holy, the Song of Songs, dealing with love between man and his wife, is the holiest of the holy."

In an article on "Married Love in Jewish Law," Dr. Leo Jung writes:

> He, Rabbi Akiba, once made a statement which on the surface is rather startling. On the last page of the Talmudic tractate "Gittin" there is a discussion of what constitutes grounds for divorce. One Rabbi said "morality" and another, "malice," but Rabbi Akiba held that if a man found another woman more beautiful than his own wife, he could divorce her. The profundity of this statement may not be immediately apparent. Unless a Jewish husband felt from the day of the wedding and beyond the Diamond anniversary that his wife remained the most beautiful woman on earth, he should grant her a divorce, for he no longer deserves

her. Curiously enough, this is echoed by Robert Ingersoll: "The essence of our attitude toward woman is that, when we have married her she must remain the most beautiful creature from now and forever."

The capacity to love makes for creative marriages. Love developed in the human relationships in marriage and family living, determines to a great extent the character and personalities of children, and in turn prepares them for their future marriages. Dr. William Menninger, psychiatrist and author of *The Human Mind* writes:

> Learning the capacity to love is perhaps one of the most difficult, and I suspect, the most important lesson the child has to learn. My own conviction is that the child does not automatically know how to love. He can only love if he is loved. . . . unless we teach our children how to love, and we in turn know how to love we never become a contributing social being.

Love is a force of many dimensions and there is always difficulty in defining the term; how much more difficult to relate it to Jewish values. Here again the Bible serves as a source to reveal two concepts of love as known to the Jewish people. One concept can be termed as modern romantic love, and the other as the aristocratic-Old-World type of love. The aristocratic approach to love is found in the biblical story of Isaac and Rebecca. It is based on the method of Eliezer, the matchmaker, who seeks out a suitable companion for his master, Isaac. After the selection of Rebecca we read the interesting sequence of events: And Isaac brought her into his mother Sarah's tent, and took Rebecca, she became his wife, and he loved her. And Isaac was comforted for his mother (Genesis 24:67).

In the aristocratic, marriage-maker approach, love comes after marriage.

The second version is that of the lovesick shepherd maiden, yearning for her lover as described in the chapters of the Song of Songs. This is love fever which comes before marriage and is the basis for the romantic concept of love in the Western world.

The romantic concept of love has been exploited by fiction and motion pictures with the theme that "they lived happily ever after." Romantic love has greatly influenced the generations of the second half of the twentieth century, causing much unhappiness and disillusionment in modern marriages. Sound marriages should have both of the elements found in the Jewish ideals of love, combining the best of the aristocratic, matchmaker marriage, and the best in the romantic-love-involved marriage.

Professor F. Alexander Magoun in his book, *Courtship, Love and Marraige,* gives this definition of love:

> Love is the passionate desire on the part of two or more people to produce together the conditions under which each can spontaneously

express his real self; to produce together an intellectual soil and an emotional climate in which each can flourish, far superior to what either could achieve alone. It is an intimate relatedness based on the mutual approval and affirmation of the character and integrity of the personalities involved. It is not a situation where two partners think more of each other than they do of themselves. It is a situation where two partners think more of the partnership than they do of themselves. It is an interweaving of interests and a facing of sacrifices together for the sake of both. It is the feeling of security and contentment that comes with the adequate satisfaction of each person's emotional needs through their mutual efforts. It is man's superlative method of self-realization and survival.

Such a definition of love as given by Professor Magoun can serve as an important perspective in the sound development in the man-woman relationship in marriage. Yet, it can be stated unequivocally that mature love comes only after marriage. A mature love resulting from a meaningful partnership finds its highest culmination in lovemaking and in the sexual act. Such a relationship is a sacred and significant part of married life. Here, as in most patterns of Jewish living, there is a sound and down-to-earth approach. Sex is not something to be condemned and feared; but the sexual relations between a man and his wife are the natural sequence in their relationship. This is seen clearly in the attitude of Jewish law and the acceptance of sex as a normal phenomenon in the life of the Jew. Sexual relations are the right of the husband and of his wife, and an essential aspect of marriage. All that Judaism demands is that these expressions be placed under moral restraints and laws, embraced in the concepts of 'Kiddushin' (sanctification). The traditions and laws of Judaism demanded that the sex life be circumscribed with the disciplines of the laws pertaining to the purity of family life and the regulations of sexual relations between a man and his wife. In the Orthodox tradition of law this is referred to as *Taharath Mishpachah* (purity of family life).

Up to this point we have examined the perspectives of the husband-wife relationship as understood and experienced in the whole framework of Jewish tradition. It has been a historic outline of the ideals of Jewish marriage and family life, as seen through the Bible, the Talmud, the Midrash and the living experience of a people over a period of four thousand years. Could any of these ideals and concepts which have come down through the ages still influence the thinking of the modern Jew? The question arises as to how these insights of the past can help to strengthen modern marriages which are being threatened by new social forces of the twentieth century. Every insight and aid ought to be brought to undergird this institution of marriage, which perhaps is one of the most difficult of all social institutions. The psychiatrist, Dr. Smiley Blanton, in his book *Love or Perish* writes:

> Marriage is of course the most difficult of all of our social institutions. Its
> success presupposes a constant process of mutual readjustment all through
> life, and this requires a great degree of individual flexibility.

The social institution of marriage requires not only constant adjustment
and growth, but also thought, work and a spirit of dedication. In Western
civilization it seems that we bring these processes to so many other institutions and professions, but fail to do so in marriage. Many in our generation
have been influenced by the romantic concept of marriage, and have forgotten the useful aspects to be found in the aristocratic matchmaking concept of marriage. Because the older tradition is based on the idea that love
comes after marriage, the importance of the dynamic process of working
at one's marriage has been stressed—a process most helpful and necessary
in contemporary marriage. This attitude of working at marriage conveys
the idea that marriage is a very sacred institution which requires dedication,
discipline and constant devotion. The traditional ceremonies and rituals of
the Jew which are built around the table and home life have much to offer
in strengthening this institution.

More than even devotion and dedication modern marriage requires that
people look upon it as a profession or as a delicate art. Such an approach
would require that men and women bring the same ingredients of skills,
techniques and processes that a teacher, a physician or a musician would
bring to their professional work. The teacher is asked to bring earnestness
to his profession, the salesman tact to his job; the surgeon skill to his delicate
work, the musician dedication to his work of music and the physician discretion to his patients' problems. In a similar way society should demand
that a man and a woman bring the same kind of earnestness, tact, skill,
dedication and discretion in creating their marriage. Today, more than
ever before, those dealing with the problems of marriage and family life
realize that there are basic ingredients that will help make marriage work,
and essential processes which can help couples gain their desired happiness.
This art of marriage requires a word of praise, a sign of appreciation. This
process of marriage demands a constant sign of wanting to give more than
one wants to receive, and above all an open channel of communication between a man and a woman.

One of the basic problems of modern marriage is the lack of communication between a husband and a wife. The inroads of radio and television in
the homes in recent decades have added more stumbling blocks to this
thorny problem. Problems of money, inlaws, sex and children can create
strains in the relationship of two people. But basic to so many marital
problems is the failure of the man to talk to his wife, or the inability of a
woman to communicate with her husband. A recent cartoon of two men

who meet each other at the bus stop on their way to work illustrates this point. One friend asks the other, "How was last night?" to which his friend answered, "Oh, it was just terrible. Our television broke down and I had to talk to my wife."

Communications between husband and wife are essential in creating the rapport and understanding so necessary in modern marriages, which are experienced in an atmosphere of stress and of strain, and ever-changing patterns of living. The Jewish home, with its age-old traditions of holiday ceremonies and table rituals, affords just such opportunities for family members to pause for warm and encouraging words, for breaking bread together and for taking time out to establish emotional ties with one another.

The four-thousand-year civilization of Judaism has not only been concerned with the ethical stance of man, but always conscious of the need to create strong family life and secure homes for its people. The teachers of Judaism engrained in the minds of their people that *Sholom Bayis* (creation of peaceful and loving homes) is to be considered as the greatest of achievements in human life. With this philosophical ideal and a genius to construct means and ways for concretizing ideas into everyday patterns of living and relationships, the guides of Judaism fortified the home and the family to meet the needs of the times. In the past, Judaism began in the home and in family life, even as Judaism begins today in home and family living. Rabbi Morris Adler of Detroit captured the essence of this strength when he wrote:

> Judaism begins at home. It doesn't begin at a meeting or a conference. It doesn't begin at a synagogue service or a philanthropic campaign. It begins in homes where Judaism lives in the atmosphere and is integrated in the normal pattern of daily life. It begins in homes where the Sabbath spreads its aura of sanctity and spirituality. It begins in homes where the Jewish words re-echo, where the Jewish book is honored, and the Jewish song is heard. It begins in homes where the child sees and participates in symbols and rites that link him to a people and a culture. It begins in homes where the Jewish etching or painting and the Jewish ceremonial object are visible and eloquently though silently exercise their influence upon those who behold them. It begins in the home where into the deepest layers of a child's developing personality are woven strands of love for and devotion to the collective life of the Jewish community. No advance in group techniques and administrative skills can compensate for the loss of home training and inculcation.
>
> Jewish organized life is short-sighted and pathetically involved in its own machinery when it does not include in its program stress upon the towering and decisive fact that Judaism begins in the home."

A home imbued with the principles of Judaism not only undergirds the marriage, but, what is as important, will give personalities involved the freedom and the opportunity to fulfill themselves and mature in their relationships. An understanding of marriage, its great Jewish ideals of love and respect, of kindness and consideration, of trust and faithfulness, can help marriages reach new levels in their development.

The traditional attitude of encouraging one to evaluate his actions and his words (taking Heshbon Hanefesh), which is rooted deeply in Jewish living, can help a married couple to follow a prescription for good marriage —one which every marriage counselor would endorse. Every marriage could be improved, each partner gain new insights and a better appreciation of his or her role, if periodically the following points would be considered:

1. Have you been able to communicate with your spouse, or have you helped your partner to reach out to this most difficult phase of married life in America?
2. Have you learned to respect your mate for what he or she is . . . and can potentially be?
3. Have you realized that you did not marry your mate to change him or her?
4. Are you aware that nagging takes the joy out of marriage?
5. Have you helped your husband be a good father, or your wife to be a good mother?
6. Are you considerate of his or her feelings?
7. Do you allow money to spoil your relations, or do you plan your financial program together?
8. Do you evaluate your marriage and relationship to your partner occasionally?
9. Do you tell your spouse how much he or she means to you—and what the marriage means to you?
10. Do you endeavor to make your physical relationship with your partner ever a wholesome and attractive experience?

To the historical perspectives of Jewish marriage and family life, and to the practical phases of modern marriage life, one should add the experience of a religious faith—so explicitly outlined by the teachers of Judaism. In brief the teachers ask for a religious faith in a living God, a faith in the soul of man, created in the image of God and a keen awareness in the most valuable of God's elements—the preciousness of every moment of time. With such a faith and understanding a husband and a wife can create great and meaningful relationships based upon human dignity and respect, human cooperation and love which could fulfill man's deepest needs. It could transform a social-legal contract in an ideal and artistic work of human endeavors. With such insights one may create a situation where two partners think more of the partnership than they do of themselves and in turn reap blessings of self-realization and survival and of security and contentment.

REFERENCES

1. BLANTON, SMILEY: *Love or Perish.* New York, S. and S., 1956.
2. FOLKMAN, JEROME D.: *The Cup of Life, A Jewish Marriage Manual.* New York, David.
3. HAMILTON, ELEANOR: Communication in marriage: endless challenge to loving. *Modern Bride Magazine,* Summer, 1960.
4. HERTZ, J. H. (Ed.) : *The Pentateuch.* London, Soncino Press, 1964.
5. *The Holy Scruptures.* New Translation. Philadelphia, Jewish Publication Society, 1964.
6. JUNG, LEO: Marriage love in Jewish law. In: *Jewish Life.* New York, The Union of Orthodox Congregations of America.
7. MAGOUN, F. ALEXANDER: *Courtship, Love and Marriage.* New York, Harper, 1948.
8. MENNINGER, WILLIAM C.: Tension in family life. *Pastoral Psychology Magazine, 4* (33) , April, 1953.
9. RABINOWITZ, STANLEY: *A Jewish View of Love and Marriage.* Judaism Pamphlet Series. Washington, D.C., B'nai B'rith Youth Organization.
10. SCHNITZER, JESHAIA: *New Horizons for The Synagogue, A Counseling Program for People.* New York, Bloch Publishing Co., 1956.
11. WEINSTEIN, JACOB J.: Isaac and Rebbekah, the Jewish conception of love and marriage as compared with the Western romantic tradition. New York, *The Reconstructionist.*

Chapter 21

THE IMPORTANCE OF MENTAL HEALTH IN THE MODERN FAMILY

THOMAS E. CONNOLLY

FAMILY IS A WORD FOR DESTINY. The family circle surrounds the globe. In our country the daily routines of 41,000,000 families generate and give direction to the driving force of democracy. In all countries, government reflects, in some degree, family patterns, hopes and aspirations.

In the past, concern with the family has varied. There have been those who have regarded the family as bedrock, and have ardently promoted its social health and longevity. Other groups have regarded the family as the stubborn, inflexible barrier to all social progress, and have sought its destruction — sometimes on a grand scale.

Inevitably, however, the family manages to survive and quietly defeats the foes. It remains the primal community, the earliest school, the basic government. It is the institution behind the community council as well as the mob, behind the university as well as the reformatory.

Presently, our churches and other community agencies see the need for strengthening the family. A united family is a defense against communism and other social and political forces attempting to change our way of life. The family unit is a weapon against attack. It strives to protect and nurture each member so that he may realize his fullest potential as a useful citizen of the community.

The family is taken for granted in our society. It does not come to public attention until it deviates from established patterns of community living.

As young married people begin to see that their feelings towards people and situations are rooted in their childhood experiences, they will need help in resisting the temptation to evade responsibility for their current behavior by rationalizing. The immature husband or wife may all too readily conclude that he is a victim of childhood experiences, and for that reason neither responsible for nor able to change his present behavior. Hence, early marriage conflicts are bound to arise. The short engagement, excessive petting and perhaps premarital sexual experience may tend to discourage the newlyweds. The glamor and romance of marriage may already be destroyed, leaving only the more practical matters. Budgets, in-laws, nights out, church attendance, association with friends — all need careful rationalization. Without complete understanding, tolerance for the other's philosophy of life and deep emotional attachment are essential to keep the couple together.

One fundamental of good mental health is that the individual must recognize the role of emotion in human life in order to understand, focus and control his feelings, and thereby achieve his own and society's goals.

He can develop that recognition in group discussions which emphasize that, in the process of growing up, one increasingly gains the satisfactions of self-realization, even though one must relinquish some of the attitudes and behavior patterns of immaturity.

It is essential to good mental health that one understand basic human emotional needs and drives and the morally and socially acceptable ways of satisfying them.

A primary, guiding principle for all the people striving for sound emotional health is that they should gain insight into themselves, their own behavior and its motivations.

Mental health received its first great stimulus in World War I. When increasing numbers of shell-shocked men were returned from the front, it became apparent that the screening they had received as draftees had been inadequate. The screening for physical fitness and gross evidence of mental illness or deficiency had excluded personality factors.

This experience, which showed that personality problems and their genesis needed exploring, gave great impetus to the mental-health movement in this country — a movement aimed at preventing mental ill-health rather than at mere diagnosis and treatment.

By World War II the Armed Forces realized that personality deficiencies can be more crippling to an individual and to the services than loss of limb. From the outset, each selectee in World War II was carefully screened for personality factors which under stress or radically changed living conditions might precipitate him into neuroses or psychoses.

It quickly became apparent that the mental-health movement, despite every effort to reach into the lives of all our people, had not as yet achieved vital significance in the homes, schools and other institutions that influence the growth and development of young people.

More than 865,000 men (17.7%) between eighteen and thirty-seven years of age were rejected for mental disease out of 4,828,000 total rejections from the beginning of Selective Service to August 1, 1945. This figure does not include rejections for neurological conditions nor for mental deficiency. Moreover, the term *mental disease* as applied to those rejected did not in all instances mean acute mental illness; it included those personality disorders that made the individual a poor risk for military service.

Since no screening process is perfect, many service people in World War

II were still to be found in military hospitals, in the guardhouse or brig — in difficulty because of deep-rooted mental habits and attitudes.

The newly married couple ideally should give careful consideration to the creation of a family. Childbirth should not be accidental. In fact, it should be carefully anticipated, financially, spiritually and economically.

The importance of the creation of a human being cannot be overemphasized. For is it not true that we plan our houses, car repairs and other essentials of today's living?

Few persons, indeed, have had the benefit of premarital instruction. Such information is available from physicians, clergymen and social workers. The Cana Conferences for Engaged Couples, sponsored by the Roman Catholic Church, are said to be most helpful. The YWCA also sponsors some good courses.

A prominent Catholic clergyman recently informed the writer that 10 per cent of engaged couples break their engagements after attending the Cana Conferences. Although the reasons vary, many couples feel they are not ready to assume marital responsibility.

The Cana Conferences are mandatory. "No punches are barred," said one priest. "We give them the works — on sex, in-laws, finances and toleration of each other. Instead of marrying on a wave of passion," he continued, "they are made to realize this is a serious business. They are procreators."

Every child brings into the world a gift from his parents — complexion, color of eyes and hair, skeletal structure, stature tendencies, facial characteristics. Some of one's father and mother, grandparents and great-grandparents — of even more remote ancestors — is in everybody's physical makeup.

But the total personality of a human being also owes a great deal to his environment. From birth, the people around a child, the care, love and protection they give him, his needs and the degree to which they are adequately (or inadequately) met — all exert their influence on his personality and his feelings towards the world.

Physical factors can affect mental attitudes and, conversely, mental attitudes can affect physical health. A well-rounded personality is easier to achieve when one has excellent health. Headaches, upset stomachs, malnutrition, poor muscle tone and fatigue may have destructive effects on one's ability to get along with people and to function at one's best.

The foundations of physical health and fitness are laid in an individual's childhood by the care and nurture he receives, by the exercise he gains by crawling, walking, running and later playing with other children, by the many health and safety measures his parents take. Later it becomes his responsibility to maintain maximum physical health and fitness. The extent to which he accepts this responsibility indicates his emotional maturity.

Family background, customs and traditions, national and community codes, economic, educational, cultural and religious patterns affect the individual as a social being and contribute to his philosophy of life.

The child's development begins as he first plays with other children and learns to know his relatives and friends. His personality is influenced by these relationships and by the things his playmates — and the adults around him — consider important. Their values cause noticeable group and social consciousness, even in a young child.

Later, the groups become increasingly important, fostering one's opinions on movies, recordings and fashion fads, one's feelings about school and one's ideas of what constitutes a good time. The attitudes of the group have cogency for the growing boy or girl and motivate much of his or her behavior.

Generally speaking, young people tend to share their parents' views on moral values. But since their friends may also influence their attitudes, young men and women need to realize that they should not buy good standing in the group at the cost of their principles. By following the group to the detriment of one's convictions, one fails to acquire a fine and mature personality.

Emotions — feelings — influence people strongly. The emotion of love, for example, influences men and women to make great sacrifices for each other. A child's love for his parents may make him carefully hoard his pennies and nickels (that might otherwise go into bubble gum or ice cream) for their Christmas or birthday presents. Mature love of country and affection for his buddies will make a man willingly risk his life in combat.

Emotions can also influence people in destructive ways. Anger can motivate harsh and cruel words or acts. Fear can create such envy and jealousy of another's success that it embitters the individual and makes him ungenerous and unkind to a competitor.

To develop a mature personality it is necessary to understand emotion and its powerful influence in one's life — an influence that can make one work for fine goals and help one in achieving them.

One often hears the expression, "He's his own worst enemy." Many people are their own worst enemies because they let emotion guide their behavior to the exclusion of reason, judgment and experience.

Fear, for example, is a normal emotion experienced by everyone. Fear can serve human beings; it alerts them to danger. But the man of proved ability who won't take a better job for fear of possible failure is allowing emotion to rule his life to his detriment.

Emotional growth is part of total personality development. It is of such vital significance in both civilian and military life that the Armed Forces consider the individual's emotional tone to be as important as his physical health and fitness. The Armed Forces try to determine the feelings of prospective recruits about people and things, and try to estimate their use of emotion to build or destroy. These determinations, brought out in initial interviews, are clues to the likelihood of an individual successfully adjusting to military life.

In much the same way, increasing numbers of civilian personnel directors are attempting to forecast (through preemployment interviews by psychologists or psychiatrists) the degree of success they may expect their employees to achieve in meeting day-by-day job responsibilities, in getting along with both colleagues and supervisors and in handling pressures and emergencies.

More and more wives are interviewed with husbands by employment counselors. Certainly the kind of wife one selects, and the "oneness" of the couple are important. The attitudes displayed by man and wife to each other can be measured to a degree, however. A wholesome family situation is more likely to aid in a good job adjustment, better production and better mental health. Hence, the role of the husband in his family situation becomes of increasing importance.

The spiritual growth of an individual is extricably tied in with his emotional growth and social development — and with his environment. His aspirations and values, creative abilities and aesthetic appreciation, and his ability to relate himself to his Creator and his fellowman will be deepened and enhanced by happy emotional growth.

Early in life a child begins to make choices of behavior, exhibiting the root development of conscience. His first choices — whether, for example, to eat a piece of candy now or wait, as his mother has said, till after dinner — are motivated by his desire to hold his parents' love and approval and by his fear that they may withdraw that love and approval.

Later the child adopts his parents' values about right and wrong and begins to use considerably more thought and judgment in making his choices. He is also influenced by the example, aspirations and ideals of his parents and other adults he admires.

As he grows up, his church experiences or his contacts in clubs and young people's groups with spiritually oriented people his own age or older continue to affect his spiritual growth and development.

One of America's most famous clergymen, the Reverend S. Parkes Cadman, left the writer with two very meaningful statements. They were delivered at public high school graduation exercises: "Faith cannot be taught, it is only caught." And, in religion, "We cannot teach, we only reach."

It becomes evident that one's spiritual life is the sum of his moral standards, his respect for his fellowman, his self-control and his belief in the God of his choice.

Mental or intellectual equipment differs from person to person. Personality reflects the way people regard their intellectual equipment and the use they make of it.

As a factor in personality, brilliance of intellect is important only to the extent to which the brilliant person uses his mind constructively and accepts brilliance for what it is — a gift he has not earned, a personal responsibility. Normal intellect must be similarly regarded as an endowment that carries personal responsibility.

No one should belittle a person of limited intellect. Everyone knows people whose kindness, consideration and generosity so far outweigh their intellectual limitations that one nevertheless respects, loves and enjoys them. Furthermore, everyone knows people who gain respect and relative success by putting their capacities and talents, however limited, to fullest use.

In contrast is the naturally gifted individual who fritters away talent because he has no worthwhile goals or ambitions. Immature or spoiled, he may believe he is superior to hard work; his philosophy may become "the world owes me a living." His mistaken self-appraisal may lead him to shirk the responsibility of his talents by lazy, wishful thinking.

The human mind, like the rest of the human organisms, responds to repeated experience, to habit. The contributions intellect makes to a mature, stable and wholesome personality depend essentially on good habits of study, reflection and thought. The best mind in the world would be like a runaway horse — out of control and even potentially dangerous — unless tempered by good habits and self-discipline.

The field of psychology has made it possible to test individual skills, aptitudes and intellectual capacities with considerable accuracy and success. Where there are large numbers of people whose capabilities must be estimated for making preliminary decisions on job placements and responsibilities, psychological testing is valuable. But testing provides only broad scale measurements, not a complete assessment of a person's capacities and ability to use himself productively.

Unfortunately, we have no test for marriage. For mating, yes, but for the many hours of social companionship in marriage, only two persons can best adjust themselves.

Money is said to be the root of all evil. And so it is in the causes given for family break-up. In earlier times families were built on faith in God, family and each other. Now, however, much depends upon one's credit potential. Such material objects as automobiles, television sets and automatic laundries are now accepted as essential to normal living. A few years ago they constituted luxuries available only to the rich. Our American system of economy has made these items available to all persons on the simplest terms. It is well that families have modern conveniences. They allow for more time together. The financial burden may have sound advantages. The young husband and father who needs to meet due dates on his bank note is less likely to loiter in bars or to seek companionship outside his home. Financial obligations, like emotional and spiritual obligations, can be compelling and therefore inspiring.

It is only when tragedy strikes, addiction to alcoholism becomes evident, or emotional interests outside the home interferes that the spell breaks. All too often, indeed, family breakdown occurs at this point. The weight of economic pressure becomes greater than mutual love and respect, and the structure is beyond repair.

It is at this point that society learns exactly what makes a family tick. Community agencies, relatives, the clergy, etc. are frequently helpless in rebuilding families. Guilt feelings supersede fond memories in their intensity. Wild recriminations lead to violent accusations and the spell of love, romance and sometimes even parenthood cannot be recaptured.

Careful economic planning is therefore important in family life. Advice of friends and relatives should be sought and used.

Family is a word for destiny? The writer still believes so. The readings completed for this document provide no blueprint for the normal well-adjusted family. Instead, many criteria are offered. How these are used depend upon the emotional maturity, intellectual capacity, spiritual balance and economic positions of the individuals involved.

Does not one's place in life depend upon the use of his potentials? Since these vary, we cannot determine the model family. Relationships between men and women are sacred and therefore not measurable. Unfortunately, again, we know little about family life until it breaks down.

The majority of American families, however, continue to survive because they are using the best equipment God gave them — spiritual, emotional, cultural and economic.

That is their destiny.

Chapter 22

RELIGION AND MARRIAGE IN TWENTIETH-CENTURY AMERICA

GERHARD FALK

I

THE INTERDEPENDENCE OF SOCIAL INSTITUTIONS is perhaps one of the most evident facts in human relationships. In fact, the very idea that a distinction between the various institutions is possible is a very recent one, derived from the development of scientific sociology and anthropology and expressed in lectures and textbooks. Thus there exists in the academic world a delineation between education, religion, family, government and economics in order to facilitate descriptive and analytic studies of these institutions. However, such a delineation does not exist in the everyday experiences of men.

Thus, religion and the other institutions had been so entwined for so long that there seemed to be no distinguishable differences between them. In fact, until the secularization of Western civilization during the seventeenth and eighteenth centuries, religious views dictated the opinions of mankind in almost all relationships, but particularly familial relationships. Thus it may now appear superfluous to examine the relationship between the institution of the family and that of religion when this relationship has for so long been so well established. However, the present reexamination of that historic relationship is necessary precisely because it has been questioned. In fact, there are those who would now presume that such a relationship does not exist or should not exist, while others point to its relaxation as the root of all the world's evils.

It is not necessary to elaborate here on the well-established functions of religion as developed by sociologists and anthropologists over the years. Such summaries have been well received (38) and have been placing the religious institution in the realm of scientific analysis since the day of Durkheim (22). It is sufficient to recall here that "all the people in the world, no matter how primitive or civilized, perceive in their environment supernatural beings and forces with which they must establish and maintain relations and to which they must adjust" (5, p. 46).

Since religion is so universal a human experience, it is evident that religious institutions influence human existence everywhere and have an effect upon that other universal institution, the family. In addition to the simultaneous, universal appearance of these institutions and their consequent

261

structural interrelationship, they are further related because they often serve overlapping functions. All social institutions are, of course, interrelated, and all interact. However, not all social institutions interact to the same degree and with the same intensity as the family and religion. The reasons may become evident to anyone who contemplates their differential functions. Thus, while there is an undoubted effect of government on family life or religious life, it is evident that such an effect is only minimal in comparison to the effect of family on religion and vice versa.

II

The most expansive of all religious functions is the designation and integration of goals and the provision of sanctions consistent therewith (57, p. 139). These are also the functions of the family. Freud, writing in *Civilization and Its Discontents* (27, pp. 21-45), claimed that religion is a manifestation of the adult's need for fatherly protection and a device whereby man protects himself from the evils of society and the dangers of nature. These manifestations are, of course, also the functions of the family.

Further evidence of such complementary functions is the sharing of educational concerns and religious teachings. Here we see a gradual shift in the center of responsibility from that of the family to the religious institution. While religious instruction of children and adults was always undertaken by religious institutions in some fashion, family life centered upon religion to such an extent for so many years that religious training was in fact a major effort in the daily behavior of every family from the Urals to America, among Christians and among Jews (21, 31).

With the progress of industrialization, the rise of commerce, the advent of science and the secularization of the family, a marked decline in religious involvement of families arose in the Western industrialized world (30, p. 254). Bible reading, which occupied such a prominent place in the family life of Jews and Protestants particularly, became less popular. Prayer, grace after meals and many other religious practices were discontinued in many homes, and moral education was relegated to the churches and schools, thus making religious instruction public issues instead of private obligations as evidenced by the recent uproar over the "prayer decisions" of the United States Supreme Court.

Today, therefore, religious instruction and almost the entire conduct of religious practices in the Western world is a church function and not one carried on by the family (30, p. 254). Even moral instruction, which was never an exclusively religious function, has been relegated largely to secondary institutions of religion and education because of the value confusions inherent in the anomic family life of industrial man. As De Tocqueville found even over one hundred years ago: "It seemed to me as if a cloud habitually hung upon their [Americans] brow and I thought them serious and almost sad, even in their pleasures. The chief reason is that the latter [Americans] are forever brooding over the advantages they do not possess" (20, pp. 712-719).

This brooding over unfulfilled expectations is also called "pleasure seeking." It is the penalty of affluence which lures industrial man with the mirage of ever-greater physical rewards. Essentially this mirage is resolved in the issue of pleasure seeking as opposed to altruism. Religions generally take the view that pleasure seeking leads to psychic pain while altruism contributes to personality stability and contravenes nervous and mental disorders (6, p. 793). An example of this religious attitude may be found in the prophecy of Micah: It hath been told thee, O man, what is good, and what the Lord doth require of thee: Only to do justice, and to love mercy and to walk humbly with thy God (37).

Family life in America was at one time similarly oriented. Certainly the Puritan family promoted an altruistic rather than a hedonistic world view, as do so many extended, rural families. In some measure, value orientations in families are a function of family size. The large families in rural and primitive societies have their household gods and family altars where ancestors are worshipped. These ancestors are believed to have some powerful influence on the living, thus serving to promote a sense of continuity for the members of the family. As the family becomes smaller, however, this religious function is pushed out into the priesthood and the church until the worship function becomes institutionalized in the church alone and becomes less and less a family affair (57, p. 149).

If we agree with the psychiatric finding that altruistic living is superior to a hedonistic mode of life because it is more productive of the well-being of others (6, p. 506), then it becomes evident that the decline in altruistic attitudes in the family, as evidenced by a decline in religious interests, deprives the family of at least one of the major means of promoting emotional security in its members. This may be seen conversely by indicating that the increase in the economic consumption function of the family has been accompanied by an increase in the anxiety factor as evidenced by the great extent of divorce, separation and delinquency (51).

The test of altruism as a superior way of life lies not only in the obligations of family members to one another, but also may come even before marriage when single people ask why sex expression should be limited to a single lifelong partner. The denial of physical pleasure by religious attitudes can then be defended by defining the "superior life" as one in which fulfillment for the individual is seen as synonymous with the production of the well-being of others (6, p. 792).

This attitude receives a good deal of support from the studies of sociologists and psychologists (12, 53, 56). Available studies relating psychological factors to marital success indicate that those who refrain from coitus until marriage find greater happiness than those who are premaritally active. The same studies also indicate that all individualistic interests, such as money, professional success and commercial entertainment are unfavorably associated with marital happiness, while love of children and home and striving toward common family goals are favorably associated with marital happiness (6, p. 506). Thus, many religious attitudes are confirmed by psychological and sociological tests so far developed. There is no reason to suspect that these tests are not valid. On the contrary, the evidence in favor of the altruistic, hence religious, attitude is supported even by such detailed statistical studies as that of the late Dr. Kinsey (34), whose work shows that the rates of nonmarital coitus for religiously devout women are only one-half that of nonreligious women, the same relationship being somewhat less pronounced for men.

A study of Catholic couples (19) showed a significant relationship between a favorable adjustment in marriage and religious instruction in the parental home, frequent church attendance and religious practice. Subjects tested in this study who had such a religious background also rated high in such criteria of happy family life as equality between marital partners, a cooperative approach in raising children, agreement on the handling of money, enjoyment of recreation and mutual friends (19).

Significant also is the finding that marital satisfaction for husbands who were church members is higher than that of husbands who were not. The same finding applies to wives. The lowest satisfaction score was recorded for husbands who never attended church (11). This could mean that the same attitudes which lead to marital happiness also lead to church attendance.

III

In view of these scientific findings the role of the clergy with reference to family life in twentieth-century industrial society should reflect a knowledge of these studies. Relying not only on tradition, clergy can now make use of these findings, provided, of course, that they become acquainted with the whole area of marriage counseling as developed by the social sciences.

Acquaintance with counseling techniques cannot restrict itself, however, to a mere knowledge of some facts and statistics. Chiefly, attitudes of the clergy toward counseling should become similar to those of responsible marital counselors if the clergy wish to have an influence upon the course of family life. This means that clergy must relinquish much of its judgmental attitude and become more accepting of parishioners' problems. Evidently, many people do not discuss their personal problems with their pastors for fear of criticism, dogmatic rejection and judgmental interpretations (41). These interpretations may depend in many instances on religious dogmas from which the clergy cannot independently deviate. Thus, the Roman Catholic belief that God is best served in isolation makes a strong case for celibacy and virginity, hence promoting bachelorhood as the greatest good. When St. Augustine called venereal pleasure sin, he gave impetus to a view that finally led to the denouncing of marriage as slavery and the lack of involvement as a superior state for Christians (21, pp. 64-79).

Such a view stands in sharp contrast to the Jewish view: Whoso findeth a wife findeth a great good (44).

Thus we see that religious interpretations of family life may be so inadequate and unrealistic that their presentation by the clergy tends toward utter abstractions which lack relevance to the lives of those who are expected to live by these dogmas. This problem is particularly acute among followers of a church whose clergy do not marry. While Roman Catholic priests are quick to answer marital questions with reference to canon law, and such concepts as "indulgence," "self-control" and "honesty" come easily to the lips of all clergy, marriage and family responsibilities reach the realities of daily life in a manner which dogma beclouds and theology confounds.

The area of interpersonal relations and family life is not the only one in which religion has lost a great deal of influence. In fact, while church attendance has grown in the past twenty years, and four-fifths of all Americans claim to believe that the Bible is the revealed word of God (3), the church is not now the agent of moral teachings in American life. This is due only in part to the attitudes of the clergy. It is also due to the beliefs of many Americans concerning the possibilities of finding satisfaction or meeting needs in the framework of religious orientation. In the area of marriage it is indicated that Americans do not expect that religion will help them in achieving greater marital satisfaction, but rather that it will help them live with marital frustration (56).

Thus, it appears that one of the reasons for the close relationship between religious affiliation and marital adjustment is not necessarily that religion promotes a better marriage, ipso facto, but rather that religion often mitigates the lack of sexual and psychological satisfaction so common in many marriages by consoling the frustrated spouse through the deprecation of bodily pleasures and the enhancement of spiritual rewards.

An example of the general distrust of religion as a source of marital aid is the experience of Wisconsin judges who had to prod many couples into a religious marriage by promising them that this would not be excessively expensive, as commonly believed. The courts in Wisconsin were swamped by couples wishing to get married there after Wisconsin law deprived justices of the peace of the authority to perform marriages in order to promote more religious ceremonies (14).

In view of this resistance, clergy must establish a sound relationship with those couples who seek their guidance before marriage if they wish to gain the confidence of their parishioners after marriage. Advice and suggestion are much more readily accepted just before marriage than afterwards. Therefore, it is during premarital counseling that the clergy can have the greatest influence on the future orientation of the engaged couple. Hence, exploration of various aspects of family life, from financial considerations to sex, will serve the clergy far better in establishing relationships with married couples than will judgmental preaching. To do this a pastor must of course experience a great deal of therapeutic growth of his own (17). Therefore, a good number of clergy have entered upon psychological training, thus achieving a less moralistic attitude than is ordinarily the case. This may eventually make it possible for religion to achieve the same anxiety-relieving function which psychiatry has attained by its nonjudgmental methods (57, p. 148).

The sum of this situation is that while at one time marriage relationships and family life tried to adjust to the requirements of religion, now religion must adjust itself to the needs of family life in mass society or lose most of its influence in this vital area of concern.

In view of this threat to the position of religion in family affairs, many church leaders have recently attempted to redefine both dogma and practice with reference to family life. One issue which gives great visibility to this effort is the attempt of Roman Catholic and other churchmen to redefine their position on birth control and sex relations. Speaking for the "liberal" group of cardinals at the Second Vatican Council, Cardinal Alfrink of Utrecht, Holland, argued that the choice of using either forbidden birth control devices or abstinence interferes in the fostering of "conjugal love" (39c). Such an attitude deviates sharply from the long-held church view that the purpose of marriage is the rearing of children and that sexual love *per se* is forbidden (39e), a view defended by Cardinals Alfredo Ottaviani and Michael Browne.

Since the social sciences have pioneered many changes in attitudes concerning sex and marriage, while churches have generally resisted such changes, many Christians and Jews in America have become alienated from their faith, feeling that religion had not kept pace with their needs (9).

IV

Recent attempts at ecumenicism led to a recognition of the need to revise some of these attitudes, as illustrated by an editorial in a leading Roman Catholic magazine to the effect that "one of the great obstacles to ecumenicism between Catholics and Protestants is still the Catholic marriage law" (2). Application of such a law is well illustrated by the Spanish marriage law which considers marriage legal only if it is in accord with canon law of the Roman Catholic church. Thus, Article 23 of Spanish law requires that even mixed marriages must be performed in accord with church law, which requires proof that the non-Catholic partner to the mixed marriage is an "apostate" (15).

It is in fact in the area of interfaith marriage that the greatest amount of friction has developed between the views of clergy and the behavior of believers. Summarily, the trend toward interfaith marriages has increased in the United States and other industrial societies. Here all religious denominations face their greatest challenge.

Occasionally it is argued that interfaith marriage can be a successful experience. Such argument generally underscores the idea that all marriages are in effect intermarriages and that diverse religions may even enrich a marriage if such differences are seen positively (8). Experience with interfaith marriage has shown, however, that the chances for a successful adjustment are not as good as is the case with endogamous unions. The chief reason for this experience is, no doubt, that theological differences also involve many differences in values and ideology which become apparent in many areas of life other than those directly concerned with theological commitment (30, p. 254). Therefore, even persons who have renounced their theological or church connections may find strong disagreements in many areas of daily life. It is for this reason that social scientists and theologians have almost universally discouraged interfaith marriage.

This drive toward endogamy has so far had telling effects in the United States. As late as 1957 the United States Bureau of the Census asked 3,500 householders over the age of fourteen to reveal their religion. It was assumed that the results of this study would be a representative sample of American experience. The study showed that 94 per cent of Americans lived in religiously homogeneous households at the time of the study. It further indicated that, in 93 per cent of households having one Jewish spouse, the other spouse was also Jewish; the same was true of 91 per cent of Protestants; and 78 per cent of households having one Roman Catholic spouse were religiously homogeneous (28).

A concomitant study of fertility rates indicated that, while Roman Catholic and Proestant fertility rates are about the same in the United States, that of a thousand Jewish women ever married is only three-quarters as high as the Christian rates. The reasons may well be sought in the highly urbanized, educated, middle-class-oriented Jewish attitudes which are, in the case of Jews, not mitigated either by the Protestant rural and Negro fertility rates or the Catholic aversion to artificial means of birth control (28, p. 22).

Although religious endogamy is today as frequent in the United States as the census study indicates, there is nevertheless reason to believe that interfaith marriages may be on the increase in the future. Conclusive proof for such a trend does not exist. However, some students of the matter believe that an increase in interfaith marriages in the United States has been in evidence since 1910. Earlier in the history of the United States it had been believed that a "melting pot" would result in the complete elimination of religious as well as nationality differences between immigrants or the children of immigrants. While such a "melting pot" theory has been well substantiated in the area of language and nationality differences, it is now also evident that the assimilation of nationalities in the United States has not crossed religious lines but has instead taken place within a "triple melting pot" of Protestant, Catholic and Jew (54). To this we add the well-documented fact that the Protestant Negro community constitutes a fourth religious subculture of considerable extent (35).

For some time now sociologists have promoted the hypothesis that the rates of interfaith marriage increase as the proportion of any religious group in the population decreases (36). This hypothesis has generally proved true, except that social distance as related to economic status has interfered with that prediction. The best American example of this condition is that of the Jews.

While European Jews were almost entirely endogamous until the end of the nineteenth century (4), a slight increase in European interfaith marriages was visible from the beginning of the twentieth century until the rise of the Hitler regime in Germany. However, this trend was not visible in the United States until after the second World War. On the contrary, historical evidence indicates that Jewish intermarriage occurred more frequently in colonial America than at any time in the United States until 1946. The usual explanations for this phenomenon were that Jews were not considered desirable spouses by non-Jews and further, that Jews had lived among gentiles so long that they had learned various techniques of resistance to intermarriage even when there were no barriers on the part of the non-Jewish population (4).

Relying on data gathered during 1937 and 1938 in Chicago, Slotkin (47) believed that Jews who married out of their faith were in fact socially and emotionally deviant and hence unrepresentative of the normal Jewish population. Thus, Slotkin identified the intermarried Jew as an unorganized or demoralized person who lived in slums and did not associate himself with the larger ethnic subculture in any manner, or as an adventurer who married a member of the "out group" as a consequence of promiscuous sex relations, or as a rebellious person who married a Christian to revenge himself on his family, or as a marginal man who married a gentile in order to escape anti-Jewish resentments and social stigmas.

By 1953, however, the Jewish intermarriage rate was estimated to have reached 5 per cent (46), a rate that increased to over 7 per cent by 1957 and reached about 10 per cent by 1964 (48). These increases could not be explained by the reasons advanced twenty years earlier. In fact, these marriages do not now serve to escape anti-Jewish sentiment, simply because such sentiment has now reached an all-time low in the United States. Nor can these Jewish intermarriages be explained as a means for improving Jewish social status, since that status has now reached an all time high (35, p. 8). In fact, by 1964, many Jews who married non-Jews had a higher social position than their non-Jewish spouses (48). The explanation for this high rate of intermarriage must therefore lie not only in the decreasing proportion of Jews in the American population, but also in a relaxation of commitment to earlier Jewish values by American Jews generally. Such values are expressed in Biblical law and Mosaic legislation, which forbid not only the marriage of a Jew to a non-Jew, but also prohibit the union of persons regarded as next of kin, i.e., mothers, sisters, daughters, granddaughters, aunts, stepmothers, daughters-in-law and others (42). The children of such prohibited unions could not marry an Israelite of legitimate birth any more than a non-Jew was allowed to do so.

In view of modern Israel's adherence to Mosaic law with reference to marriage and divorce, it is not possible for a Jew to marry a gentile in Israel today (24). In fact, the Israeli Rabbinical Council still refuses to allow the marriage of the B'nai Israel sect of Indian Jews to Jews of European descent unless the members of that sect undergo conversion. The same rule is applied to American converts who received their conversion from American Conservative or Reform rabbis whose status is not recognized in Israel (39a). American impatience with such attitudes was well illustrated when an Israeli student recently married a Christian woman in New York over the objections of his mother, who flew from Israel to prevent this union. Newspaper accounts portrayed the mother as an obstructionist who deserved to fail as "love conquered all," and a Reform rabbi officiated at the interfaith ceremony (39d).

Christian denominations face similar disaffections with rigid interpretations of intermarriage prohibitions. Thus it is estimated that nearly one-half of all Roman Catholics in America are willing to marry non-Catholics (15). This tremendous trend to intermarry has caused the Roman Catholic church to consider some serious revisions in its attitudes toward such marriages. Under the code of Roman Catholic canon law adopted in 1918, the church demanded that such unions could only be recognized by ecclesiastic authority if the non-Catholic partner agreed to raise the children in the Roman Catholic faith (15). This requirement led Protestants and others to accuse the church of encouraging the Catholic partner to view the marriage bonds lightly while placing the non-Catholic in the position of having to live with a spouse whose church either considered the marriage nonexistent or insisted that children be raised in a faith not their own (15).

Protestant resentment concerning such anti-nuptial agreements have continued even under conditions of ecumenical goodwill. In June, 1964, an Episcopal priest performed a joint wedding ceremony with a Roman Catholic priest in St. Louis. While many hailed this development as a significant step toward Christian unity, the Episcopal bishop of Rhode Island, John S. Higgins, complained that this ceremony was a "capitulation," since the Episcopal priest had officiated at a wedding which required the Episcopalian spouse to agree to raise all children in Roman Catholicism (16).

Perhaps partly stimulated by such resentments, the Second Vatican Council recently debated proposals permitting the marriage of Catholics to persons of other faiths without requiring an ante-nuptial pledge from the non-Catholic Christians (39b). In the main, this proposal would allow Roman Catholics to marry members of the Eastern Orthodox communion according to the Greek rite. Such marriages are to be considered valid but not "licit," a semantic difference which will no doubt escape most believers in both communions (39b). If accepted by the Pope, only the Roman Catholic spouse will have to pledge to raise the children in that faith unless the non-Catholic is not a Christian, in which event the ante-nuptial agreement will presumably continue (39e).

Such changes in Roman Catholic attitudes toward interfaith marriages should tend to facilitate such marriages in the future and promote their increase. It is therefore worth noting that the outcome of interfaith marriages is not as often a happy one as is the case with endogamous marriages. This is particularly true of intermarried Jews and Roman Catholics, whose mental health is reportedly poorer than that of intermarried Protestants and whose self-image is evidently less flattering than that of intermarried Protestants (29). Evidence for a higher dissatisfaction score among intermarried couples of all religious affiliations are such criteria as lack of friends, isolation from families and a high proportion of children having difficulties in school (29). This is not surprising, since interfaith marriages create some very severe identity problems for children of such unions (26), particularly when the interfaith marriage concerns Jews and Christians. In such cases, clergy of many denominations recommend that one of the spouses be converted to the religion of the other. This may be a fair solution to insure tranquility in the home. However, its psychological consequences can be very traumatic. Other attempts to adjust to this dilemma have been the abandonment of all religion, or the acceptance of a third religion, new to both spouses. Both of these attempts to find an area of religious neutrality have some merit, but are very difficult to achieve by all but the most mature minds. Perhaps it is accurate to observe here that most religious thinking falters upon the rock of maturity in any event. This would be even more true if the religious sentiment is not given an adequate opportunity to develop (1, p. 7), as is the case with those who believe that children should not be given religious instruction because they ought to choose their own religion on reaching adulthood.

As a result of the difficulties besetting interfaith marriages, on the one hand, and the ever-increasing opportunities to meet and date members of other faiths, on the other hand, a great deal of ambivalence has developed among Americans concerning interfaith marriage. An example of this ambivalence is the finding that many more people are willing to date persons of another faith than are willing to marry such persons (18), a differential which is even more pronounced with women than men. This ambivalence is further illustrated by the finding that many more Christians attend church than are in agreement with Christian doctrine, while there are twice as many Jews who are in agreement with Jewish doctrine, but are unwilling to attend synagogue, as there are Jews who are willing to attend synagogue (18). A study conducted at the University of Idaho showed (43) that 97 per cent of students were willing to date out of their faith. However, only one-half were willing to marry on an interfaith basis.

V

In addition to needed adjustments in religious attitudes toward inter-faith marriage, changes concerning Christian attitudes toward divorce are now also in evidence. It is in this area that long-honored beliefs are facing their greatest challenge in the form of contemporary practice in the United States. For four hundred years, since the Council of Trent in the middle of the sixteenth century forbade all divorce and also prohibited the remarriage of separated persons, this decree has received only the divided loyalty of Christians (49). Instead of strict adherence to this rule, various means have been devised to escape from its bounds. Among Roman Catholics the escape mechanism has consisted chiefly of the use of annulments on the grounds that the marriage was not consummated or that one party was not baptized or for a host of other legal, religious or moral issues (45).

While the Greek Orthodox and Anglican churches have generally promoted the same views on divorce as the Roman Catholic, both churches have been more ambivalent in their interpretation of this rule. Thus, in 1958, the Anglican Archbishop, Dr. Fisher, declared that marriage is indissoluble, and divorced persons can not remarry during the lifetime of both partners (45). That same year, however, the Bishop of Exeter, Arthur

Winnett, pointed to the considerable division of opinion on that subject among Anglicans and declared that the church should discourage divorce but not prohibit it (58).

Interested laymen have suggested a thoroughgoing review of the Christian attitude toward divorce. Thus, it has been proposed that divorce can be accepted by Christians without fear that the prestige of Christianity would thereby be weakened, since numerous other examples of departures from Christian teachings exist which did not weaken the faith, but merely served to adjust Christian thinking to changing circumstances. Further, it is argued that the evidence indicates that many second marriages after divorce are quite successful and therefore deserve Christian sanctification (52) as practiced by many Protestant denominations already.

It has also been suggested that all churches refrain from solemnizing legal marriages until such legal marriages have been established at least five years. It is hoped that this would avoid the embarrassing position in which churches find themselves now, when they find that the claim that God has joined man and wife together forever proves wrong.

There are many other issues which religion must face in short order. Chief among these is the stand of various denominations on birth control in face of an ever-rising population and increasing severe poverty.

VI

This survey of the relationship of those two great social institutions, family and religion, has served to indicate that the relationship is not only deep, but is intertwined in such a manner that separation is inconceivable. While religion was for many years the dominant partner in this relationship, the present century has seen a reversal of these roles, particularly in America. Religion is today forced to alter its stand on many issues in which family practice and the teaching of churches do not coincide. These issues range from abortion to divorce and the rearing of children (50). In all these areas, and many more, religion for centuries provided the guidelines for family conduct. It now appears that that conduct has escaped religious strictures, and therefore that the present and the future will be concerned with some major adjustment in the conduct of the family and the teachings of religion so that that ancient institution may once more serve to give marriage its sanction and the family its counsel.

REFERENCES

1. ALLPORT, GORDON W.: *The Individual and His Religion*. New York, Macmillan, 1961.
2. Editorial: "Mixed marriage obstacle. *America, 111*:Sept. 19, 1964.

3. BAKER, LUTHER G.: Changing religious norms and family values. *Journal of Marriage and the Family, 2:*February, 1965.

4. BARRON, MILTON L.: The incidence on Jewish intermarriage in Europe and America. *American Sociological Review, 11:*Feb., 1946.

5. BELL, EARL H.: *Social Foundations of Human Behavior.* New York, Harper, 1965.

6. BENSON, PURNELL H.: *Religion in Contemporary Culture.* New York, Harper, 1960.

7. BERTOCCI, PETER I.: What makes a Christian home? *Christian Century, 76:* May 6, 1959.

8. BLACK, ALGERNON D.: If I marry outside my religion. *Marriage and Family Living, 17:*August, 1955.

9. BLACKBURN, HENRY J.: Religion as Reaction. *Hibbert Journal, 54:*Oct., 1955.

10. BLANSHARD, PAUL: Ecclesiastical justice in Spain. *Christian Century, 76:* September 23, 1959.

11. BURCHINAL, LEE G.: Marital satisfaction and religious behavior. *American Sociological Review, 22:*June, 1957.

12. BURGESS, ERNEST W., and COTTRELL, LEONARD: *Predicting Success and Failure in Marriage,* Englewood Cliffs, Prentice-Hall, 1939.

13. CHANCELLOR, LOREN E.: Preferences and Mixtures in Marriages and Divorces. *American Journal of Sociology, 61:*November, 1955.

14. Editorial: Civil judges urge church wedding. *Christian Century, 77:*September 28, 1960.

15. Editorial: Marriage Laws Create Interfaith Conflict. *Christian Century, 79:* Mar. 14, 1962.

16. Editorial: Ecumenical jaywalking. *Christian Century, 81:*Oct. 28, 1964.

17. CRESSMAN, CHARLES P.: Ministers and marriage instruction. *Social Forces, 20:* March, 1942.

18. CHRISTOPHERSON, VICTOR A.: Responses of Protestants, Catholics and Jews concerning marriage and family life. *Sociology and Social Research, 43:* Sept., 1958.

19. CURTIS, JACK H.: A pilot study in the prediction of success in Catholic marriages. *Marriage and Family Living, 18:*May, 1956.

20. DE TOCQUEVILLE, ALEXIS: Democracy in America. In Broom, Leonard and Selznick, Phillip: *Sociology,* 3rd Ed. New York, Harper, 1963, Chapt. 13.

21. DURANT, WILL: *The Age of Faith.* New York, S. and S., 1950.

22. DURKHEIM, EMILÉ: *The Elementary Forms of the Religious Life.* London, Allen & Unwin, 1915.

23. DYER, DOROTHY T.: Religious affiliation and marital happiness. *Marriage and Family Living, 23:*Feb., 1961.

24. Editorial: Goal of Orthodox parties in Israel. *Economist, 186:*Jan. 18, 1958.

25. *Ezra 10:*10-11.

26. FELDER, ELEANOR K.: My child: Jew or Christian? *Commentary, 14:*Sept., 1952.

27. FREUD, SIGMUND: *Civilization and Its Discontents.* New York, Norton, 1961.

28. GLICK, PAUL C.: Intermarriage and fertility patterns among persons in major religious groups. *Eugenics Quarterly, 7:*Mar., 1960.
29. HEISS, JEROLD S.: Interfaith marriage and marital outcome. *Marriage and Family Living, 23:*Aug., 1961.
30. HERTZLER, J. O.: *American Social Institutions.* Boston, Allyn & Bacon, 1961.
31. HERZOG, ELIZABETH, and ZBOROWSKI, MARK: *Life Is With People.* New York, Schocken, 1952.
32. KARDINER, ABRAM: *The Psychological Frontiers of Society.* New York, Columbia, 1945.
33. KERNS, JOSEPH: The theology of marriage. *Commonweal, 80:*June 5, 1964.
34. KINSEY, A. C.; POMEROY, W. B.; MARTIN, C. E., and GEBHART, P. H.: *Sexual Behavior in the Human Female.* Philadelphia, Saunders, 1953.
35. LENSKI, GERHARD: *The Religious Factor.* Garden City, Doubleday, 1963.
36. LOCKE, HARVEY: Interfaith marriages. *Social Problems, 4:*Apr., 1957.
37. *Micah, 6:*8.
38. NOTTINGHAM, ELIZABETH K.: *Religion and Society.* New York, Random, 1954.
39. *New York Times:*
    a. September 1, 1964; b. October 16, 1964; c. October 31, 1964; d. November 9, 1964; e. November 21, 1964.
40. NOVAK, MICHAEL: Marriage: The lay voice. *Commonweal., 79:*Feb. 14, 1964.
41. OATES, WAYNE: The Pastor as Marriage Counselor. *Living, 17:*Feb., 1955.
42. POPPERS, H. L.: The declasse in the Babylonian Jewish community. *Jewish Social Studies, 20:*July, 1958.
43. PRINCE, ALFRED J.: Attitudes of College Students Toward Interfaith Marriage. *The Coordinator, 5:*Sept., 1956.
44. *Proverbs, 18:*22.
45. SANDELL, WILLIAM L.: Marriage, Divorce and the Church. *Hibbert Journal, 56:*Apr., 1958.
46. SHANKS, HERSHEL: Jewish-Gentile intermarriage: Facts and trends. *Commentary, 16:*Oct., 1953.
47. SLOTKIN, J. S.: Jewish-Gentile intermarriage in Chicago. *American Sociological Review, 7:*Feb., 1942.
48. SKLARE, MARSHALL: Intermarriage in the Jewish future. *Commentary, 37:* Apr., 1964.
49. SOWARDS, J. KELLEY: *Western Civilization.* New York, St. Martins, 1964.
50. Editorial: *Spectator, 187:*Nov. 2, 1951.
51. STEIN, MAURICE R.: *Identity and Anxiety.* Glencoe, The Free Press, 1960.
52. SYKES, NORMAN: Marriage, society and the church. *Spectator, 189:*Sept., 1952.
53. TERMAN, LEWIS L.: *Psychological Factors in Marital Success.* New York, McGraw, 1938.
54. THOMAS, JOHN L.: The Factor of religion in the selection of marriage mates. *American Sociological Review, 16:*Aug., 1951.
55. TIGUE, ARTHUR M.: The minister's role in marriage preparation and premarital counseling, *Marriage and Family Living, 20:*Feb., 1958.

56. WALLIN, PAUL: Religiosity, sexual gratification and marital satisfaction. *American Sociological Review, 22:*June, 1957.

57. WINCH, ROBERT: *The Modern Family.* New York, Henry Holt, 1952.

58. WINNETT, ARTHUR R.: Divorce and remarriage. *Spectator, 201:*Oct. 3, 1958.

Chapter 23

KNOWLEDGE AND LOVE IN RABBINIC LORE

LEO JUNG

KNOWLEDGE AND LOVE HAVE BEEN from the very inception of Judaism twin goals of individual and collective life. But their foundation throughout has been justice as social morality. "The righteous man *(Tsaddik)* is the basis of the world." The pedagogical device of promised reward and punishment threatened — serving as the means of accustoming men to choose good and shun evil — indicates the universal validity of justice as the vital principle of life, an everlasting foundation (Proverbs 10:25). This is what Moses had taught: "Judge the people with righteous judgment. . . . Justice and only justice shalt thou pursue [in J. H. Hertz's version] that thou mayest live and inherit the land" (Deborah 16:18-20). Judgment, truth and peace are interdependent: If judgment is executed, truth is vindicated and peace results.

Among the notable encounters with God *(moade Hashem)* reported in the Hebrew Bible are a number of dialogues, from Abraham to Job, each of which deals with one of the aspects of His revelation. The double meaning of *Tsedek* (both "love" and "justice," *mishpat u-tzedakah*) forms the *a priori* basis for these dialogues. To Abraham, His pioneer ambassador, life without rock-bottom assurance of God's justice loses all meaning: "Shall the Judge of all the earth not deal justly?" To Moses, our Teacher, only His forgiving mercy will give meaning to his own life: "Otherwise, blot me, pray, from the book Thou hast written!" Jonah ben Amittai, the young man on the way to become a prophet, is being shown His all-embracing loving justice and just love: "And shall I have no pity upon great Niniveh, its myriads of people and its very cattle?" Despairing Job, unyielding in his plea of innocence and undeserved affliction, learns of His abounding love in the unending panorama of nature, man and beast in His world (40-41).

But it is in the prose paragraphs of Halakhah that the *kaloskagathos* of His fair love shines forth in unique splendor.

Love between husband and wife, to deserve the term *kiddushin* (sanctity) must partake of both qualities. Occasional overpowering affection is not enough. The Shulhan Arukh insists that there must be not only consent *to* marriage, but, for the dignity of both and the high level of love, there must be consent *in* marriage. In Jewish law the husband's conjugal rights do not include that of approaching his wife without her consent. He must woo her (Eben ha-Ezer 15) throughout the years of married life; only the *am-haaretz* ("brutal ignoramus") would ever transgress this basic prohibition. The love of fellowman, too, does not envisage a never-never land, a vacation dream of complete abandonment of one's rights and possessions, but fair and loving care. The Hafetz Hayyim in his "Ahavat Hessed," describes its operation: "As the folios of the Talmud and the account books of *kehillot,* the minutes of congregational or communal meetings (*pinkassaot*) reveal them: Love of one's fellowmen creates such institutions as: "Society for Hospitality to Wayfarers"; "Society for Palliative Momentary Help"; "Free Loan Society," enabling a craftsman to obtain raw materials for the development of his economic security; "Society for the Dowering of Poor Brides," so that they may not grow old with frustration; "The Society for Visiting the Sick"; *Linat Hatzedek,* the society for providing constant vigil at the bedside of persons dangerously ill; The Holy Society for taking care of the dead and providing those who had no relatives or friends with free burial and grave. *Maskil El Dal* Society (literally, "dealing wisely with the poor") was meant to safeguard the self-respect of the recipient by bestowing its aid in utter secrecy. The Talmud reports about a heedless person offering in public his coin to a needy person. Said the sage who observed it: "You would have performed a greater mitzvah had you not shamed him thus" (Hagigah 10A).

In some communities a beautiful custom served the same purpose. Anyone "sitting Shiva" would receive from the office of the local Jewish Welfare Society two boxes, one filled with money, the other empty. The rich would fill the empty one, the poor would empty the full one. The boxes would be sent back to that office and only the executive official would know what had happened.

Membership in the societies mentioned above was a hallmark of nobility to which every citizen of the Jewish collectivity aspired. Love for the fellowman resulted in market laws and the right of collective bargaining which prevented unfair competition and every form of exploitation from the Labor Relations Board (*minhag ha-medinah*) already in force in the time of the Mishnah to the ordinances prohibiting the truck system (whose baseness is described in John Steinbeck's *Grapes of Wrath*). Almost two thousand years ago the prohibition of this system and the establishment as recorded by Josephus of the right to a job was an obligation of state and society. In these laws social justice is the matrix and love the creative, crowning element. Rabbinic rules, indeed, present the legal commentary and the concretization of this love-crowned justice and justice-based love.

Gedolah deah shenitnah ben shte otipot ("Great is that knowledge which includes two aspects of God's being: the omniscient power and infinite mercy"). Only God has these qualities. *Ke E-l deot Hashem* ("God's alone is the power of complete knowledge"). Therefore He knows the motivation of actions. As omniscient God, He knows where an act is beneficial without being truly good and when a good act might be stillborn in spite of noble intention. A million dollar building for an orphanage or a hospital may be a beneficial act from the point of view of the many it serves with its skills, its teachers and physicians. But it may not be a good act as far as the giver is concerned, as his motives may have been the expectation of reward, of public approval or of the acquisition of a good name. God's knowledge, composed of both omniscience and mercy, will judge the frustrated humanitarian as if he had completed his task. For example, if his plans for similar benefaction miscarried from a sudden change in his financial fortune or from an unwise choice of means, God's merciful knowledge will assess the motivation of the person who does a beneficial act for ulterior motives. By him, attitudes and motivations are valued and accounted.

There are three sources within the limits of human capacity of what may be called his knowledge of his Creator. It will be found, however, to embrace His work rather than His essence. Of the latter, man knows only that which His revelation has conveyed to him. The cosmos, in all its massive beauty, infinite greatness and undeviating conformity to law and order, has given man — both emerging from primitiveness and civilized — a never-failing sense of divine power. The sequence of day and night, winter and summer, sowing and harvesting, as they spell His providence, have widened and deepened the knowledge of His works.

The study of God's mind, where accessible to human questing in progressive intuition as found in the deepest thought of every generation, represents an endeavor to fathom all possible motivations of His law — especially in the *Mitzvot Maassiyot*. Rambam has warned us that our interpretation of the *ta'ame hamitzvot*, encouraging and enlightening as they may appear to us, must never be taken as final or exhaustive of the divine intent. The search in every age opens up new vistas and spurs new endeavor on the road to a wider and deeper understanding. It is the process, no less than the achievement, which is meritorious and promising of ever-greater horizons.

In general, both His Torah, our inferences from the beauty of His world and the teachings of His prophets and disciples enable us, all distance off the goal notwithstanding, to achieve conviction as to God's moral character, His control of the universe and the purpose of His creation.

Our knowledge of God, however, remains exceedingly insecure wherever individual experience, fate and destiny are concerned. At no given moment can we tell with any degree of certainty the meaning of any particular event in the life of an individual. The finger of God in history will always depend on our reconstructive ingenuity. His very Torah proclaims it: "And I appeared to Abraham, Isaac and Jacob as God Almighty."

They had seen Him, worshipped Him as the omnipotent creator of heaven and earth and human potentialities.

"But in my name as God of history I was not known to them."

It was only generations later that saw the blossoming of His promise, the election of Israel as His ambassador to mankind and the fulfillment of His pledge to bestow the Holy Land upon them. Isaac Arama, in his commentary, thus explains the enigmatic verse: "Thou shalt see my back, but my face may not be seen."

Long after, figuratively speaking, God has turned His back upon an action or event, man may be able to trace an eventual end result of development as it were, God's finger in history: the connection between apparently insignificant seed and full harvest. Thus, the dream of Joseph was the first in a chain of divinely planned happenings that brought about: exile in Egypt; the revelation of Mt. Sinai; the conquest of Palestine; and the vision of the Messianic age.

The Hebrew word for friendship, *re-ut* (according to the revelatory verse in the Psalms: *Attah yodata shivti vekumi banta le-re-i* [literally, "Thou knowest my lying down and my rising up. Thou understandest my thoughts from afar"]) , implies the sharing of ideas and ideals, a type of comradeship in noble causes. But man's love of God can neither be beneficial to Him in the usual sense of the word, nor can we in our terrestrial limitations be said to share anything with Him. It really spells a complete identification with what man considers most important. To illustrate it, I should like to refer to an apparently paradoxical prayer recited by the faithful every morning. It starts thus: *Ahavah rabbah ahavtalu* ("With great love has thou loved us. Exceeding mercy hast thou bestowed upon us. Merciful Father, all merciful, have mercy upon us") . After this introduction one would expect something like: "Save us from the lion's den. Rescue us from the jaws of death." But what follows sounds anticlimactic: "Have mercy upon us and put it into our hearts to teach, to learn, to observe, to do and to fulfill the mitzvot of your Torah." Why must we implore God's mercy three times for that? The answer lies in the last word of that portion of the prayer — *b'ahavah* ("with love") — to learn with love, to teach with love, to fulfill in the love of God, to observe for the love of God. These are rare assets for which we need a special spirit of steadfast dedication. What we really ask for is the divine help to aid us in the quest for complete identification with God's name, in order that whatever we say, do or fulfill may be a true expression of this utmost devotion. If the supreme form of love is identification with the beloved, so the supreme love of God must be a similar identification. "But God is in heaven and we are on earth, and therefore let our words be few." How can we aspire to such identification with Him, no matter how genuine our love is?

To make that point clear we may well use the comment of the Midrash Rabbah on the second verse of the first chapter of the Bible: *veruach E-lohim merahefet al pne hamayim,* which in literal translation means, "The spirit of God hovers over the face of the waters." Said our sages: *ruho shel Mashiah,* which literally means, "the spirit of the Messiah." They want to suggest that in the very act of the creation of the world, the Lord had in mind the ultimate achievement, construction, consummation of the world of the Messiah, of a life free from prejudice, envy, hatred, and one lived in justice, brotherhood and security. What we are asking in that great prayer is to be given spiritual asset of identification, and we also refer to the way it can be achieved: "enlighten our eyes through Thy Torah — for the love of Thee — an identification with Thy message." *Dabbek libbenu bemitz-votekha* ("A complete attachment to Thy laws, training us in that identification with the ultimate aim of humanity, the eternal era or realm of right-eousness and mercy as the fruit of such consistent effort"). *Ve-yahed levavenu* ("Unite our hearts to love and revere Thy name").

It is the boldest prayer, the most potent quest to our Father in heaven to allow us, within the limitation of human nature, that love of complete identification which will spell our own moral fulfillment, happiness, securi-ty and achievement of a world which He had planned in the spirit of the Messiah, as He created the ineffable boon of light upon cosmos.

There is a basic difference, often ignored, between two states in human relations: falling in love and loving. The first is the result of the sudden impact on one's senses or mind of an enchanting face or figure, of intellec-tual excellence or, on the lowest level, of material affluence.

To have fallen in love means to have been overcome by that impact to the exclusion, consciously or unconsciously, of every other consideration. How long this state lasts will depend upon the particular personality. It is essentially an ego-oriented condition. Modern Hebrew reveals its essential quality by using the reflexive *hitahev,* normally translated as "falling in love," but literally meaning "loving one's self." The person who has fallen in love has, by ignoring them, abrogated all other facets because he or she expects benefits — physical, spiritual or material, from the person with whom he or she has fallen in love. It is what the Mishna in Abot calls *Ahavah Teluyah Bedavar.* The person who has fallen in love may fall out of it when his objective is achieved, may crawl out of it in the progressive stages of disillusionment, may leap out of it by sudden intuition of its worthlessness or as a result of a new powerful stimulus. Falling in love, one may be driven by unbridled desire into excesses of error or extreme. An altogether different state, condition or attitude is that of love. Love implies or presupposes a complete evaluation by the lover of the whole personality of the beloved. That sentiment is most likely to be more stable and enduring.

It is not due to the upsurge of sudden emotion, nor is it overwhelmingly dictated by self-interest. It results in the determination to dedicate one's knowledge, power and very being to the beloved one. Being in love may be due to either of the two conditions. A superficial man or woman will experience a short period of being in love as he or she recovers from having fallen into it. A deeper one may continue being in love because of genuine dedication to the other person.

The Talmud (Sanhedrin 7a) puts it thus: "When our love was strong we could have slept on the edge of a sword. Now that our love is no more strong, a large abode would not be enough for us."

Love as the expression of identification creates intense loyalty to party, the ideals of which one shares, to the country with whose history and destiny one feels closely connected, to universal humanity whose misery (*weltschmertz*) one is unable to bear and towards whose peace and happiness one feels impelled to work. The will for unity with all man is the ultimate expression of that identification with the present and the potential high level of peace and happiness of every human being.

God's love of man manifested itself in that He did not present him with a ready-to-use world but with an emergent creation. He bestowed upon him the great blessing and task of being a partner in the work of the beginning. God warned man "to work the earth and to guard it," to use both the raw material He had placed at his disposal and the mind and the skill with which He had endowed him. In the process, the world would remove accidental impediments and those due to man's folly or quest for power.

God's love kept the high path toward happiness, security, perfection before man's mind. The evil consequences which followed upon his abuse of his free will were meant to keep luminous before him the joy and the benefit of following the divine road. Every error of man, every selfish act, every short-sighted plan for self-aggrandizement without care for the improvement of the whole not only kept man's moral stature down, but kept God's world on a lower level.

For man to hear the voice of God and the direction for fulfillment of security and worthwhileness He chose the family of Abraham, whose *raison d'être* should be the proclamation of this right way, who should be a blessing to the world and who should (in Nachmanides' version) graft the ideal upon the physical constitution of mankind. God wanted man to grow with each chapter in the world development. His love gave him a religion not of contentment and relaxation, but of constant challenge. God's love, as it were, was pained by man's zigzag course, but though he would let him suffer the consequence of his folly of wickedness, he never allowed the vision of the ultimate to disappear from his view.

When the Chosen People became victims of their human nature and listened to lower schemes of happiness, the Lord sent them His spokesmen (the prophets) whose messages in language both tender and ruthless taught the inevitable consequence of waywardness and the assurance of the eventual end when the earth will be full of the knowledge of God.

The dynamic quality of social imagination is the single hope for the gradual humanization of humanity. The challenge of a peaceful, classless society of brothers and sisters aiding each other out of love and giving each other the benefit of the doubt out of love should be answered through an abiding sense of interdependence bringing about the highest level of human life.

The elite of mankind was ever-fired by that imagination, and the righteous people among the nations of the world earned divine acceptance by listening to His voice and taking it to heart.

Thus, God's love to man extends to all ages through the happy times of contentment as well as the despondency of defeat, never changing its tone, never ceasing its admonition, never diminishing the power of the beauty and sweetness of the ultimate accomplishment of a humane society. To the world of today, God calls to use its ample blessings, its gifts of mind and beauty, its reservoirs of scholars, scientists and research men to bring health and hope to all His children, to raise the submerged two-thirds of mankind to a level where they can fill their vital needs, be assured of their rest, and happy in the consciousness that back of all the bewildering variety of phenomena is the Rock of Ages, whose voice has sounded from millennia and who will gather His people into His arms of mercy, when they are wise and good enough to heed His call, to abolish power dreams, tariffs and immigration quotas to lift the hearts of mankind up to the everlasting hills of God-created, man-earned, man-worked salvation.

God's love for man is permanent, beneficial and ever-manifest. Man's love for God is much more difficult of fulfillment. For our normal love takes the form of endearment, tenderness and of bestowing kindness and benefits. But we cannot bestow any benefit on God. He is above the world of physical things to whom our efforts could bring comfort or aid. Yet in a way He awaits our benefactions. As He created the light of the world, the rabbis said, He had in mind the light of the Messiah. The age of justice, genuine brotherhood and unlimited love — any move in this direction brings the world of His original vision nearer. There is no noble, gentle, unselfish human attitude lost in His world. Every genuine movement in the direction of His guidance, the Torah, helps to benefit His plan for a happy humanity. No matter how high our scientists will reach in their space flights, they won't be able to practice righteousness or mercy in the interstellar space, to love God with all our heart and mind and soul means to be dedicated to the principles and ideals He has given to us in His self-revelation.

His revelation means the uncovering of His character to His children of all ages and climes — the true, the only God, as far as human beings can comprehend it. It is manifest in His care and acts of justice and mercy. So that we love God truly by serving justice not for applause or gain or afluence or position, but because they are His qualities.

What we call the ceremonials, what laws and practice serve as symbols, are but a system of training for gradual habituation to righteous and merciful thinking, approaching and acting.

This love of God binds us to no particular clime, limits us to no particular territory. It raises us above the humdrum meaningless individual world to a level where we act and live in the contemplation of His ultimate goal. As we love His goal, we love Him; as we approach by our consistently selfish effort His goal, we approach Him. As our whole life becomes merged in the chorus of the voices calling for holiness which means reverence, righteousness and mercy, we become merged in the total scheme of things. It is man's tremendous boon to be able to love God and to find his own highest level in the thoughts and practice thereof.

"The Lord has in this world only the four cubits of Halakhah," which means that God's ideals, His reality, become concrete in the life of the individual who serves Him selflessly, nobly, righteously and lovingly.

Righteousness and kindness are mandatory from every human being toward every human being, but complete dedication is closest among those held up by the conviction that they are serving together the love of God.

God's love of man expresses itself also in the built-in protection against such accidents as sickness and other mishaps: antibodies, the organic defense against invasion, the immunity against infection such as the medical journals describe in ever-increasing detail. On the principle of *Imitatio Dei,* imitation within the human framework of God's love, we should take care to provide a built-in protection of human happiness, peace and security. It has been, however, our most lamentable failure.

Even in our day, two-thirds of mankind are still living on a subhuman level. Our capacity for producing food, shelter, education for all human beings is almost unlimited. But our love of man has lagged miserably behind that capacity. Most of the revolutions of bloodshed and hatred of the modern world are due to this stupid selfishness of homo sapiens.

Wherever a catastrophic consequence of indifference to our brother's plight is not properly perceived, impetuous attacks are being made on God's justice "because He allows so much human sorrow." In this connection, an experience of the present writer may not be irrelevant:

A few years ago I had delivered the invocation at an annual meeting of an American medical association. When it was over, a physician, sitting next to me on the dais said, "Rabbi, this was a beautiful, poetic address, but how can you explain God's love in the light of what we know about the ravages of cancer?" This was my answer: "We are sitting in the financial capital of the richest country in the history of the world. This year's budget for the expenditures of past, and the prevention of future wars, amounted to many billions. In the last generation modern research and devotion have succeeded in stamping out most of the deadly diseases that have ravaged mankind. Our annual expenditure for cancer research does not yet amount to a few million. Had we spent 1 per cent of what our budget devotes to war for the establishment and maintenance of institutions for the study of cancer, we might be now, with the help of God, and as the harvest of widespread thoroughgoing effort, have discovered the nature of cancer, its cause and cure. God's love, by endowing us with great mental ability, has provided us with the means of achieving it. We must never permit ourselves to argue against His province for our failure to live up to His divine command."

"Work this potential Garden of Eden and guard it." For this earth was given to us, not only as a gift but as a task. Today, initial plans have been laid for providing future fuel needs by the human race through atomic power. There is as yet another inexhaustible source of energy — that which at present causes the disaster of earthquakes. One of these days, human research devoted not to gain alone, but to making this world a source of peace and abiding security, will learn how to channel the billions of heat energies in the crust of our globe, to provide through them the needs of all God's children who now shiver in cold and suffer the pangs of hunger and are deprived of those vital benefits which the omniscient, omnipotent, all-loving Father of mankind, has stored in this planet, charging the wisdom, the character and the benevolence of its best minds and hearts to capture, hold and employ for all people.

God's love of man both in its positive and negative aspects still deserves to remain the major concern of mankind.

This love of God for man manifests itself in granting him the capacity for moral judgment. The last chapters of the Book of Job describe His tender care for all life. Undoubtedly, animals have consciousness and awareness, but it is only man that can be aware of harmony, whose artistic sense makes him thrill to a wondrous sunset, achieve profound happiness through Beethoven's symphonies and lose himself in the contemplation of Michaelangelo's Moses.

His imagination describes to him not only uncharted chapters of his future, but his social awareness creates in him a profound sense of sympathy, empathy and oneness with his fellowman everywhere. His studied judgment creates moral values, truth and beauty from Abraham's blessing for all mankind to the preview of Isaiah's time of the Messiah.

Saadia Gaon eliminated from his Siddur the last lines of the *I'E-I barukh,* the words *or hadash al Tzion ta-ir,* feeling that that prayer was addressed to the Universal Giver of light and should not be narrowed to the light of Zion, no matter how glorious. Saadia was logically right and psychologically wrong, for it has been the genius of our sacred literature to integrate the national with the universal, to find God's love in the beauty — physical or moral — of any human being, in the vision of the ocean of snow-capped peaks on any continent, in the Cedars of Lebanon, in the dew on Mt. Hermon or in the wondrous formation of the mountains near the Dead Sea.

God's love of man manifests itself in his unfolding before us the marvels of His universe, the mathematical perfection of the astral world, the unconquered vista of the Himalayas, the majestic sweep of the Amazon River and the incredible, functional perfection of the human body.

The mystery of pain has evoked deep meditation and has been the subject of many books and pamphlets to justify the ways of God and explain the discipline of sorrow. But the greater mystery is that of utter painlessness. In spite of the elaborate physical and chemical processes involved in food intake, metabolism, digestion and absorption, we suffer neither pain nor discomfort.

God's love of man is especially manifested in the pleasures — physical and emotional — derived from the satisfaction of his biological needs of eating, drinking, sleeping and loving. Childbearing used to be the exception, but its pangs promise to be eliminated in the near future by a judicious and skillful use of drugs and program of exercise. (Indeed the original meaning of *be-etzev teldi banim* usually translated as "in pain shalt thou bring forth children" in the progressive revelation of the Biblical texts seems due for a new interpretation. The word *etzev* — as seen from a comparison with authentic Arabic philology of the prophetic phrase *habbur atzavim Efrayim* — indicates its root to mean "creative, aesthetic work," so that future commentators may translate the verse to read: "for creative work of fashioning their personalities shalt thou bring forth children"). But whatever pain parturition has involved in the past was more than compensated for by the ineffable joy the young mother felt as she saw, touched, listened to the words of her baby, fruit of her own body that held intimate promise for his future.

God's love of man is shown also in the happiness derived from purposeful work. When Adam was ejected from Paradise, he was profoundly despondent. But, say the rabbis, when he heard the divine order, "in the sweat of thy brow shalt thou eat thy bread," his mind became calm and contented. Great is work, says the Talmud, for it honors man as it warms him. From the farmer's deep satisfaction with the harvest of his toil to the scientist's serene contemplation of the stellar world through the instruments he has devised or improved, there is the exquisite happiness of achievement.

For a long time the world view has been geocentric no more. Today we recognize our earth to be only one of the globes, of which there are countless numbers in the intimate galaxies of the world. Man continues to be the center of things. Life is still anthropocentric and will stay so until we are invited to a meeting in outer space of the interstellar academies, including all the imaginable scientists on other planets and stars, unless the scientists turn out to be robots equipped with detachable, exchangeable and illimitable facilities and physical power. We are the heirs and beneficiaries of God's great love, which is the source of the ingenuity of human minds and the stirring challenge to the noblest hearts of every age, from Moses, Isaiah and Hillel in the Jewish history, to Lincoln, Newton and Ghandi in the larger world.

God's love of man in granting him understanding of spiritual awareness, in keeping him cognizant of classless and warless humanity, inspires him with hope under most adverse circumstances. It helps him to defeat life's shadows by the conviction of an ultimate guiding light.

I

Concerning five kinds of love were the children of Israel commanded in the Holy Torah:

The love of God in Debarim VI:5;
The love of Torah in Jeremiah XVI:11;
The love of the Holy Land in Debarim VIII:10;
The love of the people of Israel in Vayikra XIX:18;
The love of the fellowman in Vayigra XIX:26.

II

"Thou shalt *know* it today and take it to thy heart that the Eternal is The God in the heavens above and on the earth below. There is none else."

Debarim IV:39

"Thou hast been made to see so that thou mayest *know* that the Eternal is The God, there is none else."

Debarim IV:35

"Thou favorest man with *knowledge* and teachest mortals understanding."

The Amidah of the Siddur

"And the earth will be full of the *knowledge* of God even as the waters cover the sea."   Isaiah XI:9

Immanuel Kant, in his "Theory of Ethics,"[1] makes this statement: "Morality is not properly the doctrine how we should make ourselves happy, but how we become worthy of happiness . . . . A man is worthy to possess a thing or state when his possession of it is in harmony with the *summum bonum* (the supreme good). All worthiness depends on moral conduct." "The moral laws lead to religion, i.e., to the recognition of all duties as divine commands." Long before, the first Hebrew, Abraham, had proclaimed justice as the basis of life *(tsaddik yessod olam)*, in his bold challenge of his Lord: "Shall the Judge of all the earth not do justly?" Without Him, as source and guardian of justice, life has no meaning.[2]

The Kantian overemphasis on justice implies a denigration of love: "One must live a moral life only out of a sense of duty." In the Torah, justice forms the basic assurance of a minimum to every human being, on which a maximum of *hessed* ("kindness") and *rahamim* ("unselfish love;" literally, "mother love") shall be developed, forming together the synthesis of *Imitatio Dei* (the imitation, within the human frame, of His qualities). The distinction between love not based on justice, and the latter as the foundation of the good life, is hinted at in Proverbs (XIV:34) : "Justice [as basis] uplifts a people, but love of nations [unsecured as to its objectivity and permanency by justice] will stay a failure."

Justice is objective, an all-embracing, ever-valid principle, the minimum assurance of fair play and security, the minimum demand for individual worth and collective culture. Justice is not only, as with Thomas B. Macaulay, "far-sighted policy," a type of diplomatic cleverness, statesman-like sound investment or profitable attitude. "Its power is greater and its behest is independent of anyone else's reaction." Whether our neighbors repay our own fair treatment of them by righteous dealings with us, or subject us to ruthless power politics — whether our just behavior elicits similar conduct from fellow humans or not — justice must be pursued at all costs! Even "an eye for an eye"[3] in its original Semitic meaning represents a tremendous advance on the normal heathen reaction which demanded the eyes of all the alien tribe for the loss of one eye sustained by one kinsman. Only "one tooth for a tooth" and not the fascist's "one set of teeth" for one lost by a party member! In Jewish law, however, that ancient phrase, "An eye for an eye," has completely different meaning. It stipulates financial compensation for the loss of one eye, for the loss of one tooth. On the basis of justice there must be exact valuation, neither partisan exaggeration of the monetary loss sustained by an insider, nor discriminatory devaluation — of a Negro's, a heathen's, any outsider's damage sustained. The overriding fundamental principle is justice.

On the basis of justice for all, "the stranger and the home-born, the rich and the poor," on the achievement of universal rectitude, one may build up one's personal love, a subjective sentiment. The Torah's timeless teaching, *ve-ahavta le-reakha* ("love thy neighbor"), derives from the constitutional fact, *kamokha*, that "he is like thee," created in the image of God-designed equality, entitled to fundamental, unalienable rights and privileges.

"Eye for Eye" in Mosaic Law

Further, nothing can illustrate the fundamental difference of the legal systems of these two peoples better than their different application of the law of talion, or the rule of "measure for measure." The enunciation of the principle of "life for life, eye for eye, tooth for tooth" is today recognized as one of the most far-reaching steps in human progress. It means the substitution of legal punishment, and, as far as possible, the exact equivalent of the injury, in place of wild revenge. It is the spirit of equity. The Church Father, Augustine, was one of the first to declare that the law of talion was a law of justice, not of hatred; one eye, not two, for an eye; one tooth, not ten, for a tooth; one life, not a whole family, for a life. The founders of international law — Hugo Grotius, Jean Bodin and John Selden — all maintain that the rule "eye for an eye" enjoins, on the one hand, that a fair and equitable relation must exist between the crime and the punishment, and, on the other hand, that all citizens are equal before the law, and that the injuries of *all* be valued according to the same standard. "It is a law appropriate only for free peoples," said one of the pioneers of modern Bible exegesis, John D. Michaelis, "in which the poorest inhabitant has the same rights as his most aristocratic assailant . . . . It deems the tooth of the poorest peasant as valuable as that of the nobleman; strangely so, because the peasant must bite crust, while the nobleman eats cake." Of course, in primitive society there was great danger of this principle becoming petrified into a hard-and-fast rule of terrible cruelty. In the Mosaic law, however, monetary commutation had already begun. This is seen from the prohibition of accepting money compensation for malicious murder: "Ye shall take no ransom for the life of a murderer, that is guilty of death" (Numbers XXXV: 31). The literal application is "eye for eye, tooth for tooth" was excluded in rabbinic law; and there is no instance in Jewish history of its literal application ever having been carried out.[4]

Love, as a superstructure on the rock of justice, is capable of tremendous achievement, culminating in self-sacrificing devotion to another human's happiness. Love, as the basis of life, by its very subjectiveness, uncontrolled by the ideal of the *summum bonum* of righteousness, (the divine principle) would inevitably tend to arbitrariness, according to the taste, viewpoint, prejudices, traumas of the individual, resulting in the Greek scene in Plato's three classes of citizens and in the arbitrary distinctions and discriminations consequent on such classification.

Thoroughly schooled in its disciplines, Jehudah Halevy,[5] in his *Kuzari*, emphasized the limits of philosophy and castigated the self-satisfaction of his colleagues. The following excerpt from the text of the *Kuzari* is illustrative:

63. The Rabbi: There is an excuse for the Philosophers. Being Grecians, science and religion did not come to them as inheritances. They belong to the descendants of Japhet, who inhabited the north, whilst that knowledge coming from Adam, and supported by the divine influence, is only to be found among the progeny of Shem, who represented the successors of Noah and constituted, as it were, his (Noah's) essentiality. This knowledge has always been connected with this core, and will always remain so. The Greeks only received it, when they became powerful, from Persia. The Persians had it from the Chaldeans. It was only then that the famous (Greek) Philosophers arose, but as soon as Rome assumed political leadership they produced no philosopher worthy of the name.

64. Al Khazari: Does this mean that Aristotelian philosophy is not deserving of credence?

65. The Rabbi: Certainly. He exerted his mind, because he had no tradition from any reliable source at his disposal. He meditated on the beginning and end of the world, but found as much difficulty in the theory of a beginning as in that of eternity. Finally, these abstract speculations which made for eternity, prevailed, and he found no reason to inquire into the chronology or derivation of those who lived before him. Had he lived among a people with well-authenticated and generally acknowledged traditions, he would have applied his deductions and arguments to establish the theory of creation, however difficult, instead of eternity, which is even much more difficult to accept.

16. Al-Khazari: Now I understand the difference between *E-lohim and Adonai*, and I see how far the God of Abraham is different from that of Aristotle. Man yearns for Adonai as a matter of love, taste, and conviction; whilst attachment to E-lohim is the result of speculation. A feeling of the former kind invites its votaries to give their life His sake, and to prefer death to His absence. Speculation, however, makes veneration only a necessity as long as it entails no harm, but bears no pain for its sake. I would therefore, excuse Aristotle for thinking lightly about the observation of the law, since he doubts whether God has any cognizance of it.

III

Hasdai Crescas,[6] connoisseur of both Aristotle and his disciple, Maimonides, offered trenchant criticism of the former and affectionate disagreement with the latter.

Many of our people have presumed a vision in dreams and foreign vanities. Even the great ones among our sages have been attracted to their (the philosophers') words and have adorned themselves with their argu-

ments and proofs. Among them the sublime master, our Teacher, Rabbi
Moses ben Maimon, who, notwithstanding the greatness of his mind and
his all-embracing knowledge of the Talmud, found good reasoning in the
works of the philosophers and their statements. Indeed, they enticed him,
so that he made of their weak premises veritable pillars and fundamentals
of the Torah.

I should like to make clear however that the Master does by no means
oppose the bases of the faith. But whilst we love his words and even his
causeries, we love truth more! (from the introduction to his magnum opus).

In Halevy's animadversions, as in Crescas' respectful strictures, the basic
point of discussion was the relation between knowledge and love in man's
association with his fellowman, as well as in man's connection with his
Creator.

To the categories of *Shilton ha-Sekhel* ("the rule or primacy of the intellect") and *Shilton ha-Yosher* ("the rule or primacy of righteousness"),
one might fitly add *Shilton ha-Ahavah* ("the rule or primacy of love") as
they appear in that perennial debate.

In the sacred literature of our people, prophecy complemented the work
of the intellect. Intellect alone would never have penetrated even the periphery of the mystery of God. Only through the sources of divine love was the
prophet able to gain an understanding of ultimate verities and ethicospir-
itual values. Crescas' *Or Adonai* complements Rambam's *Moreh* and *Deot*
alike. In the dramatic Midrashic elaboration of the verse in Mishle (Proverbs),[7] God consults the Torah before the creation of the world (potentially the fulfillment of His plan for the humanization of humanity). Was
it an academic consultation on the divine level? Or was it divine social en-
gineering? Or was there the prevision of *Hashgahah peratit* ("providence"),
guiding man, without forcing him, in the direction of ultimate messianic
harmony?

The intellectualist Rambam did not envision the problem as Crescas
embraced it: "To the omniscience of the perfect God, no particular 'purpose
or project' could have arisen at any particular time." In the Maimonidian
coinage, such a positive attribute of God would have been implied in our
attempt to comprehend His "project," and would therefore ascribe anthro-
pomorphic qualities to Him.[8]

Crescas sees creation as an endless process and infinite harvest of His
love. Indeed, the *Imitatio Dei* ("imitation of God"), which the Torah demands, described only the attitude of such creative love towards every one
of His children. Such creative love, an emanation of Godlike power, of the
Godlike property of every soul, knows no limitation, geographical, racial
or social.

Rav Ashi had that in mind, when, in reaction to R. Hamnuna's anger against Babylonian oppressors of his people, he confessed: "I do not understand my colleague's sentiment; I bless them all, Jews and non-Jews, even the cruel heathen."[9]

Crescas quoted both commandments — *"Thou shalt love the Lord thy God"*[10] and *"Thou shalt know Him"*[11] — and did not hesitate to ascribe primacy to the first, even as Rambam did not hesitate to define it in intellectual terms, called much later the "intellectual love of God."

Thomas Aquinas, who, through his teacher, Albertus Magnus, owed much to Rambam,[12] nonetheless followed Crescas in his declaration that to love God is better than to know Him. When Diotima[13] told Socrates that love is a philosopher, she may have essayed a compromise. Plato's *Symposium* stressed with precious clarity that just as the lover craves harmonious union with the one he loves, so does the "knower" seek intellectual union with the subject of his knowledge.

The Hebrew language, through encouragement of the full apprehension of *one* word, suggests the depth of the problem. *Heahez* means to "possess something" and to "be possessed" by it: As one reaches mastery of affection or apprehension, one is mastered by the object involved. How poor, in comparison, sounds Aristipp's boast about the woman of his love: *Echo ouk echomai* ("I have but I am not had"[14]).

The rabbis, from the time of the Mishnah to the author of *Hafetz Hayyim* of our century, have striven to achieve knowledge as love of God, even as they have endeavored, in their personal lives and letters, to know their fellowmen and to love them.

The relation between these two, love and knowledge, is the subject of the present study and may, perchance, serve as an epilogue to *Heroes of the Spirit,* the last of the three biographical volumes of *The Jewish Library.*

The knowledge of God may come as the result of contemplation, prolonged and concentrated; as an appreciation of His infinite wisdom, derived from the phenomena and processes of His infinite world; as an intuitive revelation, vouchsafed in moments of ecstasy; as the harvest of devout immersion in the timeless texts of our sacred literature. King David found such knowledge in the marvelous order of the astral world ("When I behold thy heavens, the work of thy hands . . .").[15] Rabbi Israel Meir ha-Cohen of Radin (the saint and sage, venerated as the author of *Hafetz Hayyim,* one of the noblest works of rabbinic literature) cherished it as the spirit of the Lord, revealed in the sublime level of Jewish social ethics.[16]

Neither mind nor heart, unsided, could offer enough light in the quest for such knowledge. Only the combination of intellectual and emotional approaches, within their limitations, could lead to some rewarding goal in the progress towards *Da'at Elokim* ("the knowledge of God"). The mind would search for every avenue that may widen or deepen the horizon for an ultimate comprehension of the glory of God, while the heart would crave a vision of His justice, mercy and creative love to bless its hopes, stir its resolves, and spur its ceaseless longing for an embracement of His spirit.

One may, by painstaking study of the character and personality of another, reach such total appreciation of the object of his thought that the ensuing predictability of his conduct, crowning the original appreciation, leads to a relationship that may be termed "love." Thus the sentiment of love may be derived from a profound and steady awareness of a strong, noble character. Frequently, love springs from the synthesis of intellectual admiration and emotional acceptance. Abstractly, one person may love humanity; concretely, one individual may love another. Abstract emotion is found in the happy affection an adult feels for childhood, since this represents in charming form a universal group experience during which there is a feeling of man's infinite potentiality. The optimistic prediction would emphasize the hope that, under normal circumstances, the children will become adults possessed with ultimate moral and spiritual decencies. Moreover, the love of children generically, or the love bestowed upon an individual youngster, frequently presents a compensatory expectation of personality fulfillment, most salubrious to the sorrow of one's private or public frustrations.

Normal love between men or women has intellectual or emotional roots and represents personality appreciation. The question of primacy is not vital, because a simultaneous inner movement towards total affection, in which both share, is quite within the range of possibility. The highest form of love between members of different sexes has both elements that are bridged by the unity of ethical or spiritual values. This unfailingly results in a camaraderie, engendered by the endeavor to achieve these values, whether they be academic, social, patriotic or artistic. The unavoidable resignation of mature persons may often be due to deep awareness of the discrepancy between their actual position and the goal towards which they are striving. However, as they work together toward that distant goal, their attachment for each other is deepened. Potent intellectual or emotional elements may manifest themselves as the man and the woman become immersed in their reverence for the cosmos, the shared Socratic *daimonion,* or the revelation of the interdependence of human happiness, justice and eternal peace. Intuitive awareness of the uncharted regions of a man or woman's personality may open up a vista, a total or vital comprehension, which would be denied to any piecemeal search of a probing mind. The Greek *prosopon*[17] presumes a universal human type, whose naturalized form, the Jewish *partzuf,*[18] in the rabbinic adage, insists on the utter uniqueness of every child of God. Therefore, before one can accept or reject a fellow human being, he must have an understanding of him. Therefore, knowledge and love would appear postulated as partners.

Love may move from the level of sex attraction to the selfless devotion of *rahamanut* or "motherliness," which seeks to spend its powers, understanding and knowledge for the benefit of the helpless infant; it may grow from passionate desire to passionate self-sacrifice. As *Imitatio Dei*, such *rahamanut* is accorded the supreme quality of *Kedushah,* or holiness, whose ingredients are reverence for personality, righteousness of act and attitude, and the crowning glory of mother love.

What Seneca had proclaimed about knowledge — "Were wisdom granted to me on condition that I keep it to myself, I would refuse it!" — applies doubly to the quality of love. Baco of Verulam's *Tantum enim possumus quantum scimus* ("Our potency is limited to our knowledge"), could fitly be applied to love: Only insofar as we love, do we undersand God or man or even animals. For *rahamanut* ("unselfish motherly love") extends to all life. Knowledge may be the result of search propelled by love, and the Talmud emphasizes[19] the consequence — the prohibition, on biblical authority, of any unnecessary infliction of pain on the animal, for "His mercies are over all His creatures,"[20] the decisive word, *rahamav,* emphasizing the devoted care that would prevent cruelty to any living thing.

IV

The knowledge of God has been the perennial subject of philosophical and theoretical interest.[21] Its relation to the love of Him has challenged and enchanted commentators on Holy Writ, students of the Talmud of all ages and, in particular, the masters of medieval Jewish thought, as well as scholars of the last few centuries. The "marvel of self-love" has been investigated also by the great teachers of Hassidism, with *Israel Ba'al Shem Tov* at their head. How remarkable is the devotion, the indefatigable sustained effort of an individual for what he considers his welfare! Yet he is not unaware of his shortcomings, of the trickery he employs in the advance of his aims, of the uncontrolled temper he displays when he even only suspects an assault on his possessions or his dignity or his comfort: "This is the meaning of the radical law, 'Love thy neighbor as thyself',"[22] said Rabbi Israel. "Ignore his shortcomings as you ignore your own! Go to all lengths to excuse, or explain, or account for, his action or attitude which at first displease you, even as you find reasons, excuses, justifications for your own acts or attitudes which obviously are far from right! Try to know him in his frailty as you know yourself, and thus extend love to him!"

The love of man for woman is referred to in the fourth chapter of Bereshith in these words: "And Adam knew his wife Eve and she became a mother and bore a son."[23] They have ever been animadverted, illustrated and compared with biblical texts on this subject. The mystic adumbrations of Torah and prophet, the symbolical interpretations of the "Song of Songs," the sage and reverent observations of the rabbis in Talmud and Midrash, have all deepened and broadened the understanding of love. But, above all, it has been the relation of man's love for woman and his understanding of her, in their interpenetration, that have challenged and enriched the searcher and have been of enduring influence upon throughtful lovers and students of love in all ages.

In the fabric of the patterns of religious life there has been an unchanging analogy: love of man, knowledge of fellowman, of man for woman and woman for man on one level; and love of God, knowledge of God, understanding of His way with man, on the higher one.

Righteousness as the law of life (in all nuances — from conformity to moral law to a steady endeavor to bridge the gap between the legal paragraph and the postulates of equity) depends on some basic knowledge of both matter and manner, some fundamental understanding, even in every business enterprise. The technical term again is *da'at,* meaning, literally, "knowledge," and spelling here "agreement as to fundamentals," a meeting by the minds of purchaser as well as buyer as to their intention and mutual desire to consummate the deal on the basis of shared knowledge and understanding as to what, when and how is to be sold.[24] Such *da'at* is essential also for the validity of labor contracts, as of communal, national or international negotiation.[25] The very term *re'a* (fellowman), one of the major contributions of our sacred heritage to the common treasury of man, and at the very base of the Torah's social ethics, etymologically implies community of thought, *da'at.*[26] The knowledge of the human situation, conveying sympathy through empathy, is meant to lead to concrete measures, in law and social custom, for the correction of communal abuses and the promotion of communal harmony. The obligation to remain conscious of this goal, as well as of the well-nigh impassable distance of its achievement, is meant to offer challenge and promise to those of His children as love the Lord of the universe and seek to know the Father of every human being.

V

To seek to know the mind of God, asserts Saadya,[27] amounts to no less than to seek to be God. For His mind and His knowledge are not only quantitatively, but especially qualitatively, different from, and unreachable by, human beings. The emphasis on His moral qualities, as revealed in the theophanies which Moses, Isaiah, David, and Job were granted, prepares for the interrelation, if not interdependence, of knowledge and love.

Which is primary? In the deepest sense, one ensues from, encourages the other. Love serves as a fountain of intuition, cognition, growing awareness, occasional ecstatic vision.[28] Knowledge seeks the nearness, penetrates the approach, yearns for concrete embracement, of His mind, His infinite goodness, His pervading and elusive Essence. For the interhuman situation there is a fascinating analogy, in man-woman seeking, knowing, loving. In the light of that analogy, the timeless interpretation of the "Song of Songs" as a dialogue between the loving, searching bride, the chosen people and the loving God as Israel's Friend and Guide, as Creator of their philosophy of life, seems less abstruse and evidences a deeper comprehension of that indeneification than millennial epistemological adventures have ever achieved.

All the mystery of the human personality notwithstanding, an ultimate understanding between loving husband and wife is well within the realms of probability.

Here love and knowledge result in an interpenetration of emotional and intellectual fulfillment. But in the other realm, that of God-seeking, God-loving, God-knowing, there remains an unbridgeable gap because of which full achievement stays beyond the levels, no matter how high, of the human mind. The *Imitatio Dei*, even in the moral and spiritual sphere, is the supreme goal that can but summon His children, which they, indeed, feel bound to reach for, but the complete attainment of which, by even their noblest, wisest, deepest personalities, stays impossible. However, it is never a hopeless enterprise, for the very process of that quest exerts profound influence on the devout climbers towards the peak of that "mountain of the Lord." There remains a solid good: Whilst a perfect human personality has not as yet appeared, the search for God, on the wings of love for Him, may extend and deepen, far beyond present levels, a vision or even a calm perception of the absolute, perfect, timeless Being.

Man will be forced to resign himself to the great gap between him and the knowledge of God, His nature or His essence.

VI

Genuine love implies self-identification with the beloved.[29] It is empathy in its deepest form. Total response to another releases intuitive energies, opens up new horizons and leads to a fuller knowledge of an essence than otherwise possible. The intimate relation between the object seen, the act of seeing and the personality of the observer[30] may serve as illustration, however imperfect. In the confluence of intellectual and emotional love, through the interaction and interdependence of the persons, or person and object, involved, the frontiers of love and knowledge coalesce.[31] On that level, the love of God and the love of one's fellow human, including the love between members of the two sexes, invite analogy, if not identification. Both the mystery and the rational approach are found in Ibn Ezra's interpretations of the "Song of Songs," a nontheological, but philosophical and philological reading of that *megillah*.[32]

The love of the adult for an infant derives not only from the wonder of its body, its incipient movements, its efforts to penetrate with tiny fingers into reality, but from conscious, half-conscious or unconscious indentification, to some degree, with the infinite potentialities of every baby — partly as compensation for one's frustration,[33] as inchoate hope for the solution of the problems perceived in maturity, but more so out of realization of the need to resign oneself to a distance off one's own goals and to attach oneself to the as yet unspelled-out expectation that the chances for self-fulfillment or self-realization will increase for the personality unfolding with the infant's every hour. The contemplative awareness of this untapped energy, not-yet-arrived opportunity, of his emergent intellectual and emotional riches, becomes a subterranean source of the emotional energies which feed the love of general and individual infancy and childhood. Here again, the line between intuition and rational enterprise is thin, indeed, and they promote each other.

Mature love between the sexes, too, is the fruit of knowledge: a kind of revelation of personality, conveyed through eyes, ears and the thinking processes, which eventually integrates sensation into judgment. Just as vision, appreciation and depth-knowledge of character call forth love, so is the search for knowledge that is comprehensive and penetrative the fruit of love.

The passionate and persistent seeking of a deeper apprehension of God's attributes, as accessible to human search and yearning, has its human counterpart in the zealous exploration of every facet of the beloved person, so that love may end and reach fulfillment in the full knowledge of, dedication and surrender of oneself to the beloved. For the interpretation of this total search, the languages and the images of philosophy, poetry, mystic vision and rational definition are complementary. Only the sum of all the ways of love and knowledge in search and aid of each other will represent the whole beauty and power of the polar tendencies meeting in the mystery.

The normal assumption that knowledge leads to love has its variations from Plotinus's ecstatic vision to Bergson's intellectual sympathy.[34] The awareness that love leads to knowledge has its mystic approach as well as its erotic assertion. The biblical "And Adam knew his wife Eve and she bore a child" has evoked the latter interpretation. The translation of Socrates' *Ethos* into Plato's *logos*[35] stimulated similar consideration. The vision of transcendent beauty is as much the fruit of the former as of the latter. In the myths of the latter's dialogues and epistles, the two realms are at least adumbrated, at best portrayed with rare insight and brilliance.[36] It is knowledge which opposes sophistry through the love it begets. It is love which encourages the search for the *summum bonum,* the vision of which has rendered it more dynamic.[37] The pursuit of both is an ongoing process, a *birkhat gomlin,*[38] *hashpa-at gomlin,* impervious, on its proper level, to both the cynic's sport and the boor's clumsiness. The good and the beautiful may be reached by parallel ways meeting in the infinity of the *kalos kagathos*. The platonic opposition to dualism and to a superficial monism seems to stress the essential need of this check-and-balances program on the way towards knowledge leading to love and based on knowledge.

Max Scheler[39] quotes Goethe's dictum: "One does not acquire knowledge except of that which one loves, and the deeper and fuller the knowledge is to become, the stronger, more powerful and more vivid, must the love thereof, yea, the passion thereof be." Scheler also quotes Leonardo da Vinci, who states that love is the daughter of a great perception (intuition or knowledge). The primacy varies from the former to the latter. Pascal,[40] on grounds as emotional as philosophical, identifies love with reason. Judgments as to ethical primacy, too, will affect the cause-and-effect suggestion in the achievement. (Scheler's brief but profound essay on the subject should offer fresh light, although his interpretation has some neophyte tendencies in need of correction.)

The Hebrew *heahez*,[41] as indicated above, suggests that we possess what we love and are possessed thereby, a pregnant interpretation of the mutuality of the love-knowledge relation.

Erotic love, a source of perpetuation, may promote the chances of perfect knowledge through the observation of the child's movement towards refinement, the increasing perception thereof strengthening the lover's awareness, assets and position. The "collective unconscious" of Carl G. Jung,[42] the Hindu idea of love as the intellectual recognition of the unity of being,[43] the trend towards each other of the lovers' originally unseparated entities, all represent nuances in the search for expression of the primeval relation. One may perchance find anticipation of this idea in the Midrashic concept of the original androgynic man.[44]

VII

Man in his love of God seeks to complement his own happiness by more knowledge through love, more love through increasing knowledge. But God's love of man, as recorded to Moses, as emphasized by the prophets and by their disciples, the sages of the Agadah, has only one purpose: the promotion — without determinative affection of his freedom of will — of man's happiness through increasing perfection of character and personality. The divine element in man is to lead not only the individual Jewish soul toward ever-higher levels, but to aid every fellowman in such an upward climb. The supreme human vision of God will hence be achieved not by intellectual effort, but through identification with, dedication to and consistent striving after, God's aim for the happiness and moral self-realization of man. That principle has been the essence of Jeremiah's radical assertion: All search for the essence of God must remain ever unsuccessful, both because of the limitations of the human mind and the utter inaccessibility, to time-and-space-bound endeavor, of the Creator. No world-escaping hermit is granted a deeper vision; no philosopher worshipping the Absolute can penetrate the mystery of His being. The knowledge of God, within the frame of human potentiality, is achievable only through the imitation of His ethical qualities conveyed through His revelation, even justice and compassion. The word *Tzedek* is a homonym, including both. Both are manifested by the assumption and discharge of social responsibility, by dynamic, wise love of one's fellowman, by loving identification with his problems and by empathy with his fallible weakness. Righteousness governs not only one's actions as to personal honest, normal juridical relations, it also stirs up and sustains profound indignation, protesting and battling every manifestation of *hamass* ("violence" or "oppression" in any form). Compassion again creates and sustains attitude and conduct on the levels of *Lifnim mishurat ha-Din* ("generous equity"), *Kiddush hashem* ("morally sublime action inspired by the purpose of sanctifying His Name" — a unique and supreme Jewish virtue), *ahavat hinnam* ("general love of humans without specific cause," "gratuitous love"), because of one or all of which a person would forgo his or her legal or technical advantage for the love of God and man, the fruit at once of pure altruism and pure worship of God.

One will never know God through either mere intellectual endeavor or through mere emotional identification with His spirit. It is only by passionate love of and work for the widow and the orphan, the alien and everyone else who is underprivileged that one's knowledge of Him may reach the human peak. There were the twelve precious jewels attached to the four rows of the breast plate of the High Priest. The Four *Turim* ("rows" or "volumes") comprising the totality of Jewish law find their crowning complementation in the *Hoshen Mishpat,* "The Breastplate of Justice," the last part of the authoritative but ever unfinished "Prepared Table" (*Shulhan Arukh*), Rabbi Joseph Karo's Code.

Righteousness alone, all its assets notwithstanding, will not bring about, nor express, full knowledge or love of Him. Just as epistemology, with all its keen and wholesome insights, as its ultimate harvest, offers essentially but a sense of our mental limitations, so mere righteousness does not encompass the full program of the Holy Torah.

Optimistic views as to cause and effect in political affairs may endorse the merit, essential and timeless, of right conduct. It is true that, to the student of the Torah, justice is much more, indeed, the basic principle of religion and of the good life it enjoins and inspires. Nor is it necessary to emphasize again that without justice neither religion nor human existence are left with any meaning. But justice is only a basis, and its very flowering depends upon the steady functioning, in thought, sentiment and practical conduct, of other ethical potencies.

VIII

It is the expected mutuality of justice which we have recognized as at once its major asset and its major liability. For teaching *Tzaddik yessod olam* ("the righteous is the foundation of the world") in all its interpretations, which abound in rabbinic literature, emphasizes that even if no mutuality were expectable, even when the just person would meet with dismaying ingratitude or unrighteous response to his righteous action, for him the principle must retain all its pristine cogency and power, and his actions must remain righteous and compassionate. On the common level, as a mere wise policy, we have seen it as essentially selfish because reward-promising. Since Bahya ibn Pakudah, we have accepted his position, i.e., that for the development and achievement of an ethical personality one must recognize rewards and punishments, with all their solid attractiveness and deterrent effect respectively, as but a device of an educational method for the morally as yet immature, most intelligible and appreciated in the light of the Aristotelian principle of the process of habituation, but both nonvital consequences of conduct and both of negative effect on the fruition of moral ideals.

The just person who is aware and hopeful of proper reaction to, or reward for, his equitable and/or charitable deeds does not possess a knowledge of God's character sufficiently dynamic to achieve the requisite quality and measure of *Imitatio Dei*. For God's mercy is self-propelled, an expression of His moral Being, absolute, because it is above any expectancy of reward or possibility of benefit or improvement through such recompense for His goodness and justice. The prophet Isaiah proclaimed it in one verse (50a) : *Ha-e-l ha-kaddosh nikdash bitzdakah* ("The Holy God is sanctified by His righteousness") .

In is only through dedicated attention to the helpless, the sick, the forlorn, that fuller awareness of His goodness is evidenced. It is only when the human act or attitude is "absolute," which in this context above all means "independent of, above and untouched by any positive or negative reaction," that man reaches out towards His revealed quality.

Finally, this knowledge of God is the only true chance for self-knowledge. As striving and triumphant, or defeated and frustrated, angry or satisfied humans, we know only part of our own potentiality. A mother, genuinely *rahamanah,* discovers bottomless qualities in herself. Serenity is the fruit of the pleasure of a good deed. The patient attitude and consistent loyalty in performing a good deed open up new horizons of one's personality and reveal new depths of understanding. Intellectual achievement, too, gives one pleasure. Emotional excitement has its own satisfactions, but the consciousness of having succeeded in solving the problems of one's fellowman by our unselfish endeavor, of having corrected his errors with a minimum of embarrassment and a maximum of encouragement for him, widens and deepens one's sense of human interdependence and quickens one's *joie de vivre*.

It is the creative quality of mercy that crowns justice and, through the buoyant effect on fellowman, reveals his, as it does one's own, fuller stature.

There seems to be a congenital inconsistency in many thinkers. Speaking in rabbinic terms, they will reject on principle as *pshat*[51] (*"simple"* meaning of the text) what they will admit as *derash* ("homiletical" or *"ad hoc"* interpretation). In the effort to establish the simple text meaning, for the definition of principle, they will often be harsh and uncompromising philologists, only to employ the emotional, homiletical, metaphysical interpretation in another connection. Elsewhere,[52] I have shown it in connection with R. Simeon bar Yohai's interpretation of Genesis VI:4. One may find it in R. Jacob Emden's apparently ambivalent attitude to the book of Zohar.[53] I should like to point out a not-too-dissimilar phenomenon in the fifth book of Spinoza's *Ethics* as compared to his strictly mathematical method in the rest of his book. An interesting instance may be found as one compares Rambam's *Moreh,* III:51 with the note at the end of Chapter 54.[54] As against the emphasis on the intellectual love of God in the former, the last part of the classic work stresses the knowledge of God through the contemplation and imitation of His ethical qualities.

This is how the text reads in Friedlander's accurate translation:[55]

> We are thus told in this passage (Exodus XXXVIII) that the Divine acts which ought to be known, and ought to serve as a guide for our actions, are *hesed* ("loving-kindness"), *mishpat,* ("judgment") and *tzedakah* ("righteousness"). The object of the passage is to declare that the perfection in which a man can truly glory is attained by him when he has acquired — as far as this is possible for man — the knowledge and love of God. Having acquired this knowledge, he will then be determined always to seek loving-kindness, judgment, and righteousness and thus imitate the ways of God.

In his *Iggeret ha-Kodesh,*[56] Rabbi Shneur Zalman of Liady states that *Tzedakah* in its other meaning, "charity," is the greatest of all the *mitzvot,* and that[57] Israel will be redeemed only through (the practice or merit of) *Tzedakah,* and that the love of God flows from the very depth of the heart and is superior to knowledge (of Him).

IX

Rambam's emphasis on the knowledge of God as the primary duty of the faithful[58] and Shneur Zalman's stressing of *Tzedakah* as the noblest *mitzvah* ("commandment," "good deed") represent two apparently, though not necessarily, contradictory views.[59]

The prophet, as God's spokesman, makes timeless pronouncements. The faith in, as the mystery of, their origin will remain an ever-dynamic source of metaphysical discussion. But their message has been found applicable in all lands, with all configurations, social, religious, local or universal.[60]

The philosopher — for enlightenment or criticism — sums up the meaning of events or systems of thought and endeavors to include all nuances and facets for a complete statement.

The pietist probes to the very depth of human potentiality. He is profoundly aware and humbly conscious of Divine power and of the benign wisdom and abiding unity in the changeless source behind the various aspects of the universe. The philosopher's definitions, as well as the pietist's intuitive reactions to the validity of these definitions, have often been foreshadowed by the prophetic message.

What the philosopher achieves as the fruit of prolonged meditation or fast bold abstraction, what the pietist finds in his self-abandonment to the One, the Eternal, the source at once of meaning, hope and challenge, the prophet, in cases without number, has long ago summed up in his "Thus said the Lord" revelations.

Maimonides, in the first and second chapter of *Hilkhot Yessode ha-Torah* (*The Laws Concerning the Basic Principles of the Torah*) makes the following statement:

> The fundamental of all the basic principles, the pillar of all sciences, is to know that there is a First Being who brought all existing things — celestial, terrestrial and intermediate — into being, and that all of which exist only because of His own real existence. One will be led to love and reverence of Him through the contemplation of His great and wondrous works and creatures, which affords one a glimpse of His incomparable, limitless wisdom. The Torah expresses this thought in its text: "There is none besides Him,[61] i.e., no being truly like Him. Did not David say: "When I behold thy heavens, the work of thy fingers — what is man that thou art mindful of him and the son of man that thou thinkest of him?" In accord with these words, I shall explain the works of the Sovereign of the Universe that they may serve the man of discernment as a door to the love of God. For, this God, honored and awesome, it is our duty to love and revere.

To seek to know God, in the view of Maimonides, is the supreme, the first and foremost *mitzvah*. There are two ways for fulfilling it. One is the study of nature. The Talmud[62] puts it thus: "One who knows the science of cycles and planets (astronomy) and does not follow it, concerning him Scripture says: 'But they regard not the work of the Lord, neither have they considered the operation of His hands'."[63] The other pathway is the study of His revelation, the *Torah* (or "guidance") to goodness, worth-whileness, happiness and peace. In particular is it the process of the study of *Taame ha-Mitzvot* ("the possible motivation of His commandments") that may grant one a glimpse of the divine mind. Hence Rambam's pre-occupation, especially in the third book of his *Moreh Nebukhim* (*Guide of the Perplexed*), with the search for the motivation of every *Mitzvah,* in which a human being may seem to catch a reflection of His set of values and ideas. Such discovered "cause," however, no matter how fascinating to the particular searcher, is but the fruit of his individual investigation, and must not be assumed to be the ultimate or full divine motive. Nor may confiormity to His *mitzvot* ever be made dependent on the discovery of some personally satisfactory reason. Therefore, the search for an ever-fuller, deeper appre-hension of His unfathomable mind remains the supreme *Mitzvah,* and the resulting *Shilton ha-Sekhel* (no matter how far from the ultimate goal), one of the greatest consummations achievable by His loyal ambassador to the rest of mankind: the studious, steadfast students of the Torah among all the children of Israel. The accent throughout is on intellectual endeavor, al-though its rigid insistence is relaxed in the last chapter of the *Moreh*[64]:

> The prophet does not content himself with explaining that the knowl-edge of God is the highest kind of perfection; for if this only had been his intention, he would have said, "But in this let him who glorifieth himself, find glory, that he understandeth and knoweth Me," and would have stop-ped there, or he would have said "that he understandeth and knoweth Me and knoweth Me that I am One," or "that I have not any likeness," or "that there is none like Me" or a similar phrase. He says, however, that man can only glory in the knowledge of God and in the knowledge of His ways and attributes, which are His actions, as we have shown (Part I, liv.) in expounding the passage, "Show me Thy ways" (Exodus XXXVIII:13). We are thus told in this passage that the Divine acts which ought to be known, and ought to serve as a guide for our actions, are *hessed* (loving-kindness"), *mishpat* ("judgment") and *tzedakah* ("righteousness"). An-other very important lesson is taught by the additional phrase, "in the earth." It implies a fundamental principle of the law; it rejects the theory of those who boldly assert that God's providence does not extend below the sphere of the moon, and that the earth with its contents is abandoned, that "the Lord hath forsaken the earth" (Exodus VIII:12). It teaches, as has been taught by the greatest of all wise men in the words, "The earth is the Lord's" (Exodus IX:29), that His providence extends to the earth in accordance with its nature, in the same manner as it controls the heavens in accordance with their nature. This is expressed in the words, "That I am the Lord which exercises loving-kindness, judgment and righteousness in the earth." In a similar manner we have shown (Part I,

liv.) that the object of the enumeration of God's thirteen attributes is the lesson that we should acquire similar attributes and act accordingly. The object of the above passage is therefore to declare that the perfection in which man can truly glory is attained by him when he has acquired — as far as this is possible for man — the knowledge of God, the knowledge of His creatures in their production and continued existence. Having acquired this knowledge he will then be determined always to seek lovingkindness, judgment and righteousness, and thus to imitate the ways of God.

X

An apparently contradictory emphasis is found in the writing of Lubavitch, Rabbi Shneur Zalman of Liady. He does stress the love of God as a primary commandment, and, following earlier thinkers, bases it on a sense of gratitude for His endless bounty, but his major praise is unconnected with the processes of an inquiring mind or the results of such uninterrupted quest. He quotes the sages of the Talmud,[65] who insisted: "We must be more careful about the mitzvah of *Tzedakah* ('charity') than about any other positive commandment, for it is of importance equal to all the *Mitzvot* of the Torah,[66] and brings redemption nearer."[67] Not a cloistered hermit, but a dynamic shepherd of his people, Rabbi Shneur Zalman had learned about the pangs of poverty, so that the potent expression in the Talmud about the merit of relieving it had his comprehensive understanding. He found fault with earlier and contemporary teachers whose praise of the silent, solitary life, dedicated to worship of God, to the contemplation in utter loneliness of His greatness and mystery, had dimmed their sense of the glory of *Tzedakah*, quick, delicate, warm aid to the suffering. They knew too little about the misery of the masses who lived shut out from comfort and unable to supply their primitive needs. More than once did Shneur Zalman forsake his court for lengthy visits to the drab, bitter houses of the unemployed, to "God's quartet": the widow, the orphan, the sick, the stranger at the gate.[68] To him, the life of lonely prayers and frugal study in the woods stayed bereft of a God-given opportunity for blissfulness — *Tzedakah*. A *tzaddik*, he felt, is not merely a righteous man. To deserve that appellation one must give *Tzedakah*, ("charity") of what one has, of what one knows, of what one is.

In his *Iggeret ha-Kodesh*[69] (*Letter of Holiness*) he expands his teaching:

> *Tzedakah* is the greatest of all *Mitzvot*. Israel will be redeemed only through the practice of *Tzedakah*.[70] Did not Rabbi Shimeon proclaim that he who gives *Tzedakah* to the poor sanctifies God's name every day? The reward of sowing *Tzedakah* is the quality of truth. Remember: "The work of *Tzedakah* shall be peace and the effect of *Tzedakah* quiet and confidence forever!"[71]

When Isaiah described how *He* (*the Lord*) *put* Tzedakah *as a coat of mail and as a helmet of salvation upon His head*,[72] our sages of blessed memory commented: "Just as in a coat of mail, every small scale joins with the others to form one piece of armor, so does every *perutah* ('penny') spent on charity combine with the rest to form a large sum."[73] Whilst the bases of the Jewish life are HaBaD (*Hakhmah, Binah, Deah* ["wisdom," "understanding," knowledge"]), there is no *mitzvah* more noble than *Tzedakah*: "*Tzedakah* fashions a garment of glory for the soul, emanating from the light of God and embracing all the worlds. A *tzaddik* first gives the coin to the poor and only then offers his prayer: "*Only through the act of charity do I see Thy face,*[74] for the grace of God looms over those who revere Him from everlasting to everlasting." "*Let* Tzedakah *well up as a mighty stream,*[75] for it is the spark of divinity in his own soul, stemming from the sublime Wisdom of heaven."

XI

It was the passionate servant of God, the ruthless denouncer of evil, the loving Jeremiah, who, thousands of years earlier, had offered the endorsement of both Maimonides and the Rav of Liady in a synthesis of *da'at* and *ahavah,* priceless in its simplicity[76]:

Did not thy father eat and drink, and do justice and righteousness?
Then it was well with him.
He judged the cause of the poor and needy;
Then it was well.
Is not this to know Me? saith the Lord.

NOTES

1. Para. 5.
2. Beresh. XVIII:28.
3. Shem. XXI:23.
4. Hertz, J. H.: *Pentateuch,* p. 405.
5. *Kuzari* I:4.
6. *Or Adonai.*
7. Midrash Mishle *ad loc.*
8. See Kaufmann, David: *Attributenlehre* IV: 4c, VII:3.
9. Beresh. 57b.
10. Deb. VI:5.
11. *Ibid.* IV:39.
12. Jellinek, A.: *Thos. Aquinas.*
13. *Symposium* 201.
14. *Shulhan Arukh,* Eben ha-Ezer XXV, and also Seneca, *Epistles* IX:6 — for a polar attitude.
15. Ps. VIII:5.
16. *Ahabat Hessed,* Introduction.
17. *Iliad* XVIII:25.
18. Babli San. 7a, Yer. San. IV:13.
19. Baba M. 32b.
20. Ps. CXLV:9, Jonah IV:11.
21. See Da'at Eloh. in *Otzar Yissrael* and the corresponding article in *Jewish Encyclopedia.*

22. Vay. XIX:18 and 34.
23. Beresh. IV:1.
24. Kidd. 48b, Baba B. 83b.
25. B. Baba 8b and comment, *ad. loc.*
26. Ps. CXXXIX:2 where *re'a* means "thought," also Targ. Onkel. on Bam. XVI:28.
27. *Emunot ve-Deot*, Introduction.
28. MacTaggart, J.: *Plotinus;* and Heineman, Fritz: *Plotinus, passim.*
29. *Symposium, loc. cit.*
30. Aristotle, *Physics* III:4.
31. Maximus of Tyre, Dissert. XV.
32. Introduction to his Commentary, *ad loc.*
33. Adler, A.: *Guiding Human Misfits.*
34. *Les Dounees Immediates de la Conscience*, 1888.
35. Greene, W. C.: *Moira*. Cambridge, Harvard.
36. Consult the index in A. J. Taylor's famed volume.
37. The various definitions are found in D. Runes' *Dictionary of Philosophy.*
38. Ketub. 8b.
39. *Liebe und Erkenntnis* 5f.
40. *Provincial Letters* III:12.
41. In S. R. Hirsch's ingenious commentary on Beresh. XIVII:27.
42. *Modern Man in Search of a Soul*, also, *The Integration of Personality.*
43. Gupta, S. D.: *Hindu Mysticism*, III:f.
44. Beresh. Ra. XII:14.
45. Throughout the Tanakh.
46. Baba M. 16b.
47. Berak. 20a, Pess. 53b.
48. Rabbi A. I. Kook's precious phrase.
49. Prov. X:25.
50. Hov. ha-Levavot III.
50a. Isaiah V:16.
51.. Frankel, Israel: *Peshat*. Toronto, 1956.
52. *Fallen Angels*. Dropsie College, 1926.
53. His *Mitpahat Sefarim* versus his edition of the Siddur.
54. IX:6.
55. XII:7.
56. 3, 4, 6, 12.
57. Yer. Peah I:1.
58. Yessode ha-Torah I.1.
59. Teitelbaum, M.: *ha-Rav mi-Liady* I.
60. Rambam on Prophecy, Kobetz II.
61. The Alenu prayer.
62. Shabbat 75a.
63. Isaiah V:12.
64. III:54.
65. Baba B. 10a.
66. *Ibid.*, 9a.
67. *Ibid.*
68. Deb. XV and XVI.
69. See Note 56.
70. Baba B. 9-10a.
71. Isaiah XXXII:17.
72. *Ibid.*, LIX:17.
73. Baba B. I:c.
74. Ps. XVII:15.
75. Amos V:24.
76. Jer. XXII:15, 16.

Chapter 24

HOME BACKGROUND FOR SEX INSTRUCTION

REV. GORDON LESTER

Explaining sex to a child is always a delicate matter, simply because sex itself is a delicate matter. It is one of the areas of human life which enters deep into the heart of the human person. Almost instinctively we know that when we are treating sex we are treating something fragile. Sex can be beautiful and delicate and precious when it is kept whole and intact as part of the personality. It can be shattered into fragments of lust and selfishness, of brutality and coarseness, of fear and frigidity, when it is thoughtlessly or foolhardily mishandled.

Sex is like a sweet and lovely girl. A girl has within her the rich capacity to love, to give herself. She has within her the haunting need to be loved, to mean more than life to someone who will understand and care for her. Deep in the heart of every woman is the desire to find someone to whom she can give herself. Without the thought ever forming into words, without the desire ever quite getting into the picture, a girl knows that her body is the gift by which she can give herself as a person, the offering by which she can belong to a man.

Sex is one of the most important areas in which she can find her value as a human being, the key by which she can fulfill her life — giving herself and producing life, delivering herself under the caressing hand of a man and into the hands of God the Creator working within her. This is the picture of the meaning of sex as expressed in the soul of a woman. One of the causes of our society being so out of gear today is that both men and women have been led to look upon sex from the male standpoint exclusively.

If a woman makes the mistake of giving her love to a man who is selfish or coarse or brutal, a man who will take her body and never meet her person, this sacred and fragile gift of sex can be shattered forever; or it can be ruined by faulty education which freezes and locks up this treasure forever; or scarring experiences of being victimized in youth can cause it to be brutalized and held in contempt as no more than something the lustful and the lecherous want to rob from her and then throw away with contempt.

A girl can be glorified or crushed by what happens to her in the area of sex. This is why it is so important to teach a girl and to teach a boy what sex was meant to be in the design of God. The girl must know the treasure she possesses and its capacity for happiness or sorrow. The boy must know the treasure entrusted into his hands for him to bring to fulfillment, giving life and maturity to the human being who depends upon him in the design of God.

Parents have the responsibility of opening the eyes of their children to the mystery and the beauty of sex and of guiding this power in its development to the full, flaming force of expressing love and of creating and caring for human life.

That, if you want, is the poetry, the truth. The problem is to see the poetry in the practicalities of life, to discover the truth in the acts and situations of daily life.

The most important part of teaching is the attitude of the teacher. Teaching is not some kind of commercialized passing along of information. Teaching, really, is the opening up of one's mind and heart. It is pouring out of oneself all that one knows, all that one is. It is letting truth come through oneself, no doubt colored, no doubt shaded by one's own reflection, but that is the best any of us can do, being somewhat less than God, only an image of the truth and not Truth Itself. Truth is the avenue to the mind of God; the teacher is the guide along the way.

You do not teach your children so much by sitting them down and making them listen to a man-to-man or woman-to-woman lecture, necessary as this may be from time to time. You teach them much more by how you live your life in your home and with your relatives and friends. Most of all you teach them by what you are as persons. Children, especially your own children, are not impressed by a line. They go right to the heart of a person, and, first of all, to their parents.

The awareness of this fact can be frightening to any sensible person. Parents, however, should have complete confidence that they are the best-qualified people in all the world to be the teachers of their children about human life — simply because they have been chosen by God to produce images of themselves in His image and likeness — simply because they have been chosen by God to teach their children about Him and about His way of life. Parents have one chief responsibility — to teach their children to be what God wants them to be. Anything else is secondary to that.

Regarding sex, parents, as teachers, must see it according to the reality it has been given in the plan of God. They must be the guides on the avenue of truth to His mind. Sex is meaningless except as an expression of love between a man and a woman, in the sight of God, with a willingness, at least, to accept a life He may create while they give themselves to each other. Love is a human power by which two persons give and unite themselves to each without losing their own identity as individuals. Love is a union of persons, not just of two bodies, not just of passions, but of two complete persons.

Love is not a way of dominating or absorbing another person. Love creates a third reality — a two in one flesh. It does not destroy or lessen a person. Sex, then, is the human power by which two persons express their total love to each other in a personal, intimate, unselfish, passionate and tangible way. As a person is made of body and spirit, so sex is an expression of the person in love, in body and spirit.

It is by the parent's attitude of mind that they create an atmosphere in their home. The atmosphere is the second great factor in forming the mind and character of their children. All the words in the world cannot flood over the impression made by the atmosphere. If the atmosphere is not in harmony with the words, the words will stand out like lies to the simple, direct minds of children. (This, I think, is what is most responsible for the rebellion of youth against authority and morality today. They detect the lie of the words in contrast to the atmosphere adults have created.) It is what you are as persons, the way you express yourselves in the way you live, that establishes the atmosphere of the home.

There will be disagreements between mother and father, simply because they are two distinct persons, each with a mind, each with feelings. The children, like any normal human beings, can survive that. But an atmosphere of constant bickering and disrespect between mother and father is going to make words about love sound phony.

There will be misunderstandings and hurt feelings in any family. This is no more than a normal suffering of life that must be undergone in any situation of life. But an atmosphere of distrust and suspicion cannot exist with love.

There will be hard decisions and insistence on authority in any home. We all have to live with the realities of life. But an atmosphere of hate and cruelty can only crush the person or arouse the anxiety to escape.

In any life and in any love there is going to be some selfishness. Even a child can recognize the basic goodness of a person lying under surface faults. But the atmosphere of selfishness where the other persons are twisted to fit one's own whim or advantage, or where the other persons are ignored, never given any personal sign of attention or appreciation, completely destroys any chance of a home pervaded with love.

Creating the right atmosphere in the home involves three things: first, a deep respect, almost a worship, if you will, of the human persons who make up the family; second, the signs of affection which are the natural and universal language of love on every level; third, the family familiarity which puts into healthy focus the physical and human facts of life.

The human person is the greatest of all creations. Honoring the person is honoring God, who designed and brought into being the person as the peak of His creation. In our materialistic world, there is a continually lurking danger of letting concern for money and the things money can buy outrank the persons of the family in one's talk, in one's desires and in one's attention.

Signs of affection include not just lovemaking, which is intimate and secret, but all the little public signs of attention and thoughtfulness and decency and politeness and charity in the personal relationships of the family. These are just signs of the esteem in which the person is held. The signs express and stimulate this esteem.

The family familiarity should show the normal, take-it-for-granted attitude of living between men and women, boys and girls. It means modesty without fear, common sense without exhibitionism, privacy without panic. This balances out knowledge without letting it become morbid curiosity, a sense of controlling one's senses without thinking that every sight and sound and touch is a matter for confession.

Defects in a home are likely to cause defects in a person. Defects in a person will cause defects in love. Defects in love will cause defects in sex. This is merely being realistic, not sounding an alarm. We all have some defects. Most of them can be handled. I mention it here just because the above is more or less the ideal to be striven for. But above all else, perhaps, is the need to teach children to adjust to the realities of life — to know the ideal and to want it, but not to expect it or to be crushed because it is not always present or within reach.

Parents should not be content with giving their children biological or physiological information. Such information is, of course, a necessary step. But the final goal and the ideal are not physiological facts. Rather the goal and the ideal should be an appreciation of the psychological "facts of life." That is what we mean by chastity, the virtue which keeps sex in its place as an expression of genuine love.

The concentration of parents should rather be on forming a solid person. No sex instruction will ever be complete unless children are taught to be people with a sense of unselfishness and a sense of responsibility. How else can a person express love through sex in a way that lives up to what God had in mind when He created it? It takes unselfishness to love at all. It takes a sense of responsibility to realize that sexual expressions of love can never cut God out entirely and by design. God's providence, it must be remembered, desires to work through human love to create new life.

God is always willing to step in with His supernatural help in the matter of making children capable of genuine love and genuine sex, despite the defects in the home which may seem on the surface to be the dominant influence. With daily prayer, frequent confession and Communion, one can keep in constant contact with Him. Parents should be praying most of all to know His will, how to handle the problems of life, what decisions to make, how to bear up under the burdens, to know all that He wants of them as persons and to have the courage to accept and follow His will. He knows they do not have the wisdom or the strength to do the job perfectly themselves. So He knows they need help and He wants to give it. That is why He has made contact with the divine power so available. Prayer and the frequent reception of the sacraments continually reestablish and maintain contact with the divine source of light and strength in the fulfillment of the tremendously important vocation of parenthood.

Beyond that it is simply a matter of putting reality into words. It is a matter of facing problems with equilibrium, trying to create the needed balance. No one can draw the blueprint for this; no one can prefabricate the words. One can only strive for the needed good sense and good judgment under the grace of God.

Chapter 25

MARITAL AND PREMARITAL COUNSELING WITH INTERRACIAL COUPLES

HUGO G. BEIGEL

To AVOID MISUNDERSTANDINGS, let me emphasize that a study like this inevitably treats with problems; people who are not bothered by problems do not consult a marriage counselor. The ideas developed here, therefore, must not be interpreted as a judgment on interracial relations altogether.

To some extent, however, the problems of people who select their partners from a race lower or higher in social prestige than their own are different from those of couples who are similar in race because factors related to race have caused frictions, or because at least one of the parties attributes certain marital or premarital difficulties to the racial and cultural dissimilarity.

Interracial marriages in this country amount to less than 1 per cent of all marriages, according to estimates based on local statistics (2). Our knowledge in this field is scanty; duration is completely unexplored, and couples whose marriages were unsuccessful usually do not give interviews (3). I have endeavored to obtain as much data as possible from couples of this kind, among this data such that refers to their selection motives, partly because this knowledge appeared to be of possible value for the solution of the immediate problem, partly because, in premarital counseling, it may reflect on the advisability of a marriage.

The materials at my disposal are the cases of seventeen couples. Seven of them were married to each other; ten were unmarried, and, of the latter, two were married to third persons whom allegedly they intended to divorce.

As will be pointed out in greater detail later, seven of the counselees were in doubt as to whether to continue the relationship on its present basis; three were worried because the partner appeared to seek its termination; two couples sought advice regarding the advisability of marriage; and five were in consultation regarding other problems that had evolved in the relationship.

Let us briefly point to the counselor's situation. It is — considering the currents and countercurrents whirling around interraacial marriages — more precarious than the usual one in which racially homogenous couples present their hopes and fears for evaluation. Even in those states in which the law does not interfere with such unions, the sentiments of a large portion of the population oppose them (5, 7). This portion includes not only the

majority of the high-prestige group, but also a large section of the discrimi-
nated-against minority group (4). Indeed, many people who in principle
tolerate such bonds object to one that involves their own families.

Such reactions do not necessarily stem from prejudice. All serious writers
on the subject mention the social and economic disadvantages to which the
low-prestige groups are subject (1, 6) and which naturally affect the situation of the spouse. Others mention discrepancies in mores and background
(8, 10).

Obviously, in dealing with couples intending to marry, the counselor
cannot neglect the question regarding awareness of these facts. In doing so,
however, he lays himself open to the suspicion that he wants to dissuade one
of the partners. Two cases will show the subjectivity of the reproaches.

Case 1

During his stay in Germany, a Negro sergeant in the American occupation forces had married a German girl. After four years of marriage she
wanted a divorce. Her husband persuaded her to see a counselor before she
took the final step. The woman, Gertrud, was not in an easy position. Her
husband was, as she admitted, a kind, quiet and considerate man, but she
said she simply could not stand this kind of life any longer. Being a for-
eigner, she had neither relatives nor friends to whom she could talk in
his absence. If they went some place — which they rarely did — they went
to places where only Negroes congregated or to his relatives. These relatives apparently disliked her, and she herself felt that she had nothing
in common with them. Gertrud admittedly had married to be relieved
of the postwar misery, but now she longed to go back to a "normal relationship."

When, after so many cons, the woman was reminded of some of the
pros, she became angry and accused the counselor of favoring mongreliza-
tion of the race. Her boss, a white man, had promised to marry her, and
she was not going to waste her life in the miserable union with a colored
man.

As in this case I was accused of being biased for miscegenation, in a
second one I was accused of being prejudiced against Negroes.

Case 2

Calvin, a Negro musician, lived with a white girl. For three years he
had returned to his home in the suburbs only for short daytime visits. At
the time of our first contact, Evelyn, the girlfriend, rebelled against the
perpetuation of this setup. She was no longer content with Calvin's assurance that he loathed his wife and that for years he had not had intimacies with Felicia. He had promised a long time ago to divorce Felicia
and to marry Evelyn. From time to time Evelyn rebelled. She was tired
of the delay and the changing excuses for it. One such occasion caused

Calvin to request an appointment with me. He was a handsome, well-spoken man, about 30 years old. Evelyn had just left him. What should he do to get her back?

Evelyn actually returned, induced by a repetition of his promise. Yet Calvin knew that this did not solve the problem. Thus we had several sessions in which he — in a mixture of truth and fiction — unrolled an unending account of complaints and complications. He was determined to marry Evelyn; he loved her; he could not live without her; he had out-grown his uneducated wife; he shuddered at her touch; he never went near her; he never spoke to her; he had asked her for a divorce, but she wouldn't give him one. Liars had told Evelyn that he had been seen with his wife at a Negro affair; could I calm her down? His wife had found snapshots of him and Evelyn, and she threatened with divorce. Could I dissuade her? He did not want a divorce because that would mean separation from his children, a son and a daughter; separation from them would kill him. Then, one day, he came to inquire whether I knew an abortionist, for his wife was pregnant. First he insisted that he could not be the father, later he admitted the possibility — no more than that, of course.

Calvin's nerves and his work suffered under the impact of these constant excitements. When I suggested for him to give up his double life, he be-came furious and told me that I was prejudiced against Negroes. For this reason, I was trying to separate him from the white girl.

Unfortunately, the counselor cannot avoid the suspicion of bias by keeping aloof of the race issue. The argument that all the problems, doubts and complications result merely from a temporary attitude of society is a moot one; nobody knows when a total change toward tolerance will occur, and in the meantime a not-too-sturdy relationship may break to pieces. More important still, the heavy waves of racial enmity in the past has left sediments in the personalities involved, sediments and sentiments that affect both selection and treatment of the partner in an interracial relationship.

Gertrud, the German girl (Case 1) is not likely to arouse sympathies on either side. Nonetheless, her plight was a serious one. It was not merely the difference in individualities that made her unacceptable to her husband's relatives or let their talk and thinking appear alien to her and their inter-acting repulsively coarse and undisciplined. It is possible that a white girl of a similar class background may not have minded the narrowness of their concerns, but the impossibility to balance this drought of cultural interest by establishing contact with people of a similar background is definitely inherent in the social segregation of the two races.

In a discussion of this problem, a Negro student characterized Gertrud's behavior as "white arrogance." This judgment lacks insight into human emotions and needs.

Case 3

Gertrud's problem is no more trivial than that of the Negro, Jerry, who planned to marry Hortense, a white girl. He was a city employee; she had only recently moved to New York and worked as a typist-secretary. In spite of his original proposal, Jerry suddenly appeared to be reluctant to legitimize the bond. He explained that he wanted children, but was not sure that a white mother would treat them right if they turned out to be dark skinned. The girl indignantly replied that Jerry was merely looking for a pretext to break up a relationship of which he had tired.

In an interview from which Hortense was absent, Jerry granted that he had no evidence for distrust. It had occurred to him as a hazard, but more than by this prospect he was worried by another: How would either white or dark children react to him? Would not white children look down on him, an almost-white one would hate him for the stain he had burdened him with? Would not a black child turn against him because he had sold out the race?

The counselor can counter such apprehensions by citing families who are occasionally shown on television or quoted in magazines and newspapers, but can he really mitigate them? Or should he, knowing that these worries are not completely unwarranted? Or knowing that with some couples the race issue remains so sensitive a spot that they blame on it whatever goes wrong in the family life.

Case 5

Joe, a Negro, and Vera, his white wife, were worried about their 16-year old son. He was grouchy, hostile, shy and withdrawn. They made his negroid appearance responsible for his behavior. Their guess may have been correct; but then it may have been wrong, for the observed symptoms did not differ from the not-unusual phenomena of adolescent troubles and adolescent rebellion. Yet, despite their otherwise well-functioning marriage, the parents blamed themselves.

In premarital counseling, in particular, the counselor therefore is faced with the almost unmanageable task of judging from the personalities and motives the couple's capacity to cope with such perplexities.

Concern about appearance or the reaction of children entered in three cases altogether (Cases 3, 5 and 6), not counting Calvin (Case 2). The couple in Case 6 were Melvin and Patricia. Patricia was a Chinese-American. Melvin came to ask for information on an "absolutely guaranteed safe" form of birth control. For, he said, thinking that his future children might have Asiatic features like the baby of Patricia's sister made him nauseous. We shall hear more about this man later.

In six instances it became known that the parents of one of the young people objected to the contemplated marriage on racial grounds. Only in three instances, however, did this resistance attain some measure of significance for the young couple.

Case 4

In one of the latter, Beula, a white college student, 19 years old, wanted to hear an outside opinion. She had participated in freedom rides and civil-rights demonstrations. During the exciting months in Mississippi she fell in love with a Negro who was three years older than she. On her return home she declared that they had agreed to marry. The parents — people who favored the ideas of desegregation, integration and equality — impressed upon their daughter the drawbacks of such a marriage, especially to a man like her lover, who had neither schooling, trained skills nor, apparently, aspirations toward either studying or working. Beula in return prophesied the young man a splendid career as a politician, but she let herself be persuaded to seek professional advice. Although she ridiculed her parents' timidity, her enthusiasm was somewhat dampened, so that she did give her sentiments for her parents some weight before she made a final decision.

Case 17

The second instance concerned the marriage of an American-Japanese, Helen, to Sidney, an electrician. She was 17 years old and pregnant. Sidney was ready to marry her. Her parents, however, advised an abortion. They were against the marriage because of what he had done to their girl and because he was a Jew. Helen looked for guidance as to whose advice she should follow.

Case 15

Benjamin's dilemma was his mother's objection to his plan to marry Anna, a Puerto Rican, two years Benjamin's senior. He was close to 40. Benjamin was completely dominated by his mother, and Anna wanted to put an end to his vacillation.

In the other three cases the parents' opposition had already been discounted by the candidates. Gertrud (Case 1) had gone ahead despite her parents' misgivings.

Case 6

Melvin's situation was more complicated. His father was an outspoken white supremacist. But Melvin, who felt rejected by his father, tried to get back at him. He married into the "inferior races" in defiance of his father's ideas, thus proving himself superior to the "old reactionary."

At the same time, however, this step signified self-humiliation and acceptance of his father's opinion of him: He was no good and could assert his
need for superiority only on a member of the "lower races." By the time
Melvin came for a consultation, the marriage had lasted two years. Apprehension with regard to future offspring was not his only worry. He feared,
for instance, that his marriage to an Oriental would interfere with his
career. He had scorned society — that is, his family's social set; would he
ever be reaccepted in good circles?

Case 7

As the last illustration in this group, Lester and Marietta should be
mentioned. Marietta was a dark-skinned, very pretty Puerto Rican. She
was married. Though she was a Catholic, she was determined to divorce
her husband. He drank excessively, failed to provide for her and her
1-year-old child, and mistreated her. She had moved back with her mother.
She maintained an extramarital relationship with a medical student,
Lester. Lester and she planned marriage. Marietta's parents disapproved,
partly for religious reasons, partly because Lester was Jewish.

In many instances, the people who choose a racially different mate or
lover claim ideological reasons or an irresistible attraction. In view of the
popular expectations implied in such motives, it may be amazing that in
ten out of our seventeen cases one of the parties considered or appeared to
consider the renunciation of the mutual commitment. In four instances,
these people were married; in six they had contemplated and promised
marriage. Three of them were white females; three of the seven males were
Negroes, and four were white. Among the three white females were Gertrud (Case 1) and Lora (Case 8). Whether Beula (Case 4) should be included is not quite certain, since she came upon her mother's urging.
However, she did so against the explicit objection of her lover, and the
impression she gave suggested that the familial conflict only strengthened
doubts about this affair which had already been in her mind. Even while
she took the side of her boyfriend, she seriously criticized his scheming and
some of his attitudes. She resented his making fun of her "boss-class fancies"
such as literature, art, music, higher learning and the like. But to forsake
him appeared to her as a betrayal of the cause.

Case 8

The third white female was Lora. She said that she would have left
Alan a hundred times if she did not love him so much. But she was not
sure that she could stand his jealousy and abuse much longer. Whenever
she used makeup, he suspected her of preening herself for another man.
He examined her dresses and underwear for traces that might indicate
sex relations, and one day he made a big scene because there was, by his

estimate, less contraceptive jelly in the jar than there should have been. She must have been with a man, he concluded. He was sure that her secret lovers were white men, and that she had white men on her mind when she did not respond to him ardently. He never took her out because white men would make remarks when they saw him with a white girl or spit at him and then he would "have to kill one." Lora wanted to marry Alan, but she faltered when she thought of giving up the few friends she had. Yet she would have to; Alan considered them "prejudiced," and had told her not to invite them to their home.

Among the white males, two were married.

Case 6

One was Melvin whose ambivalence regarding racial matters we discussed above. Patricia was an intelligent, lively woman. Her face was in no way striking, but Melvin called it ugly. He developed a resistance to kissing her. He disliked her body. It was too "thin" for his taste. He wanted her to develop bigger breasts, and forced her to eat fattening food until she vomited. He said she was dirty, but corrected himself: It was just that all colored people appeared dirty to him.

Case 11

The second white man, Donald, was married to Terry, who was partly Indian. At age 35 he was drawn into an extramarital affair, about which he felt terribly guilty. However, he was unable to discontinue it, because, he said, he needed to sleep with a white woman again. Donald played with the idea of a divorce and argued that his wife's racial heritage affected her entire style of living and made it impossible for her to understand his ideas and intellectual interests.

The two unmarried men were Bob and Ned.

Case 9

Bob came to New York to be an actor. Destitute and drunk, he was picked up a few years later by June, a Negro girl. She supported him. He attempted suicide, and she paid for his therapy. Recovered, at the age of 26 he started working and proved to be a rather efficient salesman. But now that he made money, he tried to break free from June. He couldn't get anywhere, he rationalized, with a Negro wife, and he would lose his job if he lived with a mistress.

Case 12

Beth, a rather attractive Negro singer had two problems: She couldn't hold a man and she was unable to enjoy sexual relations with anyone. All the men with whom she had had affairs, except the very first one, were white. They all had discarded her rather quickly. With Ned, a white government worker, she had engaged in intimate relations for several months. She had discussed marriage with him, but all of a sudden he had withdrawn, giving as a reason that she was cold, unaffectionate and hence a continuous frustration for him.

Among the Negroes one was married and two were single.

Case 10

Dan and Sue were a very handsome couple, but would have been as incompatible if both had been white or both Negro. The girl was lazy, unwilling to work either in their home or in a job, disorganized and un-educated, whereas he was proud of his college education and was stiffly dignified; he affected British manners and mannerisms. Sue was whimsical with regard to their sex relations. To cure her, Dan proposed a three-month separation. During that time she was to support herself. If, after the probation period, she had improved, he would take her back; if not, he would have the separation legalized.

The two Negro men who were torn between the wish to keep up the relationship with their white girls and to evade a commitment have been mentioned before. They were Calvin (Case 2) and Jerry (Case 3). Calvin, in addition to the sentimental reason that he presented — his children — also had material reasons not to push for a divorce. A divorce would impoverish him. To Evelyn, he outlined plots on how to catch Felicia in a compromising situation. To the counselor he conceded that the idea of a second marriage frightened him. What if Evelyn, too, would divorce him? He wouldn't have enough money to eat. His fear was not unfounded, for Calvin led a rather promiscuous life. His wife, apparently, had long ago given up to check on his whereabouts. But Evelyn was "demanding"; she expected to be at his side wherever he went.

The relative frequency of rejection in the interracial sample challenges us to examine the applicability of a theory by which some writers have tried to explain the discrimination against Negroes in the United States (4, 5, 6, 9). According to this theory, white men fear and hate Negroes because they envy them their virility and dread their competition. By repetition and elaboration this concept has grown into a myth: The Negro male — all Negroes without exception, apparently — is sexually superior to the white male and immensely attractive to white women. Hernton (4), for instance, holds that all white women are constantly "fighting the feeling of attraction" for Negroes, for, in their minds, "the Negro is a superior sexual animal," whom she "desires to touch her, indeed to rape her."

Our sample confirms neither the overwhelming sexual attraction nor the insuperable captivating power of this mythical virility.

The seven Negroes in our sample were all physically normal persons, some more, some less attractive than others. But there was only one instance in which sexual attraction was a decisive factor in selection, and possibly the reason for the continuation of the otherwise not-harmonious relationship (Case 2). Even in this instance neurotic forces became evident that probably accounted for much of this gravitation. In addition, Calvin and Evelyn often went for weeks without sex relations. The girl insisted that she did not miss this type of affection; she resented only the probability of Calvin seeking satisfaction elsewhere.

Gertrud (Case 1) found her white lover more exciting than her husband. Jerry and Hortense (Case 3) seemed to avoid copulation toward the end of a relationship that had lasted several months. This may, however, have happened on Jerry's initiative rather than on hers. Sex relations in Case 5 were normal and moderate, as could be expected after seventeen years of marriage. Between Alan and Lora (Case 8) sex relations apparently were satisfactory and as frequent as their quarrels permitted. Both, however, agreed that the man always had been the initiator to intimacies, and the girl had occasionally refused them. Dan (Case 10) was restrained, according to Sue. But she apparently was equally controlled, since she used her offers and her denials of sex — unsuccessfully — to gain advantages or to punish him. She had indeed been attracted by him, she related, not by his sexual aura, but by his dignity, his impressive mind and his attention for her. As regards Beula (Case 4), she had been introduced to sex by her boyfriend. She held his impatience against him. She tolerated sex with him just as she would probably have tolerated it with any other man. To withhold it, she felt and had been told by the man, would have indicated a residue of race prejudice.

What, then, were the actual motives that caused these people to enter into generally disapproved relations?

In several of our cases, material motives stand clearly in the foreground. The members of the prestige-group were in circumstances in which their need for material security was unlikely to be satisfied by someone of their own kind. Gertrud (Case 1) is typical of a type that comes close to prostitution. In distinction to her, Vera never forgot what she owed the man who was the first to take an interest in her when she, an immigrant with neither parents nor command of the language, lived on charity and poorly paid temporary jobs. Except for minor complications, the marriage worked out all right, but Vera did not deceive herself about her original motive: She liked Joe, she respected him, but she had never been ardently in love with him.

Bob's relation to June was purely exploitative on his part.

A strong tendency in this direction also marked Sue's attachment to

Dan (Case 10). There was one important difference, however. She was not fighting for a living, but for a life of comfort without work. Coming from a poor environment, she dreamed of a man to provide her with luxuries. Several contributed their small share, but none would marry her. When she met Dan, she felt that he was more likely than a man of her race to worship her and "treat her like a princess" (his phrase).

The limitation of a free choice proved to be instrumental also in another form. Some of the people in our sample seemed to have attached themselves to partners of the low-prestige group because these were expected to be less critical and demanding in their requirements than members of the opposite sex belonging to the high-prestige group were assumed to be. This reasoning goes for both sexes. It influenced the selection made by men in the Cases 7, 13 and 16.

Case 7

Lester was conspicuously short, of Jewish extraction and suffered from premature ejaculation. He had at one time contemplated suicide because of this defect.

Case 13

George, divorced on the grounds of sexual incompatibility, was not impotent with his Japanese ladyfriend as he had been with his wife and other white women. His very race-consciousness apparently was helpful in this respect. He had found himself for the first time functioning normally in the arms of a Japanese prostitute in Tokyo. This memory had consciously influenced his choice.

Case 16

Jack had been unhappy for many years because of his short stature and his underdeveloped genitals. Consuela, his Mexican wife, had taught him the pleasures of sex. She said she didn't mind. And this was true to some extent, for the reason for Jack's consultation was the discovery of his wife's adultery.

Case 15

Benjamin was blind on one eye, stuttered and was rather ugly even by the most tolerant standards. In addition, he had difficulties attaching himself to a female. The separation from his mother seemed easier under the guidance of a Puerto Rican, who in addition was a nurse, full-bosomed and older than he.

Case 6

Melvin's selection of a non-Caucasian mate was in the first place motivated by his feeling of unworthiness. He compensated his intense feelings of inferiority by overemphasizing his superiority. "I probably married her because it is easier to treat a colored woman as a slave than a white one," he said.

Two of the white girls labored under similar psychological handicaps. Both had had incest experiences — actual or imaginary — with their fathers, and both had incest wishes even as adults and felt consciously guilty about them.

Case 8

Lora, in addition had been sexually misused by an older brother and felt desecrated. She desired marriage and children as a veneer of reputableness and normality, but was sure deep inside herself that no man would marry her. She therefore endured patiently the sadistic moods with which Alan tortured her.

Case 14

Rachel — white, Jewish, 27 years old — was a psychotic borderline case. Her problem was whether to marry or not to marry a white man of low social and economic status. Since she embraced radical left-wing ideas, his status would have suited her, but as she fancied herself a high-caliber intellectual she was apalled by the man's disinterest in political ideology. Furthermore, she could not leave her father, who was old and sick. With the mother in a mental hospital, the father had taken care of her upbringing, her education and her physical needs. The girl alleged that on her twenty-first birthday he had offered to deflower her. She had refused. Gradually she regretted having thus offended her father; but by the time she got around to the idea that she might "give him some fun" by playing with him, he had, so Rachael explained, lost the power of and the interest in sexual activities. She took lovers. All of them were non-Caucasian. She wanted to let them know that not everybody despised them.

Rachel herself was handicapped by her physical appearance, a conspicuous clumsiness and slowness of all her movements, an odd manner of dressing and strange gestures. She empathized with "these beautiful vilified people," since she too was stared at and made fun of on the street and had been eased out of every political group which she had joined.

These experiences suggest that in many instances members of the high-prestige group attach themselves in intimate relations to members of a low-prestige group in an attempt to satisfy a material or a psychological need if they have little or no hope of satisfying it with a high-prestige group member. Not all the shortcomings are immediately noticeable, of course; where they are, however, it must be assumed that the low-prestige partner either does not mind the particular defect or that there are compensations in such relationships that cause him (or her) to make concessions, or that appear to complement a need of his (or her) own.

Some of these compensations would be the same as in homogenous marriages: conspicuous beauty; status prestige; or relative material affluence. In interracial relations status prestige is represented through belonging to the culturally leading race and serves the elevation of self-value. The need for confirmation of their own worth tends in the indicated direction in persons who see their own value threatened by the alleged deficiencies of their group. Calvin (Case 2) is an example of this. Economically, he had never suffered from his racial status. He made good money and had adjusted his life to white upper-middle class standards. He lived on the fringe of a suburban Negro community. This he resented. He belabored the cultural standards of his neighbors, the dirty children, the noisiness and practically every bad quality that the stereotype accuses the low-class Negro of. This judgment included his wife and her parents. He boasted of his many affairs with white women, even though some of these were prostitutes. He did not acknowledge Jews as "real whites." He resented his mother's marriage to his father, because she "could almost have passed as white." Dark skinned though he was, he occasionally hinted that he might be the product of his mother's adulterous relations with a white man.

Dan (Case 10) differed — as regards character — enormously from Calvin, but his basic motive for marrying a white woman resembled Calvin's closely. He, too, acknowledged the white stereotype of Negro qualities, suppressed in himself rigidly anything that might remind of them, and completely rejected his race. He crowned his "otherness" by his marriage.

Beth (Case 12) was his female counterpart. She did not mind being a Negro, she said, but she endeavored to be one to whom neither the stereotype nor the realities of the dark ghetto applied. She was a perfectionist with regard to punctuality, cleanliness and honesty. She impaired her sexual functioning by the rigid suppression of tempting feelings. Occurrences in her own family — father deserting the mother and sister having an illegitimate child — caused her to break with her family. She loathed Negro men because of their violence, their unreliability and their loafing. She left her church because the "ministers were adulterers" and became a convert to Catholicism. It attracted her for two reasons. For one, the priests were celibates, and secondly, she was the only Negro in a white parish.

Despite her frigid aversion to sex and her fear of childbirth and children, Beth had sex relations — but only with Caucasians. She disliked Jews, because they were sensual. She did not enjoy her sex relations, but she opined that she had to "do that" to catch one for marriage.

It may be amazing that Dan (Case 10) selected a wife whom he characterized as a slut. But she was not only white and goodlooking; she also gave him an extra chance to assert his superiority — doubly indeed, since she was a white woman, whom he controlled, scolded, punished, corrected and tried to educate.

In Alan (Case 8) this need for asserting his self-value was combined with sadistic trends. He took revenge on the white race, whom he feared beyond the limits of rationality, by making one of their kind his slave. He tortured her with his accusations and whims; he tore her dresses to pieces if they appeared too sexy to him; he had her wait on him and for him. He explicitly said that if it were manageable he would keep her in a cage.

In all three cases, the women submitted out of their masochistic needs. Lora's and Sue's histories have been alluded to (Cases 8 and 10). Evelyn (Case 2) had witnessed brutal scenes in her mother's and her sisters' marriages. She feared men and marriage. Wanting to be different from the people in her environment, she ran away from home, took and lost lowly jobs, was almost raped by a fellow worker, became pregnant by a man whom she did not like, but with whom she went because she was starved for company. She had met Calvin before that. After a self-induced abortion she separated from her unloved lover and called up the Negro whom she first had rejected. He seemed to be more qualified for leaning on than the men she had known before, his faults notwithstanding.

If personality disorganization forced these white women to seek balance in a disapproved form of personal relationship, it helped Patricia, Melvin's slave-wife (Case 6) to endure her husband's sadistic strivings for self-assertion. She picked up everything that would make her appear as a true American. She disliked everything foreign, including her descent. The severest disappointment for her was not that Melvin ridiculed her Asiatic characteristics, but that his father refused to receive her in his home.

The seventeen cases discussed here naturally neither exhaust the varieties of problems typical of interracial marital and premarital relations, nor do they represent all the motives leading to such marriages. Even in these cases, some of the people involved became known to the counselor only through their partners' descriptions. These were the males in Cases 1, 4, 12 and 14, and the females in Cases 3 and 13. Among those whom I got to know, a relatively high number were emotionally insecure, unstable or worse. This applies to both partners in Cases 2, 6, 7, 8, 10 and 16. Only the white males can be so characterized in the Cases 11, 13 and 15; only the white female in Case 14. Among the nonwhite females, Beth (Case 12) must be so classified, and possibly Helen, the Japanese-American girl who became pregnant at the age of seventeen.

In both groups, the one ranking high and the other ranking low in prestige, rejection of and rejection by one's group of origin have been found as motivating or as contributing factors in thirteen instances. A related

motive may be operative if other studies point to the relatively high percentage of white people of Jewish religion who seek intimate interracial
relations (7). Since in our sample only five people (2 males, 3 females) were
Jewish, it neither confirms nor denies such a hypothesis. The most conspicuous factor about this sample in comparison to counseling cases unaffected
by the race issue is the relatively great number of premarital cases. Obviously, this added element tends to raise doubts more frequently, and, from the
view of the low-prestige partner, makes the mate more precious. Since an
unusually great portion seem to use the interracial attachment as an outlet
for the personality complexes, the question arises whether the motivating
forces will undermine or strengthen the subsequent marriage.

REFERENCES

1. ALLPORT, GORDON W.: *The Nature of Prejudice.* Garden City, Doubleday-
    Anchor Books, 1958.
2. GOLDEN, JOSEPH: Characteristics of the Negro-White intermarried in Phila-
    delphia. *Am. Soc. Rev., 18:2,* 1953.
3. GOLDEN, JOSEPH: Patterns of Negro-White intermarriage. *Am. Soc. Rev., 19:*
    2, 1954.
4. HERNTON, CALVIN: Sex and Racism in America. Garden City, Doubleday,
    1965.
5. LEWIS, ANTHONY: Race, sex and the Supreme Court. *New York Time
    Magazine, Nov. 22, 1964.*
6. MYRDAL, GUNNAR: *An American Dilemma.* New York, Harper, 1944.
7. *N. Y. Times*: "Negro-White marriages." Oct. 18, 1963, page 1.
8. REISS, IRA L.: Premarital sexual permissiveness among Negroes and Whites.
    Am. Soc. Rev., 29:5, 1964.
9. SMITH, LILLIAN: *Killers of the Dream.* Garden City, Doubleday-Anchor Books,
    1963.
10. WESTIE, FRANK R.: Negro-White status differentials and social distance.
    Am. Soc. Rev., 17:5, 1952.

Chapter 26

MORAL ISSUES IN MARITAL COUNSELING

ROBERT A. HARPER

Moral issues in marital counseling are usually most effectively dealt with by transforming them into nonmoral issues. Does this mean, then, that the marital counselor contributes to the undermining of morals in marriage? No; it means only that we must spend some time at the outset of this chapter in defining the terms we shall use in trying to understand moral issues in marital counseling.

Morality is that quality of behavior that makes it right or wrong. *Morals* is a term which refers to the alleged rightness or wrongness of specific standards or of concrete behavior. When we label certain behavior of an individual or group as *moral,* we are judging it to be in accord with a code of conduct with which the individual or the group is identified.

One of the difficulties in contemporary American society, composed of persons from widely varying cultural backgrounds, is that morality is a very complicated matter. It is difficult or impossible for the marital counselor who serves a heterogeneous group of clients to be a *moralist* — that is, a student and teacher of morals, one who moralizes. So to function he would have to be an expert on the widely varying moral codes of the persons who consult him. Moralists usually must confine themselves to their own particular constituency: The rabbi of an Orthodox temple may be in a sound position to give moral advice to Orthodox Jews, but his moral counsel may not be well received by Reformed or Conservative Jews, let alone gentiles; the minister of Missouri Synod Lutherans does not pass muster as a moralist for even other brands of Lutherans; and so on. Obviously, a marriage counselor cannot wear all sorts of moralistic cloaks for persons of various religions, nationalities, social classes and other groups of varying moralities.

Even if it were possible, however, for a marriage counselor to be the expert defender of all the multitudinous varieties of moral codes, it would not be desirable. For the greatest effectiveness of help in marital counseling, we would contend, the atmosphere is not desirably moral, immoral, unmoral or amoral, but *nonmoral.* Let's look at the important distinctions in these terms.

We have already discussed *moral* marriage counseling. *Immoral* marital counseling would carry the meaning of recommending that individuals violate whatever moral codes to which they subscribe. This is obviously as difficult (and more undesirable) for the marital counselor as trying to be a positive moralist.

Unmoral marital counseling would be the kind provided by a person who lacks understanding of morality. The fact that the marital counselor can function most effectively by not being a moralist does not mean he lacks understanding of the nature and importance of morality in human behavior, nor that he lacks sympathetic understanding of moral conflicts of his clients.

Amoral marriage counseling would be the sort in which the counselor would advocate or function in accordance with a doctrine that exalts the right of persons to disregard moral codes of all kinds. This would be the Nietzschean superman type of counseling, a type which, so far as we know, has never been advocated by any sane professional person.

Nonmoral marital counseling, however, simply contends that the criteria of right and wrong are not appropriately or helpfully applied to the problems presented in the counseling setting. A request the writer has heard many hundreds of times from couples in marital counseling is: "Just tell us which of us is right and which of us is wrong." And the appropriate answer invariably is that there is no right side or wrong side in marital disagreement — just *different* sides.

Why is this nonmoral position so important? The practical reason is that in marital counseling we are looking for *solutions* to problems. *Differences* between couples can, with the help of the counselor, be understood, reduced, compromised and sometimes even removed. But so long as we look for right and wrong, we remain stymied by moral judgments rather than problem solutions. When the husband and wife, along with the marriage counselor, try to understand, rather than judge, differences can usually be dealt with effectively.

It is important for the reader to realize that the very nature of a moral judgment is such that there is nothing to be understood: The matter is either right or wrong and the person is either being good or bad. Negative moral judgments toward others come out in the form of contempt, condescension, scorn, ridicule, and even horror and loathing; and toward oneself in the form of guilt, shame, defensiveness and inferiority feelings. Positive moral judgments toward others are expressed in uncritical admiration, fawning, idealization of character traits and flattering judgmental generalizations; toward oneself in smugness, conceit or pride.

Both negative and positive moral judgments, then, are obviously not to be encouraged in a situation where a marriage has encountered problems. Such feelings as those we have just listed block understanding of the ongoing process in marriage and prevent husband, wife and counselor from working out daring and imaginative ways of improving the relationship.

Because marriage counseling is no place for making moral judgments does not mean, however, that there are not many moral issues to be dealt with in the process of counseling. If the counselor does not moralize, how can he help with these issues? He can encourage the clients to engage in rational evaluation, realistic appraisal and critical conceptual thinking, instead of looking for moral edicts which cover their problems.

In actual counseling situations, such rationality and realism must be geared to the specific situations faced by the particular couple with whom the counselor is working. It should be of some value for us in this chapter, however, to look critically at some of the general issues of morality, particular expressions of which are encountered in actual counseling circumstances. As we do so, we shall be able to observe some of the differences in perspective between this method and one based on uncritical moralizing about the same issues.

The reader's attention is called at this point to the understanding that the questions raised and the assertions made about moral issues in the rest of this chapter are to be taken as stimulating to his critical conceptual thinking. They are not to be considered new moral dogma, but a challenge to develop creative, flexible, reality-oriented attitudes about some of the moral issues which occur in many contemporary marriages.

The three broad areas of moral issues that we shall now consider are divorce, parenthood and sex. These are probably the three foremost clusters of long-standing moral judgments which have beclouded critical conceptual thinking about marriage.

DIVORCE

Although the morality about divorce is gradually changing in many subgroups of our society, a large percentage of Americans have been indoctrinated from a very early age in home, school, church and various other settings to feel that any person who gets a divorce is a failure and a sinner. To their conditioning regarding failure and sin are added a jungle of legal technicalities and outright humiliations for many of the hundreds of thousands of American couples who seek divorce each year. When, then, some of these men and women indicate anxiety, confusion and other emotional disturbances, the moralists like to point to such symptoms as proof of their thesis that divorce is automatically and inevitably a terrible thing.

Obviously, the marriage counselor's role is to help people to think through whether or not divorce is for them a more desirable course of action that a continuatioin of their particular marital relationship. It is relevant, then, to ask ourselves if, from a nonmoralistic point of view, divorce must be inherently "a terrible thing."

A rational study of divorce would seem to suggest that divorce might be thought of as an essential component of democracy. Just as there should be, in a democracy, no major abridgements of freedom of speech, assembly and worship (including, as some moralists like to forget, freedom *not* to worship), just as there should be no attempt to prevent a person from *responsibly* taking and quitting a job rather than remaining forever in his first job, so, a critical conceptual judgment would seem to tell us, there should be no interference with a person's *responsibly* entering or leaving a marriage, rather than remaining forever in his first marriage.

All human freedoms are subject to irresponsible misuse, and divorce is certainly no exception. In the hands of the irresponsible, divorce can be cruel, exploitative, tragic. In the hands of the responsible, divorce can be humane, kind, spirit-freeing. No one wants to abolish or drastically curtail the use of automobiles because they can produce tragedy in the hands of the irresponsible. Some can be prevented from using automobiles because they are permanently too irresponsible; others can be educated to use them responsibly. Most people can probably be educated to use both marriage and divorce responsibly. This is one of the marriage counselor's functions.

It is sometimes contended that divorce is always irresponsible for a couple who has children. If moralistic attitudes are put aside, however, it is difficult to find a marriage which, on realistic grounds, should be maintained strictly *because* of children. When two people have reached a point where their marriage has for them lost all possible positive value and is steadily accumulating negative values, what of a constructive nature is likely to accrue for children by the maintenance of that marriage?

Many moralists point to statistics about delinquency and broken homes. There are a number of fallacies concealed in such statistics, but the fact most relevant here is that when two people have decided that their marriage is dead and that they will stay married *only* for the children, that home is already broken in an emotional sense. There is no evidence to support the assertion that it is the physical parting of the parents that hurts the children. Or, put differently, there is no evidence that emotionally estranged parents who stay physically in the same house for the sake of their children really do their children any favor.

Faced with the moral issue of impending divorce with children involved, the marriage counselor can often help the couple to remove or reduce some of the undesirable effects of the earlier emotional break in the marriage and to protect the children from some of the unnecessary consequences of the physical break of separation and divorce. To help in this way the marital counselor will have many specific things to work out with the couple regarding their particular children, but certain general understandings can also be helpful.

One helpful understanding is that we have been so propagandized by the picture of children who are mourning their departed parents that we often overlook certain counterbalancing pieces of reality. For example, children are very conservative, for they are — reasonably enough for chronological children — quite insecure in the world. Hence, they tend to oppose anything that strikes them as a threat to their security systems, as a major change in the status quo. If Daddy has been little more to the children than an emotional stranger seen only briefly on weekends or holidays, they will nevertheless fight bitterly, forlornly, tragically, to retain his fleetingly familiar presence. But once Daddy is gone, even if he has been a more constructive influence than the father just described, children quickly adjust to life without father. They adjust *unless* Mother indicates (and perhaps Daddy, too, in the course of his visits with them) that something horrible has happened. "This is a terrible, terrible tragedy," say the parental emotional messages.

Children are, of course, excellent emotional mirrors. It is probable that we could reinforce in our children the feeling that *any* kind of change in the status quo is tragic, calamitous, unbelievably awful, providing we gave them the same sort of treatment we often do on the matter of divorce. Most of us, by way of illustration, have seen children temporarily indicate every bit as much disturbance over some such situation as a rip in a teddy bear as over a parent's departure from the home. The main difference is that they do not get the same reinforcement of their feelings of great tragedy from the adults around them on ripped teddy bears as they do on broken marriages. Hence, teddy-bear tragedies tend to be transitory, and parental divorce tragedies tend to get lasting reinforcement not only from their parents, but from neighbors, teachers, clergymen and others.

Marriage counselors can do a great deal, then, even in the unfortunate situations where emotional divorce has already occurred, in helping parents to overcome some of the emotional damage they have already done to their children, and in helping them to avoid doing additional damage with separation and divorce. Responsibly and intelligently planned divorce need not be terrible and tragic, even when children are involved.

PARENTHOOD

Even in the face of the ever-more-threatening problems associated with excessive world population, and with tremendous deficiencies in the genetic quality and environmental training of high percentages of human beings born year by year, moral myths about parenthood go relatively unchallenged in our society. To stimulate critical thinking about the usually unquestioned points of view about parenthood, the marriage counselor must sometimes strongly state radically different views. The following assertions are beliefs held tentatively by the writer (subject to correction by much-needed research), but they are made in the form of rather unqualified assertions for the sake of clarity, readability and, hopefully, startling challenge to prevail-ing prejudices about parenthood.

1. The only time reproduction is truly desirable for the children, for the married couple and for the general society is when: (a) The husband and wife are considerably above average in such traits as mental and physical health, intelligence, emotional and social maturity, and creative and adap-tive skills; (b) the marriage is a happy one; and (c) both the husband and wife not only want children in a sentimental sense, but are eager to make parenthood a main enterprise in their lives, and include in their eagerness a realization that this task means a lot of hard study, hard work and sacrifice of many other satisfactions. While some of these parental traits are not easily determined by existing evaluative methods, just the setting up of even roughly determined standards of the sort described would help to combat the moral myth that parenthood is a process to be entered into by the relatively stupid, ignorant and undedicated.

2. Very few people meet all three of the foregoing criteria (a), (b) and (c). There is a fair number of healthy, intelligent, mature, creative, adaptive people who are quite successful in business or professional activities but think that marriage and parenthood can be successfully pursued as an avo-cation to which they give little time and attention and for which they have little or no preparation. The facts are that, in order to be even moderately successful in marriage and parenthood, under contemporary social circum-stances, a great deal of time and energy and skill are required. Often indif-ference, at worst, or unskilled goodwill, at best, are all basically competent people offer family life: They have already given most of their available time, energy and talent to out-of-home careers.

3. The minority of couples who do fairly well in fulfilling the standards mentioned are likely to have their happy marriages made happier by children. In fact, for this minority, the joyful labors of parenthood probably bring as deep a sense of creative achievement as is available in life.

4. Under present-day social conditions, ancient conceptions about *duties* or *rights* about having children are quite inappropriate. "Be fruitful and multiply" is exceedingly poor advice with increasingly excessive world overpopulation and accompanying problems. Concerning the matter of *duty,* married couples who choose not to have children are being much more dutiful citizens in the light of contemporary realities than those who do have children. The former are at least not adding to the overall weight of popula-tion or of the social and psychological problems which tend to arise from duty-inspired offspring. As for any *rights* that genetically, sociologically and psychologically unqualified people may have to enter parenthood, these are privileges which have been socially granted and which may be socially

removed. All individual rights are subject to the limitations set by the welfare of the society to which the individual belongs. And the welfare of the world society — that is, of all of mankind — it becomes increasingly clear, depends upon drastic reduction in quantity and improvement in quality of population.

5. Just from their own vantage points, happy couples who do not prepare themselves seriously and well for the hard work and real sacrifices of parenthood are often in grave danger of having their previously sound marriages undermined by the arrival of children and the accompanying increase in life's stresses. Couples who have consulted the writer as a marriage counselor not infrequently mention that their troubles either began with or were markedly increased by the arrival of children.

6. Even more definitely, couples who were already quite unhappy prior to children are likely to find that the additional burdens of parenthood bankrupt their marriage and broaden and intensify their unhappiness.

7. Many of the people who urge married couples to have children and try to make them feel guilty if they do not are actually resentful of the freedom and enjoyment of life indicated by some childless couples. "I am tied down with a life I find difficult and not very enjoyable with children (doing my duty); why shouldn't you be likewise?" are the thoughts which often lie behind the spoken "Nothing like children to make life worthwhile." Such propagandists for reproduction are malefactors, not benefactors, of the couples, of children thus reproduced, and of mankind in general.

Such observations as the seven just made are apt to be judged as very radical and misanthropic by some persons, but any less severe approach to the responsibilities of parenthood seems to the writer to disregard current social reality. Realistic perceptions of existing world circumstances add up to the generalization that whenever parenthood is an involuntary function and/or one for which the individual is grossly unsuited, ill effects are very likely to ensue for all parties concerned.

Both the matter of desire and competency for parenthood are, however, relative. No parent is wholeheartedly happy about his role as a parent, and certainly no parent is perfectly equipped for the responsibilities of parenthood. But surely people who are functioning as parents predominantly contrary to their wishes and skills do injustice to themselves, their children and their society.

There is a condition which accompanies some brain injuries and diseases psychiatrically referred to as *anosognosia*, the denial of illness. A patient with anosognosia may be paralyzed in his right arm, for example, and yet stoutly deny the existence of the paralysis. He apparently so reorganizes his perception that he is able to "remove" the paralyzed limb from his field of perceived reality. He is afraid to face the reality of paralysis; he feels comfortable in denying reality.

The denial of the difficulties, the burdens, the displeasures of parenthood (or, at least, the denial of their very formidable nature), we would suggest, involves much the same psychological process as the denial of illness in the brain-injured. This might be considered an instance of *moral anosognosia*. Many people are afraid to face the unhappy realities of parenthood; they feel more comfortable in denying these realities, in believing the myth that having children is a sure route to happiness and the good life.

SEX

The traditional moral outlook on sex, of course, is more irrational than that on any other single topic with which the marriage counselor has to deal. In critically rethinking some of the moral issues connected with sex, the reader will find in the following assertions about sex an outlook that differs radically from the conventional ones.

1. Realistic evidence seems to point to the desirability not only of fully educating children about sex, but of making contraceptive and prophylactic information and equipment completely available to all persons who reach the age of possible fertility. The writer does not mean making it discreetly possible for the young person of more than average intelligence to worm such information and equipment out of the sexual black market. He means that it would be desirable to encourage young people to procure contraceptive and prophylactic knowledge and equipment. It is difficult to see what other purpose unwanted pregnancies and venereal disease serve in our society today than to punish or threaten to punish people who sexually function contrary to the ancient superstitions which constitute our premarital moral code.

It is undoubtedly true that some of the more guilt-ridden and faint-hearted youth are deterred by fear of pregnancy, of venereal disease and of the alleged wrath of a vindictive Jehovah from engaging in premarital sexual intercourse. But they then often pay the lifetime price of anxiety and guilt about even marital sex that seems a peculiar reward for touted virtue. Other costs of the deterrence program on young people who proceed with premarital sex are such things as: untreated venereal disease which fans out in a wide circle of infection; illegitimate children; guilt-ridden, resentment-filled shotgun marriages; sojourns in humiliating, morality-dripping homes for unwed mothers; illegal abortions; and a number of other priceless products of puritanism. It is only because we keep reciting rigidly to ourselves the moral ditty about the catastrophic nature of premarital coitus that we

cannot even clearly see, let alone do anything constructive about, our completely unnecessary, utterly idiotic premarital sexual morality.

2. The writer thinks it would be desirable to educate young people
frankly in how to use sex as an important part of their skills in interpersonal
relations. The suggestion here made is not only to stop teaching them that
premarital sexual intercourse is bad, but to teach them how to exercise
their own critical faculties about deciding under what sorts of circumstances
and with what sorts of partners it is likely to be functionally desirable for
all parties concerned. We should try to educate them to develop the kind
of maturity and experience and the kind of love and understanding of themselves and others to work out their widely varying self-guides for sex functioning along with other kinds of social functioning. The writer would
trust young people, thus educated, to have considerably superior judgment
in such matters to the second-hand judgments that come to them from
the ready-made codes of moralists.

3. If we take a critical and rational look at abortion, here, too, we
shall emerge with different ideas than the moralistic one that "to take a
human life is always bad." We shall question, first of all, whether the life
to be taken may be correctly considered human in light of what we know
in modern sociopsychological terms regarding the postnatal development
of human nature out of interpersonal relations. We shall ask, further, what
is most desirable for all parties concerned in a specific situation: the potential human being, the mother, the father and other people directly involved?

Under such changed approaches to abortion, our answer would at times
be, if we were thinking instead of moralizing, that the greatest practical
desirability would be to destroy the embryo or fetus. At other times, let
it develop. But we would be humanizing the concept of therapeutic abortion
to take into account the social and psychological, not just the physical, consequences of both continued and interrupted pregnancies.

Such a view of abortion, moralists say, would bring about loss of respect
for human life. The writer believes it would do quite the contrary, in other
words, increase respect for human life and for every human representative
of that general life. Entrance into human life would become less the product
of unhappy chance and increasingly the product of man's well-worked-out
plans, his best critical judgment.

4. A sex ethic should be constructed solely for the welfare of living and
future human beings and not to please our ancestors or any assumed supernatural beings or functions. What Moses, Jesus of Nazareth, Freud and
other respected figures from the past had to say should be taken into account
for any leads they may provide us, but their points of view should be subjected to the same rational inspection as any other points of view. And any

scientific evidence available (which in a sexually rational environment would become increasingly so) should take precedence over opinion from any source.

5. A rational sex ethic would be based on principles that derive from our knowledge of psychological, sociological and biological facets of human behavior, and would not concern itself with moral edicts or mystical or spiritual observations. Since our present empirical observations, including the growing clinical information of motivations outside the individual's conscious attention, are still crude and relatively unsifted, our sex values need to be particularly tentative and flexible, subject to change as we acquire new knowledge about human behavior and as social conditions alter human needs.

6. Our system of values for sex would in no way unfairly discriminate against males or females. It would be basically the same for both sexes with differences, if any, designed strictly for the necessary protection of the males or females.

7. The system of values would likewise obviously exclude any other type of discrimination, such as that of race, creed, religion, color or socio-economic status.

8. A rational sex code would likewise not discriminate against children and adolescents except in instances where their welfare is demonstrably involved, where their sex-love activities need to be limited for the actual protection of *their* health and well-being, and *not* for the protection of adult moral prejudice.

9. A realistic system of values regarding sex must take into account the fact that reproduction is a natural, though fortunately relatively infrequent, result of human sexual activity. Marriage and family laws under such a system would be primarily concerned with the encouragement and enforcement of proper care and protection of children, rather than with the hemming-in of adults with rules which do not bear on anyone's welfare.

11. Such a system of values would be based on the biopsychological fact that sex is fun for human beings. Nature has provided the healthy male and female with sexual dynamisms, which, unless restrained and perverted by social conditioning, provide the user with great pleasure. Probably more consistently enjoyable sensations proceed from the relatively unhampered erotic relationship of a man and a woman than from any other life activity. Any system of values which fails to take into account the outstanding fact that sex is pleasurable will be unrealistic, irrational and contrary to human welfare (much of our conventional sex morality is testimony to this point).

11. The kind of system of values we have been discussing would view as criminal and legally punishable only those forms of sex activities in which one individual forces his attentions on an unwilling participant,

willfully harms another, annoys others with his activities or takes advantage of a minor. Other sexual deviations than these, however neurotic, should be considered eccentricities or illnesses, not crimes.

12. Finally, a system of values for sex, along with those for parenthood and divorce which we barely touched upon, must be woven into an all-encompassing system of values which helps each individual toward increasing fulfillment of his various capacities, especially his capacity to love. Mature love means the development of concern, understanding, esteem and responsibility for all human beings, including oneself. No one achieves such love perfectly, but our efforts urgently need to be directed toward helping more individuals to progress in loving themselves and others.

The basic moral issue in marriage counseling is to help clients to free themselves from a stagnant and unrealistic morality which blocks progress in love. Many self-styled God-fearing people in our various social groups are also thought-fearing, love-fearing, science-fearing and life-fearing people.

Although the social system of the West contains in many respects the same destructive components as the social system of the Communist East, we are still permitted greater individual freedom and nonconformity. It is still possible, although difficult, for persons who have feelings of concern, understanding, esteem and responsibility for the human race to use opportunities within such institutions as the school, the home, the church, industry, labor and government to foster the growth of love and care and their necessary companion, critical conceptual judgment.

As marriage counselors we have not only opportunities but profound responsibilities to stimulate ourselves, our clients and others with whom we relate to question, to think, to examine the reality of our social life — including the marriage and family mores to which we have so stubbornly, so unthinkingly, so compulsively, locked ourselves in what may well be a death embrace. These moral matters take priority, in the writer's opinion, over many of the other issues with which we have concerned ourselves as marriage counselors, for these matters are near the core of our continued existence as a civilization.

SECTION III
MARITAL COUNSELING:
SCIENTIFIC FACTORS

Chapter 27

SEX ATTITUDES IN MARRIAGE

LEO WOLLMAN

Each marriage partner enters into the marriage situation with fixed ideas of sex based on his individual upbringing plus his accretion of life experiences. It therefore seems reasonable to aver that any generalization in the area of sex attitudes in marriage should be eschewed. However, before one can deal with specifics, it is necessary to establish certain overall patterns in marital behavior.

Happy marriages do not come to the attention of the marriage counselor. Therefore, we deal only with defective marriages. The marriage counselor is, in a sense, the matrimonial repairman. The success of his endeavors is largely attributed to his empathy and understanding of his clients' problems. An important aid to success is the objectivity of the counselor and his ability to project assurance that a solution to the problem is possible.

In the author's opinion, the majority of marital problems involve some sexual misunderstanding on the part of either or both marital partners. An illustration would be the case of a woman who received a puritanical and prudish upbringing in relation to sex. During her childhood sex instruction was completely avoided. The patient received the impression that sex was unclean and certainly not a subject for social conversation in the home or elsewhere (1). Marital discord in this case revolved around the inability of the wife to enjoy sexual intercourse. It would seem that reeducation in matters of sex would be indicated here. However, too much misinformation had been ingrained too deeply for effective results. Counseling was not enough. The combined efforts of a gynecologist, psychiatrist and marriage counselor were needed to overcome the frigidity which brought about the marital discord. The patient learned to enjoy sexual relations with her husband, and the marriage was saved.

The sexual drive is not very well understood. It has been said, periphrastically, that two people who are in love and marry recognize that libidinal impulses are reciprocal and therefore integrate their individual erotic drives to bring them within the same frame of reference (2). The love relationship which is the basis for most marriages may be impaired if the love-image is weakened by misidentification. An unhappily married customer's man sought aid from a marriage counselor for an impotency problem. He related that while he was on his honeymoon his mother, to whom he was strongly attached, suddenly died. The emotional impact of this loss was accentuated by a feeling of guilt. The guilt was occasioned by his absence at the time of death, and this was reinforced because he was on his honeymoon enjoying a pleasant sexual experience. The misidentification of his love-images could not be resolved except by the onset of impotency. Thus, a sadomasochistic withdrawal into impotency provided him with the only solution toward an expiation of his sense of guilt.

Other types of psychological impotency which affect the marriage relationship adversely are situational anxiety, failure anxiety, neurotic anxiety, hostility anxiety, acute and chronic depression and homosexuality.

As an illustration of situational anxiety, we may mention the squeaky springs of a marital bed in the home of inlaws. The greater the activity in bed, the louder the squeaking and more complete will be the failure of erection in the sensitive male (3). This condition may be made worse by a feeling of inadequacy. It may be alleviated by oiling the spring or moving.

Failure anxiety is an extension of situation anxiety. The degree of worry is intensified after failure of erection occurs and guilt feelings appear.

Neurotic anxiety results in impotency in an individual who will also manifest other neurotic complaints, e.g., fears, obsessions, imaginary aches and pains, etc.

Hostility impotency results from anger directed towards one's wife. The husband shows how much he despises his mate by failure to complete the marital act. He may have an orgasm *sine* ejaculation, or ejaculatio praecox, which represents unconscious revenge for an earlier rejection. Thus does he get even with her for a fancied or real complaint.

There occasionally is an impotence-prone personality type known as the passive man or "mama's boy," who has a weak sexual drive. This man may have an overidealized image of women, based on his strong love for his mother. To him, intercourse represents a forbidden act of defilement. Intercourse with any woman thus becomes taboo.

The depressed impotent patient is usually morose and uncommunicative and often complains of a variety of symptoms such as constipation, loss of appetite, inability to sleep, headaches and a host of other physical complaints of emotional origin. He is completely disinterested in sex of any kind. Treatment should be psychiatric and intensive.

The homosexual patient is impotent with females because he prefers male partners. There are, however, some bisexual individuals who are equally potent with both sexes.

Some comments by the woman in the conjugal bed which may lead to impotency in the male are: "Come on, *dear,* get it over with!" "Look out, you're mussing my hair!" "Don't squeeze my breasts so hard, you're hurting me!" "Not now, the children may hear." "I'm not in the mood, I think I'm getting a headache!" "I have some ironing to do now." "I want to watch the Late, Late Show." "What kind of an animal are you, you just had it yesterday!" "I'm too tired, let's wait until tomorrow." "When would you like to make love, before or after dinner?" (thus taking away the spontaneity of the act of love). The above remarks are calculated to reduce the sex urge in any man, and may serve to illustrate one type of frigidity in the female.

A second type of frigidity is attributed to a physical cause — the hooded clitoris. Dehooding the clitoris surgically exposes the sensitive glands and eventually results in clitoridauxe. An orgasm in this individual is then possible with penile penetration, rather than digital manustupration.

A third frigid type is the "total mother" type. She has no sexual response, but is happily married, devoted to her husband and a wonderful mother to her children. She not only mothers her children but mothers her husband as well. There are some husbands who prefer the mother type of wife. This symbiotic union encourages domestic felicity. *Pax in conjugale* is thus assured by the fortuitous combination of two neurotics who satisfy each other's neuroticism (4).

A fourth type commonly occurs during the honeymoon experiences. An unsophisticated bride whose initial contact with a crude and inconsiderate groom produces an emotionally traumatic and painful experience may experience honeymoon frigidity. This syndrome may be ephemeral, but is more often of a longer-lasting duration and can seriously cripple an otherwise happy union.

The fifth type is fearful of becoming pregnant too soon after a previous pregnancy. This type of wife discourages her husband's advances, is always tired at the end of the day, has bedtime headaches, and frequently retires to her bedroom before her husband, feigning sleep when he gets into bed. She is not afraid of coitus but is afraid of cyesis.

The sixth type of frigidity may be termed postpartum frigidity. A previously responsive wife now becomes cold, distant and difficult to stimulate sexually. Previously pleasurable experiences are now painful. It should be noted that dyspareunia may be frigidity disguised by a physical complaint which renders it more acceptable to the patient. The attitude of the patient toward her symptom may be the pertinent differential diagnostic point. If a physical cause is sought, it may be found sometimes as a neuroma in a healing or recently healed episiotomy site. In addition to the above there are some organic causes leading to frigidity, such as congenital atresia of the vagina and dysgenesis of the ovaries in a chromosomal abnormality.

Frigidity can be considered to be a syndrome of the total personality rather than a symptom of the genital organization.

Two relatively uncommon sexual disorders which may contribute to marital disharmony by confusing sex attitudes in marriage are nymphomania and satyriasis.

Satyriasis is a sexual aberration rarely seen. It appears as an uncontrollable desire to have sexual intercourse frequently. It is associated with a psychological deficiency. As a clinical entity it may be treated by intensive psychotherapy which is not always successful. One patient, a professional person, manifested this "Don Juanism" to such a degree that he seduced friend, patient and relative with equal facility. He was such a perfectionist in lovemaking that no seductee ever complained.

The nymphomaniac has an uncontrollable desire to have intercourse, but she does not enjoy the release of an orgasm. This troubled female is constantly searching for sexual fulfillment. She is usually an aggressive female who cannot remain happily married. (It would be interesting to speculate what the outcome of a nymph-satyr union would be.)

One should consider that an aggressive person wears a facade which harbors a neurotic coward. A compulsive compliant person may become aggressive and beat down, physically or verbally, his espoused partner.

A couple requested counseling for an unusual set of circumstances which was wrecking their marriage. He had a malignant hypertension and she had a rigid impenetrable hymen. For years, their apareunic marriage had been barren. Cohabitation by extragenital means had proven unsatisfactory. A combined treatment of surgery and hypnotherapy provided a means for salvaging an otherwise "lost" marriage (5). The husband had a sympathectomy performed, and the wife had a hymenectomy. Both responded satisfactorily to a course of hypnotherapy which was given individually and, at times, to both jointly.

It is pertinent to mention that sex attitudes of marital partners may easily be influenced by hypnotic techniques skillfully applied to the suggestible client (6, 7, 8). A well-trained competent adviser, experienced in the art of hypnosis and the science of counseling, is qualified to utilize the resources and advantages of clinical hypnosis within the sphere of his own competence. Altering attitudes thus becomes more of a reality than a theoretical possibility. In the author's experience, the female is more susceptible to sex-attitude change by hypnosuggestion than is the male. Perhaps a female marriage counselor would have more effective results with the male partner of the marriage tandem.

Early marriages, which are on the increase (9) (241,683 teenage married girls in the United States in 1959), more frequent teenage pregnancies (600,000 in 1963) (10) and the statistical fact that 50 per cent of these teenage marriages terminate in divorce (9) emphasize the growing awareness that sex attitudes of the married teenager need drastic revision. Sociologists and sex scientists have known that an increasing number of adolescents engage in sexual activities before reaching emotional maturity (10). Kinch, of the University of Western Ontario, London, Canada, concludes that "by the age of 18, at least 25% of single girls will have already indulged in sexual intercourse." Sexual relations are initiated usually before the emergence of romantic feelings; and new families are started before material independence has been attained. With sex attitudes like these, it is no surprise that the number of divorces in teenage marriages is so high.

Sex attitudes of partners in common-law marriages vary greatly. As a rule, the mutual need for sex and companionship is so symbiotic that the arrangement benefits both parties. In one case where the living together as man and wife had lasted twenty-four years, the couple decided to get married officially because, as he stated it, "I want her to have everything after I die, not to be cheated out of my money by my——family." Should the common-law arrangement be tied by looser emotional bonds or be a temporary affair between two alcoholics, the sex attitudes are more superficial and the union less likely to persist any prolonged length of time. Common-law marriages in those over sixty are on the increase; and some factors which help to explain it are loneliness, fear of the premarital blood test, economic insecurity, need for one to share room rent and food expenses, spurt of sexual interest after years of continence and the dislike of a permanent psychosexual relationship.

"Marriages" between homosexuals are arrangements of convenience, and are not usually mentioned in marriage manuals or in marriage-counseling books. Perhaps because this subject is considered taboo, one is moved to note certain sex attitudes common to these so-called marriages. The lesbian union between "butch" and "frau" is easily overlooked because society does not frown upon two females sharing an apartment. Only when disharmony from jealousy erupts into violence does the setting cause police intervention.

The domestic relationship—"marriage"—of male homosexuals is more complicated. If the buddy system is evoked and each of the duo cruises on his own, then there is less likelihood of sex violence arising. In this arrangement, the boys share all home living expenses and have their sex experiences elsewhere outside of their living quarters. Should the sexual attraction be mutual, then the sex game "who will be doing what to whom tonight?" becomes playable. Because these arrangements are usually made between emotionally immature or disturbed personalities, they are commonly brief and turbulent.

The marriage of a homosexual male with a genetic girl is often meant to be a social facade to protect the male from social castigation. Meanwhile, he is free to enjoy a homosexual relationship with his boy friend ("wife") in one apartment and his "normal" heterosexual marriage in another apartment with his married spouse. One or both of these relationships is bound to suffer after a period of time, but it has not been my experience as yet to have such a presenting complaint offered to me as a marital counselor.

The sex attitudes of these homosexuals are little understood by the average medical or legal practitioner; and the individual homosexual is wont to lead a hounded existence.

The marriage of transvestites or cross-dressers differs from that of the homosexuals in several ways. In the main, unless the transvestite is fetishistic, the sex part of the marriage arrangement is negligible (11, 12). There are exaggerated opinions among the uninformed about the extent of homosexuality among the transvestites. In the case of transvestite males who share an apartment, the purpose is usually one of convenience. Rent expense is shared and, more important, the urge to dress as a woman can be indulged in more often without fear or ridicule or the need to hide. If homosexuality is a factor, then the transvestite pair may be considered in the true category of homosexuals rather than the more esoteric grouping of transvestite.

Transvestite females usually pair off with docile and ofttimes indolent girls. The masculine attire and the aggressive male mannerisms of the "dressed" female transvestite fit in very neatly with the passive acceptance of the "feminine" female. Usually the transvestite (or TV) conducts her sex play with a "dildo" or artificial phallus, being more concerned with helping her partner reach a satisfactory orgasm. Most of these unhappy people are virgins, never permitting themselves to be "penetrated" by any male. Male sex-hormone therapy enables them to carry out their chosen masculine role by causing complete cessation of menses, and by encouraging hirsute supralabial and pogonial attributes.

The most interesting sexual aberration is transsexualism, a name coined by Harry Benjamin in 1953 (13). A transsexual is one who desires eventually to have his physical sex changed by surgery. His motives may be one or more of four major types—sexual, social, gender and legal—according to Dr. Benjamin (14).

The definitions of these terms are as follows: *sexual*—to satisfy his needs (if a genetic male) to have sexual relations as a woman, to be the passive partner, to be penetrated by a male organ; *gender*—to be accepted (if a genetic male) as a woman, i.e., he feels like a "woman imprisoned in a male body"; *social*—to be the female in genital fact rather than to appear and act as a feminine male; *legal*—to avoid the constant fear of arrest for impersonation, and be able to marry and live in domestic felicity as a housewife.

Unfortunately, few states are liberal enough, at this writing, to grant altered birth certificates to these psychic hermaphrodites who have undergone surgical removal of the male genitalia and the formation of a vaginal sheath. A court order by a knowledgeable and understanding judge is the only recourse these transsexuals (TS) have to obtain a passport or a proper birth certificate for marriage.

Many of these surgically created females had previously been married and fathered children. It is not too rare for one to see two individuals, dressed as women, with a child who is their offspring. Sexual relations between these two married partners usually cease. In one instance, while under psychiatric treatment, a couple continued to live together and admitted that they experienced a new relationship. The new female, formerly the male, would by manipulation provide sexual satisfaction for the other female, formerly the wife. While engaged in this sex play, she (previously he) would experience a sense of subtle sexual satisfaction.

It has been found that almost all transsexuals either refuse any psychotherapy outright or willingly enter therapy but do not continue for long. In the case just mentioned, the former male partner was receiving psychotherapy to enable him to accept his role as a woman while his wife was concurrently receiving hormone therapy for her menopause.

One of the most unusual cases that I have seen for marital counseling involved a feminine-looking female who is a genetic male. "Her" vagina was created by involuting the penile skin after surgical castration. Her ample breasts were implants. Her Adam's apple was scraped to become less obvious. She had had two years of feminization by hormone therapy. She looked, walked, talked and acted typically feminine, and even admitted to having a type of orgasm during sexual intercourse with a male which she described as "sweating in the vagina."

The husband, six years younger, never previously married, complained of his wife's dry vagina and sexual ardor. He was unaware of her previous masculinity. He believed she was childless and amenorrhoeic because of a vaginal hysterectomy. Both were unhappy but unwilling to separate. Marital counseling for this unusual couple provided a challenge for the counselor. The sex attitudes in this marriage are adequate, but the background is provocative.

Sex attitudes in marriage are an important factor in determining the longevity of a marriage and in predicting its future happiness. It has been truly said that a marital counselor must be a combination of Freud, Jonah, Einstein and King Solomon. In fact, he may sometimes have to be even a little better than that!

REFERENCES

1. WOLLMAN, LEO: Hypnosis in marriage and divorce. In: Greenhill, *Some Syndromes of Love*. Impact Press, New York, 1965, p. 149.

2. WOLLMAN, LEO: Sexual problems encountered in hypnotic procedures. *Journal of the American Society of Psychosomatic Dentistry and Medicine, 10* (4) :96, 1963.

3. WOLLMAN, LEO: Hypnotism and impotence. *Sexology, 29* (7) :440, 1963.

4. WOLLMAN, LEO: Hypnosis: Cure for frigidity. *Sexology, 31* (8) :517, 1965.

5. WOLLMAN, LEO: Sexual disorders managed by hypnotherapy. In: Caprio, *How To Solve Your Sex Problems With Self-Hypnosis.* New York, Citadel, 1964, p. 213.

6. WOLLMAN, LEO: Hypnosis as a clinical technique. *Pre-Med, 11* (2) :21, 1962.

7. WOLLMAN, LEO: The role of hypnosis in the treatment of infertility. *British Journal of Medical Hypnotism, 11* (3) :42, 1960.

8. *Roche Medical Image,* April 1966, p. 20.

9. WOLLMAN, LEO: Brief statistics on female adolescents. *Journal of Sex Research, 2* (1) :25, 1966.

10. Adolescence in America. *The Sciences, 6* (1) :9, 1966.

11. WOLLMAN, LEO: Transvestism and hypnotism. *British Journal of Medical Hypnotism, 15* (3) , 1964.

12. WOLLMAN, LEO: Transvestism and hypnosis. *Turnabout, 1* (4) , 1964.

13. BENJAMIN, HARRY: Transsexualism and transvestism as psycho-somatic and somato-psychic syndromes. *Amer. Journal of Psychotherapy, 8* (2) :219, 1954.

14. BENJAMIN, HARRY: *The Transsexual Phenomenon.* New York, Julian, 1966.

Chapter 28

MARRIAGE AS DYNAMIC EQUILIBRIUM:
IMPLICATIONS FOR RESEARCH

ROBERT PLUTCHIK

FOR EVERY SIX MARRIAGES THAT TOOK PLACE in 1930 in America, there was one divorce. In 1960, the ratio had been reduced to four-to-one. These simple facts suggest that marriage is an unstable institution and is becoming increasingly so.

Stability, however, is not an all-or-nothing concept, and obviously depends upon a variety of conditions related to such sociological variables as race, religion and economic status. But one may consider the question of stability from another point of view. A cup of coffee sitting on a table is described by the physicist as being in a state of stable equilibrium. This means that the weight of the cup is exactly balanced by the force exerted upward by the table. This kind of situation is contrasted with one such as balancing an egg on its end. With infinite patience it is possible to achieve a balance, but the slightest tremble will send the egg rolling. This is unstable equilibrium. To borrow an image: Marriage is a cross between a cup of coffee and a smashed egg.

In general, marriage is a set of changing relationships in a state of dynamic balance or equilibrium, a balance which is constantly shifting. The significant fact to recognize is that a dynamic equilibrium implies the simultaneous existence of oppositely directed forces. Some of these forces act to increase the stability of a marriage and some act to increase its instability. When the instability reaches a certain point, couples separate or divorce.

This conception of marriage as a state of dynamic equilibrium, implying a balance of forces, has a number of research implications. It implies, first of all, that a description be given of the forces making for both stability and instability in any marriage; it implies also that formal evaluation procedures be established for judging the relative strengths of these forces; and, finally, it implies the need to develop specific methods for modifying the equilibrium. This chapter will outline these various issues briefly.

THE MAJOR FORCES IN THE EQUILIBRIUM

There are undoubtedly many ways of categorizing the major forces that produce the dynamic equilibrium of marriage. The suggestions that follow do not represent any definitive listing, but are primarily to be considered a point of departure. The emphasis will be on contemporary events. Previous life history is significant insofar as it tends to raise or lower the likelihood of a reaction. In other words, given a certain kind of current frustration or set of circumstances, some individuals, because of their past histories, react to it with mild irritation; others react to it with rage; and still others might react to it with anxiety. The emphasis in this list will be on current interactions, and not on the historical or sociological origins of these interactions. The remainder of the chapter will describe some important sources of stability and instability in marriage and will then show the therapeutic and research implications of the view of marriage as dynamic equilibrium.

SOURCES OF STABILITY

One of the major sources of stability is the existence of *shared social involvements*. This may involve friends, relatives, members of the community, social and charitable organizations, etc. Another kind of shared social involvement concerns the daily interests of the couple, the sharing of hobbies, knowledge and topics of interest. To paraphrase a current advertising slogan: "The family that plays together stays together."

A second source of stability is the existence of continued physical attraction. If one or both of the married partners becomes overweight or physically ill, there is often a shift in the overall dynamic balance in the marriage.

A third source of stability is the existence of sexual availability and satisfaction. A number of studies have shown that there is a positive correlation between sexual satisfaction and happiness in the marriage, although no one has clearly proven which came first. Sexual availability is not to be underestimated as a source of stability.

A fourth basis for stability is the existence of children in the family. Divorce rates are known to be inversely proportional to the number of children. It is well known that many women, in a desperate effort to save a dissolving marriage, suddenly become pregnant. Whether they succeed or not depends upon the relative strengths of the other forces in the equilibrium.

A fifth basis for marriage stability is the existence of similar religious beliefs. Divorce statistics reflect the fact that both the type of religion and the strength of belief affect the stability of a marriage.

Last, but not least, a factor making for stability is the relative cost and difficulty of getting a divorce. People will sometimes remain in an unhappy marriage if getting out of it creates more problems than staying in.

I assume that these six factors are the major contributors, in the current life of an individual, to stability in marriage and that personality variables, Oedipus complexes and family histories (among others) act primarily to affect the relative sensitivity of the individual to influence by these factors (6).

SOURCES OF INSTABILITY

Since marriage has survived as an institution for a long time it is reasonable to assume that normally, in a society, the factors making for instability are fewer and weaker than the factors making for stability. Although this is generally true, there is a variation from time to time in the relative importance of these factors, and the divorce rate which more or less reflects the equilibrium that is reached will vary year by year and certainly by decades. Such factors as war, economic depression and material prosperity all affect marriage and divorce statistics.

The first of the sources of instability concerns problems of control. As Haley (2) has so aptly put it: "Marriages often flounder over the question of 'who tells who what to do when'." Haley has shown beautifully how much of a marriage deals with the question of who is in charge. The particular content of a conflict may vary widely, but often the underlying theme concerns the matter of who is in control. Quite often the most stable marriages are the traditional ones where the husband is completely in charge of everything. Many of the most successful marriages are those in which the wife is yielding and emotionally dependent (7). It is quite likely that the increased emphasis in our society on "democratic" marriages has increased the instability of the relationship by increasing conflicts over the matter of who controls whom. In a marriage where husband and wife both have a 50 per cent vote on all issues, stalemate is frequently inevitable. The increasing financial independence of women also undoubtedly contributes to conflict over matters of control. Sometimes, physical symptoms may represent "symptomatic" behavior designed to control, indirectly and involuntarily, as it were, the behavior of the spouse. This is done by regulating the amount of time the couple is together, by determining expressions of concern and by regulating certain kinds of interactions such as sexual relations.

A second major source of instability is the existence and degree of disappointed expectations. Each of the partners brings into the marriage a series of expectations, some verbalized and some not, some conscious and some unconscious. These often reflect patterns established within the families of each spouse. Although psychoanalysis tends to focus upon the unconscious expectations of the individual, we should not underestimate the importance of conscious but often unverbalized expectations that are present. All too often even in a fairly stable marriage, the spouses are not aware of each other's expectations on many issues.

Marriage counselors frequently encounter marriages where some of the conflicts concern such apparently trivial matters as: who takes out the garbage; whether the wife should have a night out with the girls each week; who should take care of writing the checks to pay the bills, etc. The psychoanalyst might describe the matter of expectations in terms of the concepts of ego-syntonic (behavior which fits one's expectations) or ego-alien (behavior which does not fit). If enough of these expectations are not in harmony, the dynamic balance of the marriage may begin to tip precariously.

The third major source of instability relates to the fact that in all familiar relationships there is a relative lack of novelty. A less polite way of saying this is that people get bored and restless and frequently develop "seven-year itches" even in marriages that are stable. This is a perfectly normal phenomenon, and is significant only if the overall balance of forces is significantly altered.

In one case where this factor seemed to be important, a husband in one of the professions took a job in a small community. Although his work was interesting and satisfying to him, his wife became increasingly restless and bored with small-town life. Finally, she thought of divorce as the only way out of the situation. The boredom was one factor which gradually changed the dynamic equilibrium so that other forces (of dissatisfaction, frustration, etc.) achieved a new importance which they had not previously had.

Any situation that acts to change this balance affects the stability of a marriage. This may occur in a variety of ways. For example, changing job or home, completing an education, losing physical attractiveness, having in-laws move in, finding or losing religion, meeting another man (or woman), having a child, losing parents or entering into psychotherapy, etc., all contribute in one way or another to this complicated dynamic balance. When the shift is large enough, friction breaks out into the open; when it is larger yet, separation or divorce may occur.

THERAPEUTIC IMPLICATIONS

In order to change a dynamic equilibrium several approaches are possible: (a) one may strengthen the sources of stability; (b) one may weaken the sources of instability; or (c) one may do both simultaneously.

Many marriages exist where enough friction develops to raise the possibility of divorce. Just as surely, in many such cases, tactful advice or suggestions may be sufficient to rebalance the marriage. It should not be assumed that, in all cases of marital difficulties repressed unconscious conflicts must exist. Instead of looking into the childhood history of each spouse, it is often sufficient to focus on the immediate relationship and the many factors that are influencing its expressions. But most therapists prefer not to give advice. They tend to focus usually on the sources of instability: control conflicts, disappointed expectations, sexual problems, financial difficulties, etc. Rarely do they give any attention to directly strengthening the sources of stability in a marriage, and thus they leave this area of therapeutic effectiveness, by default, to the pastoral and vocational counselors. Several exceptions to this are Alexander Herzberg (3), a psychoanalyst who introduced the use of "tasks" for his patients, and Albert Ellis (1), who has used a similar approach. By encouraging the patients to try to acquire new skills as well as new ways of looking at problems, they foster the development of competence and change the balance of forces in the marriage in a desired direction.

In connection with some of the other sources of instability, Haley has most fully described methods for dealing with the problem of who controls who in a marriage. He has pointed out that conflicts may develop over any one or more of three control problems: (a) what rules to follow in the marriage; (b) who sets the rules; and (c) what happens when some rules turn out to be incompatible. This latter point would be illustrated by the kind of wife who wants to be treated like an equal at the same time that she insists on being dependent on her husband. Such an incompatibility may last for years before some shift in the marriage equilibrium, due to an entirely different reason, suddenly precipitates this into the foreground as a problem.

Haley suggests that the therapist take several roles in his effort to help the individuals in the marriage. His first role should be that of a fair participant in the interaction between the spouses; he cannot be used by one of them to condemn the other. By trying to be a fair and impartial participator, the therapist gradually becomes a model to be imitated by the spouses in their interaction with each other. In addition, the therapist tries to relabel or redefine the behaviors that the spouses show toward each other. If, for example, a wife complains that her husband is spending too much time at work and that she hardly sees him anymore, the therapist might raise the question of whether this might not be considered a sign of an increasing feeling of responsibility toward his family. Negative connotations should be avoided.

Kadis (4) has also emphasized the point concerning the multiplicity of roles the therapist takes. "He will at times need to be active, passive, spontaneous, encouraging." In order for the therapist to be encouraging, however, he must have some idea of what behaviors are desirable and should be encouraged. This also implies a value commitment.

In general, stable marriages are those in which conflicts over matters of control are minimal. If therapy is successful, there will be less and less concern over who is in control of the relationship.

Although the problem of disappointed expectations sometimes relates to the matter of control, it is by no means identical to it. In every unstable marriage there are disappointed expectations and they may relate to almost any aspect of the marriage. A man may find that his wife does not cook as well as he had hoped; she might not be as sexually responsive as he had assumed; or she might be sloppy in her personal habits. A woman may find that her husband drinks more than she had realized, or that he is financially irresponsible. Quite obviously, most of these expectations are formed in the bosom of an individual's own family, but it does not follow that one must explore, in all cases, the childhood family constellation in order to help the present marriage. After all, many divorces occur *after* an individual has been through his own psychoanalysis. In many cases, what is necessary in helping to deal with disappointed expectations is a clearer sense of values concerning what is more important to one's own life and what is less important. This can sometimes be accomplished by a careful exploration of all the current aspects of the marriage plus a discussion of the alternatives which are available. In addition, since the therapist acts as a person who is capable of accepting most things, this fact has "paradigmatic" value for the spouses, to use the term proposed by the Nelsons (5) .

Occasionally, divorces occur because the couple have grown tired of one another. Although the therapist is inclined to want to look behind this statement, there is an important truth in it if taken at face value. People do get bored with one another if thrown into constant contact. Anna Karenina's lover eventually grew tired of her when he had her constantly by his side. The troubadours of the Middle Ages believed that love flowered most when it was unrequited. Dante never touched Beatrice, though he wrote beautiful love sonnets to her. In a successful marriage, passionate love changes to tenderness and concern, and the many shared interests of the marriage prevent lassitude from appearing. The less stable marriages are sometimes those in which the spouses see too much of each other. In any case, the therapist should examine the extent to which this problem is a factor in the disequilibrium.

RESEARCH IMPLICATIONS

The view that has been outlined here of marriage as a state of dynamic equilibrium has a number of implications for research. It suggests first of all that formal procedures be developed for evaluating the state of balance of a marriage. The value of having a formal scheme is that the therapist will be encouraged to look at many issues rather than only the ones that he is predisposed to examine. (It is a truism to point out that each therapist has his personal predilection about what kinds of things he wants to talk about or concern himself with.)

A second value of a formal approach to marriage counseling within the framework of this scheme is that much useful general information will be obtained about marriages, which may in turn suggest alternative formulations.

Thirdly, the conception of marriage as dynamic equilibrium directs our attention toward those forces which need to be modified, and therefore clarifies the problem of therapeutic intervention. Under certain conditions, a "depth" approach is necessary, while under others an advice-giving, information-giving approach is perfectly satisfactory, depending upon which forces are most significant in modifying the current equilibrium. It should not be assumed that anyone has yet found the optimum means for accomplishing these ends.

REFERENCES

1. ELLIS, A.: *Reason and Emotion in Psychotherapy.* New York, Lyle Stuart, 1963.
2. HALEY, J.: *Strategies of Psychotherapy.* New York, Grune, 1963.
3. HERZBERG, A.: *Active Psychotherapy.* New York, Grune, 1947.
4. KADIS, ASYA: A new approach to marital therapy. *Int. J. Soc. Psychiat., 10:*261-265, 1964.
5. NELSON, MARIE COLEMAN, and NELSON, NELSON B.: *Paradigmatic Approaches to Psychoanalysis: Four Papers.* New York, Stuyvesant Polyclinic, 1962.
6. PLUTCHIK, R.: *The Emotions: Facts, Theories and a New Model.* New York, Random House, 1962.
7. THARP, R. G.: Psychological patterning in marriage. *Psychol. Bull., 60:*97-117, 1963.

Chapter 29

EMOTIONAL PROBLEMS OF DIVORCE*

EMILY H. MUDD *with* HILDA M. GOODWIN

What Is the Definition of Divorce?

THERE ARE ESSENTIALLY two forms of divorce: (a) an absolute legal dissolution of the marriage bond; (b) a judicial separation of man and wife,
or termination of cohabitation, without dissolution of the marriage bond
(limited divorce or divorce from bed and board).

How Many People Are in This Group in the United States?

The Census reports, for 1960 (1), 2,814,000 divorced persons in the
United States: 1,106,000 men; 1,708,000 women.

Estimated national total of divorces and annulments granted in 1959
was 395,000. This represents an increase of 7.3 per cent over the 1958
figure of 368,000.

Do These Statistics Differ From Those in Other Countries?

The report of the British Royal Commission on Marriage and Divorce
(1955) (2) gives figures on divorces per thousand of the population for
1950 as follows:

New Zealand and Australia	.86
Sweden	1.19
Denmark	1.55
United States	2.48

Are These Statistics Changing?

The number of divorces granted in a single year reached an all-time
high in 1946, immediately after World War II, of 610,000. It decreased
annually after that year until 1951. Since 1951, the rate has been relatively
stable, ranging from about 370,000 to 396,000. Although the divorce rate
is fluctuating slightly from one year to the next, it is clear that the divorce
trend is still upward (3).

Does Our Cultural and Psychological Climate Induce Divorce?

Marriage is today, as it has always been, a part of the social fabric, and
its structure, strengths, weaknesses and values arise out of the particular
cultural and psychological climate in which we live. In a society or group

---

*Reprinted with permission of the authors from *The Encyclopedia of Mental Health*, New York,
Watts, 1963, pp. 483-497.

where divorce carries little social sanction or moral stigma, it seems probable that, given conditions of unhappiness and tension, the possibility of divorce as a solution will arise in the individual's thinking more quickly that it would were divorce still regarded as it was in our own country fifty years ago.

Does the Cost Affect the Rate of Divorce in Lower-Income Groups?

The cost of divorce undoubtedly affects the rate of divorce in lower-income groups. This does not, however, offer a true picture of the amount of family disorganization or marital disharmony existing within this group. In many instances where cost is prohibitive and there is a desire on the part of one or both parties to escape the unhappiness of the marital bond, either separation by mutual agreement or desertion by one partner takes place. Permanent desertion has been characterized as "the poor man's divorce." Deserted wives (and wives are more often deserted than husbands) frequently are handicapped both by lack of legal knowledge and by the lack of financial means for obtaining a divorce. In consequence, we have no way of knowing the extent of desertion, whereas divorce statistics are available for most states and for the country as a whole.

What Are the Main Legal Reasons Given for Divorce Today?

It is a well-known fact that the legal reasons given for divorce in the United States often bear little resemblance to the marital problems involved (4), but represent the conditions under which divorce is obtainable within the particular governmental jurisdiction. In general, the rule in such suits is that the legally most effective and morally least accusatory grounds are asserted in the suit. The United States has a very confusing system of divorce legislation. Until 1949, South Carolina did not allow divorce on any grounds. Legal terms are often defined differently in various states, a good example being desertion. Some of the more familiar charges for divorce are desertion, adultery, bigamy, cruelty, habitual drunkenness, nonsupport, fraud and duress. Impotence and insanity at the time of marriage are also grounds in some states.

What Are Other Reasons for Divorce in the United States?

Marriage today, as contrasted with marriage some fifty years ago, has as its primary values mutual love and affection, including sexual satisfaction, equality of the partners and freedom for personal development. Anything that disturbs the mutual sympathy and love between husband and wife creates serious tension when marriage is based on a presumption that it must offer individual happiness. If happiness is not attained, the marriage is regarded as a failure. Since marriage for love has become the basic pattern in our country, unhappiness in marriage is often blamed on a faulty choice of mate, rather than on a faulty adjustment between the two partners. Divorce or separation, with choice of another partner, may be seen as a possible solution. Essentially, marriage is a vulnerable human relationship composed of the feelings, attitudes, values, behaviors and demands that flow back and forth between the partners. Each acts as both cause and effect within this relationship. The difficulty that disrupts the relationship lies in a destructive interaction between the two partners. The focus of their difficulty may be a mother-in-law, sexual incompatibility, money, etc., but the basic problem is the failure of each to meet the other's emotional needs to a satisfactory degree.

Is the Woman Likely To Be the One To Desire Divorce First?

It is difficult to get conclusive evidence on this question. William J. Goode, in his book, *After Divorce* (5) found that 62 per cent of the women stated that they first suggested the divorce, 13 per cent stated it was mutual, and 25 per cent said it was the husband who wanted it first.

William Goode felt, however, that it was more often the husband than the wife who first wished to terminate the marriage. This would agree with the prevalent theory that the wife has a greater social and emotional investment in the marriage and would as a consequence be more concerned about preserving family ties.

Are There Certain Groups Which Show Higher Divorce Rates Than Others?

Yes, there are. Because information on religion is difficult to obtain, no question regarding religious affiliation has been listed on the decennial census, nor, with one exception, have any of the states or territories ever included the question on the marriage or divorce records.

Catholics, because of their doctrinal opposition to divorce, are underrepresented in the divorced group.

Jews are generally reported to have a lower percentage of divorce than their representation in the population.

Studies of divorce records indicate that upper occupational groups are underrepresented; middle occupational groups are proportionately represented; and the lower groups are overrepresented in the divorced population (6). However, a study of 4,500 divorce cases in Iowa found that farmers had the lowest divorce rate:

Farmers	1.5
Professional—proprietors	3.4
Clerical	4.5
Salesmen	6.9
Skilled	7.8
Semiskilled	8.3
Labor—service	18.7

For marriages which ultimately end in divorce, the breakup, actual and legal, is most likely to occur in the one- or two-year period immediately following marriage, the disruption percentage showing a subsequent yearly decline from that time on (7).

Does Divorce Tend To Run in Families?

Marital discord and divorce tend to run in a family. For example, in about two-fifths of the 1,422 divorces granted in the Toledo Family Court in 1953 (8), one or both partners, or members of their immediate families, had been parties previously to one or another form of matrimonial action.

Is a Marriage That Has Produced Children as Prone to Divorce as One That Has Not?

William Goode thinks: "For the married population as a whole, the childless couples are about twice as prone to divorce, but most analysts feel that the same factors that lead to postponing children also lead to divorce. That is, the decision to have children is for many a decision that the marriage is good enough to continue; or, negatively, since the marriage is not going well, there should not be any children just yet" (9).

Is the Divorce Rate Among Second Marriages Higher Than First Marriages? What Might This Indicate?

According to Jessie Bernard, in *Remarriage* (10), the divorce ratio increases with each subsequent divorce; that is, partners once divorced are more likely to divorce again than those never divorced. Any marriage requires adjustments, and for the remarried there may be many more complicating factors. In addition to the kinds of conflicts that may arise in any family, Jessie Bernard lists the following issues likely to split families of remarriage: (a) competition; (b) mutually incompatible values, standards, role conceptions or principles; (c) money or property.

Is the Young Marriage as Likely To End in Divorce as One Where the Participants Are in Their Middle or Late Twenties?

There is a close relationship between early marriage and instability of marriage. This is especially true of those who marry below the age of twenty-two. The proportion of divorced and remarried women, according to the United States Census, among those who first married below the age of eighteen, was about three times as high as that for women who first married between the ages of twenty-two and twenty-four years (11).

Does the Fact That Divorce Laws Are Becoming More Lenient Have an Effect on the Divorce Rate?

The fact that divorce laws are more lenient may have some slight bearing on the trend, but marriage and divorce are part of a very complicated and changing cultural pattern. The functions and expectations of marriage are changing, calling for new and untried adjustments, and separation and divorce may seem to many to be one form of adjustment of conflicting wants and values.

In Contemplating Divorce, What Fears May Be Aroused in the Woman? In the Man?

Loneliness is probably the most omnipotent and painful fear for both man and woman. Frieda Fromm-Reichmann (12) states that the degree of a person's need to depend on others, and the degree of anxiety aroused in him by the threat of isolation, depends upon personal development, but the fear of isolation and loneliness is present in everyone. Marriage is at once the most intimate of relationships and embraces more facets of an individual's personality than do other adult relationships. Loss of this relationship, by and large, therefore, represents a loss of a great number of human satisfactions. Failure in any human relationship, in our culture, carries with it some stigma of shame for the failure, some guilt and question about oneself and one's adequacy.

For the woman, there may be loss of adequate support and the necessity once more to earn her own living and to help in the support of her children. Usually the woman is responsible for the day-to-day rearing of the children, and this imposes a dual burden. She is again faced with the possibility of competing in the marriage market.

In addition to loneliness and the lack of home care, a man may face complicated problems in the financial field. It is more expensive to support two domiciles. Should he marry again, he may be faced with supporting two families, neither adequately. If he remains unmarried, his opportunity for building a sustained and satisfying emotional relationship is limited. His relationship to his children must, of necessity, be piecemeal and unsatisfying. In many instances a man feels unduly and unfairly treated by our divorce laws.

Does Age Have an Effect on the Adaptability of the Partners to Their New Single Lives?

While the adaptability of the individual is not necessarily related to age, but tied in more closely with his total personality structure, the possibilities for finding satisfactions within the social situation differ within the varying age-groups. Obviously, a man or a woman who divorces in the early twenties may find more available partners for a second marriage than will a woman or man in the middle years or later life. Establishing a new way of life, perhaps finding employment after years of being a housewife and finding new friendships present greater problems for the older person.

Are Most Divorced Individuals Emotionally Disturbed?

"Emotionally disturbed" is a very vague characterization with no clear scientific criteria. Everyone is emotionally disturbed in varying degrees during periods of stress. Studies indicate that divorce is the result of tension and conflict in a relationship between two people, where each fails to meet the needs of the other to a satisfacatory degree. This may be due to many different combinations of factors, e.g., differing cultural backgrounds, differing attitudes, values and ideals.

If People Are Emotionally Disturbed After a Divorce, Is It a Result of the Divorce, or Could They Have Been Emotionally Disturbed Before? Is the Death Rate, Suicide Rate or Illness Rate Higher Among Divorced Persons Than Among the Widowed or Married?

The ability of an individual to handle his life situation constructively is related to the degree of flexibility, stability and maturity he possesses. In many instances partners bring into marriage unresolved or unsatisfied needs from childhood, which impose too heavy a burden on the marriage relationship. For these persons, divorce represents another failure to secure wanted satisfactions and adds to the unhappiness.

We have not been able to ascertain any reliable statistical information as to whether the death rate, suicide rate or illness rate is higher among divorced persons than among widowed or married persons.

When Might Divorce Be Considered a Rational, Nonneurotic Course?

Leon Saul (13) defines a neurosis as "essentially a persisting disturbed childhood emotional relationship to the parents (and perhaps siblings)," which influences other relationships. A nonneurotic course of action would thus be one that is determined by the reality factors involved in the specific situation. When two individuals have some understanding of their interpersonal difficulty, and their own part in it, with recognition that it is impossible or improbable that sufficient change will be made to create a satisfactory relationship, a decision to divorce may be essentially healthy and mature.

Is It Possible That Divorce Might Have a Better Effect on a Child Than Would the Continuance of the Marriage?

Yes. It is not possible for parents in serious conflict to create a happy home without undue tensions, simply by willing to do so. Where couples have tried in all possible ways to effect a solution to their difficulties and have not been able to do so, it is probable that the child would be less traumatized by living with one parent in a home relatively without conflicts.

In a study by Paul H. Landis ("The Broken Home in Teenage Adjustments") (14) on adolescent adjustment, the data suggested that children from divorced parents may not have, on the average, a higher number of problems than children from separated homes.

Is It Possible That the Decision To Reject Divorce as a Way of Dealing With Marital Problems Might Be Quite Abnormal?

Yes. If either one or both marriage partners have made every effort to understand and change an unhappy or destructive relationship with no success, and there is no cultural or religious conflict regarding divorce, a desire on the part of one or both to remain in the situation might indicate a neurotic need to suffer or to inflict pain. In other instances, a determination of one partner to hold the other in the marriage despite unhappiness might have as an underlying motivation very deep and immature dependency needs, or a desire to punish the partner for rejection, or a need to possess (rather than love) the partner, or complete self-centeredness which does not recognize another's wants or needs.

How Do Parents Who Are Planning a Divorce Explain to Their Children the New Relationship?

It would be most helpful to the children if the parents could talk with them together, that is, as a unit, explaining: that it seems best for them as man and wife to live separately, and that they will be getting a divorce; that this does not mean, however, that either parent will feel differently toward the children; and that the father, if he is the one who will be living elsewhere, will plan to see the children regularly and will still be their father when they want or need him. Since children often feel that they are responsible for the separation of the parents, because of imagined or real behavioral difficulties, it is important to let the children know that the reason for the divorce is the feeling between the mother and father rather than anything the children have done.

If Either Parent Has Custody of the Children, What Problems Are Likely To Arise in Bringing Them Up?

Children need to feel loved and wanted, to have a feeling of belonging and security. Before divorce has taken place, the security of the child may be badly shaken (15). When one parent leaves, the child may feel deserted, and this, in turn, may increase his feelings of rejection and insecurity. The child may long for the absent parent and feel that the parent with whom he is living is to blame for his loss. Each time the parent visits the child, the child may live through the separating process anew. The parent who has custody may feel that he has the greater burden and may resent this. For the child the question of sexual identity may be hindered, as children learn how to be men or women through identification with the parents of the same sex.

Also, the capacity to relate to the opposite sex may be damaged through unresolved feelings of rejection or anger, and intermittent relationships. Many practical problems arise, such as care of the child while a parent works, discipline, social affairs requiring a particular parent and the child's feeling that he is different from others of his peer group.

Do Substitute Parents Such as Friends or Relatives Provide Satisfactory Adjustments for the Children?

No. Friends or relatives may ease the problem, but as a rule they cannot replace the basic parent-child relationship.

How Is It Possible for the Parent To Make New Relationships With the Opposite Sex Without Arousing Unhappiness or Confusion in the Children?

Children depend for their security and maturation upon the steadiness of warmth, love and understanding of the adults around them, rather than necessarily upon the sole possession of the parent's attention. If the child can be given this kind of understanding and environment by the parent, it is probable that any new relationship with the opposite sex may be handled without major emotional difficulties. Certainly the children will have a reaction and will need an explanation that the new partner is not replacing the father or mother *per se,* but is another person who may be an interested and loving friend to the child. At the same time the child needs assurance that the addition of a new person in the life of one parent will not necessarily change the parent's love or acceptance of the child.

If the Wife or Husband Remarries and the Original Spouse Still Has Visiting Rights, How Can This Be Handled Properly for the Best Interests of the Child?

An effort to help the child understand that the new spouse does not take the place of his own mother or father, but will be an added interested and caring person, is an essential first step. If it is possible for the real parent to visit with the child without the immediate presence of the new spouse, less tension and conflicts will be created for the child. This might be arranged through visits at the home of relatives or in a nonemotional setting.

Do More Men Remarry Than Women? What May Be the Resasons for This?

According to Paul Glick in *American Families* (16): "Divorced and widowed men had higher remarriage rates than divorced and widowed women. Remarriage rates were higher for white women than for nonwhite women during the late 1940's among widowed and divorced women in each age-group under fifty-five years old. An analysis of vital statistics data on the number of divorced in the early 1950's and census data on the previous marital status of persons who had remarried during the same period suggests that about one-half of the divorced women remarry within five years after divorce and that two-thirds will eventually remarry. About three-fourths of the men who obtain a divorce eventually remarry."

Some of the suggested reasons for the differential rate of remarriage between men and women are: (a) If a first marriage has been unhappy, the divorced woman may fear a repetition, or if happy, that it would be disloyal to the previous mate; (b) a woman receiving an income that will stop at remarriage may hesitate to remarry; (c) an older woman may fear that in marrying an older man she will have an invalid to care for; (d) a woman may not want to share her children with another man, or risk the possibility of an unhappy relationship between a new husband and her children; (e) a woman who has had an unsatisfying sexual relationship in marriage may prefer to remain unmarried.

Do Many Divorced Persons Marry "on the Rebound"? How Successful Are These Marriages?

It is impossible to answer this question accurately because no statistics are available on this subject. It is probable that some do marry because of loneliness or hurt, or desire to prove that they are capable of attracting and securing love from the other sex. Census figures indicate that during the period January, 1950, to April, 1953, 12.1 per cent of divorced persons remarried in less than one year after their divorce (17) .

Does the Divorced Man or Woman Engage in More Frequent Sexual Activity Than He or She Did in Marriage?

This question cannot be answered statistically, because no facts are available. It has been conjectured that a high proportion of divorced men and women have sexual relations with their future spouses before remarriage.

Why Does It Seem That a Divorced Woman at the Age of Thirty Has a Better Chance for Remarrying Than a Single Woman at the Same Age Has To Marry for the First Time?

There are many probable factors involved (18). A girl who has reached the age of thirty without marriage may well have some intrapersonal conflict that has fought against marriage, i.e., fear of the male sex, fear of a close relationship, unwillingness to leave the parental home and assume mature responsibilities, or a strong drive toward independence and personal achievement in a career. The divorced woman has, at least, been able to move toward a heterosexual relationship and has had some experience in living in an intimate relationship. Culturally, the girl who has been "chosen" would represent a more desirable person to the American male.

What Problems Does a Divorcée Have in Her New Life as a Single Woman?

The specific problems would depend upon the individual's living situation and personality. Generally, the following problems exist: a changed economic situation; a change in social status, and probably the necessity for developing a different kind of social life; dealing with the problems presented by the children as a one-parent family; need for companionship and affection, including sexual expression; perhaps returning to work, or completing an education as a prelude to working; handling the community's attitude toward divorce; and the often predatory attitudes of both married and single men toward a divorced woman.

What Might Be the Fears of a Divorcée in Contemplation of a Second Marriage? Of a Divorced Man?

The primary fears of each would be: of failure in another marriage; concern about the attitudes of the children toward the new partner; economic problems because the man may be obliged to divide his income between two family groups; feelings of the new partner toward the former spouse, with some lingering doubts about the new partner's involvement with his former spouse. Depending upon the situation, there might be concern about each spouse's own family or the community attitude toward remarriage, especially in certain religious groups.

Is There a Relationship Between Divorce and the Juvenile Delinquent?

The relationship between divorce and behavioral problems is not at all clear, because no adequate studies have been made. The study most frequently quoted, *Unraveling Juvenile Delinquency*, by Sheldon and Eleanor Glueck (19), relates juvenile delinquency to several types of broken homes: (a) divorced; (b) widowed; (c) separated. It is not clear, however, what problems the delinquency may have raised in the divorced and separated homes, or how much conflict and disorganization existed in the marital relationship prior to the divorce. On the other hand, there is no question that a child needs the father (who is usually the absent parent) as an object of love, security or identification, and separation from him would tend to create problems in adjustment and conflict for the child.

Is the Divorced Man Looked Upon Unfavorably by Those Who Have Influence on his Business Career?

The question concerning a divorced man would, in business, by and large, be related to his stability as a person and the reasons for his divorce, rather than disapproval of divorce *per se*. Divorce occasionally creates a job hazard.

Does Society Still Tend To Put a Stigma on the Divorced Woman More Than on the Divorced Man?

Divorce is strongly tied to several sets of value systems in our culture relating to the family. Moral proscriptions against divorce are generally weaker, but marital stability is morally approved of as a desirable social value, and culturally the woman is expected to provide the greater degree of stability in the family. Conversely, when a woman is divorced, she is usually subject to greater scrutiny and more severe judgment on conduct than is a man in a like situation.

Is a Divorced Man "a Poor Risk"?

The fact that a man is divorced does not in and of itself constitute a basis for considering him a "poor risk." The reasons for the divorce, the degree of responsibility he continues to exhibit in caring for his children, financially and emotionally, his general behavioral pattern and his reliability in work would all have some bearing on his reputation and thus on his capacity to form new relationships of a satisfying nature (20).

What Part Might Friends and Relatives of a Divorced Couple Have in Helping Them Adjust to a New Life?

William J. Goode, in his study, *After Divorce* (21), points out that there are no ethical imperatives for relatives or friends that would make them feel constrained to furnish material or emotional support during the crises and afterward to the divorced man or woman. Relatives and friends can help with the period of adjustment and afterward through attitudes of understanding and support, through assistance in finding new friends or jobs when necessary, and with the economic and emotional problems of the children in a new and divided home.

Of What Use Are Social Clubs Specifically Designed for the Divorced Man or Woman?

Usually an individual's social life is subject to considerable change after divorce. Friends may find it necessary to choose one partner to the exclusion of the other, and either partner may find that his previous social life offers no opportunity for meeting prospective partners for remarriage. Social clubs specifically designed for the divorced man or woman offer an opportunity for meeting others with like problems, a group with which both the divorced man or woman may identify and a resource for potential future mates. Divorcée Anonymous, Inc., Single Parents, Inc. and Parents without Partners have served as very real sources of help to divorced persons in those communities in which these groups are organized.

Does the Fact That More Men and Women Are Achieving Higher Education Influence the Divorce Rate?

Inasmuch as there is less divorce among persons of college education than among persons of lesser education, the increase in the number of college-educated persons might tend to influence the divorce rate. The recent trend, however, has been for men and women to marry while in process of education, and thus at a younger age, and there is a close relationship between early marriage and instability of marriage.

Does the New Emphasis on Educating Young People in the Nature and Hazards of Marriage Influence the Divorce Rate?

It is hoped that an understanding of the roles and responsibilities, attitudes and feelings, of man and wife may have a beneficial effect on the stability of present-day marriage. Education for marriage has been in existence, largely on the college level, for the past fifteen to twenty years, so that there has been insufficient time to form conclusions.

What Effect Does Psychotherapy Have in Solving the Emotional Problems of One or Both of the Partners Who Are Contemplating Divorce?

Psychotherapy may be helpful to the individual partner, depending upon the kind and intensity of problems he or she has. Uncovering sources of unconscious hostility, guilt and fear, and clarifying their influences on the marriage, may contribute to a more satisfying marital relationship. It is also possible for an individual to secure help with his own conflicting feelings without in any way stabilizing the marriage. The marriage relationship is a complementary and reciprocal one, in which both partners contribute either to the constructive and healthy relationship, or to the destructive one, and usually it is necessary for each partner to secure help with his part in the difficulty before beneficial change occures in the marriage.

What Success Has Marriage Counseling Had in Keeping Potentially Good Marriages Together?

Marriage counseling has as its primary concern an understanding of the way in which each partner projects his attitudes, feelings, wants, needs and daily behavior into the marital relationship. As each partner comes to understand and wants to change his part in the difficulties between them a potentially good marriage can be stabilized and strengthened. We find that in approximately 65 per cent of the couples counseled, the marriage is strengthened and stabilized through a constructive resolution of the problems presented; in another 30 per cent little or no constructive change results; and in the remaining 5 per cent there is retrogression.

What Success Has the Advice of Friends, Relatives and Ministers Had in Helping a Marriage To Stay Together?

This is a question that cannot be answered factually. However, it has been our experience that "advice" usually does not contribute to the stability of a marriage to any great extent. Since the difficulties in marital unhappiness lie within the interpersonal relationship, help, to be effective, must encompass an understanding of the individual and the interpersonal dynamics within the marriage, and be geared toward assisting each partner to gain an understanding of his or her part in the difficulty, and how to change it. Such marriage counseling is a professional task.

What Agencies or Institutions Are There in the Community Specifically Concerned With the Problems of Divorce?

There are many social agencies throughout the country offering help with marital problems and divorce. There are family-service agencies in more than two hundred cities, offering skilled marriage counseling services. Some family courts now have a staff of trained counselors. The American Association of Marriage Counselors has a list of qualified members living in various communities throughout the country. The National Council on Family Relations, 1219 University Avenue, Minneapolis 14, Minnesota, also carries on an extensive program of public education and research. Information concerning resources may be secured by writing to the American Association of Marriage Counselors, 27 Woodcliff Drive, Madison, New Jersey, or to the Family Service Association of America, 44 East 23rd Street, New York 10, New York.

BIBLIOGRAPHY

1. "Marital Status and Family Status," Bureau of The Census, Current Population Reports, Series P-20, No. 105, March 1960.
2. Report of British Royal Commission on Marriage and Divorce, London, 1955.
3. National Office of Vital Statistics, Public Health Service, Vital Statistics of the United States, 1959, Section 2, Marriage & Divorce Statistics, Table 2A.
4. BRIDGMAN, RALPH P.: The processes of Discord and Estrangement, Divorce and Reconciliation. Family Court Center, Toledo, Ohio.
5. GOODE, WILLIAM J.: *After Divorce.* Glencoe, Illinois, The Free Press of Glenco, 1956.
6. MONAHAN, THOMAS P.: Divorce by occupational level. *Marriage and Family Living,* November 1955.

7. KEPHART, WILLIAM M.: *Family, Society and The Individual.* Boston, Houghton Mifflin Co., 1961, Table 15.

8. See Reference #4.

9. See Reference #5.

10. BERNARD, JESSIE: *Remarriage.* New York, The Dryden Press, 1956.

11. U. S. Bureau of the Census, Current Population Reports, Series P-20, No. 67, Table 13.

12. FROMM-REICHMANN, FREIDA: "On Loneliness." *Psychoanalysis and Psychotherapy.* Selected papers of Frieda Fromm-Reichmann, edited by Dexter M. Bullard, University of Chicago Press, 1959.

13. SAUL, LEON: *Emotional Maturity.* Philadelphia, J. B. Lippincott Co., 1947, Second Edition, 1960.

14. LANDIS, PAUL H.: "The Broken Home in Teenage Adjustments," *Rural Sociology Series on The Family,* No. 4, Pullman, Washington.

15. DESPERT, LOUISE J.: *Children of Divorce.* New York, Doubleday, 1953.

16. GLICK, PAUL C.: *American Families.* U.S. Bureau of Census, p. 136.
    Glick, Paul C., Ibid, p. 139.
    BERNARD, JESSIE: *Remarriage.* New York, The Dryden Press, 1956.

17. National Office Vital Statistics, Vital Statistics, Special Report, Vol. 39, No. 3, Table 4.

18. TERMAN, L. L.: *Psychological Factors in Marital Happiness.* New York, McGraw-Hill, 1938.

19. GLUECK, SHELDON and ELEANOR: *Unravelling Juvenile Delinquency.* Cambridge, Harvard University Press, 1950.

20. *Remarriage,* op. cit. 59, Ref. #16.

21. *After Divorce* (see Ref. #5.)

Chapter 30

THE PRINCIPLE OF DUALITY IN MARRIAGE

EDWARD F. GRIFFITH

APART FROM TWO GREAT WARS, the loss of millions of men and women, the rise and fall of many states and tremendous scientific advances, the first sixty years of this century witnessed great changes in three spheres of human culture: family planning; marriage guidance; and psychosomatic medicine.

My early experiences as a doctor soon introduced me to the problems surrounding the first, from which I rapidly moved into the second, eventually gravitating towards the third — psychosomatic medicine — which not only embraces the other two, but opens the way towards a fourth — a consideration of the ultimate values by which we live and have our being, for without a deeper understanding and acceptance of these values, balanced psychophysical health seems to be impossible.

In this age in particular we have become aware that the interrelationship between the psyche and the soma — between spirit and body, between the hidden and the concrete — is so close that any neglect of or interference with the one is sure to cause some degree of disharmony and disunity in the other, which, if not corrected, may lead to considerable disunity of the personality or even total disintegration, to say nothing of the wider effects which may put our whole social structure in jeopardy.

What is true of our psychophysical health applies with equal relevance to our relationship with others — with man or woman, family or society, and necessarily includes problems of religion and morality which cannot be ignored when trying to evaluate the factors which contribute to our total well-being and, in particular, to the stability of marriage.

The pattern of life we lead today is quite different to that led at the beginning of this century. It was a strange world in which people lived — apparently stable, but really built on foundations whose insecurity we are only now beginning to understand. Its morality was austere, rigid and one-sided — more so, in fact, than it had been for many centuries. Certain things were done, and other things were not done. You either conformed or you did not. If you conformed, well and good; if not, things quickly went wrong.

Such a life pattern was bound to lead to difficulties and conflicts. That is inevitable, however; it is the law of progress. Only so can we face the challenge of the destructive forces of collectivism which beset us as we travel along the evolutionary way.

Being made up of so many different components, psychophysical health only becomes possible for the individual when he discovers the means whereby he can bring about a synthesis of these contending opposites.

It is perhaps the magnitude of our present dilemma which appalls us; the tensions and contentions seem so great — the path so twisted and narrow — though our parents seemed to know what they believed and where they were going. For them, morality seemed quite straightforward. For us, the matter is not so simple.

MORALITY

What, then, is morality? How is it related to our psychological structure or our physical health? How does the one affect the other?

Morality is concerned with conduct, with what we call "good" or "bad," with values relating to behavior, with man's adaptation to society, with religious beliefs, inner feelings and attitudes and, indeed, with much that is hidden, intangible and difficult to understand. Ultimately it is concerned with the conflict between the "I want" attitude to life and the "thou" attitude — with the manner in which my behavior affects those around me and, in particular, those who are near and dear to me.

Many a good business or professional man makes an awful mess of his personal relationships, showing that there is a division or dichotomy hidden within himself: one part — the outer, logical side — works well; the other part, which is concerned with the inner hidden values, with emotions and instincts, does not work at all well, often causing much conflict both within and without.

While the "I want" attitude to life is basically self-seeking, the "thou" attitude touches a deeper level, because it is concerned with the sacredness of personality, with the dignity of human relationships and everything that is to do with Being, that is to say a full, total and complete personality, aware of one's opposites, one's weaknesses and one's strengths.

An amoral person is an individual whose life pattern is so hostile to society that he is not really concerned with the values that make for living and relationship. He has no need of them, for he finds value only in himself. If others suffer through his behavior he is not really aware of it. He has no insight and is completely ruthless. Because he feels no guilt or anxiety he has no conflict and is therefore amoral — a psychopath, in fact.

For morality to exist, therefore, there must be opposites, and where there are opposites there must be conflict; that, too, is a healthy law of life.

The psychoneurotic, on the other hand, is aware of the conflict. Some of his hostility being turned onto himself in the form of symptoms, many of them of a physical nature, he feels the pain, hostility and guilt, though he may not be aware of the relationship between these various physical factors and his inner needs.

I would define the psyche as the total mind — consciousness and unconsciousness — while soma covers everything to do with body, nature and the things we can see, the material values. One might say that the neurophysical mechanism by which these two systems interact is made up of the brain which "thinks" and the sympathetic nervous system which "feels."

Psychosomatic medicine studies the problems and conflict arising from the interrelationship between these two, and endeavors to find ways of minimizing the negative effects which often arise when they get out of balance. It cannot, therefore, avoid considering the problems of morality. Thus the role of priest and physician must overlap. The need to revive a healthy cooperation between these two in the healing role is very necessary.

If man is a psychophysical individual, he is also a psychospiritual one. So do we reach the concept of what is frequently termed flesh and spirit and can extend our principle of duality to that of expression and repression, love and hate and also to that of Logos and Eros, Logos being equated with masculine consciousness and Eros with the feminine opposite. Jung describes Logos as discrimination, judgment and insight, and Eros as the capacity to relate (1).

Though it is becoming well recognized now that if our love relationship when young has been disturbed in some way we are likely to become psychologically hurt, and therefore react with hate and aggression (which, in a sense, is the emotional expression of hate), it is not yet so fully realized that this situation can extend itself to marriage and therefore become the underlying cause of much unhappiness and disharmony which, on the physical level, often manifests itself by disunities and upsets in the sexual sphere.

Both Eros and Logos have to do with love, Eros being basically concerned with the physical and the erotic, and Logos more concerned with the spiritual and creative side of the same drive. If, for the individual, Eros is the god of love, then the erotic dominates. If Logos is love, then the spiritual dominates. If I understand the matter rightly, the Christian religion teaches that both are necessary to mankind — flesh, or human nature, and spirit, or divine nature. The one is complementary to the other, and each is essential to the other if the totality of the personality is to be fully expressed (2). This I believe to be a psychospiritual fact of great practical importance today in dealing with problems of marital disharmony, because one finds that this relationship is usually out of balance.

It is for such reasons that the psychotherapist has a great part to play in the treatment of many difficult marital problems. One may say that many bodily illnesses, and certainly many sexual difficulties, together with a multitude of physical symptoms, are but pointers to this underlying disharmony and frequently require careful and prolonged treatment by psychotherapy.

Many people find it difficult to understand this interrelationship between body and psyche, partly because they cannot see it, and partly because they can only experience it. As such, and because it is largely hidden, they are frightened of it. Thus does such a person go merrily on his way until something happens which makes him suddenly realize his life is lopsided. Some business or matrimonial catastrophe is often a pointer to this inner disharmony, though large numbers of people fail to recognize this warning. It is within man's unconscious, however, that his life roots lie, and he who separates himself from them does so at his peril. To seek conscious understanding of the unconscious, therefore, is neither introspective nor morbid. On the contrary, it is the opposite which is true; not to make contact with these forces, both negative and positive, is the best way to develop a neurosis.

We may say that the research carried out by Freud, Adler and Jung at the turn of the century, to mention but a few of the pioneers, has provided us with working tools to help us understand and combat in some measure the enormous increase in psychosomatic problems which now confront us.

THE REJECTION OF FEMININITY

In the sphere of marriage this conflict of opposites is often reflected on the sexual level: in men who are sexually maladjusted and, in particular, in women who so often say that they do not achieve a satisfactory orgasm. The immense amount of literature that has been poured out on this subject during this century is, I think, a pointer to the deeper psychological conflicts with which woman is confronted at this time.

If we accept the fact that the clitoris is a homologue of the penis (3), and therefore carries or symbolizes masculine values, and that the vagina is essentially a feminine organ carrying feminine values, we can extend our concept of duality and, therefore, of the possibilities of conflict, to the orgasm situation, the clitoral being essentially an expression of a masculine approach and the vaginal one of feminine acceptance, just as the penis is a penetrating and taking organ and the vagina a receptive and giving one. Any woman who has had a full vaginal orgasm will most certainly appreciate the difference. Add the two together and the result is completion.

This is not to say that the clitoral orgasm is not fulfilling: Of course it is, and should be accepted and appreciated fully. Nevertheless, the difference exists and it is interesting to consider why this is so.

My analytical experience leads me to conclude that the women who fail to achieve a vaginal orgasm usually have a background pattern of identification with negative father values, i.e., they feel angry with their fathers.

Though this reaction is usually deeply repressed, it prevents them from relaxing and flowing to the man onto whom they project this hidden resentment. How can a woman flow creatively to man if there is something inside her psyche which rejects him? Such a woman is, in fact, a mixture of fear, anger, resentment and desire, which she does not understand and cannot assimilate because she is not sufficiently conscious; it is all hidden away in her unconscious. Consequently, she can neither flow to man emotionally nor fully accept his sexuality. In other words, her Logos and Eros values are not in harmony. This often leads to a great deal of trouble in the home because the woman often projects these resentments and angers onto others, and particularly on to the husband, in the form of what Jung has termed animus opinions. Such a woman is always right, always knows the answer and always has the last word. This naturally makes for disharmony in the home and is reflected in her attitude to sex, more especially as she often blames the man by saying or implying that it is his fault — that he is unable to give her an orgasm. This naturally upsets the man, who is quite likely to accept her diagnosis, in which case he, too, develops various inadequacies, such as premature ejaculation, thus contributing to the total picture of disharmony.

PSYCHOPHYSICAL CONTENTMENT

I first came across this problem in 1922 when I was house surgeon to the gynecological department of my training hospital. This was the year that the first two birth-control clinics were opened in England, Margaret Sanger having opened the first clinic in the United States in 1916.

I soon discovered that orgasm inadequacy was a matter of major concern to a large number of women, though they rarely mentioned it until encouraged to do so, when a flood of repressed emotion, anxiety and anger was released. To them, the problem of satisfaction, as they termed it, was a major issue. They realized that it caused a great deal of disharmony, but of course they had been brought up to regard the subject as unmentionable. I came across similar situations continually when I started general practice. In those days the medical student was given practically no help or teaching on this matter; one had to discover it all for oneself. Even then I realized that there was a relationship between orgasm, sexual intercourse and fear. Only much later did I realize the immense importance of the psychological factor. The continuous anxiety created in the lives of these women, together with the repressed resentment, caused much unhappiness and even illness, and it seemed to me to be a matter of major importance. So impressed was I by these experiences that I soon started two clinics where I practiced, hoping to relieve the situation in some small measure. After a while, I made an analysis of my cases, reporting my findings to a conference in London in 1933 and later in two or three articles in the medical journals (4). I had thought that by giving a woman a reliable contraceptive method she would automatically experience orgasm, but I was soon to discover that this was not so. While about 50 per cent were considerably relieved and obtained varying degrees of sensation, there remained a further group who were not so helped.

What information I had obtained in my student days about orgasm had led me to believe that is was largely a physiological response to stimulus and happened automatically in both partners when the man ejaculated. In other words, I thought its origin was about 80 per cent physical and 20 per cent psychological. Now I would reverse these figures and say that 80 per cent of the marital difficulties we come across — particularly in the realm of orgasm — are basically due to psychological causes. So impressed was I by the ignorance that I saw around me that I wrote *Modern Marriage* (5). Even then I was impressed with the need for a woman to achieve a vaginal orgasm although I realized that a great many people did not do so, and many authorities felt that this was not fully necessary. What I was really interested in was why this did not come about, and it was only when I became much more psychologically orientated and had my own analysis about twenty years ago that I began to understand the underlying psychological causes. Since then, I have written several more books illustrating the psychological brakes which prevent the achievement of a vaginal orgasm, showing how these can be removed by psychological means, even when physical treatment has failed (6). I came to the conclusion that many of the difficulties women experienced at this level were due to ignorance, which could be eliminated by effective marriage preparation and an adequate contraceptive technique. I discovered that these women quickly attained a satisfactory vaginal orgasm without having a lot of clitoral foreplay, and very soon after the marriage had been consummated — one or two months perhaps.

In speaking of marriage preparation I should include the husbands because it is essential that they should understand these matters as much as the woman. I am also of the opinion that it is quite unnecessary for women to have previous sex experience, that this often makes matters worse rather than better and that excessive and prolonged petting fixes the emotional response at the clitoral level.

THE DEVELOPMENT OF DISHARMONY

I also came to the conclusion that while a number of marriages seem to work reasonably well for some years, somewhere in the late thirties, that is to say in the second half of life, a feeling of frustration and disharmony often creeps into the relationship, and the sex life becomes upset. Why is this?

Among many possible causes it seems that in many of these cases there has been no depth of inner relationship between the couple, the woman often being fully occupied in producing and raising a family, while the husband is taken up with his business. Cohabitation therefore takes the place of cooperative endeavor, and the underlying disharmony is gradually brought to the surface, either because the children are growing up and the wife becomes bored or because they have left home and she has nothing to occupy her. If the original relationship was based largely on a sexual attraction which has dwindled away, nothing much is left. As a result, conflict develops and the basic problem — that of the husband-wife relationship — is brought into the open.

It is an unfortunate fact that when these situations arise the couple often discover that they hardly know what to say to each other, either because they have grown so far apart or because they never had really grown together.

Then again the sexual pattern has probably altered. From being very strong and important, its meaning may have dwindled for one and not the other, who very possibly begins to look elsewhere, or gets caught up in some outside infatuation. The question now arises as to whether the couple will face up to the fact that certain aspects of their personalities have been left behind in the developmental race and now clamor for attention; or will they ignore that fact and try and deal with the whole problem on a practical and somewhat superficial level; or do they simply turn and run, bringing the marriage to an end as quickly as possible? Whatever the cause may be, it is essential that they should face the fact that because each has only partly related to the other, thus leaving behind some hidden part which is now clamoring for attention, this problem can only be brought to the surface and resolved by psychotherapeutic means.

The husband, for instance, may have become so engrossed in his business that he may be living on the extroverted thinking and practical level, thus tending to ignore the inner values of feeling and intuitive awareness which he expressed at the beginning of the marriage and has now forgotten, but which may have attracted his wife to him originally. Or the wife's business or social affairs may have become so important that she may have turned the management of the house over to servants — if she can get them — and the children to a nurse; or she may have devoted herself entirely to the children and rather let the other interests go. So, one way or another, there is no true harmonious relationship between the couple. If they are wise they will seek help, accepting the fact that marriage is one continuous challenge to grow up — to pass from one stage of development to another;

that the relationship does not look after itself, but needs careful and continuous tending, each hurdle being faced and taken together. And, sometimes — because one usually grows faster than the other — one may have to wait and be patient and even suffer very considerably until the other has caught up. I must stress, however, that this reassessment of values cannot be done without outside skilled help, whether from marriage-guidance counselor, priest or psychotherapist. That, at least, is my experience, and one can only speak from experience when one is talking and writing about such matters.

It follows, therefore, that though many marriages appear to be happy and successful on the superficial level, they have no basic foundation; there is no fundamental strength of relationship between the couple on the deeper levels. They have practiced a kind of psychological self-deception for so long that it comes as a shock to them to realize that neither has really understood the needs and feelings of the other — that each has hurt and avoided the other. Such people often develop a sense of failure and emptiness and feel that they are now too old to do anything about it. If they do settle down to deal with the situation they are likely to develop a more fully integrated life. If the problem is avoided the unconscious is likely to present the individual with some other problems — an illness, perhaps — in an endeavor to make him face up to his basic situation.

It is well to remember, however, that there is much evidence to show that there is in the unconscious a self-regulating mechanism which tries to keep the two halves of our personalities — the light and the dark, as it were — in harmonious apposition, so that the wheels turn together in a perfect balance rather than grinding round without there being any real intercommunion at all. This is a subject to which Jung has paid considerable attention (7).

If the couple will not face up to their difficulties then it may be necessary to terminate the marriage.

Human life and development is rooted in the family, which is the kernel of the community and should be the prime concern of society. Disturbed family relationships breed distrust, insecurity and aggression among the children and, ultimately, within society itself. Without the basic stability of healthful family life the state would be meaningless. An unhappy and one-sided family background, especially if it is not recognized, is the best breeding ground for an unhappy marriage later on. It is for such reasons that much more attention should be paid to marriage preparation.

SEXUAL ADEQUACY IN MARRIAGE

Freud drew our attention to many of these problems a long time ago (8). Writing in 1894 about the causes of anxiety neurosis, he made it quite clear that a certain degree of direct sexual satisfaction was necessary for most people, frustration of this need leading to illness, and I see no reason to change this opinion, though one might add that an overaccentuation of the physical — of what he termed direct sexual satisfaction — frequently produces exactly the same degree of frustration and unhappiness, more especially if it is devoid of those other intangible elements which go to make relationship.

We must ask ourselves therefore what is the exact meaning of the term "direct sexual satisfaction"? Is it to be interpreted as a mere biological relief of tension, as occurs so often in the indiscriminate relationships which we come across so frequently nowadays, or does it mean something deeper and more lasting? While increased knowledge and understanding has its values, and is indeed essential for the development of the mature family relationship in a mature society, increased sexual freedom does not, by itself, provide the satisfaction to which Freud and others are obviously drawing attention — pleasure perhaps, but not a more permanent state of happiness, contentment and maturity.

The phrase "direct sexual satisfaction" must refer therefore to the whole man and not merely to his physical makeup. It should include that satisfaction which will only be found on the higher levels of the personality. Sexual activity is a psychophysical experience and, as Freud said in his paper, if it is to be satisfactory on the physical level it must be accompanied by acceptance by the psyche.

I fail to see how this further development is likely to become established until men and women learn to know each other as equal personalities, respecting their differences and encouraging the development of inner strengths which each needs to obtain from the other. Looked at from that angle, sexual activity can no longer be regarded as a mere copulatory act.

Nevertheless, it must never be forgotten that the sex drive is neither moral nor immoral; rather is it amoral — that is to say, a force which can be directed into positive or negative channels. It is one of the most potent forces which we have within us, and is capable of transformation onto most positive and creative levels. Used indiscriminately it will never provide the fundamental satisfactions which are so essential to our nature and for which we are usually seeking. Men and women have to learn to become companions, not merely sexual playmates, but companions in friendship, love and mutual understanding. Only then will the double standard be replaced by a more mature pattern of relationship, so enabling woman to achieve a satisfactory orgasm within the context of the oneness and friendship which should exist as a basis.

Only within comparatively recent times has the distinction between the mating and reproductive aspects of the sex impulse been clearly recognized, and only still more recently has it been possible to give effective expression to both in marriage. This naturally opens up further problems, because it now becomes possible for one to be used without the other. Here again, therefore, we find ourselves living in a transitional age in which we are being challenged to achieve greater insight and understanding, greater maturity and greater conscious regulation of our instinctive life, not by repression but by redirection.

All this demands considerable thought as to how young people are to be educated to reach a mature relationship in marriage. It is probable that we are now entering an era when much more attention will have to be given to the problem of education in its widest sense, starting in infancy almost, certainly progressing through the various different ages of school and university, up to the time of marriage preparation. And within this educational system we shall be wise if we devise means of educating the parent population, because a clear interchange of views between parent and child, in the spirit of love and toleration, will enable young people to grow to a greater maturity before marriage, thus having a greater chance of establishing fulfilling homes themselves. So do we enter an era when we need to develop a much greater consciousness.

THE DESTINY OF MAN

In a recent article on the destiny of man, Sir Julian Huxley discussed matters which are relevant to this theme and may be shortly summarized (9).

> Natural selection is an ordering principle of life and is the essential mechanism which directs the force of evolution. In the light of our modern knowledge of genetics and mutation, we can study it scientifically and measure its force; it takes the disorderly material provided by random or chance variations, and guides it into ordered paths of change, thus producing biological efficiency and higher levels of organization. It has also led to an increasing development of the mental and psychological capacities of life and an increasing awareness of all kinds. This surprising fact is in itself a disproof of all exclusively materialistic interpretations. The improvement and awareness of these factors is just as significant as that of our material structure and physiological organization.
>
> Of many so-called dominant groups, man is the latest. His striking evolutionary success is due entirely to his improved brain and mind, which gave him the capacity for rational and imaginative thought, for true speech, with words and symbols denoting things and ideas, instead of merely sounds and gestures expressing feelings and emotional attitudes. This enabled him to transmit experience and awareness cumulatively from generation to generation.
>
> He is thus provided with a second mechanism of heredity over and

above the genetic system of his chromosomes; a mechanism for transmitting knowledge and ideas instead of material particles like genes. Man is indeed a new and unique kind of organism and has stepped over the threshold of a quite new phase or sector of the evolutionary process. We can call it the human or psycho-social phase. He is the sole representative of a new realm or grade of being — shall we call it the psychozoa? — equivalent in importance to all the rest of the animal kingdom. In this sector, evolution is no longer purely biological but primarily cultural. What evolves is human social institutions, laws, arts, sciences, educational systems and codes of morals.

Man alone is capable of anything big in the way of further evolution. Major evolution has come to an end, except in one direction, that of better brains and minds. Only man has been able to cross the biological barrier into the new psycho-social domain. The setting up of values and the exercise of moral judgments is an inevitable consequence of these new capacities. Values are new products of past psycho-social evolution and can influence its future course. They are the products of our human awareness; they evolve in relation to the enlargement of our understanding.

The time is now ripe for an intensive and scientific study of man's destiny and psycho-social evolution, for he is to be the instrument of further evolution on earth. This evolution could be regressive or progressive. It is up to us to find the right direction; to discover and realize new and richer possibilities for life and thus, greater fulfillment for ourselves. This is our privilege but also our grave and almost frightening responsibility.

As I said in the paper from which I have quoted these extracts, these stimulating ideas put the relationship between psychology, religion, sociology and morality in its proper setting (10). They show and, indeed, demand recognition of the fact that man is now confronted with two tasks: personal individuation and psychosocial organization. Huxley insists on the importance of values — of subjective reality as being essential in the development of man's mind. He is, in fact, underlining in his own way Jung's concept of the self. Consider, therefore, what Jung has to say:

> In studying the history of the human mind, one is impressed again and again by the fact that the growth of the mind is the widening of the range of consciousness, and that each step forward has been a most painful and laborious achievement. One could almost say that nothing is more hateful to man than to give up even a particle of his unconscious (11).

In order to leave the unconscious, however, we have to return to it. This paradox is one of the most difficult things for the ordinary individual to accept. It seems ridiculous to suggest that in order to advance to further conscious awareness we have to return to our inner life to find what has been left behind and come to terms with those aspects we do not like, because we have been deprived or hurt, whether they be tie-ups in the personal unconscious or archetypal situations or, more probably, a combination of both.

For the majority of people seeking psychological help, the problems of the personal unconscious are so strong and, in particular, the parental tie-ups are so vivid, that much time and labor has to be borne before the ego is free to live its own life, unhampered by the fears, guilts, resentments and various subjective physical conditions which absorb so much of the individual's energy that he has very little left for the advancement of his life's task in his own way and according to his own nature. The point is that the problems which trouble the individual are unconscious, so that he is, in fact, unaware of their real origin because they are buried and not allowed entry into consciousness. All that he is aware of are his symptoms: his moods, frustrations and various physical ills. He does not know their cause. Nevertheless, he worries about them continually and becomes introspective so that his friends and relations, seeing only the stupid and irrational manner in which he behaves, tell him to pull himself together, instead of taking the symptoms seriously and advising him to seek psychological help. That, they say, is the last thing he needs; he is too introspective already; much better see a specialist!

Nevertheless, as Freud constantly insisted, his background has to be worked over and accepted before he can hope to progress towards a real discovery of the self, which concept is probably Jung's greatest contribution to the thought of our age, opening up as it does an immense vista of future development along the lines Huxley has indicated.

For many, however, these ideas are still too airy-fairy, too nebulous and too devoid of reality. It is probable, however, that any advance toward the deeper understanding of the problems of physical health or of spiritual insight will have to pay far more attention to these psychological factors than has been done in the past. We are, I believe, on the verge of new understanding in this realm, just as we are in the more objective and practical sphere of material and scientific advancement.

It seems possible, therefore, that the increased tensions we suffer from today are a measure of the possibilities for further advance which lie ahead. The problem, of course, is to find the reconciling factor. The closer co-operation of priest and doctor in the field of psychophysical medicine should be one of these factors, providing we can agree that man's natural instinctive drives are as pleasing to God as his spiritual ones, that each, indeed, is a reflection of the other, as the Egyptians believed six or seven thousand years ago, while the acceptance of the need for help in finding the way to a greater maturity should be the contribution of each one of us. We need psychological help in order to grow up more fully, just as we need spiritual in-

sight to learn, not because we are ill, but because this is the next state in
the cultural and evolutionary development of which Huxley speaks: "The
setting up of values and the exercise of moral judgments being an inevitable
consequence of the new capacities of man."

THE RECONCILIATION OF OPPOSITES

Much of our trouble today is due to the fact that the feeling values, so
closely linked to the soma and naturalness of the body, have for too long
been made taboo. That, I think, was the tragedy of our puritanical upbringing at the beginning of this century when we lived under the aura
of sanctity and a misguided morality imposed from without. Our problem
today is to discover how to develop this morality within, for only so shall
we be able to find that greater consciousness we so much need — a consciousness that can recognize the opposites and hold the tensions.

Morality, says Jung, is a function of the human soul, as old as humanity
itself; it cannot be imposed upon people from outside. "We have it in
ourselves from the start — not the law, but our moral nature without which
the collective life of human society would be impossible. That is why morality is found at all levels of society. It is the instinctive regulator of action
which also governs the collective life of the herd" (12).

Our need today is to bring these dark instinctual forces into the light
of day — into consciousness — for they are the basis of our psychic life.
Symbolically, as I have tried to show, they are represented by the Greek
god, Eros. To my mind, Freud's major contribution to our times is that he
made us face the significance of the erotic. He did not say that disturbances
in the sexual sphere were the sole cause of a neurosis, but rather, as one
writer puts it, that "difficulties in the sexual sphere are a revealing index
to a neurotic personality and can be looked upon in that light" (13).

Jung, I think, takes the matter further. Eros, he says, has two sides to
his nature. "He belongs on the one side to man's primordial animal nature
which will endure as long as man has an animal body. On the other side,
he is related to the highest forms of the spirit. But he only thrives when
spirit and instinct are in right harmony. If one or other aspect is lacking to
him, the result is injury or at least a lopsidedness that may easily veer towards the pathological. Too much of the animal distorts the civilized man
and too much civilization makes sick animals. This dilemma reveals the
vast uncertainty that Eros holds for man" (14).

Our task, therefore, is to build a new and more creative philosophy of
life which, while satisfying the adventurous spirit of man, will be directed
towards cultural pursuits that are peaceful and cooperative. Love and
tenderness, faith, hope and charity can never be provided by the state, but
only by man's personal endeavor and insight. Man's stability necessitates

the establishment of a balanced equilibrium between his environmental background, his psychophysical needs and his spiritual foundations.

In the furtherance of this evolutionary task, religion and medicine, priest and doctor, will have to find new insights and understandings of the problems and attitudes of the other. To this end, more people will have to travel the psychotherapeutic path.

Maybe the cataclysm of this century has been the birth pangs of a new venture, in which case the churches will have to teach their truths in a new way with the help of the psychotherapist. By this means the healing of psychosomatic illness, while embracing every possible scientific and material advance known to us, will include a new evaluation of the symbolic and a greater appreciation of the workings of the spirit, so that all these forces can work together in accordance with the age-old laws of nourishment and love given to us by the great healer of all time — the father and mother of us all, as the Egyptians used to call the Divinity.

REFERENCES

1. JUNG, C. G.: *Mysterium conjunctionis, C. W., 14*:179, 1963, p. 179.
2. TEMPLE, WILLIAM: *Readings in St. John's Gospel.* New York, Macmillan, 1950, Ch. I.
3. HAMILTON, BOYD, and MOSSOM: *Human Embryology.* Cambridge, Heffer, 1962, pp. 298, 311.
4. GRIFFITH, E. F.: The medical aspects of marriage guidance. *Lancet,* Feb. 1, 1947.
5. GRIFFITH, E. F.: *Modern Marriage,* 26th Ed. London, Methuen, 1964.
6. GRIFFITH, E. F.: *Marriage and the Unconscious.* Secker & Warburg, 1957. New and Revised Edition; Springfield, Thomas, 1967; and *Ups and Downs in Married Life.* London, Methuen, 1966.
7. JUNG, C. G.: *The practice of psychotherapy. C.W., 16*:123, 1954.
8. FREUD, S.: *The Anxiety Neurosis, C.P., I*:95 ff, 1894.
9. HUXLEY, JULIAN: *The Destiny of Man.* Hodson, H. V. [Ed.], Editor of the *Sunday Times,* to both of whom the writer is grateful for permission to quote.
10. GRIFFITH, E. F.: Psychosomatic medicine. Guild of Pastoral Psychology, 108, 1959.
11. JUNG, C. G.: *Contributions to Analytical Psychology.* Kegan, Paul, [Ed.], 1945, p. 340.
12. JUNG, C. G.: *Two essays. C.W., 7*:26, 1953.
13. WEISS, E., and ENGLISH, O. S.: *Psychosomatic Medicine.* Philadelphia, Saunders, 1947, p. 11.
14. JUNG, C. G.: *Two essays. C.W., 7*:27, 1953.

Chapter 31

CONJOINT MARITAL COUNSELING

GEORGE CALDEN

THERE HAVE BEEN MANY PROCEDURES used in the counseling of maritally troubled people. One of the major ways of dealing with the disturbed marriage has been the individual counseling or psychotherapy for only one of the spouses. In Eisenstein's *Neurotic Interaction In Marriage* (3), for example, the individual psychoanalysis of one of the marriage partners is almost the exclusive form of treatment.

Another procedure for handling disruptive interaction is through concurrent counseling or psychotherapy. The most common form of concurrent marriage counseling is that in which one counselor sees the husband and wife in separate, individual sessions. This appears to be the procedure of choice among marriage counselors. A survey of the techniques utilized by members of the American Asociation of Marriage Counselors, as reported in *Marriage Counseling: A Casebook* (1), indicates that a majority of the marriage-counseling cases were conducted in this manner. A second form of concurrent marriage counseling occurs when one counselor or therapist counsels the husband in individual sessions, while another counselor meets with the wife. Usually the counselors work independently of each other, or they may compare notes fleetingly during a busy lunch period. Occasionally, as in the Martin and Bird (8) "stereoscopic technique," the husband's therapist and the wife's therapist hold regularly scheduled conferences, at which time each therapist presents his version of the behavior of the marriage partners. The two versions are then viewed together in order to detect the distorted perceptions of either or both partners.

A third procedure that is being used increasingly is that of conjoint marriage counseling in which the same counselor sees the husband and wife together in joint sessions. At appropriate times the husband and wife also are seen in separate meetings. In this form of conjoint counseling a much greater emphasis is placed directly on the disturbed marital interaction itself, although the intrapsychic forces within each individual spouse are not ignored.

Conjoint marriage counseling has received its major impetus from the increased use of family therapy techniques, as well as from the studies of Jackson and Weakland (7) on family interaction and communication. Several recent expositions of conjoint treatment of marital disturbance are those of Bach and Alexander (2), Haley (6), Watson (10), Geist and

Gerber (5) and Sherman (9). Conjoint marriage counseling has a number of unique features. With the marriage partners present, one can immediately observe and deal with the distorted perceptions and defensive behavior that characterize so much of the marital interaction. Since the theater of operations of the marriage is in full view, the counselor can readily see the biases, distortions and destructive behavior of each participant and can bring them to their attention. Conjoint counseling also offers the possibility of reducing the time and expense involved in treatment.

The aim of this chapter is to describe several aspects of one form of conjoint marriage counseling. One may debate whether this approach should be called marriage counseling or marriage psychotherapy. If one arbitrarily views counseling as a procedure that focuses primarily on reality-oriented problem solving and psychotherapy as psychodynamically oriented, this counseling procedure can be viewed as a combination of both.

This approach has been proven fruitful in helping couples who have been referred to the writer specifically for marriage counseling. In most instances, a legal action for divorce or separation has either been initiated prior to the counseling or has been seriously considered. A minority of referrals are for persons with neurotic or psychosomatic symptoms such as depressions, anxiety reactions, peptic ulcers, asthma, back pain, headaches or sexual disorders. The referring physician usually senses that the aggravated marital situation plays a crucial role in the etiology of the symptoms. In each of these cases, the patient's spouse is asked to participate fully in the counseling. A further source of referral is from other psychotherapists who have seen the husband and wife in individual or concurrent therapy, without success, and who wish to try an interactional approach.

THE NATURE OF DISTURBED MARITAL INTERACTION

Counselors who have worked with marriage partners know that the disturbed marital interaction is an unusually complex and dynamic one that varies from couple to couple. In listening to husbands and wives express their unhappiness, however, one hears, over and over again, regardless of the specific interacting personality dynamics, three basic interweaving themes rising above the discordant notes. These themes, which occur with an almost deadly monotony, involve three major frustrations in the marital relationship:

1. *The mutual frustration of each other's psychological needs.* There is a mutual sapping of each other's feelings of self-worth and self-liking, resulting in a vicious circle of mutually destructive fight-flight interactions. Each partner behaves as if he and she were on a seesaw. By downgrading the spouse each hopes to be elevated at the other's expense. Each pushes the

other down, on the psychological seesaw, or jumps off while the other lands with a thud.

2. *The frustration of effective communication.* As a consequence of the ego-destructive relationship, constructive communication has broken down. Husband and wife are unable to talk to each other or react in a reasonable fashion. Through selective inattention or overattentiveness, projection or distortion, there is a chronic misinterpretation of the partner's actions and motives and a continual anticipation of being belittled or ignored by the partner. It is not the voice of the turtle that is heard, but rather the voice and actions of the angry, hurt or indifferent spouse.

3. *The frustration of each other's marital expectations.* Even more significant than the disappointments in the conscious expectations are the frustrations of unconscious marital hopes. These hidden expectations are based on each spouse's childhood or adolescent experiences within his or her family constellation. The most common expectations of this kind are the unconscious hope for a spouse who would either be like or unlike a significant parental or sibling figure, or for a spouse toward whom one can compulsively act out an unresolved conflict.

The specific techniques of this form of conjoint marriage counseling are aimed directly at reversing these frustrating marital relationships. In a direct, active fashion the partners are helped to avoid the excessive personalization of the spouse's defensive behavior. They are helped to minimize the destructive, fight-flight interactions and are urged to enhance their own and each other's feelings of self-worth. The counselor aids them in improving communications and helps them realistically to assess and modify their marriage expectations.

The major focus of this presentation will be on the counseling techniques utilized for dealing with the first central theme, i.e., the mutual frustration of each other's psychological needs. The other two themes will be alluded to in a secondary way.

THE FRUSTRATION OF PSYCHOLOGICAL NEEDS
"Right" and "Wrong"

During the first introductory session, each partner is seen both separately and together. Although the conjoint meeting is the predominant mode, partners generally are seen separately for one or two counseling sessions during the early stages of treatment in order to give each partner an opportunity to express his or her feelings about each other as well as to discuss their individual backgrounds and marital expectations. Usually a great deal of feeling is expressed during these early sessions. Anger, tears, righteous indignation, self-pity, hurt silence, despair and hopelessness are among the most frequent emotions on display. The delightful perceptual relationship, typified by the statement, "Love is blind," has long disappeared. Instead, the opposite expression, "Hate has sharp eyes," rules the roost. The sharp, critical lenses of each partner's psychological camera is zeroed in on each other's behavior.

In contrast to individual counseling or psychotherapy, where the disturbed person comes to treatment with an awareness that there is something wrong with himself, the typical partner in the marriage case will try to convince the counselor that there is something essentially "wrong" with the spouse. Each partner will insist that the spouse is predominantly responsible and to blame for the marital failure. In characteristic ego-defensive fashion, each partner will point to the corroded rust in the personality armor of the spouse, while trying to impress the counselor with the glow of his or her own shining armor, tarnished only as a result of the onslaughts of the partner. The refrain, expressed implicitly or explicitly, of "I am right and he is wrong," or "I am right and she is wrong," is repeated over and over again like a stuck phonograph record.

During the early sessions each partner expects the counselor to be a sort of Court of Human Relations judge or referee who will see the "rightness" of his or her behavior and the "wrongness" of the spouse's conduct. After the counselor "sees the light" and is convinced of the "rightness" of one partner, he is expected, in a relatively few sessions, to "straighten out" the other partner and persuade him to follow the path that is "right," i.e., each partner's notion of what is "right." Many couples do not even have these expectations. They feel, in despair, that their partner is hopeless and beyond redemption, and will never learn to behave in the "right" way.

When the partners are seen together, toward the latter part of the first session, the counselor expresses his awareness and concern for their hurt, angry and disappointed feelings. He indicates, however, that they have this unhappiness in common, and that they are faced with a common problem that requires the participation of both of them for a solution. At no time does the counselor reinforce the notion of blaming either partner, but encourages each one to see their disturbed marital interaction as a *mutual problem* that can be worked out by both of them. Each partner is urged to explore the ways in which *he* or *she* can improve it.

The counselor also openly discusses some of the patient's distorted notions of what the counseling or therapy is supposed to consist of. He tries to correct these notions by pointing out that his intention is not to be a partisan who will ally himself with one of the partners against the other. His goal is not to "straighten out" either partner according to the other's conception of what is "right." The counselor further points out that the most important "right" that the participants will be concerned with is "what is the most effective, most satisfying way of relating to each other," and how to achieve this. This is to be the overriding "right." What is "right" for both of them is the goal to be worked for. The counselor adds that a disturbed marriage may not have been caused by the husband and wife having selected the "wrong" partner, but may have been brought about by their not having learned effective ways of relating to each other.

An illustrative example is given to the partners of two auto drivers who are approaching an intersection at right angles to each other. The driver who has the right-of-way observes, to his horror, that the other driver, who is in a great hurry, has ignored the stop sign and continues to drive ahead. The couple is then asked which is the more important "right" in this situation. Should each driver insist he has the right-of-way and crash into the other? Or is there a more important "right"; namely, how can *both* of them or either one of them avoid the head-on crash?

By reviewing the actual interpersonal crashes of the couple, stress is placed on each partner bearing a responsibility for solving problems, regardless of who appears to be "right" on the surface. Rather than perseverating or blaming each other, the partners are repeatedly encouraged to de-emphasize the individual "rightness" or "wrongness" and to view their divergent attitudes as mainly differences of opinion to be resolved constructively.

To illustrate:

Mr. and Mrs. K. are being seen in their third joint-counseling session. The husband has had a high-school education and runs a small store. The wife, who appears quite domineering, works as a cleaning woman. She has had only an eighth-grade education. They review a fight they have had during the week. They had quarrelled originally over a disagreement concerning their children's homework. The husband had insisted that his wife should review the children's arithmetic homework to make sure that it is done correctly before being turned in. His wife, however, maintained that parents shouldn't put too much pressure on their children to have their homework done absolutely right. She felt that the children should be encouraged to do their best, and that it is the teacher's responsibility, not the parents, to correct any mistakes. This dispute led to violent shouting and incriminations. The husband responded with a flight reaction. He stalked out of the house, went to a local tavern and returned home late, more belligerent than ever. As the husband and wife related the incident, each turned to the counselor for reassurance that he or she was "right" and the other was "wrong."

At this point the counselor remarked, "Well, each one of you thinks he's right about how to deal with the children's homework. But was your way of settling your differences "right"? Did your way of solving this disagreement bring you closer together or did it push you further apart? Was your way of going about it right?"

The couple initially completely ignored the counselor's statements and continued to discuss the merits of each other's "rightness" about homework.

The husband declared, "Our children's education is very important and they should get the best help from their parents."

The counselor countered this with "Yes. Stopping for stop signs is important, too. But what happened between you is extremely important too. That is why you are here. What actually did happen between you?"

The wife sheepishly stated, "I guess we crashed."

The husband was taken aback by her temporary nondefensive attitude and expressed his agreement. "Yes, we crashed."

The wife then blurted out, with considerable feeling, "How do you expect me to help them with this new arithmetic? I've only had an eighth-grade education." The wife then revealed her feelings of inferiority about book learning. It turns out that the entire area of helping her children with their homework was highly threatening to her and made her feel inferior to her husband, who had had more schooling. The husband, now in a placating mood, stated that he had never been aware of this.

He declared, "Had I known this I wouldn't have gotten so sore to begin with."

They ultimately decided to solve this problem by the husband agreeing to spend more time with their children's arithmetic while the wife agreed not to sabotage his efforts.

In this episode, the couple was given a small, but significant experience in modifying their relationship. As the saying goes: "One experience is worth a thousand words." By focusing on the wrongness of their relationship, rather than being fixated on the "rightness" of their individual positions, they were able to diminish slightly the three basic frustrations. They were able to: (a) become less defensive; (b) become more communicative and understanding of each other; and (c) partially open the door to explore the wife's unconscious expectations in the marriage. Later in counseling it was learned that she had been raised by a strict, abusive father. She unconsciously had hoped for a husband who would either be docile and submissive or against whom she could retaliate for the abuses she suffered from her father. In marriage she was overly sensitive to, and ready to, attack any trait in her husband which suggested superiority, in this case, superiority in arithmetic.

In addition to the above, the couple was helped in a small way to adopt a *problem-solving* attitude, rather than a problem-creating one. This not only produced a temporary, amicable solution to the homework problem, but also helped to offset some of their feelings of futility concerning the future of their marriage. This technique of focusing the partner's attention on the wrongness of their relationship, and insisting that they work out a constructive solution, is used again and again. Couples are given an opportunity to face and solve problems directly, instead of being derailed by ego-defensive battles. A consistent application of this problem-solving attitude helps considerably in building a sense of self-esteem and worthwhileness in both husband and wife.

The Vicious-Circle Pattern

During the early sessions, the counselor didactically explains the three basic themes of marital frustration to the couple, and indicates that a major portion of the treatment will be concerned with helping them to reduce these frustrations.

Concerning the first theme, i.e., the mutual frustration of each other's psychological needs, the counselor explains to the couple, in fairly simple language, that all of us have two basic psychological needs: the need to feel worthwhile and the need to feel likable. We all wish to feel self-respect and self-appreciation. When each marriage partner feels likable and worthwhile, they both feel happy. Psychologically, each one is in an excellent position to convey to the spouse that he or she is also worthwhile and likable. However, if the opposite occurs, namely, if one or both partners is led to feel uncared for and unworthy, they often find it extremely difficult to convey liking and worthwhileness to the other. Faced by feelings of being blamed, rejected, downgraded, ridiculed and nagged, each partner becomes defensive. Feeling unliked and unworthwhile, they defend themselves through *fight-flight* techniques. Each partner, in an "eye for an eye" fashion, will either withdraw or attack the spouse in the one thousand and one ways couples devise for hurting each other and destroying each other's feelings of self-worth. The most common "fight" reaction is to verbally blame, criticize or ridicule the spouse. The most common form of "flight" reaction is to escape into one's own shell of silence and noncommunication by sexual withdrawal. In this cold war each one nurtures his own hurts and angry feelings, or tries to dispel feelings of unworthiness by fantasies of revenge or fantasies of the "suffering hero" variety. Some married people escape into work by working late hours. In this manner, they seek ego-satisfaction through work, and at the same time they retaliate against their spouse through their absence from home. Some escape into the ephemeral, ego-enhancing state of drinking. Others escape into the arms of another man or woman who "really appreciates" them, i.e., in whose eyes they read the message, "You are a worthwhile and likable human being."

When either partner indulges in fight or flight, the other partner interprets this and feels unworthy or unwanted, and resorts to his or her favorite retaliatory fight-flight reactions, and the vicious circle is on. Soon each one starts to anticipate the ego-destructive behavior of the other and will often interpret the most harmless and even constructive behavior of the spouse as being critical, downgrading or insincere. The couple behaves like the proverbial pair of porcupines who are trying to make love. Each yearns for love and respect in marriage. But instead, their inadequate ego-defensive behavior, like porcupine quills, produces the expectations and the actual fulfillment of mutual pain. We will refer to this mutual conveying of feelings of unworthiness as the *vicious-circle pattern*.

One simple example of the unfolding of the vicious-circle pattern will suffice:

> A husband feels under considerable pressure at his job. One day, before returning home from work, he joins a friend for a "short beer" at a local tavern. His wife, feeling frustrated, rejected and *unworthwhile* at her husband's late homecoming (and the spoiling of the supper meal), attacks him bitterly for his inconsiderateness. Feeling *unworthy and unliked* by her onslaught, he becomes resentful. First he shouts back (fight) and then stalks out of the house (flight), leaving his home-cooked meal still uneaten. Later in the week he drops in at the tavern and returns late again. Apparently, the congenial nonthreatening atmosphere of the tavern gives him a much greater feeling of ego-enhancement than the atmosphere at home where his "nagging" wife awaits him. She, in turn, feels even more uncared-for and unworthy at his late homecoming and his preference for being out with the "boys." She punishes him by resorting to more blaming, nagging and shouting. And so the vicious circle continues and spreads, each person reacting to his own feelings of unworthiness, feelings triggered by the behavior of the spouse.

> One Sunday morning, before going to church, the husband senses his wife's irritable mood, personalizes it and decides to escape his wife's impending wrath momentarily by playing an early game of golf. He promises to be home by 10:30. By 11:00 he has finished his golf but is in the tavern having a few friendly beers with his golf partners, again partially to escape his wife. She, in turn, senses where he is and angrily phones the tavern, commanding the tavern keeper to send her "no-good husband" home immediately. The husband, feeling completely humiliated, tries to prove to his friends that he is not henpecked. He simply doesn't return home all day. And so the mutual ego-destructiveness rolls on until each partner becomes allergic to the other's behavior. Each responds by spreading the ego-destructive pollen even further.

Examples of such vicious-circle relationships can be cited *ad nauseum*. A major emphasis in this form of conjoint counseling is to discuss, with the partners, this state of holy deadlock in terms of each one's contributions to the vicious-circle pattern. Over and over again, their behavior is reviewed, both individually and jointly, and they are helped to see how each worsens the vicious-circle pattern. Regardless of who appears "right" or "wrong," couples are urged to pursue constructive ways of relating in order to break the vicious circle. They are helped to see that each partner's insistence on being "right" is part of the hot and cold war of the vicious circle.

In the above case, the wife was asked in an individual session whether *her* technique of shouting at him and phoning the tavern had either changed his behavior or had improved the relationship. She admitted that it hadn't. After a few minutes of defending her behavior, she was asked to look at her own and her husband's action in terms of the vicious-circle pattern. She was helped to see how much of his conduct was defensive in nature, and how her own defensiveness and blaming attitude simply perpetuated his behavior and deepened the vicious circle. She agreed to try to reverse the approach. She reported, a week later, that one morning she had spoken to her husband in a pleasant manner. She expressed to him her realization that he was under considerable pressure on his job and she understood his need for a relaxing glass of beer after work. She added that she hoped he would come home early for supper, but continued to express empathy for his need to go to the tavern. That evening, to her surprise, the husband returned home directly from work. He had his "short beer" at home! The wife later stated in treatment, "I used to put all the blame on him. Now I realize how much I've driven him to it."

The husband later expressed himself as follows: "When I came home, she used to cut me down. She made me feel like an 'aught.' I realized that fighting back didn't help, so I decided to spend my time at the tavern. Now I realize that drink was an anesthetic. I sure was bowled over when she told me it was all right for me to have a few drinks. For the first time I felt I was not an 'aught.' "

During counseling sessions, arguments and fights between couples, which have been viewed traditionally as purely destructive and to be avoided, are for a time permitted to continue. Then the counselor "rings the bell," so to speak, for the end of the round. The couple is firmly requested to view their fighting in terms of the "what is right for the relationship." If the couple at any time resumes the ego-destructive fight, the counselor again "rings the bell" and insists on their concentrating on a positive solution to their relationship.

Arguments and fights which occur between counseling sessions are reviewed and discussed in the same way, in the presence of both husband and wife, or with one alone. A wife, for example, reported that she had been ill with the flu that week. When her husband came home, she had responded in characteristic ego-defensive terms. She already had anticipated that her husband might say, "Are you sick again?"

The wife continued, "Before he could even open his mouth, I shouted, 'Yeah, I'm sick again. But it doesn't make any difference since you don't care anyway.' " The husband reacted to this remark by going into his room, slamming the door and ignoring her for three days.

During the discussion of this incident, the wife was able to see how her proneness to feeling unworthy and her blaming and criticizing behavior contributed to the vicious circle. She then was asked what alternative behavior might have been used.

After a pause, she answered, "I could have said 'I've got the flu and you know how touchy it makes me.' "

When asked what she could have done even *after* her self-pitying and blaming remarks had been uttered, and after her husband had left the room, she replied, "I could have left a card on the breakfast table or taped to the bathroom wall, saying 'I'm sorry' or something. He always behaves better when he knows I'm trying to be nice."

This same couple had been sleeping in separate bedrooms for the past two years. This situation had begun originally when she had reacted in "flight" fashion to his reading late in bed with the night light on. After this couple had resolved a number of disputes in the therapy sessions, the bedroom situation was discussed. The problem was resolved simply by a suggestion made by his wife. She decided to return to his bed and wear an eyeshade!

After obtaining insights into their vicious-circle reactions, couples learn to employ diverse ways of coping with their ego-destructive behavior either in advance of threatening situations or afterwards. One woman patient found it effective, when she momentarily felt humiliated by, or angry at, her husband, to retreat to her room and pray. This action reduced her feelings of anger, restored her feelings of self-respect and helped her to view her husband's behavior in a less blaming way. Another woman, who had grasped the significance of the vicious-circle pattern, decided to do something to enhance her husband's feelings of self-worth. One day, after she and her husband had quarreled, she decided to bake a unique cake for him. Instead of inscribing the top of the cake with the familiar "Happy Birthday" she wrote "Happy Worthday" on it! Some marriage partners would signal to each other in advance that he or she is in a touchy mood and prone to displace hostility on to the partner. In this fashion, a wife going through her menstrual tension, or a husband upset about his work situation, would communicate to the partner that his or her irrational behavior is not to be personalized by the spouse.

FRUSTRATION OF COMMUNICATION

Couples who have lived for years in a chronic state of noncommunication and indifference learn to express mutual respect by being more open with each other and by having more, rather than less, fights. Partners are encouraged to avoid "letting the sun go down on their wrath," and to develop techniques of "making up" and resolving their disputes after their anger has been dissipated. Conjoint counseling sessions can serve as models for developing techniques for "making up." For example, one couple hadn't spoken to each other for a week before appearing for the joint meeting. Earlier in the week, the wife, who was Catholic, had brought home a palm branch after a Palm Sunday service. Her Protestant husband, in his compulsive zeal to "clean the mess" out of the living room, had scooped up the palm leaf and sundry other objects and had thrown them into the wastebasket. When the wife discovered that her palm leaf was thrown out, she angrily attributed his action to his religious bigotry. In retaliation, she removed his favorite model sailing ship from the mantel piece and put it in a dusty corner of the basement garage. When the husband discovered what had happened to his ship, he also retaliated in characteristic fight-flight fashion. He refused to speak to her for a week. After the couple was given an opportunity to air their grievances during the counseling session, they were helped to clarify their misconceptions of each other's motives and to see how each one was acting according to the seesaw, fight-flight pattern. When the counselor asked them how they could "make up," i.e., reverse the fight-flight pattern, they mutually agreed to eat out that night and go bowling afterward.

Conjoint meetings help to bring out the distortions and misapprehensions which so often stultify effective communication. Such sessions are especially valuable where verbal communication has broken down. For example, the "cold war" between one couple ended when the wife was told by her salesman husband, during a conjoint session, that his cutting remarks a few nights ago did not mean that he was angry at her. He explained that he had been emotionally upset by his inability to "tell off" his customers and therefore was very "touchy" and irritable at home. Conjoint meetings also offer couples the opportunities to obtain a clearer notion of what actually bolsters the partner's feelings of self-worth. One wife, for example, explained to her husband that his flattery concerning her attractiveness and his purchase of gifts for her had relatively little ego-significance for her. She let him know that his praise for her accomplishments did much more to enhance her feelings of self-worth.

Negative transference reactions, in which either spouse may blame or attack the counselor, is responded to by the counselor in ego-enhancing fashion, by positive regard and empathy, rather than in the expected manner of counterattack, withdrawal or by excessive rationalization and defensiveness. The counselor thus serves as a model spouse toward whom the couple can identify. The counselor is consistently nonblaming and non-partisan, but frequently points out or helps the partners to explore, how each one is contributing to the destructive marital interaction. The counselor consistently stresses the positive. He frequently asserts that each partner is trying to achieve a better relationship, but is going about it in the wrong way, or is being misunderstood. When a partner keeps emphasizing the negative aspects of the spouse's behavior, the counselor points out the many positive features of the spouse under discussion. For example, a husband complained that his wife was being "snooty" because she brought up "high-brow, intellectual" discussions at the dinner table. The counselor indicated that his wife was making an effort to communicate and share her thoughts and activities with him, and that her intentions were not being fully appreciated by him. When there has been an improvement in the marital relationship, followed by an eruption of the fight-flight pattern, the counselor indicates that this is to be expected, and that there will be continued progress, despite occasional setbacks.

An indispensable counseling technique, which is used repeatedly to curtail the vicious circle, improve communication and to minimize unrealistic marital expectations, is a variant of the "A-B-C" method proposed by Ellis and Harper (4). Each partner is helped to learn that his own "irrational sentences" concerning how the spouse "ought to" and "should" behave, as well as his own overpersonalized interpretations of the spouse's acts, are producing his feelings of frustration, anger and self-worthlessness. By discussing the couple's fight-flight patterns, as they occur in daily incidents, each partner also begins to appreciate how his *own defensive actions* are contributing to the spouse's retaliatory behavior. When the husband or wife begins to observe the spouse's defensive fight-flight reactions more objectively, he or she is less inclined to personalize such previously intolerable conduct. Instead of feeling angry or hurt by the spouse's name calling, for example, the partner learns to say, "His name calling is really *his* defensive, 'fight' reaction. I am going to avoid being caught up in the vicious circle. I am going to do all I can not to personalize *his* defensive name calling by either avoiding any fight-flight retaliatory acts on my part or by doing or saying something that may make him feel more worthwhile."

FRUSTRATION OF MARITAL EXPECTATIONS

Exploration of each partner's childhood background and of the unconscious marital expectations which underlie the marital discord are discussed either in individual or joint sessions. The major focus, however, in such discussions is on determining how past events influence the partner's present attitudes and perceptions, and how these attitudes contribute to the current fight-flight conflicts. A husband, for example, was helped to realize that he had expected his wife to behave in a manner that would be totally unlike his mother's actions. In the past, he had strongly resented his mother's stifling overpossessiveness. As a consequence, whenever his wife showed even a mild amount of warmth and affection toward him, he would withdraw from her. He misperceived her affectionate gestures as being comparable to the actions of his overpossessive mother. His wife, in turn, would personalize his withdrawal and feel rejected. In retaliation, she began finding fault with him. Soon the vicious circle of faultfinding – withdrawal – further fault-finding, was on in full force. When the husband developed some insight into his behavior, i.e., when he realized that his aloofness from his wife stemmed from his prior unpleasant reactions to his overpossessive mother, he made attempts at withdrawing less from her affectionate advances. His wife, in turn, became more tolerant of his aloofness after she became aware of his early relationship to his mother. She became less inclined to personalize his "rejection" and less prone to indulge in retaliatory faultfinding.

Partners often use insights into each other's childhood backgrounds as weapons to attack each other. One woman, for example, knew that her husband was raised by an overprotective mother who pampered him. In the marriage, whenever her husband made any request at all, she would accuse him of being "spoiled." She felt that this insight gave her complete justification to attack most of his acts. When this occurs the counselor points out how insights are being used destructively. He encourages the partners to utilize insights in a constructive fashion in order to resolve the destructive seesaw interactions.

DOUBLE-BIND RELATIONSHIPS

Many couples show marked improvements in their interactions entirely as a result of the application of methods and the adoption of attitudes that reverse the vicious, fight-flight circle. Others have greater difficulty, particularly those who have a double-bind relationship. The double-bind relationship, "the bind that destroys," occurs where one partner attempts to satisfy a request or a need of the other partner. This constructive effort then will not be greeted by approval or appreciation from the spouse, but will be rebuffed. For example, during one session in conjoint therapy, a wife complained that her husband never complimented her, whereas he often complimented friends. The husband decided to make an effort to compliment her. That evening, he praised her because of the wonderful meal she had prepared. Whereupon she replied, "Yeah, that's all I'm good for – a cook." Another woman had complained that her husband never spent any time doing things with his family. A few days later, however, when the husband proposed that the entire family go out and play miniature golf together, she replied sarcastically, "A fine time you pick to want to have fun. I have all the ironing to do tonight." One wife had for years urged her husband to attend church, but without success. After several counseling sessions, the husband decided that his church attendance might help the marital situation. When he reported to his wife that he had gone to church that Sunday, she retorted caustically, "I'm just fed up with your boasting." The husband's immediate reaction was, "You can never win," and he was ready to give up all further attempts at change.

In the examples given above, the wives resisted their husband's constructive efforts at bettering the relationship, and persisted in maintaining the familiar fight-flight pattern. During counseling sessions, the positive actions and efforts on the part of one of the partners and the rejection of these efforts by the other partner are brought to the spouse's attention. The spouse is urged to avoid the infuriating double-bind trap by responding more positively and appreciatively to the partner's constructive efforts.

In one instance, a husband made valiant efforts to avoid his characteristic withdrawal and flight reactions, despite his wife's provocative, destructive remarks. He repeatedly attempted to resort to constructive efforts at improving the marriage. When his wife finally became aware of his changed attitudes and actions, she turned on him, during the counseling session, shouting, "For God sakes, why did you wait seventeen years before you began behaving decently? Why weren't you this way seventeen years ago?"

When the counselor asked the husband how he felt about his wife's outburst, he replied, "I feel like crawling into a hole."

The counselor then turned to the wife and asked, "What do you think is going on here?"

She paused for a while, then answered sadly, "Yes, I see what's going on. For seventeen years I've been fighting and he's been fighting."

The husband then responded with, "I can't change the past seventeen years, but I can try to do better now."

An additional example of an attempt by a couple to resolve their double-bind relationship was observed during a joint counseling interview. In this case, it was the wife who had been making efforts to change, while the husband had been rejecting these efforts. One morning, the husband planned to take a taxi to the airport in order to catch an early plane for a business trip. Ordinarily, his wife, who was a habitually late riser, would never have dreamed of driving him to the airport in the family car. However, since she was determined to convey a feeling of worth to her husband, she awoke that particular morning before he did, and drove him to the airport. During the subsequent counseling session, the husband recalled this incident and stated, "I couldn't help getting the feeling, when she drove me to the airport, that she was coming along in order to put a bomb on the plane. But during the flight I thought of some of the things we talked about here. When the plane arrived safely, I phoned her and expressed my appreciation."

SUMMARY

A method of marriage counseling is presented in which the husband and wife are seen by the same counselor predominantly in joint sessions. This form of conjoint marriage counseling focuses directly on the disturbed interaction of the married partners.

The following three basic themes have been observed in most disturbed marital relationships: (a) the mutual frustration of each other's feelings of self-esteem, resulting in a vicious circle of destructive fight-flight interactions; (b) the frustration of effective communication; and (c) the frustration of each other's marriage expectations.

The specific counseling techniques are aimed directly at alleviating and reversing these three major frustrations. Through direct confrontations of their vicious-circle fight-flight, seesaw, "right and wrong" interactions, couples are helped to pursue mutually ego-enhancing behavior and positive solutions to their daily problems. They are aided in improving communications, resolving "double-bind" relationships and in realistically assessing and modifying their marriage expectations.

BIBLIOGRAPHY

1. AMERICAN ASSOCIATION OF MARRIAGE COUNSELORS: *Marriage Counseling: A Casebook*. New York, Assn. Pr., 1958.
2. BACH, G. R., and ALEXANDER, SHANA: *Intimate Enemy*. New York, Doubleday, 1967.
3. EISENSTEIN, V. W.: *Neurotic Interaction in Marriage*. New York, Basic Books, 1961.
4. ELLIS, A., and HARPER, R. A.: *Creative Marriage*. New York, Stuart, Lyle, 1961.
5. GEIST, J., and GERBER, N.: Joint interviewing: A treatment technique with marital partners. *Social Casework, 41:*76-83, 1960.
6. HALEY, J.: Marriage therapy. *Arch. Gen. Psychiat., 8:*213-234, 1963.
7. JACKSON, D. D., and WEAKLAND, J. H.: Conjoint family treatment. *Psychiatry, 24* (Suppl. 2) :30-45, 1961.
8. MARTIN, P. A., and BIRD, H. W.: An approach to the psychotherapy of marriage partners. *Psychiatry, 16:*123-127, 1953.
9. SHERMAN, S. N.: Concept of the Family in Casework Theory. In: *Exploring the Base for Family Therapy*. New York, Family Service Association of America, 1961.
10. WATSON, A. S.: The conjoint psychotherapy of marriage partners. *Amer. J. Orthopsychiat., 5:*912-922, 1963.

Chapter 32

THE LANGUAGE OF SEX

WARREN R. JOHNSON

In THE COURSE OF MY MANY years of teaching and counseling in the sex-education field, I have been impressed by the acute and chronic role that language plays in molding, as well as reflecting, human sexual attitudes and behaviors.

First of all, there is the obvious problem that language concerning sex reflects and helps maintain Judeo-Christian man's long-awkward association with sex. Our profoundly conflicting sex attitudes are reflected in our fascination with the language of sex at the same time that we consider this language taboo. In what other area is language such a barrier to thought, communication, research and education? Historical explanations of this strange situation may be found elsewhere (for example, see my own brief discussion of it in Reference 2; see also the encyclopedia in Reference 3). Among other things any teacher or counselor in this area has to deal with the frustration of communicating with people by means of words that are strongly emotionally charged — very possibly for the teacher or counselor as well as for his audience. Significantly, these words and this language are capable of arousing measurable psychophysiological upset to varying, but marked, degrees. In light of the fact that emotional upset lowers the level of functioning intelligence, the individual is likely to be less able to cope with sex-related problems than with other problems of concern to him.

In this last regard, consider the relatively tame word "prurient," which is not even a "dirty," four-letter word, but is associated darkly with "obscenity" — e.g., that which "appeals to the prurient interest." I recently asked a group of interdenominational clergymen what they thought of having literature that appeals to the "prurient interest" available to young people. Apparently, all present thought this a very bad thing and their feelings about it were noticeably strong. I then asked what the word "prurient" means — and they were startled to realize that they did not know. It was a negative verbal stimulus without intellectual significance, but quite capable of arousing strong emotion and very possibly, in some cases, punitive action.

Various authors, including Ellis (1), Sagarin (4) and MacDougald (3), have discussed the problem of our specific "dirty" words associated with sex and other bodily functions. Among other things, they have demonstrated that our attitude toward these words represents an incredible hypocrisy imposed upon us by the Puritan tradition and deprives us of some extremely useful and direct means of communication on the subject. It is not my intent to review the material covered by those authors — although I would like to go on record as being in agreement with them that we are making a grave mistake when we perpetuate negative attitudes concerning sex by a faulty use of language concerning it. Rather, the discussion which follows is in the spirit of general semantics and has to do with ways in which our language influences, molds and frequently retards our efforts toward rational, adaptive behavior.

Our language has come to us out of the past and, like a great conveyor belt, automatically brings the past to us by way of meanings that we associate with it. So automatic is this process that we generally fail to notice it at all and suppose that our feelings and behaviors are somehow "natural" to us. Little do we suspect the influence of this great conveyor belt of language in this whole business. What a shock to learn that our standards of "naturalness" as crystalized in our sex laws and morality were creations of: (a) the ancient, struggling, Jewish people of the Middle East; (b) the sex-obsessed, sex-hating, woman-hating Christian Church Fathers, especially the enormously influential St. Augustine (Tertullian: "Woman, you are the devil's doorway;" St. Chrysostom: "Among all savage beasts none is found so harmful as woman;" and St. Augustine declared that there is no real difference between sex with one's wife and sex with a whore, both being unclean and sinful) ; and (c) the Puritan tradition, which began in the sixteenth century, intensified the antisexualism of the earlier Christians and undertook to *cleanse the language* of sex. So formidable an assault has the Judeo-Christian tradition maintained upon sex that, in comparison with other areas of knowledge, we are quite literally still in the Dark Ages, and only now are we beginning to feel relatively free to examine and understand this most crucial aspect of ourselves. And language, it would seem, has been the major, unnoticed means of this remarkable, societal masochism. Perhaps we should look to it for some of our therapy.

Let us examine a few of the many particulars of this strange situation in which language plays such a prominent, usually unnoticed, role.

There is the whole range of blacklisted behaviors which are tagged with dark labels under the general rubric of "perversions." Among the ancient Jews there was enormous and realistic pressure to maintain and, if possible, build up the population. All sexual expression which was not reproduction-oriented tended to be outlawed. The full weight of religion was brought to bear to discourage such nonprocreative behaviors, and the wrath of an omnipresent God stood as a constant threat to the disobedient. Homosexuality, bestiality, coitus interruptus and, by implication, masturbation were viewed as crimes of utmost gravity against the people and God himself. The point is that although these kinds of behaviors no longer are punished by death, they are still profoundly taboo in spite of the fact that the circumstances which gave rise to the taboo are now generally nonexistent. A vengeful God seems ever watchful. Thus, expressions like "unspeakable crime against nature" continue to be sufficient grounds for severe legal penalties. People are jailed regularly for committing "sodomy" — which can mean any of a range of acts other than vaginal coitus with the man on top. To most people, and certainly before the law, the so-called perverted sexual acts are by definition bad, unspeakable and simply not done by any but "abnormal," the "perverted," "inferior" and otherwise "bad" or "sick" people. We base few of our other value judgments upon the rules of a tribal people. But in regard to value judgments about sex, we accept the ancient Jewish rules as modified by the early Christians with a blind devotion — as they are dumped unnoticed upon us by the conveyor belt of language and other symbols. (Be it noted that I am not here discussing homosexuality, bestiality, sodomy, etc. I am simply pointing out that primitive tribal rules do not preside over our modern medical, dietary or traffic practices; and I question whether ancient, primitive, tribal, sexual rules, as such, are necessarily the best for us today.)

It is not possible for people to deal rationally with unspeakable or unwritable things. Thus, for example, during and following World War I, neither the United States Army nor the public-health authorities could make any progress in the control of syphilis because almost no one, including medical doctors, were willing to use the word. Only when it gradually became possible to use the word and thereby educate people on the subject did progress in combating the disease occur. I am told by present-day public health authorities that the word has again become taboo to a surprising extent, and that this is surely a factor in our current failure to reverse the upward trend of the disease. This same kind of phenomenon is to be seen in connection with the so called "deviant" sexual behaviors, in that society demonstrates its ability to tolerate the problem but *cannot tolerate the language* associated with it. We fail to come to grips with a whole range of sex-related problems in a rational kind of way because of this incredible, self-perpetuating language barrier.

Incidentally, as an educator I find it depressing to have to add that educators are probably among the worst offenders in this matter of permitting language to block social progress. Instead of seeing the need to help the young reevaluate our use of language so as to create an educated citizenry competent to deal rationally with its problems, educators tend to reaffirm the traditional verbal taboos and deal rationality out of the game.

With regard to sex, among other things, people in our tradition have been living in a make-believe world composed of words for many centuries.

Revelation of this fact was the great shocker of the Kinsey reports. For example, we attempt to adjust to a sexcentric world which is simultaneously a profoundly sex-rejecting world. Moreover, we pretend to adjust to the nonsense that childhood is a period of nonsexuality and that after childhood nice people do not permit sex to "rear its ugly head" unless marriage occurs, after which people live happily ever after. We also pretend that older people are not sexual creatures. Like children, they are led to believe that their sexuality is a mistake and that they should be content to live in the word-world which is conveniently free of sex. This illusory word-world is more real than the "real" world to most people, it would seem.

Some relatively recent developments may illustrate the problem of bringing language into harmony with current facts. Following are some examples. It has been only little more than half a century that respectable college women could participate in sports. Consequently, it is not surprising that our language related to female behavior is from an earlier era. To be called a "female athlete" is not likely to be taken as a compliment. Traditionally, when a boy has played hard and aggressively, it has been said that "he is playing like a man." When a girl plays well, hard and aggressively — which is to say successfully — what can one say she is playing like? "Like a man"? Hardly. But then playing "like a woman" does not seem quite right either.

Every year a great deal of youthful behavior is controlled by the expression, "Get married and have children." This is without regard for the fact that, although historically men and women have badly needed each other in a marriage relationship and both have been dependent upon children to serve as free labor, a fighting force, perhaps, and sickness and old-age insurance, the fact is that today fewer and fewer men and women have such a practical and pressing need to marry. And children, as such, no longer have economic value whatever. Increasingly, women as well as men are capable of self-support and may marry or not as they choose; and if they do so choose, they have the further choice of whether or not to have children. However, we continue to think and talk of "marriage" and "the family" as though these changes were not taking place under our very noses.

We also continue to use the words "male" and "female" and "masculine" and "feminine," as though present-day male and female roles were the same as they have been traditionally. Just how is a boy supposed to act as opposed to how a girl is supposed to act? Just what are "masculine" as opposed to "feminine" behaviors? I am not prepared to say; but many of the traditional criteria do not seem very applicable, and the language of sex roles has yet to catch up.

The increased education of women along with increased encouragement to *think* has led to a variety of language confusions. For example, is it a compliment for a woman to be told that she "thinks like a man?" How would a man feel if he were told that he thinks like a woman? Due to the conveyor belt of language, we tend to have surprising difficulty recognizing that thought and language do not necessarily have a sex and that our concern is more likely to be with the *quality* of communication, its rationality, clarity and so forth, and that this can come from a disciplined, objective mind, regardless of the sex of its possessor.

An interesting contrast may be seen when we compare the conveyor belt word "wife" with the largely nonconveyor belt word "secretary." Whereas "wife," in consequence of being an ill-defined role today, is an ill-defined word, "secretary" has a definite meaning in relation to a specific function. There is little question in any experienced person's mind what is expected of a good secretary. But the well-trained and excellent secretary commonly steps daily from her well-structured, clearly defined office role and becomes lost in the ambiguities of the wife role when she goes home. She knows who and what she is when on the job. Similarly, when a woman is a prostitute, she knows quite accurately what her role is and how she is to play it. Her job is to satisfy the customer. Like the competent secretary or dental hygienist, she is trained to do the job — just as women used to be trained effectively for "women's work." The wife, on the other hand, generally has no such clear-cut idea of her role in or out of bed. In fact, a sexually sophisticated wife, or one who attempts to become such, may be rejected by her husband for lacking in virtue or proper modesty.

Teachers and counselors concerned with marriage would, I believe, be wise to bear in mind that when people marry, they generally are being wedded to a symbol delivered to them in considerable part on the great conveyor belt of language. The husband feels that he has a right to expect the wife to exhibit certain kitchen behavior, bathroom behavior, living room behavior, garden behavior. This symbol is quite rigid; and although it is inevitably violated in actual practice — which is to say in real life — its violation exacts its cost in suffering on the part of both male and female, for both accept the same symbol and really expect about the same behavior of "a wife." The wife who, due to circumstances is likely to be more preoccupied with such things, is often more disillusioned than her husband by her own failure to come pretwisted to the dimensions of what she considers the wife symbol to be. This is not a happy situation either, since the symbol-ideal as commonly conceived is all but impossible to achieve today. Her concern about it is more likely to give rise to frustration, depression and/or hostile behavior than to her "mending her ways." The wife, too, marries a symbol constructed of words — the dominant, aggressive, achieving, mature, providing, understanding, inexhaustibly-sexual-but-out-of-the-

home-infalliably-restrained, masculine male. (There's a nice trick for anyone. Can you define "masculine" in a way that is appropriate to today rather
than to Wyatt Earp's or King Solomon's day?)

Of course, the husband expects certain masculine behavior of himself
because the conveyor belt sets his word-structured, self-criteria; and he is
naturally profoundly undermined by his almost inevitable failure to "measure up" to the symbol. It seems of little importance that few besides professional athletes and actors — viewed from a distance — do measure up.

Clearly, the many discrepancies between what couples expect of each
other and of themselves in marriage are among the things that drive them
to marriage counselors, psychiatrists and the like for help. They want to
glue the great symbol of "marriage" back together again in a Humpty-
Dumpty kind of venture. Now I do not pretend to know just how the
authority on marriage should tackle these situations. Obviously, the odds
favor his success, since it is just those people who would be lost without the
large and small symbols associated with marriage who go to counselors for
help in reinstating the symbols. Still, I am under the impression that many
a counselor would benefit from a study of the conveyor belt of language.
They need — as do we all — to be careful to distinguish verbal and other
behavior that is under the control only of arbitrary authority of tradition
from that which is under the direction of rationality. (Of course, that which
is "old" or traditional is not necessarily irrational!) If all manner of problems — ranging from sex-related "guilt," "sin," "obscenity," male-female
sex roles, premarital sexual intercourse, incest, rape, homosexuality, nudity,
abortion and so on — can be pulled off the conveyor belt of language and
confronted in the light of rationality, people may be helped to greater self-
understanding and social responsibility. And perhaps a new and healthier
language of sex may in time emerge.

In this discussion I have attempted to present at least a hint of the
enormously important but generally unnoticed role of language in relation
to sexual attitudes and behaviors. Much has been neglected, undertreated
or even omitted. For example, we have not even examined the implications
of why we instantly know that a joke labeled "dirty" is almost certainly
about sex (see references). Sex and dirt — that we have such an attitude
towards the source of new life and one of life's greatest pleasures is as weird
and frightening as the fact that when we want to insult or embarrass someone badly we tell them they are "acting like a child." Badness and childhood — what perverse attitudes are reflected and transmitted in such language! Surely these matters should be of utmost concern to those responsible
for counseling or teaching others about human sexuality and human relations generally.

REFERENCES

1. ELLIS, ALBERT: An impolite interview with Albert Ellis. *The Realist,* May 1960.
2. JOHNSON, WARREN R.: Language as a factor in sexual behavior and sex education. In: *Human Sex and Sex Education: Perspectives and Problems,* by W. R. Johnson. Philadelphia, Lea and Febiger, 1963.
3. MACDOUGALD, JR., DUNCAN: Language and sex. In *The Encyclopedia of Sexual Behavior,* Vol. II, edited by Albert Ellis and Albert Abarbanel. N. Y., Hawthorne Books, 1961.
4. SAGARIN, EDWARD: *The Anatomy of Dirty Words.* New York, Lyle Stuart, 1962.

Chapter 33

MARITAL COUNSELING OF THE CHRONICALLY ILL AND DISABLED

MORTON A. SEIDENFELD

INTRODUCTION

MARITAL COUNSELING IS PERHAPS one of the most difficult and complex areas of the entire counseling field since it involves the integration or disintegration of a minimum of two people's lives and may, of course, involve many more if there are children and other family members involved. In a similar fashion the counseling of the chronically ill and disabled individual is filled with complexity since it involves not only the affected individual but his family and his community. Obviously, any attempt to deal with these two areas when they are superimposed one on the other can hardly be expected to be anything but difficult. This is often the most frustrating type of counseling situation.

In spite of inherent difficulties, this appears to be one of the most significant areas for effective marital counseling. The seriously ill individual faced with a lifetime of special concern over his illness, the disabled young person who must face the frustrations and dissatisfactions of being physically limited by deformity or malfunctioning body structure — all experience sexual drives and sexual needs that can no more be ignored than can those of their physically or mentally normal peers. Yet, strangely enough, this problem is one of the least-mentioned topics in the entire literature of the care, treatment and rehabilitation of the disabled and chronically ill. If it is considered at all, very little serious attention is given to how marital counseling can be used properly.

While no one can hope to cover all the intricacies and complexities of this problem in any brief discussion, it is desirable to consider at least some of the most significant aspects of the problem, and to suggest some useful approaches that may prove helpful to the marital counselor who is dealing with clients who have significant physical and/or mental disabilities.

Though the marriage vows of most religious faiths contain some reference to such concepts as "love, honor and cherish (obey)," "in sickness or in health," "for richer or for poorer," "for better or for worse," etc., the participants in the ceremony, either because they are optimists or because

---

*This chapter was written by the author in his private capacity, and no official support or endorsement by the Vocational Rehabilitation Administration of the Department of Health, Education, and Welfare is intended or should be inferred.

they believe "it can't happen to me," are inclined to avoid thinking about the negative aspects of their vows and "accentuate the positive." Perhaps it is proper that they do approach their marital relationships with a healthy, moderately euphoric and mildly unrealistic attitude, since in the youthful days of marriage they frequently must encounter the difficulties of learning to live together, sharing the daily tasks of living and facing the economic restrictions of the early years of life.

When illness or accident occurs, leaving in its wake not only the effects of the stresses and strains created by the unforeseen acute impact of this event but, in addition, residual disability of relatively long duration or even permanent nature, almost all marriages are taxed to some degree, some close to the breaking point and a few beyond the endurable level. These marital problems may often represent some of the most trying experiences that the counselor may encounter. They may tax his insight, his judgment and his skills in aiding his clients to the very utmost since the relationships and underlying dynamics are so often marked by real and imagined social demands which call for behavior that one or the other or both marriage partners feels unable to carry out.

The marriage counselor may roughly classify the problems of his disabled clients in a number of ways:

In terms of *onset of disability* (of one or both marital partners).

1. *Prior to marriage.*
   a. Congenital.
   b. Onset during childhood.
   c. Onset during adolescence or adult life.
2. *After marriage*
   a. Illness.
   b. Accident.

In terms of *type of disability.*

1. Disability associated with deformity.
2. Concealed disability.

In terms of *severity of disability.*

1. Very severe (restriction of function and inability to maintain socio-economic status).
2. Severe (restriction of function with only slight ability to perform activities of daily living).
3. Moderate (some restriction of function, can perform activities of daily living and can contribute to socioeconomic status).
4. Mild (limited restriction of functions, capable of independent action, moderate limits on socioeconomic status capacity).
5. Minimal (little restriction of functions, completely independent, capable of complete socioeconomic status capacity).

In terms of *family constellation* involved.
1. Self.
2. Spouse.
3. One or more children.
4. Other members of family in varying state of socioeconomic dependence.

Let us consider these problems as they are categorically listed:

ONSET OF DISABILITY AS A FACTOR

There is an amazing indifference or even avoidance of the discussion of the marital problems of the disabled individual who has endured physical or mental disability since birth or early childhood, perhaps because it is assumed that many of these people avoid marriage entirely, or if they do get married that their problems closely parallel those found among the nondisabled.

To some extent there is indeed great similarity between the problems in adaptation to married life of the able-bodied in contrast with those who are disabled. To whatever extent this is true, we shall not try to recapitulate the approaches to, or the solution of, these matters.

There are, however, some unique aspects of the disability problem that may be expected to play a role in intramarital relationships. These deserve to be delineated, for they may place special stress on the marriage counselor to exert efforts in a somewhat different manner than would be true were such disabilities not present.

First, it is important to realize that the limitations imposed on the physique and psyche of the disabled do inevitably have a real and often profound effect on the individual. If he has undergone proper treatment and has been effectively rehabilitated, the disabled individual should, with the passing of time, learn how to manage his life along lines that for the most part fit his felt-needs as fully as possible.

Most of the time these efforts at preparing the disabled for living with their disability tend to place emphasis on the rather broad generalities of getting along with others, as well as on the relatively superficial levels of association in the work situation, the family and community. All too seldom does the counseling and/or training program prepare the young individual to face up to the long-term and enduring one-to-one relationship of marriage.

Seldom, if ever, is any significant amount of time spent on determining or discussing the sex drives and sex needs of the disabled individual with him. Seldom do we even consider the marital plans of the disabled unless he makes a special effort to call his concern to our attention. He may even feel that our avoidance of the topic in our discussion with him indicates our lack of concern or our inadequacies in dealing with such problems. Perhaps he is correct. All too seldom we fail to refer him to a marriage counselor — partly because we do not know to whom to send him, and partly because we have doubts in our own minds that the marriage counselor has the experience or information regarding the disabled to meet successfully the demands of the situation.

Do the disabled ever think of sex? Do they ever think of marriage? The answer to both questions is, obviously, they do. Each year many physically disabled persons and many who have had mental disabilities have found their way to the altar. A sizable proportion of these marriages succeed in the sense that the couples remain together, bear children and maintain the marriage about as well as their nondisabled counterparts. Others who lack courage, who are less secure or who doubt their ability to assume the role of spouse find it impossible to meet or accept the challenge of living with another in a marital partnership, and instead elect to remain single rather than to face matrimony. While this decision may be the wisest one, many of these young people could enjoy a fuller, more satisfying and better-adjusted life if they were counseled appropriately and given the opportunity to have the benefits of a good marriage.

What Information Does the Unmarried Disabled Individual Need Prior to Marriage?

There would seem to be certain information that the marital counselor could give to the disabled potential spouse. This includes:

1. Specific information on the extent, degree and nature of sexual limitations he may anticipate as a result of the functional alterations of physical and/or psychological conditions associated with his disability;
2. Understanding of how he can adapt himself physically and psychically to overcome these deficits;
3. Appraisal of his personality (as it has been influenced by his disability), and what he may anticipate as necessary alterations in his behavior pattern if he is to reach a comfortable marital relationship with his spouse;
4. Provision of suitable guidance for the spouse which includes full treatment of what the disabled spouse's limitations mean to their sexual life, special problems in which the spouse must be prepared to cooperate, and awareness of the effects that will be necessary to avoid further traumatization of the disabled spouse's personality while at the same time preserving her own ego-needs against undue trauma.
5. Guidance that both members of the marital couple should share jointly which will lead to their common understanding of their col-

lective and shared individual problems, leading to a sound relationship with understanding of the special nature of the give-and-take
relationship when one spouse is disabled and the other is not, or
when each has a disability problem.

Each marriage counselor may have his own concepts regarding the order
or the manner of presenting such information. No adherence to a specific
order is predicated — it is only essential that each of the marital partners
receives the information they need to insure that they possess the knowledge
that will aid them to both self- and mutual-understanding and the ability
to meet their problems successfully without being overwhelmed by them.

Where Can the Counselor Obtain Information About the Specific Problems of Disability?

To counsel the disabled individual effectively the marriage counselor
will need a detailed description from his client's physician regarding just
what the physical and/or mental limitations are — both from the standpoint
of the actual alteration of body function and from the self-imposed restrictions made by the disabled persons.

Counseling the disabled calls for all the skill and knowledge at the
counselor's command. This means he must be fully *au courant* with the disabled counselee's medical and psychic history, his rehabilitation status and
as much as he can know about his adaptability potential. In many instances,
if not in all, the counselor will need to be in communication with the physician, the vocational rehabilitation counselor, the social worker, the psychologist and others who can provide both objective and subjective information
on the characteristics of the disabled client, and in some instances even
about the spouse.

Disability Existing Prior to Marriage

When the disability existed in your client before marriage you will, of
course, be concerned with how long before? If the disability occurred at or
very soon after birth, it is likely to have had a considerably different influence on the individual than if it occurred later in childhood, or in youth or
adult life.

As a rule, those who were born with a disability or acquire it very early
in life before they had completely or nearly completely adapted their
behavior to an intact physique are likely to have made a better adaptation
than those who have to relearn a mode of living that is at variance from
the more or less common patterns of ordinary behavior. In such an individual we may anticipate no difficulty in learning to live with his disability
since he has really known no other way of life. This does not imply, how-

ever, that he will not have experienced frustrations, dissatisfactions or stress — for he too quickly learns that this is a world in which most people expect all the people to act as though they could do anything that any "ordinary" person can do. In some situations this may be highly stress-producing, because he cannot perform in such a manner. It may be even more stressful than in those disabled after they have learned to carry out such activities, since he has never learned how to do what is expected of him. On the other hand, there are probably advantages that accrue because of being unencumbered by preconceived ideas of skills that he cannot possess, and he may have a more realistic appreciation of his potential.

With such clients, depending upon their adaptability and general personality characteristics, we might expect that marital problems would be just as traumatic, less related to their disability and more likely to be based on conflicts typically found in the nondisabled segment of married society. One must be prepared, however, for many marital problems to be ascribed to the disability which on close scrutiny will prove to result from factors only very peripherally related to physical factors originating in the disability. In somewhat more rare circumstances among the early-onset group one may find a marital discord related direcetly to the disability.

Those whose disability occurred in late childhood, youth or adult life are somewhat different since they began life as intact individuals who learned to live in the world of "average" men, developed biases and prejudices and stereotypic techniques for maintaining their own ego-strength by the common means of gaining stature through the value reduction of peers. It is inevitable that, when illness or accident creates disability, such people tend to devaluate themselves, mourn their physical and/or mental losses and become discontented, dissatisfied, frustrated people. No disabled person probably ever escapes this completely; but, fortunately, many, if not most, of them appear to be able to liberate themselves successfully from major evidence of this sort. A few cannot overcome this effect effectively, and almost none can rid themselves completely of this form of psychic disturbance. When such men and women decide to marry (and a good many avoid doing so) , they find not only all the problems of two people learning to live together harmoniously, but they also find that the additional frustrations of their disability may often serve as a real and/or imagined factor of interference with connubial well-being.

At times some of the disabled seek in marriage and their marital partner what the general society or even their own familial group has failed to provide them. Much of the need for understanding, acceptance and approval operates so far below the level of consciousness that the disabled person is not aware that he is asking of his mate or mate-to-be more than they will find themselves able to give. While this is not a foregone conclusion, and there are those who are quite capable of meeting these rather drastic requirements, it is not likely that one can anticipate its frequent occurrence.

The ability to maintain socioeconomic independence is a highly important factor in the success or failure of the married disabled individual, to an even greater extent than in normal able-bodied marriage partners. The successful maintenance of independence, a sense of personal worth, a feeling of adequacy, are essential to all human beings who live in a social milieu where these characteristics sort the failures from the successes. To the disabled person, attainment of security in our society is intimately bound up with work, economic success and status.

In ordinary life situations many marriages founder on the rocks of economic failure, unemployment, inadequate motivation to work and vocational incompetence. With disability present, the socioeconomic attainment level may fall to a low or inadequate level, with resulting loss of self-security and a serious drop in peer-status to the point where the disabled person feels he is worthless. As a result, his marriage and the maintenance of his marital responsibilities become problems with which he can no longer cope. The disabled person becomes frustrated beyond tolerance, and his marriage partner no longer can face a spouse who either becomes completely dependent or so maladapted that nothing is ever right.

This problem is not one that involves the male disabled spouse alone. It is equally significant when the female spouse is the disabled one who may find herself inadequately equipped to carry on work in a vocationally competitive field or in the household. We seldom think of the work around the home as a competitive form of employment, yet indeed it is, for the selection of a wife is seldom made without the male at least having given thought to one or two potentially appealing candidates. To the disabled wife this means she must not only compete in terms of her "sex appeal," but also what she can do in contributing to the socioeconomic stability of the home, either directly in maintaining the home or indirectly as an earner contributing to this goal.

The problem is well known enough to marriage counselors to require no further expansion. The solution, unfortunately, is often less adequately recognized or is dealt with in a more peripheral manner. The need for the marriage counselor to encourage and make referral to a vocational rehabilitation agency for the evaluation, counseling, training and placement services this resource can supply is all too often overlooked. This service can help the disabled person, in most if not all cases, to better understanding of his or her vocational problems, and can assist them in getting the help they need in preparing themselves for a vocation in keeping with their physical or mental abilities. In the interim the marriage counselor can provide help for the nondisabled spouse in restoring better perspective to the mate's problems, and by communication with the vocational rehabilitation counselor can prepare the mate for the kind of adaptation that will help the disabled husband or wife to regain confidence, independence and vocational security.

Disability Occurring After Marriage

We have been discussing many problems that exist in the marital life of marital partners, one or both of whom were disabled prior to their marriage. To a significant degree the marital difficulties of those who become disabled after marriage will closely parallel those already described. They will differ perhaps in degree and extent, but with certain notable exceptions we may expect many of the characteristic difficulties to be very much alike.

One of the significant exceptions that will concern the marriage counselor is the fact that when the couple was married they had not, in all likelihood, anticipated the illness or accident which produced disability. As a result, they are often, if not always, unprepared for the impact of this catastrophe on their lives. In the past minor ups and downs may have been met with fortitude or with some dissatisfactions. There may or may not have been some serious marital conflicts. The couple probably met adversities as well as they could, and problems were at least of relatively brief duration. Now the couple is faced with problems that are bound to be of long duration or even permanent, and they cannot face the future together on a *laissez-faire* basis any longer.

To the chronically ill or disabled spouse this represents a serious ego-threat, an economic tragedy, a threat to sexual competence and a host of other traumatic possibilities. If the marriage has been going well, the disabled spouse may gain some security from this, but even under the best of circumstances the disabled individual must inevitably question, in his mind, how long he can hope for this to continue. There is bound to be fear that his or her physical and/or mental limitations must lead to inability to carry out his or her share of the marital contract to support, maintain and sustain his spouse (and any progeny). If the marriage was not moving along smoothly prior to the onset of illness or accident, the disabling condition often supplies the needed spark to further aggravation or complete dissolution. In more rare instances it may cause improvement in the immediate situation due to sympathy or guilt feeling in the uninjured party or a dependent reaction in the injured, but marital counselors readily recognize that this hardly provides a very satisfactory outlook for the future of the marriage.

For the nondisabled spouse this new situation poses a new and long-enduring threat for which there has been little or no preparation. Economic problems connected not only with the maintenance of the home and family situation but the added burdens of medical care and postdisability expenses may be overwhelming. All these newly developed, frightening problems added to the burden of predisability marital difficulties may well prove to be the straw that breaks the camel's back.

Accident and illness alike are frequent producers of guilt feelings both in the disabled and their spouses, since so often the events that follow are often interpreted in a superstitious or quasi-religious fashion as being due to punishment for real or imagined wrongdoings. Such feelings, when they do exist, may be related to marital problems. When they occur, more complications invariably result.

The marriage counselor will find it necessary to explore these problems and their satellite complications in much the same manner as he deals with similar matters in the physically and mentally healthy subject. He need only be aware of the more profound effect and greater duration of these difficulties and the necessity to help the marital partners to eradicate or alleviate them at the earliest possible moment. Oftentimes they may be so strong as to make it virtually impossible to overcome them, especially in couples where the marriage has been close to the breaking point prior to the occurrence of the disabling condition.

TYPE OF DISABILITY AS A FACTOR

While the time of the onset of the disability plays a significant role in the marriage state, it is far from the only important factor. This type of disability may have serious implications for the disabled spouse and/or his nondisabled mate. The types of disability can be classified into two major groups: (a) those in which the disability is visible and in which some alteration in body function and/or appearance can be detected by the observer; and (b) those in which the disability is concealed or nonapparent.

Disabilities That Are Visible and/or Associated With Deformity

We are generally inclined to identify disability as a term with conditions that are more or less readily apparent to the observant. While this, of course, is not always true — as in the case of the lower-limb amputee who has been successfully fitted with a prosthesis — even this individual cannot very well conceal his disability or body deformity from his spouse.

One may wonder what impact the presence of obvious disability and/or deformity has on the marital relationship. In some marriages where the marriage partners are fully aware of the presence of this condition before marriage, perhaps this may indeed prove a very small matter. The problems that do arise in these instances are more closely related to personality conflicts which arise from, or independently of, the disabling condition, as discussed earlier. In other instances, the full effect of the presence of bodily distortion or alteration on the nondisabled spouse (or even when both partners are disabled) is not fully manifest until the prolonged intimate relationships of marriage have made these characteristics the source of personal reaction. Again, the nature and degree of reaction that may occur is difficult to anticipate in general terms.

For some, any unfavorable responses may rise to a peak rapidly and then diminish steadily until they no longer have any effect on either the observer or the observed. For others, negative reactions may persist, and the efforts to conceal them from the disabled mate may cause them to worsen to such a degree that they may seriously contribute to psychic disturbance. In between these extremes we may anticipate a wide variety of degree, extent and duration of negativity toward the apparent disability that run all the way from reluctance to be seen in public with the disabled mate, but no particular reaction when away from public scrutiny, all the way to complete inability to be with the disabled spouse.

Here again the marriage counselor will be faced with a complicaed and, unfortunately, often a frustrating counseling problem. When the disability and/or deformity is present before marriage and the counselor is consulted for premarital advice and assistance, he will, of course, want to ascertain the degree of readiness and the capacity of the future married couple to tolerate both the superficial reactions to gross bodily defect and the profound reactions regarding the importance of bodily perfection in appearance and function.

In those instances when postmarital advice is sought, the problem becomes one of relieving, when possible to do so, the feelings of the married couple regarding these visible distortions and of providing them with a more positive focus upon the values each brings to the other. This is much more easily said than done, and the marriage counselor may find it important to consult with medical, social work and vocational rehabilitation counselor colleagues in order to obtain a clearer vision of just what the disabled person can do to overcome his own reactions to his disability and the role that his mate is playing in reacting to the disability.

Disabilities That Are Not Readily Apparent to the Observer

Complicated as the apparent and readily observable disability may be, the invisible or the less readily observable disability may prove even more difficult to handle in the marital-counseling situation.

The problem here lies in the fact that the disabled partner has a disability that others, including his mate, cannot observe; hence, the demands made upon the disabled person are often either far more or far less than he can be expected to perform. This is because all of us tend to expect of the apparently intact individual all that we expect of a normal person. This often forces the disabled person to act either as though completely able to perform in such a manner or to reduce his contacts and thus minimize the demands made upon him. Either choice may prove to be physically and/or mentally deleterious to him.

Visibility of the disability often protects the individual from embarrassing demands of society. Sometimes it tends to overprotect him, but it does provide him, in a sense, with the opportunity more or less to set his own pace without having to explain why. Invisibility of disability tends to make the disabled person want to live up to what normal healthy peers do, even when he knows he should not do so. The diabetic who fails to watch his diet, the precardiac or prestroke patient who already has had his "warnings" but who insists on disregarding his condition by doing too much in the way of activities he has been told to avoid, the deaf or hard-of-hearing person who tries to hear what he cannot hear or who will not wear a hearing aid that might help him but which makes apparent their limitation — all are familiar examples.

In marriage, these hidden or well-disguished disabilities may be expected to create other problems. Such individuals may engage in excessive sexual activity to prove to themselves and their mate that they are healthy and normal. They may reverse the procedure and avoid sexual activity to protect themselves, while their mate, unaware of the significance of this behavior, interprets it as indifference or altered affection. In social life they may overindulge or underindulge themselves and their spouses. Vocationally, they may work excessively hard to attain goals well beyond their capacity, or they may quit their jobs and remain about the home while their mate fails to be aware of the cause of such behavior.

Obviously, this becomes a source of serious marital disharmony with neither spouse being fully aware of just what is happening. Oftentimes the uninformed or inadequately advised spouse makes demands that only serve to create a further rift between the marital partners.

These problems, when presented to the marriage counselor, may likewise not be fully appreciated if the counselor merely takes the health of the individuals for granted. It is well to make a careful check of the general health of both clients before going into discussion of the immediate and secondary causes of their marital conflicts. Too often the disabled client may either conceal or be unaware to what extent his disability is contributing to his difficulties in the marital relationship. Even when he is aware of the disability he may choose to avoid mentioning it as a possible factor.

Here, again, the marriage counselor may be confronted with a very complex situation in which he will need the advice and help of his medical, social-work and vocational-rehabilitation-counselor colleagues to aid him in providing optimal assistance to his clients.

SEVERITY OF DISABILITY

Another complication that the marriage counselor may anticipate in aiding the couple with one or both partners disabled is that concerned with the extent and degree of severity of the disability. These may be roughly categorized as very severe, severe, moderate, mild and minimal, and are briefly discussed.

Very Severely Disabled

The very severely disabled individual is greatly restricted functionally, and in general has minimal-to-zero capacity for independent behavior and maintenance of socioeconomic status. Such a person, when married, must inevitably become somewhat of a burden on his spouse unless economically they are so well-to-do that virtually continuous care is available, or placement in a suitable care situation is possible. In most instances, such an individual has little or nothing with which even the most skilled physician or his colleagues can work to bring about significant rehabilitation outcomes. (At least this has been the case in the past.) However, modern rehabilitation medicine in collaboration with the biophysicist and the biomedical engineer have begun to achieve great advances in the preparation of assistive devices to such a degree that if the patient has even a bare minimum of effective intact neuromuscular mechanism, one may bring the patient to at least some degree of self-care. Time and know-how will undoubtedly bring far greater advances.

Immediately, however, the nondisabled or relatively less severely disabled spouse may find himself or herself faced with a problem which cannot be coped with.

Here the marriage counselor must surely seek the best rehabilitation medical advice available in order to present intelligently the problem and suggest ways and means for the couple to cope with this trying situation. Fortunately, such problems will not be likely to occur with any frequency, and must be met, when they do occur, on a highly individualized basis.

Severely Disabled

The severely disabled differ qualitatively from the very severely disabled in that the functional capacity, though considerably restricted, does not preclude some ability to attain movements compatible with a limited amount of self-care (e.g., feeding movement with hands and/or arms). Furthermore, many of these individuals can, with suitable orthotic appliances, gain even more mastery of at least a few of the activities of daily life.

From the standpoint of the marital situation, the outlook for independence of action is still greatly limited, and economic support of self or spouse would be decidedly limited, except in the few instances of the highly creative individual who can communicate to others his thoughts and ideas, and by virtue of this carry on some activity that does not require much more than the use of his mind and knowledge. This form of productive activity would of necessity be limited to those who possess this quality of intellect, who have a broad background and who can operate on a highly creative level.

As has already been noted, however, the future may hold a great deal more for these people, since in most instances they have some residual neuromuscular capacities that may be hooked up with electronically operated devices that will aid them in supplanting many of their lost physical mechanisms. But much will depend on future developments in the orthotic field.

Fortunately, this again is a rather small group. Together with the very severely disabled they constitute only about 5 to 7 per cent of all disabled people. The marriage counselor may indeed run across an occasional marital problem from within these two categories, but it will be the exceptional situation, and calls for the close cooperation with colleagues in related fields of medicine and rehabilitation.

Moderately Disabled

In this group, together with the one to follow (mildly disabled), the marriage counselor is likely to find the major portion of his disabled clients. Among the moderately disabled, the marriage counselor will find the disabled individual whose physical and/or mental limitations may be somewhat restrictive, reducing his functional level below the level of the average person of his age, sex and intellectual competency, but who can in many areas of cognition and performance do as well (with the provision of necessary rehabilitation training and the use of suitable assistive device, when required) as many normal individuals.

Within this group it is likely that the counselor may have to deal with the many psycho-social-economic problems that have been discussed in the earlier sections of this chapter.

In addition to the more usual marital problems, these individuals will bring to the counseling situation all the complications that physical and/or mental malfunction have added and for which they lack the knowledge, the motivation or the courage to obtain needed help that would lead them to a restoration in full, or at least in part, of those competencies of which their disability has deprived them.

This situation requires the marriage counselor to make full use of his referral privileges and to see that his disabled client and spouse not only be aware that services capable of reducing the disability are available but also to see (insofar as possible) that he or she receives these services and gains all that is possible from them. In the meantime, the marriage counselor will be able to apply his own knowledge and skill to help resolve conflict and frustration within the marital complex as fully as circumstances will permit.

Mildly Disabled

Within this group of disabilities will be found the many disabled people who have very modest degrees of limitations functionally, who are quite capable of more or less complete independent action, but who often over-restrict themselves due to fear, lack of motivation and insecurity. Among these individuals are often found those whose motivational gradient was always rather low, who, for want of a better term, have little ambition and who have not been very successful in coping with life. The tendency is to blame all this on a disability; and there is often great resistance to any efforts made to bring the individual up to optimal performance levels.

It is likely that within this group will be found not only the most difficult cases for the marriage counselor, but also for the physician, the vocational rehabilitation counselor and many others interested in restoration of individuals to healthful and productive living. The record will often bear testimony to failures that existed in the life experience even before the onset of his disability. Often, marriage has been used as a shield rather than as a cooperative, mutually beneficial partnership.

The marriage counselor knows these problems well, for he has encountered them frequently among the nondisabled. They are not likely to be very different when found among those who have become disabled and are now using their disability as a new and even more protective device.

The responsibility of the marriage counselor is to ascertain the actual significance of the disability from appropriately competent resources. The counselor will need objective discussions with the physician, social worker, vocational rehabilitation counselor, etc., if he is to maintain proper perspective regarding the actual significance of the disability as a factor in the life of the disabled individual and in his adaptation to the responsibilities of marriage. With this information at hand, judgment on the role of the disability can be properly appraised. This will help avoid the ever-present pitfall of aiding and abetting the disabled client's efforts to use his disability for secondary gains in the resolution of all his life problems.

Minimal Disability

This final category includes all those disabilities which leave very little limitation of function. Such an individual has generally made complete, or virtually complete, recovery and the only significant residual effect is often largely that of psychological disturbance over the traumatic events of the past, weakening of motivation, reduced tolerance for frustration and the

like. Dependency persisting long after the actual illness or disabling experience is probably one of the worst residues.

These individuals also follow a pattern of using their past illness in a
"sick" fashion. They use the past as a weapon to provide for the present
and future. They may be reluctant to part with their symptoms, for they
find them valuable shields against the buffeting and tossing of the destructive waves of life.

Difficulties in the marriage status may have been temporarily resolved
during illness, and now the formerly disabled individual is making the
effort to continue this status even after good health has been restored.

Here again the marriage counselor needs to be aware of these possible
defense mechanisms. He must, of course, avoid making *a priori* judgments —
and instead make full use of objectively supported evidence in combating,
or at least in trying to combat, such psychologically dangerous procedures.
But he must be equally certain that he is not labeling this behavior as
pseudo-illness or pseudo-disability when in reality the reported difficulties
are factually true. Only full use of supportive information from those
competent to supply such information can be relied upon to provide the
necessary evidence.

DISABILITY IN THE FAMILY CONSTELLATION

We shall bring this chapter to a close with a discussion of some of the
marital problems that may arise when chronic illness and/or disability occurs in other members of the family than the marital partners. There are
two major categories of individuals involved here, namely: (a) one or more
children of the marriage; and (b) relatives of the family residing with them.

Disability in Children

The problems which children may contribute to the marital discord are
already well known to the marriage counselor. When one or more of the
children are born with or develop during life, physical and/or mental disorders, they may create new, complex and often very traumatic effects on
their parents.

Prenatal and natal disabilities in the child almost without exception
create serious guilt feelings in one or both parents. These vary all the way
from the concepts of "the sins of the parents are visited upon the children"
to the continuing folklore of "marking of the child" through looking at
some noxious visual stimulus such as snake, a spider, a crab, etc. Obviously,
most of these concepts are factually nonsensical. Occasionally, a disability
that occurs as a result of failure of the mother to get proper medical advice
or treatment may result in disability — but here again the resultant condition is due to ignorance, poverty or some circumstance beyond the control

of the mother or father, rather than through willful disregard. No matter what the cause, nothing can possibly be gained for parents or child when such "guilt" feelings are allowed to persist. Only further serious damage to the family can result from the continuing climate of guilt in the home.

Postnatal disabilities may also be expected to produce guilt feelings in many parents. This results from the parents' conviction that something they might have done, some precaution they might have taken, some oversight they have committed, has resulted in their child or children having become the victim of an accident or illness leading to disability.

There is a wide variety of other parental reactions that may arise when marital discord is linked with some change in their child or children. Among these may be included such reactions as: (a) considering the loss of physical perfection in the child as a reflection on parental status; (b) the inability (actual or assumed) of the child to meet the demands of parental ambition (e.g., inability to attain goals desired by the parent); (c) the disabled child as a source of economic drain on the family economy; (d) stigmatization of the child as a source of parental stigmatization (e.g., in mental retardation, epilepsy, severe bodily disfigurement, etc.). These are but a few of the more commonly encountered parental reactions which may be overt, or even more frequently covert, and can be found only when one begins to explore the basis for parental behavior toward their sick and/or disabled children.

The parents who are experiencing marital discord not infrequently make use of their child's disability as a primary or secondary basis of accentuating their differences. They fail to recognize that this is often merely an additional excuse for their interpersonal conflicts rather than the actual cause for them.

The impact of such behavior on the disabled child or children can hardly be overestimated. Parental discord is traumatizing enough; but when the child's disability is used as the apparent source of these marital reactions, it is bound to have significant effects on the child's psyche.

The marital counselor will need to consider these matters carefully and use information he can gain from his colleagues, the physician, social worker, psychologist and others, to strengthen his approach in resolving the marital problems of the parents. Parents who fail to understand fully what they are doing to their children can neither correct their own difficulties nor aid in the rehabilitation of their ill or disabled children.

A sick or disabled child or children may indeed constitute a severe drain on the family pocketbook — especially so when the parents find themselves unable to accept medical opinion relative to limitations on what can be done to further reduce or alleviate the disability and/or deformity in the child. Thus may begin a long and expensive "shopping" process which seldom helps the child's condition but may cause serious harm to his personality and his own ability to accept the limitations of his condition. It may readily create the impression that his parents will not accept him as he is, that they can only do so if he becomes "perfect" and "intact" again. The saddest aspect of this whole situation is that parents may resent the costly nature of these efforts and readily transfer their feelings, often hostile ones, to the involved child or children.

Parents who have marital discord are often likely to have experienced intense, personal frustration in their own occupational ambitions. This is especially true among parents who married before they reached social or vocational goals or objectives. Often they blame (and sometimes correctly so) their marriage — failing to recognize that their own actions were often the cause of these events. Such individuals frequently try to resolve these problems through goals they set for their children. The girl who was on her way to a career as a singer or an instrumentalist, the boy who wanted to become a physician or a lawyer, are examples of such adults who look upon their marriage as the block which can only be resolved by one or more of their progeny attaining the identical goal. The unfairness of such an approach being imposed on the child is well known to the marriage counselor. But the added insult of being angry, disappointed or further frustrated by the child who, because of illness or disability, is barred from satisfying parental ego-needs can hardly be overstressed.

Finally, the parent who feels his child's disability casts a reflection on the "purity" of his or his spouse's genetic or congenital contribution is again blaming the child for what is hardly the fault of the child. Children with epilepsy, cerebral palsy, diabetes, mental retardation etc., represent not only problems in general community understanding, but often the family community has an identical viewpoint which seriously prejudices their own attitudes.

All of these feelings, prejudices, biases and attitudes damage both the marital relationship and the welfare of the disabled individual. The gamut of such faulty attitudinal state is too large to encompass here, but the marriage counselor can cite many others from his own experience.

The problems raised by such factors are numerous and generally difficult to overcome. Actually, marriage counseling may be delayed until the marital partners can gain insight and understanding of the views, and means can be found to reduce and control these emotionalized reactions. To ignore these problems would be to court failure in dealing with many of the marriage problems. Their resolution may help to minimize a primary source of difficulty and at least reduce the damage done to the disabled child.

Full use should be made of available expertise on the prognostication of the child's medical, psychological, social and vocational future in helping to readjust the parental reactions. Disability has many psychological components as well as physiological ones, hence the counselor will need all the information that the medical-paramedical expert can supply regarding the child's potential for recovery and the expectations for his rehabilitation. By using this information, the counselor may not only be able to aid parents in reviewing their marital adjustment, but also may be able to begin to participate in the restoration of their child to a well-adjusted life.

Disability in Other Members of the Family

Illness and accident leading to disability may occur with considerable frequency among other members of the family no less than with the married couple and/or their children. Often the mother, the father or a sibling of the husband or wife may be living within the fold of the family. Occasionally there may be two or even more of such relatives in a single dwelling.

Every marriage counselor is all-too-well acquainted with the difficulties that may arise when two or more generations attempt to live in one domicile. ("Inlaw" jokes have persisted in humorous and not-so-humorous literature for too long to allow us any doubts that it is often a very serious component in marital discord.) While this by no means is an absolute "law" of marriage, it is at least a safe hypothesis that the conflict/nonconflict ratio is almost certain to increase when inlaws are too intimately involved with a married couple.

If, in addition to personality conflict situations, we add the presence of physical and/or mental disability in one of these members of the family constellation, it becomes apparent that only in exceptional circumstances can one expect to avoid worsening of intrafamilial relationships. This is likely to reach inordinate levels when the sick or disabled individual seriously taxes the family economy or becomes a source of social, psychological or vocational disturbance. The marriage counselor may find such situations among the more frustrating ones he must help to alleviate or reduce. Since the disabled individual is usually a relative of only one of the marriage partners, his or her presence creates further grounds for marital discord. If, for one reason or another, circumstances do not permit the removal of the disabled individual from the conflicting family environment one may anticipate that it will remain a persistent and often worsening influence on the marriage scene.

The combinations and psychological permutations that may occur when there is a disabled relative in the family in which there is also either disability in either a spouse or in a child hardly need discussion here.

One of the most common sources of disturbed family relationship is the aging process which is likely to create disability of some degree in the parents of the married couple. Since this is an inevitable occurrence in most instances, the couple should have planned with the parents on just how it was to be met when it occurred. Unfortunately, it is a problem that few younger individuals want to bring up with their parents — so it is often relegated to the scrapheap of forgetfulness until it can no longer be avoided. By the time serious thoughts are given to the matter, much emotional reaction is involved. The attainment of a mutually satisfying solution is relatively rare. It remains to be seen whether the new social services, including medicare for the aging, will provide adequate solutions.

The marriage counselor may anticipate considerable difficulty in aiding the couple to satisfactory solutions. The best he can do is to encourage full utilization of available community services for the relatives needing such help and do all that his skill will permit to reestablish a sound perspective in his clients toward their marriage. This is not likely to be an easy task due to the long period in which discord may have been allowed to develop.

SUMMARY

It has not been possible to treat all of the possible sources of marital discord that are influenced directly or indirectly by the presence of prolonged or severe illness or accident resulting in disability and/or deformity. Like the marital discord itself, the disability may be highly visible or may be hidden. It may involve one or both marital partners, their children, and/or their close relatives. Generally, the disability involved is not the sole factor in the troubled marital scene. Often it is a secondary factor, but used as though it were the principal difficulty.

Whatever the source, whatever the actual significance of disease or disability to his clients, the marriage counselor needs to be fully aware of its presence, and must be prepared to make full use of the available physicians, social workers, vocational rehabilitation counselors and others who may be able to provide needed specific information and who can deal with problems that may not be properly within the domain of the marriage counselor. Willingness to refer clients to other community resources for the resolution of difficulties that impinge on the marriage relationship may often help the marital counselor in a more effective solution of the couple's marital conflicts.

Chapter 34

INTERMARRIAGE AND PSYCHOLOGICAL ADJUSTMENT

VICTOR D. SANUA

THE MARRIAGE RATE IN THE United States is considered to be one of the highest in the world, since Americans tend to marry at an early age. The present emphasis on college education for everyone does not seem to make for a postponement of marriage.

Another major characteristic of marriage in the United States is the increase in rate of mating of individuals belonging to different cultural, religious and, to a lesser extent, racial backgrounds. This has become of such magnitude that religious leaders, in particular, have often met to discuss ways and means of reducing the increasing rate of these marriages. When the separate immigrant generations held to their traditional ways of thinking and customs, the rate of intermarriage was low; but the younger generations, being "homogenized" by a similar environment, have not always been willing to abide by the parental strictures of limiting their associations to individuals of the same culture, faith and race. The school and university, the recreation patterns, geographical and economic mobility, together with the emphasis on romantic love, are all factors that have contributed to this increase of intermarriage.

Opposition to intermarriage arises from two major considerations: One is based on the desire of every group to survive as an entity and to perpetuate its values; and the other comes from a practical consideration that intermarriage rarely works out. After the initial romantic period wears off, it is often assumed that numerous difficulties crop up, particularly in those cases where young individuals jump headlong into marriage, with little forethought or thorough discussion of the handling of religious differences.

These are some of the questions which usually plague the mates: Will each maintain his own religious identity? How will the children be raised? In the case of one of the mates being Catholic, will birth control be practiced? However, even if such questions are discussed frankly prior to marriage, it is no reassurance that solemn promises, or formal promises in the case of a prenuptial agreement, will be maintained after marriage. One of the mates might possibly recant on these promises at a later date, which will lead to conflicts, bitterness and unhappiness. The usual support that each spouse would receive from his own family will add to the conflicts and weaken any tendencies for compromise. We are well aware that all marriages are bound to encounter various difficulties, but intermarriage represents an additional source of conflicts that will add to these difficulties.

The question which we expect to raise in this chapter is whether the major research papers that have dealt with these problems have found a confirmation of these contraindications; hopefully, we will derive some general formulations based on such objective data.

How is intermarriage usually defined? When two individuals differing in cultural, religious or racial background marry, it is called an *intermarriage*. However, sometimes the words *mixed marriage* are used when both mates maintain their religious identities. In reviewing the research material, it is to be noted that researchers, by and large, do not seem to make much use of the variable of conversion and nonconversion, and therefore use the blanket word of *intermarriage* to cover all the contingencies. A question may be raised about using the word *intermarriage* for mates who belong to different Protestant denominations. While one would be less inclined to consider such marriages as intermarriages, they are still considered intermarriage, particularly in those cases where the two Protestant denominations may be somewhat far apart in their values and family ethos.

In this chapter we emphasize religious intermarriages, but will cover some research on interracial marriages. We shall discuss studies pertaining to marriages between Protestant, Catholics and Jews, since these are the three major religious groups in the United States. Needless to say, each of these groups is comprised of numerous subgroups, particularly in the case of Protestants, with the numerous denominations. Among the Catholics, we have the numerous nationality groups involved, such as Irish-Catholic, Italian-Catholic, etc. Thus, both religious and national characteristics may be involved, such as an Anglo-Saxon-Protestant marrying a Polish-Catholic. With regard to the Jewish groups, while marriage between a Reform and an Orthodox, or a Sephardic and Ashkenazi, cannot be considered as religious intermarriage, some elements of intermarriage may enter into the mating of such couples coming from different backgrounds.

Practically all of the studies which we shall review tend to use the gross classifications of Protestant-Catholic, Protestant-Jewish, Catholic-Jewish. Marriages could also be classified according to the sex of each mate, thus doubling the possibilities of classification. However, only in very few instances has the sex factor been considered. While religion has been used as a differentiating variable, it must be kept in mind, as pointed out by Bossard and Boll (7), that religion is different from church membership. They indicate that every religion includes the following:

1. A system of beliefs about God, life and man;
2. Established forms of worship;
3. A set of observances in the lives of its followers;

4. A number of attitudes, life values and behavior judgments;

5. A conception of life, now and in the Hereafter, the relative importance of now and Hereafter, the purpose of life, and the role of unseen forces and factors in life.

Thus, according to Bossard and Boll, interfaith marriage is not merely the union between two people who are professing allegiance to some church, but represents the union of two different cultures which are pervasive in everyday behavior.

We are discussing in this chapter, under different rubrics, the rate of increase of intermarriage, research studies which have concentrated on the type of persons who enter into intermarriage and the consequences of intermarriage. Since divorce and separation are considered to be the major index for failure, they will receive a separate treatment. The last section will deal with attitudes of students towards intermarriage.

RATE OF INTERMARRIAGE

There is no question that the rate of intermarriage has been increasing in recent decades; the problem is to get an accurate estimate. Unfortunately, no one knows for sure the exact rate of intermarriage in the United States. Applicants for marriage licenses and divorce are not required to provide such information. Therefore, what is available, mostly, are estimates of intermarriage rates, arrived at by various research techniques. It is only in the State of Iowa that complete statistics are available, since it is compulsory to provide information on religious background. While the State of Iowa is not representative of the United States, it provides us with useful information on the magnitude of the problem.

Before data on intermarriage are presented, we must point out that there are two different statistical rates of intermarriage: one involving marriages and the other involving individuals. Rodman (32) has discussed this confusion which he has found in the literature. For example, in six homogeneous Catholic marriages and four mixed Catholic marriages, two types of rates are possible. We can say that 40 per cent of the Catholic marriages are mixed, or that four Catholics out of sixteen have entered into mixed marriages, and the rate would thus be 25 per cent. Unfortunately, it is not often clear from the literature which rate is being used by the author. However, if details are given, it is possible to transform one rate into the other, and the formula has been provided by Rodman. It is to be noted, moreover, that the change is necessary only if there is a need to specify intermarriage in a specific religious category, but if one is interested to know the total number of intermarriages in the society at large, the percentage does not change.

Another problem which enters into the statistics is the role that religious conversion plays in reporting intermarriage. If one of the mates converts any time prior to the survey, this marriage is considered to be homogeneous. Since very little work has been conducted as to the frequency of conversion, such data which does not take into account this factor of religious conversion would underestimate the rate of intermarriage, if we define intermarriage as the mating of individuals who were brought up in different religions.

Thomas (40), a Catholic sociologist of St. Louis University, who examined the records on intermarriage among Catholics, estimates that during the past two decades, intermarriages account for one-fourth to one-third of all valid Catholic marriages. However, since many Catholics intermarry without the sanction of the Church, the conservative figure which he offers is that there is approximately a 50 per cent intermarriage rate in Catholic marriages. Chancellor and Monohan (11), using the Iowa statistics, reported that 42 per cent of all marriages involving a Catholic in 1953 were mixed.

As for the Protestant group, Bossard and Letts (6) found on a nationwide investigation of marriages contracted by members of the United Lutheran Church of America, in 382 congregations in twenty-eight states, that 58 per cent of the Lutherans who married found mates outside the Lutheran Church; one-fifth marrying Catholics; one-fifth marrying nonchurch members; and three-fifths marrying members of other Protestant churches. The percentage of those who married Jews and other non-Protestants was very small.

Regarding the Jewish group, Rosenthal (32) reviewed a series of studies on intermarriage, and analyzing the Iowa statistics, came to the conclusion that the future growth of the Jewish population is seriously affected by the increasing degree of intermarriage in the group. His important finding is that in approximately 75 per cent of the cases the children of such marriages are not identified as Jews. In one specific study in Greater Washington, it was found that intermarriage rises from one generation to the next, from 1 per cent for the foreign-born, to 10.2 per cent for the native-born of foreign parents, and 17.9 per cent for the native-born of native-born parents. In the Iowa statistics, he found that "during the period of 1953-1957, 42 per cent of all Iowa marriages involving Jews were intermarriages." However, Rosenthal cautions that this finding pertains only to Jews living in small Jewish communities, and small-town Jews are more exposed to a higher degree of interaction with individuals of different religions. In cities the rate was 34.2 per cent, and in towns and rural areas the rate was about 65 per cent.

Massarik (28) was also able to substantiate the influence of the size of the Jewish group on the frequency of intermarriage. He found that the rate for intermarriage in San Francisco proper was 17.2 per cent; on the Peninsula it was 20 per cent; while in Marin County it was 37 per cent.

However, even in such a large city as New York, where there is a high concentration of Jews, the rate seems to be very high, as revealed by a small-scale study conducted by Sanua (34) on the attitude of 229 Jewish college students towards intermarriage. In the questionnaire used, the following item was included: "If any member of your family (including yourself) is married to a person of a different religion than your own, please check which . . . brother, sister, uncle, etc. . . . none . . ." Approximately 85 per cent of the male college students attending a secular or Jewish Orthodox college checked none. With girls attending secular colleges, the percentage was 56 per cent, and with those attending the Orthodox Jewish college, it was 83 per cent. The striking finding, particularly in the case of families who send their children to Orthodox Jewish colleges, is that they do not seem to be immune to intermarriage. The above-cited small study seems to indicate that intermarriage has occurred in more than 15 per cent of the families. We could also add that even such a rate might be underestimated, since the margin of error, due to lapse of memory or to the fact that there might be more than one intermarriage per family, would tend to increase the rate.

Not all studies have confirmed this increase in intermarriage. For example, Kennedy (22) found from an analysis of marriage records in New Haven that there has been assortive mating, rather than random intermarriage since 1870. She formulated the "triple melting pot hypothesis," which specified that, instead of America representing the single "melting pot," popularized by Zangwill, the country is shaping up into a "triple melting pot"; that is, while nationality differences are disappearing, Catholics tend to marry Catholics, Jews tend to marry Jews, and Protestants tend to marry Protestants. Such finding was reinforced in a later study by Hollingshead (18), who interviewed 437 white couples in New Haven, where he found an intermarriage rate among Catholics of 6.2 per cent. Hollingshead concludes that "Kennedy's and our data show we are going to have three pots boiling merrily side by side with little fusion between them for an indefinite period." It is to be noted that Hollingshead's figure is strikingly different from the one given by Thomas. However, Thomas's rate is that of Catholic marriages, while Hollingshead gives the rate based on Catholic individuals.

Likewise, in 1946, Barron did not find an increasing rate of intermarriage. He felt that the Jews, during centuries of existence in proximity

to Gentile majorities, have developed attitudes and techniques of intermarriage resistance long before they arrived in the United States. However,
as indicated earlier, more recent statistics do not seem to support this view.

Thomas (40) took issue with the triple melting pot hypothesis. He
presented data to show that the rate of intermarriage in New Haven is considerably below the rate for Connecticut and for the United States as a
whole. Thomas points out that there are three factors which are associated
with marriage between Catholics and non-Catholics: (a) relative proportion of Catholics in the total population; (b) the presence of ethnic subgroups; and (c) socioeconomic class of the Catholic population. He predicts that mixed marriages will "go on increasing gradually for some time
to come."

Further evidence is given by Locke, Sabagh and Thomas (27) to support Thomas' contention. An analysis of the official Catholic Directory
which reports on intermarriage in each parish revealed that there was a
high negative correlation (−.86 in 1955) between the frequency of interfaith marriage rates and the percentage of Catholics in the population for
the forty-eight states. For example, in New England, where Kennedy and
Hollingshead have conducted their studies, and where the Catholic population as a whole is 47 per cent of the total population, the rate of intermarriage was 22 per cent. In the South Atlantic States, where Catholics
represent 5 per cent of the population, the intermarriage rate was 50 per
cent. These authors suggest that besides percentage of Catholic population,
other cultural factors may enter in determining the rate of intermarriage,
such as the social distance between the two groups, and cohesiveness and
economic status, which are somewhat similar to the variables given by
Thomas.

INTERMARRIAGE AS A SIGN OF MALADJUSTMENT

Both sociological and psychological reasons have been given as causes
of intermarriage. The reports now to be reviewed have tried to provide
psychological formulations, primarily, to explain its dynamics. One of the
earliest attempts was made by Resnick (31). Slotkin (38), after interviewing eighty-seven families of mixed marriages and examining the records of
social agencies for ninety-six intermarried families, found eight different
types of individuals who intermarry: (a) the unorganized or formerly delinquent person; (b) the promiscuous person who goes outside his group
for fear of "entangling alliances," but who succumbs at the end into marriage with the outgroup; (c) the adventurous person who seeks stimulating
experiences outside the group; (d) the socially isolated, detached individual; (e) the rebellious person who questions the validity of his group

customs and tends to adapt the culture of the outgroup; (f) the marginal person who seeks status by amalgamating with members of the dominant group; (g) the acculturated person; (h) the emancipated person — when the individual has lost awareness of his descent. Slotkin found that 64 per cent of the intermarried cases he examined could be categorized as emancipated, rebellious, marginal and acculturated. However, the validity of these categories is to be questioned, since so many of them seem to overlap. Furthermore, the fact that he took more than half of his cases from social agencies does not provide him with a representative sample of the intermarried population.

Hunt and Colley (21), after interviewing twenty males of Philippine-American marriages, found that there was a considerable degree of family disorganization (70%) in both mates. He felt that since family ties in general have disrupted, these individuals did not feel the pressures towards endogamy. Freeman (13) found that individuals who intermarry show a sense of alienation toward their own group after they feel that they have been rejected. They often show a record of conflict with their parents, and an idealization of some alien culture. Dating and mating selection follow identification with the new group.

Mayer (29) furthermore found that those who intermarried against the wishes of their parents were not only attracted by their mates, but also supported by mutual friends who approved of the relationship. Here the reference group played an important role. Levinson and Levinson (25), in their intensive sociopsychological study of twenty intermarried couples, did not find that all intermarriage necessarily could be explained on the basis of some pathology on the part of the partners. They found two major groups of Jewish individuals who marry outside their group. One group, which they labeled "reluctants" — individuals who had a strong Jewish identity and great dependence on their mothers — through intermarriage had attempted to establish adult independence and escape the past. They called this type "neurotic exogamy." For the second group, intermarriage was not found to be symptomatic of a neurosis, but resulted from a weakening of identity. The traditional Jewish values have no more meaning to them. They were called the "emancipated." Their mates, while of a different religion, tended to have similar goals and personality. Since the sample was based on twenty couples, this typology has yet to be corroborated by further studies.

One of the most adequate studies to date regarding the characteristics of the religiously intermarried was undertaken by Heiss (16), based on the data he obtained from the Midtown Study of Rennie, Srole, *et al.* (39). Out of a sample of 1,660 cases studied, Heiss was able to analyze the data on

304 intermarried respondents and 863 intramarried respondents. This study represents a decided improvement on others, since he was able to have a control group.

The rate of intermarriage was found to be 21.4 per cent for Catholics, 33.9 per cent for Protestants and 18.4 per cent for Jews. Heiss formulated six hypotheses, which he tried to test. Those who are likely to intermarry have the following characteristics:

1. Parents with weak religious ties;
2. Early "unsatisfactory relationship" with parents;
3. Early experience of "strifeful family life";
4. Tenuous family ties to their immediate and extended families when they were young;
5. "Emancipation from parental influence" at time of marriage;
6. Parents who had a "difficult time."

The above information was obtained from the respondents in the course of a long interview, and obviously depended upon the recall of long-past events.

The results show that only parents having a difficult time did not differentiate between the intermarried and the intramarried groups. Three hypotheses, "early unsatisfactory relationship with parents," "early experience of strifeful family life," and "emancipation from parental influence at time of marriage" (2, 3, 5) were found to be present with the intermarried Catholics and received strong support, with "tenuous family ties" (4) receiving some support. With the Protestant group, "parents with weak religious ties," and "tenuous family ties to their immediate and extended families when they were young" (1, 4) received some support. With the Jewish group, only "tenuous family ties to their immediate and extended families when they were young" (4) received strong support, and "emancipation from parental influence at time of marriage" (5) received some support. Thus, only one hypothesis seems to hold in all three groups, and that is "tenuous family ties to their immediate and extended families when very young."

In another study by Hey (18), negative results were found. Despite the fact that he had selected interfaith couples who had applied for marriage counseling, he found little difference between the characteristics of those couples and a matched group of same-faith couples. He found, however, that conversion of one spouse results in a greater amount of disagreement and intensity of disagreement. His conclusion was that differences in religious backgrounds of marital partners do not distinguish them from couples of the same faith when both groups are well matched.

In a doctoral dissertation, Besancecy (5) explored the influence of "anomic situations" which might weaken religious endogamy, such as war-time marriages, rural-urban migration, vertical occupational mobility. In general, he found that his theoretical scheme was more predictive of Catholic than of Protestant intermarriages, which supports Heiss' study. For both groups, parents and relatives were the most significant agents of social control. The church control was found to be more effective for maintaining membership in church for those who attended Catholic schools than for forestalling intermarriage. Occupational mobility, upward and downward, was the only "anomic situation" which showed a significant but weak relationship with interfaith marriage.

Sklare (37) provides us with a short review of intermarriage. He concludes that the notions of the causes of intermarriage are beginning to look outmoded. The rate of intermarriage may not only be increasing because Jews in increasing numbers are moving into the general society, but also because tastes and ideas such as liberalism, always preferred by Jews, are becoming more prevalent among non-Jews, and, as a result, Jews are becoming more acceptable as marriage partners. Chancellor and Monahan (11) previously had stated that the greater prevalence of intermarriage may be due to a more tolerant attitude of the American public. It would seem, according to them, that church affiliation may not be as important as other factors.

OUTCOME OF INTERMARRIAGE: SOCIAL AND PSYCHOLOGICAL MALADJUSTMENT

The question which is raised now is whether intermarriage in itself causes problems of adjustment in both mates, provided there are no patent personality problems. Are the sources of conflict of the intermarried due purely to differences in their religious upbringing? Any study intended to answer this question is bound to have some serious methodological problems, since it would be difficult to separate the sources of friction due to personality differences from those conflicts which are provoked primarily by religious differences. There is no question that there is an interaction between these two sources of conflict.

Another complicating factor is that the researcher who studies intermarried couples is likely to study those who have remained married. He may thereby exclude from his research those who have been divorced or separated, thus eliminating major research data needed to test the hypothesis. It is thus possible to find intermarried couples who, through the positive aspects of their personalities, have remained together despite difficulties, and therefore would not represent the "average intermarried couple." Another problem would be to find criteria to classify and discriminate between successful and unsuccessful marriages.

There have been a number of studies pertaining to adjustment of the intermarried. Baber (1) collected data on 325 cases of mixed marriages suggested by his students. They were rated on a five-point scale as to their degree of happiness. Out of a possible combination of six types of marriage among the three major religious groups he found that the Jewish-Protestant marriage has a considerably higher average happiness rating. To his surprise, he found happy marriages outnumbered unhappy marriages three to one. He was well aware of the limitations of the study, since there may have been an unconscious desire on the part of the students to select only those happy cases. Furthermore, while the mates appeared to be happy to the outside observer, they may have kept their quarrels private. One significant finding, however, is that the happier couples were more similar in cultural and racial characteristics.

Two other studies, one by Schnepp and Masako (36) and another by Golden (15), likewise have not found the expected unhappiness among intermarried couples. Schnepp's study of twenty American-Japanese war marriages in St. Louis found that neither mate had regrets or serious inlaw problems. He found that cooperation and adaptation was common, and that stability was characteristic of these couples. Golden (1958) likewise, in another sample of Negro-white couples, felt that their marriage had a good chance to survive. He found that they usually marry at an older age and that a sizable number had previous marriages, which, according to Golden, may have led them to have some forethought before undertaking another marriage. It is possible that, in both instances, selectivity may have entered to give biased samples. Schnepp has studied only war marriages in the States, after the initial adjustment in Japan. It may be true that there were no serious problems in these twenty married couples, but we have no idea about the number of war marriages that went on the rocks in Japan or even in St. Louis. Furthermore, since Golden had only interviewed couples who were willing to be interviewed, it could be assumed that those who had refused to be interviewed included a high percentage of unhappy marriages.

In none of the above studies was a control group used. Heiss (17) felt that no valid answer can be obtained unless the investigator has a control group. To determine whether any marriage type (inter- or intramarried) determines outcome, it is necessary to compare intramarried and intermarried couples on similar premarital characteristics. However, contrary to the usual assumptions that interfaith marriages are heterogeneous, Heiss hypothesized that interfaith marriages may be just as homogeneous as intrafaith marriages. He felt that if two adults of different backgrounds are willing to intermarry, there must be some homogeneity of views, attitudes and values. For example, prospective spouses may not subscribe to the traditional positions of their ingroup. Examining the same sample used in the Mid-Town Study, Heiss compared 304 intermarried and 863 intra-married couples. No attempt was made to distinguish the various subtypes of intermarriages. The findings are based on a number of questions which were included in the long questionnaire. The extent of life satisfaction was measured by seven questions. An example is: "In general, would you say that most of the time you are in high spirits, good spirits, low spirits or very low spirits?" Other questions included: "Do you worry about marriage?" and "Can the unmarried person be just as content as the married one?" Another measure of satisfaction was the final mental-health rating on these couples that was given by the psychiatrists. Other areas investigated include children, importance of religion and interpersonal relationships, to mention only a few of the highlights of the findings.

For all intermarried Catholics, the outcome is consistently poor in the items measuring satisfaction. Surprisingly, the intermarried Protestant group had a more satisfactory score than the intramarried. The intermarried Jews see their relatives less regularly, and more of them feel, significantly, that the unmarried can be just as content as the married. If any conclusion is to be drawn from such data, it is that intermarriage is more likely to be deleterious to Catholics and Jews, and has no effect on Protestants, pro-vided, of course, that the matching has ruled out selective factors. Since the findings did not agree with his hypotheses, Heiss indicated that it may be possible that he overestimated the degree to which interfaith marriages are homogeneous.

INTERMARRIAGE AND MENTAL HEALTH

In the two sections preceding, we have tried to provide summaries of studies which have given data on the premarital personalities of the mates and their subsequent marital adjustment. Such studies, in general, have been carried on with small samples, by single investigators or a small team of investigators. Some had to rely on subjective evaluations of happiness and personality adequacy, some using more objective methods than others. In one study, responses to a questionnaire were provided by mates. To our knowledge, no data are available on the prevalence of mental illness and the suicide rate for the intermarried, as compared to the intramarried.

In the second volume of the Midtown Study, Langner and Micheal (24) have selected a number of independent variables which were believed to be related to the mental-health status of the respondents. One of them was religious heterogeneity, which could be a potential source of marital stress, which would, in turn, lead to strain, and even mental disturbance. They found that persons who married a partner of a different religion showed no greater risk than those who had spouses of the same religion. Only in the case of individuals belonging to the middle class was there some increment in mental disturbance. What seemed to be significant in the study is that the rate of intermarriage among those high on the socioeconomic level was 34.9 per cent, for the middle class 26.1 per cent and for the low class 23.2 per cent. They feel there is some evidence that the higher the socioeconomic status of the individual, the more he is inclined to marry outside his religious group. Ethnic, religious and other values are of less importance to this group, and are replaced by other aspects of the American ethos. Since in this study there was no breakdown of types of marriages, some subgroup differences may have been obscured by using only a large, heterogeneous sample of intermarried and intramarried.

A recent report by Saucier (35) presented data on the role played by psychological factors on interethnic marriages among people who have been diagnosed as psychiatrically ill. He felt that a study of psychiatric cases may help in understanding better the phenomenon of intermarriage in general. The sample included fifteen couples where the mates were Catholics and one mate was of French-Canadian background, while the others were of Irish, English, Scottish or Welsh descent. He found that intermarriage seems to be more psychiatrically damaging to the female spouse; or more women who are susceptible to mental illness are attracted by intermarriage. He found that most intermarried patients came from families where the mother was perceived as the most powerful parent and as the main disciplinarian. Hypothesizing on the intervening variables between the two situations, Saucier indicated that a domineering father would induce in his children the maximum ethnic barriers and differences, whereas a domineering mother would minimize the ethnic boundaries, which would not inhibit marriage outside the community. Another major finding was that there was a greater tendency towards depression in intermarried subjects, and an occurrence of deep trouble in their relationship with their children. In regard to the relationship between intermarriage and psychiatric disturbance, Saucier assumed that the individual marrying outside the community as a workable solution to his emotional problems caused by an overdominating mother discovers, after a number of years of intermarried life, the illusory aspect of this hope. This study is unique in its approach to the problem of intermarriage, since it has provided intensive clinical information on intermarried couples. This should set the stage for expanding the study to many different kinds of interethnic marriages, and those marriages which could cause even greater problems, such as interreligious marriages, or even interethnic marriages with mates of different religions.

INTERMARRIAGE AND DIVORCE

We have discussed some of the research and the resulting theories which have often been formulated to explain why people embark on intermarriage.

We have also discussed some of the problems which may arise specifically from differences in religion and race between intermarried couples. Both of these variables should be considered as independent variables. There is no question that there is an interaction between what the mates bring to a marriage and the resulting adjustment. While the independent variables may be difficult to evaluate, the dependent variable, such as divorce or separation, can easily be computed. Though divorce may be considered a more accurate measure, it has its limitations. Married couples may not go as far as divorce and separation because they are unwilling to abrogate some religious or traditional values. The fact that some couples stay married cannot be used as a criterion for marital happiness. Nevertheless, studies of divorce and separation are of importance, and, with reservations they provide interesting information as to the precariousness of such marriages.

A number of studies have dealt primarily with the frequency of divorce among different types of marriages. Bell (4) found that the divorce rate in Maryland for intermarried Protestant and Catholic couples was 15.2 per cent. In Week's findings (41) in the state of Washington the rate was 17.4 per cent. Landis (23) administered a questionnaire to 4,108 college students who were to report on the marriage of their parents. From such information, it was possible to establish a relationship between interfaith marriages and divorce rates. Landis found that the highest rate of divorce occurred when the husband was Catholic and the wife was Protestant (20.6%), and the lowest rate (4.4%) when both parents were Catholic. It should be noted that in this study information was obtained only on interreligious marriages when there were children. Thus, information on childless couples could not be included in the study. In all of the aforementioned studies, it was found that those who were unwilling to identify with any religion had the highest rate of divorce.

While Landis relied on the reports of students, Monahan and Kephert (30) relied on the divorce and desertion testimony records in Philadelphia. They found that while strong prohibition against divorce for Catholics holds down the rate of divorce, it does not prevent the occurrence of family disorganization, as the high desertion figure for Catholics indicates.

A most thorough study on the rate of divorce has been conducted by the Iowa State University. As we have mentioned earlier, Iowa is the only state that requests information on religion. The following are some of the major findings by Burchinal and Chancellor (9), who directed the project:

1. There was no difference between homogeneous Protestant marriages and denominationally mixed Protestant marriage types;
2. Contrary to Landis' finding, differences in the marital survival rates between the Catholic wife-Protestant husband marriage and Protestant wife-Catholic husband marriage was quite small;

3. The lowest survival rate of interreligious marriages was derived mainly from the marriage of Catholics to individuals who were not affiliated with any Protestant denomination. Thus, it would seem that
the rate of broken marriages was more influenced by the lack of
religious identification of the non-Catholic partner than by a clash
of religious values and beliefs.

Hawaii has been an area of research that has provided much sociological
data, in view of its racial fusion in recent decades. Cheng and Yamamura
(12), in a study of the divorce rate on the island, have found that it varies
according to the different degrees of ethnic and cultural ties of the intermarried couples. They found that when four Oriental groups, Japanese,
Chinese, Korean and Filipino, cross the race line their total outmarriage
divorce rate is 21.5 per cent. However, when Orientals married non-
Oriental mates, the outmarriage divorce rate increased further to 27.4 per
cent.

Most of the studies reviewed have found that more interfaith marriages
tend to end in divorce than same faith marriages. However, there is one
study which dissents with these findings. Locke (26) found that when
comparing two hundred divorced couples and two hundred married couples,
religious differences were not found to constitute a significant factor in the
divorced group.

INTERMARRIAGE AND CHILDREN

Another major aspect of the problem in intermarriage is its consequences
on the psychological adjustment of the children. Except for some anecdotal
reports discussing some of the maladjustment problems of children of intermarried couples, we have not been able to locate studies which compare
children of intrafaith and interfaith couples. On the other hand, some of
the studies which we have reviewed include a number of findings as to the
problems incurred by intermarried parents with their children.

Baber (1) found that half of the conflicts reported by Protestant-Catholic marriages were over the problem of religious training of the children.
In Heiss' (17) studies, intermarried Catholics were found to have more
difficulties with their children than other religiously intermarried groups.
Landis found that the chief source of friction centered around the religious
training of the children. It was already pointed out that promises made prior
to marriage under the antenuptial agreement insisted upon by the Catholic
Church are sometimes reneged upon by the Protestant and Jewish parent.
To support this, Landis states that in 50 per cent of the cases of Catholic-
Protestant marriages, the children were raised as Protestant. Landis found
that another source of conflict is the intervention of the grandparents in the

religious education of the grandchildren. Parents may be torn between the demands for a compromise to assure their marital happiness and the intrasigent demands of their own parents.

Undoubtedly, the question of religion for the children represents a major stumbling block in intermarriages. While conversion of one parent may reduce this problem, any other solution is rife with conflicts. For example, if all the children are reared in the religion of one of the parents, their relationship with the other parent cannot be entirely normal. A barrier is bound to exist between parents and children when they belong to different religions. In some instances, the parents decide beforehand that religion of the child will depend on the sex; that is, a girl will be raised in the mother's religion, and a boy in the father's religion. This solution seems somewhat cruel and rife with danger for family harmony. If the parents decide to let the child choose his religion when he grows up, it places too much of a burden on the child, since he is bound to have conflicts of allegiance towards his parents, besides enduring the conflicts of self-identity. Even if parents promise to have a religious vacuum in the house, it is hardly possible for either parent not to influence, consciously or unconsciously, the religious outlook of the children to his own religion. These various solutions are bound to confuse the child and make him insecure, since normally he needs the support of both of his parents. For more detailed information about the types of problems which the children incur, the reader is referred to Bossard and Boll (7) and Gordon's (14) books on intermarriage, where these authors have devoted special chapters to this aspect. Gordon feels quite strongly about the consequences of intermarriage on children. He writes: "For that reason, if for no other, such mixed marriages are to be discouraged. They are unfair to children, the innocent victims of often well-intentioned parents."

INTERMARRIAGE AND THE FUTURE

Some of the studies we have reviewed give evidence that the rate of intermarriage has been increasing in the past few decades. The question arises: What are the expectations, the prospects of intermarriage in the United States in years to come? In other words, it is important to learn more about the attitude of our young people towards intermarriage.

In a sudy published in 1960, Burchinal (8) administered a questionnaire to Protestant high-school and university students. He found that there was a negative attitude towards religious cross-dating and intermarriage, which correlated positively with religiosity. Furthermore, the higher the social status, the greater the negative attitude. Females were less favorable to intermarriage, as compared to males.

Bealer *et al.* (3), in a large-scale study of Pennsylvania rural youth, administered a social-distance scale to fourteen religious groups, pertaining to intermarriage. The religious groups were ranked in their presumed sect or church likeness as measured by the degree of structural formalization. Except for Roman Catholics and Mennonites, exogamy exceeded endogamy. The authors concluded that in many social situations in contemporary American society, religious affiliation is not important.

A major book on intermarriage is that written in 1964 by Gordon (14), a rabbi and social scientist. The book represents a most comprehensive survey on attitudes of college students towards intermarriage. Since Gordon did not separate the Jewish students from the various religious groups in his sample of 5,407 students, Sanua (34) undertook a replication of the study, with 229 Jewish college students attending secular and religiously oriented colleges, as a sample. The following represents a selection of the results, comparing Gordon's and Sanua's findings:

SELECTED RESPONSES

	Gordon's Sample All Colleges	Sanua's Sample Jewish Secular	Jewish Religious
1. Parents disapprove of dating person of different religion	28%	82%	93%
2. I never date a person of a different religion.	10%	60%	90%
3. I would break off at once if it developed that I loved someone of a different religion than mine.	8%	37%	67%
4. If a brother or sister would marry "out of the faith," I would strongly disapprove.	14%	43%	75%

The above figures show that, particularly in the case of the 5,407 students studied by Gordon, intermarriage is not regarded as too objectionable. While the Jewish group seems to be more inclined to be endogamous, quite a significant percentage of them, even those attending religious schools, would not object to intermarriage.

Gordon also administered to students an adaptation of the Bogardus Social Distance Scale to assess the desirability of a number of religious, nationality and racial groups as marriage partners. We have to bear in mind that 47 per cent identified themselves as Protestants, 31 per cent as Catholics and 12 per cent as Jewish, the rest belonging to other religious groups or having no affiliations; 86 per cent were white, 12 per cent Negroes; and 2 per cent were neither white or Negro. The following represents his findings as to the desirability of each group:

ATTITUDE TOWARDS CROSS-DATING AND INTERMARRIAGE OF GORDON'S SAMPLE
OF 5,407 COLLEGE STUDENTS

	I Would Date, or Allow a Son or Daughter To Date a . . .	*I Would Marry A . . .*
Protestant	83%	74%
Italian	76%	65%
Irish	77%	64%
Polish	72%	61%
Catholic	73%	56%
Greek	64%	50%
Jew	60%	37%
Mexican	45%	31%
Negro	24%	29%
Japanese	46%	24%
Filipino	42%	24%

As expected, Jews, Mexicans, Negroes, Japanese and Filipinos were least desirable as marriage partners, while students, except for the Negro group, would be more tolerant to dating outside their groups. The conclusion which was drawn by Gordon from his study is that acceptance of intermarriage appears to be growing. These students are well familiar with intermarriage, since 40 per cent of them had indicated that intermarriage existed in their own family. The major question that is raised by Gordon is whether these attitudes constitute a threat to the well-being of the individual, society, family and organized religion. He feels that intermarriage represents a decided threat.

SUMMARY AND CONCLUSIONS

In this chapter we have tried to cover a number of empirical studies which have dealt with the problems of intermarriage. The following represents some of the generalizations which we have derived from these studies:

1. With few exceptions, all studies indicate that the rate of intermarriage is increasing in the United States, and is expected to increase. Fifty per cent of Catholics marry outside their faith. The percentage for Protestants seems to be just as high. For the Jewish group, it is approximately 17 per cent. A number of investigators have found that such sociological variables as the relative proportion of the religious group, economic status and group cohesiveness influence strikingly the rate of intermarriage.

2. There seems to be contradictory evidence as to the frequency of prior pathology in intermarried couples. Some researchers have found definite psychological disturbance in the intermarried, while others have not found it. In one study by Levinson and Levinson (25), the intermarried were found to be in two groups: those who sought intermarriage as a solution to

personality problems and those who had lost their identity toward the in-group.

3. As to difficulties arising from intermarriage, here again we have contradictory evidence. However, the data show that intermarriage may affect the three religious groups differently. Intermarriage among Jews and Catholics seems to have more serious repercussions than intermarriage among Protestants.

4. All studies show that the intermarried have a high risk of divorce. There is some evidence that the rate may change for the worse if the husband is Catholic and the wife is Protestant.

5. A number of studies indicates that the rearing of children of inter-married couples represents a serious source of conflict. There are, however, no studies which compare the personality of the children of intermarried couples and the children of homogeneous parents.

6. The data reveal that college students, except for Jewish students, do not object so strongly to interreligious dating, or interreligious marriage, if they fall in love, or to a sibling marrying outside the group. However, the degree of dating and marrying outside the group is strongly influenced by the religion and ethnicity of the partner, with the Protestant being in the most favorable position and the Filipino being in the most unfavorable position. The position of the Jew is seventh in the eleven categories.

What conclusions are we to draw from these findings? First of all, we must be aware that in most studies all types of intermarriages were lumped together. In view of the complexity of the variables involved, each inter-marriage represents a unique combination of two individuals. Some may succeed, but the probability is that these will carry an added burden which will manifest itself in later years, particularly at the time when the religious education of the children is to be decided. If young people decide to embark on intermarriage, education for the children has to be discussed thoroughly, since it will reveal where each stands on this most delicate and crucial ques-tion, and may possibly give rise to second thoughts. While a thorough dis-cussion is not a guarantee that the marriage will be successful, it might minimize, in certain instances, the serious problems which may arise.

Since we have seen that many young people today do not find it ob-jectionable to marry outside their religion, one of the greatest challenges both for parents and religious bodies is to encourage young people to marry within their faith.

REFERENCES

1. BABER, R. E.: A study of 325 mixed marriages. *American Sociological Re-view, 2:*705-716, 1937.
2. BARRON, L. M.: *People Who Intermarry.* Syracuse, Syracuse, 1946.

3. BEALER, R. C., *et al.*: Religious exogamy: A study of social distance. *Sociology and Social Research, 48*:69-79, 1963.

4. BELL, H. M.: *Youth Tell Their Story.* Washington, D.C. American Council on Education, 1938.

5. BESANCENY, P. H.: Factors associated with Protestant-Catholic marriages in Detroit area: A problem of social control. *Dissertation Abstracts, 25*:2656, 1964.

6. BOSSARD, J. H. S., and LETTS, H. C.: Mixed marriages involving Lutherans. *Marriage and Family Living, 18*:308-310, 1956.

7. BOSSARD, J. H. S., and BOLL, ELEANOR S.: *One Marriage, Two Faiths: Guidance on Interfaith Marriage.* New York, Ronald, 1957.

8. BURCHINAL, LEE B.: Membership groups and attitudes towards cross-religious dating and marriages. *Marriage and Family Living, 22*:248-253, 1960.

9. BURCHINAL, LEE B., and CHANCELLOR, L. E.: Survival rates among religiously homogamous and interreligious marriages. *Social Forces, 41*:353-362, 1963.

10. CAHMAN, WERNER J. (Ed.) : *Intermarriage and Jewish Life in America.* New York, Herzl Press, 1962.

11. CHANCELLOR, L. E., and MONAHAN, T. P.: Religious preference and interreligious mixtures in marriages and divorces in Iowa. *American Journal of Sociology, 61*:233-239, 1955.

12. CHENG, C. K., and YAMAMURA, D.: Interracial marriage and divorce in Hawaii. *Social Forces, 36*:77-84, 1957.

13. FREEMAN, L.: Homogamy in interethnic mate selection. *Sociology and Social Research, 39*:369-377, 1955.

14. GORDON, A. I.: *Intermarriage: Interfaith, Interracial, Interethnic.* Boston, Beacon, 1964.

15. GOLDEN, J.: Patterns of Negro-White intermarriage. *American Sociological Review, 19*:144-147, 1954.

16. HEISS, J. S.: Premarital characteristics of the religiously intermarried in an urban area. *American Sociological Review, 25*:47-55, 1960.

17. HEISS, J. S.: Interfaith marriage and marital outcome. *Marriage and Family Living, 23*:228-233, 1961.

18. HEY, R. N.: Dissimilarity of religious background of marital partners as a factor in mental conflict. *Dissertation Abstracts, 34*:3877, 1963.

19. HOLLINGSHEAD, A.: Cultural factors in the selection of marriage mates. *American Sociological Review, 15*:619-627, 1950.

20. HOOVER, H. F.: *Attitudes of High School Students Towards Mixed Marriage.* Washington, D.C., Catholic University Press, 1950.

21. HUNT, C., and COLLEY, R.: Intermarriage and cultural change: A study of Filippino-American marriages. *Social Forces, 35*:223-230, 1957.

22. KENNEDY, RUBY J.: Single or triple melting pot? Intermarriage trends in New Haven, 1870-1940. *American Journal of Sociology, 49*:331-339, 1944.

23. LANDIS, J. T.: Marriages of mixed and non-mixed religious faiths. *American Sociological Review, 14*:401-407, 1949.

24. LANGNER, T. S., and MICHAEL, S. T.: *Life Stress and Mental Health,* Vol. II. New York, The Free Press of Glencoe, 1963.

25. LEVINSON, MARIA, and LEVINSON, D. J.: Jews who intermarry: Sociopsychological bases of ethnic identity and change. *Yivo Annual of Jewish Social Science, 12*:103-130, 1958-59.

26. LOCKE, H. J.: *Predicting Adjustment in Marriage*. New York, Holt, Rinehart & Winston, 1951.

27. LOCKE, H. J., SABAGH, G., and THOMES, MARY: Interfaith Marriages. *Social Problems, 4*:329-333, 1957.

28. MASSARIK, F.: Report of the Jewish population of San Francisco, Marin County and the Peninsula. Jewish Welfare Federation of San Francisco, Marin County, 1959.

29. MAYER, J. E.: *Jewish-Gentile Courtships*. Glencoe, The Free Press, 1961.

30. MONOHAN, T. P., and KEPHART, W. M.: Divorce and desertion by religious and mixed religious groups. *American Journal of Sociology, 59*:454-465, 1954.

31. RESNICK, R. B.: Some sociological aspects of intermarriage of Jew and non-Jew. *Social Forces, 12*:94-102, 1933.

32. RODMAN, H.: Technical note on two rates of mixed marriage. *American Sociological Review, 30*:776-778, 1965.

33. ROSENTHAL, E.: Major determinants of the future size of the Jewish population in the United States. In: *Future Directions of American Jewish Life*. New York, Jewish Welfare Board, 1964, pp. 49-63.

34. SANUA, VICTOR: Attitudes of Jewish adolescents and college students of different ideologies towards intermarriage. Unpublished paper, 1965.

35. SAUCIER, J. F.: Psychiatric aspects of interethnic marriage. In: *Trans-cultural Psychiatric Studies*. Montreal, Canada: Allan Memorial Institute-McGill University, 1965.

36. SCHNEPP, G. J., and MASAKO YUI, AGNES: Cultural and marital adjustment of Japanese war brides. *American Journal of Sociology, 61*:48-50, 1955.

37. SKLARE, M.: Intermarriage and the Jewish Future. *Commentary, April*:1-7, 1964.

38. SLOTKIN, J. S.: Jewish-Gentile intermarriages in Chicago. *American Sociological Review, 7*:34-39, 1942.

39. SROLE, L.; LANGNER, T. S.; MICHAEL, S. T.; OPLER, M. K., and RENNIE, T. A. C.: *Mental Health in the Metropolis*, Vol. I. New York, McGraw, 1961.

40. THOMAS (S. J.), J. L.: The factor of religion in the selection of marriage mates. *American Sociological Review, 16*:487-491, 1951.

41. WEEKS, H. A.: Differential divorce rates by occupation. *Social Forces, 21*: 334-347, 1943.

Chapter 35

MORALITY AND MARITAL COUNSELING*

HIRSCH LAZAAR SILVERMAN

Behavioral scientists, as well as psychologists, ought to recognize the essential fact that a psychologist functioning in the role of a marriage counselor is a professional scientist dedicated to the principle of helping to create a world of satisfying interpersonal relations and mutual enjoyments — a world dedicated to the continuous realization and growth of personality.

In the broad sense this may be termed adjustment process in marital counseling — "adjustment" implying responses that are mature, satisfying, efficient and wholesome. While in the constant pursuit of truth there is such a thing as objective truth, which can be understood by the logical mind, adjustment in marriage is of course relative, not absolute in character; for, we must realize, there is no such thing as a *perfectly* adjusted person. This is a world only striving toward perfection.

Adjustment in regard to marriage counseling must be judged and evaluated in terms of an individual's capacities to change and to meet the demands imposed on her or on him; and we know that these capacities will vary with the individual's personality and with his developmental level. Adjustment is again relative — most assuredly so in marital counseling, because its qualities vary to some extent with the society or culture in which it occurs, and also because of certain individual variations.

We know that every person in marriage has his or her uncertainties and limitations in matters of adjustment; and there are times when mental conflicts even resist resolution. Also, to be sure, even the best adjustment in marriage is not necessarily final or pervasive. For no one of us can meet all the exigencies of life with skill, insight, efficiency and emotional equilibrium at all times.

This, then, brings us to the nature of our immediate analysis: the "moral issues" in marital counseling. The use of words like "good" and "bad" in reference to marital counseling and adjustment to marriage may be almost anathema to psychological practitioners because such terms are essentially and paramountly ethical in nature; and the psychologist prefers, in his scientific approach, not to be placed in the position of making value judgments regarding human behavior.

---

*A lecture delivered at the 73rd Annual Convention of the American Psychological Association, in Chicago, Illinois, 1965, under the auspices of the Academy of Psychologists in Marital Counseling.

443

For myself, I believe that ethics and morality certainly have a definite and specific role in marital counseling. But terms like "good" and "bad" need not be specifically peculiar to morality or to ethical science. (When, for example, we speak of one's health being "good" or "bad," we are most certainly not concerned about moral implications *per se*. We are stating a fact, or an attitude, or a feeling, or a belief, or a point of view.)

Supplementarily, it should be pointed out, just as maladjustive behavior in humans is not necessarily morally "bad," we know that the well-adjusted person is not necessarily a paragon of virtue. Adjustment in or out of marriage is not the same thing as virtue, just as marital maladjustment is not the same thing as sin. There are sociological and religious aspects to this evaluation, as there are psychological, to be sure.

When we speak of morality, what we essentially are dealing with, in great part at least, are *moral considerations,* in effect pertaining to or concerned with *right conduct* or the *distinction* between right or wrong. In this sense, we may well be concerned with the *principles* or *rules* of right conduct; and we may be expected to express or convey truths or *counsel* as to right conduct. Scientifically, then, marital counseling is founded on the fundamental principles of right conduct, rather than on enactment or custom, implying at the same time, as a logical corollary perhaps, the virtuous individual, or being virtually or practically such through the effect on the mind or feelings, or on results generally. Accordingly, I am indicating the multifaceted areas involved in marital counseling on a psychological level, involving an almost orthopsychiatric emphasis multidimensionally.

Further, "moral issues" in marital counseling depend in sufficient part upon what is objectively and comprehendibly observed of human nature and actions, or of things generally, rather than upon mere demonstration, or what is deemed to be *moral evidence*. Here, too, we have legal factors, as well as psychological, in evaluating this area fully enough.

In essence, then, in the psychological sense "morals" and "ethics" refer to rules and standards of *conduct* and of *practice,* with "morals" referring to generally accepted customs of conduct and *right living* in a society, and to the individual's practice in relation to these, with "ethics" implying high standards of honest and honorable dealing, of methods used and of quality of product.

Obviously, all of these concepts have basic relevance to the field of *marriage counseling as an ethical science and art.* "Ethics," then, has a sound role in psychology when understood as the implementation of the principles of morality, *including both the science of the good* and *the nature of the right.* At this point I hope that the relevancies to living more maturely are patent.

To my way of thinking, "morality" and "marital adjustment," again, are closely related; for wholesome adjustment, taken in its fullest psychological meaning, includes moral soundness. Just as "sin" committed in a marriage relationship is primarily a moral evil, while certainly secondarily maladjustive, so is "maladjustment" primarily a psychological evil, and is morally bad in those instances where the response is moral as well as psychological. The psychologist in this regard then functions as a logician, philosopher, humanist and scientist.

In the practice of marital counseling, time and time again it has been established that moral laws are an important aspect of reality in living; and morality itself is an essential part of the functioning of human nature. I would therefore emphasize the importance of moral principles for effective living and mental health. The individual with an intelligent sense of morality is the person with a volitional disposition to *accept* and to *act* in terms of *self-imposed* moral laws and principles.

In conclusion, then, "moral adjustment" in the best and fullest sense of the term, in or out of marital counseling, for that matter, requires: (a) acceptance, introspection and continuous development of moral values, ideals and principles, all of which are necessary to the growth of a mature, personal, and subjective morality (1, 3) ; (b) integration of sensory impulses, desires and cravings with these moral values and principles (5) ; (c) constant application of values and principles to the effective resolution of mental conflicts, the reduction of the tension of frustrations and the expression of truly moral conduct (4) ; (d) integration of moral values and principles with religious and spiritual values (6) ; and (e) a high degree of self-discipline by means of which values, principles and ideals can be effectively expressed in moral conduct (2) .

Summarily, the concept of marital adjustment, in terms of the moral issues involved in the counseling process, refers essentially to the art of living effectively and wholesomely within the framework of responsibilities, relations and expectancies that constitute the state of marriage, coupled with appropriate and intelligent compatibility of sexual, psychological and religious factors, consistently requiring continuous personal growth, predicated on respect, love, trust, autonomy, recognition and integrity in the lives of each of us as human beings.

REFERENCES

1. ALLPORT, GORDON W.: Conscience and mental health. *The Individual and His Religion*. New York, Macmillan, 1950, Chapter IV.
2. LINDWORSKY, J.: *The Training of the Will*. Milwaukee, Bruce, 4th ed., 1929.
3. MAGNER, J. A.: *Personality and Successful Living*. Milwaukee, Bruce, 1944, pp. 52, 53, 64-66.

4. Moore, T. V.: *Personal Mental Hygiene*. New York, Grune, 1944, pp. 134-135.
5. Schneiders, Alexander A.: Personal and social adjustment. *Personal Adjustment and Mental Health*. New York, Rinehart, 1955, Chapter 15.
6. Silverman, Hirsch Lazaar: Religion, philosophy, and psychology. Oregon State University, *Improving College and University Teaching*, XI (3), Summer, 1963.

Chapter 36

A DIFFERENTIAL APPROACH IN MARRIAGE COUNSELING WITH THE DISTURBED CLIENT

HILDA M. GOODWIN

ALL OUR LIVES LONG, EVERY DAY AND EVERY HOUR, we are engaged in the process of accommodating our changed and unchanged selves to changed and unchanged surroundings" (2). This statement, made some sixty years ago by Samuel Butler, while no less true today of the individual, has a peculiar application to the marriage counselor or social agency offering a helping service within the community. Marriage Council of Philadelphia has been working with troubled marriages for over a quarter of a century, and offers individual counseling for premarital or marital partners, and since 1958 has added group marriage counseling. Twenty-five years ago the greater number of clients coming to Marriage Council of Philadelphia were essentially healthy, young, premarital couples asking for educational or counseling help with problems of physical and interpersonal adjustment to marriage. Today a greatly increased number of individuals and/or marital partners, one or both of whom may be described as "borderline," "suffering with severe ego defects," "severe personality disorders" or "prepsychotic" come seeking help. Although many terms are used to describe the psychological disturbances of persons with poor capacity to function socially in interpersonal relationships and environmentally, their chief characteristic may be considered as a severe ego defect involving various areas of their functioning.* Usually there is no clear break with reality in the form of delusions or hallucinations, although occasionally, after the prepsychotic person has developed considerable trust in the relationship, bizarre material may break through momentarily and must be handled.

Today, through the use of drug therapy combined with other methods of treatment, many postpsychotic persons† are returning to the community. In attempting to adjust to life in their family setting, they, too, seek help with their marital problems. A brief study of current applications at Marriage Council reveals that approximately 35 per cent of applications are from individuals who are now or have been involved in psychiatric treatment.

---

*This group of persons suffers from an impairment in secondary ego processes, such as faulty reality perception, inadequate reality testing, poor judgment, inadequate control of aggressive and sexual impulses and a resultant incapacity to form satisfying interpersonal relationships.

†This group is comprised largely of persons suffering from the schizophrenic disorders.

447

This group breaks down into three categories: those clients who recognize a need for help with intrapersonal problems, and may have utilized psychiatric treatment for a better self-adjustment, but have not yet resolved their marital difficulties; those clients who have broken with reality, have spent some time in an institution, and are again living with their families, but with difficulty; and those clients who may have had contact with psychiatric resources for varying degrees of help, but whose present adjustment in marriage, in job or in other relationships is conflicted and unhappy.

Giving effective help to this group of clients calls for treatment radically different from that which has been traditional in many settings. We do not feel it appropriate, with this specific group, to use the type of uncovering approach which moves back into early history and early developmental study as a means of helping the individual to understand the genesis of his present difficulties and, hopefully, through insight gained, to begin to resolve them to some degree.

Although there are some distinctive features in the personality structures of the "borderline," the prepsychotic and the postpsychotic person, the counseling approach in these situations is essentially the same. The emphasis, timing and the range of techniques that the counselor uses may vary with the individual client and his specific needs, but the underlying principles guiding the treatment are the same. Treatment is not directed toward change in the personality structure, but toward improvement in ego functioning. Thus, the goal is to help these clients adapt more successfully to both the situation and interpersonal aspects of his environment.

Before moving into further discussion of the counseling process with these clients, it might be useful to consider briefly some of the feelings and characteristics common to many of these individuals. Consideration must be given, of course, to individual differences in degree of intensity and relative dominance of the various characteristics mentioned. Despite the different ways in which these clients may present themselves, one finds, in varying degrees of intensity, the following feelings and characteristics:

The first is *strong feelings of loneliness and isolation.* These clients express a deep need for closeness with another human being, but an equal fear and distrust of closeness, and, by their behavior, tend to alienate others.

Mrs. X, a 40-year-old married woman, after a period of hospitalization, complained bitterly of her loneliness. Despite efforts of her church group and of her husband, her distrust and fear and the insatiable quality of her need, with consequent frustration and resulting hostility, made it impossible for her to form any close, meaningful relationships.

A second characteristic is a *deep well of anger,* of which the client may or may not be aware. If he is aware, he rarely sees his aggressive or hostile behavior as related to his anger, but tends to feel it was "for the benefit of the other," or was "righteous indignation." Anger may be expressed in disguised form, perhaps in feeling that the other person is angry with him, or in a suspicion and distrust of the other's motives or intentions. These clients are afraid of expressing anger, even when it is appropriate, but tend to feel unconsciously that any expression of anger will be extremely destructive to themselves and to others. If angry feelings erupt, extreme anxiety may result.

> Mrs. J, feeling very angry with her ungiving husband, an individual whose resources for meeting need in others were extremely limited, was unable to recognize or express her anger directly, but became extremely anxious when it threatened to break through. She displayed a phobic reaction to her kitchen so that she could no longer prepare meals for herself and husband, thus punishing Mr. J and giving expression to her anger without permitting herself to recognize or be responsible for it.

A third common characteristic is the *very strong ambivalence* felt in many areas of living. Often these individuals feel strongly pulled in diverse directions, so they may be caught in their feelings of love and hate, trust and distrust, and inability to move in any direction.

> Miss X had been engaged to a young man for eighteen months. Although she expressed her feeling that she was alive and happy only when he was present, at the same time she expressed her fear that marriage to him would be equivalent to death, and she was unable to come to a decision concerning marriage.

A fourth characteristic of these clients is their *fear*, not only of other people and the possibility of hurt or rejection, but that they will be unable to control their own sexual or aggressive impulses.

> While Mr. Z was in the armed forces, Mrs. Z became involved in an extramarital affair. Mr. Z, who was a passive person, unconnected with his own hostility, denied any strong feelings toward Mr. X, but became very anxious lest Mrs. Z's paramour be killed in a car accident. He stated that he had never felt angry since, as a small boy, he hit another child with a bat and laid open the child's head.

A fifth characteristic is *confusion* about many things. Often these individuals cling to quite contradictory values, or may be uncertain of what they believe. This may be revealed in a too-positive attitude, in an inability to express any choice or in contradictory choices.

> Mr. D insisted that his children attend private schools, although this was creating extreme financial stress in the family. At the same time, he was very active in writing about and stressing the values to be found in a

public-school education and actively challenging other families in his neighborhood for their failure to send their children to the public schools.

A sixth common factor lies in such clients' *use of words* or phrases, or vague generalities, as a way to escape, to conceal or to avoid having other people know what they really think or feel, either because they are not in touch with their own feelings and ideas, or because they find these feelings and ideas too frightening.

> Miss X frequently spoke of her need for "liberty," "creativity" and a "mature love relationship." When the counselor attempted to help Miss X be more specific about the meaning of these statements, it became obvious that Miss X had no clear conception of what a "mature love relationship" involved. These expressions were her way of concealing her very real lack of emotional involvement and connection with her feelings.

A seventh factor relates to *perceptiveness* of the other person's feelings and attitudes, and sensitivity to the slightest indication of rejection or non-acceptance by the counselor.

> On this date Miss Y explained that she had visited her fiancé in Chicago, and had stayed at the usual hotel. Mr. X, since his home was nearby, did not secure a room at the hotel, but decided to stay in her room overnight. She was fearful that the hotel management might find this out and an embarrassing situation ensue. During the course of the interview, we talked of various ways of dealing with the situation in the future.
>
> When Miss Y returned for her next counseling interview, she was very anxious and guarded. After a few minutes she was able to let the counselor know that she felt the counselor had been angry with her fiancé and would not want her to marry him. The counselor had felt angry with Mr. X, admitted this, relating it to concern for Miss Y's welfare. Following this Miss Y was again able to involve herself more fully in the interview.

Since these clients perceive and feel their problems in terms of social maladjustment, either interpersonal or situational, their choice of a source of help may well be a counselor or a social agency. Others may be referred by the psychiatrist who has treated them during the acute stages of their illness, or, in other situations, a doctor, psychiatrist or clergyman may feel that marital counseling might be a more helpful approach at a particular time. Often these clients hope or believe that the solution to their problems lies in a change in the external situation or a change in the nature of an important relationship. Rarely does the individual recognize or seek help with his basic problems.

Counseling in these situations is primarily focused on helping the individual to perceive and to adjust to his social (interpersonal) reality, with specific reference to the marital relationship in this setting and to his environment in a way that will afford him at least minimal satisfaction.* Our approach is an ego-supportive and a reality-oriented one. The establishment of a working relationship is an important factor in any type of treatment. However, in attempting to work with this group of clients it is of paramount importance that a positive-feeling communication be established as soon as possible. This is not easy to achieve since these clients trust less, are more fearful of sharing, are more withdrawn and more perceptive than most clients. They are quick to pick up any feelings of rejection, non-acceptance or lack of honesty on the part of the counselor, and they are especially sensitive to nonverbal cues. The counselor's recognition and control of his own feelings of rejection, of impatience or of anxiety aroused by these clients is of major importance. Their heavy dependency needs, their fear and expectation of rejection from an uncaring world, combined with their aggressive and hostile impulses, their lack of accurate reality perception plus their great inner perceptiveness makes management of the counseling relationship a matter of delicate balance. If, however, the counselor is receptive, flexible, responsive and able to move as slowly as these clients need to, and can handle stressful situations without undue anxiety, a bridge may be established over which real communication may take place. These clients find it difficult to work with a passive, monosyllabic counselor, as this tends to increase their feelings of isolation and aloneness. Equally, the reflective therapeutic approach, i.e., the counselor acting as a screen on which the client may project feelings and attitudes, which the counselor then restates in order to emphasize their emotional significance, is detrimental to the forming of an ongoing relationship with these clients. Since these clients struggle with some confusion about their feelings and are fearful of being overwhelmed by them, this approach tends to confuse the client, and the apparent distance of the counselor may be felt as lack of caring, and the attempted "insight" as criticism.

The basic counseling approach which we have found most helpful with this type of client is a reality-oriented, nurturing one, with an active reaching out and interest in helping, and with genuine responsiveness, within professional limits, to the feelings of the client. The counselor needs to take an active responsibility to keep their work together focused toward solving the external problems with which these clients are struggling, and for the development of an implicit atmosphere of the counselor and client working together.

Inevitably these clients need to test out the counselor's interest and good will as part of their total reality testing. Thus, we do not, as we might in

---

*Individual counseling involves separate interviews weekly with each marital partner and occasional joint interviews with both spouses present.

other situations, turn questions or criticisms back to the client nor try to relate these to persons in the client's past. Instead, the counselor needs to give serious thought to the criticism within the interview hour, considering whether or not it is valid without becoming defensive, and, within professional limits, if he has felt rejecting or angry, admitting it. These clients quickly perceive any falsification of feeling or attitude, and will trust the counselor less. On the other hand, if these clients feel understood and supported, they may put out very positive feelings toward the counselor. Again, the feelings are accepted and respected, and *then* related to the reality of the client's situation, i.e., his loneliness and isolation, and his beginning to reach out toward others. Personal questions are answered matter-of-factly.

These clients do not react to the environment as it is, but rather as they see it, and their misperceptions cause them to react in ways that affect the response of the environment to them. Part of the counseling effort is, therefore, directed toward helping these clients come to know more clearly *what* they feel, and to connect their ways of behaving with the responses they receive. This is to be distinguished from attempting to help these clients through an historical approach to understand the *why* of their behavior. Any *why* of behavior would be related to the current situation and would depend upon the degree of trust in the relationship to the counselor. The counselor's perception and expression in a matter-of-fact way of what these clients seem to be feeling helps them to connect with their feelings, and indicates subtly that these feelings are within the "normal" range as the counselor recognizes them. The difference is a "talking to" feelings as contrasted with delving or probing into the feelings of the client and the possible origins of them.

The effort throughout is to support those defenses that serve the clients helpfully, not to pick up or deal with fantasy material that may break through, but to refocus on his current reality situations. It is equally important to help the client develop more facility in reality testing. This is especially important with the client who is distrustful and suspicious of his partner. The counselor needs to accept that he feels this way and go over the situation step by step to understand what facts might make the client feel as he does. Then, without implication of criticism, he must tentatively raise questions as to whether there might be other possible explanations.

Since these clients have trouble managing external affairs, such as time and money, it is important that the counselor maintain reasonable time limits and set fees realistically.

Group marriage counseling offers another resource for help for many of these couples. However, all clients are seen initially in individual interviews, and an initial joint interview is arranged to make decisions concerning ongoing treatment. The group experience focuses on conflict on an interpersonal level rather than on intrapsychic conflicts. Reality testing and clarification are an intrinsic part of the group process. The group atmosphere offers both support and expectation of willingness to look at one's own behavior in the marriage. No pressure is placed on a couple to participate verbally until they are ready, in order that they have an opportunity to move into the group as slowly as needed. Focus within the group is on the reality of the ongoing interaction of the spouses with each other. Since both partners are present, there are more opportunities to connect with distorted perceptions. Thus, the group offers its members an opportunity to experience emphatically and to see portrayed vividly an externalization of the same needs, feelings, frustrations and behaviors with which they are attempting to deal. Through this externalization, they may be able to connect with their own feelings and behavior with less anxiety. Couples are usually moved into a group in which one of the cotherapists has been their individual counselor. The relationship to the counselor supports these clients in moving into the group, but the relationship becomes diluted as the group affords emotional satisfaction and support. This enables the individual still caught in the dependency-independency struggle to differ violently with the cotherapists, and, as the cotherapists are able to respond nondefensively and the group faces the individual with his projections, he is able to resolve some of his conflict and perceive other adults more clearly. Essentially the group enables each individual within the limits of his fixed intrapsychic structure to modify his adaptive patterns in a safe setting as he comes into realistic contact with social values and patterns of social relations acceptable to the group. Many of the same processes and techniques that prevail in the one-to-one relationship in counseling are present in the group setting, used less intensively and with a different balance, i.e., relationship, acceptance, universalization, reduction of hostility, guilt and feelings of anxiety.

CONCLUSIONS

In attempting to counsel with clients suffering from severe ego defects, we believe that a differential use of relationship and techniques is indicated as follows:

1. Treatment depends upon the early establishment of a nurturing relationship, in which the counselor actively reaches out to involve the client.

2. Because of the specific nature of the difficulties with which these clients struggle, it is important that the counselor have a genuine responsiveness to the feelings of the client. Feelings, either negative or positive, arising within the process of counseling, are dealt with realistically within the counselor-client relationship, and no effort is made to relate them to the client's earlier life situation.

3. The focus is actively held toward solving the problems with which

the client is currently struggling, with minimal discussion of early history or dynamics.

4. An attempt is made to help the client connect with how his way of behaving in current situations evokes the responses that he gets. Effort is not directed toward assisting the client to understand the early genesis of his pattern of behavior.

5. Sustaining techniques are used throughout, and defenses that serve the client helpfully are supported.

6. Reality testing is encouraged. Situations are reviewed step by step, as counselor and client work together to understand what happened and other possible ways of dealing with the situation.

The basic principles underlying this methodology are:

1. Treatment is not directed toward effecting any change in the client's basic conflicts or personality structure;

2. Personality is a balance of forces, thus an improvement in ego functioning may be enough to enable the individual to make changes in his total social functioning;

3. Through the use of an ego-supportive and reality-oriented approach, certain definite improvements may be realized, i.e.: improvement in client's perceptions of reality; improvement in his reality testing; some shift in use of defenses and in reaction to the demands of the superego; and some reduction in the intensity of his chronic hostility and dependency.

This approach tends to diminish the client's anxiety, increase his capacity to perceive reality, lessens the breakthrough of fantasy, and, as he is able to take on suggestions from the counselor, he may be able to change his adaptive patterns somewhat, thus effecting a more satisfying way of meeting his needs.

REFERENCES

1. AMERICAN PSYCHIATRIC ASSOCIATION: *Diagnostic and Statistical Manual, Mental Disorders,* 1952.

2. BUTLER, SAMUEL: *The Way of All Flesh.* New York, Dutton, 1903.

3. FARBER, LAURA: Casework treatment of ambulatory schizophrenics. *Social Casework, XXXIX* (No. 1) :January, 1958.

4. FLINT, ARDEN A., JR.: Some dynamic factors in marital group psychotherapy. *International Journal of Group Psychotherapy, 12* (No. 3) .

5. FROMM-REICHMANN, FRIEDA: On loneliness. *Psychoanalysis and Psychotherapy,* Ed. by Dexter M. Bullard. Selected Papers of Frieda Fromm-Reichmann, University of Chicago Press, 1959.

6. STUART, RICHARD: Supportive Casework with Borderline Patients. *Social Work,* Vol. 9 No. 1) : January, 1964.

Chapter 37

A PSYCHOLOGICAL APPROACH TO
SEXUAL NORMALITY AND SEXUAL HEALTH:
A CRITICAL APPRAISAL FOR THE COUNSELOR
IN MARITAL PROBLEMS

HENRY GUZE

INTRODUCTION

THE COUNSELOR OR PSYCHOTHERAPIST dealing with marital problems is frequently called upon to discuss with his patients the meaning of sexual health and sexual pathology. That this area is most complicated is attested to by the fact that almost all authors writing on the subject present a clearly personal view, a statistical picture or a cultural relativism. The concept of sexual health, therefore, must be reorganized in such a way as to anchor it firmly in biological reality on a cross-cultural basis. In approaching this subject from the standpoint of the psychobiologist, one must not, however, neglect the significance of the need for a meaningful ethical code which, nonetheless, does not overlook the fact that man is an animal. The following presentation is meant to be thought provoking to the marriage counselor while offering him guidelines toward an understanding of the reality of biological phenomena.

Recent studies such as those of Masters and Johnson (20) have focused, in an objective and scientific way, on the descriptive physiology of the human sexual response. Their data are of such nature that it may be assumed that these reactions to sexual stimulation are pertinent, regardless of the culture being examined. If this is so, then one might say that interference with this pattern of reaction to sexual stimulation could be deleterious to the organism. Unfortunately, Masters and Johnson (20) do not elaborate adequately on the psychological concomitants of the sexual response. Another criticism perhaps lies in the fact that their data are based upon a volunteer population and that sex behavior was observed and experimentally induced.

Except for a few pioneers such as Dickinson (5), whose detailed studies reveal perspicacity and courage, historically, physicians, psychologists and biologists have contributed very little to the understanding of human sexual anatomy and physiology. The medical scientist, the psychologist and the marriage counselor must avail himself of realistic information with regard to what happens with the genitalia and the rest of the body during sexual experience. The physiological elaborations of Masters and Johnson pertain to a pattern of changes of muscular, glandular and vascular nature induced by a variety of stimuli. Their researches indicate that four phases are present in the temporal pattern of a complete sexual response: excitement, plateau, orgasm and resolution. The evidence leads to the presentation of a single pattern for the male and three different patterns for the female, women seemingly demonstrating greater variability of sexuality than males.

It is clear that the marriage counselor or psychotherapist must be able to utilize information from this type of study and from other biological evaluations of man to set up principles defining healthy sexual behavior. The historic relativistic positions of the cultural anthropologist, and views such as those of Szasz (25), are open to critical examination. Despite their contributions to the study of human behavior, they do not help to establish diagnostic criteria. This chapter, therefore, is an effort to derive some absolute principles with reference to sexual health.

DISTINCTION BETWEEN STATISTICAL NORM AND PATHOLOGY

The statistical norm is a measure of variability, and the normal curve frequently includes both pathological and nonpathological behavior. However, it is not clear as to where the pathology falls in the curve. The abnormal, from a statistical standpoint, is quantitatively deviant from the average, and is presumably less frequently present in nature than the normal. It is important to recognize that the majority determines normality. Honigman (14) has emphasized this fact in his discussion of communities where nearly everybody has tuberculosis or syphillis: ". . . and such communities," he says, "are not unknown — those diseases would would be normal. The fact that the majority may be pathological is a serious comment on the fads and fashions of what is healthy behavior."

In a careful analysis of the concept of what is sexually healthy as described in the medical literature, Guze (8) found that the medical approach reflects the layman's folklore very much, as does the literature of the layman. What is sexually healthy is probably very different from what is sexually normal, statistically. However, because deviation from approved social values may create intrapersonal conflict, the sexual deviant, although not pathological in terms of sex behavior as such, may develop neurotic fears of social reprisal.

The statistical picture is relative to the culture, and the culture may be pathological; thus there is a violation of the concept of "healthy," if by "normal" one means healthy. While external manifestations of sexual behavior differ considerably, perhaps the question may be asked whether the acts, under scrutiny, are psychobiologically fulfilling and nondisruptive.

Frequently, introduction of the "civilized way" changes the manner of expression of a biological act. For example, the development of instruments for the purpose of eating may have changed the appearance of this behavior in a more complex society, as compared to a primitive culture. However, it is assumed that the biological process of eating and its psychological implications are not interfered with by the changes in the manner of expression of the behavior.

Part of the question, then, is whether the sexual act, as operationally manifested is psychobiologically adequate and gratifying to all individuals concerned, without being harmful. Thus the repertoire of sexual expression cannot be taken at face value. It must be examined from the standpoint of its implications, both intra- and interpersonally.

It is erroneous to interpret the Kinsey (15) data or similar studies as the criteria for healthy behavior. This error, as previously indicated, is related to the substitution of statistical variability for evidence of biological "naturalness" or healthy behavior. By the same token, the appearance of murder as a universal act would imply that it is a healthy act if only it is done frequently enough. Obviously, if done frequently enough, murder, as in warfare, might be so "healthy" that the species could be seriously threatened. There are, indeed, those biologists who would interpret these data as evidence of the wisdom of nature and the survival of the fittest.

The Kinsey data, particularly, have acted to induce a kind of strange iatrogenicity — people may be worried if they have not, for example, been involved in adultery or in some other type of activity frequently occurring in the population.

Socially, the appearance of extramateship liaisons is widespread, as indicated by Ford and Beach (7), beyond our own culture. In fact, in some societies, so long as the incest rules are observed, adultery is even encouraged. While the sexual behavior described is encouraged, albeit regulated, there is evidence that in some societies — the Toda, for example — men occasionally resent sharing a mate with a second man. This is so even though "immorality" attaches to the begrudging husband. The experience of the act by the persons involved would seem to be extremely important in determining whether an act is healthy or not. The sexual act is experienced in several ways: (a) bodily change and the return to homeostasis following reaction; (b) the perception of the experience and the internal feelings about it; and (c) the awareness of the cultural attitude and the feelings relating thereto. Thus, there may be conflict because of cultural regulations relating to a given type of sexual expression. Cultural approval, or even advocacy of a given act, does not necessarily make for personal comfort or health.

IS THERE A UNIVERSAL MEASURE OF PATHOLOGY?

Perhaps the first problem to be faced is whether indeed there is an entity which can be defined as sexual pathology, distinct from other psychopathology. It seems to this writer that such distinction is invalid. If it is invalid, then sexual pathology is the same as pathological reaction of the organism in wider aspects of psychobiology.

What are some of the criteria for pathology as discussed here? Honigmann quotes Masserman (18), who attempts to develop a relatively culture-free definition of psychopathology. If the species we are dealing with is characterized by the same biological mechanisms, then a description of those mechanisms will be the same, regardless of the culture. Honigmann, following Masserman, suggests the following response patterns as evidence of psychopathology.

1. *Anxiety* is regarded as the initial indicator. It is manifested by: a racing, pounding heart; rapid, shallow or difficult breathing; trembling; a sweaty, flushed or pale skin; incontinence, and a feeling of impending catastrophe and panic that has been labeled "fear of catastrophic breakdown."

2. *Disorders of affect* range from mild to serious depression and include emotional blunting or disproportionate excitement.

3. *Reality distortion* involves the denial of the commonly accepted awareness of "things as they are"; an inability to distinguish between the associative, or "dream," quality and that of the objective, communicable datum.

4. *Regression* includes behavior which is "analogous to the responses of the unsocialized child, involving extreme passivity, profound withdrawal from social relations, extreme aggressiveness, and open masturbation or soiling"; control is very inadequate.

5. *Disintegration,* without showing the qualities of regression, may be marked by inability to keep under control hostile, erotic and other impulses.

6. *Dissociation* is shown by any acute or chronic inability to perceive, interpret or manipulate reality; a loss of consciousness, as in a trance state.

In addition to this list of pathology, one might suggest total lack of feeling, a kind of internal anesthesia marked by verbal awareness, but experiential denial.

ARE THERE DEGREES OF PATHOLOGY

While the experience of pathology may be the same, regardless of the culture, the external expression may vary. Deviance, while defined by the community, may only become obvious if the behavior becomes drastic and dangerous. It is also true that even extreme behavior, such as self-injury, may be socially acceptable in some societies, i.e., among the Doukhobors of

British Columbia, arson and dynamiting of their own houses are approved means of social expression (11). The larger surrounding society, however, regards this behavior most negatively. A recent and provocative example of such behavior is the immolation of Buddhist monks in Vietnam (23). Under these circumstances it would appear that the behavior is approved and encouraged by a considerable segment of the Buddhist population. It is neither statistically normal nor biologically healthy, insofar as it is brutally self-destructive. What goes on psychodynamically in the individual destroying himself by burning, and in his approving observers is a crux question with respect to psychopathology.

How does one determine the "amount" of pathology, if one can speak of such? It seems that pathological ideation is present in all persons at some time (10). Pathologic ideation would be that kind of internal thought process which, if converted to overt expression, could be seriously injurious to the person or his environment. It seems to be of an hallucinatory nature, such as the image of raping someone, as opposed to any physical expression of that image. It should be noted that so-called pathological images appear to be present universally in human experience. The real problem lies in the handling of such images. The sexual impulse, phylogenetically, is not marked by the cerebral restraints acquired in ontogeny by the human being. Thus there is a threshold problem at the human level. It seems to be the problem of learning and cortical adequacy in the experience and expression of sexual pattern. Sexual expression may be related to the plasticity of the person as limited by his learning capacity.

WHAT ARE SOME ASPECTS OF THE EXPRESSION OF SEXUAL PATHOLOGY?

1. The development of sexual responses to nonsexual situations. This type of situation is one which is so divested of closeness to the primary stimulus (the body of a person of the opposite sex or the same sex) that members of the species ordinarily do not respond to it. Fetishes fall into this category when they replace totally the "unconditioned stimulus" to which they were originally associated. This type of response constitutes psychopathology because of the unreality of the stimulus situation.

2. Sexuality derived from degrading the partner constitutes a displacement whereby the feeling of arousal is brought about by an emotional pattern that can be injurious. By definition, an injurious sexual response is pathological.

3. Sexual responses which are purportedly natural expressions of psychobiological changes in the person may become an economic occupation, as in prostitution. Thus a biological act is performed on command, without reference to psychobiological changes. This is analogous to eating on com-

mand, for monetary reward rather than for the satisfaction of hunger or appetite. The act of prostitution appears to be socially normal, but biologically pathological.

4. Exclusiveness (6) or narrowness of function may be developed, such as sexual gratification from masturbation only. This type of behavior might be regarded as pathological only because of its inadequacy for the full expression of a person's potential. On the other hand, it may be, under many circumstances, the adjustment of choice. The need for variety of expression should always be examined in terms of the person and his available field.

5. It must not be assumed that an uncontrollable drive for variety is an indication of behavioral health. The fact that certain pleasant experiences may become sufficient is not an indication of pathology. As in the case of food selection, if one has never tried seafood and chooses not to do so, he cannot be considered emotionally ill unless he would starve without it. Since sexual starvation is usually preceded by more drastic problems, a mere switch from homosexuality to heterosexuality is not necessarily a sign of good adjustment. This does not deny the probability that homosexual behavior may at times fulfill a sexual need in a way that cannot be regarded as pathological.

Psychopathology expressed in the sexual sphere may often be due to the learning of conflicting sexual attitudes, that is, conflicting with the cultural pattern of acceptability or with the personal attitudes of an individual. It is unfortunate that at the present time the best way of teaching young people about sex is not clearly known. Thus, Oliven (24) says: "Children's reaction to nudity appears to be largely conditioned by the attitude of the total environment." He adds: "In our civilization, with its long tradition of genital concealment, deliberate individualistic over-frankness by the parent in this respect is almost bound to have unfavorable effects of some kind on the child."

WHAT CAN BE LEARNED ABOUT NORMAL SEXUALITY FROM INFRAHUMAN BEHAVIOR

There have been many studies in recent years dealing with the nature of sexuality in animals below man. Frequently the observer assumes that the discovery of human-like patterns in an infrahuman setting means that man's sex pattern should include all the behavioral trends of the lower animals. An interesting example of sexual versatility is *Truncatus Tursiops* (the porpoise) (21). This joyous mammal lives among the fishes, perhaps to be close to some roving mermaids. He is truly polymorphous perverse. If there is no female porpoise available, a turtle will do. Should man be guided by this child of nature?

Granted that the animal here referred to is a very intelligent mammal, and that man has a repertoire potentially as great, still man's learning and thinking both increase his scope of experience and delimit the randomness of his behavior. There seems to be a general tendency for discrimination and selectivity of response. The problem is to decide when man's selectivity and discrimination become inhibition and deprivation.

How does man differ from other mammals in what is sexually healthy? While the impulse pattern may be similar, the forcing of another person by a human being is undesirable; this is so because the primary sexual act for man might then become a hostile gesturing. Aggression and sex behavior might become indistinguishably intertwined, as in rape for example.

Biologically it is self-protective that man avoid force, lest he elicit force as a reaction. Such reaction would interfere with the natural completion of the sexual act. A distinction must be made between force and the dominant-submissive interplay in sexuality (1). The latter, below man, is regulated often by seasonal or cyclic aspects.

At the level of man it would appear that an act should be mutually agreed upon (or agreeable), with a full understanding of its significance for both parties. This position does not conflict with the essence of experience as such. The biological spontaneity of the sexual function as a personal and an interpersonal occurrence is enhanced by mutual acceptability.

A contact of a sexual nature between man and the lower animals would appear to result from an inability to establish adequate contact with other human beings. This might be in some cases evidence of severe pathology. One might ask further about the biological ethics of forcing oneself upon a lower animal, perhaps unduly hurting or injuring it. Even compliance by the animal is an act of violation, because the animal is not capable of deciding about the personal value of the involvement. Furthermore, the sexual act becomes, under such circumstances of man-beast contact, a denial of complete interpersonal cooperation and awareness as part of sexual experience.

Is it biologically acceptable that man torture animals below him for sexual gratification? There are, indeed, people who gain complete sexual gratification by such acts as may be most painful to a helpless animal. For example, one man experienced erections when he threw animals he captured into a fire. This is an act which denotes a serious disturbance in the mechanism for empathy. Yet many (basically nondisturbed) persons might respond to a variety of brutal acts with sexuality. This may be a biological "spill-over" from one emotion to another. It is probably likely that this overlap occurs frequently in nature. The development of a habit, however, of purposive hostile response as a source of arousal is undesirable. It is likely, by means of a conditioning mechanism, to cause a displacement of "gentle" erotic response by overly aggressive reaction.

The fact that a given reaction is possible and appears both in ontogeny and phylogeny does not make it an act that is, therefore, nonpathological. Furthermore, the "same" act of behavior carried out by different organisms or by the same organism at different times in its own life is not necessarily the same, but may be equivalent.

Thus the estrus of a rat is not the same as the human menstrual cycle, although hormonal factors operate in both cases and sexuality is present in both animals. Apparently there is evidence "that the functional activity of various endocrine glands in mammals is affected by stimulation derived from other individuals of the same species" (12). Heape, as early as 1901, observed that in various species the female is brought to estrus by the presence of the male, and the male is brought to rut by the presence of the female (12). It is not clear as to how much this effect of one sex on the other is present in man but there probably is, under normal conditions of intermingling, a basic and constant "undercurrent" of arousal. Such "undercurrent" is, under circumstances of nonpathology, an energizing and rarely interfering aspect of successful living. This is drive as a force and a *raison d'être*.

ARE THERE ANATOMICAL LIMITATIONS TO SEXUAL BEHAVIOR?

If the parts of the body involved show a nonrelationship anatomically, then pursuit of the sexual act (on this basis) may be defined as pathological. Thus, for example, a vaginal orifice blocked by a hymen that cannot be broken in intercourse (without surgical intervention) must be regarded as an abnormal place of entry for the penis. The forced pursuit of such act is evidence of indwelling problems about sex and sexuality.

One may wonder about oral acts where the thrusts of the penis cause gagging by blocking the tracheo-esophogeal area. Is this really a sexual act as such? Masters (19) quotes a German prostitute who said that one had to learn not to choke on it and not to bite the "partner." Furthermore, the lips and mouth seem to get tired because of the involvement of muscles ordinarily not utilized. This complaint has often been made by patients of the writer (including homosexual men). While oral contact with the penis seems to be pleasurable and gratifying to both participants, it is questionable as to whether the mouth can be regarded as a natural orifice for the complete expression of the sexual activity of the penis.

Anal intercourse, in spite of the anal sensitivity to stimulation, may be anatomically contraindicated as such. The anal canal is externally terminated by a slit-like orifice, the anus, controlled by the corrugator cutis muscle. The canal is 1.5 to 3 cm in length to the pectinate line, and is very sensitive to stimuli that are pain producing. This is in contrast to the rectum, which is not sensitive to pain stimuli. It is of importance to remember that the pectinate line consists of a number of projections, or papillae (5 to 8), connected by thin, semilunar folds at their bases (the valves of Morgagni). Cantor (3), after whose description the above anatomical picture is organized, says: "Sodomists commonly demonstrate a relaxed sphincter and all gradations of proctitis." If there are anatomical and functional changes because of the insertion of the penis *in ano,* and if these changes are in a negative direction, then such contact is contraindicated as pathological. This does not negate the sexual meaningfulness of anal stimulation.

While the above negative admonition is challengeable, a case example from this writer's practice is that of a male who had fantasies of entering his penis into the auditory canal. Aside from the operating psychodynamics, the anatomical issue is clear; that is, that most penises do not fit into the ear.

The introduction of objects into the anus for sexual gratification is a frequent occurrence and can be considered in the realm of psychopathology because of the biological danger to the person. There are many cases on record where objects used for anal masturbation have slipped into the rectum and could not be removed except by surgical means. The fantasy factors in this type of behavior may be far from primary in a sexual sense, and may involve strong sadomasochistic imagery or ideation.

To declare again that some acts are probably part of a pathological process does not deny anal sexuality as being part of the natural sensitivity involved in sexual play. However, it is important to remember that any sexual act is a function of a total person, and that often a judgment of pathology depends on an examination of a complete relationship rather than an act *per se.* Sometimes a writer on sex does not make clear his reason for relegating some acts to "perversity." For example, Oliven (24) says: "A husband's preference for anilingus is evidence of psychosexual pathology." Oliven fails to describe what he means by "preference" in a quantitative sense. Does he mean preference to other sexual acts? Furthermore, he fails to make clear why it is a husband's preference rather than a wife's preference or a mutual preference. Finally, psychosexual pathology in this case is not clarified. This type of statement is all too frequent in the literature on sexual hygiene.

IS IT POSSIBLE FOR AN ACT TO BE PARTIALLY HEALTHY?

While observable behavior may be nonpathological, or may appear to be even desirable, there may be pathological psychological reasons for this behavior. Thus the willful exposure to "unwanted" pregnancy may on the surface appear as healthy sexuality.

Since it is assumed that pregnancy is a natural desire, we tend to forget that it may be used in psychological ways other than for the simple reproduction of offspring.

A sexual act may take place because it is fashionable to indulge. Thus the act itself may be acceptable, but the motivation behind it may be highly questionable. A culture may become so oriented that all girls of a certain age must have engaged in intercourse. This would assume such behavior whether or not the individual is emotionally prepared for it.

Henry (13), in describing child sexuality in Pilagá culture, emphasizes the free release of sexuality among these people, particularly among the children. It is curious that sexuality among the Pilagá forms the basis for much insult and hostile expression. It is never really clear as to whether the sexuality of childhood is not very often more of a hostile than a sexual form of behavior.

The sexual activity gives the impression of being healthy, and is to the extent that it is culturally acceptable and biologically natural. Consequently there are no "neurotic" conflicts within the person, purportedly. However, persons may find that even though their behavior is socially approved, the tax upon them is too great. An act may be contrary to a person's basic temperament or personality organization.

CAN ONE DISTINGUISH THE PATHOLOGICAL ACT FROM THE PATHOLOGICAL PERSON?

If we assume that a pathological act is a function of a responding human being, then there are no pathological acts as such. It is a reification to separate the act from the person, except insofar as one is examining interindividual sexual variability. Thus studies such as the Kinsey (15, 16) reports can throw light on the sexual mode of expression in a given biological organism, man, in a specific society. It cannot cast light on pathology which is intraindividual.

If acts themselves cannot be judged, one cannot arrive at the contradiction that normal, or healthy, people do pathological or sick things.

One may raise the question about such acts as lynching, which are mass activities engaged in by presumably average citizens.

It seems to be possible to sway a whole group of people into temporary pathology, even against their so-called "will." Surely the excited citizens who ran madly to escape the "War of the Worlds" were seriously disturbed people, even if only temporarily (4). (The "War of the Worlds," it will be recalled, was a radio broadcast on the evening of October 30, 1938. Its theme was an invasion from Mars.)

Any "act of pathology" is potentially in the repertoire of the human being, provided that the emotional tone of the situation is such as to suppress those controls which prevent randomness and unbridled emotional expression. Too much control and the complete suppression of emotion are also evidence of pathology.

Pathological expression in any given person seems to be related to the manner of dealing with the suggestions from the inner and outer world (9). The fact that different persons carry out the same suggestion differently from each other, and often consistently so, is evidence of individual differences in impulse handling. This point emphasizes the idea that environment is a subjective rather than objective entity. The same environment differs in the experience of the beholders. Guze has indicated that ". . . of two subjects told to respond to a male experimenter as if he were a female, one does so directly and bluntly; the other, with much wavering and misgiving. A third person given the same suggestion smiles childishly and attempts to partake of the joke, meanwhile avoiding the behavior." Such responses appear in the hypnotic state as well as in the waking state — perhaps more sharply in the former.

The repertoire of expression depends upon individual differences in consitution and learning acting together. Learning is a selective process based on the previous history of a person and the current field forces, as outlined by Lewin (17). The role of very early experience in later sensitivity has been defined recently in the increased attention given to the effects of imprinting and "critical periods" (22).

WHAT HYPOTHETICAL CRITERIA CAN BE ESTABLISHED TO DISTINGUISH SEXUAL HEALTH FROM SEXUAL PATHOLOGY?

Any act which is gratifying to the individual and which is not harmful biologically or psychologically to himself or any other individual may be regarded as healthy behavior. It should be noted that the so-called pathological images appear to be present universally in human experience. The real problem lies in the handling of such images (10).

How does one determine the psychological aspect of observable behavior? This question is concerned with an elaboration of the intraindividual component of overt action, the so-called covert correlate. If overt behavior is neither the cause of, nor the result of, the criteria for psychopathology (as indicated above), one may assume that the person is functioning in a healthy way. An interpersonal relationship is healthy only if neither of the parties involved experiences unreality.

What if the act is harmful only to the self in a psychological way? This becomes a problem of "civil liberties." It might be stated as follows: Does a person have the right, if he does not trespass on others, to be self-destructive emotionally? Aside from the civil liberties issue, which poses a problem in Western ethics and law, self-destructive behavior cannot be regarded as healthy under any circumstance. This does not exclude the fact that self-destruction may at some time be unavoidable, necessary or the lesser of two evils.

An act is sexually healthy if it is consistent with the biological level of the organism. Thus one assumes that what is normal for the dog may not be normal for man, behaviorally. The human being, having the capacity for some rational behavior and foresight, might show an awareness of consequences which is not shown by lower animals. If man fails to perceive the implications of at least some of his behavior, he may then be regarded as functioning pathologically. For example, in view of the increasing population density, a couple that has a large number of children is increasing the population pressure and thereby doing harm to themselves and to other people. This is a clear lack of foresight and an indication of unrealistic behavior.

It may be noted that this position does not imply that the basic drive must be suppressed. There is, rather, the suggestion that one take cognizance of the impulses related to drive and extend them so far as they are harmless in their effect psychobiologically.

The criterion of the effect upon the individual, rather than the social or statistical criterion, should dominate in the determination of whether an act is healthy or pathological. A person may find that some types of behavior are contrary to his self-consistency, even though his culture may encourage them. How such deviation from the culture occurs is a basic problem in the understanding of personality development.

Sexually healthy behavior shall thus be of such nature as to show a unity between the act and the attitude toward the act, provided such act is not contrary to the psychobiological well-being of the self and of others.

A sexually healthy act should be realistic in terms of the outer (sensory) and the inner (fantasy) world. The presence of fantasy or imagery seems to be universally ongoing at all times in the individual (10). It is, however, suppressed during stimulation from the outside environment. It is hypothesized that, ideally, sex relations are accompanied by a minimum of extraneous fantasy. On the other hand, the fantasy component, since it is almost always present, must be recognized as basic to the development of sexuality. If it does not become distorted by becoming associated with hostility to, and degradation of, the sexual object, it is usually part of the expression of healthy sexuality. If it does not interfere with outward sexual expression, and if a person can handle the impulses that it represents in terms of nondestructive and noninjurious behavior, it may then be regarded as a concomitant of healthy sexual experience.

The sexually healthy act is one which permits the building up of tumescence within the individual and permits release at an appropriate time in such a way as to be tension reducing. In lieu of research about sexual feeling as such, it is not known whether Burton's (2) assumption that man is sad following sexual release is generally correct. If it is, it may be that it is only applicable to the male, and not to the female. Furthermore, it may be an artifact of Western culture. There are indeed sparse data available.

The sexually healthy act is neither forced on the self, nor on a partner, nor on a social observer. It is basically spontaneous, a feeling experience rather than an intellectual experience. Thus the person who feels that he must indulge in sex behavior of a certain kind because his peers do so may be behaving in a pathological manner. By the same token, the acceptance of a "sexual experience" for which one is not prepared may be tantamount to a forced experience. It is likely to result in emotional disruption in both the person who is forced and the one doing the forcing. Furthermore, the person doing the forcing is probably pathologically motivated. One must remember that there is a difference between force and seduction. The latter is pathological only if the seduced is incapable, for some basic reason (i.e., mental retardation), to gauge the consequence of behavior. One might say that extreme sexuality clouds a person's judgment even if one is ordinarily capable of gauging consequences. However, such clouding is qualitatively different from the vulnerability of the psychobiologically incompetent.

After evaluating the above criteria of sexual health, a significant conclusion comes to the fore. It is that in the final analysis there are probably no pathological sexual acts as such. To assume that there are would be to reify an abstraction. Behavior is a person behaving. Therefore it follows that there are pathological people — people who function in an emotionally harmful way, whether to themselves or to others. Most likely, injury to either the self or to another person is the same in terms of the implications for psychopathology. It may be concluded, in this sense, that sexual pathology is psychopathology, and that psychopathology is a psychopathological person. Thus the functional unity of the organism is maintained, and imbalance of any aspect of the psychological being involves imbalance of the total person.

THE NATURE AND FUNCTION OF THE PATHOLOGICAL PERSON

As indicated in the previous section, it is unwise to speak of pathology as an abstracted entity. Therefore some remarks must be made to define that aspect of the psychopathological person which may manifest itself in disturbed sexual functioning.

Such person may feel a compulsiveness about sexual expression which spills over any control in terms of impulse handling. Contrariwise, he may have developed such defensive controls that he cannot respond to any situation which has arousal characteristics. In the first case there may be irresponsible psychopathic sexuality, attempts to express a total genital impulse without regard for personal danger or that of others. The individual is mostly inward, but acts upon, rather than with or because of, the outside world. In the second case there is little if any overt expression. The individual suppresses or represses the arousal from the outside world and functions mostly solipsistically. He may manifest anxiety, fear, anger and immobility.

Both types described above are not capable of realistic manipulation of the outside world in such a way as to avoid injury to the self or to others. There may be an overflow of hallucinatory experiences, sexual confabulation and, finally, the probability of delusional reaction to the hallucinatory component. The persons in the first category may respond with paranoid panic if there is any external block to their expression. The second group may remain merely in the delusional range or withdraw into immobility. The development of imagery which is inconsistent with cooperative and harmless sexuality may appear in both categories. In the first category, overt violence may supplant sexuality. In the second, a masochistic component may lead to sadomasochistic fantasy which becomes a basis for guilt feeling and ideas of reference and persecution. That there is some kind of continuum between the two categories described above, and that gradations lie between them, makes possible a variety of pathological types.

In the final analysis, the particular sexual act is a function of a given individual who manifests specific and describable psychodynamics. If the members of a given culture are statistically similar in their attitudes, it is possible for those people to be behaviorally similar as a result of similar patterns of psychodynamics. The fact that human beings are more similar to each other than different makes such a statement possible on the basis of the biology of homo sapiens. Perhaps this is what is meant by the French proverb *Honi soit qui mal y pense* — "the source of evil is in the thoughts." An act is the resultant and can be judged in terms of its impact on the self or on others, whether it is beneficial, neutral or harmful.

REFERENCES

1. BEACH, F. A.: *Hormones and Behavior*. New York, Hoeber, 1962.
2. BURTON, R.: *The Anatomy of Melancholy*. New York, Empire State, 1924.
3. CANTOR, A. J.: *Ambulatory Proctology*, 2nd Ed. New York, Hoeber, 1952.
4. CANTRIL, H., GAUDET, HAZEL, and HERZOG, HERTA: *The Invasion From Mars*. Princeton, Princeton Univ. Press, 1940.
5. DICKINSON, R. L.: *Atlas of Human Anatomy*, 2nd Ed. Baltimore, Williams & Wilkins, 1949.
6. ELLIS, A.: *The American Sexual Tragedy*. New York, Twayne, 1954.
7. FORD, C. S., and BEACH, F. A.: *Patterns of Sexual Behavior*. New York, Harper, 1962.

8. GUZE, H.: Sexual Attitudes in the Scientific Medical Literature. *J. Int. Sexol.*, 1-5, 1951.

9. GUZE, H.: Hypnosis as wish-fulfillment - a projective approach. *Br. J. Med. Hypnotism*, 2:6-16, 1951.

10. GUZE, H.: *Toward a Theory of Schizophrenia and the Schizophrenic Process: The Borderlines of Hypnosis.* In: M. V. Kline (Ed.), *Psychodynamics and Hypnosis.* Springfield, Thomas, 1966.

11. HAWTHORN, H. B.: *The Doukhobors of British Columbia.* Vancouver, University of British Columbia, 1955.

12. HEAPE, W.: The "Sexual Season" of Mammals and the Relation of the "Proestrum" to Menstruation. *Quart. J. Micr. Sci., 44*:1-70, 1901.

13. HENRY, J.: The social function of child sexuality in Pilagá Indian culture. In: P. H. Hoch and J. Zubin, [eds.]: *Psychosexual Development in Health and Disease.* New York, Grune, 1962.

14. HONIGMANN, J. J.: Toward a Distinction Between Psychiatric and Social Abnormality. *Social Forces, 31*:274-278, 1953.

15. KINSEY, A. C.; POMEROY, W. B., and MARTIN, C. E.: *Sexual Behavior in the Human Male.* Philadelphia, Saunders, 1948.

16. KINSEY, A. C.; POMEROY, W. B.; MARTIN, C. E., and GEBHARD, P. H.: *Sexual Behavior in the Human Female.* Philadelphia, Saunders, 1953.

17. LEWIN, K.: *Principles of Topological Psychology.* New York, McGraw, 1936.

18. MASSERMAN, J.: *Principles of Dynamic Psychiatry.* Philadelphia, Saunders, 1946.

19. MASTERS, R. E. J.: *Forbidden Sexual Behavior and Morality.* New York, Julian, 1962.

20. MASTERS, W. H., and JOHNSON, VIRGINIA J.: *Human Sexual Response.* Boston, Little, 1966.

21. McBRIDE, A. F., and HEBB, D. O.: Behavior of the captive bottle-nose dolphin, tursiops truncatus. *J. Comp. Physiol. Psychol., 41*:111-123, 1948.

22. MOLTZ, H.: An epigenitic approach. *Psychol. Rev., 70*:123-138, 1963.

23. NEW YORK HERALD TRIBUNE: Another fiery Buddhist protest - at Saigon Cathedral. October 28, 1963.

24. OLIVEN, J. F.: *Sexual Hygiene and Pathology.* Philadelphia, Lippincott, 1955.

25. SZASZ, THOMAS: *The Myth of Mental Illness.* New York, Harper, 1961.

Chapter 38

PATTERNS OF THERAPY FOR THE FAMILY

WILLIAM L. CARRINGTON

Progress, man's distinctive mark alone,
Not God's, and not the beast's;
God is, they are,
Man partly is, and wholly longs to be.
                    ROBERT BROWNING, "A Death in the Desert"

THE HUMAN SPIRIT APPEARS TO BE blessed with a creative discontent, which, combined as it is with a perennial curiosity, incites men and women to search continually for something better in human living. The evolution of therapy through human history provides a vivid demonstration of these two great human urges, to know more and to do better, yet the goal is as far away as ever.

Patterns of therapy for the family are most appropriately considered in the general perspective of progressive community projects for the promotion of mental health, and these same two urges can be seen clearly in the working out of this whole enterprise. The urge to know more is to be seen in the progressive widening and deepening of insights into the many-sided complexities of the problem, and the urge to do better in the equally progressive expansion of therapeutic "teamwork." This expansion has been so rapid that many overlapping roles of different kinds of therapists have not yet been adequately delineated.

The limitation of the present subject to the family, however impossible, is appropriate, because the family is being seen more and more clearly as the true unit of the community, the arena in which most of the strains which affect society so deeply can be seen most clearly and dealt with most effectively. As Gardner Murphy (1) points out: "Conflicts in the home find a way of giving rise to conflict in group after group. So all that is meaningful in community life may need to be seen in a psychoanalytic light in terms of the reliving of early family experience."

The subject may be considered under two main headings: first, the main patterns of therapy which seem appropriate to the needs of the family; and second, the different kinds of therapists and their overlapping fields of work.

PATTERNS OF THERAPY APPROPRIATE TO POSSIBLE NEEDS OF THE FAMILY

For the purpose of the present discussion these patterns will be considered in five groups — psychiatric, medical, social, religious and domestic

— which necessarily overlap to some extent. In considering them as appropriate to possible needs of the family it would seem necessary to think beyond the family as a group of people to its individual members. Any disorders affecting them bear on the family; any therapy carried out with them affects the family; and any improvement of family relationships and general welfare will contribute to the health and welfare of individual members. It is significant that it is only in relatively recent times that the family has been given representation to any relevant degree in most of these patterns of therapy. This has come about because of the growing conviction that the family cannot be insensitive to any serious trouble in any of its members, nor free from responsibility in the complex patterns of causation of many personality disorders in them.

The Psychiatric Patterns of Therapy

These patterns are distinguished from the others by the fact that the predominant focus of therapy is on the ineffective functioning of various inner dynamic urges, conscious and unconscious, of individuals, however much attention may also need to be given to consequent disturbances of personal relationships and personal conduct, and to etiological factors concerned with environment or with personal relationships.

They range from intensive and prolonged psychoanalysis (sometimes including narcoanalysis or hypnoanalysis), through extended or brief psychotherapy, to more superficial counseling, interviewing and supportive therapy. They seek assistance, where it seems appropriate, from various kinds of "physical therapy" (such as electroconvulsive therapy and leucotomy), from chemical therapy (such as that provided by insulin or other endocrine products, stimulants, sedatives, tranquilizers or relaxants), from occupational therapy, physiotherapy, "social therapy" (the "therapeutic community"), from "spiritual therapy," (as offered more and more by trained chaplains and ministers) and from "domestic therapy" given by marriage partners, parents, relatives, neighbors and friends.

Whether any of the psychiatric patterns are carried out in hospitals or other institutions, for brief or prolonged "full-time" stay, in public or private "clinics" or "consulting rooms," or in patients' homes, they are being brought more and more into relationship with the family, and beyond that with society. This is happening in many very significant ways. Mental hospitals are being progressively rescued from their remoteness and brought into closer relationship with the families of the mentally ill and with society in general, through increased facilities for visiting, through "open days" for the community, through auxiliaries, full-time chaplaincies, increasing publicity and the general education of the community. In these and similar ways the age-old social stigma of mental illness is being overcome steadily, and this is of the greatest importance for the family. At the same time more attention and scientific study is being given to the criminal, the delinquent, the vandal and the alcoholic. This is also bringing some of the psychiatric patterns of therapy into closer relationship with the family and with society.

Within mental hospitals and some other institutions there is now much more freedom than formerly. This is made possible by better medical understanding and skill and by the use of tranquilizers. Such "community" activities as "group psychotherapy," "sociodrama" and "therapeutic social clubs" are helping to equip the mentally and socially ill for better human relationships on discharge, and this constitutes a valuable form of therapy for the family. With these advances there are increasing facilities for rehabilitation of the mentally ill from the hospital to their homes and families, their jobs and, generally, into society. But there would appear to be much more that needs to be done in this, and in the related project of helping other members of the family to live creatively with the mentally ill at the beginning of an illness and after discharge from hospital, so that admission or read-mission to hospital may be diminished. This is being assisted to some extent by the opening up of some "day hospitals," as well as through convalescent hospitals and mental hygiene clinics. "Night hospitals" have also been opened in some countries to enable people to have treatment while carrying on their daytime occupations. All of these are most valuable for family welfare.

This expanding relationship of the psychiatric patterns of therapy with the family and with society is less obviously, but more profoundly, expressed in the fact that many insights born of psychiatric experience and psychiatric and related research have spread and are spreading more and more into the everyday life of people, individual and social. This is helping to bring about better ways of prevention of mental and social illness, and promotion of better mental and social health through education, training, and earlier and more efficient diagnosis and therapy.

It seems clear that for the further widening of influence of the psychiatric patterns for therapy, and for the further promotion of mental and social health, the psychiatric facilities will need to be brought more and more closely into geographical and professional relationships with families. Geographically there is still a dearth of psychiatric facilities in many out-of-town areas, even in some closely populated ones, and an unnecessarily great distance between some mental hospitals and clinics and many families which they serve. Professionally, while there is a growing amount of effective teamwork between psychiatrists and members of other professions in hospitals and clinics, there would seem to be a need for closer liaison between psychiatrists in private practice and such other professional "therapists" as family doctors, social workers, ministers and marriage counselors outside the hospitals and special clinics, if the best interests of the family are to be served.

It is clear from these and similar developments that the psychiatric patterns of therapy, important and central as they are for the mental and social health of the family and the community, cannot of themselves attend to more than a part of the total need. It is therefore necessary to give some consideration to other possible patterns of therapy for the family, and to see how they can interrelate with the psychiatric patterns and with each other.

The Medical Patterns of Therapy

In one sense, of course, the medical patterns of therapy include the psychiatric, but for present purposes it would seem appropriate to think of them as focused on the total health and fitness of each member of the family in terms of their influence on the general welfare (in its broadest sense) of the family. Any serious or prolonged disturbance of health or fitness of any member of a family constitutes a strain on the whole functioning of the family, a strain which in some cases may precipitate its actual breakdown. At the same time, any effective therapy applied to any member of a family exerts an influence far beyond the particular person.

As with the psychiatric patterns, the medical patterns of therapy have a wide range. They cover all kinds of therapy from specialized medical and surgical treatment, through the whole range of specialties, to the simplest "general" medical and surgical treatment, with all the varied therapeutic resources of general hygiene, dietetics, physiotherapy, radiotherapy, occupational therapy, psychotherapy and nursing, again not forgetting the contribution of "spiritual therapy" from a trained chaplain or minister and "social therapy" from a kind neighbor or relative or friend.

The medical patterns may also be considered from the point of view of the different medical therapists — specialists, family doctors, resident medical officers of hospitals, medical officers attached to schools, industries, all kinds of institutions and official departments, and medical administrators. All of these may have an important part in the promotion of family health. There is an increasing amount of medical teamwork, most obvious in hospitals and other institutions, but also carried out widely and effectively in private medical practice. This teamwork involves a wide range of medical talent and medical resource — for diagnosis as well as for therapy — radiologists, biochemists and pathologists — plus the help of psychologists, almoners and social workers, and other nonmedical persons.

As with the psychiatric patterns there is also an increasing spread of this teamwork into society. With shorter periods of stay in the hospital for many disorders, the help of relatives and friends at home has become more generally necessary, and, with increasing publicity and general education of the public in medical matters, there is more interest and concern on the part of other people (including employers and administrators of accident and sickness benefits) in the ills and injuries of people.

In addition, the increasing incidence of "stress disorders" of all kinds has greatly altered the whole nature of medical practice. These strains and stresses are much less susceptible to "quarantine" and other kinds of "isolation" than are the causative agents of infectious diseases which they have largely replaced in the "epidemiology" of medical practice. The stresses and strains come in large degree from conflicting interpersonal relationships, and inevitably exert a considerable influence on such relationships. For these reasons, and also because the emotional stresses are matters of universal concern, more and more "medical" matters are being brought into close relationship with community life as well as with family living.

It is now generally recognized that considerable numbers of the symptoms that bring people to their doctors for help, and to their chemists for "magic," are of emotional origin, and also that such commonly prescribed remedies as tonics, sedatives, stimulants and tranquilizers are generally of partial and temporary, if any, value unless the patient can also unburden his deeper concerns, even those of which he feels ashamed or otherwise self-conscious, to someone who is, in the best sense of the term, a good listener. There is need for much greater training of medical practitioners for effective "family counseling," an art in which the traditional "family doctor" often came to considerable competence, through temperament and experience more than through specific training. The many and prevalent emotional and personal factors in people's disorders could then be given more and better therapeutic attention. It is important to emphasize that this extra family counseling, largely through good "creative listening" would not necessarily involve the busy doctor in much more time-consuming work. In most cases it would enable him to use the time he already spends with any patient much more effectively. It is the experience of many doctors who have cultivated this "family counseling" that their work becomes very much more effective, as well as interesting, and that, ultimately, much otherwise fruitlessly spent time is saved. When it is realized that the family doctor is often the first to come into contact with the early symptoms of mental as well as physical illness, the value of even minor psychotherapy at this stage can well be imagined. He also may come into contact with many disturbances of family relationships long before they become of sufficiently obvious intensity to bring the people to seek help, and here again he has the most far-reaching opportunity for help and for the prevention of later difficulties and of tragedies involving the children. Here is a medical pattern of therapy for the family which would appear to have almost unlimited prospects for the future if it is more fully accepted and carried out by medical practitioners, with any other assistance that may seem appropriate.

It seems obvious that, in this field of personal relationships and personal stresses and strains, there are more therapeutic needs than could ever be coped with by all the likely psychiatric resources of the foreseeable future. The trained psychiatrist will have an increasing participation in this field as a consultant, and there are many obvious advantages to psychiatrists, family doctors and specialists, and to their patients, if psychiatric help is backed up by the support of a referring doctor, however little part he may have in the details of the psychotherapy.

The Social Patterns of Therapy

This is a wide and expanding group of patterns of therapy for the family, centered primarily on the trained social worker, and the psychiatric social worker, whose training is even more specialized. The history of social casework has demonstrated a progressively deepening application of help from the "symptomatic treatment" of making available any needed food, clothing, shelter or money, to the discovery and handling of deeper personal inadequacies, emotional injuries and other disorders. At the same time it has deepened in therapeutic philosophy and method, from admonition and advice to appropriate forms of "client-centered counseling," in which people's own actual and potential inner resources and strengths are brought to awareness, encouraged, mobilized and channeled into positive application. Modern social casework is "family-centered" whether it seems to be applied to the difficulties of an individual or to the many and complex troubles of the "multiproblem family."

In this evolution of social casework it has been inevitable that social workers should come to grips with many of the inner dynamic urges of individuals, and thus overlap into the field of the psychiatrists, to some extent. The training of social workers, and particularly that of psychiatric social workers, has been adapted to meet this and many other needs which have been made evident in their expanding work. Any psychiatric doubts as to the wisdom of this overlapping have been dispelled, both by the extent to which the demands exceed all the psychiatric resources, and by the obvious success of the social casework carried out apart from, as well as in conjunction with, psychiatric services.

As this evolution of social casework has proceeded, other specific needs in the social field have become more and more evident, and other social patterns of therapy have been developed to meet them. The increase in numbers of clinical psychologists and their range of work is one example of this. From psychological testing and other diagnostic and research activities, clinical psychologists have found themselves unable to avoid overlapping into the therapeutic field, partly because the personal relationships created in the diagnostic work are inevitably therapeutic, and partly because the rapport which comes about in that work often puts them in the best position to offer effective therapy. In some cases, also, they become involved in therapy simply because no other competent person happens to be readily available.

This applies also to some extent to such other social patterns of therapy as those provided by probation officers and a variety of other workers in social welfare organizations and agencies. Modern industry has also found it necessary to institute such social services as those of personnel officers, and modern educational institutions have for similar reasons appointed student counselors to give personal help where it may be needed. All of these services are indirectly, and often directly, of considerable therapeutic value for the family.

But in all of these social patterns of therapy, and in spite of all that they can offer to the family, it has been found that disturbances of the actual relationships within the family were not being offered adequate help on anything like a sufficient scale. Disturbed and disrupted family living seems to have increased in amount and intensity to an extent beyond the capacity of the general resources of the community (psychiatric, medical, religious and social). At the same time the increasing awareness of the consequences of domestic failure in mental, physical and social illness has added to the realization of the extent and urgency of the need. The increasing realization of the depth and complexity of the intimate relationships of family life has combined with the other insights to bring about the creation of a further social pattern of therapy which is focused directly on the family itself, and particularly on the marital relationships so crucial to family welfare.

Beginning in America in 1929, in England in 1938 and in Australia in 1947, professional people from various related disciplines have been developing a social pattern of therapy which is primarily focused on the marriage relationship, and which takes the form of what is called marriage counseling. In most cases it naturally extends, or is ready to extend, beyond marriage counseling to family counseling, and services of this kind are now in existence, to a varying degree and with some variation in type, in almost every country of the civilized world.

In America, marriage- and family-counseling services have been given predominantly by professional people with special additional training, either privately or in nonprofit social agencies. In Great Britain, Australia, New Zealand and other countries, the demands for help have from the beginning exceeded the available money or professional manpower. "A new resource," as Dr. David Mace described it, had to be discovered, mobilized, trained and put to work. Volunteers were enlisted, put through a rigorous selection process by highly qualified professional people and given a very comprehensive theoretical and practical training. After a further assessment, those who were regarded as competent were accepted as part-time voluntary counselors, to work as a team under very close professional supervision, and backed by a panel of professional consultants.

With these safeguards carefully administered, this kind of marriage-counseling service has proved its value and effectiveness wherever it has been carried out. It makes no attempt to discount or displace other therapeutic services for the family. It is inevitable and valuable that such other marriage- and family-counseling services should continue to be carried out, both as private professional services for those who wish to use them, and as public community professional services through social casework agencies, and medical, psychiatric and child-guidance clinics. But alongside and in cooperation with all of these services, at least in Great Britain, Australia and New Zealand, there has been proof in abundance of the need for the specific voluntary social therapeutic service of marriage counseling, carried out by selected, trained and supervised people, with and without basic professional training apart from that given for this particular work. The already heavy demands on these services are progressively increasing as they have become better known and more widely available.

Throughout all of these patterns of therapy there is a deep and growing conviction, in the minds of all who take part in them, that however important it is to offer such therapy, it is still more important to find better ways of prevention of mental, physical and social ill health than exist at present, good and widespread as these are. In one sense, of course, most of the therapy helps to prevent further disorder and disaster (especially in future generations) as well as to relieve the present trouble. But there is a growing conviction of the need for much more widespread and comprehensive education and preparation for marriage, parenthood and family life than has ever existed before. This is a very large and complex project, far beyond the scope of the present discussion, but it cannot logically be separated from any consideration of patterns of therapy for the family, because it would certainly equip parents and future parents much more fully to carry out what will later be referred to as the domestic patterns of therapy, which are in some ways possibly the most important of all. Such a project involves a very close and integrated teamwork between many kinds of professionally trained people, and it will need to develop on a scale beyond anything so far attempted, and to utilize the services of many people without specific professional training under competent professional leadership.

The Religious Patterns of Therapy

These patterns are distinguished from the others by the fact that the predominant focus is on the ultimate loyalty of people, the dynamic inspiration which generates and sustains their power to give of themselves, regardless of any apparent response, because what they are doing is seen as creatively worthwhile for its own sake, because they are conscious of having received from life, or from God the Creator, Director and Sustainer of life, far more than they could ever deserve; and they seek, therefore, in loving gratitude, to serve others. It is expressed briefly and clearly in some words of Jesus: "Freely ye *have* received, freely give" (Matthew 10:8). This is the main underlying power behind the highest and most creative forms of love, through which men and women may be inspired to love even the unlovable, the unattractive and the unresponsive, who in fact are, of all people, most in need of it.

The religious patterns of therapy seek to cooperate with the natural healing forces in people at this level of ultimate values and creative energies which we call the spiritual. In general, this attempt at cooperation may be considered from three points of view: the creation of a spiritual environment of outgoing unselfish love "without strings"; the offering of what we might call "spiritual nourishment"; and the attempt to expose and liberate people from any spiritual hindrances to health, such as "envy, hatred and malice, and all uncharitableness," as it is eloquently described in the Litany in *The Book of Common Prayer*.

The spiritual environment, the first "channel" of spiritual therapy, can be thought of as "the fellowship of the Spirit" (Phillippians 2:1), or in simpler terms as "an environment of love." The therapeutic value of love has been rediscovered by psychologists and psychiatrists, and it is generally agreed that the genuine unselfish, wisely and consistently administered love of parents to children is the main factor in the generation of a healthy personality. And when any child has the misfortune to grow up in a home and family in which this love is not available, his whole future health may depend on the availability of some comparable environment of love outside the home. A therapeutic resource of this kind which has not yet been adequately recognized or developed is the church congregation, together with smaller groups of church members. By offering genuine unselfish love and acceptance to the love-starved, rejected and lonely, they will be exerting a greater therapeutic influence than they may realize. This is, of course, being done on a fairly wide front now, but there seems room for more awareness of its therapeutic value, and more deliberate cultivation of this kind of therapeutic service, possibly at first by special groups of people in some church congregations, under the leadership of ministers who are fully aware of the deeper implications of the project.

"Spiritual nourishment," the second channel of spiritual therapy, may include the whole range of religious worship, prayer, the administration of the sacraments, the "laying on of hands" and anointing with "consecrated oil" or "holy water." These are universal "means of grace," the value of which is enhanced when those who participate do so in the true spirit of worship — an offering to God for His own sake, and not primarily for what benefit may be received. Any self-centered faith is psychologically as well as spiritually inadequate, because it cannot help being "neutralized" by fear that the hoped-for results may not happen. This is a vast subject beyond the scope of the present discussion, but it represents an important pattern of spiritual therapy, which may be provided mainly, but in no sense entirely, by ministers and religious leaders. It is open to all people to study and to practice, and it also lends itself to group study and practice.

The liberation of people from spiritual "poisons," the third of the channels of spiritual therapy, is an important part of the "pastoral" work of the church. In dealing with such "poisons" as have been mentioned, and their symptoms, such as resentment, guilt, fear and anxiety, this pastoral pattern cannot avoid overlapping with many of the others, but the spiritual therapy is seen in an extra dimension of the ultimate meaning and purpose of life, beyond such matters of expediency as "adjustment" to society and "inner peace." This is so whether the pastoral work is carried out by minister or layman, and it is becoming more fully realized that teamwork between a minister and at least a group of his congregation adds much to the value of the whole work.

The Domestic Patterns of Therapy

These are distinguished from the others by the fact that they are specifically concerned with the application of domestic relationships, husband-wife, parent-child and sibling relationships, and relationships of any member of a family with others in or associated with the home. If the term "therapy" is taken to include the promotion of health, it is likely that these domestic patterns are the most fundamental and important of all, in that the foundations of mental, physical and social health are laid, for good or ill, mainly in the home and family. All projects for education, for marriage, parenthood, family life and, indeed, for education for citizenship in the broadest sense need to take into account the predominant influence of parents, as educators for life, healers of all kinds of trouble, and sources of inspiration and power to love and serve other people. Education, psychotherapy and religion, the three great forces which can mold and transform man's internal character structure, and thus "assist him to bring forth from within himself the resources for changing the patterns of contemporary civilization" (2), all have their first and most ultimately influential application through what may be regarded as domestic patterns of therapy, patterns in, as well as for, the family.

In addition to these patterns of therapy in the family which exist in their own right, there are patterns of therapy which cooperate with any or all of the first four patterns dealt with. The psychiatric patterns may assist disturbed people to disentangle and make better use of their intrapersonal dynamic urges, but these people live in families, and are strongly influenced for good or ill by domestic attitudes, as in turn they influence the domestic scene. In some countries the experiment of using good private homes for the housing and care of mentally ill patients is proving of the greatest value. The members of such families are giving valuable service and at the same time learning much about human nature and human relationships.

Similarly, the medical patterns, the social patterns and the religious patterns must depend on the quality of domestic relationships for much of their effectiveness, not only for therapy but often for the earliest recognition of trouble.

It seems clear, therefore, that the more effective and comprehensive any therapy for the family may be, the more it is equipping one of the most influential of all therapeutic agencies to do its healing and even more its health-promoting work. It was suggested at the beginning of this discussion that the family is the arena in which many of the strains which affect society so deeply and widely can be seen most clearly and dealt with most effectively. Is there a central principle of human relationships which can be seen clearly and applied effectively in the family as a kind of "working model" of community relationships? Possibly the most fundamental insight in this regard is that only those who have had the experience of being genuinely loved can develop the capacity to love themselves wisely and to love their "neighbors" as themselves. As a corollary to this, an essential element in the "therapeutic" quality of love is the full acceptance of other people's (and particularly children's) feelings, though not necessarily of their conduct. This principle of personal relationships has been illuminated and clarified through the experience and research of almost all "helping" disciplines, and it seems destined to bring about a great advance in child care and in almost every other kind of human interaction. To reject or attack other people's feelings is to reject or attack other people, and that, focused down into its simplest terms, is war. To accept them in the spirit of "live and let (or help) live" is to encourage community, and that, focused down into its simplest terms, is health, mental and physical, to some extent, as well as social.

This acceptance of other people's feelings is also the essential principle of living with disturbed, distorted and even disrupted other people in such a manner that they will exert the least harmful influence, and that they will be given the most steady dependable personal environment for their own growth and healing. This again is a very large and complex subject, beyond the scope of the present discussion.

For the most effective therapeutic influence within the family, parents and others need more than education. They need the capacity to love as well as the knowledge of what love is. For this capacity they may need to be healed, to be liberated from deep emotional tensions and conflicts; and they also need to be loved so that the capacity to love can be generated and developed within them. Preparation of people for the responsibilities of family life, and above all for family "therapy," thus needs the cooperation of healthy education, healthy psychotherapy and healthy religion, a richly creative kind of teamwork which is therapeutic for members of the team, as well as those whom they serve.

THE DIFFERENT KINDS OF "THERAPISTS" AND THEIR OVERLAPPING FIELDS

It is clear from this consideration of the different patterns of therapy that there has been, still is and will be, considerable exchange of insights between the different disciplines involved in them. This, of course, is an essential principle and condition of good teamwork. There are also many common elements in all the different patterns, the most fundamental of which is the therapeutic importance of the therapist-client (or patient, relative or friend) relationship, expressed mainly through what is called "communication." In considering the different kinds of "therapist" it is therefore necessary to think of the specific, possibly somewhat exclusive, contribution of each, and the general contribution which may be closely related with and even identical with, that of some other kinds of "therapist."

The exclusive contribution of each therapist is fairly clear at the center, but often vague and variable at the periphery. For example, the psychiatrist has an exclusive responsibility for the main direction and administration of treatment in frank and serious disturbances of the intrapersonal dynamics of individuals, whatever help he may need or receive from others, or whatever he may delegate to others. His work cannot help spreading out to the coverage of many interpersonal matters, and often to social environmental factors, in which it overlaps with that of the social worker, the psychiatric social worker and many other kinds of therapists. It seems impossible to lay down "rules" or criteria at present, but decisions about "who shall attempt what" are mostly made on a basis of competence, availability, "rapport" and possibly results.

The exclusive contribution of the medical practitioner (family doctor or specialist) is the diagnosis and the specific treatment of disease and the general promotion of health. But again the doctor's work will often spread out to many fields which are not in any sense "medical," and many other people carry out much minor medical and surgical "diagnosis" and "treatment," often, but not always, with considerable efficiency. Attempts to fence off close professional "preserves" are notoriously unsuccessful, except at the center, where special competence is necessary. The same applies to the minister, whose special field of work has been dealt with already, and whose general field may overlap many others.

The social worker also has a fairly definite range of work in which special knowledge and competence are necessary, but his work is at any time likely to spread out beyond any suggested boundaries, and may often be overlapped by that of other kinds of "therapists." In fact, the social field is of great variety and complexity, and it is being covered by such "therapists" as ministers, teachers, probation officers, lawyers, police, psychologists, sociologists, "home economists," visiting nurses, public servants (in pensions, benefits and other "welfare" departments) , politicians, marriage counselors and many others.

The field of work of the marriage counselor, one of the newest of the social "therapists," needs some consideration in this discussion of patterns of therapy for the family. Marriage counseling in the first place is not so much a profession in itself as an art, a therapeutic service which may be common to people of many professions, and to some without specific background professional training. This is partly because of the universality of marriage and family relationships. The actual field of work of the marriage counselor is gradually being delineated through the experience gained in carrying it out. At the center of the work, the marriage counselor's main attention is on the interpersonal relationship between husband and wife and, to some extent, on the total family relationship. In this it is impossible to avoid some contact with the intrapersonal dynamics which underlie so many interpersonal relationships, but when these appear to be a large factor in the trouble the counselor will generally refer the client for psychiatric help. The marriage counselor as such is neither trained, nor does he desire, to treat a mentally ill person. He may be drawn into the situation to help the partner of such a mentally ill person cope with the task of living with him, and in this way may be of considerable help to the psychiatrist who may be treating him.

Wherever the community service of marriage counseling is operating it has drawn together, in increasingly effective teamwork, men and women from a variety of professions — doctors, ministers, social workers, teachers, lawyers, probation officers and others. It has also, at least in Britain, Australia and New Zealand, drawn in other carefully selected and trained people without professional background, but with real experience of marriage and family life. Unmarried and divorced people are not generally accepted in these countries as voluntary marriage counselors, not because they are necessarily unsuitable — many of them may be very competent indeed — but because at present it is too difficult to assess their suitability unless they have demonstrated their competence in actual professional training and practice. Each of the fields from which counselors are drawn has a contribution to the rich teamwork, and the more the counselors can work together, the more effective the total work is found to be. An essential part of their training is that marriage counselors should learn to recognize their limitations and be prepared to refer clients to a person of special competence when it seems necessary, and this is made easier when the work of counselors is properly supervised by a professionally trained "casework supervisor" in full-time attendance at the marriage-counseling agency. This, and the provision of a representative panel of consultants, would seem to be absolutely vital for the proper working of any such agency.

The criteria for selection, the details of training, and the principles of "accreditation" and supervision of marriage counselors are now clearly laid down in most countries, and they are continually open to further modification in the light of experience. This experience is also likely to offer help to members of many professions in what has been termed "the art of professional conversation," the central concern of all helping professional relationships, and, ultimately, as the basis of all patterns of therapy for the family, one of the universal resources for the promotion of mental, physical and social health.

REFERENCES

1. MURPHY, GARDNER: *Menninger Quarterly, XIII* (No. 3) :14, 1959.
2. ROBERTS, DAVID E.: *Psychotherapy and a Christian View of Man.* New York, Scribner, 1950, p. 7.

Chapter 39

THE MARITAL PROCESS

JULES BARRON

AN ADEQUATE UNDERSTANDING of marriage comes of total rather than fragmented or segmented study.

Each human relationship can only truly be seen in terms of its own uniqueness. Whatever label the relationship bears, it provides a particular frame of reference, an orientation, a mental set. The label, whether it be marital, friendship, professional, etc., carries for each person special meanings borne of his experiences. These meanings pertain to rules, limits, cultural, social and personal implications.

To understand process in a relationship is more complex and more dynamic than that which merely involves behavioral change and description. In process we do not deal with a segment of behavior or life. It is not cross-sectional or static. It involves change, movement, shifts on an ongoing basis. In the study of process we need to be able to focus on a moving target, as it were. We require a personal pliability or facility to follow the course of the relationship, to experience its evolution, its growth and its regressions.

Charting the currents of the relationship is as if we are traveling Oceania with all of the natural and human forces that affect the experience; with all of the viscissitudes of nature and man. There is an admixture of calm and turbulence, high and low tides, experienced waters that are shallow and those that are deep, areas of light and of darkness, safety and danger.

A process approach to marriage is marriage *in* process. Obviously and consciously it involves two people. Much less conspicuously and less consciously it includes a kind of corporate structure. Each partner brings a multifaceted person that represents incorporations of premarital significant others. These influential shadows are often multiplied and magnified by the penetrating forces of culture and society. The rapidity of change in a society in revolution with regard to the psychosexual role adds to the whole and results in a kaleidoscopic pattern that is most challenging.

Needless to say, the confines of a single chapter can only permit a humble effort. It is an effort to regard the flow of human relatedness within the framework of a single society and within the context of a relationship that comes under the highly charged title of "marriage." If we were to merely examine the definitions, expressions or words that are commonly used with reference to marriage one would derive some sense of the specialness of this human arrangement. The jokes and jibes provide more attestations to the feelings and attitudes that pervade this condition. It is a relationship between a man and a woman, profoundly and singularly characterized by a legal bond that is superimposed upon a union evolved out of an emotional matrix. Whatever the course of premarital events and motivations, once formed, the marriage is, by definition, an institutional state. Therefore, in addition to the predisposing factors that will affect the nature of the marital relationship, there is the special consideration of the institutionalization of the relationship that is significant and meaningful.

The ubiquitous existence of the marital state is itself evidence that it is a form of relatedness significantly necessary to our human economy and security operations. Its popularity points out the need of one person for another. Even the nature of its unpopularity, paradoxically confirms its specialness.

Marriage is a special form of attachment between two people. In its broadest conception, which is beyond the scope of this writing, it may be non-legal, non-institutional and non-sexual. For example, it is sometimes said that one is married to his job. There are people of the same or opposite sex with an intimate ongoing bond without legal status or license. Generally it suggests an interconnection or correspondence that is tied together by some human need for another. When the marriage takes on the added dimension of being vested with the juristic quality, it is, as we more conventionally think of this social institution. The relationship now becomes part of the establishment that comes under special laws and customs. Obligations, duties and responsibilities, however volitionally assumed and executed, have the added character of coming under the aegis of the law. Historically the marriage has been easily entered into. Exit has been another matter and could be found only with great difficulty involving all kinds of practical and emotional stresses. For many it is a feeling of "No Exit." Indeed, one's conceptions of and attitudes towards marriage and divorce, unity and separateness cannot be disengaged from the nature of the marital dyad. Similarly, the relationship cannot be considered apart from the social climate with its expectations, prohibitions and morality. Even more, the entire structure of the individual including his images, needs, judgments are dramatically portrayed in the marital unit. Undoubtedly the very nature of man is intimately bound up in the process. A thorough study would necessarily involve the fields of anthropology and sociology as well as psychology.

With this in mind, we will regard the significant factors connected to the marital process and several possible ontogenetic courses of the nuptial union. For the purpose of this writing, the area of interest will be confined to some of the ways in which the *Two* move through the relationship. I will address myself to the processional character of marriage and the forces that facilitate or hinder this movement.

Think of several stage settings, each one permitting us to exercise our voyeuristic inclinations. It is like looking through the glass windows of human encounter. In each setting there is the common denominator of a couple with props, scenery and an interaction that is unique and peculiar to their balance.

Each interaction has its own struggles, strainings, stresses and strivings towards and away from growth.

Each member of the pair made his selection for both conscious and unconscious reason. Each one brought his hopes, dreams, illusions and particular sense of reality. Each has his health or lack of it. Both are seeking to form such an amalgamation out of some degree of health and pathology as it exists at the time wedlock is initiated. The view of concern here is not just in terms of where the couple begins and what they are at the time of the wedding but what happens from there.

My philosophic orientation is that each person has a growth potential which may be activated or aborted; that it is the responsibility of the person to determine his direction. Although the past, significantly, has permeated and influenced our lives and personality structure, we are not at its mercy. Hence we are capable of changing the nature of our existence. A total attitude of determinism may be defeating and permit a justification for perpetuating pathology at the worst, and a lack of growth at best.

The oft used term to describe the marital interaction is "compatibility." Usually, to be compatible is thought of as good and to be incompatible is regarded as bad. It is descriptive and judgmental rather than explanatory. Actually, compatibility is an existential phenomenon and can only be sustained as long as those involved either grow or do not grow together. It is an interplay between human energies and vectors. It is the nature of movement or the process working between the significant two. It is neither based on health nor pathology but on the harmonious balance that can be obtained and maintained in the relatedness. Its character can be rhythmical or dysphoric. It demonstrates point and counterpoint. It develops its own scores and orchestral mosaic. If the partners establish a merger of synchronous illusions the survival of the marriage will depend on the ability of both persons to either hold onto their illusions or give them up. If there is a contract founded on the principle of reality, it will remain valid insofar as each person of the diad can so accommodate himself without marked discrepancy or divergence. Generally, the progression of their experiences must approximate the same course and direction. A relative state of congruency must exist. There may be a mutuality of togetherness or separateness, of agreement or disagreement or any other forms of relatedness that are mutually ego syntonic for each person. Finally, in the marriage, an alliance is made where the two achieve an actual or pseudo-relatedness. The union may be borne of a real investment of the authentic self that generates a true sense of oneness, sensitivity and experiential communication. In this, there is encounter, fusion, and openness. Each partner participates actively in the growth process to foster the marital integration and preserve the integrity of each. Or, the liaison may be cast of egos that come together with the intent of sustaining a state of alienation. This may occur through modes of behavior that are polar opposites. That is, the state of disunited union may be found in the superficial relatedness or paradoxically managed by the symbiotic design of intense absorption. It seems clear that the architectural schemes under which marriage can lie are manifold.

It would be cardinal negligence to speak of any human relationship without the consideration of love and sex. It is probably fair to say that "love" existed long before relationships became institutionalized. It is undoubtedly accurate to assume that sexual behavior solidly laid its claim as a significant means of intercourse from the earliest beginnings of living time. I suspect that our civilizations and increasingly complex societal developments helped to create many layers of confusion with regard to the meaning and expression of human need in both love and sex. It is no enviable part of our heritage to try to disentangle the many and assorted webs thus woven. It is our task to understand the multiple levels of function and purposes intertwined with the experience of love and sex.

In our world it is somewhat rare to find the couple who did not marry out of love or, at least, under the banner of love. If the motive for marriage is not regarded with favor by society and not consistent with society's expectations, it frequently becomes important to use the acceptable reasons as excuses. As marriage must be connected with love as the more noble motive, sex, for its acceptability, must also be affiliated with love. Even more insistently, sex must find its respectability by its limited association with marriage. Perhaps this is what Don Juan had in mind when he said that marriage must be a licentious institution for it to be so popular. This triumvirate is, in the most literal sense, an outgrowth of society and the civilization of man. The literature is vivid testimony of the rules that triangulated marriage, love and sex in a bed of repressive strangulation. It is sanctioned that love and sex be discussed as part of the marital arrangement and considered unseemly or sacrilegious to deal with such matters or to give advice or consent to those outside of the institutional state. To write of sexual responsibility in human relations and, more so, to write of sexual responsibility in the non-marital state, is regarded as being in unquestionably poor taste. On the other hand, writing of sexual responsibility in marriage is of finer stuff. The "logic" of these attitudes become fairly well set in the very grain of our thinking and feeling process. Our motives, from wherever they came or whatever they are in the real context of our psychobiological beings, are funnelled appropriately into the camp of love, sex and marriage. One becomes the justification for the other where it does not actually exist. The triumvirate that can be a process of beauty becomes used as the jug into which all manner of wishes are poured.

By virtue of the social artifacts, contradictory encumbrances, unnatural rules and beliefs, it is without amazement that marriage is pervaded by hypocritical behavior, conflict and guilt, and trapped in the motif of the double-bind. Compounding the problem is the profound inculcation of divorce as an act of culpability. This only intensifies the tensions existing in marriage. Laws can justly be used to protect the individual from the destructive acts of others. Laws, edicts or rules can never legislate genuine relatedness. We cannot be allowed to choose between creative or destructive behavior. We must be permitted human choice with respect to love, sex and marriage. With choice is implied a deep sense of responsibility. The lack of choice more likely produces the kind of reactions that result in a counterreaction of anger and defeating behavior.

Even in such a cursory examination as this writing, one can only be bewildered, not by the extent of marital disharmony, but by the fact that harmony exists at all.

What seems to keep society together and marriages as well, very often in sickness and in health, in artificial, illusional and a variety of disturbed states, as well as in the bond of genuineness and authenticity, is man's need for another. All this is evidence of the basicness and strength of this need. That man will seek human contact even as he must protect himself from it.

For the practical purpose of illustration I will describe several forms of marital arrangements, each reflective of a different process. It is necessary that process is regarded both existentially, dialectically and relativistically.

In existential terms, the man, the "I and the Thou" and the marriage are what they are at the particular moment of space and time. In dynamic terms, they have come to be where they are through a series of experiential phenomena involving encounters with their external and internal worlds. At the moment of where they are, there is an inherent choice and responsibility. Choice and responsibility are related to the balance of forces operating in a relative period of time and to one's sense of being and integrity.

In dialectical terms, the unity of the marital relationship is a function of and relative to the nature and Gestalt of all existent forces pressing towards synthesis. Since change may be regarded as ongoing and universal the relationship in the marriage is temporal. Temporality, therefore, is an essential aspect of process. It is the dynamic shift or nature of movement.

In a finite segment of infinite and objective space and time each member of the marriage interacts with a particular uniqueness.

With the introduction of relativity in the understanding of the process of marital relatedness, the process receives further clarification as a totality in which the elements of the whole are forming new arrangements with each other. These changing arrangements may occur without alterations in the basic ingredients or elements and are produced by a combination of external and internal vectors which result in the new or different pattern of relatedness. In short, the elements within the marriage are relative to each other and are modified by shifts in time and space. In turn, the configuration of these elements in time and space, which is the nature or character of the marital relationship, affects all those arrangements that lie within its social sphere of influence.

Within this framework the course of marriage is inseverable from the life process. Its movement reflects the alterations and adjustments of each partner. The process in marriage, its changes in role relationships, its balances and imbalances, is determined by the condition of each of the marital pair. The condition involves factors of identity, ego synthesis and integration.

While the significant diad has been referred to as consisting of an I and a Thou, it is more complicated than this. It should be recognized that there are two I's and two Thou's in each diad, for each person is both and I and a Thou. This has importance in seeing each person as both the subjective subject and the subjective object, as both a receiver and a giver. The ability to move appropriately into either role is basic to the psychological homeostasis of relatedness. It is in this ability that interactive mutuality may be achieved.

Now for some illustrative examples which, for convenience, I have categorized in several ways. Again, I want to note that compatibility is not to be thought of as synonymous with either health or pathology; with relatedness or unrelatedness. It is but a state of harmonious coexistence. As long as each diadic member doesn't diverge significantly from the marital contract, the marriage will exist.

First I will present some compatible interactions. Whenever any couple is in trouble it is because their balance is threatened.

1. Parallel Unidirectional Relatedness

The direction itself is unimportant. It is important that movement of the two is in the same direction. The emotional contract is based on an agreement of distance or separateness that is to be maintained. This permits the security of a social and pseudo-relatedness without the risk of personal involvement. Such persons are likely to be alienated, ideationally oriented people with or without the mask of feeling and sensitivity. They are in accord with the expectation that the marital ship not be rocked by waves of emotionally induced volleys toward each other. In a therapeutic experience with these people, the therapist need find some way of stirring the pot. If this couple enters therapy it is more likely to come about because of the anxiety created by something that is threatening their pseudo-involvement. They will protest about the lack of relationship and communication at this time as a defense against any change.

2. *Periodic Contact-Separateness*

Periodic Contact-Separateness is actually a modification of Parallel Unidirectional Relatedness. In this kind of patterns the twosome largely keeps their distance from each other. However there are brief and widely spaced moments when the spouses require a sense of reality and involvement to alleviate the anxiety of aloneness and isolatedness. However, the contact-involvement creates its own anxiety and cannot usually be sustained. In psychotherapy this kind of couple is less difficult and the contact periods can be utilized for further growth.

3. *The Quicksand-for-Two Relatedness*

Here, the *unad*, if I may be permitted to coin a term, involves a complete absorption of one into the other with confusion and loss of identity. It is a psychical schemata in which the two egos hide in each other within a human capsule as a security operation against the threat of a world perceived as hostile. They lose themselves and really do not have each other. It is a plight of two human beings being pulled deeper into a quicksand of the non-living. This would be differentiated from the two drowning souls who may combine their strengths to survive. The survival can only occur then because of a willingness and ability to temporarily let go of their clawing grasp of each other and unwrap their clinging bodies; for one to allow the other to reach out to a branch or solid piece of the world. This *unad* consists of two infantile beings in undifferentiated mass. Even implication of separation is a great threat. It is this manner of threat that may precipitate this person into therapy. And, in therapy, the effort will be made to draw the therapist into the same kind of quicksand.

4. *Paradoxical Human Relatedness*

I am using the term, Paradoxical Human Relatedness, to describe the mutuality of oneness and separateness. This is truly a diadic relatedness wherein the egos maintain a separate identity and at the same time merge in a union of sharing, communication and sensitivity. It is an emotional involvement where there is the strength to be open and risk vulnerability and hurt; the strength to stand and the strength to lean; the strength to be strong and the strength to be "weak." There is merger rather than absorption, unity rather than incoporation. There is an ability to enjoy togetherness and accept separateness. It is possible for one to lose himself in the other without losing his sense of integrity. Although this relationship is not to be regarded as psychotherapy, it is therapeutic in a life producing and growth potentiating sense.

Needless to say, purity in or of anything is a myth. So be it with the above stated marital patterns. Disturbed relationships in marriage are not always disturbed. Healthy interactions are not always healthy. Hence, we can only gain real perspective by observing the process, the patterned course of the marriage rather than by studying a dissected piece out of context. The dissected kind of approach is frequently used by the members of the marital diad when it is necessary to create smokescreens for the real nature of their motives and wishes. Isolated incidents or sections of the process are produced as evidence and cause of their dissatisfactions while they are "enjoying" the security of unreality. The protests and the resounding noises of battle are used to drown out or silence the sounds of the inner selves.

From the time of inception the marriage is formed and re-formed. The ontogeny of the marriage is a recapitulation of the pattern that occurs in the ontogenetic development of the individual. Whether we speak of the process in the person, the marriage or society we are speaking of the nature of growth and the life process. In each case there is the potentiality of evolution. Growth is not steady and smooth. It has its plateaus and regressions, its syntheses and disintegrations. The equilibrium in marriage, as in life, is ever-changing. As life is a process that matures towards termination, so is the marriage a similar experience. Within the experiential plasm of life and the marriage, the course of life and death is experienced in many ways. We can see the ebb and flow, birth and rebirth. Each experience of termination of an old balance is a kind of death which can be a true ending or a new beginning. Each new balance comes of an old one that has changed or died.

Basic to the marital process is the development of an establishment wherein the man and wife are functionally related to each other in a mode of operation that insures a minimal fulfillment of each others needs. The equilibrium involves a primary state of stability amidst the shifting forces within the marital edifice and in relation to the unstable pressures of the outer worlds. At the same time there need be an ability to expand and create. Each person, within his limitations and the limitations of the marriage, requires a personal expressiveness and sense of being creative. If life itself can be seen as a creative force then this power need be expressed in the marriage. If none of this is achieved in reality, survival must hinge on a state of illusion or pseudo-relatedness and pseudo-creativity.

When man and woman take each other for better or worse, for pleasure or pain, in sanity or insanity, it is a striving, in the deepest sense, to achieve a sense of organic unity which is life in its search for unity. The unification of two appears to be basic to the unity and integrity of the one. It is as though there can be no I without a Thou and no Thou without an I. The ego finds its relative wholeness and completeness to the degree that relatedness is managed. Living is a process of relating. The marriage, within our culture, provides the only opportunity where the most complete union may be formed with a minimum amount of difficulty with regard to the social customs and mores. At the same time because of archaic attitudes and laws it becomes the ground for the seeds of disunion. In essence, the marital arena provides the potential area for both the greatest unity and greatest disunity.

Another way in which we may regard the marital arrangement in the institutional state is as a bridge designed and engineered between two pieces of ground. The bridge is the structure across which travels the flow of experiential traffic of each mate. It is a marital bridge founded on a contract whereby the party of the first part and the party of the second part shall be sole owners in possession of and in control of the traffic. The tolls to be paid are for them and between them. The bridge is their land, not to be trespassed upon without due authority given by the owners. The marital bridge may vary in its architecture and strength but always is intended as a special crossing for the particular Two.

I have spoken of the compatible relationships in marriage. The reader may well be wondering about those that are incompatible. These have no special categories for they include any marital bridge that has collapsed or been broken. The incompatible marriage is the one where the equilibrium has been thrown into chaos without the ability to create or find a new state of balance or form of relatedness. The break may not always be legal but is, without exception, an emotional one. The emotional break or the state of disharmonious coexistence may begin and end in many possible diadic conditions. A marriage may originate in any one of the four primary categories mentioned earlier. It may then change course and move into another. That is, the relatedness may be Parallel Unidirectional, Periodic Contact-Separateness, the Unadic Quicksand-for-Two or Paradoxical Human Relatedness.

In the Parallel Undirectional Marriage the catastrophic break would occur when the separateness cannot be sustained by one of the spouses. The husband or wife, through his personality changes, may have gradually taken a new and different direction which is now producing inadequate satisfactions, an interaction that shakes the stability quotient and brings it below the level of frustration tolerance and threatens the state of being of one or both. For example, one mate may have moved towards a new personal state of Periodic Contact-Separateness and perhaps, growing further towards Paradoxical Human Relatedness.

In every marriage occasional shifts may occur from one kind of relatedness to another. These fluctuations may be temporary regressions or spurts of growth. As long as each person returns to the original contractual arrangement or changes together the contract will remain intact.

Where the marital agreement says that "we shall allow each other only moments of real contact" as in the Periodic Contact-Separateness, the schism may be reached when one member either reaches out for a more sustained encounter or turns away towards the Parallel Unidirectional Relatedness where the twain must never meet.

In the Unadic or Quicksand-for-Two Relatedness, the truly diadic direction is forbidden unless the Two agree. Absorption is the rule and never the twain shall part.

When two people are signers to the contract of Paradoxical Human Relatedness they have attained a true communion between relatively healthy persons. They are in a process of conjoint, concordant and rhythmic dialogue. Here, if splitting occurs it may evolve out of a pace discrepancy between the Two where one's growth sufficiently surpasses the other as to create a distance between the couple. Or, each partner may continue to grow but in different directions from each other. A third possibility is that one person of the marriage may be significantly breaking his vows by a regressive process towards one of the other categories of Relatedness.

We see, then, that a breach in the marriage, be it via emotional and/or legal divorce, may be out of health or pathology. This, of course, is contrary to our social and legal attitudes which, at the very least, imply that marital schisms are wrong, bad, or sick. It also becomes evident to this observer that the marriage will not remain intact if there are any unilateral movements or changes in the primary agreement set forth in the unconscious court of the couple. If the unconscious marriage had a Justice of the Peace with contractual vows significantly discordant with the reality of consciousness, the bridge is largely in a precarious and brittle mold. It is rather difficult to maintain the requirements of two divergent contracts at the same time. The probability of unilaterality of movement is greater. Generally, the common denominator of all contracts states that "Thou shall not be vastly healthier or sicker than I." If there is any such discrepancy, it must be of such a nature that does not markedly affect the sense of union or basic security of either person.

It has been pointed out that the marital process is best seen in the context of the life process for it is an integral part of the living experience which is Relatedness. The natural condition of life as we know it is characterized by growth and regression, synthesis and disintegration, oneness and separateness, living and dying. All of these experiences are most appropriately applied to and invaluably helpful in our understanding of the marital diad.

In the psychotherapeutic experience we have learned well that the process of regression is essential to the growth of the patient. In every day experiences our observations can illustrate that fragmentation or disorganization of the individual often precedes periods of new growth, accelerated expansion, or creative functioning. As in psychotherapy or other life experiences, the disorganization in the marriage is not necessarily pathognomonic of chaos and destruction. It may be the result of a breaking down of old systems or structures to prepare for new patterns and further growth. Again, whether the resultant disequilibrium leads towards a more creative process in the marriage or severs its bonds will be a function of the Two moving together or apart.

The frequently unrealistic and idealized pictures painted of the good marriage by authoritative as well as unauthoritative sources make it very important that we do not view the marital experience as disjoined from our knowledge of growth and development. All forms of relatedness are woven of emotional attachment. The tapestry of marriage is bordered, edged, and blessed with legal sanctions and prohibitions. In our era of revolution and in all areas of living, we are in a period of transition. Nations, groups and individuals are fighting for the right to exist; for their right to be themselves; for self-determination. We hear more about sexual revolutions, crusades and movements to change laws affecting divorce and abortion. Our society and the world at large has been in the throes of upheaval in three most controversial fields of human experience — sex, politics and religion. It seems that, phylogenetically, we are adolescing. Knowledge of oneself from the nation to the individual is being sought. There is much questioning and introspecting. Fragmentation and divisiveness have loomed large to turn our senses and provoke anxiety about the nature of man and his institutions, the meaning of his condition and of life and death. We are caught in the grips of the problem of survival. Separateness or isolatedness is less than ever a matter of choice. There are dramatic scenes of disintegration and synthesis going on in this twentieth century. It is a matter of growth versus regression and the decline of civilization; oneness of the world or alienation; living or dying. It is a world in crisis. Whither we go from here can only be forward or backward but we cannot sit on fences or even on walls lest we suffer the fate of Humpty Dumpty. We cannot stand still.

Our disintegrating process can be a forerunner to new syntheses or the termination of experience.

Within this context of history, the marital interaction, too, in its process, has its tides, currents and whirlpools. The marital field has a uniqueness which is subject to the field of forces that bombard it from within and from without. The interplay is constant and insistent. The nature of the process in marriage is not affected only by attitudes toward and about marriage, in the field of social space and time. As the human institutional care of the family and society, the connubial association has the characteristics of the business partnership as well as the important qualities of a spiritual merger. There is probably no institution that is as influenced by as many variables as are extant in the world at large, either directly or indirectly. Consequently, the marital process is also a function of attitudes directed towards premarital relatedness, non-marital and post-marital status, attitudes towards masculinity and femininity with their respective roles, and the value systems that pervade our human sphere. Economics, politics, religion, sex, war and peace are all waves that break upon and lap at the foundations of marriage. They are also, and at the same time, undertows that pull at its footings.

In summary then, the marital process is an integral part of human life process. As the core institutional arrangement that binds people together, it is the basic fabric of social structure. If the weave is too tight it may create stress factors that result in a break. If the pattern is too compressed it may lack breathing space and decay. If the weave is too loose it may fall apart from lack of substance. Statistically, about one out of four marriages culminate in legal divorce. Non-statistically, a much larger number of marriages close in emotional divorce. This knowledge of the frequency with which the marital process runs a terminal course to a condition of alienation or disjointedness has been manifested in reevaluations of our traditional values and a search for new understanding and meaning with regard to both marriage and divorce. On a deeper level people are groping and grasping for meaningfulness in relatedness; for apprehension of relatedness, oneness and separateness; for a sense of integrity in an inferno of contradictions, hypocrisies and illusions. If this seems highly critical, it is so intended as an expression of hopefulness. For this is part of the process of disintegration and growth. Old tissue may die in order that untapped potential may be drawn upon and new life generated. This is the dialectic. Old syntheses which, at one time, were valid in their time and space may become antithetical to growth and, therefore, to the process of life and living. If a new synthesis were, then, not be found, it would be tantamount to death.

Viewing the edifice of marriage, with at least one dialectic eye, permits comprehension of process rather than a static and singular way of seeing.

Hence, despite the wide assortment of negative attitudes and feelings about marriage, the problem with marriage is not marriage. The problem lies in the nature of the process as created by human need in a particular and temporal assemblage of evolving, shaping and altering forces. The nature of these forces with its strains, thrusts and presses determine and reveal direction. The significant forces are largely human in a complicated network of paradoxical structures struggling for existence in a cosmos of polar and tensional states, beginnings and endings, illusions and realities. No better example of this is found than in the ontogenetic process of marriage. The marital process is not a divine creation, nor are its rules and character of superhuman origin. It is a creation and reflection of man. Its highest sanctification is human need for another with the possibility of a productive and loving communal connection.

In conclusion, I would say that while process is most difficult to study because it is life in motion, it can bring us closest to the truth and reality. In view of this it is important to approach process through several theoretical pathways almost simultaneously. Process in marriage, as process in psychotherapy, need be understood existentially, dialectically and relativistically as well as dynamically. Living truth cannot be found in compartments of knowledge. Life be not so proud for us that we hesitate to use all available tools to breach our walls of ignorance.

SECTION IV
SUMMARY
COMPREHENSIVE EVALUATION:
MARITAL COUNSELING CONCEPTS

Chapter 40

SUMMARY OF CONTRIBUTORS' VIEWPOINTS: ABSTRACTS OF CONTENTS

HIRSCH LAZAAR SILVERMAN, Ph.D., D.Sc.

T HE CONTENTS OF THIS VOLUME are multifaceted, diverse and various. The contributors have written as individuals, each a specialist in his own discipline. The result, it is hoped, will add to knowledge in the broad area of marital counseling. The editor in this concluding chapter briefly summarizes, in abstract, each of the chapters. To avoid any semblance of partiality, the abstracts appear alphabetically by contributor.

★　　★　　★

Marital counseling as an important aspect in the general field of counseling needs its own ideology, according to Anand (Chapter 13). One of the various important questions raised is: What should be the goal of marriage counseling — family unity or individual happiness? Anand's thesis is that, in general, the goal of marital counseling is family unity *with* individual happiness. In certain cases the approach of the counselor is to be determined by balancing his different roles as psychologist, private practitioner, marriage counselor and expert attached to a certain agency, and as a member of a certain sociocultural system. Also to be considered in balancing the approach are his responsibilities to the client as an individual, as part of the unit — the couple and the institutions of marriage and family — to the agency to which he is attached and to society at large. In some cases individual happiness may have to be given priority, according to Anand again. But such cases are exceptions to the rule. As a general rule, then, the choice is not either family unity or individual happiness, but family unity with individual happiness.

★　　★　　★

Barron (chapter 39) writes comprehensively to clarify the nature and significance of process in the marital relationship. Through a study and an understanding of process, it is possible to achieve a more realistic perspective of the 'specialness' of this institutionized form of relatedness, both in terms of itself and in terms of its interconnectedness with the world of space and time in which it functions. Barron discusses the internal and external forces, values and attitudes that affect the course of the marital arrangement. The ontogeny and evolution of marriage in process is examined and several types or categories of relatedness are introduced. These categories are dynamic and fluid rather than static or segmental. They are used to illus-

499

trate the nature of growth and regression in the life process of which
marriage is an integral part within the framework of our culture, society
and civilization. It is explained that a multiple theoretical approach is
necessary to our study of process. To be sure, process is most difficult to
study because it is life in motion. In view of this it is important to approach
it through several theoretical paths simultaneously. These paths include
not only a dynamic orientation but also an existential, dialectical and relativistic approach. Living truth cannot be found in compartments of knowledge: This makes a multi-theoretical study mandatory.

★   ★   ★

IRT Therapy, in Bassin's view (Chapter 10), refers to the application
of Integrity, Responsibility and Transparency, as defined and explained by
William Glasser (*Reality Therapy: A New Approach to Psychiatry*), O.
Hobart Mowrer (*The New Group Therapy*), and Sidney M. Jourard.
Bassin's chapter explains the concepts and describes case situations and
examples wherein the treatment approach is appropriate in the marriage-
counseling field. In essence, the viewpoint as presented concerns the general
inadequacy of conventional Freudian-based concepts in the field, and pro-
poses treatment procedures and philosophy which can be applied not only
to individuals involved in marital difficulties, but to all situations calling
for a return to responsible behavior to meet the basic needs of people for
love and self-regard.

★   ★   ★

Seventeen cases of interracial marriages and premarital relations are
discussed by Beigel (Chapter 25) with regard to the problems specific to
the race issue and the motivation leading to selection. All males in the
sample discussed by the author are either white or Negroes; the females are
white, Negro, Mexican, Japanese, Chinese and Indian. Material reasons —
loneliness in a strange environment and self-rejection — are among the
prominent motives of white women and men; prestige strivings and rejection of one's group are among those of the nonwhite group.

★   ★   ★

Brussel (Chapter 4) discusses love and relates sex to love. He writes on
heterosexual adjustment and the adjustment of a stable life. Having a
"stable life, with established home and family" may be "a goal to be
sought," but whether this is necessarily love is questioned.

Whether in the limited sense of the sex act or in the lofty sense of
reverence for the Supreme Being, the human phenomenon called "love"
has captured the imagination of poets, philosophers, moralists and even
scientists from time immemorial, says Brussel; and he presents various concepts of love, such as the love between husband and wife, between parents
and children, etc., but he concentrates primarily on the former. He traces

the role of love in various times and social structures from the Egyptians to the present day, showing the introduction of the "double standard" and the concept of sin.

Since love in psychiatric usage is "associated with heterosexual adjustment" and the concept of love today "may be estimated as somewhere between sentiment and sex without inhibitions or excessive restrictions," the author naturally spends most of his time discussing the relation of sex to love. He regrets the fact that "sex is too frequently set apart from love" in so many of our current books, plays and movies, because such an emphasis on sex alone does not provide an atmosphere for love, as can be seen by our rising divorce rate.

Finally, Brussel presents a guide to the raising of children in a happy home atmosphere where sex is treated naturally and where love is present, and where the children grow up to have a healthy attitude towards sex and love, enabling them to enter into a meaningful love relationship.

★ ★ ★

Calden (Chapter 31) presents a method of treating disturbed marital interaction through the direct involvement of both partners in conjoint counseling sessions.

Three basic themes have been observed, according to Calden, in most disturbed marital relationships: (a) the mutual frustration of each partner's self-esteem, resulting in a vicious circle of mutually destructive, fight-flight interactions; (b) the frustration of effective communication; and (c) the frustration of unrealistic marital expectations.

The counseling techniques described by Calden are intended to help the partners obtain insight into how each one contributes to the three major marital frustrations. Through direct confrontations of the partners' fight-flight, "right-wrong" and double-bind interactions, they are helped to gain experience in problem-solving solutions to their daily problems. The conjoint sessions aid in improving communication and in more realistically appraising and modifying their marriage expectations.

★ ★ ★

In spite of the fact that the family is the arena in which many socially destructive forces can be seen most clearly and dealt with most effectively, it is only in relatively recent times that the family has been given its appropriate place in therapeutic programs, according to Carrington (Chapter 38).

Five overlapping patterns of therapy applicable to the needs of the family are considered: psychiatric, medical, social, religious and domestic. This is followed by discussion of the different kinds of "therapists" and the necessary teamwork between them.

The special work of marriage and family counseling is discussed as it has developed in response to the realization that disturbances in the actual personal relationships within the family have not been offered sufficient help through the other available resources. As one of the social patterns of therapy, this service has an important and essential part in the total therapeutic project.

The importance of the domestic patterns of therapy in the whole program is emphasized by Carrington, and particular consideration is given to its influence in the promotion of mental and social health in any community.

★   ★   ★

Connolly (Chapter 21) deals specifically with the family; and feels that as an institution, sociologically and essentially, the family remains for all time the primal community among humanity. It is his view that the spiritual growth of the individual in the family structure is tied in most assuredly with his emotional growth and social development, as well as with his environment.

★   ★   ★

Disturbed marital interaction arises, in Ellis' view (Chapter 7), when a marital partner is neurotic or psychotic in his own right, and when he consequently has unrealistic expectations of what his mate's behavior should be. Whatever the original source of these irrational premises may be, the important thing is that an individual usually does not clearly understand what they are, and, even when he does, he stubbornly refuses to work against them and give them up. Basically, therefore, he is a "drifter," according to Ellis; and his disturbed marriage will usually continue until he realizes that "cognitive goofing" simply does not pay, and that there is no way out of individual and relationship human dilemmas other than work.

★   ★   ★

Marital discord and breakdown of communications between husband and wife show a highly significant coappearance. It seems highly desirable, therefore, according to Eisenstadt (Chapter 18), to examine the nature and elements of language and communication, how they may be misused and what can be done to rehabilitate marital communication and establish harmony via a linguistic and semantic approach.

Language is not synonymous with communication, for it consists largely of a code of signs, signals and symbols which are used in the attempt to express or transfer emotions, thoughts and desires. In addition, a subconscious language of which neither sender nor receiver are aware has been tentatively identified, in Eisenstadt's view. Errors of word usage, improper frame of reference, disorganized material, contradictory tonal and verbal signs, and hyperemotional coloration impair the linguistic code.

Communications include thought, purpose, message formulation, transmission, reception, reaction, feedback and consequent verbal behavior.

Barriers of intellectual, cultural, emotional and mechanical origin may alter or hinder effective communication. According to Eisenstadt, the marriage counselor can study and utilize contemporary findings on language and communication in order to (a) improve his own interview and counseling skills; (b) glean considerable diagnostic material from the communications characteristics of his clientele; and (c) suggest certain improvements in the linguistic and transfer techniques of his client which may relieve tensions and help establish marital rapport.

★   ★   ★

A close relationship between religion and the family has existed throughout the history of civilization. This relationship functioned for a long time to promote family stability. In view of recent social changes, however, the relationship is no longer functional, according to Falk (Chapter 22)," as illustrated by the lack of confidence in the clergy, the high interfaith marriage rates and deviations from religious teachings in the areas of divorce, birth control and child rearing."

In order to maintain its influence upon family life, religion is making some major adjustments in its teaching and its dogmas. This has become necessary because the practices of believers in the areas of marriage and family life do not coincide with the dogmas advocated by their churches. Illustrations of this attempt to adjust religious belief to family practice may be found in the discussions at the Vatican Council, the ambiguities in Protestant attitudes and the alienation of Jewish practices from the Jewish tradition, in the viewpoint maintained by Falk.

★   ★   ★

The historical antecedents of the social and legal institutions of divorce are traced by Foster (Chapter 15), in order to help explain the gap between statute and "living law," and to give some insight into the current ambivalence regarding matrimonial law. It is found that most of our law of marriage and divorce emanates from religious dogma and principles rather than from pragmatic experience, which was the source of the common law. Theologians rather than lawyers shaped our divorce law, hence divorce, according to Foster, has become institutionalized so as to adapt to the values of our time and place. Reform of the law is urgently needed so that courts may adopt a helpful approach to family breakdown and discard the traditional emphasis upon rewarding virtue and punishing sin.

★   ★   ★

Marriage places people in the most intimate relationship known to modern life. The immediate result of this is to prompt some of our most spontaneous self-expression. Although this is of great psychological value potentially, the facts of our marital behavior frequently leave much to be desired, in Fromme's interpretation (Chapter 6). Among the reasons for this, our lack of experience with intimacy, except in a dependent parent-child relationship, figures prominently. Even more important, marriage is more than a mere romantic liaison; it is a very grown-up relationship. This means that only grown-ups are ready for it. Developing an adult personality is by no means guaranteed by our growth in years. The result of marrying when we are not emotionally ready is finding ourselves in a less desirable situation than we expected. Instead of freely giving our best to each other, an emotional free-for-all emerges which, oddly enough, serves the purpose often of preserving us from developing psychological symptoms. We blame freely instead of loving freely, *per* Fromme. So we remain unhappy, but enjoy the secondary gains of a sense of self-justification. The more truly *adult* people are, the more capable they are of grown-up relationships. Marriage offers the possibility of greatest self-fulfillment for those adult enough for, and ready for, it.

★   ★   ★

People of every psychological type and of every degree of psychic normality or abnormality may suffer from marital conflicts, indicates Goldberg (Chapter 9). Consequently, the marriage counselor must be trained and competent to recognize severe mental disturbance in his clients. Referral for psychiatric diagnosis and possible treatment may be appropriate; at other times, marital counseling may still be very appropriate, even in the presence of deep intrapsychic disturbance in one or both spouses. Many combinations of marital counseling and individual therapy are possible and appropriate in handling certain situations. The counselor must be particularly alert to the presence of depression or other psychiatric conditions predisposing to suicide in his clients. Marital counseling and joint psychotherapy offer new insights and perspectives on many psychiatric problems, in Goldberg's view.

★   ★   ★

"Borderline" clients, or clients suffering from various degrees of ego defect, today constitute a large proportion of the clients who come to social agencies for help with their problems of interpersonal difficulties. Invariably the problem is perceived as a situational or interpersonal one, with little awareness of the part played by intrapsychic difficulties. Goodwin (Chapter 36) attempts to delineate one way of working, within a social-agency framework offering marriage counseling, with this group of clients. Since these clients are struggling with a high degree of ambivalence, are apprehensive, distrustful of relationship and have frequently been disappointed in prior attempts to secure therapeutic help, the management of the counselor-client relationship assumes great importance. Because of the weak ego strength of the client, focus within interviews is kept on solving the current reality and relationship problems with which the client is struggling, and efforts are directed toward improving ego strength. An historical or interpretative approach is utilized very sparingly, according to Goodwin. The differential approach described in her chapter might be utilized to some degree by counselors or therapists working within other services and settings.

★ ★ ★

In this century considerable changes have taken place in the pattern of human relationships. We have become aware of the interaction of the psyche and the soma, and there is a need to reassess the values governing our lives.

Progress involves changing attitudes to moral concepts and the need to be aware of the conflicting opposites — the concern for oneself *versus* the concern for others, according to the thesis maintained by Griffith (Chapter 30).

Man's human and spiritual natures are complimentary, and both need to be understood and expressed. In marital disharmony the balance is often upset, and the conflict may be reflected on the sexual level. Where conflicts have been repressed, psychotherapeutic help is necessary. Marriage preparation and education should enable an individual to recognize these problems when they arise.

Evolution in the future is likely to be in the realm of the mind, *per* Griffith. We need to develop a morality within and a consciousness that can recognize the opposites and hold the tension.

★ ★ ★

Guze (Chapter 37) concerns himself with an effort to establish the difference between sexual "health" and sexual normality. He emphasizes the facts that pathology is really cross-cultural, and that there are biologic foundations for the determination of what is sexually healthy and what is sexually pathological. His interpretations are based on the premise that what is physically or emotionally harmful to the individual is essentially behaviorally pathological. Concomitantly, he feels that an act which is not harmful to the participants in sexual behavior — or to any one in direct contact with them — is regarded as healthy or nonpathological.

★ ★ ★

A moralistic approach to the problems of marriage is inappropriate in counseling, in Harper's view (Chapter 26). It is essential for the marital counselor to help the couple realistically to understand their differences and to work toward rational solutions rather than determining the right and the wrong of problems and positions.

Just because moralizing is to be avoided, however, does not mean that moral issues are not important in marital counseling. The three outstanding areas of such issues are divorce, parenthood and sex.

Divorce, viewed realistically instead of moralistically, is a basic human right to be exercised for correction of marital errors. Responsibly handled, according to Harper, it need not bring tragedy or misery. Parenthood and sex both have many false moral assumptions associated with them. It is one of the most important functions of the marriage counselor to stimulate critical and realistic thinking about some of these assumptions. The questions raised and the assertions made in Harper's chapter are designed to serve as such stimulation.

★   ★   ★

The purpose of Herz's emphasis (Chapter 17) is to point up inconsistent, differing and confusing value systems, leading to conflict that marital partners bring to a marriage as a result of background exposure to either the authoritarian or democratic family setting.

Herz discusses the development of the socioeconomic factors in early American history and how they shaped interpersonal family relationships of that period, compared to the twentieth century urban cultural setting with its own type of familial interaction.

Both periods have their own sets of values and corresponding family patterns. The early eighteenth-nineteenth century American family was placed in a patriarchal-authoritarian setting with a background of familism. Due to historical-social factors, including the shift from a rural to an urban society, American families have become more democratically-individualistically oriented.

Confusion and conflict, stemming from changing family patterns in this transitional period, have a marked effect upon marital stability, in Herz's view.

★   ★   ★

In recent years there has been an increasing recognition on the part of marriage counselors that values are both implicitly and explicitly operative in the counseling relationship. The very notion of counseling implies a value system. The particular theoretical orientation of the practitioner carries with it certain value assumptions, Hudson states (Chapter 14). The circumstances under which the therapy occurs may denote certain value considerations which are functioning for both therapist and client. The value issues with which marriage counselors are faced become increasingly complex when the therapy involves a married couple.

The value position of the marriage counselor is probably more complex than that of any other individual working in the helping professions. With the implementation of standards of training and the establishment of training centers, the professional marriage counselor is coming into his own. Hudson maintains that marriage counseling is evolving from an educational, advice-giving, conscious, reality-oriented service to a scientific, highly specialized form of psychotherapy.

★   ★   ★

Language plays a chronic and acute role in molding and reflecting human sexual attitudes and behaviors. Our conflicting sex attitudes are reflected in a fascination with the tabooed language of sex. Emotional upset engendered by this language is likely to affect the effectiveness of the counselor as well as the client.

Many ill-defined words and hypocritic attitudes towards "dirty" words confuse and/or block easy and rational communication on the subject of sex. Moreover, regulations of the ancient Jews and the antisexual, antifemale attitudes of the early Christian fathers are still delivered to us daily in the language of sex, and are most sharply and formally apparent in our sex laws and sexual morality, according to Johnson (Chapter 32).

Even more insidiously, our language of male and female roles, of "marriage and the family," of childbearing, etc., is attuned to the past rather than to the changing present. A major stumbling block in marriage is the fact that people think that they know what the word means and the fact that people marry symbols (i.e., preconceived male and female role-players) rather than persons.

Counselors and educators need to distinguish verbal and other behavior that is controlled solely by the arbitrary authority of tradition from that which is controlled by rationality. In this area, rationality is constantly threatened by traditional notions associated with such words as sin, morality, guilt, obscenity, male, female, homosexual, perversion — and sex. A rational approach to human sexuality and to the language of sex may, in time, in Johnson's argument, give rise to a happier and healthier pattern of sexual behavior, an aspect of which would necessarily be a new and healthier language of sex.

★   ★   ★

Love as a superstructure on the rock of justice, in terms of rabbinic lore, in Jung's viewpoint (Chapter 23), is capable of tremendous achievement, culminating in self-sacrificing devotion to another human being's happiness. The sentiment of love, then, may be derived from a profound and steady awareness of a strong, noble character; and love springs from the synthesis of intellectual administration and emotional acceptance. Only insofar as we love do we understand God or man, in Jung's evaluation; and, additionally, in the fabric of the patterns of religious life, there has been an unchanging analogy: love of man, knowledge of fellow man, of man for woman and woman for man on one level, and love of God, knowledge of God, understanding of His way with man on the higher one.

Genuine love, then, in the final analysis, implies self-identification with the beloved. It is empathy in its deepest form. Mature love between the sexes is the fruit of knowledge; and just as vision, appreciation and depth, and knowledge of character call forth love, so the search for comprehensive and penetrative knowledge is the fruit of love. Thus are combined philosophy and religion and psychology.

★   ★   ★

Sex is the most intimate expression of human love, while love is the total expression of the human person, Lester (Chapter 24) points out. Sex, to him, expresses the depth or exposes the shallowness of the person who loves. All that shapes and colors the person will influence the personal power of sex.

Insofar as love is walled in by selfishness, sex will use another person — a violation of all that love means. Sex cannot be true without sensitivity for and understanding of the value of the other person.

Teaching young people to know and appreciate the meaning of sex, therefore, is much more a matter of teaching them how to be an authentic person than acquainting them with anatomical terms and physiological facts.

Furthermore, in Lester's view, sex is not a technique to be learned by charts. It is a power and a talent to be opened up by learning how to live life with love. The Creator designed the power of sex to express the power of conjugal love. Only in following His design will the riches of sex be found and possessed.

★   ★   ★

Marriage counseling is presented by Luckey (Chapter 11) as a process which includes aspects of both education and therapy, and which demands special skills and areas of knowledge from the counselor, regardless of his theoretical orientation (four of which are reviewed). The key to all counseling is the counselor himself — his knowledge and use of himself in establishing an effective relationship with his clients. Specific techniques of marriage counseling, as contrasted with individual counseling, include three sets of perceptions and expectations (of self, of spouse, of self as perceived by spouse). Goals to be achieved, in Luckey's emphasis, are perception and understanding of self, of spouse, of the dynamics of the relationship between the two and the establishment of effective communication.

★   ★   ★

Private practice is an appealing idea. It holds as much attraction for marriage counselors, clinical psychologists and psychiatric social workers as it does for physicians and lawyers, and there are very good reasons for this. To many, it appears as an ultimate goal. Yet, because the mental-health field is unique in a number of ways, private practice in this field has characteristics of its own that cannot be ignored by any one aspiring to practice for himself, according to McGinnis (Chapter 19).

There are other important attractions of private practice besides the ones of self-satisfaction, prestige and income. Perhaps the strongest attraction of all is the broadened opportunity to give service which private practice offers.

The mental-health disciplines are rather new, professionally. Yet, few if any other professions require as intensive training and extensive experience for successful solo private practice. The chapter by McGinnis takes the position that the most important single factor indicating this readiness is personal maturity and a healthy emotional adjustment.

Future expansion of group practice and solo private practice, which can develop concurrently, offers an ideal intermediate step towards ultimate solo practice. One profession — "psychotherapy" — practiced by "psychotherapists" will finally blend the essentials of all the mental-health areas, McGinnis feels. This psychotherapist will be qualified to treat the whole person and all his problems (exclusive of medical ones) at whatever therapeutic level is appropriate.

★   ★   ★

Sexual maladjustment, children, infidelity, money, inlaws, are some of the problems that are the cause of marital difficulties according to Mudd and Goodwin (Chapter 3). Supplementarily, basic to adjusting to different temperaments, values, desires and ideals is an acceptance by each partner of the right of the other person to be different. Moreover, jealousy not founded on fact is the outward manifestation of a deep insecurity of a jealous partner in his or her sexual role and in his or her concept of self. Essentially, too, each person brings to marriage a need for maintaining his own identity and a need for a complementary relationship with another. Finally, Mudd and Goodwin feel that breakdown of communication between partners is frequently one of the first symptoms of a disturbed marital relationship.

★   ★   ★

Family caseworkers, over and beyond their assistance in helping the troubled person mobilize his or her inner resources, have a primary obligation to seek out community resources needed by their clients. Lawyers are often essential to the welfare and future stabilization of husbands, wives and children immersed in family conflict, Mudd feels (Chapter 16). Frustrated and angry clients may threaten impulsive action which may jeopardize their legal rights. Caseworkers need orientation to legal problems, although they should never give specific legal advice. Through mutual trust and constructive communication between the two professions, cooperative efforts in resolving conflict and settling disputes outside the courts might be tried, argues Mudd. Other preventative approaches might include premarital counseling, longer waiting periods between license and marriage and community concern for the needs of families at all stages of the family cycle.

★   ★   ★

Tension and conflict precede divorce. Everyone is emotionally disturbed in varying degrees during such periods of stress. However, if sufficient change in a marriage to create a satisfactory relationship is impossible or improbable, the decision to divorce may be essentially healthy and mature, in the view held by Mudd and Goodwin (Chapter 29). Before, during and after divorce, decisions concerning the children are stressful to all. For the marital pair, loss of the marriage relationship represents the loss of a large number of human relationships. Fears of loneliness and isolation are probably the most omnipotent and painful emotions for both men and women. Moreover, divorce is evidence of failure and carries with it a stigma of shame and guilt. Confidence in one's adequacy in interpersonal relations is shaken. Most divorced persons eventually remarry — men more often than women. A potentially good marriage can be stabilized and strengthened, with timely, competent, professional help, through constructive resolution of the marital conflicts.

★   ★   ★

Neubeck (Chapter 12) addresses himself to the marriage therapist who, in order to deal with problems involving his clients' extramarital relations, must understand the real meaning of the "extra" in extramarital.

An attempt is made to describe the norms of marital relations and to see what limitations upon freedom and spontaneity these norms impose upon spouses. The incident of extramarital relationships is linked to relative needs for freedom and spontaneity of the partners and to the degree marriage itself can meet these needs. Social psychology theory is used by Neubeck to conceptualize the use of marital space.

★   ★   ★

Marriage is understood by Plutchik (Chapter 28) as a set of relationships in a state of dynamic equilibrium, but one in which the balance point is constantly shifting under the influence of various forces. Some of the forces, such as the existence of physical attraction, act to keep the balance stable. Other forces, such as conflicts over who is in control, act to increase the instability of a marriage. These various forces are briefly described by Plutchik, with the emphasis being placed on contemporary factors in the lives of the individuals, rather than historical sources. From this point of view, marriage counseling is considered to be a set of techniques and strategies designed to modify the balance of forces in the marriage in a desired direction. This view also has some research implications. It suggests the need to develop formal procedures for evaluating the state of balance of a marriage. It also directs the counselor's attention toward those forces which are most likely to be effective in changing a given equilibrium.

★   ★   ★

Casual, unconventional marriage counseling has existed from time immemorial, perhaps for as long as the institution of marriage. But professional marriage counseling is no more than three or four decades old, having its origins with the investigations and teachings of Ernest R. Groves and with the almost simultaneous founding of several marriage-consultation centers, Reevy points out (Chapter 1). The pioneers in marriage counseling were deeply interested in fostering the emergence of the new profession and steering its growth. And so they were involved in all sorts of interlocking pursuits related to the founding of a new profession, as in the founding and directing of the first marriage-consulting centers, the first professional organization representing the new discipline, and the showing of their concern with the problem of developing standards of education and training in this new field.

From the start the pioneers gave much thought and planning to this matter, which has been a continuing concern with leaders, particularly of the leaders of the American Association of Marriage Counselors. Largely under the aegis and leadership of the Association, standards of education and training for marriage counseling have been established and upheld. As a result, marriage counseling today is an interdisciplinary field representing a number of professions such as medicine, psychology, sociology and social work. There have been, for a few decades, a number of training programs giving the type of education and training approved by the Association; and it seems likely that the number of these training programs will grow and flourish so that marriage counseling will be an even more viable profession than it is now. Evidence of this is shown in the fact, according to Reevy, that the membership of the Association has tripled in the last ten years and, further, some professions (as medicine and psychology) are showing a marked interest in marriage counseling as a speciality.

★   ★   ★

Although the patient often views the physician as the first helping person to whom he can turn with personal problems involving sex, marriage and the family, medical training has rarely prepared the physician to deal with such clinical situations, Resnik indicates (Chapter 2). Often a socially constricted, sexually inhibited intellectual, the physician has little personal experience or supervised learning process in dealing fully with the wide variety of marital and sexual relationships. When married himself, the physician must become aware of the reciprocal needs of his wife and family before he is in a position to give therapy to his patient with marital difficulties, as well as with organic ones. A program for including marriage counseling in medical school curricula is also outlined by Resnik.

★   ★   ★

Intermarriage has been on the increase in the United States because of the high degree of acculturation attained by immigrant groups. Sanua (Chapter 34) surveys the literature on intermarriage, particularly with reference to the relationship between intermarriage and psychological adjustment. Topics covered include intermarriage as a sign of maladjustment, conflicts resulting from intermarriage, the relationship between intermarriage and mental health, intermarriage and the divorce rate, problems encountered in raising children when parents are intermarried and attitudes of college students towards intermarriage.

It is estimated by Sanua that the rate of intermarriage is highest among the Catholic group and lowest with the Jewish group. There is contradictory evidence as to prior pathology in intermarried couples, and also regarding the difficulties resulting from intermarriage. It would seem, however, from the little evidence available, that intermarriage by Jews and Catholics seems to have more serious repercussions on their psychological adjustment than intermarriage by Protestants; and that college students today tend to accept interreligious dating and interreligious marriages readily, particularly when love is involved.

The general conclusion that may be drawn from the empirical studies cited is that intermarriage may succeed, but the risks are that it will carry an added burden which will manifest itself in later years, particularly when the religious education for the children is to be decided.

★   ★   ★

The most serious psychological crisis in contemporary society is the identity crisis, which reflects the changing structure and function of the family, particularly in America, as well as the rapidly shifting pattern of society. Other factors contributing to this crisis, in Schneiders' view (Chapter 8), are the industrial revolution, modern educational theory, psychoanalysis and similar influences. In addition, the changes in family size and composition are known to have a direct bearing on personality development and on role definition.

Both the identity crisis and the problem of role definition have important implications for marriage and marital success. Roles and role definitions are also reflected to an important extent in the values created by affluence, by changing feminine status and by social values. Family income, the status of the husband and interpersonal relationships in marriage are all seriously affected, Schneiders holds, by these continuing changes. These value changes have in turn affected the deepest identities of both men and women, and have created problems for children as well as for family living.

Thus, a clear-cut definition of roles in marriage becomes increasingly difficult. The problems of personal identity and of role definition are two sides of the same coin. All commitments in the marital relationship hinge upon the successful completion of these two tasks by both husband and wife. The various roles that both must learn to define and to assume effectively cannot be achieved successfully in the absence of either sex identity or self-identity.

★   ★   ★

Schnitzer (Chapter 20) deals with a historical perspective of the man-woman relationship as seen through the Bible, the Talmud and the Midrash, the parables and stories as told by the rabbis and sages of old. The Bible and the Talmud considered marriage as the highest ideal in Jewish life, and the Hebrew term for marriage, *Kiddushin* meaning "making holy" or "sanctifying," served as a criteria throughout history. To love one's wife, to honor one's mate and to consider a good wife far more precious than rubies was man's obligation upon assuming the privilege of marriage.

The capacity to love makes for creative marriages. Judaism always extolled the place of love in marriage. Rabbi Akiba, the great sage, considered the love between a man and his wife as the holiest of the holy. In the civilization of Judaism one finds two versions of love. One, the aristocratic approach, is found in the biblical story of Isaac and Rebecca. It is based on the method of Eliezer, who seeks out a suitable companion for his master, Isaac. The second version is that of the lovesick shepherd maiden yearning for her lover as described in the chapters of The Song of Songs. Sound marriages should have both of the elements found in the Jewish ideals of love, combining the best of the aristocratic matchmaker-marriage; and the best of the romantic-love-involved marriages, Schnitzer insists.

To the historical perspectives of Jewish marriage and family life, and to the practical phases of modern marriage life, one should add the experience of a religious faith. A faith in God, in the grandeur of man's soul and the keen awareness of the preciousness of time can transform this social-legal contract into an ideal and artistic work of human endeavors — an ideal marriage.

★   ★   ★

Marital counseling generally takes place in an atmosphere that involves disturbances in socioeconomic, sexual, emotional and religious differences, or some combination of these. These problems are seldom simple, and the addition of severe physical or mental disability merely serves to compound the already complicated marriage relationship. Perhaps this is the reason that physicians, social workers, psychologists, marriage counselors and many others often appear to avoid steadfastly even discussing the effect of chronic disability with their patients or clients on such matters as marital discord and the responsibilities of the disabled mate *versus* the nondisabled. Seidenfeld (Chapter 33) presents some of the major aspects of physical and mental disability on the disabled spouse, his disabled or nondisabled mate, their children and their immediate family constellation.

Many factors play a role in the marital adjustment of the disabled, just as they do with the nondisabled. In addition, however, the disability may play a direct or indirect part in further influencing many of the aspects of married life. Such factors as the severity of the disability, the nature of the disability and the time of onset in relation to the married state may tend to influence the marital relationship and to create problems that require the marriage counselor to seek advice and cooperation from other professional disciplines.

Because of the immense complexity that physical or mental disability presents, the marriage counselor needs to familiarize himself with some of the major changes that may occur as a result of disabling conditions. These have been discussed by Seidenfeld with particular reference to what role they play in affecting the married couple and what may be done to help reduce or even eliminate them as factors in marital discord.

★   ★   ★

In an idealistic sense, Silverman (Chapters 5 and 35) writes on morals in marriage, and womanhood, in terms which are perhaps more philosophic in emphasis than truly objective. His views are a combination of philosophic interpretation with psychological insight into human nature, relative to matters of marriage counseling. He tends to optimism in psychological thought, while realizing well enough that human beings are "human," with their faults and imperfections, their virtues and attributes. Not only psychologically and sociologically but philosophically, Silverman implies that there is in man's very being a flowing equilibrium between good and evil, the noble and the base, the sublime and the ridiculous, the weighty and the trivial. For in marriage factors as related to human beings, the future in terms of happiness and contentment belongs to independence, not domination, to diversity, not conformity, to freedom, not servitude.

★   ★   ★

Each marriage partner enters the marriage contract with fixed ideas of sex, based on his individual upbringing plus the accretion of his life experiences, in Wollman's view (Chapter 27). Counseling should take into consideration the idea that the emotional impact of the love relationship will tend to bolster a sagging love image and provide a basis for sexual compatibility. Sex attitudes in the suggestible client may be enhanced by hypnotic techniques in individual or group setting.

The sex attitudes of the teenager in marriage are then briefly discussed by Wollman within the framework of reference of marital counseling; and mention is made of the complex sex attitudes of the married transvestite and transsexual. Homosexual "marriages" and heterosexual marriages of homosexuals are also discussed.

AUTHOR AND CONTRIBUTOR INDEX

SUBJECT INDEX